ROTISSERIE®
LEAGUE
BASEBALL

ROTISSERIE® LEAGUE BASEBALL

1996 Edition

Edited by
Glen Waggoner

The Rotisserie League
Lee Eisenberg • Rob Fleder • Peter Gethers
Daniel Okrent • Michael Pollet • Cary Schneider
Robert Sklar • Cork Smith • Harry Stein
Glen Waggoner • Steve Wulf

Little, Brown and Company
Boston   New York   Toronto   London

Contents

Introduction: Lovin' the Spoonful   1

1. The Inner Game   5
Play Ball! • Roti-Trek, The Next Generation • How to Spell
R-E-L-I-E-F • Final Innings • The Rules, Simplified

2. Scouting Report   23
1996 Player Ratings • Behind the Plate • At the
Corners • Up the Middle • In the Outfield • Designated
Hitters • On the Mound • Out of the Bullpen

3. By the Numbers   195
Stat-Pak • League Leaders • Top Position Players
• Post All-Star Leaders

4. Down on the Farm   229
A Long Night's Journey into Day • The New World Order
• 1996 Farm System Prospects

5. Front Office   261
How to Keep Score • Roti·Stats! • The RLBA
Wants You! • Roti·Stats Top Teams of 1995
• Roti·Stats Tightest Pennant Races of 1995

6. Ground Rules   275
Official Constitution • Rotisserie Ultra • Rotisserie Lite

7. Postgame Shower   309
A Yoo-Hoo to Arms

Appendix: Final 1995 Averages   315

ROTISSERIE® LEAGUE BASEBALL

Introduction

Lovin' the Spoonful
by Steve Wulf

The Walkman lay in pieces on the ground. It lay there—housing shattered, headphones horribly twisted, batteries scattered every which way—not as a metaphor for the game, which had indeed seemed irreparably broken a few months before, but rather as a reminder that the national pastime, i.e., Rotisserie League Baseball, was once again whole.

Before our literary juices take us any further along this purple path, perhaps we should back up a little. Let us return to that Saturday in May when a desultory group assembled in Beloved Founder and Former Commissioner-for-Life Dan Okrent's dining room for the annual, one and only, original Rotisserie League Draft.

We were depressed for several reasons. Commissioner-for-Life Cork Smith had sold his East Side home, complete with its Arthurian dining room, so we had to assemble in the unfamiliar, modern, albeit pleasant surroundings of the Okrents' West Side apartment. Steve Wulf was 15 minutes late, and he would have had a good excuse—he muttered something about working till four a.m., serving breakfast to four children under the age of eight, coaching two Little League games, making one trip to the OTB for Kentucky Derby bets and another to the liquor store for the Maker's Mark that was essential to mint juleps—except that Wulf is always 15 minutes late for the draft.

Then there was the baseball season itself, which sprang not from a sense of *rapprochement*, not from the realization by both Labor and Lord that they were destroying the game, but rather from a judge named Sonia. Besides, the season was several weeks late and 18 games short, thus ensuring us of another incomplete game.

Replacement baseball might have been more appealing, if only because we longed to hear those magic words, "Rick Lancellotti, thirty-five dollars."

There were other factors involved in our depression, as well, long-simmering ones that we'll try to convey a little later.

The crowning moment of the 1995 draft came when one of our owners, who shall remain nameless lest this embarrass him—you can thank us later, Cary—threw his Trevor Wilson autograph-model colostomy bag on the table just as the bidding was about to begin. Fortunately, it was empty at the time. But for some reason, the pumpernickel bagels didn't seem quite as appetizing after that.

So it was, with heavy hearts, bitter sentiments and queasy stomachs, that we held our annual auction. Records were set for the most expensive non–base stealer in history (Fred McGriff, $52), the most expensive starting pitcher in history (Greg Maddux, $34), and the most expensive nephew of Dwight Gooden in history (Gary Sheffield, $44). John Littlefield returned in the person of Brad Clontz ($28), and Ebenezer Scrooge returned in the person of Harry Stein, who still had about $120 to spend when the draft ended.

For occupational therapy, we took a Painter, a Butler, an Abbott, a Prince, a King, a Barber, a Groom, a Walker, a Miller, a Cooper, a Parent, a Counsell, and a couple of Sanderses. Yet we found nothing the least bit amusing about the '95 draft. Eleven angry men left that room murmuring, "I hate my team."

The lone smile was on the face of Jay Lovinger, proprietor of the Lovin' Spoonful. For this, his third draft since taking over the compost heap that was the McCall Collects, Jay had lovin'ly assembled a nice corps of players from two years of dumping: Todd Jones, Todd Hundley, Chuck Carr, Andres Galarraga, Barry Bonds, Tom Henke, Chipper Jones, Ron Gant. He was a man with a plan, and when he needed a starting pitcher, he forked over the $34 for Greg Maddux.

In the weeks immediately following the draft, Jay made some very canny trades: Chipper Jones to the Wulfgang for Randy Myers, Chuck Carr to the Fleder Mice for Quilvio Veras and Bret Saberhagen, and Tim Pugh, Marvin Freeman, and Daryl Kile to a certain team that shall remain nameless lest we embarrass the owner—you're welcome again, Cary—for Dave Justice.

In real life, it was a fairly interesting season. (Yeah, sure, you knew Pete Schourek was going to win 18 games.) But the actual races were nowhere near as exciting as the Rotisserie race. As we moved into August, it appeared as though Lovinger, not to mention Justice, might prevail. Spoonful pitching was less than impressive—Glen (The Bar Mitzvah Boy) Dishman, Pete (Hardi-har) Harnisch, Tommy (Sickly Shade Of) Greene—but Jay kept telling anyone who would listen that his pitching philosophy had been borrowed from the Hippocratic Oath: First, do no harm. That was easy for him to say, what with Myers and Maddux.

"If I win this thing with my horrible pitching," Jay would muse, "that will prove just how good Greg Maddux is."

When Saberhagen, who also knows Cy Young, was traded from the moribund Mets to the mile-high Rockies, the Spoonful seemed a lock. Most of the rest of the league was behind Jay—in more ways than one. He is a mensch among mensches, he had never tasted Yoo-Hoo, he had doted on his club, and he was not Lee Eisenberg, owner of his nearest competitor, the perennial powerhouse Eisenberg Furriers. The Furriers are about as beloved in the Rotisserie League as they would be at a PETA meeting.

First, do no harm. The motto would come back to haunt the Spoonful. And which pitcher would do the most harm? As it turned out, it was Saberhagen. As soon as the ace was traded to Colorado, he started pitching like Bret

Somers. (An obscure reference perhaps, but Somers was a sharp-tongued actress once married to Jack Klugman, who did portray the quintessential sportswriter, and, more pointedly, she once sat next to Don Sutton on the panel of *The Match Game*. You can't pay for information like this, can you?)

Suddenly, Lovinger was looking at these incredibly ugly pitching lines next to Saberhagen's name. In one game against the Cubs, which the Rockies lost 26–9, Saberhagen gave up home runs to Mark Grace and Sammy Sosa, both of whom were members of the Furriers.

And that, friends, brings us to the shattered Walkman. With two weeks to go in the season, Jay decided to activate Tommy Greene of the Phillies when he learned he would be pitching against Dave Telgheder of the Mets. As Jay sat in the backyard of his palatial home in Pelham, N.Y., listening to the Mets game on the radio, Greene proceeded to issue bases on balls to five batters, including Telgheder, in the second inning—talk about your Walkman. When five earned runs had crossed the plate, the usually mild-mannered Lovinger flung his Sony to the ground and stomped on it, in full view of his astonished wife and daughter.

You might ask, How did this act symbolize the healing and renewal of the Rotisserie League? (More likely, you would ask, What kind of a putz would ruin a perfectly good Walkman because of Tommy Greene? But that question would not serve our purposes here.)

The answer is this. With the trashing of that radio, Lovinger restored the passion and electricity and, yes, lovin' that had been missing from the Rotisserie League since even before the strike.

Truth be told, we original pioneers had lost our spirit over the years. The game wasn't our be-all and end-all any more. We had families, to be sure, and reasonably responsible jobs, but we also arrived at each successive draft with the clearer realization that thousands, then millions were playing a game that only 10 people had once played. And with that realization came the growing resentment that we had not become rich men because of the Rotisserie League.

In fact, the piddling money that Little (We'll say!), Brown (Not Green) gives us for this book—split 12 ways—is about all we have to show for starting a movement that has found its way into every law firm and firehouse and sports department in the nation. Perhaps that is why our annual draft had become about as exciting as Bud Selig testimony before Congress, about as passionate as a Don Fehr press conference, about as interesting as one of Murray Chass's baseball columns.

"Fred McGriff, $52," someone would say. "Big hairy deal," most of us would think.

But that was before we all got caught up in Jay's quest. When the Lovin' Man threw down his Walkman, we all felt his pain. When the Furriers made their final-week charge, we rooted for the Spoonful to hold them off. We knew it would come down to ratio, so when Saberhagen took the mound on the final day of the regular season, we were right there beside Jay and all those Rockies fans, who were desperate for a wild-card spot. Surely, Bret would summon up his dormant pitching power. Surely, the Spoonful would get what they deserved.

Well, the Rockies won. But the pitching line on Saberhagen that day read like this:

IP	H	R	ER	BB	SO
2	7	8	6	1	0

That pretty much clinched it for the Furriers. Jay still had to wait another 24 hours before the official stats were crunched. When the fax came the next day, he saw that the Spoonful was just one point behind the Furriers, one point that Saberhagen could have given him, one point behind the 1995 Rotisserie League title—had he and Eisenberg tied, Lovinger would have won by virtue of leading in more categories. The next day, the O.J. verdict came in. And the day after that was the always depressing Yom Kippur, the Day of Atonement.

So what did Jay do the day after the day after the day after the day after the day after? He called around to see if anyone would be interested in Mickey Morandini.

That, dear readers, is the true, revived spirit of the Rotisserie League. When the gang got together to give Lee his Yoo-Hoo shower—not to mention a big, fat check—last November, they also presented Jay with a little gift. A Sony Walkman.

Big hairy deal, you say. Hey, it just about blew our book advance.

1

The Inner Game

Play Ball!

If art imitated life instead of vice-versa, a chapter called "The Inner Game" would contain a deep, probing inquiry into the heart and soul of the National Pastime. There would be a balanced, detailed analysis of last winter's impasse over a new Basic Agreement, a sober assessment of last spring's flirtation with "Replacement Baseball," a cautiously upbeat account of last summer's brave attempt to table basic differences and get on with the game, and a sombre reminder of last fall's realization—it came to everyone somewhere between the last out of the World Series and the arrival of the box score for Tom Glavine's brilliant performance the next morning—that the game is still in deep trouble, that no real progress had been made, that there was no evidence of movement on either side, and that another season was in jeopardy.

Okay, tell the truth. When did you nod off, between spring and summer? Or did you make it all the way to "deep trouble" before falling into a deep snore?

That's the way we feel. We've had quite enough of Bud Fehr and Donald Selig, thank you very much. We don't want to hear from small markets vs. big markets. Revenue sharing, luxury taxes, sharing of ancillary income—go away! Salary caps? Let's talk *baseball* caps!

Look, by the time you read these words, the people who control our game will have cut a deal—or not. Either way, the only "Inner Game" we want to read about is the one played by pitchers and batters, not lawyers and accountants. If we're all in the same ballpark on that score, we think you'll be happy with what follows.

Our first correspondents, **Mark Batterman** and **Ken Kuta**, have been here before. Actually, sometimes it seems that they've been here forever, like that wart on your mother-in-law's chin. Batterman has determined to devote his life to correcting the Founding Fathers' many errors—conceptual, structural, and otherwise. A couple of years ago he proposed an overhaul of our sacred scoring categories, proposing that Strikeouts be substituted for Ratio. (We still get a chuckle around the clubhouse about that one.) Last year, Batterman teamed up with Kuta, his obedient houseboy and dark angel. The result: a diatribe that wheeled around Rotisserie owners' most common mistakes, some of which were originally patented by the Batterman-Kuta battery.

This year, together again, they eschew the piecemeal approach to re-creating the game in their own image in favor of a more ambitious scheme—in "Roti-Trek, The Next Generation" they lead us in search of the perfect Rotisserie League. With the utmost humility, of course.

Great, you may be thinking right about now, but what am I going to do about my bullpen? You took the words right out of our mouth. And so, as a growing number of us do when faced with Rotisserie puzzlers like this, we turn to **John Benson**.

No, you haven't inadvertently fast-forwarded to Chapter 4, John's customary hole in the batting order, where his "Down on the Farm" scouting report has become a Rotisserie staple. And don't panic—he's there again this year, telling us what new names to think about for this year and beyond. But John's also here, offering valuable tips on building a bullpen in "How to Spell R-E-L-I-E-F."

Batting third in the order this year is **Sally Small**. A farmer by summer and a writer by winter, Sally is a baseball fan all year around. She and her husband claim to raise pears and apples in the Sacramento delta, but in fact they spend most of their time along the third-base line at Oakland–Alameda County Stadium, where they are A's season-ticket holders.

Although Sally played a mean first base on her high school softball team, she doesn't play Rotisserie baseball, a character flaw we decided to overlook after reading "Final Innings," an article of hers that first appeared in *The New Yorker* (and is reprinted here with that magazine's kind permission).

"I sent the piece directly to Roger Angell and asked if he would be interested," Sally told us when we tracked her down after the last pears had been picked last fall. Angell, a longtime editor at *The New Yorker* and a Hall-of-Fame baseball writer, was definitely interested: "He told me he had been planning to write something about Walter Haas, the owner of the A's, but wanted to run my story instead."

Over the years, Sally had submitted 24 short stories to *The New Yorker*, all of which had been rejected—some by Angell, the magazine's senior fiction editor. "Final Innings" was her first hit. In our book, it's a grand slam.

TIME OUT!

Not so fast there, Rookie. (And only you know if you are one.) Before stepping up to the plate in The Inner Game, take a close look at The Rules, Simplified (see pages 19–21). Then memorize the sacred Rotisserie Constitution in Chapter 6 (pages 277–294). Only then, after you have a glimmer of what madness lies ahead, should you proceed. This announcement is brought to you as a public service by the Founding Fathers of Rotisserie League Baseball. Don't come around later saying you weren't warned.

Roti-Trek, The Next Generation
or, The Search for the Perfect
Rotisserie League
by Mark Batterman & Ken Kuta

Certain moments are frozen in time. January, 1994. The gut-wrenching night when Los Angeles was torn asunder by powerful forces of nature, exploding the world as we knew it apart. After a night of sheer terror, standing amidst the rubble and dust, a sickening realization set in: Nothing will ever be the same—that which was solid and secure when we innocently toddled off to bed had irrevocably shaken itself apart. Nope. None of us in Southern California who lived through it will ever forget exactly where we were the moment the Farrah Fawcett-Major League broke up.

Yes, the legendary Farrah Fawcett-Major League, its vaunted status as Roti-Stats League No. 101, its storied history, the time-honored, unbroken, spring-to-spring, blood-to-blood ritual, the renowned bank account drain and source of a million marital conflicts, all gone in the blink of an eye.

Tough luck? Nah. When push comes to shove, if the players and owners of the national pastime can't be bothered worrying about the integrity of the game, who were we? Hell, we know a golden opportunity when we see one. No stupid little thing like no league to play in was going to stop us. We didn't skipper our two franchises, The Marks Brothers and The Kuta Kintes, to pennants, *b-i-i-i-g* money, and Yoo-Hoo showers over our eleven Roti-years by outstandingly good looks alone. The Baseball Gods had handed us a gift—hey, maybe not Tim Salmon on a long-term contract at $11—but a gift just the same, and we were not going to start peeing into the wind of fortune now.

Finally, after years of bitching, here was our chance to create a league in our own image. Yes, our mission (and we chose to accept it) was to form the *perfect* Rotisserie League!

Crafty analysis told us that any league was only as good as its people and its rules. Because we're "People ... People who need People" people, we tackled the people part first.

We started with a simple premise: All Rotisserie Owners Are Created Equal. Then we dumped it. Egalitarianism is a fine and noble thing, but we'd have to put up with these guys (and maybe gals) in late-night trading sessions in smoke-filled rooms. We needed a special kind of player. So, we sat down and made two lists: "Owners We Like to Play With," and "Owners Who Suck."

The second list raised its hand first. For starters, no dickheads. Look, we're not starting a new branch of the Major League Baseball Players Association. Okay? And, no sociopaths. We're not playing Strat-O-Matic. And while we were at it, we opted against sitting at the table with a bunch of twitchy, sweating types who demand to play for full stakes but have to finish in the money to pay their rent. So, no deadbeats.

And—this was really important—no whiners. It's not that we don't care that if you hadn't bought Billy Ashley for $32 you might have been in the money. (We feel your pain.) It's just that we're still dealing with our own grief over spending a total of $98 on Dave Hollins, Marquis Grissom, and Steve Avery.

Also, no old college buddies who don't know the difference between Albert Belle and Albert Brooks, who think Piazza is a public square in an Italian village, and who won't trade unless it's to their fellow alumni. (The old Tom Glavine and Jeff Bagwell for Pat Gomez, Ryan Hawbitzel, and an Ultra pick because he's building for next year's trade.)

For sure, no one whose wife drops the phone with a tart, "Oh, dear, it's one of your little baseball friends," like you just asked her to sign our "Reinstate Bob Packwood" petition.

Finally, no hockey fans. Okay, you can be a fan, but no hockey season ticket holders. And don't even think of asking us to hurry up the draft because you've got great center ice seats for a hot playoff game between the Ducks and the Whales. On second thought, no hockey fans.

So, who would make up this brave new Roti-world? What sterling qualities were we looking for in ownership besides a love of tobacco juice and grass stains, combined with a solid TRW report? The truth is, we could deal with almost any non–hockey fan as long as one of them was strong enough, forthright enough, and stupid enough to be the **Commissioner**.

What makes a good Commissioner? Ah, if you asked us, we could write a book. Our Commissioner would have to be as virtuous as Honest Abe. No more worrying if the guy fielding the FAAB calls was cherry-picking the bids so he could slip in David Wells for $26. And we're tired of disputes being rough and bumpy; we're ready for a smoother ride. He'd need great steering in how he handled the group and come equipped with leather upholstery in his office's roomy conference room. Also, we needed someone who could form a bridge between two sides, never went on vacation, had way too much time on his hands, had ready access to a fax machine and a photocopier, liked talking on the phone, and, above all, would handle the daily nonstop traffic of player moves and trades without overheating or running out of gas.

In short, we were looking for Lincoln: The Man, The Car, The Tunnel.

Okay, we had ourselves and a Commissioner, at least on paper. But what about the rest? Besides a few good men (and women), we needed a certain special Roti-mix, beginning with a **Trader**. A straw to stir the drink. A guy who bounces around more than a Tim Wakefield knuckler. You know, a guy who's alone in first by 16 points in mid-August but still calls you at 9:52 on Sunday night because, heck, he's just gotta have Mesa as his third closer.

That would bring the league up to four. Since we're in a major league city, we had to have **Someone with Great Season Tickets**. And, damn it, every league needs a **Cubs Fan**. It's just not a Roti-draft unless someone wears a faded blue cap and bids Rey Sanchez up to twenty bucks. How about a couple of earnest **Rookies** to pluck. Plus, a really big guy named **Bear**. Finally, we needed at least one really funny guy, a **Comic**: After all, this is supposed to be fun. Isn't it? Well, someone told us it should be. Oh come on, it should be fun on occasion, shouldn't it? The hell with it, that's our job.

When we added it up, it all came down to this: We wanted to play with people we actually might want to hang with and share a brewski or two. Is that too much to ask? We thought not. Throw in a **Nice Guy** to finish last and we'd be happy.

The easy part was done. We knew who we wanted. We hadn't actually found anybody to join us. But conceptually we were batting 1.000, so now the real work began. We grabbed our chaw, stuck a big wad between our cheek and gums, and . . . immediately started gagging. (Have you ever actually *chewed* tobacco?) After we cleaned ourselves up, it was time to tackle the rules.

Attempting to fill the void left behind by the spirited "Tastes great! Less filling!" discussions that once occupied our lives, we started by sitting down and shouting at each other for a week over Rotisserie Ultra vs. Rotisserie Classic. Classic won, but only because Batterman is writing the final draft of this.

Next, overwhelmed by the enormity of our task, we decided to seek the counsel and wisdom of a better mind than ours. A games genius, a master of strategy, the Duke of Rules. Alex Trebek has an exclusive with Merv Griffin, so we called Glen "Iron Horse" Waggoner. "Son," he said to both of us, sounding like Spencer Tracy in *Boys Town*, "buy the book." We subsequently learned that this is what he says to everybody, no matter who they are or what they want.

Well, he was right. Did you know there's a lot of great stuff right there? Including, in the 1994 edition, a vigorous, insightful, and compelling article called "The K-Factor" by Mark Batterman about dumping the antiquated Ratio category and replacing it with Strikeouts, thereby making Rotisserie baseball more fun and challenging, while also restoring starting pitching to its rightful place of importance? Well, there is.

But we wanted more. A clear philosophy that expressed our own particular bent on this game we call Rotisserie. (Heck, that egalitarianism thing worked out okay.) So we channeled Abner Doubleday, Bart Giamatti, and Bo Diaz (don't ask us, it was a mystical experience) and came up with this: All things being equal, it should be possible for anyone to win this game. Pretty heavy, huh? But, you should be able to win it two different ways: by putting a winning team together at the Draft Table or by managing your way to the pennant during the season, through trades, savvy pick-ups, and pure dumb luck.

It's long been our pompous, holier-than-thou attitude that some Roti-rules keep the rich richer and poor poorer. No more. In this best of all possible Leagues, we would level the playing field, ease the anti-dumping rule, and allow for the sane replacement of any player, injured or not, who is clogging up your pipeline to the pennant.

The glue that holds this in place is The Revenue Neutral Rule. When

---

you claim a player out of free agency or off of waivers, why should you make a profit? Well, that's what happens when you use the $10 salary called for in the Official Rules. Ten smackeroos is a nice round number, but the average player should cost $12. (Okay, $260 divided by 23 players is $11.30. We rounded up a little. You caught us!)

By boosting the call-up salary by just two measly bucks these players become just a tad harder to keep. Since a few more players who are on the bubble are released, more players become available in the draft. Think about it: Chad Fonville at $10 . . . Chad Fonville at $12.

See what we mean? The richer the talent pool, the more opportunities for all teams at the auction draft. (Egalitarianism forever!) You don't have to be loaded going into the auction draft to be a winner coming out.

Now, we're not so radical as to say do away with Anti-Dumping. We are not immoral anarchists. But we don't have a problem saying, "Tweak the sucker." We just want to acknowledge the concept of supply and demand. Accordingly, "Asterisk Players" start at $30. "Asterisk Pitchers" start at $25. This allows for bottom feeders to belch up an over-priced gem or two to a contender at a price that is more realistic. Ha! Suddenly it's possible to trade for the pennant.

And finally, we conceived the "Bite It for $30 Rule." You've got Scott Cooper for $22. No, they're not saying "Cooooo!" They're saying "Booooo!" This guy stinks and he's killing your average! Big problem in Rotisserie Classic. No problem at all in Rotisserie Perfect. Just pony up thirty bucks, put Booper . . . ah, Cooper on waivers, and dip into the free agency pool for a real third baseman. Excuse us for sounding like George Steinbrenner, but if a hurt-you player doesn't have the courtesy to blow out a knee or a rotator cuff, we should be able to chuck his butt off our team, anytime we want. This helps everyone, whether you're chasing the flag or screwing the pooch.

It was time to play ball. The blueprint for Roti-greatness was in our hand! We picked up the phone and began our task. Two years later, we've survived baseball's Time of Troubles and two down-to-the-wire, hard-fought battles for our new league's flag—including a nightmare finish in the first year in which the Xtra Strength Anesons snatched the crown away from our new team, the K-Mark Shoppers, on the last day before the @#$%& strike.

"So," you're undoubtedly poised to exclaim, "you guys did it, you formed a more perfect union, you revamped the Official Rules, streamlined the game, opened it up, made it more egalitarian, found ten like-minded owners, and put together a Perfect Rotisserie League!"

Get real. We joined the 12-year-old California Dreaming League. Who has the time to form the perfect anything nowadays? Idealism was a fine thing in the '60s, but we're in the '90s now, Buckwheat.

Besides, it's a great group of guys, we hold the vaulted status of Roti-Stats League No. 103, and there's this guy, John Inferrera, who is not only crazy enough to be the Commissioner, he's an attorney with this great conference room. . . .

How to Spell R-E-L-I-E-F
by John Benson

It doesn't seem all that long ago that I bought Doug Jones for $5.

He was a fading 30-year-old journeyman with a grand total of nine major league saves and a ten-year resume that bore an eerie resemblance to a Trailways bus schedule. Facing early retirement if he didn't figure out some way to get batters out, he had given up any thought of adding velocity to his lukewarm fastball. He decided instead to concentrate on adding deception to his change-up, which already moved like molasses.

The idea worked. Jones found a place in the Cleveland bullpen in late 1987, and then achieved dominance at Ponce in Puerto Rican winter ball, crafting a 0.51 ERA and even becoming a strikeout king in a league where everybody swung at everything. For five bucks I got 37 saves in 1988 and 75 more in 1989 and 1990.

Successes like that tend to remain eternally fresh in your memory, while mistakes like paying $16 for Jim Traber—which I did in the same draft— get quickly erased from the gray cells to make room for more vital information, like dental appointments and things you meant to say to your boss but didn't.

Scouting for saves paid off big time back in 1988. *Baseball America* was just being widely discovered. Winter league stats, if they attracted any scrutiny at all, were regarded with suspicion. There was no *Baseball Tonight*. *Baseball Weekly* wouldn't appear on the newsstands for another three years. Heck, even the *Benson Baseball Monthly* didn't debut until 1989.

People actually had secrets going into their drafts!

Times have changed. If you enter draft day 1996 with a bullpen strategy based on finding a 30-save guy cheap, *i.e.*, for under $20, you are going to have your heart broken, even in an "easy" league. Everybody now has access to so much of the same information—such as who got saves during September last year, and who just blossomed in winter ball—what you need now is a better way of using all that commonly available information.

The emergence of more and better information isn't the only big change that's affected bullpen strategies. The other major development is a wider understanding of Rotisserie economics. Different people react to these realities in different ways, but certain fundamental truths ought to be self-evident to everyone:

(1) Saves are the scarcest of all Rotisserie scoring commodities. One win for a pitching staff is precious enough to keep owners awake until the final West Coast box score comes across the AP wire. But a save is twice as rare. Every game produces a win for some pitcher, but only about half of all games yield a save.

(2) Saves are concentrated in a small number of pitchers. While wins

are spread among five starters on each team, with a significant trickle-down to various middle innings toilers, saves are handed—through the control of the manager—almost exclusively to one or two anointed closers.

(3) The combination of points (1) and (2) means that ace relievers are—surprise! surprise!—extremely valuable in Rotisserie baseball.

You would howl with laughter if I tried to convince you that a 30-save man is worth as much as a starter who gets 60 wins, so I won't. Yet the possibility of a Grade A closer being worth two or three times as much as a good starter isn't really all that far-fetched, and the notion underlies our auction draft behavior. There are some esoteric concepts at work, such as the diminishing marginal utility of a save after you get near the top of that category, and mundane concerns like the minimum innings rule. But it's an economic fact, one experientially verified, that ace relievers commonly sell for $35 or more, while starters—Greg Maddux and Randy Johnson notably excepted—rarely crack the $25 ceiling.

(4) Finally, and most troublesome, if you follow points (1), (2), and (3) and pay the logical price of $40 for a stud reliever who then gets a sore arm, your whole year is ruined. Ask anyone who had Duane Ward in 1994. This dilemma unfolded gradually, giving astute Rotisserians time to formulate and test various new strategies reacting to it. People often ask me which of these new strategies works best. The short answer is that it depends on what your league is like, and whether your goal is to finish first (or bust while trying), or just to be respectable year after year.

Here are the major theories, the circumstances in which they may be useful, and some advice for implementing each:

1. Pay Full Sticker Price

Getting saves the old-fashioned way, by paying for them at retail, is still the surest method for many teams. For example, if you have a strong freeze list and plenty of money to spend, why scrimp on the saves department? Paying the full price for the best available ace can also work nicely if your draft has a large supply of ace relievers being returned to the available pool—fully half of the supply/demand function will be in your favor. Finally, the method that appears to be the least imaginative may in fact be a clever contrarian policy, if enough owners in your league convince themselves to adopt one of several "dump saves" strategies. Prices will drop when everyone flees the saves market, leaving bargains behind.

Once you have made the budget decision to shell out for top quality, the next issue is minimizing risk. Obviously you prefer a pitcher who has never been on the disabled list. That caution wouldn't have saved you from Duane Ward's shocking collapse, but it would have helped you avoid Bryan Harvey and numerous other expensive mistakes of recent years.

Finally, make sure your top gun is viewed as such by his real major league team. Choose a well-established veteran with a fat long-term contract, and you won't get stuck with too many Ken Ryans or Brad Clontzes.

2. Dump Saves I: The $5 Bullpen

Seeing that it takes about $45 to score big in the saves category, and noting that, with eight categories to cover and $260 to spend, $32.50 per category seems like the right budget, many owners would just as soon put as little as $5 into their bullpen, and shift $30 or $40 into a more secure market like star hitters. The $1 relievers can be low-risk lefty-lefty matchup specialists like Rick Honeycutt (much safer than your typical $1 starter). And you might even get lucky; Tony Castillo went for $1 in most leagues last year and ended up with a nice pile of saves. In the National League, take any Braves reliever for $1; they all get used wisely, pick up occasional wins, and sometimes emerge like Greg McMichael did in 1993.

One caution for any "dump saves" strategy (or any dump-a-category method) is that relying on a subset of categories will work only in a *tight* league. If your league has a diversity of owners ranging from sharks to fish, and the winner typically accrues 75 to 80 points, you need to score something in every category. Giving up saves may help you finish third, but not first. In a balanced league where 58 or 59 points can take the Yoo-Hoo most years, then dumping a category can make more sense.

3. Dump Saves II: The Nine-Man Rotation

Following the same logic as the no-saves reliever method, this strategy differs by taking the money from saves and putting it into more and better starting pitchers, instead of hitting. Personally, I think this method gets more credit than it deserves. It works best in leagues that deviate from the Standard Eight categories by adding strikeouts or innings pitched, and/or by taking away Ratio and replacing it with one of the common pitching volume measures.

The big problem, especially in a league that uses both ERA and Ratio, is that those $1 filler starters are likely to kill you. In every case I've seen, where someone pursued this strategy and won, it has coincided with one or more of the following phenomena: (a) hitting so strong that mediocre pitching doesn't matter, (b) having Greg Maddux, or (c) outrageous luck in choosing $1 starters. In all three of these situations, the deliberate pouring of more money into starting pitchers has been irrelevant.

Yes, the owner pursued the strategy. And yes, he won. But the two weren't necessarily connected.

4. The Setup Strategy

Here's one I like! Rather than chasing one of those $40 aces, you can buy five high-quality setup men for an average of $5 to $6 each. You can save $10 or $20, stay under the $32.50 per category budget, help your ERA and Ratio immensely, and give yourself five chances to get lucky in saves. The nicest thing about top setup men is that they often turn into closers, giving you both the saves you need now and some gem keepers for the future. The likes of Dennis Eckersley, Duane Ward, and Rob Dibble were in this group not so long ago, as were Rod Beck, Robb Nen, and Trevor Hoffman more recently.

I have it on good authority, in fact, that the Farley Grangers of

Tony's Italian Kitchen League in New York once threw a $1 middle-innings reliever and occasional starter into a mid-season deal with the Waggoner Wheels. The pitcher in question? Dennis Eckersley, the year he made the transformation to closer.

If you plan to pursue the Setup Strategy, look for hard throwers with a strikeout/walk ratio over 3:1, and you can sit back and wait for nature to take its course. Better still, ring up the Farley Grangers and talk trade.

5. Let's Make a Deal
One of the commonest misconceptions in Rotissestrategy is that you have to field a complete team on Opening Day. In Rotisserie you can come out of the draft with no speed, or no power, or no starting pitchers, or even no bullpen, and fill in the gaps later. There is no prize for "balance" in June. If the price of saves is too high on draft day, then some other commodity must be selling cheap—and that's what you want to buy. So you can stock up on hitters, or starting pitchers, or whatever is being neglected, and trade your surplus later. And if you really want that $45 ace reliever, it can be a lot easier to pick him up after the owner who bought him has fallen out of contention, because he didn't consider any of these alternative strategies.

6. Have a Lot of Pure, Blind, Dumb Luck.
Of all the strategies I have tried in over a decade of playing Rotisserie baseball, this one works best.

CHEAP RELIEF IN 1996

You won't find any Dennis Eckersleys for $1 in these two lists—at least I don't think you will—but you will find pitchers who will pick up some wins, post good numbers, and notch a few saves as setup men or number two closers. And each is good enough to step up and be the main man if his team's designated closer falters or is injured.

NATIONAL LEAGUE

Ron Villone (Padres)
A first-round pick in 1992, he made conversion from starter to reliever by gaining command of a blow-'em-away fastball. Looked shaky at times in majors last year, but logged 0.61 ERA and 13 saves in Triple-A tune-up. He's the reason for all the trade rumors concerning Trevor Hoffman.

Ricky Bottalico (Phillies)
A "closer of the future" who's moving steadily toward his destination. For long stretches in second half of 1995, he was clearly more effective than the anointed closer, Heath Slocumb. Manager Jim Fregosi didn't think it wise to change their roles in midstream, but that was last year.

Tim Scott (Expos)
Dodgers gave up on him in 1990 when he didn't show enough progress coming back from arm surgery. It's taken time, but he's recovered completely, now throwing well over 90 MPH and keeping hitters off balance with a good splitter. He's got closer stuff and just needs an opportunity.

Xavier Hernandez (Reds)
Slated to be Yankees' closer in 1994, the X-man fell on hard times—his control deserted him after an elbow bruise and hitters feasted. Last year he regained command of his good splitter. Look for a sackful of wins and a few saves in a setup role he's proved he can handle.

Doug Henry (Mets)
A one-pitch closer for the Brewers, he lost his job when the fastball became a little too straight and much too predictable. Now he's added a slider, a forkball, and a straight change. Also, the fastball's moving again. Another thing to consider: he's eight years younger than John Franco.

AMERICAN LEAGUE

Troy Percival (Angels)
Big guy who seems to have found control and confidence to go with his big fastball. The only factor separating Percival from 30 saves in 1995 was the presence of Lee Smith in the Angels bullpen. Pretty big presence, but surely Smith is going to get old one of these years. Isn't he?

Stan Belinda (Red Sox)
So long as Rick Aguilera's around, Belinda's the second fiddle in Sox bullpen—and that's just as well. The former Pirates stalwart and Royals washout has closer's stuff but not the makeup: he performs better in setup role. On a team like Boston, that translates into 7–10 wins and a handful of saves.

Jeff Nelson (Mariners)
Finishing a long apprenticeship in a setup role, Nelson has blossomed nicely. The side-armer has been an effective closer in winter ball and is ready for that job in the majors when given a chance. Resurgence of Norm Charlton blocks his road to becoming Seattle ace, but he's a great No. 2.

Mike Timlin (Blue Jays)
When Duane Ward first developed arm trouble in 1994, Timlin looked like the natural choice to take the closer's job in Toronto. Although it turned into a long struggle, he was finally doing that job in the final days of 1995. Could be a big factor in Toronto's bounce-back this season.

Matt Whiteside (Rangers)
Touted as a "closer of the future" way back in 1992, Whiteside took a couple steps backward before finally taking a step forward in 1995. He has a history of arm problems when used excessively, but others (like Robb Nen) have come through similar struggles to arrive at a happy ending.

Final Innings
by Sally Small

Baseball-team "appreciations" have become a standard late-season P.R. ritual, designed to bring out a few hundred extra fans on the final weekend home date, but the ceremonies out at the sunstruck Oakland Coliseum a week ago Sunday were something else. The appreciation was not for the fans or the team but for its owners, the Walter Haas family, who for the past fifteen years have been the flip side of George Steinbrenner: a shining model of altruistic, self-effacing, and successful sports-franchise ownership. Now the A's have been sold to a couple of businessmen, Steve Schott and Ken Hofmann, and although the team will stay put, the crowd of thirty thousand, one hundred twelve fans seemed to know that they were probably saying goodbye to a tenor of baseball enjoyment that had been set by Walter A. Haas, Jr., himself, the shy and smiling Levi Strauss proprietor, who bought the club in 1981 as a means of doing something positive for the economy and the spirits of the city. Haas, who had been in declining health for months, was not present, but his son, Walter J. Haas, who is the team's chairman and chief executive officer, was forgiven some tears when the club's gift to its owner was announced: every man and woman in the Athletics' front office (well over a hundred); the manager, Tony LaRussa, and his seven coaches; and all thirty-two players on the roster had pledged fifteen hours of service apiece to the Oakland community.

The A's won a World Series and three league pennants during Haas's stewardship, but with him, pleasure in the day always outranked winning, and this game (against the Minnesota Twins) had the atmosphere of a company picnic. The players sat on folding chairs in the infield, with their wives beside them and their younger children on their laps. The stands were also crowded with families and kids, and there were plenty of large baseball caps resting on small, sunburned ears, and ponytails poking out the backs. The Athletics' home-uniform cap has a yellow bill, and the youngsters in the lower stands, seen from the upper deck, looked like flocks of ducklings waving enormous baseball gloves at each nearby foul ball. In the bleachers and outer stands, there were a dozen-odd hand-lettered signs thanking the Haas family: "THANKS FOR HAASPITALITY," "HAASTA-LA-VISTA," "HAAS #1," and the like.

The Oakland Athletics have retired only two players' numbers (as against the Yankees' overbearing thirteen), and when the newest yellow jersey was unveiled on the right-field wall, across from Catfish Hunter's No. 27 and Rollie Fingers's No. 34 in left, there was no number on it at all. But the name "Haas" spelled out across the back in green letters brought the crowd to its feet in a spontaneous roar. The players stood and cheered, too—and in an instant, it seemed, everyone was up again and yelling, this time for Mark McGwire's four-hundred-and-sixty-five-foot home run in the second inning, *way* back into the left-field bleachers: a shining meteor sent up, everyone knew, for Walter Haas. Three days later, he died.

The Rules, Simplified

1. Rotisserie League teams are made up of real, live major league baseball players who are selected at an auction draft that takes place at the beginning of the season (typically on the first weekend following Opening Day).

2. Each team in a Rotisserie League is composed of 23 players taken from the active rosters of National or American League teams. A Rotisserie League drawn from National League or American League players should have 12 teams. You can, however, have fewer teams.

3. A team consists of five outfielders, two catchers, one second baseman, one shortstop, one middle infielder (either 2B or SS), one first baseman, one third baseman, one corner man (1B or 3B), one utility man (NL) or designated hitter (AL), and nine pitchers.

4. Players are purchased at an open auction. Spending is limited to $260 per team. (If you don't want to use money, call them units or pocorobas or whatever. The point is resource allocation.) Teams may spend less. The first bidder opens the auction with a minimum bid of $1 for any player. The bidding then proceeds around the room (at minimum increments of $1) until only one bidder is left. The process is repeated, with successive owners introducing players to be bid on, until every team has a complement of 23 players.

5. A player is eligible to be drafted for any position at which he appeared in 20 or more games the preceding year. If he did not appear in 20 games at any one position, he is eligible for the position at which he appeared the most times. Once the season starts, a player qualifies for a position by playing it once. Multiple eligibility is okay.

6. Trading is permissible from Auction Draft Day until midnight August 31. After every trade, both teams must be whole—that is, they must have the same number of active players at each position that they had before the trade.

7. If a major league player is put on the disabled list, sent to the minors, traded to the other league, or released, he may be replaced by a player

---

from the free agent pool of unowned talent. Replacement must be made by position. The original player may either be released or placed on his Rotisserie team's reserve list. A team may not release, reserve, or waive a player without replacing him with another active player.

8. Cumulative team performance is tabulated in four offensive and four pitching categories:

   - Composite batting average (BA)
   - Total home runs (HR)
   - Total runs batted in (RBI)
   - Total stolen bases (SB)
   - Composite earned run average (ERA)
   - Total wins (W)
   - Total saves (S)
   - Composite ratio: walks (BB) + hits (H) ÷ innings pitched (IP)

9. Teams are ranked from first to last in each of the eight categories. For example, in a 12-team league, the first-place team receives 12 points, the second-place team 11 points, on down to one point for last place. The team with the most points wins the pennant.

10. Prize money is distributed as follows: 50% for first place, 20% for second, 15% for third, 10% for fourth, and 5% for fifth. Even more important, the owner of the winning team receives a bottle of Yoo-Hoo—poured over his/her head. (See Chapter 7, Postgame Shower, pages 309–313.)

●   ●   ●

"Do I have to play for money?" No. We do, but unlike the big league version, Rotisserie League Baseball can be played for very little money, or none at all. You can play for pennies, Cracker Jack prizes, or nothing at all and still have fun. Just be sure to keep the ratio of "acquisition units" to players at 260:23 for each team on Auction Draft Day.

"What do I do if it's May 15 and I've just gotten around to reading this book? Wait till next year?" Absolutely not! That's second-division thinking! You can start anytime! Put your league together, hold your auction draft, and deduct all stats that accrue prior to that glorious day. Next year, start from scratch.

The rest of your questions are dealt with in the pages that follow. We hope. If not, write us c/o **Rotisserie League Baseball Association, 82 Wall Street, Suite 1105, New York, NY 10005**. Or call at **800-676-7684**. We'll do our best to get you playing what we still modestly call The Greatest Game for Baseball Fans Since Baseball.

2

Scouting Report

1996 Player Ratings

The only bad thing about the 1995 season was that it was too short. Yes, we were deprived of Spring Training. We had to put up with a threatened insult known as "Replacement Baseball." And it did take most of us a good little while before we got over being pissed off and started being fans again. Even so, by any measure except length, 1995 was a Hall of Fame season.

Greg Maddux pitched better than any right-hander since Walter Johnson—and Randy Johnson pitched as well as Greg Maddux, once you factor in what the DH does to an AL pitcher's ERA. And what about Mike Mussina and Pete Schourek? Jose Mesa? Mark Wohlers?

Dante Bichette had an MVP-calibre year—who cares that it would have only been a journeyman's year had he played his home games anywhere but Coors Field? Jay Buhner had the quietest huge season in modern memory, while teammate Edgar Martinez led the league in batting average and on-base average. Matt Williams hit 62 homers in 161 games—it's just too damned bad they were spread over three seasons. Kenny Lofton was the most thrilling player in the World Series—next to teammate Omar Vizquel, who blatantly defied the law of gravity in turning double plays. Watching Mo Vaughn strike out was more exciting than watching most guys hit home runs—good thing, too, because Mo's 150 Ks led both leagues.

You had great comeback seasons (Ron Gant, Tim Wakefield), great rookie seasons (Chipper Jones, Hideo Nomo, Garrett Anderson), and break-out seasons from new triple-threat stars (Reggie Sanders, Tim Salmon).

True, there were a few blemishes. Tony Gwynn slumped to .368. Barry Bonds had such a lousy year for him—33 HR, 104 RBI, 31 SB, .294 BA—that he talked about retiring. And we'll never know what heights the All-Bad Breaks team—Junior Griffey, Jeff Bagwell, Matt Williams, Gary Sheffield, Mike Piazza—might have reached if they hadn't missed 291 games.

Speaking of Mike Piazza, he pretty clearly established that he's the best-hitting catcher in baseball history, didn't he? (Yes, *including* Johnny Bench.)

Albert Belle became the first member of the 50-50 Club with 50 homers and 52 doubles. Mark McGwire had the best HR/AB of anyone in baseball history. (Yes, *including* Babe Ruth.) Eddie Murray got his 3,000th hit. Don Mattingly got a taste of the postseason. And Cal Ripken played in a lot of games.

The Wild Card and another round of playoffs had a lot of people, us included, worried that baseball was going to turn into hockey. Instead, we saw the most exciting playoff series in who-remembers-when, and . . . (What's that? You didn't get to see the Mariners-Yankees series? Guess that's why they call it the Regional Pastime) . . . and the two best teams in baseball *still* ended up in the World Series.

The baseball year began with Tom Glavine hearing boos every time he took the mound in Atlanta because of his role in the strike. And it ended with Tom Glavine, World Series MVP, parading down Peachtree Street to a standing ovation.

That pretty much sums up the 1995 season. And now?

Let's play two.

NEW! POST ALL-STAR STATS!

Want to know who finished strong last season? Who took a nosedive? Uncertain about keeping a veteran player and want to see if he showed signs of slipping? Want to find out whether a certain rookie who started hot and then went cold warmed back up in the second half?

You came to the right place. This year you'll find **Post All-Star Stats** for all position players and pitchers evaluated in this chapter—yet another scouting tool to help you build a Yoo-Hoo team.

Salary projections are predicated on a start-from-scratch auction draft. In continuing leagues that carry over players from year to year, auction day prices will be skewed by the quality and quantity of available talent.

Players traded from one league to the other during the season appear in the league in which they finished the year. Thus, look for Bobby Bonilla among AL corners and David Wells among NL starters.

Once again, former RLBA GM John Hassan was in charge of American League scouting. If all Red Sox players seem wildly overpriced and ridiculously overhyped, blame him.

STATS, Inc. is responsible for the numbers in this chapter, for the Rotisserie Stat-Pak in Chapter 3, and for the final 1995 averages at the end of the book. The STATS team, with Steve Moyers leading off and John Dewan batting cleanup, is strictly major league. Check out page 264 for a full list of their publications and services, all of which will help you solve the really important mysteries of life.

HITS. RUNS. NO ERRORS.
ROTI•STATS
CALL 800-676-7684

Behind the Plate

NATIONAL LEAGUE

Catchers
pp. 27–41

Corners
pp. 41–62

Infield
pp. 63–82

Outfield
pp. 83–113

DH
pp. 114–118

Starters
pp. 119–157

Relievers
pp. 157–193

BRAD AUSMUS   Age 26/R $11

The Padres still think he can be a 10- to 15-homer kind of hitter. If that ever happens, he becomes a steal. And speaking of steals, his 16 stolen bases last season were 13 more than the next-best NL catcher. *That's* why Rotisserie hearts go pitter-patter when his name comes up in the draft.

Year	Team	Lg.	Pos.	G	AB	R	H	HR	RBI	SB	BA
1993	San Diego	NL	C	49	160	18	41	5	12	2	.256
1994	San Diego	NL	C	101	327	45	82	7	24	5	.251
1995	San Diego	NL	C	103	328	44	96	5	34	16	.293
Post All-Star				54	167	22	50	4	22	10	.299

PAT BORDERS   Age 32/R $1

The sun keeps setting on former north-of-the-border heroes like this one, who has gone from 1992 World Series MVP to likely career oblivion.

Year	Team	Lg.	Pos.	G	AB	R	H	HR	RBI	SB	BA
1992	Toronto	AL	C	138	480	47	116	13	53	1	.242
1993	Toronto	AL	C	138	488	38	124	9	55	2	.254
1994	Toronto	AL	C	85	295	24	73	3	26	1	.247
1995	Kansas City	AL	C	52	143	14	33	4	13	0	.231
1995	Houston	NL	C	11	35	1	4	0	0	0	.114
Post All-Star				27	77	3	12	0	1	0	.156

DARREN DAULTON   Age 34/L $16

Unless your group medical insurance is a whole lot better than ours, factor in major DL time to the price you bid for him. He celebrated a season that never got started with reconstructive surgery to one knee, the 8th operation to another, an exploratory procedure on his shoulder, and a bone scan of his wrist. What did you expect, Buffalo wings from Hooters? A class act and significant run producer, he has also become a major physical risk.

Year	Team	Lg.	Pos.	G	AB	R	H	HR	RBI	SB	BA
1992	Philadelphia	NL	C	145	485	80	131	27	109	11	.270
1993	Philadelphia	NL	C	147	510	90	131	24	105	5	.257
1994	Philadelphia	NL	C	69	257	43	77	15	56	4	.300
1995	Philadelphia	NL	C	98	342	44	85	9	55	3	.249
Post All-Star				38	129	15	38	3	24	0	.295

STEVE DECKER   Age 30/R $1

Backup catchers in Florida aren't likely to produce much for the remainder of this century. For the reason, see CHARLES JOHNSON below.

Year	Team	Lg.	Pos.	G	AB	R	H	HR	RBI	SB	BA
1992	San Francisco	NL	C	15	43	3	7	0	1	0	.163
1993	Florida	NL	C	8	15	0	0	0	1	0	0.000
1995	Florida	NL	C	51	133	12	30	3	13	1	.226
Post All-Star				34	100	9	23	3	12	0	.230

ANGELO ENCARNACION   Age 22/R $1

The Pirates think he's destined to be no better than a backup, especially with prospect Jason Kendall close to being ready. But the Pirates have been wrong before. And anyway, wouldn't it be a kick to get up at your draft and let his melodious name roll off your lips?

Year	Team	Lg.	Pos.	G	AB	R	H	HR	RBI	SB	BA
1995	Pittsburgh	NL	C	58	159	18	36	2	10	1	.226
Post All-Star				44	123	14	23	2	7	1	.187

TONY EUSEBIO   Age 28/R $12

No one knew. Not us, for sure. Not even the Astros. "Hell, if we knew he was this good, we never would have got Wilkins," said a contrite Houston official. Yeah, we liked his bat well enough season before last to pencil him as the Astros' starter last year. But we didn't figure on a .300 BA or on the run production. Indeed, what impressed the most was that he held his offensive production steady throughout the season. And the scouts think there will be more power down the road. Now they tell us.

Year	Team	Lg.	Pos.	G	AB	R	H	HR	RBI	SB	BA
1994	Houston	NL	C	55	159	18	47	5	30	0	.296
1995	Houston	NL	C	113	368	46	110	6	58	0	.299
Post All-Star				62	209	25	60	4	29	0	.287

DARRIN FLETCHER   Age 29/L $11

All you need to know about the Expos' predicament is that they fear this solid, slightly above-average catcher might be too expensive to keep. Isn't it time to admit that there is no word for baseball in French and bid Montreal a fond *adieu*?

Year	Team	Lg.	Pos.	G	AB	R	H	HR	RBI	SB	BA
1992	Montreal	NL	C	83	222	13	54	2	26	0	.243
1993	Montreal	NL	C	133	396	33	101	9	60	0	.255
1994	Montreal	NL	C	94	285	28	74	10	57	0	.260
1995	Montreal	NL	C	110	350	42	100	11	45	0	.286
Post All-Star				59	194	27	57	5	23	0	.294

JOE GIRARDI   Age 31/R $9

Hidden amid all those mile-high bombers, he is in a perfect spot to provide some of those quiet numbers that make the shrewd shopper look like a genius.

Year	Team	Lg.	Pos.	G	AB	R	H	HR	RBI	SB	BA
1992	Chicago	NL	C	91	270	19	73	1	12	0	.270
1993	Colorado	NL	C	86	310	35	90	3	31	6	.290
1994	Colorado	NL	C	93	330	47	91	4	34	3	.276
1995	Colorado	NL	C	125	462	63	121	8	55	3	.262
Post All-Star				65	236	35	54	6	25	1	.229

CARLOS HERNANDEZ   Age 28/R $1

You've spent serious money on Mike Piazza and have a buck left for his backup. So take the plunge and bleed Dodger Blue.

Year	Team	Lg.	Pos.	G	AB	R	H	HR	RBI	SB	BA
1992	Los Angeles	NL	C	69	173	11	45	3	17	0	.260
1993	Los Angeles	NL	C	50	99	6	25	2	7	0	.253
1994	Los Angeles	NL	C	32	64	6	14	2	6	0	.219
1995	Los Angeles	NL	C	45	94	3	14	2	8	0	.149
Post All-Star				16	31	1	6	1	3	0	.194

Catchers
pp. 27–41

Corners
pp. 41–62

Infield
pp. 63–82

Outfield
pp. 83–113

DH
pp. 114–118

Starters
pp. 119–157

Relievers
pp. 157–193

TODD HUNDLEY   Age 26/B $13

Only injuries have kept him from being mentioned in the same breath with all the other young Mets who are being ticketed for stardom. He is the best of all worlds—a switch-hitting catcher with 25-homer potential. And what's utterly startling is last year's BA: for Ty Cobb's sake, this guy came into last season batting .219 lifetime! If he can stay off the DL, Hundley takes over from Darren Daulton as the best power-hitting catcher in baseball—except for that pizza guy in Hollywood, of course.

Year	Team	Lg.	Pos.	G	AB	R	H	HR	RBI	SB	BA
1992	New York	NL	C	123	358	32	75	7	32	3	.209
1993	New York	NL	C	130	417	40	95	11	53	1	.228
1994	New York	NL	C	91	291	45	69	16	42	2	.237
1995	New York	NL	C	90	275	39	77	15	51	1	.280
Post All-Star				32	102	16	32	3	15	0	.314

BRIAN JOHNSON   Age 28/R $1

The wrong Johnson.

Year	Team	Lg.	Pos.	G	AB	R	H	HR	RBI	SB	BA
1994	San Diego	NL	C	36	93	7	23	3	16	0	.247
1995	San Diego	NL	C	68	207	20	52	3	29	0	.251
Post All-Star				34	103	11	29	0	11	0	.282

CHARLES JOHNSON   Age 24/R $9

The right Johnson. He's one major reason why we still think that a few years from now the Marlins—not the Rockies—will be the better of the two expansion teams. Johnson's already so good a catcher that the Marlins can afford to be patient while he develops into a 20-homer, 80-RBI offensive player.

Year	Team	Lg.	Pos.	G	AB	R	H	HR	RBI	SB	BA
1994	Florida	NL	C	4	11	5	5	1	4	0	.455
1995	Florida	NL	C	97	315	40	79	11	39	0	.251
Post All-Star				38	126	17	40	5	17	0	.317

TIM LAKER   Age 26/R $1

When you leaf through the *Baseball Register* and the team notes and the media guides and the scouting reports for some added nugget of information that will help you make a pinpoint evaluation of a player, and you discover a catcher who has led three different minor leagues in errors and/or passed balls on four separate occasions, and you further discover that he has never established that he could hit for power or average, you cannot help but reach the conclusion, albeit reluctantly, that the guy is a stiff.

Year	Team	Lg.	Pos.	G	AB	R	H	HR	RBI	SB	BA
1992	Montreal	NL	C	28	46	8	10	0	4	1	.217
1993	Montreal	NL	C	43	86	3	17	0	7	2	.198
1995	Montreal	NL	C	64	141	17	33	3	20	0	.234
Post All-Star				30	72	9	21	2	7	0	.292

MIKE LIEBERTHAL   Age 24/R $1

With Darren Daulton a big unknown because his knees are made of oatmeal, the Phillies might have to catch this guy a lot more than they want to. Everybody knows that he's never going to produce Daulton-like numbers. What should worry you (and the Phils) is that there is a strong chance he might not even produce Carlos Hernandez–like numbers.

Year	Team	Lg.	Pos.	G	AB	R	H	HR	RBI	SB	BA
1994	Philadelphia	NL	C	24	79	6	21	1	5	0	.266
1995	Philadelphia	NL	C	16	47	1	12	0	4	0	.255
Post All-Star				15	46	1	12	0	4	0	.261

JAVY LOPEZ   Age 25/R $16

All you need to hear are the words of a NL general manager who said, "If you take Piazza out of the equation because he's from another planet, the best young catcher in baseball is Javy Lopez." We heartily agree.

Year	Team	Lg.	Pos.	G	AB	R	H	HR	RBI	SB	BA
1992	Atlanta	NL	C	9	16	3	6	0	2	0	.375
1993	Atlanta	NL	C	8	16	1	6	1	2	0	.375
1994	Atlanta	NL	C	80	277	27	68	13	35	0	.245
1995	Atlanta	NL	C	100	333	37	105	14	51	0	.315
Post All-Star				46	158	21	57	7	26	0	.361

KIRT MANWARING   Age 30/R $3

Just an average player who will never get better.

Year	Team	Lg.	Pos.	G	AB	R	H	HR	RBI	SB	BA
1992	San Francisco	NL	C	109	349	24	85	4	26	2	.244
1993	San Francisco	NL	C	130	432	48	119	5	49	1	.275
1994	San Francisco	NL	C	97	316	30	79	1	29	1	.250
1995	San Francisco	NL	C	118	379	21	95	4	36	1	.251
Post All-Star				62	205	11	52	3	21	0	.254

CHARLIE O'BRIEN   Age 34/R $6

For two years, he has been Greg Maddux's designated catcher, which is as good as it gets. You sit there, you put out your mitt, and he hits it every time. You don't have to worry about base runners to throw out. And the game is usually over in around two and a half hours. No wonder Charlie hits so many home runs in so few at-bats. He's the most relaxed person in the majors.

Year	Team	Lg.	Pos.	G	AB	R	H	HR	RBI	SB	BA
1992	New York	NL	C	68	156	15	33	2	13	0	.212
1993	New York	NL	C	67	188	15	48	4	23	1	.255
1994	Atlanta	NL	C	51	152	24	37	8	28	0	.243
1995	Atlanta	NL	C	67	198	18	45	9	23	0	.227
Post All-Star				40	118	7	23	4	10	0	.195

TOM PAGNOZZI   Age 33/R $4

Said one Cardinals executive late last season, "Geez, Pagnozzi makes Danny Sheaffer look like Johnny Bench."

Year	Team	Lg.	Pos.	G	AB	R	H	HR	RBI	SB	BA
1992	St. Louis	NL	C	139	485	33	121	7	44	2	.249
1993	St. Louis	NL	C	92	330	31	85	7	41	1	.258
1994	St. Louis	NL	C	70	243	21	66	7	40	0	.272
1995	St. Louis	NL	C	62	219	17	47	2	15	0	.215
Post All-Star				10	34	2	5	1	4	0	.147

Catchers
pp. 27–41

Corners
pp. 41–62

Infield
pp. 63–82

Outfield
pp. 83–113

DH
pp. 114–118

Starters
pp. 119–157

Relievers
pp. 157–193

MARK PARENT   Age 34/R $5

We don't get it. We really don't get it. Parent comes up when Slaught goes down, hits 14 homers, and is "designated for reassignment"—a shoo-in for the Euphemism Hall of Fame, by the way—when Sluggo finally comes back. Nothing against Sluggo, but we weren't aware that the Pirates were so power-packed that they could afford to ditch a guy who could deliver 15 dingers in part-time duty from the catcher's hole. How many NL catchers hit as many as 14 homers last year? Three, that's how many, none of whom were "designated for reassignment." And Parent wasn't through for the year: his "reassignment" eventually landed him with the Cubs, for whom he hit 3 more dingers. Here's a guy with 25 homers *lifetime* in parts of nine major league seasons coming into last year, and he hits 18? You gotta figure the ball was juiced when Parent came to bat, otherwise we don't get it, we really don't get it. (P.S.: We don't see him doing it again.)

Year	Team	Lg.	Pos.	G	AB	R	H	HR	RBI	SB	BA
1992	Baltimore	AL	C	17	34	4	8	2	4	0	.235
1993	Baltimore	AL	C	22	54	7	14	4	12	0	.259
1994	Chicago	NL	C	44	99	8	26	3	16	0	.263
1995	Pittsburgh	NL	C	69	233	25	54	15	33	0	.232
1995	Chicago	NL	C	12	32	5	8	3	5	0	.250
Post All-Star				39	130	12	25	7	13	0	.192

MIKE PIAZZA   Age 27/R $40

One of the four or five best players in the game. Enjoy.

Year	Team	Lg.	Pos.	G	AB	R	H	HR	RBI	SB	BA
1992	Los Angeles	NL	C	21	69	5	16	1	7	0	.232
1993	Los Angeles	NL	C	149	547	81	174	35	112	3	.318
1994	Los Angeles	NL	C	107	405	64	129	24	92	1	.319
1995	Los Angeles	NL	C	112	434	82	150	32	93	1	.346
Post All-Star				70	272	50	89	19	56	1	.327

TODD PRATT   Age 29/R $1

Arf.

Year	Team	Lg.	Pos.	G	AB	R	H	HR	RBI	SB	BA
1992	Philadelphia	NL	C	16	46	6	13	2	10	0	.283
1993	Philadelphia	NL	C	33	87	8	25	5	13	0	.287
1994	Philadelphia	NL	C	28	102	10	20	2	9	0	.196
1995	Chicago	NL	C	25	60	3	8	0	4	0	.133
Post All-Star				5	15	1	2	0	2	0	.133

JEFF REED   Age 33/L $1

Arf-Arf.

Year	Team	Lg.	Pos.	G	AB	R	H	HR	RBI	SB	BA
1992	Cincinnati	NL	C	15	25	2	4	0	2	0	.160
1993	San Francisco	NL	C	66	119	10	31	6	12	0	.261
1994	San Francisco	NL	C	50	103	11	18	1	7	0	.175
1995	San Francisco	NL	C	66	113	12	30	0	9	0	.265
Post All-Star				34	54	3	14	0	5	0	.259

BENITO SANTIAGO   Age 31/R $9

He will never be the perennial All-Star we all once thought he would be.
And he might be one of those guys who needs to look for a new team every
couple of years. But Santiago can still put up some decent stats, even if used
in intermittent duty.

Year	Team	Lg.	Pos.	G	AB	R	H	HR	RBI	SB	BA
1992	San Diego	NL	C	106	386	37	97	10	42	2	.251
1993	Florida	NL	C	139	469	49	108	13	50	10	.230
1994	Florida	NL	C	101	337	35	92	11	41	1	.273
1995	Cincinnati	NL	C	81	266	40	76	11	44	2	.286
Post All-Star				66	212	33	57	8	37	2	.269

SCOTT SERVAIS   Age 28/R $8

Wrigley Field might just be the place for him to cash in on his decent power
and give the wise buyer some very nice numbers. He is not to be confused
with the pitcher Scott Service, whose name is pronounced the same but is
not capable of producing very nice numbers.

Year	Team	Lg.	Pos.	G	AB	R	H	HR	RBI	SB	BA
1992	Houston	NL	C	77	205	12	49	0	15	0	.239
1993	Houston	NL	C	85	258	24	63	11	32	0	.244
1994	Houston	NL	C	78	251	27	49	9	41	0	.195
1995	Houston	NL	C	28	89	7	20	1	12	0	.225
1995	Chicago	NL	C	52	175	31	50	12	35	2	.286
Post All-Star				43	144	24	44	10	31	1	.306

DANNY SHEAFFER   Age 34/R $2

To continue the thought expressed under the entry entitled TOM PAG-
NOZZI, that same Cards executive added, "The trouble is that Johnny Bench
has been retired for about 15 years."

Year	Team	Lg.	Pos.	G	AB	R	H	HR	RBI	SB	BA
1993	Colorado	NL	C	82	216	26	60	4	32	2	.278
1994	Colorado	NL	C	44	110	11	24	1	12	0	.218
1995	St. Louis	NL	C	76	208	24	48	5	30	0	.231
Post All-Star				52	144	14	32	2	16	0	.222

DON SLAUGHT   Age 37/R $3

Said one of the Pirates, "Whenever we need to make a roster move and
there isn't an obvious one available, we can always fall back on disabling
Sluggo because he always has something wrong with him." Alas, we may
have lucked upon a new Rotisserie category—days spent on the DL. But
even though he is getting a little long in tooth, Sluggo can still come off his
sick bed and hit a line drive for you.

Year	Team	Lg.	Pos.	G	AB	R	H	HR	RBI	SB	BA
1992	Pittsburgh	NL	C	87	255	26	88	4	37	2	.345
1993	Pittsburgh	NL	C	116	377	34	113	10	55	2	.300
1994	Pittsburgh	NL	C	76	240	21	69	2	21	0	.287
1995	Pittsburgh	NL	C	35	112	13	34	0	13	0	.304
Post All-Star				21	63	9	20	0	5	0	.317

KELLY STINNETT   Age 26/R $1

Has found his niche. Unfortunately, that niche is for a light-hitting backup of marginal utility.

Year	Team	Lg.	Pos.	G	AB	R	H	HR	RBI	SB	BA
1994	New York	NL	C	47	150	20	38	2	14	2	.253
1995	New York	NL	C	77	196	23	43	4	18	2	.219
Post All-Star				52	139	16	27	2	12	0	.194

EDDIE TAUBENSEE   Age 27/L $8

A solid performer on a very good team. Of course, Kenny Lofton is a spectacular performer on a great team. But that's all blood under the bridge, isn't it? Baseball fans don't remember things like Brock-Broglio for more than 30, 40 years. (P.S.: Can't hit ambidextrous pitching.)

Year	Team	Lg.	Pos.	G	AB	R	H	HR	RBI	SB	BA
1992	Houston	NL	C	104	297	23	66	5	28	2	.222
1993	Houston	NL	C	94	288	26	72	9	42	1	.250
1994	Cincinnati	NL	C	61	177	29	52	8	21	2	.294
1994	Houston	NL	C	5	10	0	1	0	0	0	.100
1995	Cincinnati	NL	C	80	218	32	62	9	44	2	.284
Post All-Star				40	86	15	29	4	21	1	.337

LENNY WEBSTER   Age 31/R $1

At one point late last year he had the same number of home runs as he had thrown-out base stealers. Unfortunately, the number was one. As a Phillies coach put it, "Until he had to play, we never realized how little he brings to the table."

Year	Team	Lg.	Pos.	G	AB	R	H	HR	RBI	SB	BA
1992	Minnesota	AL	C	53	118	10	33	1	13	0	.280
1993	Minnesota	AL	C	49	106	14	21	1	8	1	.198
1994	Montreal	NL	C	57	143	13	39	5	23	0	.273
1995	Philadelphia	NL	C	49	150	18	40	4	14	0	.267
Post All-Star				31	104	14	31	4	11	0	.298

RICK WILKINS   Age 28/L $5

He was damaged goods when Houston got him, so it's only fair to suspend a final verdict. But while he was out, the Astros discovered that the catcher they already had was the real deal. And meanwhile, Wilkins is another year farther away from that season when he hit all those homers in Wrigley Field.

Year	Team	Lg.	Pos.	G	AB	R	H	HR	RBI	SB	BA
1992	Chicago	NL	C	83	244	20	66	8	22	0	.270
1993	Chicago	NL	C	136	446	78	135	30	73	2	.303
1994	Chicago	NL	C	100	313	44	71	7	39	4	.227
1995	Chicago	NL	C	50	162	24	31	6	14	0	.191
1995	Houston	NL	C	15	40	6	10	1	5	0	.250
Post All-Star				13	36	4	9	1	4	0	.250

Catchers
pp. 27–41

Corners
pp. 41–62

Infield
pp. 63–82

Outfield
pp. 83–113

DH
pp. 114–118

Starters
pp. 119–157

Relievers
pp. 157–193

AMERICAN LEAGUE

ANDY ALLANSON   Age 34/R $1

At one point, Marcel Lachemann had four catchers on his active roster and Allanson on the DL. Maybe he has a recurring nightmare involving passed balls. Or maybe he's a big *Road Warrior* fan and has a thing about the gear. Whatever. With Mark Dalesandro and Chris Turner gone, Allanson could still be around if Lachemann can live with just three catchers. But that still leaves an unanswered question: how can a guy who is 6'5" and 225 pounds play eight major league seasons and hit only 19 home runs?

Year	Team	Lg.	Pos.	G	AB	R	H	HR	RBI	SB	BA
1992	Milwaukee	AL	C	9	25	6	8	0	0	3	.320
1993	San Francisco	NL	C	13	24	3	4	0	2	0	.167
1995	California	AL	C	35	82	5	14	3	10	0	.171
Post All-Star				13	31	0	4	0	2	0	.129

SANDY ALOMAR   Age 29/R $9

Alomar as in mallomar: fragile shell, soft center, crumbly base. This guy is the main reason the Indians are thinking about changing the name of their AA team to the Canton Rehabs. Eight years in the big leagues and just one 300-AB season. Still, when he does manage to stay in the lineup, he puts up solid offensive numbers from the backstop slot.

Year	Team	Lg.	Pos.	G	AB	R	H	HR	RBI	SB	BA
1992	Cleveland	AL	C	89	299	22	75	2	26	3	.251
1993	Cleveland	AL	C	64	215	24	58	6	32	3	.270
1994	Cleveland	AL	C	80	292	44	84	14	43	8	.288
1995	Cleveland	AL	C	66	203	32	61	10	35	3	.300
Post All-Star				59	183	30	51	9	31	3	.279

JORGE FABREGAS   Age 26/L $1

Jorge accidentally (and lightly) spiked Cal Ripken about a week before Cal broke the consecutive games played record. Upon returning to the dugout, Fabregas's teammates reminded him of what he had almost done. Jorge was suitably horrified and responded with a lusty "Oh, my God!" That's what you should say if he ends up as your second catcher.

Year	Team	Lg.	Pos.	G	AB	R	H	HR	RBI	SB	BA
1994	California	AL	C	43	127	12	36	0	16	2	.283
1995	California	AL	C	73	227	24	56	1	22	0	.247
Post All-Star				40	122	7	27	0	10	0	.221

JOHN FLAHERTY   Age 28/R $8

Legitimate All-Star candidate in the first half of last year, then joined his fellow Tigers in a team-wide swoon the second half. If he starts off like a housafire again, trade him by June 15.

Year	Team	Lg.	Pos.	G	AB	R	H	HR	RBI	SB	BA
1992	Boston	AL	C	35	66	3	13	0	2	0	.197
1993	Boston	AL	C	13	25	3	3	0	2	0	.120
1994	Detroit	AL	C	34	40	2	6	0	4	0	.150
1995	Detroit	AL	C	112	354	39	86	11	40	0	.243
Post All-Star				58	182	11	35	2	14	0	.192

BILL HASELMAN
Age 29/R   **$4**

Stroked a few key, late-inning, run-producing hits last year for the Sox. Then again, who didn't?

Year	Team	Lg.	Pos.	G	AB	R	H	HR	RBI	SB	BA
1992	Seattle	AL	C	8	19	1	5	0	0	0	.263
1993	Seattle	AL	C	58	137	21	35	5	16	2	.255
1994	Seattle	AL	C	38	83	11	16	1	8	1	.193
1995	Boston	AL	C	64	152	22	37	5	23	0	.243
Post All-Star				37	95	14	20	4	17	0	.211

ERIC HELFAND
Age 27/R   **$1**

Hard to believe the A's won't be looking to improve their backup catching.

Year	Team	Lg.	Pos.	G	AB	R	H	HR	RBI	SB	BA
1993	Oakland	AL	C	8	13	1	3	0	1	0	.231
1994	Oakland	AL	C	7	6	1	1	0	1	0	.167
1995	Oakland	AL	C	38	86	9	14	0	7	0	.163
Post All-Star				22	55	6	10	0	6	0	.182

CHRIS HOILES
Age 31/R   **$17**

Another solid year, so why does his career seem so disappointing? Maybe it's because we thought 1993 was his breakout season, when in fact it was his career year. That said, double-digit dingers from your catcher is just the thing to warm a Rotisserie heart.

Year	Team	Lg.	Pos.	G	AB	R	H	HR	RBI	SB	BA
1992	Baltimore	AL	C	96	310	49	85	20	40	0	.274
1993	Baltimore	AL	C	126	419	80	130	29	82	1	.310
1994	Baltimore	AL	C	99	332	45	82	19	53	2	.247
1995	Baltimore	AL	C	114	352	53	88	19	58	1	.250
Post All-Star				57	179	25	52	9	31	1	.291

RON KARKOVICE
Age 32/R   **$8**

Probably has a good year or two left before one of the White Sox minor league catchers turns him into a backup backstop.

Year	Team	Lg.	Pos.	G	AB	R	H	HR	RBI	SB	BA
1992	Chicago	AL	C	123	342	39	81	13	50	10	.237
1993	Chicago	AL	C	128	403	60	92	20	54	2	.228
1994	Chicago	AL	C	77	207	33	44	11	29	0	.213
1995	Chicago	AL	C	113	323	44	70	13	51	2	.217
Post All-Star				55	168	22	38	6	27	1	.226

RANDY KNORR
Age 27/R   **$3**

With Carlos Delgado headed to first, Knorr will be battling Angel Martinez for playing time. Knorr's progress was delayed by a fractured thumb last year. He needs to step up and *take* the job soon. Someday one of the Blue Jays rookies will click, and he'll be just another backup. And he's better than that.

Year	Team	Lg.	Pos.	G	AB	R	H	HR	RBI	SB	BA
1992	Toronto	AL	C	8	19	1	5	1	2	0	.263
1993	Toronto	AL	C	39	101	11	25	4	20	0	.248
1994	Toronto	AL	C	40	124	20	30	7	19	0	.242
1995	Toronto	AL	C	45	132	18	28	3	16	0	.212
Post All-Star				16	46	3	7	0	5	0	.152

Catchers
pp. 27–41

Corners
pp. 41–62

Infield
pp. 63–82

Outfield
pp. 83–113

DH
pp. 114–118

Starters
pp. 119–157

Relievers
pp. 157–193

CHAD KREUTER Age 31/R $1

Someone in your league may remember his 15 homers in 1993 and give him a shot. Just hope that someone isn't you.

Year	Team	Lg.	Pos.	G	AB	R	H	HR	RBI	SB	BA
1992	Detroit	AL	C	67	190	22	48	2	16	0	.253
1993	Detroit	AL	C	119	374	59	107	15	51	2	.286
1994	Detroit	AL	C	65	170	17	38	1	19	0	.224
1995	Seattle	AL	C	26	75	12	17	1	8	0	.227
Post All-Star				2	7	0	2	0	0	0	.286

MIKE LAVALLIERE Age 35/L $1

The definitive third catcher. Remember: you only need two.

Year	Team	Lg.	Pos.	G	AB	R	H	HR	RBI	SB	BA
1992	Pittsburgh	NL	C	95	293	22	75	2	29	0	.256
1993	Chicago	AL	C	37	97	6	25	0	8	0	.258
1993	Pittsburgh	NL	C	1	5	0	1	0	0	0	.200
1994	Chicago	AL	C	59	139	6	39	1	24	0	.281
1995	Chicago	AL	C	46	98	7	24	1	19	0	.245
Post All-Star				19	47	4	14	1	12	0	.298

JIM LEYRITZ Age 32/R $7

In Rotisserie ball, a versatile and valuable player, even though the power numbers declined. In real life, an annoying cog who thinks he's a wheel. When the Yankees were spiraling out of contention last year, he told the press, "They should trade me for a pitcher." Thing is, he was right, but he made it sound like he felt Jim Leyritz was a commodity that 29 major league GMs were lining up to grab.

Year	Team	Lg.	Pos.	G	AB	R	H	HR	RBI	SB	BA
1992	New York	AL	DH	63	144	17	37	7	26	0	.257
1993	New York	AL	1B	95	259	43	80	14	53	0	.309
1994	New York	AL	C	75	249	47	66	17	58	0	.265
1995	New York	AL	C	77	264	37	71	7	37	1	.269
Post All-Star				33	100	17	25	3	15	0	.250

BARRY LYONS Age 35/R $1

Is this the same Barry Lyons who used to . . . yeah, it must be. Gosh, we thought he had retired and was managing somewhere in A ball.

Year	Team	Lg.	Pos.	G	AB	R	H	HR	RBI	SB	BA
1995	Chicago	AL	C	27	64	8	17	5	16	0	.266
Post All-Star				24	64	8	17	5	16	0	.266

MIKE MACFARLANE Age 31/R $12

Just a wild guess, but do you suppose the looming greenness in left field at Fenway might have had something to do with his hitting 27 points below his career average? Look for RBI and BA to come up this year, with homers about the same—if he stays in Boston.

Year	Team	Lg.	Pos.	G	AB	R	H	HR	RBI	SB	BA
1992	Kansas City	AL	C	129	402	51	94	17	48	1	.234
1993	Kansas City	AL	C	117	388	55	106	20	67	2	.273
1994	Kansas City	AL	C	92	314	53	80	14	47	1	.255
1995	Boston	AL	C	115	364	45	82	15	51	2	.225
Post All-Star				56	178	23	44	5	21	0	.247

SANDY MARTINEZ
Age 23/R   **$3**

Want to catch for the Blue Jays? Send them your résumé. Martinez led the Pioneer League with 24 passed balls in 1992 and the Florida State League with 14 errors in 1994, so he could turn out to be Carlos Delgado without power. But hey, the Blue Jays have to send out somebody to catch—it's a rule—and he has as good a shot at the job as anybody.

Year	Team	Lg.	Pos.	G	AB	R	H	HR	RBI	SB	BA
1995	Toronto	AL	C	62	191	12	46	2	25	0	.241
Post All-Star				54	164	11	39	1	22	0	.238

MIKE MATHENY
Age 25/R   **$1**

Competent.

Year	Team	Lg.	Pos.	G	AB	R	H	HR	RBI	SB	BA
1994	Milwaukee	AL	C	28	53	3	12	1	2	0	.226
1995	Milwaukee	AL	C	80	166	13	41	0	21	2	.247
Post All-Star				59	142	12	36	0	19	1	.254

BRENT MAYNE
Age 27/L   **$1**

Remember the Mayne? KC remembers making him a first-round pick in the 1989 draft, but no one remembers seeing any evidence since then to make it look like a good idea. Maybe it's the name. Shouldn't a guy named Brent Mayne be a lifeguard on *Baywatch*?

Year	Team	Lg.	Pos.	G	AB	R	H	HR	RBI	SB	BA
1992	Kansas City	AL	C	82	213	16	48	0	18	0	.225
1993	Kansas City	AL	C	71	205	22	52	2	22	3	.254
1994	Kansas City	AL	C	46	144	19	37	2	20	1	.257
1995	Kansas City	AL	C	110	307	23	77	1	27	0	.251
Post All-Star				61	158	12	46	0	15	0	.291

MATT MERULLO
Age 30/L   **$2**

Plays behind Matt Walbeck though their numbers are similar. In fact, Merullo has more RBI per AB. (No, it's not a new Rotisserie category, but it is evidence that we've done our homework.)

Year	Team	Lg.	Pos.	G	AB	R	H	HR	RBI	SB	BA
1992	Chicago	AL	C	24	50	3	9	0	3	0	.180
1993	Chicago	AL	DH	8	20	1	1	0	0	0	.050
1994	Cleveland	AL	C	4	10	1	1	0	0	0	.100
1995	Minnesota	AL	C	76	195	19	55	1	27	0	.282
Post All-Star				35	82	12	24	1	17	0	.293

Catchers
pp. 27–41

Corners
pp. 41–62

Infield
pp. 63–82

Outfield
pp. 83–113

DH
pp. 114–118

Starters
pp. 119–157

Relievers
pp. 157–193

GREG MYERS   Age 29/L $5

Lefty hitting catchers with a little pop always get us fuzzy headed, so we had high hopes for this guy when he came up with Toronto to stay in 1990. Were we wrong? Maybe, but on the strength of last season we prefer to think of it as prematurely right. Of course, just about everybody on that Cinderella Angels team had a good year, so maybe Myers will turn back into a pumpkin. On the other hand, he is a lefty-hitting catcher with a little pop ...

Year	Team	Lg.	Pos.	G	AB	R	H	HR	RBI	SB	BA
1992	California	AL	C	8	17	0	4	0	0	0	.235
1992	Toronto	AL	C	22	61	4	14	1	13	0	.230
1993	California	AL	C	108	290	27	74	7	40	3	.255
1994	California	AL	C	45	126	10	31	2	8	0	.246
1995	California	AL	C	85	273	35	71	9	38	0	.260
Post All-Star				48	147	16	39	5	14	0	.265

JOE OLIVER   Age 30/R $9

Joe Oliver was the name of Louis Armstrong's musical mentor when the Greatest Musician of the Twentieth Century was starting out in New Orleans. That's got nothing to do with Rotisserie, but, the season before, neither did this Joe Oliver, who spent all but six games of 1994 on the disabled list. Nice comeback.

Year	Team	Lg.	Pos.	G	AB	R	H	HR	RBI	SB	BA
1992	Cincinnati	NL	C	143	485	42	131	10	57	2	.270
1993	Cincinnati	NL	C	139	482	40	115	14	75	0	.239
1994	Cincinnati	NL	C	6	19	1	4	1	5	0	.211
1995	Milwaukee	AL	C	97	337	43	92	12	51	2	.273
Post All-Star				36	116	12	28	3	18	0	.241

LANCE PARRISH   Age 39/R $1

Parrish was the most potent power-hitting catcher of the 1980s. Somebody should whisper to the big guy that the 1980s ended six years ago. On the other hand, he had more homers than any other Toronto catcher, so maybe he'll hang around to the end of this decade. Hey, if nothing else, he could be strength coach.

Year	Team	Lg.	Pos.	G	AB	R	H	HR	RBI	SB	BA
1992	California	AL	C	24	83	7	19	4	11	0	.229
1992	Seattle	AL	C	69	192	19	45	8	21	1	.234
1993	Cleveland	AL	C	10	20	2	4	1	2	1	.200
1994	Pittsburgh	NL	C	40	126	10	34	3	16	1	.270
1995	Toronto	AL	C	70	178	15	36	4	22	0	.202
Post All-Star				26	60	6	13	1	13	0	.217

TONY PENA   Age 38/R $2

Pena's catching skills and clubhouse leadership made him a perfect role player on this great Indians team, so his second year in a row of offensive rebirth was just gravy. He's also ageless, so you can count on him again. And so long as Sandy "Ouch" Alomar is around, the Indians backup catcher is sure to get enough work to keep from getting rusty.

Year	Team	Lg.	Pos.	G	AB	R	H	HR	RBI	SB	BA
1992	Boston	AL	C	133	410	39	99	1	38	3	.241
1993	Boston	AL	C	126	304	20	55	4	19	1	.181
1994	Cleveland	AL	C	40	112	18	33	2	10	0	.295
1995	Cleveland	AL	C	91	263	25	69	5	28	1	.262
Post All-Star				36	100	11	31	2	15	1	.310

IVAN RODRIGUEZ   Age 24/R $18

Notice how you didn't hear as much about his arrogance and selfishness last season? Maybe he's growing up. Not as much power as Stanley or Hoiles, but then you look at his age and realize that his future lies ahead.

Year	Team	Lg.	Pos.	G	AB	R	H	HR	RBI	SB	BA
1992	Texas	AL	C	123	420	39	109	8	37	0	.260
1993	Texas	AL	C	137	473	56	129	10	66	8	.273
1994	Texas	AL	C	99	363	56	108	16	57	6	.298
1995	Texas	AL	C	130	492	56	149	12	67	0	.303
Post All-Star				74	281	27	79	6	36	0	.281

MIKE STANLEY   Age 32/R $21

The Yankees' season was summed up by the mid-August game in which Stanley had three HR and 7 RBI—and they still lost. In a pinch, he could still play first, third, and the outfield, the way he used to do with the Rangers, who let him walk because Rodriguez was ready. Lethal with the bases loaded. Sees a lot of lefthanded pitching. A team leader. Right now, the best backstop bet in the AL.

Year	Team	Lg.	Pos.	G	AB	R	H	HR	RBI	SB	BA
1992	New York	AL	C	68	173	24	43	8	27	0	.249
1993	New York	AL	C	130	423	70	129	26	84	1	.305
1994	New York	AL	C	82	290	54	87	17	57	0	.300
1995	New York	AL	C	118	399	63	107	18	83	1	.268
Post All-Star				65	218	35	60	11	49	0	.275

TERRY STEINBACH   Age 34/R $13

Steady, reliable, seemingly unaffected (so far) by advancing years. What you've seen is what you'll get.

Year	Team	Lg.	Pos.	G	AB	R	H	HR	RBI	SB	BA
1992	Oakland	AL	C	128	438	48	122	12	53	2	.279
1993	Oakland	AL	C	104	389	47	111	10	43	3	.285
1994	Oakland	AL	C	103	369	51	105	11	57	2	.285
1995	Oakland	AL	C	114	406	43	113	15	65	1	.278
Post All-Star				50	180	19	54	5	21	0	.300

RON TINGLEY   Age 36/R $1

His best year yet, though hardly good enough to send tingleys up your spine.

Year	Team	Lg.	Pos.	G	AB	R	H	HR	RBI	SB	BA
1992	California	AL	C	71	127	15	25	3	8	0	.197
1993	California	AL	C	58	90	7	18	0	12	1	.200
1994	Chicago	AL	C	5	5	0	0	0	0	0	0.000
1994	Florida	NL	C	19	52	4	9	1	2	0	.173
1995	Detroit	AL	C	54	124	14	28	4	18	0	.226
Post All-Star				26	63	8	16	4	13	0	.254

Catchers pp. 27-41

Corners pp. 41-62

Infield pp. 63-82

Outfield pp. 83-113

DH pp. 114-118

Starters pp. 119-157

Relievers pp. 157-193

DAVE VALLE   Age 35/R $1

Had a big power year in 1993, just like Chad Kreuter. You know it's over for a guy when they start making the Kreuter comparisons.

Year	Team	Lg.	Pos.	G	AB	R	H	HR	RBI	SB	BA
1992	Seattle	AL	C	124	367	39	88	9	30	0	.240
1993	Seattle	AL	C	135	423	48	109	13	63	1	.258
1994	Boston	AL	C	30	76	6	12	1	5	0	.158
1994	Milwaukee	AL	C	16	36	8	14	1	5	0	.389
1995	Texas	AL	C	36	75	7	18	0	5	1	.240
Post All-Star				12	19	3	6	0	2	0	.316

MATT WALBECK   Age 26/B $3

Plays in front of Matt Merullo though their numbers are similar. Tom Kelly hung in there with him, but 1995 was a lost year for the whole team, maybe for the whole state of Minnesota. Walbeck and all the Twins (except for their, ah, "pitchers") will rebound next year. Minnesota, too.

Year	Team	Lg.	Pos.	G	AB	R	H	HR	RBI	SB	BA
1993	Chicago	NL	C	11	30	2	6	1	6	0	.200
1994	Minnesota	AL	C	97	338	31	69	5	35	1	.204
1995	Minnesota	AL	C	115	393	40	101	1	44	3	.257
Post All-Star				64	224	24	61	0	26	2	.272

CHRIS WIDGER   Age 24/R $1

Widger is an example of how to bring along a young player. Instead of going out to get some ho-hum veteran backup catcher, the Mariners eased Widger into the majors, let him get his feet wet backing up Dan Wilson. (No, there wasn't a leak in the Kingdome. We were speaking metaphorically, as we are prone to do in moments of weakness.) Keep an eye on Widger in Spring Training. In the minors he showed some pop (16 homers in the Southern League) as well as some versatility (he played first base and outfield when he wasn't catching). Could he be the next Mike Stanley? If so, you read it here first. If not, we're denying we ever brought the matter up.

Year	Team	Lg.	Pos.	G	AB	R	H	HR	RBI	SB	BA
1995	Seattle	AL	C	23	45	2	9	1	2	0	.200
Post All-Star				18	34	2	5	1	2	0	.147

GEORGE WILLIAMS   Age 25/B $1

Hmmm . . . Terry Steinbach's 34, isn't he?

Year	Team	Lg.	Pos.	G	AB	R	H	HR	RBI	SB	BA
1995	Oakland	AL	C	29	79	13	23	3	14	0	.291
Post All-Star				29	79	13	23	3	14	0	.291

DAN WILSON   Age 27/R $6

Solid.

Year	Team	Lg.	Pos.	G	AB	R	H	HR	RBI	SB	BA
1992	Cincinnati	NL	C	12	25	2	9	0	3	0	.360
1993	Cincinnati	NL	C	36	76	6	17	0	8	0	.224
1994	Seattle	AL	C	91	282	24	61	3	27	1	.216
1995	Seattle	AL	C	119	399	40	111	9	51	2	.278
Post All-Star				69	231	25	67	7	36	1	.290

GREG ZAUN   Age 24/B $1

We like guys whose last names begin with a Z. Helps end the section on a note of finality.

Year	Team	Lg.	Pos.	G	AB	R	H	HR	RBI	SB	BA
1995	Baltimore	AL	C	40	104	18	27	3	14	1	.260
Post All-Star				32	80	14	22	2	10	1	.275

At the Corners

NATIONAL LEAGUE

EDGARDO ALFONZO   Age 22/R $6

Dallas Green is one of those baseball people who is not easily impressed and who hands out praise to today's players about as freely as Newt Gingrich hands out welfare checks. So when Green said last season that Alfonzo was "one of the hardest-working, fundamentally sound young players I've had in years," we took notice. One note of caution: the Mets fear that he might have chronic back trouble. (That's Alfonzo, not Green.)

Year	Team	Lg.	Pos.	G	AB	R	H	HR	RBI	SB	BA
1995	New York	NL	3B	101	335	26	93	4	41	1	.278
Post All-Star				40	142	12	44	1	19	1	.310

SHANE ANDREWS   Age 24/R $7

He whiffs on roughly every third at bat, but that's a ratio common to young sluggers in today's game. With big-time power, he might be one of those hunch bets that pays big dividends.

Year	Team	Lg.	Pos.	G	AB	R	H	HR	RBI	SB	BA
1995	Montreal	NL	3B	84	220	27	47	8	31	1	.214
Post All-Star				41	111	9	23	2	15	0	.207

ERIC ANTHONY   Age 28/L $3

Go figure. In Houston, he showed good power potential, and so you think, wow, wonder what he'd do if he ever got away from the Astrodome. Been gone two seasons now, so guess we know.

Year	Team	Lg.	Pos.	G	AB	R	H	HR	RBI	SB	BA
1992	Houston	NL	OF	137	440	45	105	19	80	5	.239
1993	Houston	NL	OF	145	486	70	121	15	66	3	.249
1994	Seattle	AL	OF	79	262	31	62	10	30	6	.237
1995	Cincinnati	NL	OF	47	134	19	36	5	23	2	.269
Post All-Star				22	52	3	11	0	4	0	.212

Catchers
pp. 27-41

Corners
pp. 41-62

Infield
pp. 63-82

Outfield
pp. 83-113

DH
pp. 114-118

Starters
pp. 119-157

Relievers
pp. 157-193

RICH AUDE
Age 24/R $1

Didn't exactly explode during the second half. Didn't do all that much in the first half, come to think of it.

Year	Team	Lg.	Pos.	G	AB	R	H	HR	RBI	SB	BA
1993	Pittsburgh	NL	1B	13	26	1	3	0	4	0	.115
1995	Pittsburgh	NL	1B	42	109	10	27	2	19	1	.248
Post All-Star				14	39	4	8	0	8	0	.205

JEFF BAGWELL
Age 27/R $35

We like him as much as any player in baseball. But shouldn't a hitter this good learn how to get away from inside pitches on his hands? Isn't there some way he could, you know, *practice* pulling his mitts back? If this thing happens again, we can only conclude that somebody in the great hall of fame upstairs just flat out doesn't like him.

Year	Team	Lg.	Pos.	G	AB	R	H	HR	RBI	SB	BA
1992	Houston	NL	1B	162	586	87	160	18	96	10	.273
1993	Houston	NL	1B	142	535	76	171	20	88	13	.320
1994	Houston	NL	1B	110	400	104	147	39	116	15	.368
1995	Houston	NL	1B	114	448	88	130	21	87	12	.290
Post All-Star				46	183	37	61	11	42	3	.333

MIKE BENJAMIN
Age 30/R $2

For five days, he was Ty Cobb. Unfortunately, for the rest of the season, he was Mike Benjamin.

Year	Team	Lg.	Pos.	G	AB	R	H	HR	RBI	SB	BA
1992	San Francisco	NL	SS	40	75	4	13	1	3	1	.173
1993	San Francisco	NL	2B	63	146	22	29	4	16	0	.199
1994	San Francisco	NL	SS	38	62	9	16	1	9	5	.258
1995	San Francisco	NL	3B	68	186	19	41	3	12	11	.220
Post All-Star				34	90	5	12	0	2	4	.133

SEAN BERRY
Age 30/R $14

An underappreciated player from whom the maximum has been extracted by Felipe Alou. However, since he'll make more than the minimum salary, he has likely become too expensive for the Expos' owners, who make no pretense anymore about wanting to win. So it might be au revoir time for yet another fine Expo ballplayer. Why does that city have a baseball team, anyway?

Year	Team	Lg.	Pos.	G	AB	R	H	HR	RBI	SB	BA
1992	Montreal	NL	3B	24	57	5	19	1	4	2	.333
1993	Montreal	NL	3B	122	299	50	78	14	49	12	.261
1994	Montreal	NL	3B	103	320	43	89	11	41	14	.278
1995	Montreal	NL	3B	103	314	38	100	14	55	3	.318
Post All-Star				57	180	22	60	9	31	2	.333

JEFF BRANSON
Age 29/L $10

Everyone was waiting for the Reds to go get a third baseman. But the platoon in which he was the key produced very solid numbers. Like everybody else, we were surprised by the amount of pop he brought to the plate last summer. We always take notice when a guy suddenly slugs twice as many HR as he's ever hit before, particularly when there isn't much in his minor league record to suggest he had it in him.

Year	Team	Lg.	Pos.	G	AB	R	H	HR	RBI	SB	BA
1992	Cincinnati	NL	2B	72	115	12	34	0	15	0	.296
1993	Cincinnati	NL	SS	125	381	40	92	3	22	4	.241
1994	Cincinnati	NL	2B	58	109	18	31	6	16	0	.284
1995	Cincinnati	NL	3B	122	331	43	86	12	45	2	.260
Post All-Star				65	187	21	44	7	26	1	.235

Catchers
pp. 27–41

Corners
pp. 41–62

Infield
pp. 63–82

Outfield
pp. 83–113

DH
pp. 114–118

Starters
pp. 119–157

Relievers
pp. 157–193

RICO BROGNA   Age 25/L $19

Count us among the skeptics who thought that his splashy 1994 debut was a strike-induced aberration. Count us among the cynics who thought he would be brought swiftly to earth by a full season of exposure to major league curveballs. Count us among the enthusiasts who now believe he's going to be a fine, productive hitter for the rest of the century. We at least had a lot of company. As one Mets executive put it, "We assumed we'd be looking for a first baseman. He's surprised us as much as anyone."

Year	Team	Lg.	Pos.	G	AB	R	H	HR	RBI	SB	BA
1992	Detroit	AL	1B	9	26	3	5	1	3	0	.192
1994	New York	NL	1B	39	131	16	46	7	20	1	.351
1995	New York	NL	1B	134	495	72	143	22	76	0	.289
Post All-Star				73	266	44	80	13	45	0	.301

KEN CAMINITI   Age 32/S $20

That was quite a little home run blitz he unleashed in September, wasn't it? Two dingers a day for three days, and about a jillion RBI. Too bad they came a little late—he'd just signed a two-year contract extension with the Padres at "only" $3 million per, a steep paycut from the $4.7 he earned last season. Caminiti's always been a solid ballplayer, a dependable run producer, and a gamer. Our only reason for restraint is that we don't believe he's going to get a whole bunch better, which is why we're giving him a salary cut too. What he is is plenty good enough, mind you, but don't look at his totals in last year's short season and project him for 30 taters this year. Something in the 18–20 range is more like it.

Year	Team	Lg.	Pos.	G	AB	R	H	HR	RBI	SB	BA
1992	Houston	NL	3B	135	506	68	149	13	62	10	.294
1993	Houston	NL	3B	143	543	75	142	13	75	8	.262
1994	Houston	NL	3B	111	406	63	115	18	75	4	.283
1995	San Diego	NL	3B	143	526	74	159	26	94	12	.302
Post All-Star				75	275	44	87	15	49	9	.316

MARK CARREON   Age 32/R $12

It's not a good sign when a solid, hardworking journeyman like this gets to be so important on your team. Ask the Giants brass, they'll tell you they wish some other guys had played well enough so that Carreon would have gotten a hundred fewer AB. That said, there's no early evidence that the Giants are going to be much better this season, so Carreon could provide excellent value again.

Year	Team	Lg.	Pos.	G	AB	R	H	HR	RBI	SB	BA
1992	Detroit	AL	OF	101	336	34	78	10	41	3	.232
1993	San Francisco	NL	OF	78	150	22	49	7	33	1	.327
1994	San Francisco	NL	OF	51	100	8	27	3	20	0	.270
1995	San Francisco	NL	1B	117	396	53	119	17	65	0	.301
Post All-Star				68	259	31	81	9	47	0	.313

VINNY CASTILLA   Age 28/R $28

Let the purists and poets sneer at Coors Field hitters like Castilla. Let them smugly point out that he wouldn't be half the hitter if he played his home games in a "real" ballpark at sea level. Sure, there's a big-ballpark effect at play with all the Rockies. But did those same purists and poets sneer at Roger Maris for jerking a bunch of cheap home runs in Yankee Stadium? Did those same purists and poets sneer at Rico Petrocelli in Fenway or Ernie Banks in Wrigley or Norm Cash in Tiger Stadium? All we know is that when he was taken in the expansion draft from Atlanta, Braves people said he'd someday be a good offensive player. That he took "good offensive player" a step further and became a Rocky Mountain Matt Williams was in major measure the product of rarefied air and terrible pitching, but a good swing has something to do with it. Enjoy the numbers.

Year	Team	Lg.	Pos.	G	AB	R	H	HR	RBI	SB	BA
1992	Atlanta	NL	3B	9	16	1	4	0	1	0	.250
1993	Colorado	NL	SS	105	337	36	86	9	30	2	.255
1994	Colorado	NL	SS	52	130	16	43	3	18	2	.331
1995	Colorado	NL	3B	139	527	82	163	32	90	2	.309
Post All-Star				71	265	41	80	15	42	2	.302

ARCHI CIANFROCCO   Age 29/R $3

Good role player.

Year	Team	Lg.	Pos.	G	AB	R	H	HR	RBI	SB	BA
1992	Montreal	NL	1B	86	232	25	56	6	30	3	.241
1993	Montreal	NL	1B	12	17	3	4	1	1	0	.235
1993	San Diego	NL	3B	84	279	27	68	11	47	2	.244
1994	San Diego	NL	3B	59	146	9	32	4	13	2	.219
1995	San Diego	NL	1B	51	118	22	31	5	31	0	.263
Post All-Star				51	118	22	31	5	31	0	.263

GREG COLBRUNN   Age 26/R $24

Years ago, the Expos thought he had the potential to be a solid power hitter in the chilly north country. And after drifting into obscurity because of pesky thumb injuries, lo and behold he became a solid power hitter in the humid subtropics. If he can keep his hands healthy, he will be a solid power hitter in all climes for the rest of the decade.

Year	Team	Lg.	Pos.	G	AB	R	H	HR	RBI	SB	BA
1992	Montreal	NL	1B	52	168	12	45	2	18	3	.268
1993	Montreal	NL	1B	70	153	15	39	4	23	4	.255
1994	Florida	NL	1B	47	155	17	47	6	31	1	.303
1995	Florida	NL	1B	138	528	70	146	23	89	11	.277
Post All-Star				74	286	44	80	15	52	7	.280

SCOTT COOPER   Age 28/L $6

It was August and the Cardinals had long ago descended into the nether regions of the 1995 season, and a top club executive was standing with a visitor in the press box as Cooper shanked another soft fly ball to left field. The executive turned to the visitor and said, "Geez, why didn't someone tell us that this guy couldn't play." Sorry, we thought you knew. Anyway, better late then never: "This guy can't play."

Year	Team	Lg.	Pos.	G	AB	R	H	HR	RBI	SB	BA
1992	Boston	AL	1B	123	337	34	93	5	33	1	.276
1993	Boston	AL	3B	156	526	67	147	9	63	5	.279
1994	Boston	AL	3B	104	369	49	104	13	53	0	.282
1995	St. Louis	NL	3B	118	374	29	86	3	40	0	.230
Post All-Star				50	143	8	27	1	9	0	.189

CLIFF FLOYD

Age 23/L **$8**

Remember years ago when Joe Theismann had his leg snapped in full view of the *Monday Night Football* cameras? Floyd's wrist injury last year, though suffered on a far smaller stage, was no less gruesome. He should be healthy this year and the Expos think he can resume realizing his considerable promise. We're dubious, because wrist injuries have a way of being devastating to hitters. Remember Bob Horner? He was never the same after his broken wrist. We wish Floyd well, in part because the guy in our league who owned him at $10 waived him and nobody claimed him, and in part because we are generous spirits who wish everybody well. No price that we set can make much sense at this stage in his rehab. Pay close attention to what he does in winter ball (if he plays) and in Spring Training. And pencil him in in the outfield, where the Expos plan to use him, and not first, where they have Dave Segui.

Year	Team	Lg.	Pos.	G	AB	R	H	HR	RBI	SB	BA
1993	Montreal	NL	1B	10	31	3	7	1	2	0	.226
1994	Montreal	NL	1B	100	334	43	94	4	41	10	.281
1995	Montreal	NL	1B	29	69	6	9	1	8	3	.130
Post All-Star				11	17	1	0	0	0	0	0.000

ANDRES GALARRAGA

Age 34/R **$32**

Just another one of those Rockies, who are so fun to have on your team for at least those 81 games a year they will play in Denver. The Big Cat is also good for double figures in SB, which is a nice bonus. By the way, it's not just the thin air that got Galarraga back on track—Don Baylor gets a big chunk of the credit as well.

Year	Team	Lg.	Pos.	G	AB	R	H	HR	RBI	SB	BA
1992	St. Louis	NL	1B	95	325	38	79	10	39	5	.243
1993	Colorado	NL	1B	120	470	71	174	22	98	2	.370
1994	Colorado	NL	1B	103	417	77	133	31	85	8	.319
1995	Colorado	NL	1B	143	554	89	155	31	106	12	.280
Post All-Star				74	296	39	80	13	51	7	.270

MARK GRACE

Age 31/L **$17**

A consummate pro, a proven hitter, an exceptional producer and quite possibly an ex-Cub. He's been so steady for so long that we're prepared to stop carping about how little pure power he brings to the table—and in Wrigley Field, yet! If he would just—please!—deliver double figures in home runs consistently, and not just every once in a while, we wouldn't ever complain again. Promise.

Year	Team	Lg.	Pos.	G	AB	R	H	HR	RBI	SB	BA
1992	Chicago	NL	1B	158	603	72	185	9	79	6	.307
1993	Chicago	NL	1B	155	594	86	193	14	98	8	.325
1994	Chicago	NL	1B	106	403	55	120	6	44	0	.298
1995	Chicago	NL	1B	143	552	97	180	16	92	6	.326
Post All-Star				75	290	51	91	6	43	4	.314

Catchers pp. 27–41

Corners pp. 41–62

Infield pp. 63–82

Outfield pp. 83–113

DH pp. 114–118

Starters pp. 119–157

Relievers pp. 157–193

MARK GRUDZIELANEK
Age 25/R **$6**

He could wind up at shortstop. He could wind up at third. He could wind up in the outfield. And his name could wind up on an eye chart. But he's going to play somewhere for the Expos, and the only question is whether he can produce more than singles. And if he lives up to the speed rep he brings from the minors, we wouldn't even fret about the singles.

Year	Team	Lg.	Pos.	G	AB	R	H	HR	RBI	SB	BA
1995	Montreal	NL	SS	78	269	27	66	1	20	8	.245
Post All-Star				31	116	9	28	0	9	5	.241

DAVE HANSEN
Age 27/L **$1**

If you want to spend your hard-earned money on a pinch-hitter without power who can't play in the field or steal a base if his life depended on it, be our guest. Just don't spend our money.

Year	Team	Lg.	Pos.	G	AB	R	H	HR	RBI	SB	BA
1992	Los Angeles	NL	3B	132	341	30	73	6	22	0	.214
1993	Los Angeles	NL	3B	84	105	13	38	4	30	0	.362
1994	Los Angeles	NL	3B	40	44	3	15	0	5	0	.341
1995	Los Angeles	NL	3B	100	181	19	52	1	14	0	.287
Post All-Star				52	104	10	31	0	8	0	.298

LENNY HARRIS
Age 31/L **$1**

You can do worse on your bench. You can also do better.

Year	Team	Lg.	Pos.	G	AB	R	H	HR	RBI	SB	BA
1992	Los Angeles	NL	2B	135	347	28	94	0	30	19	.271
1993	Los Angeles	NL	2B	107	160	20	38	2	11	3	.237
1994	Cincinnati	NL	3B	66	100	13	31	0	14	7	.310
1995	Cincinnati	NL	3B	101	197	32	41	2	16	10	.208
Post All-Star				49	69	9	14	2	5	1	.203

CHARLIE HAYES
Age 30/R **$16**

He gave the Yankees two solid years before being left unprotected in the expansion draft. He gave the Rockies two solid years before being left unwanted in the free-agent scrap heap. He gave the Phillies a solid season, and they probably won't keep him around, either. Some think it's because he's lazy. Some think it's because his numbers grow soft in the late season. But his bottom line ain't all that bad.

Year	Team	Lg.	Pos.	G	AB	R	H	HR	RBI	SB	BA
1992	New York	AL	3B	142	509	52	131	18	66	3	.257
1993	Colorado	NL	3B	157	573	89	175	25	98	11	.305
1994	Colorado	NL	3B	113	423	46	122	10	50	3	.288
1995	Philadelphia	NL	3B	141	529	58	146	11	85	5	.276
Post All-Star				73	286	31	72	5	34	3	.252

BRIAN R. HUNTER

Age 28/R   **$4**

Spent much of last year on the DL. Can still deliver a handful of dingers when he's healthy.

Year	Team	Lg.	Pos.	G	AB	R	H	HR	RBI	SB	BA
1992	Atlanta	NL	1B	102	238	34	57	14	41	1	.239
1993	Atlanta	NL	1B	37	80	4	11	0	8	0	.138
1994	Cincinnati	NL	OF	9	23	6	7	4	10	0	.304
1994	Pittsburgh	NL	1B	76	233	28	53	11	47	0	.227
1995	Cincinnati	NL	1B	40	79	9	17	1	9	2	.215
Post All-Star				15	23	0	3	0	3	1	.130

BUTCH HUSKEY

Age 24/R   **$8**

Once so fat that Dallas Green wouldn't allow him to wear a Mets uniform, once so snakebit that he separated his shoulder while hitting a home run and couldn't even round the bases, he swore off the jelly doughnuts, put his bad luck behind him, and now is again a power-hitting prospect who might get a shot to win either the third-base or left-field job at Shea Stadium. He seems like he's been around forever, but he's only 24, so we're betting he makes the grade and turns Alfonzo into a second baseman or an outfielder.

Year	Team	Lg.	Pos.	G	AB	R	H	HR	RBI	SB	BA
1993	New York	NL	3B	13	41	2	6	0	3	0	.146
1995	New York	NL	3B	28	90	8	17	3	11	1	.189
Post All-Star				28	90	8	17	3	11	1	.189

GREGG JEFFERIES

Age 28/S   **$26**

We are, of course, in the numbers business. Because of that, we have disciplined ourselves through years of hard experience not to have our opinion swayed by personalities. So what if a guy is unanimously perceived by his fourth set of major league teammates as a selfish little snot? What do we care when one of his fellow Phillies says of Jefferies, "He expects everyone to kiss his butt because he's hitting .280. Bleep him." That may be easy for someone playing next to him to say, but Rotisserie owners respond to a different drummer. We see a *four-category* selfish little snot, and we pay the price.

Year	Team	Lg.	Pos.	G	AB	R	H	HR	RBI	SB	BA
1992	Kansas City	AL	3B	152	604	66	172	10	75	19	.285
1993	St. Louis	NL	1B	142	544	89	186	16	83	46	.342
1994	St. Louis	NL	1B	103	397	52	129	12	55	12	.325
1995	Philadelphia	NL	1B	114	480	69	147	11	56	9	.306
Post All-Star				65	278	40	95	6	37	4	.342

HOWARD JOHNSON

Age 35/S   **$1**

Hey, a third of his hits were home runs. All he has to do is get 160 hits or so, and we're talking Babe Ruth–time in Wrigley field.

Year	Team	Lg.	Pos.	G	AB	R	H	HR	RBI	SB	BA
1992	New York	NL	OF	100	350	48	78	7	43	22	.223
1993	New York	NL	3B	72	235	32	56	7	26	6	.238
1994	Colorado	NL	OF	93	227	30	48	10	40	11	.211
1995	Chicago	NL	3B	87	169	26	33	7	22	1	.195
Post All-Star				47	85	14	22	2	11	1	.259

Catchers
pp. 27–41

Corners
pp. 41–62

Infield
pp. 63–82

Outfield
pp. 83–113

DH
pp. 114–118

Starters
pp. 119–157

Relievers
pp. 157–193

MARK JOHNSON   Age 28/L $6

Big-time power potential but little clue about how to hit. But he's a Dartmouth grad, so it's not like he should be unteachable.

Year	Team	Lg.	Pos.	G	AB	R	H	HR	RBI	SB	BA
1995	Pittsburgh	NL	1B	79	221	32	46	13	28	5	.208
Post All-Star				27	80	7	10	4	7	1	.125

CHIPPER JONES   Age 23/S $31

For an assessment, we turn to Bobby Cox, who has won a division title in the last five consecutive seasons. "What about Chipper? Well, he's our best third baseman, that's clear. He's also our best shortstop if that's where we want to play him. He's also our best left fielder by a wide margin. And even though we have Grissom, I'm not so sure he might not be our best center fielder. As a hitter, I look at him and see someone in a few years who is another George Brett, only he's a switch-hitter with more power than George. Plus, he's a great kid who works his tail off and is too tough to intimidate. I guess, that's about it." Thanks, Bobby.

Year	Team	Lg.	Pos.	G	AB	R	H	HR	RBI	SB	BA
1993	Atlanta	NL	SS	8	3	2	2	0	0	0	.667
1995	Atlanta	NL	3B	140	524	87	139	23	86	8	.265
Post All-Star				72	266	44	75	10	39	5	.282

ERIC KARROS   Age 28/R $32

He and Mike Piazza share a Manhattan Beach condo, which makes them the most productive Left Coast roommates this side of Demi Moore and Bruce Willis.

Year	Team	Lg.	Pos.	G	AB	R	H	HR	RBI	SB	BA
1992	Los Angeles	NL	1B	149	545	63	140	20	88	2	.257
1993	Los Angeles	NL	1B	158	619	74	153	23	80	0	.247
1994	Los Angeles	NL	1B	111	406	51	108	14	46	2	.266
1995	Los Angeles	NL	1B	143	551	83	164	32	105	4	.298
Post All-Star				75	284	48	82	18	57	0	.289

JEFF KING   Age 31/R $16

A quiet man who puts up quiet numbers in one of the quietest stadiums around. Last season he had the best season of his career. Quietly.

Year	Team	Lg.	Pos.	G	AB	R	H	HR	RBI	SB	BA
1992	Pittsburgh	NL	3B	130	480	56	111	14	65	4	.231
1993	Pittsburgh	NL	3B	158	611	82	180	9	98	8	.295
1994	Pittsburgh	NL	3B	94	339	36	89	5	42	3	.263
1995	Pittsburgh	NL	3B	122	445	61	118	18	87	7	.265
Post All-Star				71	262	38	68	12	47	4	.260

MARK LEWIS   Age 26/R $7

Former shortstop of the future in Cleveland who found a new life as the other half of Jeff Branson in Cincinnati. Now shortstop of the future in Detroit.

Year	Team	Lg.	Pos.	G	AB	R	H	HR	RBI	SB	BA
1992	Cleveland	AL	SS	122	413	44	109	5	30	4	.264
1993	Cleveland	AL	SS	14	52	6	13	1	5	3	.250
1994	Cleveland	AL	SS	20	73	6	15	1	8	1	.205
1995	Cincinnati	NL	3B	81	171	25	58	3	30	0	.339
Post All-Star				39	84	11	26	1	16	0	.310

SCOTT LIVINGSTONE Age 30/L $2

So long as you don't expect him to discover the source of the Congo or anything, not a bad spare part to have around.

Year	Team	Lg.	Pos.	G	AB	R	H	HR	RBI	SB	BA
1992	Detroit	AL	3B	117	354	43	100	4	46	1	.282
1993	Detroit	AL	3B	98	304	39	89	2	39	1	.293
1994	Detroit	AL	DH	15	23	0	5	0	1	0	.217
1994	San Diego	NL	3B	57	180	11	49	2	10	2	.272
1995	San Diego	NL	1B	99	196	26	66	5	32	2	.337
Post All-Star				57	147	22	53	4	27	2	.361

JOHN MABRY Age 25/L $9

The Cardinals like his pure swing and his work ethic. And scouts who followed him in the minors think he will eventually develop 15- to 20-HR power.

Year	Team	Lg.	Pos.	G	AB	R	H	HR	RBI	SB	BA
1994	St. Louis	NL	OF	6	23	2	7	0	3	0	.304
1995	St. Louis	NL	1B	129	388	35	119	5	41	0	.307
Post All-Star				68	231	20	71	4	28	0	.307

DAVE MAGADAN Age 33/L $3

He will always be on shaky footing, because managers like to see a lot more power in their corner men. But he's a steady hitter whose consistency with the bat keeps him employed somewhere.

Year	Team	Lg.	Pos.	G	AB	R	H	HR	RBI	SB	BA
1992	New York	NL	3B	99	321	33	91	3	28	1	.283
1993	Seattle	AL	1B	71	228	27	59	1	21	2	.259
1993	Florida	NL	3B	66	227	22	65	4	29	0	.286
1994	Florida	NL	3B	74	211	30	58	1	17	0	.275
1995	Houston	NL	3B	127	348	44	109	2	51	2	.313
Post All-Star				71	223	27	73	1	32	0	.327

FRED MCGRIFF Age 32/L $35

There was much revisionist history floating around last summer. With McGriff headed for free agency, there was talk among some of the baseball heads that McGriff produces "soft numbers" and that he wouldn't be that crucial a loss for the Braves if he should walk. All we know is that he is one of a select few people on earth for whom you can confidently write down 30 homers and 95 RBI every year. That's good enough for us.

Year	Team	Lg.	Pos.	G	AB	R	H	HR	RBI	SB	BA
1992	San Diego	NL	1B	152	531	79	152	35	104	8	.286
1993	Atlanta	NL	1B	68	255	59	79	19	55	1	.310
1993	San Diego	NL	1B	83	302	52	83	18	46	4	.275
1994	Atlanta	NL	1B	113	424	81	135	34	94	7	.318
1995	Atlanta	NL	1B	144	528	85	148	27	93	3	.280
Post All-Star				75	276	39	77	16	48	1	.279

HAL MORRIS Age 31/L $16

Look for the Reds to dump his salary and send him and his no-power bat packing. His value then will depend largely on where he lands. If it's in a

Catchers
pp. 27-41

Corners
pp. 41-62

Infield
pp. 63-82

Outfield
pp. 83-113

DH
pp. 114-118

Starters
pp. 119-157

Relievers
pp. 157-193

big-hitting lineup, he can be valuable. If he has to be counted on as one of the big guns, stay away.

Year	Team	Lg.	Pos.	G	AB	R	H	HR	RBI	SB	BA
1992	Cincinnati	NL	1B	115	395	41	107	6	53	6	.271
1993	Cincinnati	NL	1B	101	379	48	120	7	49	2	.317
1994	Cincinnati	NL	1B	112	436	60	146	10	78	6	.335
1995	Cincinnati	NL	1B	101	359	53	100	11	51	1	.279
Post All-Star				70	249	43	77	8	34	1	.309

JOSE OLIVA   Age 25/R $4

He has awesome power potential. He's also with his third team at a very young age. All we know is that his laziness and general personality so grated upon the Braves that virtually every other Braves player individually visited manager Bobby Cox to ask that the Braves get him out of the clubhouse. This is not what you might call a ringing endorsement.

Year	Team	Lg.	Pos.	G	AB	R	H	HR	RBI	SB	BA
1994	Atlanta	NL	3B	19	59	9	17	6	11	0	.288
1995	Atlanta	NL	3B	48	109	7	17	5	12	0	.156
1995	St. Louis	NL	3B	22	74	8	9	2	8	0	.122
Post All-Star				35	98	9	13	3	10	0	.133

TERRY PENDLETON   Age 35/S $14

He's everything he's always been, and with the Marlins lineup beginning to show muscle around him, he remains a valuable player.

Year	Team	Lg.	Pos.	G	AB	R	H	HR	RBI	SB	BA
1992	Atlanta	NL	3B	160	640	98	199	21	105	5	.311
1993	Atlanta	NL	3B	161	633	81	172	17	84	5	.272
1994	Atlanta	NL	3B	77	309	25	78	7	30	2	.252
1995	Florida	NL	3B	133	513	70	149	14	78	1	.290
Post All-Star				71	274	41	78	8	39	0	.285

J. R. PHILLIPS   Age 25/L $2

One Rotisserie owner of our acquaintance—we can't mention names, but he did invent the darned game—picked up Phillips on waivers in mid-season when he was hitting .180 or so, reasoning that he would end up hitting .220 or so, to do which he would have to hit .250 with a few homers over the second half. Impeccable reasoning, and it actually worked out pretty much that way. No one is more upbeat or positive than Giants manager Dusty Baker. But after watching Phillips strike out 11 times in one three-game series, even Baker was moved to say, "I can't watch this anymore." It got so ugly that at times, it even made . . .

Year	Team	Lg.	Pos.	G	AB	R	H	HR	RBI	SB	BA
1993	San Francisco	NL	1B	11	16	1	5	1	4	0	.313
1994	San Francisco	NL	1B	15	38	1	5	1	3	1	.132
1995	San Francisco	NL	1B	92	231	27	45	9	28	1	.195
Post All-Star				33	73	14	21	5	15	0	.288

STEVE SCARSONE   Age 29/R $7

. . . look like the second coming of Orlando Cepeda. (Which, just in case you were wondering, he isn't.)

Year	Team	Lg.	Pos.	G	AB	R	H	HR	RBI	SB	BA
1992	Baltimore	AL	2B	11	17	2	3	0	0	0	.176
1992	Philadelphia	NL	2B	7	13	1	2	0	0	0	.154
1993	San Francisco	NL	2B	44	103	16	26	2	15	0	.252
1994	San Francisco	NL	2B	52	103	21	28	2	13	0	.272
1995	San Francisco	NL	3B	80	233	33	62	11	29	3	.266
Post All-Star				45	135	16	31	4	13	2	.230

Catchers
pp. 27–41

Corners
pp. 41–62

Infield
pp. 63–82

Outfield
pp. 83–113

DH
pp. 114–118

Starters
pp. 119–157

Relievers
pp. 157–193

DAVID SEGUI   Age 29/B $12

He was overlooked in Baltimore, dissed in New York, and forgotten when he was sent to Montreal, where he settled in and had a fine season. The word out of Montreal is that even if Cliff Floyd comes all the way back, he will be moved to left field. Segui seems finally to have found a home.

Year	Team	Lg.	Pos.	G	AB	R	H	HR	RBI	SB	BA
1992	Baltimore	AL	1B	115	189	21	44	1	17	1	.233
1993	Baltimore	AL	1B	146	450	54	123	10	60	2	.273
1994	New York	NL	1B	92	336	46	81	10	43	0	.241
1995	New York	NL	OF	33	73	9	24	2	11	1	.329
1995	Montreal	NL	1B	97	383	59	117	10	57	1	.305
Post All-Star				71	278	42	80	9	45	1	.288

TIM WALLACH   Age 38/R $8

His back problems often made him look like a pretzel. Then he blew out his knee and insisted on playing, a hard-nosed attitude that has always made him very popular on every team for which he's played. Alas, time is also running out on one of this generation's class acts. The will is there, but the body may be just too beat up.

Year	Team	Lg.	Pos.	G	AB	R	H	HR	RBI	SB	BA
1992	Montreal	NL	3B	150	537	53	120	9	59	2	.223
1993	Los Angeles	NL	3B	133	477	42	106	12	62	0	.222
1994	Los Angeles	NL	3B	113	414	68	116	23	78	0	.280
1995	Los Angeles	NL	3B	97	327	24	87	9	38	0	.266
Post All-Star				52	173	13	45	5	21	0	.260

JOHN WEHNER   Age 28/R $2

(*Attention: Please send the children from the room—we're going to commit irony.*) This Pittsburgh native, a career utility man of marginal skills, made the last out in the final home game of last season, a game that a lot of us feared was going to be the last major league game in Pittsburgh. Now a lot of us fear the reprieve was only temporary.

Year	Team	Lg.	Pos.	G	AB	R	H	HR	RBI	SB	BA
1992	Pittsburgh	NL	3B	55	123	11	22	0	4	3	.179
1993	Pittsburgh	NL	OF	29	35	3	5	0	0	0	.143
1994	Pittsburgh	NL	3B	2	4	1	1	0	3	0	.250
1995	Pittsburgh	NL	OF	52	107	13	33	0	5	3	.308
Post All-Star				46	95	12	28	0	5	3	.295

EDDIE WILLIAMS   Age 31/R $6

We were kind of hoping for some kind of miracle follow-up to his startling debut in 1994. Didn't happen. He was plagued by nagging injuries, but the fact is he may have reached his level—about 12–15 homers, 50–60 RBI, BA somewhere in the .255–.265 range. And you know what? That's not a bad level at all.

Year	Team	Lg.	Pos.	G	AB	R	H	HR	RBI	SB	BA
1994	San Diego	NL	1B	49	175	32	58	11	42	0	.331
1995	San Diego	NL	1B	97	296	35	77	12	47	0	.260
Post All-Star				44	115	14	29	5	15	0	.252

MATT WILLIAMS   Age 30/R $40

Only one of the best players on earth.

Year	Team	Lg.	Pos.	G	AB	R	H	HR	RBI	SB	BA
1992	San Francisco	NL	3B	146	529	58	120	20	66	7	.227
1993	San Francisco	NL	3B	145	579	105	170	38	110	1	.294
1994	San Francisco	NL	3B	112	445	74	119	43	96	1	.267
1995	San Francisco	NL	3B	76	283	53	95	23	65	2	.336
Post All-Star				40	149	26	44	10	30	1	.295

TODD ZEILE   Age 30/R $17

Stardom has eluded him. If it's ever going to happen, Wrigley Field is the place.

Year	Team	Lg.	Pos.	G	AB	R	H	HR	RBI	SB	BA
1992	St. Louis	NL	3B	126	439	51	113	7	48	7	.257
1993	St. Louis	NL	3B	157	571	82	158	17	103	5	.277
1994	St. Louis	NL	3B	113	415	62	111	19	75	1	.267
1995	St. Louis	NL	1B	34	127	16	37	5	22	1	.291
1995	Chicago	NL	3B	79	299	34	68	9	30	0	.227
Post All-Star				56	203	23	42	6	21	0	.207

AMERICAN LEAGUE

MIKE BLOWERS   Age 30/R $20

A breakthrough season. Took over Seattle's hot corner and made Edgar Martinez a full-time DH, which sort of worked out okay for everybody, especially Lou Piniella.

Year	Team	Lg.	Pos.	G	AB	R	H	HR	RBI	SB	BA
1992	Seattle	AL	3B	31	73	7	14	1	2	0	.192
1993	Seattle	AL	3B	127	379	55	106	15	57	1	.280
1994	Seattle	AL	3B	85	270	37	78	9	49	2	.289
1995	Seattle	AL	3B	134	439	59	113	23	96	2	.257
Post All-Star				73	249	37	70	17	64	1	.281

WADE BOGGS   Age 37/L $18

No team in baseball got less power from the corners than the Yankees, so next year Boggs will probably move to first base so that Russ Davis can finally get his shot at third. There's no guarantee that that will help: Davis, despite his gaudy minor league record, is still a question mark, and Boggs, unless the planet time-warps back to 1987, isn't likely to deliver serious power. That's also assuming that Boggs's strong second half convinced Steinbrenner to re-sign his fellow Floridian. Wherever he lands, Boggs will still give a hitting clinic every time he steps to the plate. It will be interesting to watch him try to hang on long enough to get 3,000 hits. He is a most willful player who has always been able to get what he wants, and he's wanted 3,000 hits since he was three years old.

Year	Team	Lg.	Pos.	G	AB	R	H	HR	RBI	SB	BA
1992	Boston	AL	3B	143	514	62	133	7	50	1	.259
1993	New York	AL	3B	143	560	83	169	2	59	0	.302
1994	New York	AL	3B	97	366	61	125	11	55	2	.342
1995	New York	AL	3B	126	460	76	149	5	63	1	.324
Post All-Star				68	253	50	88	3	35	0	.348

BOBBY BONILLA   Age 33/B $29

You can't blame him for Baltimore's complete and utter collapse after his arrival. He hit for power, he drove in runs, he hit for average, he played some decent third, and he smiled a lot. After all, he thought he'd been traded to a contender. His most valuable contribution, though, was pushing Cal Ripken to take that memorable walk/run around Camden Yards on the night of 2,131.

Year	Team	Lg.	Pos.	G	AB	R	H	HR	RBI	SB	BA
1992	New York	NL	OF	128	438	62	109	19	70	4	.249
1993	New York	NL	OF	139	502	81	133	34	87	3	.265
1994	New York	NL	3B	108	403	60	117	20	67	1	.290
1995	New York	NL	3B	80	317	49	103	18	53	0	.325
1995	Baltimore	AL	OF	61	237	47	79	10	46	0	.333
Post All-Star				75	294	59	100	15	59	0	.340

SCOTT BROSIUS   Age 29/R $17

Back-to-back solid seasons. This year will make it back-to-back-to-back. Not spectacular, so he's a good bet to slide in under the radar and become a Rotisserie bargain.

Year	Team	Lg.	Pos.	G	AB	R	H	HR	RBI	SB	BA
1992	Oakland	AL	OF	38	87	13	19	4	13	3	.218
1993	Oakland	AL	OF	70	213	26	53	6	25	6	.249
1994	Oakland	AL	3B	96	324	31	77	14	49	2	.238
1995	Oakland	AL	3B	123	389	69	102	17	46	4	.262
Post All-Star				62	194	38	57	12	32	2	.294

JEFF CIRILLO   Age 26/R $9

Not bad for a guy whose main job in the field was as backup to Kevin Seitzer. In fact, this role player produced such good numbers you're kind of surprised he wasn't on the Indians. No wonder Seitzer made all those noises about retiring last year.

Year	Team	Lg.	Pos.	G	AB	R	H	HR	RBI	SB	BA
1994	Milwaukee	AL	3B	39	126	17	30	3	12	0	.238
1995	Milwaukee	AL	3B	125	328	57	91	9	39	7	.277
Post All-Star				70	209	34	55	6	31	3	.263

WILL CLARK   Age 32/L $19

We don't mean to pry, but didn't Will the Thrill used to be a home run threat? The RBI total is terrific, the jaw still juts like no other, and the official position of the Rangers is, heck, yes, we're still doggone glad we let

Catchers
pp. 27–41

Corners
pp. 41–62

Infield
pp. 63–82

Outfield
pp. 83–113

DH
pp. 114–118

Starters
pp. 119–157

Relievers
pp. 157–193

Rafael Palmeiro go to the Orioles so we could sign Clark for the same money. Funny, but by our calculations—Palmeiro has 25 more homers than Clark over the past two years—the Rangers blew it big time.

Year	Team	Lg.	Pos.	G	AB	R	H	HR	RBI	SB	BA
1992	San Francisco	NL	1B	144	513	69	154	16	73	12	.300
1993	San Francisco	NL	1B	132	491	82	139	14	73	2	.283
1994	Texas	AL	1B	110	389	73	128	13	80	5	.329
1995	Texas	AL	1B	123	454	85	137	16	92	0	.302
Post All-Star				71	262	45	83	8	56	0	.317

RON COOMER   Age 29/R $2

What do Gene Larkin, Dave McCarty, Steve Dunn, Scott Stahoviak, Dan Masteller, and Ron Coomer have in common? None has come close to being an adequate replacement—oops, bad choice of words—for local hero Kent Hrbek. Right now, it's between Coomer and Stahoviak. Okay, that's not exactly Mantle vs. Mays, but Minnesota is not exactly a big-league baseball team.

Year	Team	Lg.	Pos.	G	AB	R	H	HR	RBI	SB	BA
1995	Minnesota	AL	1B	37	101	15	26	5	19	0	.257
Post All-Star				37	101	15	26	5	19	0	.257

RUSS DAVIS   Age 26/R $8

Most teams would have done something more definitive with one of their top prospects by the time he turned 26, but the Yankees have been reluctant to roll the dice with Davis. It's just not George's way to go with good young talent possessing tremendous potential when he can spend a big-market for-tune on past-their-prime stars. But the Red Sox sat on Boggs, whom Davis should replace at third this season, until his mid-twenties, and Boggs survived nicely. So maybe Davis's long incubation will not have been in vain. If he does pan out for the Yankees, it will be testimony to Gene Michaels's perse-verance, patience, and baseball savvy. The Stick, who richly deserves a stretch of peace and tranquility after what he's been through, said no to a lot of tempting offers for Davis over the last three years. And if Davis doesn't pan out? It was Steinbrenner's fault for sticking with Stick.

Year	Team	Lg.	Pos.	G	AB	R	H	HR	RBI	SB	BA
1994	New York	AL	3B	4	14	0	2	0	1	0	.143
1995	New York	AL	3B	40	98	14	27	2	12	0	.276
Post All-Star				23	58	10	14	1	10	0	.241

CECIL FIELDER
Age 32/R   **$33**

If you calculate a dollar a dinger as a fair price, then anything in the mid-thirties you pay for the big guy is a good investment: he can still bang 'em with the best. Last season Fielder voiced his displeasure with all the losing in Detroit, and we sympathize. But until some of those vaunted Tiger prospects come through (especially the pitchers), the Big Guy will do his banging for a fourth-place team. The Tigers are still three or four position players and a starting rotation away from being a contender.

Year	Team	Lg.	Pos.	G	AB	R	H	HR	RBI	SB	BA
1992	Detroit	AL	1B	155	594	80	145	35	124	0	.244
1993	Detroit	AL	1B	154	573	80	153	30	117	0	.267
1994	Detroit	AL	1B	109	425	67	110	28	90	0	.259
1995	Detroit	AL	1B	136	494	70	120	31	82	0	.243
Post All-Star				67	243	28	56	11	31	0	.230

TRAVIS FRYMAN
Age 27/R   **$24**

The HR figure is not a typo. Are we concerned? Not a bit. Guarantee: 20 HR and 100 RBI.

Year	Team	Lg.	Pos.	G	AB	R	H	HR	RBI	SB	BA
1992	Detroit	AL	SS	161	659	87	175	20	96	8	.266
1993	Detroit	AL	SS	151	607	98	182	22	97	9	.300
1994	Detroit	AL	3B	114	464	66	122	18	85	2	.263
1995	Detroit	AL	3B	144	567	79	156	15	81	4	.275
Post All-Star				74	296	41	82	8	45	1	.277

GARY GAETTI
Age 37/R   **$26**

We wrote him off five years ago, shrewdly noting the declining power numbers and the increasing years. We were, ah, premature in reporting his baseball demise. But we don't think he can do it again—it's just flat out against nature.

Year	Team	Lg.	Pos.	G	AB	R	H	HR	RBI	SB	BA
1992	California	AL	3B	130	456	41	103	12	48	3	.226
1993	California	AL	3B	20	50	3	9	0	4	1	.180
1993	Kansas City	AL	3B	82	281	37	72	14	46	0	.256
1994	Kansas City	AL	3B	90	327	53	94	12	57	0	.287
1995	Kansas City	AL	3B	137	514	76	134	35	96	3	.261
Post All-Star				75	274	43	70	18	47	3	.255

DAVE HOLLINS
Age 29/B   **$5**

Hard to say who's had a tougher three years, Hollins or Bill Clinton. Even harder to say who's less likely to make a big comeback.

Year	Team	Lg.	Pos.	G	AB	R	H	HR	RBI	SB	BA
1992	Philadelphia	NL	3B	156	586	104	158	27	93	9	.270
1993	Philadelphia	NL	3B	143	543	104	148	18	93	2	.273
1994	Philadelphia	NL	3B	44	162	28	36	4	26	1	.222
1995	Philadelphia	NL	1B	65	205	46	47	7	25	1	.229
1995	Boston	AL	DH	5	13	2	2	0	1	0	.154
Post All-Star				15	39	5	7	2	5	0	.179

Catchers
pp. 27–41

Corners
pp. 41–62

Infield
pp. 63–82

Outfield
pp. 83–113

DH
pp. 114–118

Starters
pp. 119–157

Relievers
pp. 157–193

JOHN JAHA   Age 29/R $17

Last year we called Jaha "Wally Joyner with a lousy BA." We figure he read it, got mad, and went out and proved us wrong. Good for him. But he still has to play for Bud Selig. Bad for him. How bad is it to play for that small-minded used car saleman who did his dead-level best to run baseball into the ground? When Phil Garner had his team playing hard and in the wild card race (thus ruining the revenue sharing argument), Selig actually said publicly that it couldn't last, that they couldn't keep it up. Thanks, Bud—your team needed that.

Year	Team	Lg.	Pos.	G	AB	R	H	HR	RBI	SB	BA
1992	Milwaukee	AL	1B	47	133	17	30	2	10	10	.226
1993	Milwaukee	AL	1B	153	515	78	136	19	70	13	.264
1994	Milwaukee	AL	1B	84	291	45	70	12	39	3	.241
1995	Milwaukee	AL	1B	88	316	59	99	20	65	2	.313
Post All-Star				56	211	36	65	14	44	1	.308

WALLY JOYNER   Age 33/L $17

John Jaha with no power. Sorry, that's not being fair to Jaha. Whatever his Ro-tisserie numbers, Joyner is not one of our favorites. The minute he passed the 500 plate appearances that triggered his 1996 contract at a cool $5 million, he missed two games with a stiff back. We think he's just a stiff, period.

Year	Team	Lg.	Pos.	G	AB	R	H	HR	RBI	SB	BA
1992	Kansas City	AL	1B	149	572	66	154	9	66	11	.269
1993	Kansas City	AL	1B	141	497	83	145	15	65	5	.292
1994	Kansas City	AL	1B	97	363	52	113	8	57	3	.311
1995	Kansas City	AL	1B	131	465	69	144	12	83	3	.310
Post All-Star				68	245	33	79	7	42	1	.322

SCOTT LEIUS   Age 30/R $6

So we pencilled him in last year as a sleeper candidate for 20 dingers. So he fell a few dingers short. So nobody's perfect.

Year	Team	Lg.	Pos.	G	AB	R	H	HR	RBI	SB	BA
1992	Minnesota	AL	3B	129	409	50	102	2	35	6	.249
1993	Minnesota	AL	SS	10	18	4	3	0	2	0	.167
1994	Minnesota	AL	3B	97	350	57	86	14	49	2	.246
1995	Minnesota	AL	3B	117	372	51	92	4	45	2	.247
Post All-Star				56	169	25	45	1	16	0	.266

JEFF MANTO   Age 31/R $12

A journeyman arrives. With just 222 major league AB at age 30, Manto—a former Indians farmhand who fizzled in two shots—figured to spend the rest of his baseball career in the high minors, spear-carrying for some organization so that its real prospects wouldn't have to resort to playing scrub to hone their skills. Then a miracle happened—Manto got his Big Break, and he took third base away from Leo Gomez the way Gomez took it away from Chris Sabo. Too bad Ken Burns wasn't hanging around with his camcorder.

Year	Team	Lg.	Pos.	G	AB	R	H	HR	RBI	SB	BA
1993	Philadelphia	NL	3B	8	18	0	1	0	0	0	.056
1995	Baltimore	AL	3B	89	254	31	65	17	38	0	.256
Post All-Star				46	108	13	24	5	8	0	.222

TINO MARTINEZ   Age 28/L $28

He finally had the year he always threatened to. Welcome to the first tier of first basemen in the American League, Tino. You may take the place vacated by . . .

Year	Team	Lg.	Pos.	G	AB	R	H	HR	RBI	SB	BA
1992	Seattle	AL	1B	136	460	53	118	16	66	2	.257
1993	Seattle	AL	1B	109	408	48	108	17	60	0	.265
1994	Seattle	AL	1B	97	329	42	86	20	61	1	.261
1995	Seattle	AL	1B	141	519	92	152	31	111	0	.293
Post All-Star				73	278	50	80	13	53	0	.288

DON MATTINGLY   Age 34/L $8

Now batting for the Nippon Ham Fighters, Donnie Ballgame? Could be. Everybody knows it's over. Everybody knows the Yankees can't justify bringing him back. It's a shame his last year in New York had to be spent on an underachieving team. It's a shame about the back troubles that turned him into a slap hitter for the last half dozen seasons. It's a shame he grew bitter and lashed out at his treatment by Steinbrenner last summer. What did he expect? Yes, he was subjected to a lot of petty slights. But no, he hadn't exactly earned his $4.3 million a year this decade. For a while, though, there wasn't a sweeter hitter on the planet. Thanks, Don. And *sayonara*?

Year	Team	Lg.	Pos.	G	AB	R	H	HR	RBI	SB	BA
1992	New York	AL	1B	157	640	89	184	14	86	3	.287
1993	New York	AL	1B	134	530	78	154	17	86	0	.291
1994	New York	AL	1B	97	372	62	113	6	51	0	.304
1995	New York	AL	1B	128	458	59	132	7	49	0	.288
Post All-Star				74	265	36	79	6	29	0	.298

MARK McGWIRE   Age 32/R $37

One of the best power hitters in the game, he hasn't played a full season since 1991. Keep that in mind when the bidding starts to climb. Sure, he might swat 50 if he were healthy a whole year. The key word is "if." A classic Rotisserie mistake is to draft bench-pressers like McGwire and think "This is the year he'll be healthy." Like the bride who says "I can change him," you will be disappointed. Good news: Oakland may make him a full-time DH next year to save him from the wear and tear of actually playing his position. Half a player at 32. Way to go, Mark. This never happened to Hank Greenberg.

Year	Team	Lg.	Pos.	G	AB	R	H	HR	RBI	SB	BA
1992	Oakland	AL	1B	139	467	87	125	42	104	0	.268
1993	Oakland	AL	1B	27	84	16	28	9	24	0	.333
1994	Oakland	AL	1B	47	135	26	34	9	25	0	.252
1995	Oakland	AL	1B	104	317	75	87	39	90	1	.274
Post All-Star				36	105	25	29	15	31	1	.276

Catchers
pp. 27–41

Corners
pp. 41–62

Infield
pp. 63–82

Outfield
pp. 83–113

DH
pp. 114–118

Starters
pp. 119–157

Relievers
pp. 157–193

TIM NAEHRING   Age 29/R $12

Finally, *finally*, he stayed injury-free long enough to put together a solid
season. Yes, he made everybody forget Scott Cooper, who spent the summer
making St. Louis fans wish they could forget him.

Year	Team	Lg.	Pos.	G	AB	R	H	HR	RBI	SB	BA
1992	Boston	AL	SS	72	186	12	43	3	14	0	.231
1993	Boston	AL	2B	39	127	14	42	1	17	1	.331
1994	Boston	AL	2B	80	297	41	82	7	42	1	.276
1995	Boston	AL	3B	126	433	61	133	10	57	0	.307
Post All-Star				65	220	26	60	5	20	0	.273

PHIL NEVIN   Age 25/R $3

Has shown that he has the swagger, the me-first attitude, and the pout of a
bona fide superstar. Has yet to prove that he can hit anything but Triple-A
pitching. Keep an eye on him in Spring Training, though—if this former
Houston first-round draft pick is half as good as he thinks he is, you can
grab a surefire Hall of Famer cheap.

Year	Team	Lg.	Pos.	G	AB	R	H	HR	RBI	SB	BA
1995	Houston	NL	3B	18	60	4	7	0	1	1	.117
1995	Detroit	AL	OF	29	96	9	21	2	12	0	.219
Post All-Star				29	96	9	21	2	12	0	.219

JOHN OLERUD   Age 27/L $14

A second year of reduced power and Carlos Delgado fiddling around with a
first baseman's glove spells trouble for the next Ted Williams. (Remember
when people used to call him that?) Olerud has a lot to prove this year.
Without a turnaround, last year's rumor could be this year's trade. The Jays
need pitching and they won't wait if Olerud doesn't produce.

Year	Team	Lg.	Pos.	G	AB	R	H	HR	RBI	SB	BA
1992	Toronto	AL	1B	138	458	68	130	16	66	1	.284
1993	Toronto	AL	1B	158	551	109	200	24	107	0	.363
1994	Toronto	AL	1B	108	384	47	114	12	67	1	.297
1995	Toronto	AL	1B	135	492	72	143	8	54	0	.291
Post All-Star				70	244	42	82	5	33	0	.336

RAFAEL PALMEIRO   Age 31/R $34

It would be tough to find a more consistent, productive hitter. It would also
be tough to find a guy with numbers like these who never gets mentioned
when the best players in the game are talked about. But in Rotisserie circles,
he gets mentioned all the time.

Year	Team	Lg.	Pos.	G	AB	R	H	HR	RBI	SB	BA
1992	Texas	AL	1B	159	608	84	163	22	85	2	.268
1993	Texas	AL	1B	160	597	124	176	37	105	22	.295
1994	Baltimore	AL	1B	111	436	82	139	23	76	7	.319
1995	Baltimore	AL	1B	143	554	89	172	39	104	3	.310
Post All-Star				76	290	47	97	24	57	0	.334

DEAN PALMER   Age 27/R $26

There is a photograph of Jimmy Foxx looking at Ted Williams's skinny arms, wondering where all that power came from. Williams generated his power by using his whole body, especially his hips. Think of other great hitters like Stan Musial, Hank Aaron, Willie Mays, Andre Dawson—all had great power and relatively normal bodies. None spent his spare time pumping iron. Which brings us to Dean Palmer, who missed most of last year with a ruptured bicep tendon suffered when he swung so hard that he pulled his overdeveloped muscle off the bone. This misguided approach also plagues the efforts of Juan Gonzalez, Jose Canseco, and Mark McGwire—big men who go on and off the DL and who will be full-time DHs long before their time because of all the time they spend in the weight room. Jeez, it's enough to make you want to stretch out on the couch and take a nap.

Year	Team	Lg.	Pos.	G	AB	R	H	HR	RBI	SB	BA
1992	Texas	AL	3B	152	541	74	124	26	72	10	.229
1993	Texas	AL	3B	148	519	88	127	33	96	11	.245
1994	Texas	AL	3B	93	342	50	84	19	59	3	.246
1995	Texas	AL	3B	36	119	30	40	9	24	1	.336
Post All-Star				2	4	0	2	0	0	0	.500

CRAIG PAQUETTE   Age 27/R $12

Between Brosius and Paquette, the A's have the hot corner pretty well covered. If Brosius doesn't move to first, one could end up as trade bait.

Year	Team	Lg.	Pos.	G	AB	R	H	HR	RBI	SB	BA
1993	Oakland	AL	3B	105	393	35	86	12	46	4	.219
1994	Oakland	AL	3B	14	49	0	7	0	0	1	.143
1995	Oakland	AL	3B	105	283	42	64	13	49	5	.226
Post All-Star				56	165	25	36	5	26	3	.218

EDUARDO PEREZ   Age 26/R $2

The emergence of J. T. Snow and the acquisition of Tony Phillips has left little playing time for Perez. The Angels moved him around so much he may be valuable as a utility player someday, but probably not in California.

Year	Team	Lg.	Pos.	G	AB	R	H	HR	RBI	SB	BA
1993	California	AL	3B	52	180	16	45	4	30	5	.250
1994	California	AL	1B	38	129	10	27	5	16	3	.209
1995	California	AL	3B	29	71	9	12	1	7	0	.169
Post All-Star				7	6	1	1	1	2	0	.167

HERBERT PERRY   Age 26/R $3

Hard to imagine this guy playing much with Paul Sorrento and Eddie Murray in the way. But Eddie's getting up there, so Perry's worth picking up cheap now in the hope of him playing more later.

Year	Team	Lg.	Pos.	G	AB	R	H	HR	RBI	SB	BA
1994	Cleveland	AL	1B	4	9	1	1	0	1	0	.111
1995	Cleveland	AL	1B	52	162	23	51	3	23	1	.315
Post All-Star				43	129	16	40	0	18	1	.310

Catchers
pp. 27-41

Corners
pp. 41-62

Infield
pp. 63-82

Outfield
pp. 83-113

DH
pp. 114-118

Starters
pp. 119-157

Relievers
pp. 157-193

TONY PHILLIPS　　　　　　　　　　　　　Age 36/B　　$26

Every time you saw Tony Phillips on TV last year he looked mean and feisty, arguing balls and strikes or yelling at opponents. The nasty Tony was just what the Angels needed. Ordinarily, a player doesn't wait until he's in his mid-thirties to learn how to hit home runs. But there's nothing remotely ordinary about Mr. Phillips. Year after year, an amazing and versatile player.

Year	Team	Lg.	Pos.	G	AB	R	H	HR	RBI	SB	BA
1992	Detroit	AL	OF	159	606	114	167	10	64	12	.276
1993	Detroit	AL	OF	151	566	113	177	7	57	16	.313
1994	Detroit	AL	OF	114	438	91	123	19	61	13	.281
1995	California	AL	3B	139	525	119	137	27	61	13	.261
Post All-Star				72	275	58	67	13	24	5	.244

JUAN SAMUEL　　　　　　　　　　　　　Age 35/R　　$7

Kansas City is the wrong place for a veteran with something left. Somebody will pick him up after such a strong year. So should you.

Year	Team	Lg.	Pos.	G	AB	R	H	HR	RBI	SB	BA
1992	Kansas City	AL	OF	29	102	15	29	0	8	6	.284
1992	Los Angeles	NL	2B	47	122	7	32	0	15	2	.262
1993	Cincinnati	NL	2B	103	261	31	60	4	26	9	.230
1994	Detroit	AL	OF	59	136	32	42	5	21	5	.309
1995	Detroit	AL	1B	76	171	28	48	10	34	5	.281
1995	Kansas City	AL	DH	15	34	3	6	2	5	1	.176
Post All-Star				48	116	9	22	4	12	1	.190

KEVIN SEITZER　　　　　　　　　　　　Age 34/R　　$12

Jeff Cirillo's emergence allows Bud Selig to let Seitzer leave Milwaukee via free agency for the second time. Seitzer talked retirement briefly last year, but these numbers mean somebody will pay him nicely to stick around.

Year	Team	Lg.	Pos.	G	AB	R	H	HR	RBI	SB	BA
1992	Milwaukee	AL	3B	148	540	74	146	5	71	13	.270
1993	Milwaukee	AL	3B	47	162	21	47	7	30	3	.290
1993	Oakland	AL	3B	73	255	24	65	4	27	4	.255
1994	Milwaukee	AL	3B	80	309	44	97	5	49	2	.314
1995	Milwaukee	AL	3B	132	492	56	153	5	69	2	.311
Post All-Star				70	260	32	78	3	32	2	.300

J. T. SNOW　　　　　　　　　　　　　　Age 28/B　　$22

A very nice comeback year for a guy once traded for his teammate Jim Abbott. Snow's season is further proof that age 27 is the beginning of a player's prime. Oh, and by the way—we would be remiss if we did not point out that Snow is a former Yankee farmhand, one of the more recent in a long line of good ones that Steinbrenner has sent away.

Year	Team	Lg.	Pos.	G	AB	R	H	HR	RBI	SB	BA
1992	New York	AL	1B	7	14	1	2	0	2	0	.143
1993	California	AL	1B	129	419	60	101	16	57	3	.241
1994	California	AL	1B	61	223	22	49	8	30	0	.220
1995	California	AL	1B	143	544	80	157	24	102	2	.289
Post All-Star				75	285	43	78	13	51	1	.274

PAUL SORRENTO
Age 30/L   **$18**

Not bad for a platoon player hitting out of the seven hole.

Year	Team	Lg.	Pos.	G	AB	R	H	HR	RBI	SB	BA
1992	Cleveland	AL	1B	140	458	52	123	18	60	0	.269
1993	Cleveland	AL	1B	148	463	75	119	18	65	3	.257
1994	Cleveland	AL	1B	95	322	43	90	14	62	0	.280
1995	Cleveland	AL	1B	104	323	50	76	25	79	1	.235
Post All-Star				53	164	23	35	12	38	1	.213

ED SPRAGUE
Age 28/R   **$17**

One of the few Blue Jays who seemed to remember they were the defending champions. Toronto needs Sprague to keep it up. Bet that he does.

Year	Team	Lg.	Pos.	G	AB	R	H	HR	RBI	SB	BA
1992	Toronto	AL	C	22	47	6	11	1	7	0	.234
1993	Toronto	AL	3B	150	546	50	142	12	73	1	.260
1994	Toronto	AL	3B	109	405	38	97	11	44	1	.240
1995	Toronto	AL	3B	144	521	77	127	18	74	0	.244
Post All-Star				77	283	39	64	7	39	0	.226

SCOTT STAHOVIAK
Age 26/L   **$4**

A participant in the Hrbek Replacement Derby, he has one thing that Hrbie certainly never had—speed. Surgery for elbow chips ended his season. While they had his arm open, let's hope the doctors slipped in some power. He's shown some pop before. If it comes back, the job is his.

Year	Team	Lg.	Pos.	G	AB	R	H	HR	RBI	SB	BA
1993	Minnesota	AL	3B	20	57	1	11	0	1	0	.193
1995	Minnesota	AL	1B	94	263	28	70	3	23	5	.266
Post All-Star				43	111	12	30	1	12	4	.270

DOUG STRANGE
Age 31/B   **$1**

Late in the draft, you're tired, you've got a middle infield hole to fill, the room's stuffy, your head's feeling a little Strange ... oh, why the hell not: he's only a buck.

Year	Team	Lg.	Pos.	G	AB	R	H	HR	RBI	SB	BA
1992	Chicago	NL	3B	52	94	7	15	1	5	1	.160
1993	Texas	AL	2B	145	484	58	124	7	60	6	.256
1994	Texas	AL	2B	73	226	26	48	5	26	1	.212
1995	Seattle	AL	3B	74	155	19	42	2	21	0	.271
Post All-Star				37	72	9	19	1	10	0	.264

B. J. SURHOFF
Age 31/L   **$15**

Great comeback from a solid pro. Added bonus: he qualifies this year at C, 1B, and OF. His season must have irked his owner because Surhoff dug in and really produced at a crossroads in his career. Selig hates that, because it means he has to pay the guy what he's worth.

Year	Team	Lg.	Pos.	G	AB	R	H	HR	RBI	SB	BA
1992	Milwaukee	AL	C	139	480	63	121	4	62	14	.252
1993	Milwaukee	AL	3B	148	552	66	151	7	79	12	.274
1994	Milwaukee	AL	3B	40	134	20	35	5	22	0	.261
1995	Milwaukee	AL	OF	117	415	72	133	13	73	7	.320
Post All-Star				69	270	46	79	9	41	3	.293

Catchers
pp. 27–41

Corners
pp. 41–62

Infield
pp. 63–82

Outfield
pp. 83–113

DH
pp. 114–118

Starters
pp. 119–157

Relievers
pp. 157–193

FRANK THOMAS Age 27/R $41

Only the fifth player in major league history to have 100 RBI in his first five seasons. Even though we hate wishing any enterprise Jerry Reinsdorf's associated with well, we do hope the White Sox bounce back. Why? Because baseball needs guys like Frank Thomas in the playoffs. Check out the phenomenal .454 OB average. Also the 50% increase in stolen bases.

Year	Team	Lg.	Pos.	G	AB	R	H	HR	RBI	SB	BA
1992	Chicago	AL	1B	160	573	108	185	24	115	6	.323
1993	Chicago	AL	1B	153	549	106	174	41	128	4	.317
1994	Chicago	AL	1B	113	399	106	141	38	101	2	.353
1995	Chicago	AL	1B	145	493	102	152	40	111	3	.308
Post All-Star				79	265	53	78	19	58	1	.294

JIM THOME Age 25/L $31

Thome sweet Thome. One of the nicest swings in baseball. And he's just getting started. This year, look for 30 dingers and 90 RBI.

Year	Team	Lg.	Pos.	G	AB	R	H	HR	RBI	SB	BA
1992	Cleveland	AL	3B	40	117	8	24	2	12	2	.205
1993	Cleveland	AL	3B	47	154	28	41	7	22	2	.266
1994	Cleveland	AL	3B	98	321	58	86	20	52	3	.268
1995	Cleveland	AL	3B	137	452	92	142	25	73	4	.314
Post All-Star				74	240	48	72	8	34	1	.300

MO VAUGHN Age 28/L $39

Want a clue as to how hard he plays? Look at the SB total. As a sportswriter friend of ours says, "Mo's one of the few guys I'd pay to see if I didn't get in for free." More than Belle, more than Thomas, more than Bonds, more than anybody, Vaughn can stop conversation in a crowded bar and get all eyes turned toward the TV set just by stepping up to the plate. Listen to what Lou Piniella told Peter Gammons last summer: "There's a presence to Mo that sets him apart. He has fun, but he has that presence that says, 'Don't mess with us.' He's all *us*, something you didn't see in the past with the Red Sox." Our choice for MVP, too.

Year	Team	Lg.	Pos.	G	AB	R	H	HR	RBI	SB	BA
1992	Boston	AL	1B	113	355	42	83	13	57	3	.234
1993	Boston	AL	1B	152	539	86	160	29	101	4	.297
1994	Boston	AL	1B	111	394	65	122	26	82	4	.310
1995	Boston	AL	1B	140	550	98	165	39	126	11	.300
Post All-Star				72	288	46	89	15	66	1	.309

ROBIN VENTURA Age 28/L $29

A lot was made of his 19 errors last year. We'd like to make a lot out of the fact he hit two grand slams in one game last year. How many errors is that worth? One of the premier power-hitting third-sackers in the game.

Year	Team	Lg.	Pos.	G	AB	R	H	HR	RBI	SB	BA
1992	Chicago	AL	3B	157	592	85	167	16	93	2	.282
1993	Chicago	AL	3B	157	554	85	145	22	94	1	.262
1994	Chicago	AL	3B	109	401	57	113	18	78	3	.282
1995	Chicago	AL	3B	135	492	79	145	26	93	4	.295
Post All-Star				70	247	37	72	11	44	3	.291

Up the Middle

Catchers
pp. 27–41

Corners
pp. 41–62

Infield
pp. 63–82

Outfield
pp. 83–113

DH
pp. 114–118

Starters
pp. 119–157

Relievers
pp. 157–193

NATIONAL LEAGUE

KURT ABBOTT   Age 26/R $14

Early-season show of power got him thinking he was another Ernie Banks, which led to over-swinging and too many strikeouts. But he's an outstanding athlete who could quietly emerge as one of the better offensive shortstops in the league. And his development has—thankfully, from the Marlins' perspective—relegated . . .

Year	Team	Lg.	Pos.	G	AB	R	H	HR	RBI	SB	BA
1993	Oakland	AL	OF	20	61	11	15	3	9	2	.246
1994	Florida	NL	SS	101	345	41	86	9	33	3	.249
1995	Florida	NL	SS	120	420	60	107	17	60	4	.255
Post All-Star				70	239	33	60	9	34	1	.251

ALEX ARIAS   Age 28/R $1

. . . to the utility, fill-in status his skills richly deserve. In fact, his relegation to part-time duty underscores how the Marlins have grown away from being just an expansion team. And for that matter, the development of . . .

Year	Team	Lg.	Pos.	G	AB	R	H	HR	RBI	SB	BA
1992	Chicago	NL	SS	32	99	14	29	0	7	0	.293
1993	Florida	NL	2B	96	249	27	67	2	20	1	.269
1994	Florida	NL	SS	59	113	4	27	0	15	0	.239
1995	Florida	NL	SS	94	216	22	58	3	26	1	.269
Post All-Star				44	109	12	29	1	17	0	.266

JASON BATES   Age 25/S $8

. . . is a similar benchmark for the Rockies. He's the first product of their farm system to make an everyday dent, and he is going to get a lot better. The first thing he has to do is learn to hit lefties (.183 against them last year, vs. .291 against righties). The fact that he hit a ton better at home than on the road (.325 vs. .212) is a familiar Rockies story by now.

Year	Team	Lg.	Pos.	G	AB	R	H	HR	RBI	SB	BA
1995	Colorado	NL	2B	116	322	42	86	8	46	3	.267
Post All-Star				56	128	19	34	2	20	0	.266

DAVID BELL Age 23/R $5

Because his father is one of the all-time class acts, we could never say anything bad about him. And because Cardinals people (and Indians people before they traded him) rave about his work habits, solid skills, and ability to be a tough out, there isn't any call to say anything bad about him anyway. He worked over the winter on playing second base, and the job will be his to lose this spring. We're betting that he doesn't.

Year	Team	Lg.	Pos.	G	AB	R	H	HR	RBI	SB	BA
1995	Cleveland	AL	3B	2	2	0	0	0	0	0	0.000
1995	St. Louis	NL	2B	39	144	13	36	2	19	1	.250
Post All-Star				39	144	13	36	2	19	1	.250

JAY BELL Age 30/R $8

On the great Pirates clubs of yesteryear, he was an integral part of the mix. On the faceless Pirates teams of today, he unfortunately gets too much attention, simply because he is one of the few recognizable names. Good power from the SS hole.

Year	Team	Lg.	Pos.	G	AB	R	H	HR	RBI	SB	BA
1992	Pittsburgh	NL	SS	159	632	87	167	9	55	7	.264
1993	Pittsburgh	NL	SS	154	604	102	187	9	51	16	.310
1994	Pittsburgh	NL	SS	110	424	68	117	9	45	2	.276
1995	Pittsburgh	NL	SS	138	530	79	139	13	55	2	.262
Post All-Star				75	291	42	85	8	37	1	.292

RAFAEL BELLIARD Age 34/R $1

The Esteban Beltré of the National League.

Year	Team	Lg.	Pos.	G	AB	R	H	HR	RBI	SB	BA
1992	Atlanta	NL	SS	144	285	20	60	0	14	0	.211
1993	Atlanta	NL	SS	91	79	6	18	0	6	0	.228
1994	Atlanta	NL	SS	46	120	9	29	0	9	0	.242
1995	Atlanta	NL	SS	75	180	12	40	0	7	2	.222
Post All-Star				47	112	6	22	0	4	0	.196

CRAIG BIGGIO Age 30/R $30

While you weren't looking, he might have become the best second baseman in baseball. And yes, we do remember that there are a couple of pretty good ones over in the other league. Heck, if his power keeps developing, he might this year become the rarest of all birds—a 30-year-old 30/30 second baseman worth 30 Rotissebucks.

Year	Team	Lg.	Pos.	G	AB	R	H	HR	RBI	SB	BA
1992	Houston	NL	2B	162	613	96	170	6	39	38	.277
1993	Houston	NL	2B	155	610	98	175	21	64	15	.287
1994	Houston	NL	2B	114	437	88	139	6	56	39	.318
1995	Houston	NL	2B	141	553	123	167	22	77	33	.302
Post All-Star				74	289	68	93	12	36	21	.322

JEFF BLAUSER Age 30/R $8

A hard-nosed gamer with above-average power, Blauser arrived at free agency at a time when his wealthy organization has no other shortstops on the horizon. So the Braves gave him a big three-year contract, whereupon he plummeted to one of the worst seasons of any everyday player in the majors and became the favorite boo-target of all the tomahawk-choppers in Fulton County Stadium. We think that it was because he was pressing too hard. Relax, Jeff. There, that should do it.

Year	Team	Lg.	Pos.	G	AB	R	H	HR	RBI	SB	BA
1992	Atlanta	NL	SS	123	343	61	90	14	46	5	.262
1993	Atlanta	NL	SS	161	597	110	182	15	73	16	.305
1994	Atlanta	NL	SS	96	380	56	98	6	45	1	.258
1995	Atlanta	NL	SS	115	431	60	91	12	31	8	.211
Post All-Star				47	170	19	32	4	11	4	.188

TIM BOGAR
Age 29/R   **$1**

More useful to the Mets as a bit player in an unfolding rebuilding drama than to you.

Year	Team	Lg.	Pos.	G	AB	R	H	HR	RBI	SB	BA
1993	New York	NL	SS	78	205	19	50	3	25	0	.244
1994	New York	NL	3B	50	52	5	8	2	5	1	.154
1995	New York	NL	SS	78	145	17	42	1	21	1	.290
Post All-Star				47	93	11	29	0	13	1	.312

BRET BOONE
Age 26/R   **$14**

If you own him, you gotta love his numbers and potential for improvement. And you don't have to be concerned that everyone who plays with or coaches Boonie the Younger finds him just a tad on the cocky side.

Year	Team	Lg.	Pos.	G	AB	R	H	HR	RBI	SB	BA
1992	Seattle	AL	2B	33	129	15	25	4	15	1	.194
1993	Seattle	AL	2B	76	271	31	68	12	38	2	.251
1994	Cincinnati	NL	2B	108	381	59	122	12	68	3	.320
1995	Cincinnati	NL	2B	138	513	63	137	15	68	5	.267
Post All-Star				70	262	32	68	10	39	4	.260

ANDUJAR CEDENO
Age 26/R   **$4**

Said one veteran scout after watching him strike out three times and then nearly decapitate a fan behind first base with one of his misguided missiles from the hole: "It makes you sick to see all that ability go to waste." The Padres, however, still hope it's not too late.

Year	Team	Lg.	Pos.	G	AB	R	H	HR	RBI	SB	BA
1992	Houston	NL	SS	71	220	15	38	2	13	2	.173
1993	Houston	NL	SS	149	505	69	143	11	56	9	.283
1994	Houston	NL	SS	98	342	38	90	9	49	1	.263
1995	San Diego	NL	SS	120	390	42	82	6	31	5	.210
Post All-Star				53	150	11	26	0	5	5	.173

Catchers
pp. 27–41

Corners
pp. 41–62

Infield
pp. 63–82

Outfield
pp. 83–113

DH
pp. 114–118

Starters
pp. 119–157

Relievers
pp. 157–193

ROYCE CLAYTON

Age 26/R $11

When all around him was in chaos, he still kept driving in big runs, making all the plays at short, and stealing bases when they mattered. Now, if he would just cut down on his strikeouts, we'd like him even more.

Year	Team	Lg.	Pos.	G	AB	R	H	HR	RBI	SB	BA
1992	San Francisco	NL	SS	98	321	31	72	4	24	8	.224
1993	San Francisco	NL	SS	153	549	54	155	6	70	11	.282
1994	San Francisco	NL	SS	108	385	38	91	3	30	23	.236
1995	San Francisco	NL	SS	138	509	56	124	5	58	24	.244
Post All-Star				70	264	25	62	2	20	11	.235

WIL CORDERO

Age 24/R $18

First, he became a shortstop version of Steve Sax and started slinging every throw from short as if he were in a cow-chip hurling contest. Then the Expos tried him in the outfield, sending him into a deep sulk during which he drove in just 3 runs in over a month. So le front office canceled the experiment, sent him back to the infield, and said that he would be the starting shortstop for the Expos this year—or not be an Expo at all. We took that as a gentle hint that le front office is getting a little impatient waiting around for him to become a full-bore star. Hard to estimate the impact on a young player's morale of seeing a good team being dismantled around him.

Year	Team	Lg.	Pos.	G	AB	R	H	HR	RBI	SB	BA
1992	Montreal	NL	SS	45	126	17	38	2	8	0	.302
1993	Montreal	NL	SS	138	475	56	118	10	58	12	.248
1994	Montreal	NL	SS	110	415	65	122	15	63	16	.294
1995	Montreal	NL	SS	131	514	64	147	10	49	9	.286
Post All-Star				63	241	28	65	5	21	5	.270

TRIPP CROMER

Age 28/R $2

He comes from a baseball family—his dad is a scout and various brothers and cousins have played professional ball. Alas, none of them could hit either.

Year	Team	Lg.	Pos.	G	AB	R	H	HR	RBI	SB	BA
1993	St. Louis	NL	SS	10	23	1	2	0	0	0	.087
1994	St. Louis	NL	SS	2	0	1	0	0	0	0	0.000
1995	St. Louis	NL	SS	105	345	36	78	5	18	0	.226
Post All-Star				44	138	10	28	0	6	0	.203

DELINO DeSHIELDS

Age 27/L $18

Here's a little story that pretty much sums up the Rotisserie Experience (Downside Division). An owner in our league, convinced that DeShields would bounce back to the form he showed in Montreal in 1990–93, bought him for $26 at our draft auction last spring—coincidentally, exactly the price we had placed on him in last year's book. Smart, huh? But wait—it gets worse. Our owner stayed with DeShields, took to heart every statement by Lasorda that he was standing behind DeShields, and went down to the Mendoza line with DeShields. Then, in desperation, our owner put DeShields in a package with some great young talent for next year (Paul Wilson, others) and peddled him to another team in mid-July. Check out DeShields's second-half performance—particularly those 20 SB—if you want a true-life picture of Rotisserie Hell.

Year	Team	Lg.	Pos.	G	AB	R	H	HR	RBI	SB	BA
1992	Montreal	NL	2B	135	530	82	155	7	56	46	.292
1993	Montreal	NL	2B	123	481	75	142	2	29	43	.295
1994	Los Angeles	NL	2B	89	320	51	80	2	33	27	.250
1995	Los Angeles	NL	2B	127	425	66	109	8	37	39	.256
Post All-Star				62	172	31	47	4	21	20	.273

Catchers
pp. 27–41

Corners
pp. 41–62

Infield
pp. 63–82

Outfield
pp. 83–113

DH
pp. 114–118

Starters
pp. 119–157

Relievers
pp. 157–193

MARIANO DUNCAN   Age 33/R $8

Has gloves (and bat), will travel. The consummate role player who keeps on rolling out productive seasons.

Year	Team	Lg.	Pos.	G	AB	R	H	HR	RBI	SB	BA
1992	Philadelphia	NL	OF	142	574	71	153	8	50	23	.267
1993	Philadelphia	NL	2B	124	496	68	140	11	73	6	.282
1994	Philadelphia	NL	2B	88	347	49	93	8	48	10	.268
1995	Philadelphia	NL	2B	52	196	20	56	3	23	1	.286
1995	Cincinnati	NL	2B	29	69	16	20	3	13	0	.290
Post All-Star				43	110	21	33	4	23	0	.300

SHAWON DUNSTON   Age 33/R $16

A fine year answered any lingering questions about his full recovery from back surgery. Now the Cubs are toying with the possibility of converting him to third base. But there is also the possibility that they'll cut him loose, which would make him an intriguing commodity with the right team. Heck, put him in Denver and he'd hit 30 homers. Of course, you could put . . .

Year	Team	Lg.	Pos.	G	AB	R	H	HR	RBI	SB	BA
1992	Chicago	NL	SS	18	73	8	23	0	2	2	.315
1993	Chicago	NL	SS	7	10	3	4	0	2	0	.400
1994	Chicago	NL	SS	88	331	38	92	11	35	3	.278
1995	Chicago	NL	SS	127	477	58	141	14	69	10	.296
Post All-Star				65	250	32	65	7	33	6	.260

CHAD FONVILLE   Age 25/B $8

. . . in Denver and he might hit, well, maybe as many homers as Walt Weiss. But Fonville will probably stay in Los Angeles, where, despite his lack of range, weak arm, nonexistent power, and so-so hands, he was able to win the shortstop job. Of course, as we will see later in this section, that was not an accomplishment of epic proportions.

Year	Team	Lg.	Pos.	G	AB	R	H	HR	RBI	SB	BA
1995	Montreal	NL	2B	14	12	2	4	0	0	0	.333
1995	Los Angeles	NL	SS	88	308	41	85	0	16	20	.276
Post All-Star				72	273	38	76	0	15	18	.278

CARLOS GARCIA   Age 28/R $11

It wasn't until June that he was finally over the knee injury suffered in winter ball. The Pirates' best player. That could be construed as faint praise, but we don't mean it that way. He's good, really good, and this year's numbers will reflect it.

Year	Team	Lg.	Pos.	G	AB	R	H	HR	RBI	SB	BA
1992	Pittsburgh	NL	2B	22	39	4	8	0	4	0	.205
1993	Pittsburgh	NL	2B	141	546	77	147	12	47	18	.269
1994	Pittsburgh	NL	2B	98	412	49	114	6	28	18	.277
1995	Pittsburgh	NL	2B	104	367	41	108	6	50	8	.294
Post All-Star				49	168	17	52	3	24	5	.310

JEFF KENT   Age 28/R $17

The most unpopular player in the Mets' clubhouse, where his moodiness
and arrogance turned off every teammate. Time was, moodiness and arrogance were commonplace in that clubhouse, but last season's New, Improved
Mets are a cheerful, outgoing bunch who know that A Met is an anagram
of Team. Does this mean that the Mets will move to protect team chemistry?
Not necessarily. That offense is pretty swell coming from second base. But
if they do move him, it might not be so swell coming from third base, which
is where he'd likely end up.

Year	Team	Lg.	Pos.	G	AB	R	H	HR	RBI	SB	BA
1992	Toronto	AL	3B	65	192	36	46	8	35	2	.240
1992	New York	NL	2B	37	113	16	27	3	15	0	.239
1993	New York	NL	2B	140	496	65	134	21	80	4	.270
1994	New York	NL	2B	107	415	53	121	14	68	1	.292
1995	New York	NL	2B	125	472	65	131	20	65	3	.278
Post All-Star				65	249	39	71	10	40	1	.285

MIKE LANSING   Age 27/R $10

Solid, versatile player. A little punch, a little speed, and (usually) a little
salary.

Year	Team	Lg.	Pos.	G	AB	R	H	HR	RBI	SB	BA
1993	Montreal	NL	3B	141	491	64	141	3	45	23	.287
1994	Montreal	NL	2B	106	394	44	105	5	35	12	.266
1995	Montreal	NL	2B	127	467	47	119	10	62	27	.255
Post All-Star				74	274	25	77	5	38	23	.281

BARRY LARKIN   Age 31/R $32

So *this* is what he can do when he isn't banged up and/or on the disabled
list. He got our vote for MVP.

Year	Team	Lg.	Pos.	G	AB	R	H	HR	RBI	SB	BA
1992	Cincinnati	NL	SS	140	533	76	162	12	78	15	.304
1993	Cincinnati	NL	SS	100	384	57	121	8	51	14	.315
1994	Cincinnati	NL	SS	110	427	78	119	9	52	26	.279
1995	Cincinnati	NL	SS	131	496	98	158	15	66	51	.319
Post All-Star				70	271	54	93	9	37	29	.343

MARK LEMKE   Age 30/B $2

Says Bobby Cox: "He's the biggest pain in the neck when he sits out a game.
When he gets hurt or I rest him, I'd rather have him back in the clubhouse
because he can't sit still." All that hyperactivity, alas, does not translate into
boffo offensive production.

Year	Team	Lg.	Pos.	G	AB	R	H	HR	RBI	SB	BA
1992	Atlanta	NL	2B	155	427	38	97	6	26	0	.227
1993	Atlanta	NL	2B	151	493	52	124	7	49	1	.252
1994	Atlanta	NL	2B	104	350	40	103	3	31	0	.294
1995	Atlanta	NL	2B	116	399	42	101	5	38	2	.253
Post All-Star				65	233	24	61	3	22	1	.262

NELSON LIRIANO
Age 31/B   **$2**

Enough stick to warrant a second buck when you're filling out your bench.

Year	Team	Lg.	Pos.	G	AB	R	H	HR	RBI	SB	BA
1993	Colorado	NL	SS	48	151	28	46	2	15	6	.305
1994	Colorado	NL	2B	87	255	39	65	3	31	0	.255
1995	Pittsburgh	NL	2B	107	259	29	74	5	38	2	.286
Post All-Star				64	172	18	49	3	28	0	.285

ROBERTO MEJIA
Age 23/R   **$1**

Three strikes and you're out, right? Maybe not. We have a sneaky feeling the Rockies still haven't given up on this guy. He's still only a baby, after all, so maybe they shouldn't. You can, however.

Year	Team	Lg.	Pos.	G	AB	R	H	HR	RBI	SB	BA
1993	Colorado	NL	2B	65	229	31	53	5	20	4	.231
1994	Colorado	NL	2B	38	116	11	28	4	14	3	.241
1995	Colorado	NL	2B	23	52	5	8	1	4	0	.154
Post All-Star			000	0	0	0	0	0	0	0	0.000

ORLANDO MILLER
Age 27/R   **$6**

Often erratic in the field and sometimes too moody to reach, but the Astros still think he can develop into a solid shortstop. We do too.

Year	Team	Lg.	Pos.	G	AB	R	H	HR	RBI	SB	BA
1994	Houston	NL	SS	16	40	3	13	2	9	1	.325
1995	Houston	NL	SS	92	324	36	85	5	36	3	.262
Post All-Star				33	98	12	22	2	9	2	.224

MICKEY MORANDINI
Age 29/L   **$8**

It was All-Star Monday and the Mick sat amid Bonds, Piazza, Maddux, and the rest and drank it all in. When it dawned on somebody that teammates Darren Daulton and Lenny Dykstra had not shown up for the workout, the Mick was surrounded by the always-charming Philadelphia media pack. "Where's Dutch, where's the Dude?" they asked in unison. The Mick just shrugged and said, "How do I know? I got over here as early as I could so I could get some autographs."

Year	Team	Lg.	Pos.	G	AB	R	H	HR	RBI	SB	BA
1992	Philadelphia	NL	2B	127	422	47	112	3	30	8	.265
1993	Philadelphia	NL	2B	120	425	57	105	3	33	13	.247
1994	Philadelphia	NL	2B	87	274	40	80	2	26	10	.292
1995	Philadelphia	NL	2B	127	494	65	140	6	49	9	.283
Post All-Star				69	267	32	76	2	22	5	.285

MIKE MORDECAI
Age 28/B   **$3**

No guarantees here, but if Blauser struggles again or if no second baseman is picked up to challenge or oust Lemke, this guy, who has both solid defensive skills and some pop, could end up at either position. (No relation to Mordecai Brown, aka 3-Finger Brown, of whom it was said he always gave 60 percent.)

Year	Team	Lg.	Pos.	G	AB	R	H	HR	RBI	SB	BA
1994	Atlanta	NL	SS	4	4	1	1	1	3	0	.250
1995	Atlanta	NL	2B	69	75	10	21	3	11	0	.280
Post All-Star				42	55	6	15	2	7	0	.273

Catchers pp. 27-41

Corners pp. 41-62

Infield pp. 63-82

Outfield pp. 83-113

DH pp. 114-118

Starters pp. 119-157

Relievers pp. 157-193

JOSE OFFERMAN
Age 27/B   **$3**

Let's put it this way. When he finally was benched after his errors total started getting dangerously close to the magic 40 plateau, and after he was guilty of innumerable fundamental mistakes on the field and on the basepaths, some Dodgers were seen high-fiving when the Offerman-less lineup card was posted.

Year	Team	Lg.	Pos.	G	AB	R	H	HR	RBI	SB	BA
1992	Los Angeles	NL	SS	149	534	67	139	1	30	23	.260
1993	Los Angeles	NL	SS	158	590	77	159	1	62	30	.269
1994	Los Angeles	NL	SS	72	243	27	51	1	25	2	.210
1995	Los Angeles	NL	SS	119	429	69	123	4	33	2	.287
Post All-Star				52	178	26	47	3	17	2	.264

JOSE OQUENDO
Age 32/B   **$1**

Pretend Oquendo means "Pass" in Spanish.

Year	Team	Lg.	Pos.	G	AB	R	H	HR	RBI	SB	BA
1992	St. Louis	NL	2B	14	35	3	9	0	3	0	.257
1993	St. Louis	NL	SS	46	73	7	15	0	4	0	.205
1994	St. Louis	NL	SS	55	129	13	34	0	9	1	.264
1995	St. Louis	NL	2B	88	220	31	46	2	17	1	.209
Post All-Star				36	91	11	18	1	6	0	.198

JOHN PATTERSON
Age 29/B   **$1**

And that Patterson means "Oquendo" in English.

Year	Team	Lg.	Pos.	G	AB	R	H	HR	RBI	SB	BA
1992	San Francisco	NL	2B	32	103	10	19	0	4	5	.184
1993	San Francisco	NL	2B	16	16	1	3	1	2	0	.188
1994	San Francisco	NL	2B	85	240	36	57	3	32	13	.237
1995	San Francisco	NL	2B	95	205	27	42	1	14	4	.205
Post All-Star				48	91	12	19	1	7	2	.209

GERONIMO PENA
Age 29/B   **$1**

The Dominican Mickey Kluttz, with more time on the DL the last 3 years than time active. He's the reason that health insurance in this country is so doggone expensive.

Year	Team	Lg.	Pos.	G	AB	R	H	HR	RBI	SB	BA
1992	St. Louis	NL	2B	62	203	31	62	7	31	13	.305
1993	St. Louis	NL	2B	74	254	34	65	5	30	13	.256
1994	St. Louis	NL	2B	83	213	33	54	11	34	9	.254
1995	St. Louis	NL	2B	32	101	20	27	1	8	3	.267
Post All-Star				12	38	8	9	0	2	1	.237

JODY REED
Age 33/R   **$3**

Feisty.

Year	Team	Lg.	Pos.	G	AB	R	H	HR	RBI	SB	BA
1992	Boston	AL	2B	143	550	64	136	3	40	7	.247
1993	Los Angeles	NL	2B	132	445	48	123	2	31	1	.276
1994	Milwaukee	AL	2B	108	399	48	108	2	37	5	.271
1995	San Diego	NL	2B	131	445	58	114	4	40	6	.256
Post All-Star				73	267	31	68	3	26	4	.255

REY SANCHEZ   Age 28/R $3

Over the years, Harry Caray has called him Roy, Reed, Ralph, Orlando, Rafe, and assorted other names. Come to think of it, he does seem sort of interchangeable.

Year	Team	Lg.	Pos.	G	AB	R	H	HR	RBI	SB	BA
1992	Chicago	NL	SS	74	255	24	64	1	19	2	.251
1993	Chicago	NL	SS	105	344	35	97	0	28	1	.282
1994	Chicago	NL	2B	96	291	26	83	0	24	2	.285
1995	Chicago	NL	2B	114	428	57	119	3	27	6	.278
Post All-Star				48	152	16	36	1	8	1	.237

DAVE SILVESTRI   Age 28/R $2

A onetime Yankee prospect with some power. A reserve at best.

Year	Team	Lg.	Pos.	G	AB	R	H	HR	RBI	SB	BA
1992	New York	AL	SS	7	13	3	4	0	1	0	.308
1993	New York	AL	SS	7	21	4	6	1	4	0	.286
1994	New York	AL	2B	12	18	3	2	1	2	0	.111
1995	New York	AL	2B	17	21	4	2	1	4	0	.095
1995	Montreal	NL	SS	39	72	12	19	2	7	2	.264
Post All-Star				39	72	12	19	2	7	2	.264

OZZIE SMITH   Age 41/B $2

The Wiz wants to stay around long enough to reach 2,500 hits for his career. But his shoulder is still iffy, his range is failing, and he doesn't run much anymore. So with a heavy heart, we advise him to not hang around too long and tarnish our memory of what he once was. And being hard-headed scouts, we advise you not to invest in the past.

Year	Team	Lg.	Pos.	G	AB	R	H	HR	RBI	SB	BA
1992	St. Louis	NL	SS	132	518	73	153	0	31	43	.295
1993	St. Louis	NL	SS	141	545	75	157	1	53	21	.288
1994	St. Louis	NL	SS	98	381	51	100	3	30	6	.262
1995	St. Louis	NL	SS	44	156	16	31	0	11	4	.199
Post All-Star				25	88	10	14	0	8	2	.159

KEVIN STOCKER   Age 26/B $4

He's a long way (in BA miles) from the rookie who hit .324 to help the Phillies to a pennant. But we think the real Stocker is somewhere in between these extremes.

Year	Team	Lg.	Pos.	G	AB	R	H	HR	RBI	SB	BA
1993	Philadelphia	NL	SS	70	259	46	84	2	31	5	.324
1994	Philadelphia	NL	SS	82	271	38	74	2	28	2	.273
1995	Philadelphia	NL	SS	125	412	42	90	1	32	6	.218
Post All-Star				66	218	20	50	1	11	3	.229

Catchers
pp. 27–41

Corners
pp. 41–62

Infield
pp. 63–82

Outfield
pp. 83–113

DH
pp. 114–118

Starters
pp. 119–157

Relievers
pp. 157–193

ROBBY THOMPSON   Age 33/R $7

Makes our back ache just to think of him trying to reach a ground ball. Give it up, Robby. Time to hit the Jacuzzi.

Year	Team	Lg.	Pos.	G	AB	R	H	HR	RBI	SB	BA
1992	San Francisco	NL	2B	128	443	54	115	14	49	5	.260
1993	San Francisco	NL	2B	128	494	85	154	19	65	10	.312
1994	San Francisco	NL	2B	35	129	13	27	2	7	3	.209
1995	San Francisco	NL	2B	95	336	51	75	8	23	1	.223
Post All-Star				49	172	32	42	6	13	1	.244

JEFF TREADWAY   Age 33/L $1

Pinch-hitter and little else, should he find a job at all.

Year	Team	Lg.	Pos.	G	AB	R	H	HR	RBI	SB	BA
1992	Atlanta	NL	2B	61	126	5	28	0	5	1	.222
1993	Cleveland	AL	3B	97	221	25	67	2	27	1	.303
1994	Los Angeles	NL	2B	52	67	14	20	0	5	1	.299
1995	Los Angeles	NL	3B	17	17	2	2	0	3	0	.118
1995	Montreal	NL	2B	41	50	4	12	0	10	0	.240
Post All-Star				24	19	0	6	0	6	0	.316

QUILVIO VERAS   Age 24/B $21

A rare recent mistake by the Mets, who basically gave him away to Florida. He has developing extra-base power, big-time speed, and Alomar-esque range at second. A star in the making.

Year	Team	Lg.	Pos.	G	AB	R	H	HR	RBI	SB	BA
1995	Florida	NL	2B	124	440	86	115	5	32	56	.261
Post All-Star				64	222	45	64	2	19	29	.288

JOSE VIZCAINO   Age 28/B $8

For too long, he's been dismissed by just about everybody (us included) as just another utility man. Well, that RBI total tells a different story, and it's one that Mets front office people enjoyed hearing. That's because by season's end some Mets people were backtracking on the inevitability of Cuban-born prospect Rey Ordoñez, who didn't hit in the minors this year and who, in the parlance of scouts, is a "high maintenance type of kid." All of a sudden, Vizcaino started looking less like just another utility man and more like a plausible regular.

Year	Team	Lg.	Pos.	G	AB	R	H	HR	RBI	SB	BA
1992	Chicago	NL	SS	86	285	25	64	1	17	3	.225
1993	Chicago	NL	SS	151	551	74	158	4	54	12	.287
1994	New York	NL	SS	103	410	47	105	3	33	1	.256
1995	New York	NL	SS	135	509	66	146	3	56	8	.287
Post All-Star				71	276	36	84	2	32	5	.304

WALT WEISS
Age 32/B **$4**

If there were any questions about his power, they were answered with mile-high certainty last summer when he slammed his first home run in 750 AB. "Great!" said Larry Walker. "He's now a member of the 30-30-30-30-1 club."

Year	Team	Lg.	Pos.	G	AB	R	H	HR	RBI	SB	BA
1992	Oakland	AL	SS	103	316	36	67	0	21	6	.212
1993	Florida	NL	SS	158	500	50	133	1	39	7	.266
1994	Colorado	NL	SS	110	423	58	106	1	32	12	.251
1995	Colorado	NL	SS	137	427	65	111	1	25	15	.260
Post All-Star				69	203	32	57	1	12	6	.281

ERIC YOUNG
Age 28/R **$12**

You own Eric Young, you're always hoping his teammates get hurt. Nothing serious, mind you, just a bump or bruise that will keep them out of the lineup so Young can get a few AB. A valuable offensive player whose speed makes him a *really* valuable Rotisserie player, he doesn't have a regular position, and might not be all that useful to you if he did. After all, you don't want him thinking too much about defense.

Year	Team	Lg.	Pos.	G	AB	R	H	HR	RBI	SB	BA
1992	Los Angeles	NL	2B	49	132	9	34	1	11	6	.258
1993	Colorado	NL	2B	144	490	82	132	3	42	42	.269
1994	Colorado	NL	OF	90	228	37	62	7	30	18	.272
1995	Colorado	NL	2B	120	366	68	116	6	36	35	.317
Post All-Star				66	259	48	89	4	23	25	.344

AMERICAN LEAGUE

MANNY ALEXANDER
Age 25/R **$5**

Former shortstop prospect who blossomed on the other side of the bag. Steals should improve, along with defense, ending the platoon with Bret Barberie.

Year	Team	Lg.	Pos.	G	AB	R	H	HR	RBI	SB	BA
1992	Baltimore	AL	SS	4	5	1	1	0	0	0	.200
1993	Baltimore	AL	DH	3	0	1	0	0	0	0	0.000
1995	Baltimore	AL	2B	94	242	35	57	3	23	11	.236
Post All-Star				41	95	13	17	1	4	2	.179

LUIS ALICEA
Age 30/B **$8**

Very important cog for the Red Sox last year. Assuming they don't go out and get Alomar, as rumored, look for a slight improvement across the board.

Year	Team	Lg.	Pos.	G	AB	R	H	HR	RBI	SB	BA
1992	St. Louis	NL	2B	85	265	26	65	2	32	2	.245
1993	St. Louis	NL	2B	115	362	50	101	3	46	11	.279
1994	St. Louis	NL	2B	88	205	32	57	5	29	4	.278
1995	Boston	AL	2B	132	419	64	113	6	44	13	.270
Post All-Star				71	219	34	65	4	27	8	.297

Catchers pp. 27–41

Corners pp. 41–62

Infield pp. 63–82

Outfield pp. 83–113

DH pp. 114–118

Starters pp. 119–157

Relievers pp. 157–193

ROBERTO ALOMAR Age 28/B $35

Bad enough his team was out of it by May. This poor guy was stalked by, you guessed it, a crazed fan. May end up in Boston or LA, but it seems to be checkout time at the Sky Dome Hotel. The best second baseman, but not by as wide a margin as many people think.

Year	Team	Lg.	Pos.	G	AB	R	H	HR	RBI	SB	BA
1992	Toronto	AL	2B	152	571	105	177	8	76	49	.310
1993	Toronto	AL	2B	153	589	109	192	17	93	55	.326
1994	Toronto	AL	2B	107	392	78	120	8	38	19	.306
1995	Toronto	AL	2B	130	517	71	155	13	66	30	.300
Post All-Star				64	261	34	74	3	29	19	.284

CARLOS BAERGA Age 27/B $33

Baerga has one of the biggest heads in professional sports. We're talking hat size here, not attitude, but he could be forgiven for having a rather large view of himself. All he has to do is listen to us talk about him. Now one of the premier players in the game. If it weren't for Alomar, Baerga would be getting a lot more ink. Not as much speed as Alomar, but more power. Alomar has an edge in the field, in case you're keeping score at home. See how it is? You can't talk about one of these guys without bringing up the other—they're that close.

Year	Team	Lg.	Pos.	G	AB	R	H	HR	RBI	SB	BA
1992	Cleveland	AL	2B	161	657	92	205	20	105	10	.312
1993	Cleveland	AL	2B	154	624	105	200	21	114	15	.321
1994	Cleveland	AL	2B	103	442	81	139	19	80	8	.314
1995	Cleveland	AL	2B	135	557	87	175	15	90	11	.314
Post All-Star				68	276	44	83	4	45	6	.301

ESTEBAN BELTRE Age 28/R $1

The Rafael Belliard of the American League.

Year	Team	Lg.	Pos.	G	AB	R	H	HR	RBI	SB	BA
1992	Chicago	AL	SS	49	110	21	21	1	10	1	.191
1994	Texas	AL	SS	48	131	12	37	0	12	2	.282
1995	Texas	AL	SS	54	92	7	20	0	7	0	.217
Post All-Star				32	56	5	13	0	3	0	.232

MIKE BORDICK Age 30/R $9

A little pop, a little speed, a big heart. Good guy to have in your clubhouse.

Year	Team	Lg.	Pos.	G	AB	R	H	HR	RBI	SB	BA
1992	Oakland	AL	2B	154	504	62	151	3	48	12	.300
1993	Oakland	AL	SS	159	546	60	136	3	48	10	.249
1994	Oakland	AL	SS	114	391	38	99	2	37	7	.253
1995	Oakland	AL	SS	126	428	46	113	8	44	11	.264
Post All-Star				72	247	22	64	6	30	5	.259

DOMINGO CEDENO Age 27/B $2

Leading candidate for backup job behind Alex Gonzalez. If he can deliver 4–5 homers in that role, he's worth the extra buck as your backup middle infielder.

Year	Team	Lg.	Pos.	G	AB	R	H	HR	RBI	SB	BA
1993	Toronto	AL	SS	15	46	5	8	0	7	1	.174
1994	Toronto	AL	2B	47	97	14	19	0	10	1	.196
1995	Toronto	AL	SS	51	161	18	38	4	14	0	.236
Post All-Star				29	100	8	20	3	12	0	.200

Catchers
pp. 27–41

Corners
pp. 41–62

Infield
pp. 63–82

Outfield
pp. 83–113

DH
pp. 114–118

Starters
pp. 119–157

Relievers
pp. 157–193

JOEY CORA   AGE 30/B $8

A career year at the plate. Couple more like it and he may actually have a career. One cautionary note: Cora led all AL infielders in errors, so the Mariners may well be looking for an alternative. In fact, if it weren't for José Offerman, who is truly in a league by himself when it comes to errors, Cora would have led all major league infielders in miscues. Most of the errors came on throws, and he was a teammate of Steve Sax in Chicago, so maybe he caught something there.

Year	Team	Lg.	Pos.	G	AB	R	H	HR	RBI	SB	BA
1992	Chicago	AL	2B	68	122	27	30	0	9	10	.246
1993	Chicago	AL	2B	153	579	95	155	2	51	20	.268
1994	Chicago	AL	2B	90	312	55	86	2	30	8	.276
1995	Seattle	AL	2B	120	427	64	127	3	39	18	.297
Post All-Star				63	223	36	69	2	22	10	.309

GARY DISARCINA   Age 28/R $7

When he went down, so did the Angels. When they finally halted a nine-game September skid, he was 2 for 3 with a run scored and a stolen base. Ask anybody on the Angels, they'll tell you he is the heart and soul of the team.

Year	Team	Lg.	Pos.	G	AB	R	H	HR	RBI	SB	BA
1992	California	AL	SS	157	518	48	128	3	42	9	.247
1993	California	AL	SS	126	416	44	99	3	45	5	.238
1994	California	AL	SS	112	389	53	101	3	33	3	.260
1995	California	AL	SS	99	362	61	111	5	41	7	.307
Post All-Star				31	112	17	30	1	8	5	.268

RAY DURHAM   Age 24/B $11

Heckuva start to what looks like a nice long career. Finally, Frank Thomas can look to his right and see a real player.

Year	Team	Lg.	Pos.	G	AB	R	H	HR	RBI	SB	BA
1995	Chicago	AL	2B	125	471	68	121	7	51	18	.257
Post All-Star				63	237	31	59	4	24	3	.249

DAMION EASLEY   Age 26/R $2

First two seasons, he looked like a decent hitter. Last two seasons, he looked like an easy out. We don't like the trend line.

Year	Team	Lg.	Pos.	G	AB	R	H	HR	RBI	SB	BA
1992	California	AL	3B	47	151	14	39	1	12	9	.258
1993	California	AL	2B	73	230	33	72	2	22	6	.313
1994	California	AL	3B	88	316	41	68	6	30	4	.215
1995	California	AL	2B	114	357	35	77	4	35	5	.216
Post All-Star				61	170	17	40	0	10	4	.235

ALVARO ESPINOZA
Age 34/R $1

Played every infield position last year. Too bad versatility isn't a Rotisserie category. He even DHed a few times, proving that Mike Hargrove has a sense of humor.

Year	Team	Lg.	Pos.	G	AB	R	H	HR	RBI	SB	BA
1993	Cleveland	AL	3B	129	263	34	73	4	27	2	.278
1994	Cleveland	AL	3B	90	231	27	55	1	19	1	.238
1995	Cleveland	AL	2B	66	143	15	36	2	17	0	.252
Post All-Star				39	111	13	29	2	12	0	.261

FELIX FERMIN
Age 32/R $1

Just when things were looking up after a terrific 1994, the bottom fell out—and the timing couldn't have been worse. If you're already spotting your designated successor 13 years and a world of talent, you don't want to go losing a hundred-plus points from your preceding season's BA.

Year	Team	Lg.	Pos.	G	AB	R	H	HR	RBI	SB	BA
1992	Cleveland	AL	SS	79	215	27	58	0	13	0	.270
1993	Cleveland	AL	SS	140	480	48	126	2	45	4	.262
1994	Seattle	AL	SS	101	379	52	120	1	35	4	.317
1995	Seattle	AL	SS	73	200	21	39	0	15	2	.195
Post All-Star				40	97	11	21	0	8	1	.216

TONY FERNANDEZ
Age 33/B $3

The malcontent act grew old a long time ago; eroding skills haven't made it any prettier. With Derek Jeter ready to give the Yankees a fresh, new, positive face as they contemplate the move across the river to New Jersey, Fernandez may have to take his perpetual pout somewhere else to finish playing out the string.

Year	Team	Lg.	Pos.	G	AB	R	H	HR	RBI	SB	BA
1992	San Diego	NL	SS	155	622	84	171	4	37	20	.275
1993	Toronto	AL	SS	94	353	45	108	4	50	15	.306
1993	New York	NL	SS	48	173	20	39	1	14	6	.225
1994	Cincinnati	NL	3B	104	366	50	102	8	50	12	.279
1995	New York	AL	SS	108	384	57	94	5	45	6	.245
Post All-Star				58	193	28	48	3	20	2	.249

JEFF FRYE
Age 29/R $1

Give him the boot.

Year	Team	Lg.	Pos.	G	AB	R	H	HR	RBI	SB	BA
1992	Texas	AL	2B	67	199	24	51	1	12	1	.256
1994	Texas	AL	2B	57	205	37	67	0	18	6	.327
1995	Texas	AL	2B	90	313	38	87	4	29	3	.278
Post All-Star				49	148	19	38	4	17	0	.257

GREG GAGNE
Age 34/R $6

A baker's dozen solid years as one of the most consistent offensive shortstops in the AL. Think about it: aside from Ripken and Trammell, how many AL shortstops over the past decade have produced more from the plate than Gagne? He anchored the Royals' infield during the wild card race, so look for him to survive the KC youth movement.

Year	Team	Lg.	Pos.	G	AB	R	H	HR	RBI	SB	BA
1992	Minnesota	AL	SS	146	439	53	108	7	39	6	.246
1993	Kansas City	AL	SS	159	540	66	151	10	57	10	.280
1994	Kansas City	AL	SS	107	375	39	97	7	51	10	.259
1995	Kansas City	AL	SS	120	430	58	110	6	49	3	.256
Post All-Star				73	263	33	65	4	30	1	.247

Catchers
pp. 27–41

Corners
pp. 41–62

Infield
pp. 63–82

Outfield
pp. 83–113

DH
pp. 114–118

Starters
pp. 119–157

Relievers
pp. 157–193

BRENT GATES   Age 26/B $6

Didn't bounce back from his 1994 leg injury as well as expected, but there's still plenty of upside here.

Year	Team	Lg.	Pos.	G	AB	R	H	HR	RBI	SB	BA
1993	Oakland	AL	2B	139	535	64	155	7	69	7	.290
1994	Oakland	AL	2B	64	233	29	66	2	24	3	.283
1995	Oakland	AL	2B	136	524	60	133	5	56	3	.254
Post All-Star				71	290	32	79	3	33	2	.272

BENJI GIL   Age 23/R $7

To say Gil needs to work on making contact is sort of like saying the Grand Canyon is a ditch. He struck out 147 times last year to finish second in the league behind Mo Vaughn, who—in case you hadn't noticed—had a few more HR and RBI than Gil. You want perspective? Gil whiffed almost a third more times than *Mickey Tettleton* in about the same number of AB. All that fanning may have made life more tolerable in field-level boxes at The Ballpark in July and August, but it didn't thrill the Texas brain trust. Neither did the near–Mendoza Line batting average. They did like the punch Gil demonstrated when he did make contact, and they're hopeful that winter ball will help.

Year	Team	Lg.	Pos.	G	AB	R	H	HR	RBI	SB	BA
1993	Texas	AL	SS	22	57	3	7	0	2	1	.123
1995	Texas	AL	SS	130	415	36	91	9	46	2	.219
Post All-Star				63	192	13	37	2	17	0	.193

CHRIS GOMEZ   Age 24/R $11

Barring a trade and assuming that Alan Trammell doesn't have second thoughts about retiring, Gomez becomes the full-time SS this year in Tiger Stadium. That's fine—he has some power and he drives in runs, which Tiger fans have come to expect from their shortstop. But he does need to learn to hit RH pitching a little better: last year's 70-point differential against lefties and righties is not going to cut it.

Year	Team	Lg.	Pos.	G	AB	R	H	HR	RBI	SB	BA
1993	Detroit	AL	SS	46	128	11	32	0	11	2	.250
1994	Detroit	AL	SS	84	296	32	76	8	53	5	.257
1995	Detroit	AL	SS	123	431	49	96	11	50	4	.223
Post All-Star				65	249	21	52	4	23	0	.209

ALEX GONZALEZ   Age 22/R $9

He impressed a lot of people at the end of last year when the Jays sat him down so they could take a look at Tomas Perez. Gonzalez never complained, putting the team first. GM Gord Ash says the job is his, so he's worth a very

---

long look in winter ball and Spring Training. Has the speed to deliver 25–30 SB as soon as he learns to run against big league pitchers.

Year	Team	Lg.	Pos.	G	AB	R	H	HR	RBI	SB	BA
1994	Toronto	AL	SS	15	53	7	8	0	1	3	.151
1995	Toronto	AL	SS	111	367	51	89	10	42	4	.243
Post All-Star				56	173	24	38	5	12	2	.220

CRAIG GREBECK   Age 31/R $1

A scrapper, but he may not have the tools to earn another utility job.

Year	Team	Lg.	Pos.	G	AB	R	H	HR	RBI	SB	BA
1992	Chicago	AL	SS	88	287	24	77	3	35	0	.268
1993	Chicago	AL	SS	72	190	25	43	1	12	1	.226
1994	Chicago	AL	2B	35	97	17	30	0	5	0	.309
1995	Chicago	AL	SS	53	154	19	40	1	18	0	.260
Post All-Star				25	73	9	16	0	8	0	.219

OZZIE GUILLEN   Age 32/L $4

One of the nicest people in the game, as his support of the family of his late friend Gus Polidor reaffirmed. An off-year at the plate, but we figure that was just part of the general malaise that struck so many of the White Sox last year.

Year	Team	Lg.	Pos.	G	AB	R	H	HR	RBI	SB	BA
1992	Chicago	AL	SS	12	40	5	8	0	7	1	.200
1993	Chicago	AL	SS	134	457	44	128	4	50	5	.280
1994	Chicago	AL	SS	100	365	46	105	1	39	5	.288
1995	Chicago	AL	SS	122	415	50	103	1	41	6	.248
Post All-Star				68	229	30	50	1	17	3	.218

DAVID HOWARD   Age 29/B $1

Good news and bad news for Howard last year. The pitcher he hit the worst (Dave Stewart) retired, but the pitcher he hit the best (Mike Moore) was released. Played over 30 games in the OF, demonstrating his versatility and possibly extending his career. But not in KC, which has 4 of the best young OFs in the game.

Year	Team	Lg.	Pos.	G	AB	R	H	HR	RBI	SB	BA
1992	Kansas City	AL	SS	74	219	19	49	1	18	3	.224
1993	Kansas City	AL	2B	15	24	5	8	0	2	1	.333
1994	Kansas City	AL	3B	46	83	9	19	1	13	3	.229
1995	Kansas City	AL	2B	95	255	23	62	0	19	6	.243
Post All-Star				64	180	21	50	0	17	6	.278

DEREK JETER   Age 21/R $5

There is no reason anyone can think of why Jeter should not be the Yankees' opening day shortstop next year. Look for nice BA and a little speed. Somebody should tell him, though, that the first time he makes an error he will likely be sent back to Columbus and put under house arrest.

Year	Team	Lg.	Pos.	G	AB	R	H	HR	RBI	SB	BA
1995	New York	AL	SS	15	48	5	12	0	7	0	.250
Post All-Star				2	1	0	1	0	1	0	1.000

PAT KELLY
Age 28/R   **$5**

Hampered by injury last year, Kelly has never lived up to advance billing. Could be looking to get out of the Bronx even more than the team itself.

Year	Team	Lg.	Pos.	G	AB	R	H	HR	RBI	SB	BA
1992	New York	AL	2B	106	318	38	72	7	27	8	.226
1993	New York	AL	2B	127	406	49	111	7	51	14	.273
1994	New York	AL	2B	93	286	35	80	3	41	6	.280
1995	New York	AL	2B	89	270	32	64	4	29	8	.237
Post All-Star				62	186	19	41	1	22	4	.220

CHUCK KNOBLAUCH
Age 27/R   **$32**

Super four-category year from the best fielding second baseman in the American League and arguably the best leadoff hitter in baseball. And he's just now hitting his prime. If only he played for a major league team.

Year	Team	Lg.	Pos.	G	AB	R	H	HR	RBI	SB	BA
1992	Minnesota	AL	2B	155	600	104	178	2	56	34	.297
1993	Minnesota	AL	2B	153	602	82	167	2	41	29	.277
1994	Minnesota	AL	2B	109	445	85	139	5	51	35	.312
1995	Minnesota	AL	2B	136	538	107	179	11	63	46	.333
Post All-Star				74	285	66	100	10	40	26	.351

PAT LISTACH
Age 28/B   **$1**

Like Bill Clinton, Listach had a great season in 1992, but it's been all downhill ever since.

Year	Team	Lg.	Pos.	G	AB	R	H	HR	RBI	SB	BA
1992	Milwaukee	AL	SS	149	579	93	168	1	47	54	.290
1993	Milwaukee	AL	SS	98	356	50	87	3	30	18	.244
1994	Milwaukee	AL	SS	16	54	8	16	0	2	2	.296
1995	Milwaukee	AL	2B	101	334	35	73	0	25	13	.219
Post All-Star				54	164	16	37	0	9	8	.226

KEITH LOCKHART
Age 31/L   **$2**

To all appearances a lifetime minor leaguer, Lockhart was called up for a cup of coffee by San Diego in 1994 where he hit only slightly better than June. There was no reason whatsoever to expect that he would hold down a platoon job and hit .300 last season. But he did. We think there are several moral lessons to be drawn here, and we will retire quietly and let you draw them.

Year	Team	Lg.	Pos.	G	AB	R	H	HR	RBI	SB	BA
1994	San Diego	NL	3B	27	43	4	9	2	6	1	.209
1995	Kansas City	AL	2B	94	274	41	88	6	33	8	.321
Post All-Star				69	201	33	60	5	24	6	.299

NORBERTO MARTIN
Age 29/R   **$1**

Played five positions last year, none of them well enough to earn a regular job.

Year	Team	Lg.	Pos.	G	AB	R	H	HR	RBI	SB	BA
1993	Chicago	AL	2B	8	14	3	5	0	2	0	.357
1994	Chicago	AL	2B	45	131	19	36	1	16	4	.275
1995	Chicago	AL	2B	72	160	17	43	2	17	5	.269
Post All-Star				38	106	12	33	2	15	4	.311

Catchers
pp. 27–41

Corners
pp. 41–62

Infield
pp. 63–82

Outfield
pp. 83–113

DH
pp. 114–118

Starters
pp. 119–157

Relievers
pp. 157–193

PAT MEARES
Age 27/R   **$8**

A little pop, a little speed. Never a bad combo, particularly when it comes this cheap.

Year	Team	Lg.	Pos.	G	AB	R	H	HR	RBI	SB	BA
1993	Minnesota	AL	SS	111	346	33	87	0	33	4	.251
1994	Minnesota	AL	SS	80	229	29	61	2	24	5	.266
1995	Minnesota	AL	SS	116	390	57	105	12	49	10	.269
Post All-Star				64	209	29	54	5	28	7	.258

TOMAS PEREZ
Age 22/B   **$1**

A rule 5 draft pick from Montreal, Perez performed reasonably in the majors last year, but seems destined for a year of seasoning in Syracuse or Knoxville. Gaston likes him.

Year	Team	Lg.	Pos.	G	AB	R	H	HR	RBI	SB	BA
1995	Toronto	AL	SS	41	98	12	24	1	8	0	.245
Post All-Star				31	87	12	22	1	7	0	.253

JEFF REBOULET
Age 31/R   **$3**

Plugs holes. If you have any, he's your man.

Year	Team	Lg.	Pos.	G	AB	R	H	HR	RBI	SB	BA
1992	Minnesota	AL	SS	73	137	15	26	1	16	3	.190
1993	Minnesota	AL	SS	109	240	33	62	1	15	5	.258
1994	Minnesota	AL	SS	74	189	28	49	3	23	0	.259
1995	Minnesota	AL	SS	87	216	39	63	4	23	1	.292
Post All-Star				42	103	20	31	1	10	0	.301

CAL RIPKEN
Age 35/R   **2,131**

And counting.

Year	Team	Lg.	Pos.	G	AB	R	H	HR	RBI	SB	BA
1992	Baltimore	AL	SS	162	637	73	160	14	72	4	.251
1993	Baltimore	AL	SS	162	641	87	165	24	90	1	.257
1994	Baltimore	AL	SS	112	444	71	140	13	75	1	.315
1995	Baltimore	AL	SS	144	550	71	144	17	88	0	.262
Post All-Star				76	286	37	69	10	53	0	.241

...IGUEZ
Age 20/R   **$10**

...an young, he bounced back and forth between Seattle and Tacoma ...This is the year he stays put in Seattle and wakes everybody up ...parkling talents.

Catchers
pp. 27–41

Corners
pp. 41–62

Infield
pp. 63–82

Outfield
pp. 83–113

DH
pp. 114–118

Starters
pp. 119–157

Relievers
pp. 157–193

Year	Team	Lg.	Pos.	G	AB	R	H	HR	RBI	SB	BA
1994	Seattle	AL	SS	17	54	4	11	0	2	3	.204
1995	Seattle	AL	SS	48	142	15	33	5	19	4	.232
Post All-Star				24	68	7	14	3	10	1	.206

LUIS SOJO   Age 30/R $4

His AB will decline as Rodriguez takes over at short, but he could play a lot more second if Cora doesn't get over the throwing yips.

Year	Team	Lg.	Pos.	G	AB	R	H	HR	RBI	SB	BA
1992	California	AL	2B	106	368	37	100	7	43	7	.272
1993	Toronto	AL	2B	19	47	5	8	0	6	0	.170
1994	Seattle	AL	2B	63	213	32	59	6	22	2	.277
1995	Seattle	AL	SS	102	339	50	98	7	39	4	.289
Post All-Star				60	201	32	61	5	27	0	.303

ALAN TRAMMELL   Age 38/R   No Price

Last year, Trammell and Whitaker set an American League record for games played as teammates. Not as big a deal as Ripken, but just as representative of another era. Farewell to one of the great ones.

Year	Team	Lg.	Pos.	G	AB	R	H	HR	RBI	SB	BA
1992	Detroit	AL	SS	29	102	11	28	1	11	2	.275
1993	Detroit	AL	SS	112	401	72	132	12	60	12	.329
1994	Detroit	AL	SS	76	292	38	78	8	28	3	.267
1995	Detroit	AL	SS	74	223	28	60	2	23	3	.269
Post All-Star				31	98	7	22	0	8	0	.224

JOHN VALENTIN   Age 29/R $29

We went back and read what we wrote about Valentin last year, and boy, are we impressed with ourselves. *"Emergence as one of the premier offensive shortstops in baseball."* Yep, that was us. *"We're talking Cal Ripken–Barry Larkin numbers."* Uh-huh, we said it. *"Can't think of a single American League shortstop likely to post better numbers [in 1995]."* Hey, was there ever any doubt?

Year	Team	Lg.	Pos.	G	AB	R	H	HR	RBI	SB	BA
1992	Boston	AL	SS	58	185	21	51	5	25	1	.276
1993	Boston	AL	SS	144	468	50	130	11	66	3	.278
1994	Boston	AL	SS	84	301	53	95	9	49	3	.316
1995	Boston	AL	SS	135	520	108	155	27	102	20	.298
Post All-Star				69	263	57	82	13	60	12	.312

JOSE VALENTIN   Age 26/B $12

The other Valentin has some thump of his own and good speed, but maybe he should rethink this switch-hitting deal and play all his games on the road: last season he hit .133 against lefties and only .180 at home.

Year	Team	Lg.	Pos.	G	AB	R	H	HR	RBI	SB	BA
1992	Milwaukee	AL	2B	4	3	1	0	0	1	0	0.000
1993	Milwaukee	AL	SS	19	53	10	13	1	7	1	.245
1994	Milwaukee	AL	SS	97	285	47	68	11	46	12	.239
1995	Milwaukee	AL	SS	112	338	62	74	11	49	16	.219
Post All-Star				51	140	24	28	4	20	8	.200

RANDY VELARDE   Age 33/R $3

At some point, guys like Velarde hurt teams more by blocking the development of young players more than they help by providing some versatility and production. It's not Velarde's fault—he is what he is, a good utility man who can best help a team by coming off the bench and filling in at a number of positions. It's just that the presence of a guy like that gives a timid front office an excuse for not taking a chance on younger, untested players with bigger upsides. Still, the Yanks will miss him.

Year	Team	Lg.	Pos.	G	AB	R	H	HR	RBI	SB	BA
1992	New York	AL	SS	121	412	57	112	7	46	7	.272
1993	New York	AL	OF	85	226	28	68	7	24	2	.301
1994	New York	AL	SS	77	280	47	78	9	34	4	.279
1995	New York	AL	2B	111	367	60	102	7	46	5	.278
Post All-Star				59	193	36	56	4	27	3	.290

FERNANDO VINA   Age 26/L $2

A marginally better choice than his platoon partner, but probably not worth mounting a write-in campaign for the All-Star team.

Year	Team	Lg.	Pos.	G	AB	R	H	HR	RBI	SB	BA
1993	Seattle	AL	2B	24	45	5	10	0	2	6	.222
1994	New York	NL	2B	79	124	20	31	0	6	3	.250
1995	Milwaukee	AL	2B	113	288	46	74	3	29	6	.257
Post All-Star				61	156	20	39	1	14	1	.250

OMAR VIZQUEL   Age 28/B $13

The starting SS on the best team in baseball, with a solid offensive performance that indicates it wasn't all about his glove last year. More SB than in any two previous major league seasons. Until he turned all those double plays in the Series, who knew he could fly as well as run?

Year	Team	Lg.	Pos.	G	AB	R	H	HR	RBI	SB	BA
1992	Seattle	AL	SS	136	483	49	142	0	21	15	.294
1993	Seattle	AL	SS	158	560	68	143	2	31	12	.255
1994	Cleveland	AL	SS	69	286	39	78	1	33	13	.273
1995	Cleveland	AL	SS	136	542	87	144	6	56	29	.266
Post All-Star				70	270	44	74	2	30	14	.274

LOU WHITAKER   Age 38/L $12

Trammell's dance partner seems to have a lot more left. Don't be surprised to see him deflect any discussion of his retirement plans.

Year	Team	Lg.	Pos.	G	AB	R	H	HR	RBI	SB	BA
1992	Detroit	AL	2B	130	453	77	126	19	71	6	.278
1993	Detroit	AL	2B	119	383	72	111	9	67	3	.290
1994	Detroit	AL	2B	92	322	67	97	12	43	2	.301
1995	Detroit	AL	2B	84	249	36	73	14	44	4	.293
Post All-Star				46	127	21	35	9	26	2	.276

In the Outfield

Catchers
pp. 27–41

Corners
pp. 41–62

Infield
pp. 63–82

Outfield
pp. 83–113

DH
pp. 114–118

Starters
pp. 119–157

Relievers
pp. 157–193

NATIONAL LEAGUE

MOISES ALOU   Age 29/R $26

Playing for Dad has not always been easy. Neither have been the injuries, with which he has stoically coped. Neither has playing for ownership that makes no secret about not being interested in anything except slashing costs. The good news for the Son is that he has likely become too expensive to stay in Montreal, which should be good for his career but bad news for Dad.

Year	Team	Lg.	Pos.	G	AB	R	H	HR	RBI	SB	BA
1992	Montreal	NL	OF	115	341	53	96	9	56	16	.282
1993	Montreal	NL	OF	136	482	70	138	18	85	17	.286
1994	Montreal	NL	OF	107	422	81	143	22	78	7	.339
1995	Montreal	NL	OF	93	344	48	94	14	58	4	.273
Post All-Star				30	105	18	23	6	19	1	.219

BILLY ASHLEY   Age 25/R $5

It was a hazy Saturday afternoon in Dodger Stadium when the mighty Ashley stepped to the plate and launched a soaring shot that went completely out of the ballpark, landing in the parking lot beyond the left-field bullpen in a place no ball had ever gone in stadium history. Thus, it was a historical moment, underscoring the raw power of the mighty Ashley. What's wrong with this picture? Alas, the pitcher was Mark Cresse, the Dodgers' bullpen coach. The time was 4:30. The setting was batting practice. And until he proves otherwise, the mighty Ashley is the modern-day version of Dave Nicholson.

Year	Team	Lg.	Pos.	G	AB	R	H	HR	RBI	SB	BA
1992	Los Angeles	NL	OF	29	95	6	21	2	6	0	.221
1993	Los Angeles	NL	OF	14	37	0	9	0	0	0	.243
1994	Los Angeles	NL	OF	2	6	0	2	0	0	0	.333
1995	Los Angeles	NL	OF	81	215	17	51	8	27	0	.237
Post All-Star				21	33	1	5	0	0	0	.152

DEREK BELL   Age 27/R $30

So many RBI, so few homers. But don't worry, he should keep getting better and better. The speed is a nice bonus.

Year	Team	Lg.	Pos.	G	AB	R	H	HR	RBI	SB	BA
1992	Toronto	AL	OF	61	161	23	39	2	15	7	.242
1993	San Diego	NL	OF	150	542	73	142	21	72	26	.262
1994	San Diego	NL	OF	108	434	54	135	14	54	24	.311
1995	Houston	NL	OF	112	452	63	151	8	86	27	.334
Post All-Star				45	176	21	58	3	30	10	.330

DANTE BICHETTE   Age 32/R $41

Obviously, you have to be careful if he winds up somewhere other than Denver. Sure, you have to be concerned that he was a talented, rock-headed disappointment in California and Milwaukee prior to arriving in Colorado.

And of course, you have to worry just a little when two veteran members of the Rockies' brass privately call him "one of the dumbest players we've ever been around," and his manager seconds them—publicly. But it's pretty hard not to be blinded by the light of those numbers.

Year	Team	Lg.	Pos.	G	AB	R	H	HR	RBI	SB	BA
1992	Milwaukee	AL	OF	112	387	37	111	5	41	18	.287
1993	Colorado	NL	OF	141	538	93	167	21	89	14	.310
1994	Colorado	NL	OF	116	484	74	147	27	95	21	.304
1995	Colorado	NL	OF	139	579	102	197	40	128	13	.340
Post All-Star				72	305	59	105	27	80	7	.344

BARRY BONDS   Age 31/L $43

He will never be confused with Mr. Rogers, and he ended a frustrating season by saying something about retiring. But he's still the best player in the National League until somebody proves otherwise.

Year	Team	Lg.	Pos.	G	AB	R	H	HR	RBI	SB	BA
1992	Pittsburgh	NL	OF	140	473	109	147	34	103	39	.311
1993	San Francisco	NL	OF	159	539	129	181	46	123	29	.336
1994	San Francisco	NL	OF	112	391	89	122	37	81	29	.312
1995	San Francisco	NL	OF	144	506	109	149	33	104	31	.294
Post All-Star				75	258	57	73	17	51	18	.283

JERRY BROWNE   Age 30/B $1

The Guv remains useful.

Year	Team	Lg.	Pos.	G	AB	R	H	HR	RBI	SB	BA
1992	Oakland	AL	3B	111	324	43	93	3	40	3	.287
1993	Oakland	AL	OF	76	260	27	65	2	19	4	.250
1994	Florida	NL	3B	101	329	42	97	3	30	3	.295
1995	Florida	NL	OF	77	184	21	47	1	17	1	.255
Post All-Star				41	96	13	24	0	4	0	.250

JACOB BRUMFIELD   Age 30/R $6

Not exactly the everyday quality center fielder the Pirates were hoping for when they plucked him out of the bargain bin. But they were playing a version of fantasy baseball to expect more.

Year	Team	Lg.	Pos.	G	AB	R	H	HR	RBI	SB	BA
1992	Cincinnati	NL	OF	24	30	6	4	0	2	6	.133
1993	Cincinnati	NL	OF	103	272	40	73	6	23	20	.268
1994	Cincinnati	NL	OF	68	122	36	38	4	11	6	.311
1995	Pittsburgh	NL	OF	116	402	64	109	4	26	22	.271
Post All-Star				70	239	41	65	3	14	16	.272

DAMON BUFORD   Age 25/R $4

Destined to be no more than a fourth or fifth outfielder, so pay accordingly.

Year	Team	Lg.	Pos.	G	AB	R	H	HR	RBI	SB	BA
1993	Baltimore	AL	OF	53	79	18	18	2	9	2	.228
1994	Baltimore	AL	DH	4	2	2	1	0	0	0	.500
1995	Baltimore	AL	OF	24	32	6	2	0	2	3	.063
1995	New York	NL	OF	44	136	24	32	4	12	7	.235
Post All-Star				44	136	24	32	4	12	7	.235

ELLIS BURKS   Age 31/R $8

The Rockies aren't likely to keep him, which means you should discount his numbers before making your bid. Unless, of course, he ends up in Wrigley Field.

Year	Team	Lg.	Pos.	G	AB	R	H	HR	RBI	SB	BA
1992	Boston	AL	OF	66	235	35	60	8	30	5	.255
1993	Chicago	AL	OF	146	499	75	137	17	74	6	.275
1994	Colorado	NL	OF	42	149	33	48	13	24	3	.322
1995	Colorado	NL	OF	103	278	41	74	14	49	7	.266
Post All-Star				54	143	24	41	8	30	5	.287

BRETT BUTLER   Age 38/L $9

His sanctimonious manner can get old pretty quick, but you can't say that about his game. Miserable first half burned his pride, so he cranked it up in the second half and ended with a very Butleresque season.

Year	Team	Lg.	Pos.	G	AB	R	H	HR	RBI	SB	BA
1992	Los Angeles	NL	OF	157	553	86	171	3	39	41	.309
1993	Los Angeles	NL	OF	156	607	80	181	1	42	39	.298
1994	Los Angeles	NL	OF	111	417	79	131	8	33	27	.314
1995	New York	NL	OF	90	367	54	114	1	25	21	.311
1995	Los Angeles	NL	OF	39	146	24	40	0	13	11	.274
Post All-Star				66	258	52	89	1	16	18	.345

CHUCK CARR   Age 27/B $6

Said one Marlins executive in the season's final week, "The way baseball is nowadays, it's awfully difficult to make any guarantees. But here's one you can take to the bank. We will have a new center fielder in 1996."

Year	Team	Lg.	Pos.	G	AB	R	H	HR	RBI	SB	BA
1992	St. Louis	NL	OF	22	64	8	14	0	3	10	.219
1993	Florida	NL	OF	142	551	75	147	4	41	58	.267
1994	Florida	NL	OF	106	433	61	114	2	30	32	.263
1995	Florida	NL	OF	105	308	54	70	2	20	25	.227
Post All-Star				62	165	34	38	2	10	19	.230

DAVE CLARK   Age 33/L $4

After that scary outfield collision, he did little the rest of the year. But Clark is a solid, professional hitter who delivers a good return on a modest investment.

Year	Team	Lg.	Pos.	G	AB	R	H	HR	RBI	SB	BA
1992	Pittsburgh	NL	OF	23	33	3	7	2	7	0	.212
1993	Pittsburgh	NL	OF	110	277	43	75	11	46	1	.271
1994	Pittsburgh	NL	OF	86	223	37	66	10	46	2	.296
1995	Pittsburgh	NL	OF	77	196	30	55	4	24	3	.281
Post All-Star				28	65	11	11	0	2	0	.169

Catchers
pp. 27-41

Corners
pp. 41-62

Infield
pp. 63-82

Outfield
pp. 83-113

DH
pp. 114-118

Starters
pp. 119-157

Relievers
pp. 157-193

JEFF CONINE　　　　　　　　　　　　　　　Age 29/R　　　$32

All-Star hero, consistent run producer, and a hard-nosed gamer. The genuine article.

Year	Team	Lg.	Pos.	G	AB	R	H	HR	RBI	SB	BA
1992	Kansas City	AL	OF	28	91	10	23	0	9	0	.253
1993	Florida	NL	OF	162	595	75	174	12	79	2	.292
1994	Florida	NL	OF	115	451	60	144	18	82	1	.319
1995	Florida	NL	OF	133	483	72	146	25	105	2	.302
Post All-Star				67	256	32	73	11	57	1	.285

MIDRE CUMMINGS　　　　　　　　　　　　Age 24/L　　　$2

Looked overmatched by major league pitching, seemed lost at times in the outfield, and didn't impress Jim Leyland & Co. with his work habits. But he's still young, and goodness knows there are plenty of job opportunities in Pittsburgh.

Year	Team	Lg.	Pos.	G	AB	R	H	HR	RBI	SB	BA
1993	Pittsburgh	NL	OF	13	36	5	4	0	3	0	.111
1994	Pittsburgh	NL	OF	24	86	11	21	1	12	0	.244
1995	Pittsburgh	NL	OF	59	152	13	37	2	15	1	.243
Post All-Star				52	137	12	33	2	15	1	.241

ANDRE DAWSON　　　　　　　　　　　　　Age 41/R　　　$4

Class with a capital "C," and if he wants to come back after having his 11th knee operation in the off-season, then let him come back. Just don't spend much to have him grace your roster.

Year	Team	Lg.	Pos.	G	AB	R	H	HR	RBI	SB	BA
1992	Chicago	NL	OF	143	542	60	150	22	90	6	.277
1993	Boston	AL	DH	121	461	44	126	13	67	2	.273
1994	Boston	AL	DH	75	292	34	70	16	48	2	.240
1995	Florida	NL	OF	79	226	30	58	8	37	0	.257
Post All-Star				41	122	15	34	4	22	0	.279

MIKE DEVEREAUX　　　　　　　　　　　　Age 32/R　　　$5

Too good a player to be passed around so freely from team to team. If the Braves don't re-sign Fred McGriff and move Ryan Klesko to first base, Devo might play more in Atlanta than anyone initially believed.

Year	Team	Lg.	Pos.	G	AB	R	H	HR	RBI	SB	BA
1992	Baltimore	AL	OF	156	653	76	180	24	107	10	.276
1993	Baltimore	AL	OF	131	527	72	132	14	75	3	.250
1994	Baltimore	AL	OF	85	301	35	61	9	33	1	.203
1995	Chicago	AL	OF	92	333	48	102	10	55	6	.306
1995	Atlanta	NL	OF	29	55	7	14	1	8	2	.255
Post All-Star				65	194	29	59	7	36	4	.304

LENNY DYKSTRA　　　　　　　　　　　　Age 33/L　　　$19

Back problems, knee surgery, slowing bat, a life-in-the-fast-lane lifestyle—the Dude is one big gamble.

Year	Team	Lg.	Pos.	G	AB	R	H	HR	RBI	SB	BA
1992	Philadelphia	NL	OF	85	345	53	104	6	39	30	.301
1993	Philadelphia	NL	OF	161	637	143	194	19	66	37	.305
1994	Philadelphia	NL	OF	84	315	68	86	5	24	15	.273
1995	Philadelphia	NL	OF	62	254	37	67	2	18	10	.264
Post All-Star				16	63	14	17	2	3	4	.270

JIM EISENREICH
Age 36/L   **$11**

Because the Phillies were so Phragile, he played more than is absolutely ideal. Spotted correctly, he is a valuable. A consummate pro.

Year	Team	Lg.	Pos.	G	AB	R	H	HR	RBI	SB	BA
1992	Kansas City	AL	OF	113	353	31	95	2	28	11	.269
1993	Philadelphia	NL	OF	153	362	51	115	7	54	5	.318
1994	Philadelphia	NL	OF	104	290	42	87	4	43	6	.300
1995	Philadelphia	NL	OF	129	377	46	119	10	55	10	.316
Post All-Star				69	193	21	58	6	28	7	.301

CARL EVERETT
Age 24/B   **$15**

Oozing with talent, he had a rough time figuring out how to use it. Now with his third organization, though, and it's all finally starting to come together for him. There's a lesson here, and it has to do with patience. So many players are being rushed to the majors nowadays that there are going to be more and more cases of talented players getting moved around before finding their niche. So stay alert and keep reading.

Year	Team	Lg.	Pos.	G	AB	R	H	HR	RBI	SB	BA
1993	Florida	NL	OF	11	19	0	2	0	0	1	.105
1994	Florida	NL	OF	16	51	7	11	2	6	4	.216
1995	New York	NL	OF	79	289	48	75	12	54	2	.260
Post All-Star				62	232	38	64	9	48	1	.276

STEVE FINLEY
Age 31/L   **$18**

Wouldn't he have looked good the last few years in Camden Yards?

Year	Team	Lg.	Pos.	G	AB	R	H	HR	RBI	SB	BA
1992	Houston	NL	OF	162	607	84	177	5	55	44	.292
1993	Houston	NL	OF	142	545	69	145	8	44	19	.266
1994	Houston	NL	OF	94	373	64	103	11	33	13	.276
1995	San Diego	NL	OF	139	562	104	167	10	44	36	.297
Post All-Star				71	280	52	88	5	26	21	.314

RON GANT
Age 31/R   **$38**

We knew back in April that big things were going to happen. On an absolutely stultifying day—spring training is meant for March, not April—in that garden spot of Florida known as Plant City, Gant pumped a dozen balls into the swamp beyond the left-field fence. His muscles bulging, his face dripping, he walked out of the cage, tossed his bat away, and declared in a voice that carried across the state to West Palm Beach, where the Braves train, "I guess there now won't be any questions about whether I'm back or not." Nope. None at all.

Year	Team	Lg.	Pos.	G	AB	R	H	HR	RBI	SB	BA
1992	Atlanta	NL	OF	153	544	74	141	17	80	32	.259
1993	Atlanta	NL	OF	157	606	113	166	36	117	26	.274
1995	Cincinnati	NL	OF	119	410	79	113	29	88	23	.276
Post All-Star				55	180	28	46	9	34	9	.256

Catchers
pp. 27-41

Corners
pp. 41-62

Infield
pp. 63-82

Outfield
pp. 83-113

DH
pp. 114-118

Starters
pp. 119-157

Relievers
pp. 157-193

BERNARD GILKEY   Age 29/R $21

Just a good solid hitter who has never gotten his just due, except from us. Out of favor in St. Louis for reasons that we cannot fathom. True, catching and throwing are not his strong suits, but we suspect the fact that he feels he should be compensated at something like market rates may be a problem for the Cardinals exchequer.

Year	Team	Lg.	Pos.	G	AB	R	H	HR	RBI	SB	BA
1992	St. Louis	NL	OF	131	384	56	116	7	43	18	.302
1993	St. Louis	NL	OF	137	557	99	170	16	70	15	.305
1994	St. Louis	NL	OF	105	380	52	96	6	45	15	.253
1995	St. Louis	NL	OF	121	480	73	143	17	69	12	.298
Post All-Star				67	258	40	74	9	33	6	.287

LUIS GONZALEZ   Age 28/L $19

Solid, consistent pro who could become a fixture in Wrigley Field.

Year	Team	Lg.	Pos.	G	AB	R	H	HR	RBI	SB	BA
1992	Houston	NL	OF	122	387	40	94	10	55	7	.243
1993	Houston	NL	OF	154	540	82	162	15	72	20	.300
1994	Houston	NL	OF	112	392	57	107	8	67	15	.273
1995	Houston	NL	OF	56	209	35	54	6	35	1	.258
1995	Chicago	NL	OF	77	262	34	76	7	34	5	.290
Post All-Star				68	226	33	69	7	32	4	.305

MARQUIS GRISSOM   Age 28/R $32

The Braves were disappointed, and they weren't trying to hide it. Ditto on both counts from us. We expected a lot more. We're prepared to call it an off year and predict a big bounceback. The Braves may not be so ready to forgive and forget. Don't be surprised if he's wearing a different uniform by the time you read this.

Year	Team	Lg.	Pos.	G	AB	R	H	HR	RBI	SB	BA
1992	Montreal	NL	OF	159	653	99	180	14	66	78	.276
1993	Montreal	NL	OF	157	630	104	188	19	95	53	.298
1994	Montreal	NL	OF	110	475	96	137	11	45	36	.288
1995	Atlanta	NL	OF	139	551	80	142	12	42	29	.258
Post All-Star				73	271	40	62	5	17	15	.229

TONY GWYNN   Age 35/L $35

Our favorite number? Just 15 strikeouts in 535 AB. One of the great artists of our time.

Year	Team	Lg.	Pos.	G	AB	R	H	HR	RBI	SB	BA
1992	San Diego	NL	OF	128	520	77	165	6	41	3	.317
1993	San Diego	NL	OF	122	489	70	175	7	59	14	.358
1994	San Diego	NL	OF	110	419	79	165	12	64	5	.394
1995	San Diego	NL	OF	135	535	82	197	9	90	17	.368
Post All-Star				67	266	39	99	3	38	10	.372

GLENALLEN HILL   Age 31/R $23

The Giants are arguably the worst organization in baseball, as most of their personnel decisions the past couple of seasons reflect. Does the name Deion Sanders ring a bell? The signing of Hill was a great exception to that sorry record. So look for the Giants to turn around and trade him for Matt Nokes or somebody equally useful.

Year	Team	Lg.	Pos.	G	AB	R	H	HR	RBI	SB	BA
1992	Cleveland	AL	OF	102	369	38	89	18	49	9	.241
1993	Cleveland	AL	OF	66	174	19	39	5	25	7	.224
1993	Chicago	NL	OF	31	87	14	30	10	22	1	.345
1994	Chicago	NL	OF	89	269	48	80	10	38	19	.297
1995	San Francisco	NL	OF	132	497	71	131	24	86	25	.264
Post All-Star				67	245	41	66	16	43	12	.269

TODD HOLLANDSWORTH   Age 22/L $7

Some Dodgers people think he has a chance to turn into a solid package of high average, extra-base power, and decent speed. Injuries kept the rest of us from forming an opinion, but don't consign this name to the round file just yet.

Year	Team	Lg.	Pos.	G	AB	R	H	HR	RBI	SB	BA
1995	Los Angeles	NL	OF	41	103	16	24	5	13	2	.233
Post All-Star				33	96	16	24	5	13	2	.250

THOMAS HOWARD   Age 31/S $6

Useful spare part, but he'll always be struggling for AB on that team.

Year	Team	Lg.	Pos.	G	AB	R	H	HR	RBI	SB	BA
1992	Cleveland	AL	OF	117	358	36	99	2	32	15	.277
1992	San Diego	NL	OF	5	3	1	1	0	0	0	.333
1993	Cleveland	AL	OF	74	178	26	42	3	23	5	.236
1993	Cincinnati	NL	OF	38	141	22	39	4	13	5	.277
1994	Cincinnati	NL	OF	83	178	24	47	5	24	4	.264
1995	Cincinnati	NL	OF	113	281	42	85	3	26	17	.302
Post All-Star				63	177	27	51	2	17	11	.288

TRENIDAD HUBBARD   Age 29/R $4

Could help the Rockies in spare role. Could step into the slot likely to be vacated by Ellis Burks. And he will always be the best player ever named for a misspelled island.

Year	Team	Lg.	Pos.	G	AB	R	H	HR	RBI	SB	BA
1994	Colorado	NL	OF	18	25	3	7	1	3	0	.280
1995	Colorado	NL	OF	24	58	13	18	3	9	2	.310
Post All-Star				24	58	13	18	3	9	2	.310

BRIAN L. HUNTER   Age 25/R $31

It was mid-June, and one of the Founding Fathers—we can't say who, but his name appears on the cover of this book—was desperate, in a way that only a Rotisserie owner with pitchers named Greg Swindell, Paul Wagner, Keith Jarvis, and Joe Grahe can be. *Truly* desperate. So he called up another owner, whose team was already out of the race, and asked about starting pitching: Kent Mercker, in the last year of his contract, was available. But the desperate-for-pitching owner didn't want to give up anybody who would be useful this year; his whole point in talking trade was to breathe life into his feeble team. So he offered a minor leaguer from his farm system for Mercker. The other owner hadn't heard of his minor leaguer, so the pitching-

Catchers
pp. 27–41

Corners
pp. 41–62

Infield
pp. 63–82

Outfield
pp. 83–113

DH
pp. 114–118

Starters
pp. 119–157

Relievers
pp. 157–193

hungry owner put on the hard sell, telling the other owner how great the kid was going to be someday. Well, someday came sooner than expected. The day after the trade was consummated, the minor leaguer was called up by the Astros. Yep, you guessed it. Right next to Broglio-Brock and Taubensee-Lofton, there will be a place in the history of all-time dumb trades for Mercker–Brian Hunter.

Year	Team	Lg.	Pos.	G	AB	R	H	HR	RBI	SB	BA
1994	Houston	NL	OF	6	24	2	6	0	0	2	.250
1995	Houston	NL	OF	78	321	52	97	2	28	24	.302
Post All-Star				57	222	26	60	1	16	13	.270

CHRIS JONES   Age 30/R $4

Good player. If he were five years younger the Mets would be giving him a shot at something bigger than fourth outfielder–pinch hitter.

Year	Team	Lg.	Pos.	G	AB	R	H	HR	RBI	SB	BA
1992	Houston	NL	OF	54	63	7	12	1	4	3	.190
1993	Colorado	NL	OF	86	209	29	57	6	31	9	.273
1994	Colorado	NL	OF	21	40	6	12	0	2	0	.300
1995	New York	NL	OF	79	182	33	51	8	31	2	.280
Post All-Star				42	89	13	24	4	19	2	.270

BRIAN JORDAN   Age 29/R $34

For a time there it looked like we were going to lose him to football. But last season he started getting a handle on hitting the curve, and he began to understand just how big his future is in baseball.

Year	Team	Lg.	Pos.	G	AB	R	H	HR	RBI	SB	BA
1992	St. Louis	NL	OF	55	193	17	40	5	22	7	.207
1993	St. Louis	NL	OF	67	223	33	69	10	44	6	.309
1994	St. Louis	NL	OF	53	178	14	46	5	15	4	.258
1995	St. Louis	NL	OF	131	490	83	145	22	81	24	.296
Post All-Star				63	231	42	69	12	39	12	.299

DAVID JUSTICE   Age 29/L $31

Last season might have been an off year for him, but it wouldn't have been for most others. One of those blue-chip commodities who always pays dividends.

Year	Team	Lg.	Pos.	G	AB	R	H	HR	RBI	SB	BA
1992	Atlanta	NL	OF	144	484	78	124	21	72	2	.256
1993	Atlanta	NL	OF	157	585	90	158	40	120	3	.270
1994	Atlanta	NL	OF	104	352	61	110	19	59	2	.313
1995	Atlanta	NL	OF	120	411	73	104	24	78	4	.253
Post All-Star				73	252	40	60	14	40	2	.238

MIKE KELLY   Age 25/R $1

A bust. For lots of teams, the fizzle-out of a first-round draft pick in whom a lot had been invested would spell disaster, in part because everyone would be so reluctant to acknowledge it. Not in Atlanta. One of the things that makes the Braves such a successful organization is their relative lack of self-delusion. Kelly is a fifth outfielder at best? Okay, let's move on. The Braves never have any problem cutting their losses, because there is always more talent on the way. Speaking of cutting losses, there's the case of . . .

Year	Team	Lg.	Pos.	G	AB	R	H	HR	RBI	SB	BA
1994	Atlanta	NL	OF	30	77	14	21	2	9	0	.273
1995	Atlanta	NL	OF	97	137	26	26	3	17	7	.190
Post All-Star				37	25	7	3	0	1	2	.120

ROBERTO KELLY   Age 31/R $13

. . . one of the game's most overrated players, who gets traded with about the same frequency that Ross Perot pops up on *Larry King Live*. (And yes, we have been among those who have overrated him.)

Year	Team	Lg.	Pos.	G	AB	R	H	HR	RBI	SB	BA
1992	New York	AL	OF	152	580	81	158	10	66	28	.272
1993	Cincinnati	NL	OF	78	320	44	102	9	35	21	.319
1994	Atlanta	NL	OF	63	255	44	73	6	24	10	.286
1994	Cincinnati	NL	OF	47	179	29	54	3	21	9	.302
1995	Montreal	NL	OF	24	95	11	26	1	9	4	.274
1995	Los Angeles	NL	OF	112	409	47	114	6	48	15	.279
Post All-Star				68	235	27	64	5	32	9	.272

MIKE KINGERY   Age 35/L $7

A solid role player whose value would plummet if he were to wind up somewhere other than Denver.

Year	Team	Lg.	Pos.	G	AB	R	H	HR	RBI	SB	BA
1992	Oakland	AL	OF	12	28	3	3	0	1	0	.107
1994	Colorado	NL	OF	105	301	56	105	4	41	5	.349
1995	Colorado	NL	OF	119	350	66	94	8	37	13	.269
Post All-Star				63	164	29	41	3	18	4	.250

RYAN KLESKO   Age 24/L $31

"Look at him," said a Braves coach. "He weighs around 240 pounds, and it's all just slabs of muscles. He's the strongest SOB around here and what's even better, he's a mean SOB who hates to lose, thinks he should hit every pitch 450 feet, and is harder on himself than anyone else could be." We need no more persuasion. Whether in the outfield or at first, this is a SOB destined for stardom.

Year	Team	Lg.	Pos.	G	AB	R	H	HR	RBI	SB	BA
1992	Atlanta	NL	1B	13	14	0	0	0	1	0	0.000
1993	Atlanta	NL	1B	22	17	3	6	2	5	0	.353
1994	Atlanta	NL	OF	92	245	42	68	17	47	1	.278
1995	Atlanta	NL	OF	107	329	48	102	23	70	5	.310
Post All-Star				64	201	27	57	15	45	3	.284

Catchers
pp. 27-41

Corners
pp. 41-62

Infield
pp. 63-82

Outfield
pp. 83-113

DH
pp. 114-118

Starters
pp. 119-157

Relievers
pp. 157-193

RAY LANKFORD   Age 28/L $33

The numbers came bouncing back last year, But there remains that gnawing doubt that he may have topped out. Not a bad place to be, mind you, just not where we thought he would be by now.

Year	Team	Lg.	Pos.	G	AB	R	H	HR	RBI	SB	BA
1992	St. Louis	NL	OF	153	598	87	175	20	86	42	.293
1993	St. Louis	NL	OF	127	407	64	97	7	45	14	.238
1994	St. Louis	NL	OF	109	416	89	111	19	57	11	.267
1995	St. Louis	NL	OF	132	483	81	134	25	82	24	.277
Post All-Star				66	227	43	65	15	47	9	.286

DARREN LEWIS   Age 28/R $14

Great glove, covers a lot of ground, and steals a few bases. But he's not exactly a Rotisserie monster.

Year	Team	Lg.	Pos.	G	AB	R	H	HR	RBI	SB	BA
1992	San Francisco	NL	OF	100	320	38	74	1	18	28	.231
1993	San Francisco	NL	OF	136	522	84	132	2	48	46	.253
1994	San Francisco	NL	OF	114	451	70	116	4	29	30	.257
1995	San Francisco	NL	OF	74	309	47	78	1	16	21	.252
1995	Cincinnati	NL	OF	58	163	19	40	0	8	11	.245
Post All-Star				64	188	24	46	1	9	14	.245

TONY LONGMIRE   Age 27/L $7

For better or worse, he will likely get a shot to play every day in Philadelphia. And before he got hurt, he looked like he had turned into a legit major-league player.

Year	Team	Lg.	Pos.	G	AB	R	H	HR	RBI	SB	BA
1993	Philadelphia	NL	OF	11	13	1	3	0	1	0	.231
1994	Philadelphia	NL	OF	69	139	10	33	0	17	2	.237
1995	Philadelphia	NL	OF	59	104	21	37	3	19	1	.356
Post All-Star				19	40	8	14	1	10	1	.350

TOM MARSH   Age 30/R $3

He was injured once last year when he ran into the Wrigley Field ivy. He went down again when his head met a knee at second base and he was knocked unconscious. He hurt his knee when he tripped over a bullpen mound chasing a fly ball. In the minors, he got beaned a couple of times, went headfirst into three different outfield walls, and caught his arm on a chain-link fence. Now, none of these exploits are reasons for you to have him on your team. But it does put him a cut (not to mention a bump, bruise, contusion, and abrasion) above the average fifth outfielder.

Year	Team	Lg.	Pos.	G	AB	R	H	HR	RBI	SB	BA
1992	Philadelphia	NL	OF	42	125	7	25	2	16	0	.200
1994	Philadelphia	NL	OF	8	18	3	5	0	3	0	.278
1995	Philadelphia	NL	OF	43	109	13	32	3	15	0	.294
Post All-Star				31	72	8	21	1	7	0	.292

AL MARTIN   Age 28/L $14

Okay, he had a tough act to follow, but we find it very hard to get too excited about him.

Year	Team	Lg.	Pos.	G	AB	R	H	HR	RBI	SB	BA
1992	Pittsburgh	NL	OF	12	12	1	2	0	2	0	.167
1993	Pittsburgh	NL	OF	143	480	85	135	18	64	16	.281
1994	Pittsburgh	NL	OF	82	276	48	79	9	33	15	.286
1995	Pittsburgh	NL	OF	124	439	70	124	13	41	20	.282
Post All-Star				66	231	37	76	6	24	11	.329

Catchers
pp. 27–41

Corners
pp. 41–62

Infield
pp. 63–82

Outfield
pp. 83–113

DH
pp. 114–118

Starters
pp. 119–157

Relievers
pp. 157–193

DERRICK MAY   Age 27/L $8

Gave the Astros a shot of juice down the stretch with a number of key hits. But he's so much of a defensive liability that the only position at which he could be an everyday player is DH. Last we looked, that would mean he's in the wrong league.

Year	Team	Lg.	Pos.	G	AB	R	H	HR	RBI	SB	BA
1992	Chicago	NL	OF	124	351	33	96	8	45	5	.274
1993	Chicago	NL	OF	128	465	62	137	10	77	10	.295
1994	Chicago	NL	OF	100	345	43	98	8	51	3	.284
1995	Milwaukee	AL	OF	32	113	15	28	1	9	0	.248
1995	Houston	NL	OF	78	206	29	62	8	41	5	.301
Post All-Star				66	187	28	56	8	39	2	.299

BRIAN McRAE   Age 28/B $21

Liberated from his taskmaster dad, he seemed to fit into Wrigley Field just fine. The Cubs need to re-sign him, and even those Tribune Corporation empty suits should see the wisdom of such a move. McRae is fun to watch, both on the field and on base.

Year	Team	Lg.	Pos.	G	AB	R	H	HR	RBI	SB	BA
1992	Kansas City	AL	OF	149	533	63	119	4	52	18	.223
1993	Kansas City	AL	OF	153	627	78	177	12	69	23	.282
1994	Kansas City	AL	OF	114	436	71	119	4	40	28	.273
1995	Chicago	NL	OF	137	580	92	167	12	48	27	.288
Post All-Star				69	298	39	86	5	22	10	.289

ORLANDO MERCED   Age 29/L $17

Lo and behold, he has become a real offensive force. Considering that he was hitting in the world's most anonymous lineup, this blossoming is all the more impressive.

Year	Team	Lg.	Pos.	G	AB	R	H	HR	RBI	SB	BA
1992	Pittsburgh	NL	1B	134	405	50	100	6	60	5	.247
1993	Pittsburgh	NL	OF	137	447	68	140	8	70	3	.313
1994	Pittsburgh	NL	OF	108	386	48	105	9	51	4	.272
1995	Pittsburgh	NL	OF	132	487	75	146	15	83	7	.300
Post All-Star				75	281	46	84	9	52	5	.299

RAUL MONDESI   Age 25/R $38

Sky's the limit. Talent galore, and he's only scratched the surface. But the next Roberto Clemente? Let's have a couple more seasons like last year under his belt before we get swept away in a hyperbolic frenzy.

Year	Team	Lg.	Pos.	G	AB	R	H	HR	RBI	SB	BA
1993	Los Angeles	NL	OF	42	86	13	25	4	10	4	.291
1994	Los Angeles	NL	OF	112	434	63	133	16	56	11	.306
1995	Los Angeles	NL	OF	139	536	91	153	26	88	27	.285
Post All-Star				71	266	39	68	13	48	12	.256

JAMES MOUTON   Age 27/R $14

Speed to spare, but he doesn't look like he has the stick to be a major factor.
That's okay: speed to spare is a good thing.

Year	Team	Lg.	Pos.	G	AB	R	H	HR	RBI	SB	BA
1994	Houston	NL	OF	99	310	43	76	2	16	24	.245
1995	Houston	NL	OF	104	298	42	78	4	27	25	.262
Post All-Star				61	168	20	43	1	14	8	.256

MARC NEWFIELD   Age 23/R $6

Remember the name, because the Padres might have made a steal here.
They dealt off Andy Benes, the underachiever with the big stuff and the
bigger salary, and got this smooth-swinging prospect plus a Randy Myers
clone named Ron Villone. Newfield is a big guy (6'4", 205) who could end
up at first base.

Year	Team	Lg.	Pos.	G	AB	R	H	HR	RBI	SB	BA
1993	Seattle	AL	DH	22	66	5	15	1	7	0	.227
1994	Seattle	AL	DH	12	38	3	7	1	4	0	.184
1995	Seattle	AL	OF	24	85	7	16	3	14	0	.188
1995	San Diego	NL	OF	21	55	6	17	1	7	0	.309
Post All-Star				21	55	6	17	1	7	0	.309

MELVIN NIEVES   Age 24/B $9

Still raw, still overswings, still strikes out way too much. But he has huge
ability that could be harnessed any time now.

Year	Team	Lg.	Pos.	G	AB	R	H	HR	RBI	SB	BA
1992	Atlanta	NL	OF	12	19	0	4	0	1	0	.211
1993	San Diego	NL	OF	19	47	4	9	2	3	0	.191
1994	San Diego	NL	OF	10	19	2	5	1	4	0	.263
1995	San Diego	NL	OF	98	234	32	48	14	38	2	.205
Post All-Star				46	92	13	19	8	20	2	.207

JOE ORSULAK   Age 33/L $3

A pro's pro.

Year	Team	Lg.	Pos.	G	AB	R	H	HR	RBI	SB	BA
1992	Baltimore	AL	OF	117	391	45	113	4	39	5	.289
1993	New York	NL	OF	134	409	59	116	8	35	5	.284
1994	New York	NL	OF	96	292	39	76	8	42	4	.260
1995	New York	NL	OF	108	290	41	82	1	37	1	.283
Post All-Star				52	139	24	39	1	22	0	.281

PHIL PLANTIER   Age 27/L $11

Thud. The shoulder miseries just won't go away.

Year	Team	Lg.	Pos.	G	AB	R	H	HR	RBI	SB	BA
1992	Boston	AL	OF	108	349	46	86	7	30	2	.246
1993	San Diego	NL	OF	138	462	67	111	34	100	4	.240
1994	San Diego	NL	OF	96	341	44	75	18	41	3	.220
1995	Houston	NL	OF	22	68	12	17	4	15	0	.250
1995	San Diego	NL	OF	54	148	21	38	5	19	1	.257
Post All-Star				58	160	25	40	5	23	1	.250

LUIS POLONIA

Age 31/L   **$4**

No thanks. He hits a few singles and steals a few bases, and he never stops talking about how good he is.

Year	Team	Lg.	Pos.	G	AB	R	H	HR	RBI	SB	BA
1992	California	AL	OF	149	577	83	165	0	35	51	.286
1993	California	AL	OF	152	576	75	156	1	32	55	.271
1994	New York	AL	OF	95	350	62	109	1	36	20	.311
1995	New York	AL	OF	67	238	37	62	2	15	10	.261
1995	Atlanta	NL	OF	28	53	6	14	0	2	3	.264
Post All-Star				43	114	12	30	1	4	4	.263

BIP ROBERTS

Age 32/B   **$17**

The way we figure it, health care reform got stymied when none of the managed care organizations would agree to enroll the Bipster: too great a risk.

Year	Team	Lg.	Pos.	G	AB	R	H	HR	RBI	SB	BA
1992	Cincinnati	NL	OF	147	532	92	172	4	45	44	.323
1993	Cincinnati	NL	2B	83	292	46	70	1	18	26	.240
1994	San Diego	NL	2B	105	403	52	129	2	31	21	.320
1995	San Diego	NL	OF	73	296	40	90	2	25	20	.304
Post All-Star				21	88	12	24	1	6	7	.273

HENRY RODRIGUEZ

Age 28/L   **$6**

Good hitter, but no better than a fourth outfielder. He will get a chance to play for the Expos, though, because he has one attribute that the organization prizes above all others: a low salary.

Year	Team	Lg.	Pos.	G	AB	R	H	HR	RBI	SB	BA
1992	Los Angeles	NL	OF	53	146	11	32	3	14	0	.219
1993	Los Angeles	NL	OF	76	176	20	39	8	23	1	.222
1994	Los Angeles	NL	OF	104	306	33	82	8	49	0	.268
1995	Los Angeles	NL	OF	21	80	6	21	1	10	0	.262
1995	Montreal	NL	1B	24	58	7	12	1	5	0	.207
Post All-Star				15	30	3	5	0	0	0	.167

DEION SANDERS

Age 28/L   **$15**

Nice move the Giants made, giving up good young arms for Jerry Jones's prize attraction. Can't see him coming back to baseball, not now. Nobody on any of the teams he played for ever faulted him for lack of effort. Sure, he was only a part-timer, but when he played baseball, he played hard.

Year	Team	Lg.	Pos.	G	AB	R	H	HR	RBI	SB	BA
1992	Atlanta	NL	OF	97	303	54	92	8	28	26	.304
1993	Atlanta	NL	OF	95	272	42	75	6	28	19	.276
1994	Atlanta	NL	OF	46	191	32	55	4	21	19	.288
1994	Cincinnati	NL	OF	46	184	26	51	0	7	19	.277
1995	Cincinnati	NL	OF	33	129	19	31	1	10	16	.240
1995	San Francisco	NL	OF	52	214	29	61	5	18	8	.285
Post All-Star				55	229	32	64	5	20	8	.279

Catchers
pp. 27-41

Corners
pp. 41-62

Infield
pp. 63-82

Outfield
pp. 83-113

DH
pp. 114-118

Starters
pp. 119-157

Relievers
pp. 157-193

REGGIE SANDERS   Age 28/R $42

A flat-out stud, a dead-solid personality, a surefire superstar. The second-best all-round player in the NL.

Year	Team	Lg.	Pos.	G	AB	R	H	HR	RBI	SB	BA
1992	Cincinnati	NL	OF	116	385	62	104	12	36	16	.270
1993	Cincinnati	NL	OF	138	496	90	136	20	83	27	.274
1994	Cincinnati	NL	OF	107	400	66	105	17	62	21	.262
1995	Cincinnati	NL	OF	133	484	91	148	28	99	36	.306
Post All-Star				65	233	43	70	13	43	17	.300

GENE SCHALL   Age 25/R $6

The Phillies will likely convert him from first base and give him a look in left. He has power that they think can develop into the 15–20 homer range and enough discipline to hit .300. But remember that he's a product of a Phillies farm system that is less bountiful than the Dead Sea.

Year	Team	Lg.	Pos.	G	AB	R	H	HR	RBI	SB	BA
1995	Philadelphia	NL	1B	24	65	2	15	0	5	0	.231
Post All-Star				19	53	1	10	0	4	0	.189

GARY SHEFFIELD   Age 27/R $41

Look what he did in around a third of a season. Matured as a person, he is in his prime as a hitter. A Triple Crown would not surprise us in the least.

Year	Team	Lg.	Pos.	G	AB	R	H	HR	RBI	SB	BA
1992	San Diego	NL	3B	146	557	87	184	33	100	5	.330
1993	San Diego	NL	3B	68	258	34	76	10	36	5	.295
1993	Florida	NL	3B	72	236	33	69	10	37	12	.292
1994	Florida	NL	OF	87	322	61	89	27	78	12	.276
1995	Florida	NL	OF	63	213	46	69	16	46	19	.324
Post All-Star				22	70	19	24	10	27	5	.343

DWIGHT SMITH   Age 32/L $3

Useful.

Year	Team	Lg.	Pos.	G	AB	R	H	HR	RBI	SB	BA
1992	Chicago	NL	OF	109	217	28	60	3	24	9	.276
1993	Chicago	NL	OF	111	310	51	93	11	35	8	.300
1994	Baltimore	AL	OF	28	74	12	23	3	12	0	.311
1994	California	AL	OF	45	122	19	32	5	18	2	.262
1995	Atlanta	NL	OF	103	131	16	33	3	21	0	.252
Post All-Star				53	65	7	16	1	12	0	.246

SAMMY SOSA   Age 27/R $41

Hey, overlook the wild swings and wild throws, the often frighteningly bad fundamental plays. The guy is an awesome offensive talent and the perfect Wrigley Field player.

Year	Team	Lg.	Pos.	G	AB	R	H	HR	RBI	SB	BA
1992	Chicago	NL	OF	67	262	41	68	8	25	15	.260
1993	Chicago	NL	OF	159	598	92	156	33	93	36	.261
1994	Chicago	NL	OF	105	426	59	128	25	70	22	.300
1995	Chicago	NL	OF	144	564	89	151	36	119	34	.268
Post All-Star				75	286	52	75	21	65	19	.262

TONY TARASCO
Age 25/L — $13

Faded down the stretch, but we look for bigger and better things from him.

Year	Team	Lg.	Pos.	G	AB	R	H	HR	RBI	SB	BA
1993	Atlanta	NL	OF	24	35	6	8	0	2	0	.229
1994	Atlanta	NL	OF	87	132	16	36	5	19	5	.273
1995	Montreal	NL	OF	126	438	64	109	14	40	24	.249
Post All-Star				59	187	23	41	6	15	13	.219

JESUS TAVAREZ
Age 25/S — $3

The Marlins were looking for somebody, anybody, to replace Chuck Carr in center field, and for a while they thought Tavarez might be the answer. Now they see him as more of a fourth outfielder.

Year	Team	Lg.	Pos.	G	AB	R	H	HR	RBI	SB	BA
1994	Florida	NL	OF	17	39	4	7	0	4	1	.179
1995	Florida	NL	OF	63	190	31	55	2	13	7	.289
Post All-Star				50	151	28	47	2	11	7	.311

MILT THOMPSON
Age 37/L — $1

Fading away.

Year	Team	Lg.	Pos.	G	AB	R	H	HR	RBI	SB	BA
1992	St. Louis	NL	OF	109	208	31	61	4	17	18	.293
1993	Philadelphia	NL	OF	129	340	42	89	4	44	9	.262
1994	Houston	NL	OF	9	21	5	6	1	3	2	.286
1994	Philadelphia	NL	OF	87	220	29	60	3	30	7	.273
1995	Houston	NL	OF	92	132	14	29	2	19	4	.220
Post All-Star				49	69	7	15	2	12	2	.217

RYAN THOMPSON
Age 28/R — $12

Cockier than Johnnie Cochran, undisciplined at the plate, and under pressure from the finally blossoming Mets youth corps, he could wind up in another uniform. Might be better for everyone concerned. He's not Green's favorite player by a mile or so, and he may need a fresh start to ever come close to realizing his potential.

Year	Team	Lg.	Pos.	G	AB	R	H	HR	RBI	SB	BA
1992	New York	NL	OF	30	108	15	24	3	10	2	.222
1993	New York	NL	OF	80	288	34	72	11	26	2	.250
1994	New York	NL	OF	98	334	39	75	18	59	1	.225
1995	New York	NL	OF	75	267	39	67	7	31	3	.251
Post All-Star				43	153	17	32	2	15	1	.209

ANDY VAN SLYKE
Age 35/L — $4

The sand might be running out of his playing career, but we have a hunch that he will soon show up on the tube, making a new calling out of being witty, erudite, and insightful, either as a baseball analyst or as a regular on *Crossfire*. We can all say we knew him when.

Year	Team	Lg.	Pos.	G	AB	R	H	HR	RBI	SB	BA
1992	Pittsburgh	NL	OF	154	614	103	199	14	89	12	.324
1993	Pittsburgh	NL	OF	83	323	42	100	8	50	11	.310
1994	Pittsburgh	NL	OF	105	374	41	92	6	30	7	.246
1995	Baltimore	AL	OF	17	63	6	10	3	8	0	.159
1995	Philadelphia	NL	OF	63	214	26	52	3	16	7	.243
Post All-Star				61	208	24	50	2	14	6	.240

Catchers
pp. 27-41

Corners
pp. 41-62

Infield
pp. 63-82

Outfield
pp. 83-113

DH
pp. 114-118

Starters
pp. 119-157

Relievers
pp. 157-193

JOHN VANDERWAL

Age 29/L $3

Pinch hitter extraordinaire. If only you could figure a way to get him three or four pinch-hit calls a game, you would really have yourself something.

Year	Team	Lg.	Pos.	G	AB	R	H	HR	RBI	SB	BA
1992	Montreal	NL	OF	105	213	21	51	4	20	3	.239
1993	Montreal	NL	1B	106	215	34	50	5	30	6	.233
1994	Colorado	NL	1B	91	110	12	27	5	15	2	.245
1995	Colorado	NL	1B	105	101	15	35	5	21	1	.347
Post All-Star				54	54	5	15	2	7	1	.278

GARY VARSHO

Age 34/L $1

And not a penny more.

Year	Team	Lg.	Pos.	G	AB	R	H	HR	RBI	SB	BA
1992	Pittsburgh	NL	OF	103	162	22	36	4	22	5	.222
1993	Cincinnati	NL	OF	77	95	8	22	2	11	1	.232
1994	Pittsburgh	NL	OF	67	82	15	21	0	5	0	.256
1995	Philadelphia	NL	OF	72	103	7	26	0	11	2	.252
Post All-Star				40	35	2	6	0	5	0	.171

LARRY WALKER

Age 29/L $41

Even though he's a Canadian and all, don't you think he just might be a tiny bit happy to be out of Montreal?

Year	Team	Lg.	Pos.	G	AB	R	H	HR	RBI	SB	BA
1992	Montreal	NL	OF	143	528	85	159	23	93	18	.301
1993	Montreal	NL	OF	138	490	85	130	22	86	29	.265
1994	Montreal	NL	OF	103	395	76	127	19	86	15	.322
1995	Colorado	NL	OF	131	494	96	151	36	101	16	.306
Post All-Star				71	259	47	76	16	51	12	.293

JEROME WALTON

Age 30/R $7

One of the top five fourth outfielders in the league. And we mean that as a compliment.

Year	Team	Lg.	Pos.	G	AB	R	H	HR	RBI	SB	BA
1992	Chicago	NL	OF	30	55	7	7	0	1	1	.127
1993	California	AL	DH	5	2	2	0	0	0	1	0.000
1994	Cincinnati	NL	OF	46	68	10	21	1	9	1	.309
1995	Cincinnati	NL	OF	102	162	32	47	8	22	10	.290
Post All-Star				46	67	17	21	3	12	0	.313

RONDELL WHITE

Age 24/R $26

Can't miss. This could be his big, breakout year.

Year	Team	Lg.	Pos.	G	AB	R	H	HR	RBI	SB	BA
1993	Montreal	NL	OF	23	73	9	19	2	15	1	.260
1994	Montreal	NL	OF	40	97	16	27	2	13	1	.278
1995	Montreal	NL	OF	130	474	87	140	13	57	25	.295
Post All-Star				75	306	51	94	6	31	19	.307

MARK WHITEN

Age 29/B $9

A bust in Boston, Whiten returned to the NL and did enough for the desperate Phillies to warrant another look this year. That's fine by us, because we're always looking for reasons to justify taking yet another chance on someone who *looks* so much like a ballplayer. You see him play when he's swinging the bat well and you think, another Bonds, another Sanders (Reggie, not Deion). But when his swing goes south, it's all the way to Tierra del Fuego. We've overpaid for him before; we're prepared to overpay for him again.

Year	Team	Lg.	Pos.	G	AB	R	H	HR	RBI	SB	BA
1992	Cleveland	AL	OF	148	508	73	129	9	43	16	.254
1993	St. Louis	NL	OF	152	562	81	142	25	99	15	.253
1994	St. Louis	NL	OF	92	334	57	98	14	53	10	.293
1995	Boston	AL	OF	32	108	13	20	1	10	1	.185
1995	Philadelphia	NL	OF	60	212	38	57	11	37	7	.269
Post All-Star				65	228	40	60	11	39	7	.263

Catchers
pp. 27–41

Corners
pp. 41–62

Infield
pp. 63–82

Outfield
pp. 83–113

DH
pp. 114–118

Starters
pp. 119–157

Relievers
pp. 157–193

AMERICAN LEAGUE

RICH AMARAL Age 34/R $8

Gained new life in left field, although Vince Coleman's continued resurgence won't help Amaral's cause. A better bet to stick around in Seattle than Warren Newson.

Year	Team	Lg.	Pos.	G	AB	R	H	HR	RBI	SB	BA
1992	Seattle	AL	3B	35	100	9	24	1	7	4	.240
1993	Seattle	AL	2B	110	373	53	108	1	44	19	.290
1994	Seattle	AL	2B	77	228	37	60	4	18	5	.263
1995	Seattle	AL	OF	90	238	45	67	2	19	21	.282
Post All-Star				42	110	19	31	1	11	8	.282

RUBEN AMARO Age 31/B $1

Gives new meaning to term "marginal player."

Year	Team	Lg.	Pos.	G	AB	R	H	HR	RBI	SB	BA
1992	Philadelphia	NL	OF	126	374	43	82	7	34	11	.219
1993	Philadelphia	NL	OF	25	48	7	16	1	6	0	.333
1994	Cleveland	AL	OF	26	23	5	5	2	5	2	.217
1995	Cleveland	AL	OF	28	60	5	12	1	7	1	.200
Post All-Star				19	45	2	9	0	5	0	.200

BRADY ANDERSON Age 32/L $19

Consistent. Solid. Plays hard. Great sideburns. Status with Orioles is helped by fact that (a) he is Cal Ripken's best friend on the club, and (b) Alex Ochoa and Damon Buford now toil for other teams.

Year	Team	Lg.	Pos.	G	AB	R	H	HR	RBI	SB	BA
1992	Baltimore	AL	OF	159	623	100	169	21	80	53	.271
1993	Baltimore	AL	OF	142	560	87	147	13	66	24	.262
1994	Baltimore	AL	OF	111	453	78	119	12	48	31	.263
1995	Baltimore	AL	OF	143	554	108	145	16	64	26	.262
Post All-Star				76	298	56	79	7	33	15	.265

GARRET ANDERSON　　　　　　　　　Age 23/L　　$17

Usually you'd dismiss 12 homers, a .321 BA, and 102 RBI at Vancouver—Anderson's numbers in 1994—as, well, PCL numbers. From now on, we're not going to be so hasty.

Year	Team	Lg.	Pos.	G	AB	R	H	HR	RBI	SB	BA
1994	California	AL	OF	5	13	0	5	0	1	0	.385
1995	California	AL	OF	106	374	50	120	16	69	6	.321
Post All-Star				75	292	42	99	14	55	4	.339

KEVIN BASS　　　　　　　　　　Age 36/B　　$1

That he was so useful in a part-time role shows how weak Baltimore really was.

Year	Team	Lg.	Pos.	G	AB	R	H	HR	RBI	SB	BA
1992	New York	NL	OF	46	137	15	37	2	9	7	.270
1992	San Francisco	NL	OF	89	265	25	71	7	30	7	.268
1993	Houston	NL	OF	111	229	31	65	3	37	7	.284
1994	Houston	NL	OF	82	203	37	63	6	35	2	.310
1995	Baltimore	AL	OF	111	295	32	72	5	32	8	.244
Post All-Star				50	129	9	22	1	5	4	.171

DANNY BAUTISTA　　　　　　　　Age 23/R　　$4

His career was over before it really began. The Tigers have too many other and better OFs for this guy to be around next year, though he's young enough to grab on elsewhere. There's an outside chance he could do a Lee Tinsley/Troy O'Leary and blossom on a new team. But there's an inside chance he won't.

Year	Team	Lg.	Pos.	G	AB	R	H	HR	RBI	SB	BA
1993	Detroit	AL	OF	17	61	6	19	1	9	3	.311
1994	Detroit	AL	OF	31	99	12	23	4	15	1	.232
1995	Detroit	AL	OF	89	271	28	55	7	27	4	.203
Post All-Star				33	104	11	19	6	12	1	.183

RICH BECKER　　　　　　　　　　Age 24/B　　$2

A lot less than advertised so far. Sort of a Jeffrey Hammonds without all the DL time, but the same lousy numbers. He's young, though—he could still start getting hurt a lot.

Year	Team	Lg.	Pos.	G	AB	R	H	HR	RBI	SB	BA
1993	Minnesota	AL	OF	3	7	3	2	0	0	1	.286
1994	Minnesota	AL	OF	28	98	12	26	1	8	6	.265
1995	Minnesota	AL	OF	106	392	45	93	2	33	8	.237
Post All-Star				72	262	32	62	1	23	5	.237

ALBERT BELLE　　　　　　　　　Age 29/R　　$45

Forget about his bat being corked. We're saying the bases were juiced the year he stole 23. Actually, we wish he would use a corked bat all the time. Hit 70, 80 home runs. Give Manny Ramirez a *real* target to aim for.

Year	Team	Lg.	Pos.	G	AB	R	H	HR	RBI	SB	BA
1992	Cleveland	AL	DH	153	585	81	152	34	112	8	.260
1993	Cleveland	AL	OF	159	594	93	172	38	129	23	.290
1994	Cleveland	AL	OF	106	412	90	147	36	101	9	.357
1995	Cleveland	AL	OF	143	546	121	173	50	126	5	.317
Post All-Star				76	286	69	92	36	75	3	.322

DARREN BRAGG   Age 26/L $3

Could eke out some productive playing time as Seattle's fifth OF.

Year	Team	Lg.	Pos.	G	AB	R	H	HR	RBI	SB	BA
1994	Seattle	AL	DH	8	19	4	3	0	2	0	.158
1995	Seattle	AL	OF	52	145	20	34	3	12	9	.234
Post All-Star				7	7	2	3	0	0	0	.429

JAY BUHNER   Age 31/R $37

Could eke out some productive playing time as one of the best right fielders in baseball. We'd like to see him lose that goatee thing, though.

Year	Team	Lg.	Pos.	G	AB	R	H	HR	RBI	SB	BA
1992	Seattle	AL	OF	152	543	69	132	25	79	0	.243
1993	Seattle	AL	OF	158	563	91	153	27	98	2	.272
1994	Seattle	AL	OF	101	358	74	100	21	68	0	.279
1995	Seattle	AL	OF	126	470	86	123	40	121	0	.262
Post All-Star				75	273	57	69	29	75	0	.253

JOE CARTER   Age 36/R $26

Hung in there better than most Blue Jays, the majority of whom spent the summer molting. Last year ended a six-year streak of 100 RBIs in a season. But we're more concerned about the dropoff in dingers—eight fewer than in 1994 in 123 more AB. Joe's always been one of our favorites, but at a certain age, your bat speed starts to slow down. It happened to us, it could be happening to him.

Year	Team	Lg.	Pos.	G	AB	R	H	HR	RBI	SB	BA
1992	Toronto	AL	OF	158	622	97	164	34	119	12	.264
1993	Toronto	AL	OF	155	603	92	153	33	121	8	.254
1994	Toronto	AL	OF	111	435	70	118	27	103	11	.271
1995	Toronto	AL	OF	139	558	70	141	25	76	12	.253
Post All-Star				75	302	35	69	11	34	7	.228

JERALD CLARK   Age 32/R $3

A severely sprained knee and an influx of young players kept Clark on the DL all year. When he played OF/1B he did fine, so he'll at least get a look in spring training.

Year	Team	Lg.	Pos.	G	AB	R	H	HR	RBI	SB	BA
1992	San Diego	NL	OF	146	496	45	120	12	58	3	.242
1993	Colorado	NL	OF	140	478	65	135	13	67	9	.282
1995	Minnesota	AL	OF	36	109	17	37	3	15	3	.339
Post All-Star				1	1	0	0	0	0	0	0.000

ALEX COLE   Age 30/L $6

A horrible leg injury ended Cole's season. Find out in spring training if it ended his career.

Year	Team	Lg.	Pos.	G	AB	R	H	HR	RBI	SB	BA
1992	Cleveland	AL	OF	41	97	11	20	0	5	9	.206
1992	Pittsburgh	NL	OF	64	205	33	57	0	10	7	.278
1993	Colorado	NL	OF	126	348	50	89	0	24	30	.256
1994	Minnesota	AL	OF	105	345	68	102	4	23	29	.296
1995	Minnesota	AL	OF	28	79	10	27	1	14	1	.342
Post All-Star				3	4	0	0	0	0	0	0.000

Catchers
pp. 27-41

Corners
pp. 41-62

Infield
pp. 63-82

Outfield
pp. 83-113

DH
pp. 114-118

Starters
pp. 119-157

Relievers
pp. 157-193

VINCE COLEMAN   Age 34/B $34

The new grass in Kansas City didn't slow him down, and now he's back on turf in Seattle. Had a big September for Mariners. Second year of good behavior. Let's say he's adjusted to the AL. Now if he could only adjust to left field.

Year	Team	Lg.	Pos.	G	AB	R	H	HR	RBI	SB	BA
1992	New York	NL	OF	71	229	37	63	2	21	24	.275
1993	New York	NL	OF	92	373	64	104	2	25	38	.279
1994	Kansas City	AL	OF	104	438	61	105	2	33	50	.240
1995	Kansas City	AL	OF	75	293	39	84	4	20	26	.287
1995	Seattle	AL	OF	40	162	27	47	1	9	16	.290
Post All-Star				64	256	38	72	3	16	21	.281

MARTY CORDOVA   Age 26/R $29

From the first weeks of spring training to the end of the season, Cordova delivered what Rich Becker had always promised—power, speed, and outfield companionship for Kirby. Will be a cornerstone of Twins until they are required to pay him what he's worth.

Year	Team	Lg.	Pos.	G	AB	R	H	HR	RBI	SB	BA
1995	Minnesota	AL	OF	137	512	81	142	24	84	20	.277
Post All-Star				75	284	48	82	12	47	16	.289

CHAD CURTIS   Age 27/R $28

Curtis for Tony Phillips helped both teams; the Angels last year and the Tigers from now on. At 26, Curtis will lead this team for years. Look for a nice increase in production as he settles into Motown.

Year	Team	Lg.	Pos.	G	AB	R	H	HR	RBI	SB	BA
1992	California	AL	OF	139	441	59	114	10	46	43	.259
1993	California	AL	OF	152	583	94	166	6	59	48	.285
1994	California	AL	OF	114	453	67	116	11	50	25	.256
1995	Detroit	AL	OF	144	586	96	157	21	67	27	.268
Post All-Star				74	302	47	77	9	23	13	.255

JOHNNY DAMON   Age 22/L $12

Showed more than a flash of his potential in 40-game call-up last year. Watch the Royals. In August, they dumped some veterans and played all their kids— and ended up in the wild card race. Damon's speed and gap power make him a perfect fit in KC.

Year	Team	Lg.	Pos.	G	AB	R	H	HR	RBI	SB	BA
1995	Kansas City	AL	OF	47	188	32	53	3	23	7	.282
Post All-Star				47	188	32	53	3	23	7	.282

CARLOS DELGADO   Age 23/L $7

He's certainly not a catcher, he's probably not an outfielder, and he's not likely to be much of a first baseman. But he's still a baby, and the Blue Jays will turn heaven and earth to get his left-handed firestick into the game.

Year	Team	Lg.	Pos.	G	AB	R	H	HR	RBI	SB	BA
1993	Toronto	AL	DH	2	1	0	0	0	0	0	0.000
1994	Toronto	AL	OF	43	130	17	28	9	24	1	.215
1995	Toronto	AL	OF	37	91	7	15	3	11	0	.165
Post All-Star				23	65	5	11	2	8	0	.169

ALEX DIAZ   Age 27/B $7

Made the most out of Griffey's injury and the ensuing playing time. Mariners have a Kingdomeful of OF candidates, but Diaz's speed will guarantee him a long look in the spring.

Year	Team	Lg.	Pos.	G	AB	R	H	HR	RBI	SB	BA
1992	Milwaukee	AL	OF	22	9	5	1	0	1	3	.111
1993	Milwaukee	AL	OF	32	69	9	22	0	1	5	.319
1994	Milwaukee	AL	OF	79	187	17	47	1	17	5	.251
1995	Seattle	AL	OF	103	270	44	67	3	27	18	.248
Post All-Star				46	103	20	23	1	10	7	.223

JIM EDMONDS   Age 25/L $33

The guy had promise, but nobody, nothing prepared us for this. What did he go for in your auction draft? About ten bucks, right? That's what we're saying. Nobody saw this coming. Okay, maybe Rod Carew. Edmonds cops a bit of an attitude, so there were probably a few people who enjoyed the late-season slump that took him out of the MVP race. But slump, shlump— Edmonds had a great year. And *this* year, we see another good one coming.

Year	Team	Lg.	Pos.	G	AB	R	H	HR	RBI	SB	BA
1993	California	AL	OF	18	61	5	15	0	4	0	.246
1994	California	AL	OF	94	289	35	79	5	37	4	.273
1995	California	AL	OF	141	558	120	162	33	107	1	.290
Post All-Star				73	297	66	86	20	55	0	.290

LOU FRAZIER   Age 31/B $3

Former Expo who gave the Rangers a little speed late in the season. To put that in perspective, aside from Otis Nixon and Mark McLemore, Frazier was the only other Ranger in high single figures in SB. Nothing to get overheated about, but guys like Frazier do make scouring the transaction wire pay off.

Year	Team	Lg.	Pos.	G	AB	R	H	HR	RBI	SB	BA
1993	Montreal	NL	OF	112	189	27	54	1	16	17	.286
1994	Montreal	NL	OF	76	140	25	38	0	14	20	.271
1995	Montreal	NL	OF	35	63	6	12	0	3	4	.190
1995	Texas	AL	OF	49	99	19	21	0	8	9	.212
Post All-Star				49	99	19	21	0	8	9	.212

DAVE GALLAGHER   Age 35/R $1

Picked up from the Braves for his baseball savvy, Gallagher is a great clubhouse guy who hurt himself before he could really work his clubhouse magic on the Angels. Maybe they should all claim their late-season dive was his fault. Hey, they were going great until he showed up, weren't they?

Year	Team	Lg.	Pos.	G	AB	R	H	HR	RBI	SB	BA
1992	New York	NL	OF	98	175	20	42	1	21	4	.240
1993	New York	NL	OF	99	201	34	55	6	28	1	.274
1994	Atlanta	NL	OF	89	152	27	34	2	14	0	.224
1995	Philadelphia	NL	OF	62	157	12	50	1	12	0	.318
1995	California	AL	OF	11	16	1	3	0	0	0	.188
Post All-Star				30	59	5	16	0	1	0	.271

Catchers
pp. 27–41

Corners
pp. 41–62

Infield
pp. 63–82

Outfield
pp. 83–113

DH
pp. 114–118

Starters
pp. 119–157

Relievers
pp. 157–193

CURTIS GOODWIN   Age 23/L $16

One of the road-running Goodwins who entered the league last year. A great prospect with serious, no-kidding, beep-beep speed. Very high on himself, but so are we.

Year	Team	Lg.	Pos.	G	AB	R	H	HR	RBI	SB	BA
1995	Baltimore	AL	OF	87	289	40	76	1	24	22	.263
Post All-Star				50	154	10	27	0	9	6	.175

TOM GOODWIN   Age 27/L $30

Okay, technically he did not "enter" the league last year, but he certainly had not done much in previous cup-of-coffee stops in the majors before. Steals aren't at quite the premium they used to be in the American League, but anyone who rips 50 gets our undivided attention.

Year	Team	Lg.	Pos.	G	AB	R	H	HR	RBI	SB	BA
1992	Los Angeles	NL	OF	57	73	15	17	0	3	7	.233
1993	Los Angeles	NL	OF	30	17	6	5	0	1	1	.294
1994	Kansas City	AL	DH	2	2	0	0	0	0	0	0.000
1995	Kansas City	AL	OF	133	480	72	138	4	28	50	.287
Post All-Star				73	266	42	76	3	18	24	.286

SHAWN GREEN   Age 23/L $17

The Blue Jays outfield will be interesting to watch this spring. Will they move Carter to DH? Will they sign Devon White? What about Robert Perez and Shannon Stewart? Every one of those questions is affected by Shawn Green, who could develop into a fixture in that outfield. Look for him to throw a dozen or so steals onto his stat line this season.

Year	Team	Lg.	Pos.	G	AB	R	H	HR	RBI	SB	BA
1993	Toronto	AL	OF	3	6	0	0	0	0	0	0.000
1994	Toronto	AL	OF	14	33	1	3	0	1	1	.091
1995	Toronto	AL	OF	121	379	52	109	15	54	1	.288
Post All-Star				67	223	29	72	8	32	1	.323

MIKE GREENWELL   Age 32/L $17

Mike Greenwell as elder statesman? We figured someone would brain him with a fungo before that ever happened. But hey, we're not in the rumor-mongering, character-assassinating, ad hominem ing business. We're objective, professional analysts who call 'em like we see 'em. And what we see here are solid numbers, year after year.

Year	Team	Lg.	Pos.	G	AB	R	H	HR	RBI	SB	BA
1992	Boston	AL	OF	49	180	16	42	2	18	2	.233
1993	Boston	AL	OF	146	540	77	170	13	72	5	.315
1994	Boston	AL	OF	95	327	60	88	11	45	2	.269
1995	Boston	AL	OF	120	481	67	143	15	76	9	.297
Post All-Star				63	255	30	75	9	45	5	.294

RUSTY GREER   Age 27/L $8

About half as good as Greenwell, so we owe you 50 cents.

Year	Team	Lg.	Pos.	G	AB	R	H	HR	RBI	SB	BA
1994	Texas	AL	OF	80	277	36	87	10	46	0	.314
1995	Texas	AL	OF	131	417	58	113	13	61	3	.271
Post All-Star				69	220	28	62	7	28	1	.282

KEN GRIFFEY, JR.   Age 26/L $44

Ken Sr. teases Jr. about Dad's three rings from his Cincinnati days. Junior says he only wants one. In 1997, he may even pull a Deion and sign a one-year deal with a top team. This is the year Junior goes for the mint, a salary drive for one of the game's best players. Hold on to him or spend whatever it takes to get him, because this is going to be a lot of fun to watch.

Year	Team	Lg.	Pos.	G	AB	R	H	HR	RBI	SB	BA
1992	Seattle	AL	OF	142	565	83	174	27	103	10	.308
1993	Seattle	AL	OF	156	582	113	180	45	109	17	.309
1994	Seattle	AL	OF	111	433	94	140	40	90	11	.323
1995	Seattle	AL	OF	72	260	52	67	17	42	4	.258
Post All-Star				45	161	29	41	10	27	3	.255

DARRYL HAMILTON   Age 31/L $10

First known case of an elbow surgery affecting stolen bases. Anyway, Hamilton made a good comeback. A good third or excellent fourth outfielder.

Year	Team	Lg.	Pos.	G	AB	R	H	HR	RBI	SB	BA
1992	Milwaukee	AL	OF	128	470	67	140	5	62	41	.298
1993	Milwaukee	AL	OF	135	520	74	161	9	48	21	.310
1994	Milwaukee	AL	OF	36	141	23	37	1	13	3	.262
1995	Milwaukee	AL	OF	112	398	54	108	5	44	11	.271
Post All-Star				54	190	30	53	3	24	3	.279

JEFFREY HAMMONDS   Age 25/R $2

Don't want to jump to any conclusions, but so far he looks suspiciously like an injury-plagued underachiever.

Year	Team	Lg.	Pos.	G	AB	R	H	HR	RBI	SB	BA
1993	Baltimore	AL	OF	33	105	10	32	3	19	4	.305
1994	Baltimore	AL	OF	68	250	45	74	8	31	5	.296
1995	Baltimore	AL	OF	57	178	18	43	4	23	4	.242
Post All-Star				11	20	1	5	0	0	1	.250

SHAWN HARE   Age 29/L $1

Rabbit Maranville has a better chance of playing somewhere this year.

Year	Team	Lg.	Pos.	G	AB	R	H	HR	RBI	SB	BA
1992	Detroit	AL	OF	15	26	0	3	0	5	0	.115
1994	New York	NL	OF	22	40	7	9	0	2	0	.225
1995	Texas	AL	OF	18	24	2	6	0	2	0	.250
Post All-Star				0	0	0	0	0	0	0	0.000

RICKEY HENDERSON   Age 37/R $22

Nice for anybody not named Rickey Henderson. Missed a game last year because he wasn't "mentally available." Hey, the first step back is recognizing your problem.

Year	Team	Lg.	Pos.	G	AB	R	H	HR	RBI	SB	BA
1992	Oakland	AL	OF	117	396	77	112	15	46	48	.283
1993	Oakland	AL	OF	90	318	77	104	17	47	31	.327
1993	Toronto	AL	OF	44	163	37	35	4	12	22	.215
1994	Oakland	AL	OF	87	296	66	77	6	20	22	.260
1995	Oakland	AL	OF	112	407	67	122	9	54	32	.300
Post All-Star				54	197	32	64	4	26	15	.325

Catchers
pp. 27–41

Corners
pp. 41–62

Infield
pp. 63–82

Outfield
pp. 83–113

DH
pp. 114–118

Starters
pp. 119–157

Relievers
pp. 157–193

JOSE HERRERA   Age 23/L $1

Brought up in August from AA when Rickey hurt his hamstring while think-ing about running. Herrera is considered the best defensive outfielder in the Oakland farm system, but that's about it—hence the salary. Always available mentally, however.

Year	Team	Lg.	Pos.	G	AB	R	H	HR	RBI	SB	BA
1995	Oakland	AL	OF	33	70	9	17	0	2	1	.243
Post All-Star				33	70	9	17	0	2	1	.243

PHIL HIATT   Age 26/R $1

Sent to AAA during the great purge of August 11 (see Johnny Damon). Could resurface if the team is sold and a bunch of people who don't know what they are doing take over.

Year	Team	Lg.	Pos.	G	AB	R	H	HR	RBI	SB	BA
1993	Kansas City	AL	3B	81	238	30	52	7	36	6	.218
1995	Kansas City	AL	OF	52	113	11	23	4	12	1	.204
Post All-Star				20	41	2	8	1	4	0	.195

BOB HIGGINSON   Age 25/L $9

Had a great first half, then spent the second half learning what big-league pitching is all about. Grab him and hope he doesn't pick up where he left off.

Year	Team	Lg.	Pos.	G	AB	R	H	HR	RBI	SB	BA
1995	Detroit	AL	OF	131	410	61	92	14	43	6	.224
Post All-Star				65	211	27	43	4	15	3	.204

DWAYNE HOSEY   Age 28/B $5

The Red Sox' ride to the division title was helped out by many smart pickups by GM Dan Duquette. Hosey gave the team a boost at the top of the order in September and will certainly be a factor this year. The Royals' front office caught heat for letting Hosey go despite having so many other talented, young OFs. Keep an eye on him. One caveat: the Red Sox are Hosey's sixth team. This is not ordinarily a good sign.

Year	Team	Lg.	Pos.	G	AB	R	H	HR	RBI	SB	BA
1995	Boston	AL	OF	24	68	20	23	3	7	6	.338
Post All-Star				24	68	20	23	3	7	6	.338

MICHAEL HUFF   Age 32/R $1

No.

Year	Team	Lg.	Pos.	G	AB	R	H	HR	RBI	SB	BA
1992	Chicago	AL	OF	60	115	13	24	0	8	1	.209
1993	Chicago	AL	OF	43	44	4	8	1	6	1	.182
1994	Toronto	AL	OF	80	207	31	63	3	25	2	.304
1995	Toronto	AL	OF	61	138	14	32	1	9	1	.232
Post All-Star				38	80	10	22	0	4	1	.275

DAVID HULSE   Age 28/L $9

Change of scenery didn't energize him. Kielbasa lunches ate into his SBs. A nice complementary player, which describes every Brewer.

Year	Team	Lg.	Pos.	G	AB	R	H	HR	RBI	SB	BA
1992	Texas	AL	OF	32	92	14	28	0	2	3	.304
1993	Texas	AL	OF	114	407	71	118	1	29	29	.290
1994	Texas	AL	OF	77	310	58	79	1	19	18	.255
1995	Milwaukee	AL	OF	119	339	46	85	3	47	15	.251
Post All-Star				68	185	27	41	2	22	8	.222

STAN JAVIER   Age 32/B $17

A great third man for you. Players like Javier are keys to winning Rotisserie teams. You need two or three of them to get out of the middle of the pack. Frank Thomas, Albert Belle, and five Wayne Kirbys won't do it.

Year	Team	Lg.	Pos.	G	AB	R	H	HR	RBI	SB	BA
1992	Los Angeles	NL	OF	56	58	6	11	1	5	1	.190
1992	Philadelphia	NL	OF	74	276	36	72	0	24	17	.261
1993	California	AL	OF	92	237	33	69	3	28	12	.291
1994	Oakland	AL	OF	109	419	75	114	10	44	24	.272
1995	Oakland	AL	OF	130	442	81	123	8	56	36	.278
Post All-Star				69	226	49	67	4	38	23	.296

LANCE JOHNSON   Age 32/L $30

Lost in the horrid year of the White Sox was this great year by LJ. Just keeps getting better. The White Sox will be back and Johnson will be a big contributor.

Year	Team	Lg.	Pos.	G	AB	R	H	HR	RBI	SB	BA
1992	Chicago	AL	OF	157	567	67	158	3	47	41	.279
1993	Chicago	AL	OF	147	540	75	168	0	47	35	.311
1994	Chicago	AL	OF	106	412	56	114	3	54	26	.277
1995	Chicago	AL	OF	142	607	98	186	10	57	40	.306
Post All-Star				78	343	61	116	9	40	20	.338

WAYNE KIRBY   Age 32/L $1

Didn't really respond to the reserve role and played like the career minor leaguer he used to be. Will never start for this team, but could make modest contributions coming off the bench.

Year	Team	Lg.	Pos.	G	AB	R	H	HR	RBI	SB	BA
1992	Cleveland	AL	DH	21	18	9	3	1	1	0	.167
1993	Cleveland	AL	OF	131	458	71	123	6	60	17	.269
1994	Cleveland	AL	OF	78	191	33	56	5	23	11	.293
1995	Cleveland	AL	OF	101	188	29	39	1	14	10	.207
Post All-Star				53	98	12	19	0	5	5	.194

KENNY LOFTON   Age 28/L $40

It would be worth getting a satellite dish just to be able to watch him play center field every day. The HR have found their level but look for even more SB this year.

Year	Team	Lg.	Pos.	G	AB	R	H	HR	RBI	SB	BA
1992	Cleveland	AL	OF	148	576	96	164	5	42	66	.285
1993	Cleveland	AL	OF	148	569	116	185	1	42	70	.325
1994	Cleveland	AL	OF	112	459	105	160	12	57	60	.349
1995	Cleveland	AL	OF	118	481	93	149	7	53	54	.310
Post All-Star				59	232	50	71	2	26	35	.306

Catchers
pp. 27–41

Corners
pp. 41–62

Infield
pp. 63–82

Outfield
pp. 83–113

DH
pp. 114–118

Starters
pp. 119–157

Relievers
pp. 157–193

CANDY MALDONADO   Age 35/R $5

Wanders the earth, bat in hand, looking for teams in pennant races. Often finds them.

Year	Team	Lg.	Pos.	G	AB	R	H	HR	RBI	SB	BA
1992	Toronto	AL	OF	137	489	64	133	20	66	2	.272
1993	Cleveland	AL	OF	28	81	11	20	5	20	0	.247
1993	Chicago	NL	OF	70	140	8	26	3	15	0	.186
1994	Cleveland	AL	DH	42	92	14	18	5	12	1	.196
1995	Toronto	AL	OF	61	160	22	43	7	25	1	.269
1995	Texas	AL	OF	13	30	6	7	2	5	0	.233
Post All-Star				37	78	11	21	4	12	0	.269

DAVE MARTINEZ   Age 31/L $5

Not the best Martinez in baseball, but a nice guy to have in a backup role.

Year	Team	Lg.	Pos.	G	AB	R	H	HR	RBI	SB	BA
1992	Cincinnati	NL	OF	135	393	47	100	3	31	12	.254
1993	San Francisco	NL	OF	91	241	28	58	5	27	6	.241
1994	San Francisco	NL	OF	97	235	23	58	4	27	3	.247
1995	Chicago	AL	OF	118	303	49	93	5	37	8	.307
Post All-Star				72	208	36	70	2	27	4	.337

WILLIE McGEE   Age 37/B $3

Probably won't be in Boston this year, but proved there last year that he still has the tools to play somewhere.

Year	Team	Lg.	Pos.	G	AB	R	H	HR	RBI	SB	BA
1992	San Francisco	NL	OF	138	474	56	141	1	36	13	.297
1993	San Francisco	NL	OF	130	475	53	143	4	46	10	.301
1994	San Francisco	NL	OF	45	156	19	44	5	23	3	.282
1995	Boston	AL	OF	67	200	32	57	2	15	5	.285
Post All-Star				62	192	30	55	2	15	4	.286

MARK McLEMORE   Age 31/B $11

Our interest will sink as soon as his SB fall below 20.

Year	Team	Lg.	Pos.	G	AB	R	H	HR	RBI	SB	BA
1992	Baltimore	AL	2B	101	228	40	56	0	27	11	.246
1993	Baltimore	AL	OF	148	581	81	165	4	72	21	.284
1994	Baltimore	AL	2B	104	343	44	88	3	29	20	.257
1995	Texas	AL	OF	129	467	73	122	5	41	21	.261
Post All-Star				60	229	26	52	2	10	4	.227

MATT MIESKE   Age 28/R $9

The Bud Selig of major league outfielders.

Year	Team	Lg.	Pos.	G	AB	R	H	HR	RBI	SB	BA
1993	Milwaukee	AL	OF	23	58	9	14	3	7	0	.241
1994	Milwaukee	AL	OF	84	259	39	67	10	38	3	.259
1995	Milwaukee	AL	OF	117	267	42	67	12	48	2	.251
Post All-Star				64	160	22	38	7	25	2	.237

LYLE MOUTON
Age 26/R   **$4**

A bright spot, one of the few, for the White Sox last summer. Don't go nuts, though: there's nothing in his history to suggest that he'll turn out to be anything more than okay.

Year	Team	Lg.	Pos.	G	AB	R	H	HR	RBI	SB	BA
1995	Chicago	AL	OF	58	179	23	54	5	27	1	.302
Post All-Star				51	163	22	51	4	25	0	.313

WARREN NEWSON
Age 31/L   **$3**

Come to think of it, Mouton could turn out to be Newson, once a Chisox bit player himself. And that would be okay.

Year	Team	Lg.	Pos.	G	AB	R	H	HR	RBI	SB	BA
1992	Chicago	AL	OF	63	136	19	30	1	11	3	.221
1993	Chicago	AL	DH	26	40	9	12	2	6	0	.300
1994	Chicago	AL	OF	63	102	16	26	2	7	1	.255
1995	Chicago	AL	OF	51	85	19	20	3	9	1	.235
1995	Seattle	AL	OF	33	72	15	21	2	6	1	.292
Post All-Star				35	74	15	21	2	6	1	.284

DAVE NILSSON
Age 26/L   **$11**

Former catcher who is now a passable outfielder. Started the season on the DL with a mosquito-borne illness called "Ross River Fever," which sounds like the name of a Charlie Sheen movie. We're pretty sure Cal would have played through it.

Year	Team	Lg.	Pos.	G	AB	R	H	HR	RBI	SB	BA
1992	Milwaukee	AL	C	51	164	15	38	4	25	2	.232
1993	Milwaukee	AL	C	100	296	35	76	7	40	3	.257
1994	Milwaukee	AL	C	109	397	51	109	12	69	1	.275
1995	Milwaukee	AL	OF	81	263	41	73	12	53	2	.278
Post All-Star				67	220	35	63	10	45	2	.286

OTIS NIXON
Age 37/B   **$24**

A guy gets caught stealing 21 out of 71 attempts, you'd think he might be a little more selective. But at Nixon's age, maybe you've earned the right to run any damn time you please.

Year	Team	Lg.	Pos.	G	AB	R	H	HR	RBI	SB	BA
1992	Atlanta	NL	OF	120	456	79	134	2	22	41	.294
1993	Atlanta	NL	OF	134	461	77	124	1	24	47	.269
1994	Boston	AL	OF	103	398	60	109	0	25	42	.274
1995	Texas	AL	OF	139	589	87	174	0	45	50	.295
Post All-Star				73	301	51	91	0	22	30	.302

JON NUNNALLY
Age 24/L   **$12**

Had a great first half and then the league caught up to him.

Year	Team	Lg.	Pos.	G	AB	R	H	HR	RBI	SB	BA
1995	Kansas City	AL	OF	119	303	51	74	14	42	6	.244
Post All-Star				68	170	26	36	3	21	3	.212

Catchers
pp. 27–41

Corners
pp. 41–62

Infield
pp. 63–82

Outfield
pp. 83–113

DH
pp. 114–118

Starters
pp. 119–157

Relievers
pp. 157–193

TROY O'LEARY
Age 26/L   **$15**

Irish guys always bloom in Boston.

Year	Team	Lg.	Pos.	G	AB	R	H	HR	RBI	SB	BA
1993	Milwaukee	AL	OF	19	41	3	12	0	3	0	.293
1994	Milwaukee	AL	OF	27	66	9	18	2	7	1	.273
1995	Boston	AL	OF	112	399	60	123	10	49	5	.308
Post All-Star				58	199	30	54	3	14	2	.271

PAUL O'NEILL
Age 33/L   **$34**

One of the best outfielders in the game and a truly brilliant pickup by the Yankees, O'Neill is possibly the biggest baby in sports. Not that he isn't tough. It's those tantrums he throws whenever he doesn't do what he wants to do on the field. Helmets and bats fly. Curses soar. Scowls abound. Doesn't he know there are a lot of Little Leaguers watching his every move? Doesn't he care? (This message brought to you as a public service announcement by Rotisserie League Baseball.)

Year	Team	Lg.	Pos.	G	AB	R	H	HR	RBI	SB	BA
1992	Cincinnati	NL	OF	148	496	59	122	14	66	6	.246
1993	New York	AL	OF	141	498	71	155	20	75	2	.311
1994	New York	AL	OF	103	368	68	132	21	83	5	.359
1995	New York	AL	OF	127	460	82	138	22	96	1	.300
Post All-Star				75	275	47	74	11	57	1	.269

KIRBY PUCKETT
Age 35/R   **$29**

At 35, he's as good as ever. All those overdeveloped weight-room guys should take a look at Kirby, who, along with some games at DH, played 2B, SS, and 3B last year. Probably will stay in Minnesota because the team was encouraged by the performance of some of the players acquired for Aguilera, Erickson, and Tapani. But Kirby, just one word of advice the next time you step in against Dennis Martinez: DUCK!

Year	Team	Lg.	Pos.	G	AB	R	H	HR	RBI	SB	BA
1992	Minnesota	AL	OF	160	639	104	210	19	110	17	.329
1993	Minnesota	AL	OF	156	622	89	184	22	89	8	.296
1994	Minnesota	AL	OF	108	439	79	139	20	112	6	.317
1995	Minnesota	AL	OF	137	538	83	169	23	99	3	.314
Post All-Star				71	274	47	95	13	59	1	.347

TIM RAINES
Age 36/B   **$17**

Still a rock.

Year	Team	Lg.	Pos.	G	AB	R	H	HR	RBI	SB	BA
1992	Chicago	AL	OF	144	551	102	162	7	54	45	.294
1993	Chicago	AL	OF	115	415	75	127	16	54	21	.306
1994	Chicago	AL	OF	101	384	80	102	10	52	13	.266
1995	Chicago	AL	OF	133	502	81	143	12	67	13	.285
Post All-Star				71	255	41	69	4	35	7	.271

MANNY RAMIREZ
Age 23/R   **$37**

Has 50 major league home runs. At the same age, Mo Vaughn had 4, Albert (then Joey) Belle had 7, Frank Thomas had 39, and Barry Bonds had 41. You probably see where we're going with this.

Year	Team	Lg.	Pos.	G	AB	R	H	HR	RBI	SB	BA
1993	Cleveland	AL	DH	22	53	5	9	2	5	0	.170
1994	Cleveland	AL	OF	91	290	51	78	17	60	4	.269
1995	Cleveland	AL	OF	137	484	85	149	31	107	6	.308
Post All-Star				72	253	41	75	13	55	1	.296

KEVIN ROBERSON · Age 28/B · $1

The Mariners have too many outfielders for this guy to be in their plans. For that matter, the American League has too many outfielders for this guy to be in your plans.

Year	Team	Lg.	Pos.	G	AB	R	H	HR	RBI	SB	BA
1993	Chicago	NL	OF	62	180	23	34	9	27	0	.189
1994	Chicago	NL	OF	44	55	8	12	4	9	0	.218
1995	Chicago	NL	OF	32	38	5	7	4	6	0	.184
Post All-Star				0	0	0	0	0	0	0	0.000

TIM SALMON · Age 27/R · $39

The Angels finally got some other hitters, so Salmon didn't have to spend the summer swimming upstream the way he did in previous years. He responded with his best season yet, but we believe even better is still to come.

Year	Team	Lg.	Pos.	G	AB	R	H	HR	RBI	SB	BA
1992	California	AL	OF	23	79	8	14	2	6	1	.177
1993	California	AL	OF	142	515	93	146	31	95	5	.283
1994	California	AL	OF	100	373	67	107	23	70	1	.287
1995	California	AL	OF	143	537	111	177	34	105	5	.330
Post All-Star				74	286	64	104	19	63	3	.364

RUBEN SIERRA · Age 30/B · $23

Wonder why Tony LaRussa called him the village idiot? In the Yankees' final homestand last year, Sierra was on a tear. But more than once against the Tigers and the Blue Jays, Sierra went into a little jig at home plate before beginning his turtle-like home run trot. After one of these displays, the TV camera picked up Showalter going over to Sierra and getting in his face— not, from the fire coming out of Buck's eyes, to praise him. The message: cut out that bullbleep before you get one of our guys hurt with a retaliation pitch. Because Sierra was clearly expecting some unadulterated praise from his manager, the look of incredulity on his face was priceless. And speaking of priceless, the Yankees are stuck with Sierra for two more years and $10 million, but they still may sit him down a lot. He's not Joe Torre's kind of ballplayer any more than he was Buck Showalter's. Maybe the Yanks should trade him for Danny Tartabull.

Year	Team	Lg.	Pos.	G	AB	R	H	HR	RBI	SB	BA
1992	Oakland	AL	OF	27	101	17	28	3	17	2	.277
1992	Texas	AL	OF	124	500	66	139	14	70	12	.278
1993	Oakland	AL	OF	158	630	77	147	22	101	25	.233
1994	Oakland	AL	OF	110	426	71	114	23	92	8	.268
1995	Oakland	AL	OF	70	264	40	70	12	42	4	.265
1995	New York	AL	DH	56	215	33	56	7	44	1	.260
Post All-Star				61	234	34	61	7	44	1	.261

Catchers pp. 27–41

Corners pp. 41–62

Infield pp. 63–82

Outfield pp. 83–113

DH pp. 114–118

Starters pp. 119–157

Relievers pp. 157–193

TODD STEVERSON   Age 24/R $2

Will probably end up as Detroit's fifth outfielder this year, which is roughly equivalent to ninth outfielder on most other teams.

Year	Team	Lg.	Pos.	G	AB	R	H	HR	RBI	SB	BA
1995	Detroit	AL	OF	30	42	11	11	2	6	2	.262
Post All-Star				4	2	1	0	0	0	0	0.000

FRANKLIN STUBBS   Age 35/L $1

Will be swept out the door in a Tiger youth movement.

Year	Team	Lg.	Pos.	G	AB	R	H	HR	RBI	SB	BA
1992	Milwaukee	AL	1B	92	288	37	66	9	42	11	.229
1995	Detroit	AL	1B	62	116	13	29	2	19	0	.250
Post All-Star				19	32	3	10	2	10	0	.313

GARY THURMAN   Age 31/R $1

Nice year at Tacoma, which is very close to Seattle.

Year	Team	Lg.	Pos.	G	AB	R	H	HR	RBI	SB	BA
1992	Kansas City	AL	OF	88	200	25	49	0	20	9	.245
1993	Detroit	AL	OF	75	89	22	19	0	13	7	.213
1995	Seattle	AL	OF	13	25	3	8	0	3	5	.320
Post All-Star				4	5	0	0	0	0	0	0.000

LEE TINSLEY   Age 27/B $13

One of the first Red Sox players to play winter ball and it paid off big time. Now, winter ball is nearly mandatory for young or still-developing players in Boston. Times have changed in Beantown. If he can avoid the injury bug, Tinsley will continue to improve.

Year	Team	Lg.	Pos.	G	AB	R	H	HR	RBI	SB	BA
1993	Seattle	AL	OF	11	19	2	3	1	2	0	.158
1994	Boston	AL	OF	78	144	27	32	2	14	13	.222
1995	Boston	AL	OF	100	341	61	97	7	41	18	.284
Post All-Star				50	141	25	38	2	16	6	.270

MICHAEL TUCKER   Age 24/L $8

So let's get this straight—after *L.A. Law* folds, he loses a few pounds, goes to fantasy camp, gets spotted by a Royals scout, and . . . oh, this is the *other* Michael Tucker? Whatever. Anyway, Johnny Damon, Jon Nunnally, and Tom Goodwin have made this Michael Tucker the Royals' fourth outfielder. Still, pick him up because he'll step right in if any of the others falter.

Year	Team	Lg.	Pos.	G	AB	R	H	HR	RBI	SB	BA
1995	Kansas City	AL	OF	62	177	23	46	4	17	2	.260
Post All-Star				35	95	17	29	4	13	1	.305

TURNER WARD
Age 30/B   **$1**

"I'll throw in Turner Ward" is the most common phrase in AL Rotisserie leagues. Pick him up and start thinking trade.

Year	Team	Lg.	Pos.	G	AB	R	H	HR	RBI	SB	BA
1992	Toronto	AL	OF	18	29	7	10	1	3	0	.345
1993	Toronto	AL	OF	72	167	20	32	4	28	3	.192
1994	Milwaukee	AL	OF	102	367	55	85	9	45	6	.232
1995	Milwaukee	AL	OF	44	129	19	34	4	16	6	.264
Post All-Star				4	11	2	3	0	0	1	.273

DEVON WHITE
Age 33/B   **$17**

Probably gone from Toronto, but still worth a long look. Pay close attention in spring training to how that fractured foot is doing.

Year	Team	Lg.	Pos.	G	AB	R	H	HR	RBI	SB	BA
1992	Toronto	AL	OF	153	641	98	159	17	60	37	.248
1993	Toronto	AL	OF	146	598	116	163	15	52	34	.273
1994	Toronto	AL	OF	100	403	67	109	13	49	11	.270
1995	Toronto	AL	OF	101	427	61	121	10	53	11	.283
Post All-Star				46	194	25	52	2	20	7	.268

BERNIE WILLIAMS
Age 27/B   **$21**

Carried the Yanks last September. Didn't draw that much attention outside of the Bronx because the Pinstripes were a dozen games behind the Red Sox and only fighting for a wild card spot. Williams, though an erratic fielder, should be the Yankees' main man in center field for years.

Year	Team	Lg.	Pos.	G	AB	R	H	HR	RBI	SB	BA
1992	New York	AL	OF	62	261	39	73	5	26	7	.280
1993	New York	AL	OF	139	567	67	152	12	68	9	.268
1994	New York	AL	OF	108	408	80	118	12	57	16	.289
1995	New York	AL	OF	144	563	93	173	18	82	8	.307
Post All-Star				79	309	57	108	9	44	2	.350

GERALD WILLIAMS
Age 29/R   **$4**

Don't doze off at the auction draft and jump the bidding on the wrong Williams.

Year	Team	Lg.	Pos.	G	AB	R	H	HR	RBI	SB	BA
1992	New York	AL	OF	15	27	7	8	3	6	2	.296
1993	New York	AL	OF	42	67	11	10	0	6	2	.149
1994	New York	AL	OF	57	86	19	25	4	13	1	.291
1995	New York	AL	OF	100	182	33	45	6	28	4	.247
Post All-Star				60	103	14	23	1	11	2	.223

ERNIE YOUNG
Age 26/R   **$3**

One of many young A's who'll get a long look this spring.

Year	Team	Lg.	Pos.	G	AB	R	H	HR	RBI	SB	BA
1994	Oakland	AL	OF	11	30	2	2	0	3	0	.067
1995	Oakland	AL	OF	26	50	9	10	2	5	0	.200
Post All-Star				19	32	8	6	1	4	0	.188

Catchers
pp. 27–41

Corners
pp. 41–62

Infield
pp. 63–82

Outfield
pp. 83–113

DH
pp. 114–118

Starters
pp. 119–157

Relievers
pp. 157–193

Designated Hitters

HAROLD BAINES   Age 37/L $22

Another season for Harold Baines, another reason to keep the DH. No, wait—kill the DH, but grandfather Harold Baines. Indeed, a couple of us have become grandfathers since Harold Baines came into the league. Hit his 300th HR last year, but the team seemed to be preoccupied with some other record most of the season.

Year	Team	Lg.	Pos.	G	AB	R	H	HR	RBI	SB	BA
1992	Oakland	AL	DH	140	478	58	121	16	76	1	.253
1993	Baltimore	AL	DH	118	416	64	130	20	78	0	.313
1994	Baltimore	AL	DH	94	326	44	96	16	54	0	.294
1995	Baltimore	AL	DH	127	385	60	115	24	63	0	.299
Post All-Star				70	217	37	63	14	33	0	.290

GERONIMO BERROA   Age 31/R $26

With Berroa, on the other hand, the game would be a lot more fun if he were made to play in the field. What Dick Stuart was to first base, this guy is to left field—or was, the last time we saw him out there. Glove aside, which is where it ought to be, what a sweet hitter he is. Picked up right where he left off in 1994. Still, his playing time may be affected this year if A's move McGwire into DH slot (assuming McGwire is fully recovered from his various maladies). Pay attention to box scores in the spring.

Year	Team	Lg.	Pos.	G	AB	R	H	HR	RBI	SB	BA
1992	Cincinnati	NL	OF	13	15	2	4	0	0	0	.267
1993	Florida	NL	OF	14	34	3	4	0	0	0	.118
1994	Oakland	AL	DH	96	340	55	104	13	65	7	.306
1995	Oakland	AL	DH	141	546	87	152	22	88	7	.278
Post All-Star				72	287	41	82	10	46	5	.286

JOSE CANSECO   Age 31/R $32

If the Red Sox give Kevin Kennedy one present for winning the division in a rebuilding year, it should be the re-signing of Canseco, one of Kennedy's favorites. Jose didn't hit his promised 50 HRs—because of injuries, natch—but look at what he did in the 102 games he did play. Still can carry a team when he's on. Just don't expect a full season of it.

Year	Team	Lg.	Pos.	G	AB	R	H	HR	RBI	SB	BA
1992	Oakland	AL	OF	97	366	66	90	22	72	5	.246
1992	Texas	AL	OF	22	73	8	17	4	15	1	.233
1993	Texas	AL	OF	60	231	30	59	10	46	6	.255
1994	Texas	AL	DH	111	429	88	121	31	90	15	.282
1995	Boston	AL	DH	102	396	64	121	24	81	4	.306
Post All-Star				70	280	48	91	19	60	1	.325

CHILI DAVIS   Age 36/B $28

Most kinds of chili don't keep this long, but Davis is definitely into some kind of swell preservative.

Year	Team	Lg.	Pos.	G	AB	R	H	HR	RBI	SB	BA
1992	Minnesota	AL	DH	138	444	63	128	12	66	4	.288
1993	California	AL	DH	153	573	74	139	27	112	4	.243
1994	California	AL	DH	108	392	72	122	26	84	3	.311
1995	California	AL	DH	119	424	81	135	20	86	3	.318
Post All-Star				69	243	41	70	11	48	1	.288

KIRK GIBSON
Age 38/L   No Price

Thanks for the memories, Gibbie. Nobody ever had a better exit line: "I was traded for my family."

Year	Team	Lg.	Pos.	G	AB	R	H	HR	RBI	SB	BA
1992	Pittsburgh	NL	OF	16	56	6	11	2	5	3	.196
1993	Detroit	AL	DH	116	403	62	105	13	62	15	.261
1994	Detroit	AL	DH	98	330	71	91	23	72	4	.276
1995	Detroit	AL	DH	70	227	37	59	9	35	9	.260
Post All-Star				19	63	5	16	0	6	2	.254

JUAN GONZALEZ
Age 26/R $35

An ill-advised weight-lifting program has stunted the development of one of the best young hitters in the game. He's still young, but can you think of anyone in any sport who's recovered fully from back problems? The Rangers regret his big contract as much as they regret anything in the history of the team. On the lighter side, when Gonzalez heard that an older woman who runs the elevator in Tiger Stadium was having a hard time with the heat last summer, he bought her an electric fan. By the way, if you were impressed with what Jose Canseco did in 102 games, be aware that Gonzalez's assault and battery of American League pitching was accomplished in 97 games.

Year	Team	Lg.	Pos.	G	AB	R	H	HR	RBI	SB	BA
1992	Texas	AL	OF	155	584	77	152	43	109	0	.260
1993	Texas	AL	OF	140	536	105	166	46	118	4	.310
1994	Texas	AL	OF	107	422	57	116	19	85	6	.275
1995	Texas	AL	DH	90	352	57	104	27	82	0	.295
Post All-Star				56	215	35	66	15	49	0	.307

CHIP HALE
Age 31/L $2

Plays the infield and spells Pedro Munoz at DH. Could lose his job to a rookie that shows a nickel's worth of potential, so stay away.

Year	Team	Lg.	Pos.	G	AB	R	H	HR	RBI	SB	BA
1993	Minnesota	AL	2B	69	186	25	62	3	27	2	.333
1994	Minnesota	AL	3B	67	118	13	31	1	11	0	.263
1995	Minnesota	AL	DH	69	103	10	27	2	18	0	.262
Post All-Star				45	71	6	17	1	10	0	.239

BOB HAMELIN
Age 28/L $2

The bigger they are, the harder they fall? Yep, that seems the appropriate cliché here.

Year	Team	Lg.	Pos.	G	AB	R	H	HR	RBI	SB	BA
1993	Kansas City	AL	1B	16	49	2	11	2	5	0	.224
1994	Kansas City	AL	DH	101	312	64	88	24	65	4	.282
1995	Kansas City	AL	DH	72	208	20	35	7	25	0	.168
Post All-Star				32	85	9	13	4	12	0	.153

Catchers
pp. 27–41

Corners
pp. 41–62

Infield
pp. 63–82

Outfield
pp. 83–113

DH
pp. 114–118

Starters
pp. 119–157

Relievers
pp. 157–193

JOHN KRUK

Age 35/L   No Price

Could have been a successful designated hitter another 10–15 seasons, if only he could have had a pinch-runner starting at home plate. One of our all-time favorites. And another guy with a terrific exit line: a base hit.

Year	Team	Lg.	Pos.	G	AB	R	H	HR	RBI	SB	BA
1992	Philadelphia	NL	1B	144	507	86	164	10	70	3	.323
1993	Philadelphia	NL	1B	150	535	100	169	14	85	6	.316
1994	Philadelphia	NL	1B	75	255	35	77	5	38	4	.302
1995	Chicago	AL	DH	45	159	13	49	2	23	0	.308
Post All-Star				14	44	2	9	0	2	0	.205

EDGAR MARTINEZ

Age 33/R $39

That grand-slam homer in the fourth game of the AL divisional playoff did more to Bring Back Baseball than anything else that happened all season. Unless it was the double down the line in the last half of the ninth inning of the fifth game that sent Junior ripping around from first with the winning run. The most amazing thing about Martinez's year was that he kept the team in contention while Griffey missed two months. A right-handed Tony Gwynn, only with a lot more power.

Year	Team	Lg.	Pos.	G	AB	R	H	HR	RBI	SB	BA
1992	Seattle	AL	3B	135	528	100	181	18	73	14	.343
1993	Seattle	AL	DH	42	135	20	32	4	13	0	.237
1994	Seattle	AL	3B	89	326	47	93	13	51	6	.285
1995	Seattle	AL	DH	145	511	121	182	29	113	4	.356
Post All-Star				76	271	63	95	15	57	1	.351

PAUL MOLITOR

Age 39/R $20

A little-known casualty of the strike, Molitor was so depleted by participating in the negotiations that it took him half a season to recover. He vowed not to take part in any labor talks this off-season and will be worth a look if he stayed home all winter.

Year	Team	Lg.	Pos.	G	AB	R	H	HR	RBI	SB	BA
1992	Milwaukee	AL	DH	158	609	89	195	12	89	31	.320
1993	Toronto	AL	DH	160	636	121	211	22	111	22	.332
1994	Toronto	AL	DH	115	454	86	155	14	75	20	.341
1995	Toronto	AL	DH	130	525	63	142	15	60	12	.270
Post All-Star				72	292	32	87	8	28	7	.298

PEDRO MUNOZ

Age 27/R $24

Hobbled by injuries again, Muñoz still put up some nice numbers. Another one of those guys who can break your heart unless you factor in DL time when calculating the price you'll pay.

Year	Team	Lg.	Pos.	G	AB	R	H	HR	RBI	SB	BA
1992	Minnesota	AL	OF	127	418	44	113	12	71	4	.270
1993	Minnesota	AL	OF	104	326	34	76	13	38	1	.233
1994	Minnesota	AL	OF	75	244	35	72	11	36	0	.295
1995	Minnesota	AL	DH	104	376	45	113	18	58	0	.301
Post All-Star				53	193	18	60	6	27	0	.311

EDDIE MURRAY
Age 40/R $27

When we speak sharply about guys like Juan Gonzalez, Mark McGwire, and Jose Canseco for rampant iron-pumping, it's Eddie Murray we have in mind. Last year, Murray went on the DL for the second time in 19 years. Do you even think those weight-room guys will be playing when they are 39, let alone putting up numbers like these?

Year	Team	Lg.	Pos.	G	AB	R	H	HR	RBI	SB	BA
1992	New York	NL	1B	156	551	64	144	16	93	4	.261
1993	New York	NL	1B	154	610	77	174	27	100	2	.285
1994	Cleveland	AL	DH	108	433	57	110	17	76	8	.254
1995	Cleveland	AL	DH	113	436	68	141	21	82	5	.323
Post All-Star				53	204	31	66	9	37	3	.324

DARRYL STRAWBERRY
Age 34/L $7

Very hard to figure this guy. Played the good soldier last year in New York. Played winter ball and worked on his fielding as well as on getting his stroke back. Then again, a man with so many demons is hard to count on. Plus he's well past the typical baseball player's prime years, and for a power hitter to regain his stroke . . . well, we think he has a long road back. Could produce in a limited role in NY, or could be gone due to the fact that he and Sierra can't field and Sierra has that huge contract. Pay a little more if he signs with a team that has a chance of playing him regularly.

Year	Team	Lg.	Pos.	G	AB	R	H	HR	RBI	SB	BA
1992	Los Angeles	NL	OF	43	156	20	37	5	25	3	.237
1993	Los Angeles	NL	OF	32	100	12	14	5	12	1	.140
1994	San Francisco	NL	OF	29	92	13	22	4	17	0	.239
1995	New York	AL	DH	32	87	15	24	3	13	0	.276
Post All-Star				32	87	15	24	3	13	0	.276

DANNY TARTABULL
Age 33/R $17

In the best of all possible worlds, he would have a great year in Oakland and Sierra would have a great year in New York. Both are immensely talented and a heckuva lot of fun to watch when they get hot. Are we optimistic? Let's say we see a half-full glass in one park, a half-empty one in another, and we're not quite sure which is where.

Year	Team	Lg.	Pos.	G	AB	R	H	HR	RBI	SB	BA
1992	New York	AL	OF	123	421	72	112	25	85	2	.266
1993	New York	AL	DH	138	513	87	128	31	102	0	.250
1994	New York	AL	DH	104	399	68	102	19	67	1	.256
1995	New York	AL	DH	59	192	25	43	6	28	0	.224
1995	Oakland	AL	DH	24	88	9	23	2	7	0	.261
Post All-Star				26	93	9	23	2	7	0	.247

Catchers
pp. 27–41

Corners
pp. 41–62

Infield
pp. 63–82

Outfield
pp. 83–113

DH
pp. 114–118

Starters
pp. 119–157

Relievers
pp. 157–193

MICKEY TETTLETON
Age 35/B $25

Knees are shot, so he won't be doing any more catching. Pity. We always liked drafting a catcher good for 30 homers a year and enough strikeouts to alter weather patterns.

Year	Team	Lg.	Pos.	G	AB	R	H	HR	RBI	SB	BA
1992	Detroit	AL	C	157	525	82	125	32	83	0	.238
1993	Detroit	AL	1B	152	522	79	128	32	110	3	.245
1994	Detroit	AL	C	107	339	57	84	17	51	0	.248
1995	Texas	AL	OF	134	429	76	102	32	78	0	.238
Post All-Star				67	205	39	52	18	41	0	.254

GREG VAUGHN
Age 30/R $20

Another Brewer, another role player, but a thumper. You'll need a lot to compensate for that BA, but the power numbers are solid.

Year	Team	Lg.	Pos.	G	AB	R	H	HR	RBI	SB	BA
1992	Milwaukee	AL	OF	141	501	77	114	23	78	15	.228
1993	Milwaukee	AL	OF	154	569	97	152	30	97	10	.267
1994	Milwaukee	AL	OF	95	370	59	94	19	55	9	.254
1995	Milwaukee	AL	DH	108	392	67	88	17	59	10	.224
Post All-Star				45	160	32	44	9	25	1	.275

JOE VITIELLO
Age 25/R $7

If he shows any life at all, he should be able to put Bob Hamelin into the minor leagues for good. To be a real contributor to your team, however, he'd have to show a lot more than he did last year.

Year	Team	Lg.	Pos.	G	AB	R	H	HR	RBI	SB	BA
1995	Kansas City	AL	DH	53	130	13	33	7	21	0	.254
Post All-Star				45	119	12	33	7	21	0	.277

DAVE WINFIELD
Age 44/R No Price

He may try to catch on with somebody, but we wish he wouldn't. It's time. Indians players showed a lot of class by asking him to come along to the post-season even though he wasn't on the roster; he showed a lot of class by going.

Year	Team	Lg.	Pos.	G	AB	R	H	HR	RBI	SB	BA
1992	Toronto	AL	DH	156	583	92	169	26	108	2	.290
1993	Minnesota	AL	DH	143	547	72	148	21	76	2	.271
1994	Minnesota	AL	DH	77	294	35	74	10	43	2	.252
1995	Cleveland	AL	DH	46	115	11	22	2	4	1	.191
Post All-Star				23	62	8	12	1	1	0	.194

On the Mound

NATIONAL LEAGUE

Catchers
pp. 27–41

Corners
pp. 41–62

Infield
pp. 63–82

Outfield
pp. 83–113

DH
pp. 114–118

Starters
pp. 119–157

Relievers
pp. 157–193

JUAN ACEVEDO   Age 25/R $8

For a while the Mets feared the young fireballer they acquired from Colorado in the Bret Saberhagen deal was damaged goods. Then they decided his shoulder tenderness was just the result of too many innings compiled in winter ball, an uninspiring Colorado debut last spring, and a summer in the minors. Pay close attention in spring training: if he gets his regular turn, it means he's okay. And if he's okay, it means, well, that he's a whole lot better than just okay, because the kid has some seriously nasty stuff to go with his heat.

Year	Team	Lg.	G	IP	H	BB	SO	W	L	ERA	SV	Ratio
1995	Colorado	NL	17	65.2	82	20	40	4	6	6.44	0	1.553
Post All-Star			1	3.0	9	0	1	0	0	15.00	0	3.000

ANDY ASHBY   Age 28/R $18

While no one was looking, he has become one of the top right-handers in the league. He should remain one of them for a few years. Stumbled around the first couple of months but came on strong in the second half. The team figures to be a lot stronger this year, so 12–10 could jump to 18–4, a W-L record more in keeping with the ERA.

Year	Team	Lg.	G	IP	H	BB	SO	W	L	ERA	SV	Ratio
1992	Philadelphia	NL	10	37.0	42	21	24	1	3	7.54	0	1.703
1993	San Diego	NL	12	69.0	79	24	44	3	6	5.48	0	1.493
1993	Colorado	NL	20	54.0	89	32	33	0	4	8.50	1	2.241
1994	San Diego	NL	24	164.1	145	43	121	6	11	3.40	0	1.144
1995	San Diego	NL	31	192.2	180	62	150	12	10	2.94	0	1.256
Post All-Star			16	100.2	99	32	74	6	5	2.59	0	1.301

PEDRO ASTACIO   Age 26/R $4

The Dodgers banished Astacio to the bullpen around midseason. That's not a pretty fate for a Tommy Lasorda–managed pitcher, because it means you get to warm up six out of every seven days. If Pedro can learn how to pitch rather than throw, he can still help someone's rotation.

Year	Team	Lg.	G	IP	H	BB	SO	W	L	ERA	SV	Ratio
1992	Los Angeles	NL	11	82.0	80	20	43	5	5	1.98	0	1.220
1993	Los Angeles	NL	31	186.1	165	68	122	14	9	3.57	0	1.250
1994	Los Angeles	NL	23	149.0	142	47	108	6	8	4.29	0	1.268
1995	Los Angeles	NL	48	104.0	103	29	80	7	8	4.24	0	1.269
Post All-Star			30	32.0	31	7	29	6	1	3.66	0	1.188

STEVE AVERY   Age 25/L $15

A mystery to one and all. However, remember he's young and that his shoulder was tested out without finding any problems. Also remember that no one is better at massing bruised egos and ruffled confidence than Leo

---

Mazzone, the Braves' pitching guru. There's been talk that Atlanta might risk sending him into free agency, and that would certainly change the equation. But keep in mind that he's still just a kid in baseball years, even though it does seem like he's been around since Sandy Koufax quit. And take a look at the job he did against the Reds in the fourth game of the NLCS—maybe it just took all year for the real Steve Avery to take the mound.

Year	Team	Lg.	G	IP	H	BB	SO	W	L	ERA	SV	Ratio
1992	Atlanta	NL	35	233.2	216	71	129	11	11	3.20	0	1.228
1993	Atlanta	NL	35	223.1	216	43	125	18	6	2.94	0	1.160
1994	Atlanta	NL	24	151.2	127	55	122	8	3	4.04	0	1.200
1995	Atlanta	NL	29	173.1	165	52	141	7	13	4.67	0	1.252
Post All-Star			15	87.1	77	29	72	3	8	5.15	0	1.214

WILLIE BANKS   Age 27/R $1

Next lifetime. Maybe.

Year	Team	Lg.	G	IP	H	BB	SO	W	L	ERA	SV	Ratio
1992	Minnesota	AL	16	71.0	80	37	37	4	4	5.70	0	1.648
1993	Minnesota	AL	31	171.1	186	78	138	11	12	4.04	0	1.541
1994	Chicago	NL	23	138.1	139	56	91	8	12	5.40	0	1.410
1995	Chicago	NL	10	11.2	27	12	9	0	1	15.43	0	3.343
1995	Los Angeles	NL	6	29.0	36	16	23	0	2	4.03	0	1.793
1995	Florida	NL	9	50.0	43	30	30	2	3	4.32	0	1.460
Post All-Star			12	65.0	65	38	39	2	4	4.15	0	1.585

WILLIE BLAIR   Age 30/R $1

Moved into the San Diego rotation in the last third of the season, where he had a dozen mostly decent starts. No guarantees that he won't be pushed aside, but could be valuable on an improving team.

Year	Team	Lg.	G	IP	H	BB	SO	W	L	ERA	SV	Ratio
1992	Houston	NL	29	78.2	74	25	48	5	7	4.00	0	1.258
1993	Colorado	NL	46	146.0	184	42	84	6	10	4.75	0	1.548
1994	Colorado	NL	47	77.2	98	39	68	0	5	5.79	3	1.764
1995	San Diego	NL	40	114.0	112	45	83	7	5	4.34	0	1.377
Post All-Star			19	85.1	82	36	61	6	5	4.11	0	1.383

JAMIE BREWINGTON   Age 24/R $3

Showed promise in late-season exposure. However, we strongly advise one and all to stay away from pitchers wearing Giants uniforms. They all tend to become mediocre or injured or both. Call it the Mike LaCoss Legacy. And if they don't get hurt, they get traded in bad deals that wind up with them pitching better somewhere else.

Year	Team	Lg.	G	IP	H	BB	SO	W	L	ERA	SV	Ratio
1995	San Francisco	NL	13	75.1	68	45	45	6	4	4.54	0	1.500
Post All-Star			13	75.1	68	45	45	6	4	4.54	0	1.500

JIM BULLINGER   Age 30/R $9

He won't knock your socks off, but he's become a solid winner in an unlikely spot. The only problem with him—or with any Cubs starter, for that matter—is that you can never sleep the night before he pitches at home. At that park, a pitcher can have his good stuff and still give up five runs in the first inning.

Year	Team	Lg.	G	IP	H	BB	SO	W	L	ERA	SV	Ratio
1992	Chicago	NL	39	85.0	72	54	36	2	8	4.66	7	1.482
1993	Chicago	NL	15	16.2	18	9	10	1	0	4.32	1	1.620
1994	Chicago	NL	33	100.0	87	34	72	6	2	3.60	2	1.210
1995	Chicago	NL	24	150.0	152	65	93	12	8	4.14	0	1.447
Post All-Star			15	94.0	104	44	61	6	7	4.88	0	1.574

DAVE BURBA   Age 29/R $8

All he did after arriving in Cincinnati was turn into one of the hottest pitchers in the league. Didn't he used to be a Giant?

Year	Team	Lg.	G	IP	H	BB	SO	W	L	ERA	SV	Ratio
1992	San Francisco	NL	23	70.2	80	31	47	2	7	4.97	0	1.571
1993	San Francisco	NL	54	95.1	95	37	88	10	3	4.25	0	1.385
1994	San Francisco	NL	57	74.0	59	45	84	3	6	4.38	0	1.405
1995	San Francisco	NL	37	43.1	38	25	46	4	2	4.98	0	1.454
1995	Cincinnati	NL	15	63.1	52	26	50	6	2	3.27	0	1.232
Post All-Star			19	68.2	58	31	54	6	2	3.67	0	1.296

JOHN BURKETT   Age 31/R $11

Aces don't necessarily have to pile up Johnson-esque strikeouts. Aces don't necessarily have to pile up Maddux-esque shutouts. An ace can instead be defined as someone who piles up Burkett-esque innings. Used to pitch for the Giants, didn't he?

Year	Team	Lg.	G	IP	H	BB	SO	W	L	ERA	SV	Ratio
1992	San Francisco	NL	32	189.2	194	45	107	13	9	3.84	0	1.260
1993	San Francisco	NL	34	231.2	224	40	145	22	7	3.65	0	1.140
1994	San Francisco	NL	25	159.1	176	36	85	6	8	3.62	0	1.331
1995	Florida	NL	30	188.1	208	57	126	14	14	4.30	0	1.407
Post All-Star			16	103.0	116	28	67	8	6	3.76	0	1.398

TOM CANDIOTTI   Age 38/R $10

The novelty of the knuckleball wears thin/when you lose twice as many as you win. That's a poem, sort of, and we're in a quandary, sort of, about what to do when Candiotti's name comes up in the auction draft. His ERA's perfectly respectable—better than stablemate Ramon Martinez's, as a matter of fact—and almost the same as his lifetime mark (3.46 entering 1995), which means you know what to expect from Candiotti. But the guy hasn't had a winning season since 1990, when he was 15–11 at Cleveland. Guess that also means you know what you can expect from Candiotti.

Year	Team	Lg.	G	IP	H	BB	SO	W	L	ERA	SV	Ratio
1992	Los Angeles	NL	32	203.2	177	63	152	11	15	3.00	0	1.178
1993	Los Angeles	NL	33	213.2	192	71	155	8	10	3.12	0	1.231
1994	Los Angeles	NL	23	153.0	149	54	102	7	7	4.12	0	1.327
1995	Los Angeles	NL	30	190.1	187	58	141	7	14	3.50	0	1.287
Post All-Star			15	94.2	103	30	79	3	8	4.18	0	1.405

Catchers
pp. 27–41

Corners
pp. 41–62

Infield
pp. 63–82

Outfield
pp. 83–113

DH
pp. 114–118

Starters
pp. 119–157

Relievers
pp. 157–193

FRANK CASTILLO   Age 26/R $12

Knock us over with a feather. Who woulda thunk that by season's end he would be one of the NL's best pitchers? Not us.

Year	Team	Lg.	G	IP	H	BB	SO	W	L	ERA	SV	Ratio
1992	Chicago	NL	33	205.1	179	63	135	10	11	3.46	0	1.179
1993	Chicago	NL	29	141.1	162	39	84	5	8	4.84	0	1.422
1994	Chicago	NL	4	23.0	25	5	19	2	1	4.30	0	1.304
1995	Chicago	NL	29	188.0	179	52	135	11	10	3.21	0	1.229
Post All-Star			16	103.2	100	31	75	5	6	3.47	0	1.264

GLENN DISHMAN   Age 25/L $1

Dished out a lot of misery to a lot of Rotisserie owners. But he's young and left-handed, so what does he care? Padres must like him—they kept running him out there in the second half despite mounting evidence that he was overmatched.

Year	Team	Lg.	G	IP	H	BB	SO	W	L	ERA	SV	Ratio
1995	San Diego	NL	19	97.0	104	34	43	4	8	5.01	0	1.423
Post All-Star			15	71.0	82	30	30	3	6	5.83	0	1.577

DOUG DRABEK   Age 33/R $16

And who woulda thunk that by season's end that Doug Drabek, once one of baseball's better big-game pitchers, would be just a smidge above journeyman status? Drabek had a worse ERA than *Greg Swindell,* for Cy Young's sake! Our prediction? NL Comeback Pitcher of the Year in 1996. Meanwhile, up in Pittsburgh, Drabek's place as a big-game pitcher has been assumed by . . .

Year	Team	Lg.	G	IP	H	BB	SO	W	L	ERA	SV	Ratio
1992	Pittsburgh	NL	34	256.2	218	54	177	15	11	2.77	0	1.060
1993	Houston	NL	34	237.2	242	60	157	9	18	3.79	0	1.271
1994	Houston	NL	23	164.2	132	45	121	12	6	2.84	0	1.075
1995	Houston	NL	31	185.0	205	54	143	10	9	4.77	0	1.400
Post All-Star			16	97.1	107	23	62	6	4	4.72	0	1.336

JOHN ERICKS   Age 28/R $2

. . . Huh? All right, so the Pirates don't play big games anymore, but this guy is big, and he is a pitcher. Some Pirates people actually think he can become "a decent pitcher." Unfortunately, "decent" is not the kind of label that makes you reach for your wallet.

Year	Team	Lg.	G	IP	H	BB	SO	W	L	ERA	SV	Ratio
1995	Pittsburgh	NL	19	106.0	108	50	80	3	9	4.58	0	1.491
Post All-Star			15	84.0	93	44	62	1	8	5.14	0	1.631

JEFF FASSERO   Age 33/L $16

An established, innings-eating competitor who always keeps his team in games, a bona fide professional—in other words, someone who's become too expensive for the Expos to keep. Watch where he ends up and reap the dividends accordingly.

Year	Team	Lg.	G	IP	H	BB	SO	W	L	ERA	SV	Ratio
1992	Montreal	NL	70	85.2	81	34	63	8	7	2.84	1	1.342
1993	Montreal	NL	56	149.2	119	54	140	12	5	2.29	1	1.156
1994	Montreal	NL	21	138.2	119	40	119	8	6	2.99	0	1.147
1995	Montreal	NL	30	189.0	207	74	164	13	14	4.33	0	1.487
Post All-Star			16	101.1	114	47	79	5	8	4.71	0	1.589

SID FERNANDEZ   Age 33/L $11

Bombed in his first outing as a Phillie, but El Sid was borderline terrific most of the other times he toed the rubber. You always have to wonder when he'll fall off the wagon and eat a McDonald's—not a Big Mac, a *McDonald's*—or when his elbow will act up or when his back will go out or ... well, El Sid has never been a model of endurance or consistency. But when he is good, he is very, very good. A big reason this year? Johnny Podres.

Year	Team	Lg.	G	IP	H	BB	SO	W	L	ERA	SV	Ratio
1992	New York	NL	32	214.2	162	67	193	14	11	2.73	0	1.067
1993	New York	NL	18	119.2	82	36	81	5	6	2.93	0	0.986
1994	Baltimore	AL	19	115.1	109	46	95	6	6	5.15	0	1.344
1995	Baltimore	AL	8	28.0	36	17	31	0	4	7.39	0	1.893
1995	Philadelphia	NL	11	64.2	48	21	79	6	1	3.34	0	1.067
Post All-Star			11	64.2	48	21	79	6	1	3.34	0	1.067

KEVIN FOSTER   Age 27/R $7

Quick, which was the only NL team to have four double-figure winners? Hint: this change-up specialist was one of them.

Year	Team	Lg.	G	IP	H	BB	SO	W	L	ERA	SV	Ratio
1993	Philadelphia	NL	2	6.2	13	7	6	0	1	14.85	0	3.000
1994	Chicago	NL	13	81.0	70	35	75	3	4	2.89	0	1.296
1995	Chicago	NL	30	167.2	149	65	146	12	11	4.51	0	1.276
Post All-Star			16	87.0	75	29	75	6	6	4.45	0	1.195

MARVIN FREEMAN   Age 32/R $1

Let's just call it the Coors Effect.

Year	Team	Lg.	G	IP	H	BB	SO	W	L	ERA	SV	Ratio
1992	Atlanta	NL	58	64.1	61	29	41	7	5	3.22	3	1.399
1993	Atlanta	NL	21	23.2	24	10	25	2	0	6.08	0	1.437
1994	Colorado	NL	19	112.2	113	23	67	10	2	2.80	0	1.207
1995	Colorado	NL	22	94.2	122	41	61	3	7	5.89	0	1.722
Post All-Star			8	22.0	24	13	14	0	1	6.14	0	1.682

TOM GLAVINE   Age 30/L $25

The last winner of the Cy Young Award before the Age of Maddux began is every bit the classy, left-handed gamer he's always been. And every bit as good as he ever was.

Year	Team	Lg.	G	IP	H	BB	SO	W	L	ERA	SV	Ratio
1992	Atlanta	NL	33	225.0	197	70	129	20	8	2.76	0	1.187
1993	Atlanta	NL	36	239.1	236	90	120	22	6	3.20	0	1.362
1994	Atlanta	NL	25	165.1	173	70	140	13	9	3.97	0	1.470
1995	Atlanta	NL	29	198.2	182	66	127	16	7	3.08	0	1.248
Post All-Star			15	103.1	94	35	63	8	3	2.70	0	1.248

JOE GRAHE   AGE 28/R $1

Let's just call it the Coors Effect.

Year	Team	Lg.	G	IP	H	BB	SO	W	L	ERA	SV	Ratio
1992	California	AL	46	94.2	85	39	39	5	6	3.52	21	1.310
1993	California	AL	45	56.2	54	25	31	4	1	2.86	11	1.394
1994	California	AL	40	43.1	68	18	26	2	5	6.65	13	1.985
1995	Colorado	NL	17	56.2	69	27	27	4	3	5.08	0	1.694
Post All-Star			6	12.1	23	9	9	0	1	9.49	0	2.595

Catchers
pp. 27–41

Corners
pp. 41–62

Infield
pp. 63–82

Outfield
pp. 83–113

DH
pp. 114–118

Starters
pp. 119–157

Relievers
pp. 157–193

TYLER GREEN
Age 26/R   **$3**

For half a season, he was an All-Star and a young star in the making. Then, in the words of a Phillies coach, "We started expecting him to produce. That changed things. Producing is hard when you're squeezing the ball so tight that the stitches leave marks on your hands."

Year	Team	Lg.	G	IP	H	BB	SO	W	L	ERA	SV	Ratio
1993	Philadelphia	NL	3	7.1	16	5	7	0	0	7.36	0	2.864
1995	Philadelphia	NL	26	140.2	157	66	85	8	9	5.31	0	1.585
Post All-Star			12	44.2	77	25	27	0	5	10.68	0	2.284

TOMMY GREENE
Age 28/R   **$1**

With Bobby Muñoz, Greene was one of two poster boys for the Phillies' rotation in 1995—that is, he spent most of the season on the DL, and when he did pitch, he was horrible.

Year	Team	Lg.	G	IP	H	BB	SO	W	L	ERA	SV	Ratio
1992	Philadelphia	NL	13	64.1	75	34	39	3	3	5.32	0	1.694
1993	Philadelphia	NL	31	200.0	175	62	167	16	4	3.42	0	1.185
1994	Philadelphia	NL	7	35.2	37	22	28	2	0	4.54	0	1.654
1995	Philadelphia	NL	11	33.2	45	20	24	0	5	8.29	0	1.931
Post All-Star			8	28.1	36	19	21	0	5	7.94	0	1.941

JOEY HAMILTON
Age 25/R   **$15**

Great stuff, growing maturity, improving team behind him. Next on the agenda: a winning record.

Year	Team	Lg.	G	IP	H	BB	SO	W	L	ERA	SV	Ratio
1994	San Diego	NL	16	108.2	98	29	61	9	6	2.98	0	1.169
1995	San Diego	NL	31	204.1	189	56	123	6	9	3.08	0	1.199
Post All-Star			16	107.0	107	32	68	3	7	3.28	0	1.299

CHRIS HAMMOND
Age 30/L   **$11**

A solid left-hander on a team that is steadily improving. That's a combination that can pay some big dividends.

Year	Team	Lg.	G	IP	H	BB	SO	W	L	ERA	SV	Ratio
1992	Cincinnati	NL	28	147.1	149	55	79	7	10	4.21	0	1.385
1993	Florida	NL	32	191.0	207	66	108	11	12	4.66	0	1.429
1994	Florida	NL	13	73.1	79	23	40	4	4	3.07	0	1.391
1995	Florida	NL	25	161.0	157	47	126	9	6	3.80	0	1.267
Post All-Star			14	87.0	90	29	72	4	4	4.86	0	1.368

MIKE HAMPTON
Age 23/L   **$12**

A solid left-hander on a team that is getting ready to take a nosedive. That's a combination that can waste some serious money. And we'd be scared off if Hampton weren't so young.

Year	Team	Lg.	G	IP	H	BB	SO	W	L	ERA	SV	Ratio
1993	Seattle	AL	13	17.0	28	17	8	1	3	9.53	1	2.647
1994	Houston	NL	44	41.1	46	16	24	2	1	3.70	0	1.500
1995	Houston	NL	24	150.2	141	49	115	9	8	3.35	0	1.261
Post All-Star			15	95.2	94	37	69	5	5	3.67	0	1.369

PETE HARNISCH

Age 29/R   **$7**

The Mets like to think that he can be the kind of veteran competitor to stabilize their staff of wunderkinds. Frankly, we'd rather go with one of the wunderkinds, especially given the arm trouble that felled him last season.

Year	Team	Lg.	G	IP	H	BB	SO	W	L	ERA	SV	Ratio
1992	Houston	NL	34	206.2	182	64	164	9	10	3.70	0	1.190
1993	Houston	NL	33	217.2	171	79	185	16	9	2.98	0	1.149
1994	Houston	NL	17	95.0	100	39	62	8	5	5.40	0	1.463
1995	New York	NL	18	110.0	111	24	82	2	8	3.68	0	1.227
Post All-Star			4	27.0	22	3	22	1	1	2.00	0	0.926

GIL HEREDIA

Age 30/R   **$4**

Steady.

Year	Team	Lg.	G	IP	H	BB	SO	W	L	ERA	SV	Ratio
1992	Montreal	NL	7	14.2	12	4	7	0	0	1.84	0	1.091
1992	San Francisco	NL	13	30.0	32	16	15	2	3	5.40	0	1.600
1993	Montreal	NL	20	57.1	66	14	40	4	2	3.92	2	1.395
1994	Montreal	NL	39	75.1	85	13	62	6	3	3.46	0	1.301
1995	Montreal	NL	40	119.0	137	21	74	5	6	4.31	1	1.328
Post All-Star			26	52.0	47	6	28	2	1	2.08	1	1.019

JASON ISRINGHAUSEN

Age 23/R   **$17**

He's got it all—a nasty sinking fastball, a hard slider, improving control, physical stamina, and a cocky "I'll kick your butt" mentality.

Year	Team	Lg.	G	IP	H	BB	SO	W	L	ERA	SV	Ratio
1995	New York	NL	14	93.0	88	31	55	9	2	2.81	0	1.280
Post All-Star			14	93.0	88	31	55	9	2	2.81	0	1.280

DANNY JACKSON

Age 34/L   **$6**

Call us crazy, but we think there is a connection between the two straight productive—and healthy—seasons Jackson had in 1993 and 1994 and the fact that he had them as a Phillie, working under the wise guidance of pitching coach Jim Fregosi. Last season, few pitchers in baseball fared worse. Still, the Cardinals are optimistic about his physical condition, and you hesitate to write off someone who has had more lives than Richard Nixon.

Year	Team	Lg.	G	IP	H	BB	SO	W	L	ERA	SV	Ratio
1992	Chicago	NL	19	113.0	117	48	51	4	9	4.22	0	1.460
1992	Pittsburgh	NL	15	88.1	94	29	46	4	4	3.36	0	1.392
1993	Philadelphia	NL	32	210.1	214	80	120	12	11	3.77	0	1.398
1994	Philadelphia	NL	25	179.1	183	46	129	14	6	3.26	0	1.277
1995	St. Louis	NL	19	100.2	120	48	52	2	12	5.90	0	1.669
Post All-Star			7	37.2	42	15	22	1	3	4.54	0	1.513

KEVIN JARVIS

Age 26/R   **$1**

Couple of good early outings, but mostly he spent his summer getting hammered.

Year	Team	Lg.	G	IP	H	BB	SO	W	L	ERA	SV	Ratio
1994	Cincinnati	NL	6	17.2	22	5	10	1	1	7.13	0	1.528
1995	Cincinnati	NL	19	79.0	91	32	33	3	4	5.70	0	1.557
Post All-Star			6	9.2	11	4	7	0	0	4.66	0	1.552

Catchers
pp. 27–41

Corners
pp. 41–62

Infield
pp. 63–82

Outfield
pp. 83–113

DH
pp. 114–118

Starters
pp. 119–157

Relievers
pp. 157–193

BOBBY JONES   Age 26/R $7

Nothing flashy, just a competitor who gets the maximum out of what he has. He'll always need a lot of run support, because he doesn't blow people away with an assortment of off-speed pitches. Right-handed batters hit considerably better than do lefty swingers (.296 vs. .248), possibly because the latter are so eager to jump all over his several varieties of change-up. He's also a prime candidate to be trade bait when the Mets go shopping.

Year	Team	Lg.	G	IP	H	BB	SO	W	L	ERA	SV	Ratio
1993	New York	NL	9	61.2	61	22	35	2	4	3.65	0	1.346
1994	New York	NL	24	160.0	157	56	80	12	7	3.15	0	1.331
1995	New York	NL	30	195.2	209	53	127	10	10	4.19	0	1.339
Post All-Star			15	90.1	97	31	59	6	4	5.48	0	1.417

JEFF JUDEN   Age 25/R $2

Seems like he's been around forever, which may be why the Phillies gave up on him—they thought that surely he had to be older than their media guide said he was. Will a change of scenery help? Maybe, but consider this: Johnny Podres of the Phillies is one of the best pitching coaches in the business, while Dick Pole of the Giants is, ah, not.

Year	Team	Lg.	G	IP	H	BB	SO	W	L	ERA	SV	Ratio
1993	Houston	NL	2	5.0	4	4	7	0	1	5.40	0	1.600
1994	Philadelphia	NL	6	27.2	29	12	22	1	4	6.18	0	1.482
1995	Philadelphia	NL	13	62.2	53	31	47	2	4	4.02	0	1.340
Post All-Star			13	62.2	53	31	47	2	4	4.02	0	1.340

DARRYL KILE   Age 27/R $4

One of the major disappointments of the year. It's not as if he spent the summer pitching BP: left-handed hitters hit only .250 off him, righties just .232. But he walked over five batters every nine innings, and you just can't get away with that, not even in the Astrodome. If you like rolling the dice, the gamble is that he'll get back the (relatively) good control he showed in 1993, which at the time looked like his breakout year. Just keep in mind that 1993 may have been his career year instead.

Year	Team	Lg.	G	IP	H	BB	SO	W	L	ERA	SV	Ratio
1992	Houston	NL	22	125.1	124	63	90	5	10	3.95	0	1.492
1993	Houston	NL	32	171.2	152	69	141	15	8	3.51	0	1.287
1994	Houston	NL	24	147.2	153	82	105	9	6	4.57	0	1.591
1995	Houston	NL	25	127.0	114	73	113	4	12	4.96	0	1.472
Post All-Star			10	42.2	44	29	41	1	3	4.85	0	1.711

FREE OPENING DAY *ROTISSERIE HOT LIST*

(See page 268)

MARK LEITER   Age 32/R $11

Great story. Endured personal tragedy, painful injuries, and more downs than ups in a career that looked like it was going nowhere fast. Then all of a sudden he emerges as the ace of the Giants staff. Okay, so he doesn't trigger memories of Juan Marichal when he takes the mound, but he has guts and character, which should be good enough for 10–12 wins.

Year	Team	Lg.	G	IP	H	BB	SO	W	L	ERA	SV	Ratio
1992	Detroit	AL	35	112.0	116	43	75	8	5	4.18	0	1.420
1993	Detroit	AL	27	106.2	111	44	70	6	6	4.72	0	1.453
1994	California	AL	40	95.1	99	35	71	4	7	4.72	2	1.406
1995	San Francisco	NL	30	195.2	185	55	129	10	12	3.82	0	1.227
Post All-Star			16	114.0	101	29	89	7	6	3.63	0	1.140

JON LIEBER   Age 25/R $1

Not even if you throw in Stoller.

Year	Team	Lg.	G	IP	H	BB	SO	W	L	ERA	SV	Ratio
1994	Pittsburgh	NL	17	108.2	116	25	71	6	7	3.73	0	1.298
1995	Pittsburgh	NL	21	72.2	103	14	45	4	7	6.32	0	1.610
Post All-Star			10	17.1	22	4	11	2	0	2.60	0	1.500

ESTEBAN LOAIZA   Age 24/R $3

Rushed to the majors at least a year before he was ready, Loaiza showed flashes of why the Pirates are so high on him. With Ray Miller whispering his mantra (Throw Strikes–Change Speeds–Work Fast) in his ear, the big right-hander from Tijuana should pay a good return on a small investment.

Year	Team	Lg.	G	IP	H	BB	SO	W	L	ERA	SV	Ratio
1995	Pittsburgh	NL	32	172.2	205	55	85	8	9	5.16	0	1.506
Post All-Star			16	88.1	110	34	44	2	6	5.20	0	1.630

GREG MADDUX   Age 29/R $33

Tough on lefties last season (.194), but had trouble with righties (.198). Obviously has some work to do.

Year	Team	Lg.	G	IP	H	BB	SO	W	L	ERA	SV	Ratio
1992	Chicago	NL	35	268.0	201	70	199	20	11	2.18	0	1.011
1993	Atlanta	NL	36	267.0	228	52	197	20	10	2.36	0	1.049
1994	Atlanta	NL	25	202.0	150	31	156	16	6	1.56	0	0.896
1995	Atlanta	NL	28	209.2	147	23	181	19	2	1.63	0	0.811
Post All-Star			14	105.1	74	15	95	11	1	1.62	0	0.845

PEDRO MARTINEZ   Age 24/R $16

He's not a head-hunter—that charge is blatantly unfair and false. But he does believe the inside of the plate is his, which makes him an occasional, not exactly intentional, but de facto rib-hunter.

Year	Team	Lg.	G	IP	H	BB	SO	W	L	ERA	SV	Ratio
1992	Los Angeles	NL	2	8.0	6	1	8	0	1	2.25	0	0.875
1993	Los Angeles	NL	65	107.0	76	57	119	10	5	2.61	2	1.243
1994	Montreal	NL	24	144.2	115	45	142	11	5	3.42	1	1.106
1995	Montreal	NL	30	194.2	158	66	174	14	10	3.51	0	1.151
Post All-Star			15	98.2	88	37	89	8	5	4.01	0	1.267

Catchers pp. 27–41

Corners pp. 41–62

Infield pp. 63–82

Outfield pp. 83–113

DH pp. 114–118

Starters pp. 119–157

Relievers pp. 157–193

RAMON MARTINEZ   Age 28/R $19

The difference between 1995 and 1994? About five–six mph on his fastball that he had temporarily misplaced. Returned to rightful status as Top Martinez in his family.

Year	Team	Lg.	G	IP	H	BB	SO	W	L	ERA	SV	Ratio
1992	Los Angeles	NL	25	150.2	141	69	101	8	11	4.00	0	1.394
1993	Los Angeles	NL	32	211.2	202	104	127	10	12	3.44	0	1.446
1994	Los Angeles	NL	24	170.0	160	56	119	12	7	3.97	0	1.271
1995	Los Angeles	NL	30	206.1	176	81	138	17	7	3.66	0	1.246
Post All-Star			15	111.2	83	34	78	9	1	2.66	0	1.048

KENT MERCKER   Age 28/L $9

One outing he looks like a world beater, the next one he can't get past the fourth inning. The Braves are just as puzzled as his Rotisserie owners, but they're not ready to stick a fork in him, not yet, not with all that left-handed stuff he has when he's right.

Year	Team	Lg.	G	IP	H	BB	SO	W	L	ERA	SV	Ratio
1992	Atlanta	NL	53	68.1	51	35	49	3	2	3.42	6	1.259
1993	Atlanta	NL	43	66.0	52	36	59	3	1	2.86	0	1.333
1994	Atlanta	NL	20	112.1	90	45	111	9	4	3.45	0	1.202
1995	Atlanta	NL	29	143.0	140	61	102	7	8	4.15	0	1.406
Post All-Star			15	62.2	70	24	33	3	4	4.16	0	1.500

MICHAEL MIMBS   Age 27/L $3

We defer to one of the best scouts in the game, a veteran employed by an American League club who has seen it all and whose judgment has been uncannily accurate over the years, on the subject of Mr. Mimbs: "If he wasn't left-handed, he'd be bagging groceries." Some of those around the clubhouse think that's a little harsh, but we calls 'em like we sees 'em.

Year	Team	Lg.	G	IP	H	BB	SO	W	L	ERA	SV	Ratio
1995	Philadelphia	NL	35	136.2	127	75	93	9	7	4.15	1	1.478
Post All-Star			22	57.1	53	36	48	3	3	4.55	1	1.552

DAVE MLICKI   Age 27/R $3

An interesting case. He impressed the Mets brass with his grit and his stuff. The overall numbers weren't too impressive, but he was death to right-handed batters, who hit just .213 off him. But with Jason Isringhausen, Bill Pulsipher, a healthy Pete Harnisch, and Bobby Jones being joined by phenom Paul Wilson, there's no room in the rotation for Mlicki. Middle innings relief with an occasional start? Maybe, but a more likely scenario has him setting up Franco—or even serving as the righty half of a R-L closer platoon. Get him for small change in the auction draft and you could end up with seven–eight wins and ten-plus saves.

Year	Team	Lg.	G	IP	H	BB	SO	W	L	ERA	SV	Ratio
1992	Cleveland	AL	4	21.2	23	16	16	0	2	4.98	0	1.800
1993	Cleveland	AL	3	13.1	11	6	7	0	0	3.38	0	1.275
1995	New York	NL	29	160.2	160	54	123	9	7	4.26	0	1.332
Post All-Star			15	83.2	88	33	67	5	3	4.41	0	1.446

MIKE MORGAN   Age 36/R $5

Cubs dumped his salary on the Cards, who tried hard to pass it on but couldn't find any takers. Meanwhile, he pitched well enough to have a much better W-L record than 7-7. But hasn't that always been the case with Morgan? In 15 major league seasons, he's been over .500 exactly twice.

Year	Team	Lg.	G	IP	H	BB	SO	W	L	ERA	SV	Ratio
1992	Chicago	NL	34	240.0	203	79	123	16	8	2.55	0	1.175
1993	Chicago	NL	32	207.2	206	74	111	10	15	4.03	0	1.348
1994	Chicago	NL	15	80.2	111	35	57	2	10	6.69	0	1.810
1995	Chicago	NL	4	24.2	19	9	15	2	1	2.19	0	1.135
1995	St. Louis	NL	17	106.2	114	25	46	5	6	3.88	0	1.303
Post All-Star			13	79.0	91	22	34	3	4	4.22	0	1.430

TERRY MULHOLLAND   Age 33/L $2

Called "a pile of soot" by one Bay Area columnist, who presumably did not intend it as a compliment. Said one Giants veteran, "In all honesty, it's hard to believe anyone could get hit harder than he did this season." How hard was that? Well, Mulholland gave up 25 gopher balls, bad enough to tie Kevin Foster of the Cubs for second in the NL in that ignominious category. But Foster and stablemate Steve Trachsel, who led the league with 32, at least had the old tried-and-true "Wind Is Blowing Out at Wrigley Field Today" excuse to fall back on. (By the way, you'd expect that Colorado Rockies pitchers would sweep this category, wouldn't you? But only Bret Saberhagen with 21 HR was close to the top, and some of those taters were served up when he was a Met. Then it dawned on everybody at the Rotisserie Think Tank: Rockies starters didn't last long enough to dish up enough dingers to challenge for individual honors. Collectively, of course, Rockies pitchers topped the NL in round-trippers. Call it a team effort.) Now, where were we? Oh, yes—Terry Mulholland. Stick a fork in him.

Year	Team	Lg.	G	IP	H	BB	SO	W	L	ERA	SV	Ratio
1992	Philadelphia	NL	32	229.0	227	46	125	13	11	3.81	0	1.192
1993	Philadelphia	NL	29	191.0	177	40	116	12	9	3.25	0	1.136
1994	New York	AL	24	120.2	150	37	72	6	7	6.49	0	1.550
1995	San Francisco	NL	29	149.0	190	38	65	5	13	5.80	0	1.530
Post All-Star			18	91.1	106	20	44	3	6	5.42	0	1.380

BOBBY MUNOZ   Age 28/R $1

With Tommy Greene, Muñoz was one of two poster boys for the Phillies' rotation in 1995—that is, he spent most of the season on the DL, and when he did pitch, he was horrible.

Year	Team	Lg.	G	IP	H	BB	SO	W	L	ERA	SV	Ratio
1993	New York	AL	38	45.2	48	26	33	3	3	5.32	0	1.620
1994	Philadelphia	NL	21	104.1	101	35	59	7	5	2.67	1	1.304
1995	Philadelphia	NL	3	15.2	15	9	6	0	2	5.74	0	1.532
Post All-Star			3	15.2	15	9	6	0	2	5.74	0	1.532

Catchers
pp. 27–41

Corners
pp. 41–62

Infield
pp. 63–82

Outfield
pp. 83–113

DH
pp. 114–118

Starters
pp. 119–157

Relievers
pp. 157–193

JAIME NAVARRO
Age 28/R $15

The Cubs guessed right. The payoff? A durable, reliable innings-eater with good control who gives them a chance to win just about every time he goes out there.

Year	Team	Lg.	G	IP	H	BB	SO	W	L	ERA	SV	Ratio
1992	Milwaukee	AL	34	246.0	224	64	100	17	11	3.33	0	1.171
1993	Milwaukee	AL	35	214.1	254	73	114	11	12	5.33	0	1.526
1994	Milwaukee	AL	29	89.2	115	35	65	4	9	6.62	0	1.673
1995	Chicago	NL	29	200.1	194	56	128	14	6	3.28	0	1.248
Post All-Star			15	107.2	114	33	73	7	4	3.68	0	1.365

DENNY NEAGLE
Age 27/L $14

A lefty with pinpoint control—now that's a concept. But control is certainly the key for Neagle, who survived opponents' hitting .273 against him last season by walking fewer than two batters every nine innings. For those Rotisserie owners who owned him for a buck or two in 1993 and 1994, believed in his promise, but just couldn't take another year of heartbreak—well, that's the way the old ball bounces. And for those lucky souls who picked him up for a buck or two in last spring's auction drafts—well, we hate your eyes.

Year	Team	Lg.	G	IP	H	BB	SO	W	L	ERA	SV	Ratio
1992	Pittsburgh	NL	55	86.1	81	43	77	4	6	4.48	2	1.436
1993	Pittsburgh	NL	50	81.1	82	37	73	3	5	5.31	1	1.463
1994	Pittsburgh	NL	24	137.0	135	49	122	9	10	5.12	0	1.343
1995	Pittsburgh	NL	31	209.2	221	45	150	13	8	3.43	0	1.269
Post All-Star			15	102.0	107	24	79	4	4	3.53	0	1.284

HIDEO NOMO
Age 27/R $21

Led majors in wild pitches (19). Second in NL in permitting stolen bases (29). First in world in elapsed time of windup. More to the point, he was the toughest pitcher to hit, by a surprisingly wide margin, in the major leagues. Yes, that includes Greg Maddux and Randy Johnson. Opponents batted .197 against Maddux, .201 against Johnson (better than Maddux's mark, if you adjust for the DH), and .182 against Nomo. One cautionary note: he showed signs of arm weariness in the second half, with a decided loss in velocity of his fastball. And with Tommy Lasorda back for another year, you can be sure he will be overpitched again. At least this year there won't be a lot of wasted breath over whether he's a *real* rookie.

Year	Team	Lg.	G	IP	H	BB	SO	W	L	ERA	SV	Ratio
1995	Los Angeles	NL	28	191.1	124	78	236	13	6	2.54	0	1.056
Post All-Star			15	101.0	73	32	117	7	5	3.03	0	1.040

DONOVAN OSBORNE
Age 26/L $7

If he's over his arm problems, and it appears he is, the lefty named after two of our least favorite singers could have a breakout year.

Year	Team	Lg.	G	IP	H	BB	SO	W	L	ERA	SV	Ratio
1992	St. Louis	NL	34	179.0	193	38	104	11	9	3.77	0	1.291
1993	St. Louis	NL	26	155.2	153	47	83	10	7	3.76	0	1.285
1995	St. Louis	NL	19	113.1	112	34	82	4	6	3.81	0	1.288
Post All-Star			15	91.1	87	29	69	4	5	3.74	0	1.270

STEVE PARRIS
Age 28/R   **$1**

Jim Leyland must really, *really* like living in Pittsburgh, because managing there can't be a whole gang of fun.

Year	Team	Lg.	G	IP	H	BB	SO	W	L	ERA	SV	Ratio
1995	Pittsburgh	NL	15	82.0	89	33	61	6	6	5.38	0	1.488
Post All-Star			11	64.1	69	25	44	5	4	4.62	0	1.461

CARLOS PEREZ
Age 25/L   **$13**

A lot of fun to watch on the field. No fun at all off the field.

Year	Team	Lg.	G	IP	H	BB	SO	W	L	ERA	SV	Ratio
1995	Montreal	NL	28	141.1	142	28	106	10	8	3.69	0	1.203
Post All-Star			12	72.1	71	14	53	3	6	4.11	0	1.175

MARK PETKOVSEK
Age 30/R   **$4**

The kind of guy that scouts call "a bulldog." We'd like it better if they just called him "a good pitcher," but you can't be picky these days when looking for a fourth or fifth starter.

Year	Team	Lg.	G	IP	H	BB	SO	W	L	ERA	SV	Ratio
1993	Pittsburgh	NL	26	32.1	43	9	14	3	0	6.96	0	1.608
1995	St. Louis	NL	26	137.1	136	35	71	6	6	4.00	0	1.245
Post All-Star			17	86.0	82	20	52	3	4	3.77	0	1.186

MARK PORTUGAL
Age 33/R   **$11**

An ex-Giant, right? Some deal—Johnny Roper, who had rotator cuff surgery, and a Dallas Cowboys cornerback for the aforementioned Mr. Burba and this solid right-hander. Wonder if the Giants would be interested in this bridge we have?

Year	Team	Lg.	G	IP	H	BB	SO	W	L	ERA	SV	Ratio
1992	Houston	NL	18	101.1	76	41	62	6	3	2.66	0	1.155
1993	Houston	NL	33	208.0	194	77	131	18	4	2.77	0	1.303
1994	San Francisco	NL	21	137.1	135	45	87	10	8	3.93	0	1.311
1995	San Francisco	NL	17	104.0	106	34	63	5	5	4.15	0	1.346
1995	Cincinnati	NL	14	77.2	79	22	33	6	5	3.82	0	1.300
Post All-Star			16	90.0	94	25	43	6	7	3.70	0	1.322

TIM PUGH
Age 29/R   **$1**

Some things in this world we just do not get. Pugh, a right-hander, held lefty hitters to a puny .203 BA, but righty hitters tattooed him at a .311 clip. It isn't supposed to go that way, is it?

Year	Team	Lg.	G	IP	H	BB	SO	W	L	ERA	SV	Ratio
1992	Cincinnati	NL	7	45.1	47	13	18	4	2	2.58	0	1.324
1993	Cincinnati	NL	31	164.1	200	59	94	10	15	5.26	0	1.576
1994	Cincinnati	NL	10	47.2	60	26	24	3	3	6.04	0	1.804
1995	Cincinnati	NL	28	98.1	100	32	38	6	5	3.84	0	1.342
Post All-Star			11	33.1	30	9	13	1	4	3.78	0	1.170

Catchers
pp. 27–41

Corners
pp. 41–62

Infield
pp. 63–82

Outfield
pp. 83–113

DH
pp. 114–118

Starters
pp. 119–157

Relievers
pp. 157–193

BILL PULSIPHER Age 22/L $14

When scouts weren't raving about his live fastball, his combative makeup, and his exuberant approach to the game, they were talking about mechanical flaws in his delivery that could cause elbow problems down the way.

Year	Team	Lg.	G	IP	H	BB	SO	W	L	ERA	SV	Ratio
1995	New York	NL	17	126.2	122	45	81	5	7	3.98	0	1.318
Post All-Star			12	90.2	81	27	48	4	3	3.77	0	1.191

PAUL QUANTRILL Age 27/R $4

A control pitcher who will keep his team in the game and get his wins, he can also torpedo your team ERA. Not bad as ballast if you have a Maddux or a Glavine on board, Quantrill will never be anybody's ace.

Year	Team	Lg.	G	IP	H	BB	SO	W	L	ERA	SV	Ratio
1992	Boston	AL	27	49.1	55	15	24	2	3	2.19	1	1.419
1993	Boston	AL	49	138.0	151	44	66	6	12	3.91	1	1.413
1994	Boston	AL	17	23.0	25	5	15	1	1	3.52	0	1.304
1994	Philadelphia	NL	18	30.0	39	10	13	2	2	6.00	1	1.633
1995	Philadelphia	NL	33	179.1	212	44	103	11	12	4.67	0	1.428
Post All-Star			18	91.2	114	24	52	4	8	5.01	0	1.505

PAT RAPP Age 28/R $14

Who was the best pitcher in the NL over the last six weeks? No, it wasn't Maddux or Glavine or Nomo or either of the Martinez brothers. It was this Marlin right-hander, who was nearly unhittable over an amazing eight-start streak. Will he carry it over into a year of greatness? Probably not, but on an improving team, we do see him having a year of goodness.

Year	Team	Lg.	G	IP	H	BB	SO	W	L	ERA	SV	Ratio
1992	San Francisco	NL	3	10.0	8	6	3	0	2	7.20	0	1.400
1993	Florida	NL	16	94.0	101	39	57	4	6	4.02	0	1.489
1994	Florida	NL	24	133.1	132	69	75	7	8	3.85	0	1.508
1995	Florida	NL	28	167.1	158	76	102	14	7	3.44	0	1.398
Post All-Star			15	94.2	75	40	58	11	2	2.28	0	1.215

BRYAN REKAR Age 23/R $3

A good-looking prospect, and the Rockies are high on him. Maybe they'll restrict him to road games until he builds up his confidence.

Year	Team	Lg.	G	IP	H	BB	SO	W	L	ERA	SV	Ratio
1995	Colorado	NL	15	85.0	95	24	60	4	6	4.98	0	1.400
Post All-Star			15	85.0	95	24	60	4	6	4.98	0	1.400

SHANE REYNOLDS Age 28/R $9

Along with Mike Hampton, Reynolds was one of the two bright spots on the Houston staff last year. Good control. Even if the team goes south, and we think it will, he will produce respectable ERA and Ratio numbers.

Year	Team	Lg.	G	IP	H	BB	SO	W	L	ERA	SV	Ratio
1992	Houston	NL	8	25.1	42	6	10	1	3	7.11	0	1.895
1993	Houston	NL	5	11.0	11	6	10	0	0	0.82	0	1.545
1994	Houston	NL	33	124.0	128	21	110	8	5	3.05	0	1.202
1995	Houston	NL	30	189.1	196	37	175	10	11	3.47	0	1.231
Post All-Star			16	102.2	108	19	96	5	6	4.21	0	1.237

ARMANDO REYNOSO

Age 29/R   **$1**

The last name is pronounced Rey-NO-so. Don't forget the NO part.

Year	Team	Lg.	G	IP	H	BB	SO	W	L	ERA	SV	Ratio
1992	Atlanta	NL	3	7.2	11	2	2	1	0	4.70	1	1.696
1993	Colorado	NL	30	189.0	206	63	117	12	11	4.00	0	1.423
1994	Colorado	NL	9	52.1	54	22	25	3	4	4.82	0	1.452
1995	Colorado	NL	20	93.0	116	36	40	7	7	5.32	0	1.634
Post All-Star			15	72.0	95	26	34	5	7	5.50	0	1.681

JOSE RIJO

Age 30/R   **$21**

That Marge is a pip, isn't she? Her ace goes under the knife and is lost for the season. Come playoff time, she gives his seat on the team plane to her stupid dog and makes him—Rijo, not the dog—pay his own way. If he bounces back from the surgery, Rijo has to be considered one of the best pitchers in baseball. Too bad it's for the Dog Lady.

Year	Team	Lg.	G	IP	H	BB	SO	W	L	ERA	SV	Ratio
1992	Cincinnati	NL	33	211.0	185	44	171	15	10	2.56	0	1.085
1993	Cincinnati	NL	36	257.1	218	62	227	14	9	2.48	0	1.088
1994	Cincinnati	NL	26	172.1	177	52	171	9	6	3.08	0	1.329
1995	Cincinnati	NL	14	69.0	76	22	62	5	4	4.17	0	1.420
Post All-Star			2	7.0	7	3	7	1	0	3.86	0	1.429

KEVIN RITZ

Age 30/R   **$5**

If you really must have one Rockies starter, this is probably the one.

Year	Team	Lg.	G	IP	H	BB	SO	W	L	ERA	SV	Ratio
1992	Detroit	AL	23	80.1	88	44	57	2	5	5.60	0	1.643
1994	Colorado	NL	15	73.2	88	35	53	5	6	5.62	0	1.670
1995	Colorado	NL	31	173.1	171	65	120	11	11	4.21	2	1.362
Post All-Star			17	91.0	101	36	61	4	8	4.85	2	1.505

BRET SABERHAGEN

Age 31/R   **$15**

Let's get this straight—the Rockies brain trust are geniuses because they parlayed four guys who can hit home runs at home, a stupid new wild card system, and an abjectly mediocre division into a playoff berth in their third year of existence? Maybe, but it says here geniuses don't invest over $14 million in pitchers with the shaky medical history of this one and remain geniuses for very long. Of all the Rent-a-Pitchers acquired for the stretch drive, Saberhagen was the worst in both leagues by a wide margin. Frankly, we don't know how to peg the guy. When his arm is right, he's one of the best in the game—it's a genuine delight to watch anyone with such good control throw so hard. But you can count on his arm not being right, at least for part of the season, and then you want to cover your eyes.

Year	Team	Lg.	G	IP	H	BB	SO	W	L	ERA	SV	Ratio
1992	New York	NL	17	97.2	84	27	81	3	5	3.50	0	1.137
1993	New York	NL	19	139.1	131	17	93	7	7	3.29	0	1.062
1994	New York	NL	24	177.1	169	13	143	14	4	2.74	0	1.026
1995	New York	NL	16	110.0	105	20	71	5	5	3.35	0	1.136
1995	Colorado	NL	9	43.0	60	13	29	2	1	6.28	0	1.698
Post All-Star			11	53.0	69	15	38	2	2	5.77	0	1.585

Catchers
pp. 27–41

Corners
pp. 41–62

Infield
pp. 63–82

Outfield
pp. 83–113

DH
pp. 114–118

Starters
pp. 119–157

Relievers
pp. 157–193

SCOTT SANDERS   Age 27/R $8

An important building block in a steadily improving Padres team. This could be a big year for him.

Year	Team	Lg.	G	IP	H	BB	SO	W	L	ERA	SV	Ratio
1993	San Diego	NL	9	52.1	54	23	37	3	3	4.13	0	1.471
1994	San Diego	NL	23	111.0	103	48	109	4	8	4.78	1	1.360
1995	San Diego	NL	17	90.0	79	31	88	5	5	4.30	0	1.222
Post All-Star			3	4.1	9	1	5	0	0	8.31	0	2.308

CURT SCHILLING   Age 29/R $5

Is your health insurance paid up?

Year	Team	Lg.	G	IP	H	BB	SO	W	L	ERA	SV	Ratio
1992	Philadelphia	NL	42	226.1	165	59	147	14	11	2.35	2	0.990
1993	Philadelphia	NL	34	235.1	234	57	186	16	7	4.02	0	1.237
1994	Philadelphia	NL	13	82.1	87	28	58	2	8	4.48	0	1.397
1995	Philadelphia	NL	17	116.0	96	26	114	7	5	3.57	0	1.052
Post All-Star			2	13.0	11	3	15	2	0	4.85	0	1.077

PETE SCHOUREK   Age 26/L $21

A rare (at least in the McIlvaine Era) mistake by the Mets becomes a major find for Cincinnati. It isn't a fluke—this tall drink of water has always had plenty of stuff, and now he has the confidence and command that should make him the mainstay of that staff and one of the best pitchers in the league for the rest of the century. Which brings up the possibility that the Mets may have made a second rare mistake by giving Dallas Green that contract extension. Yes, he did a good job in flogging the Mets to a strong second half last summer. And yes, beneath all that bluster may beat the heart of a master motivator, not the ticker of a tyrant. But is he really the guy you want trying to mold a bunch of kids into men? This is the same Dallas Green, remember, who single-handedly ran Schourek out of town on a rail. Just wanted to set the record straight here, what with memories being short and all.

Year	Team	Lg.	G	IP	H	BB	SO	W	L	ERA	SV	Ratio
1992	New York	NL	22	136.0	137	44	60	6	8	3.64	0	1.331
1993	New York	NL	41	128.1	168	45	72	5	12	5.96	0	1.660
1994	Cincinnati	NL	22	81.1	90	29	69	7	2	4.09	0	1.463
1995	Cincinnati	NL	29	190.1	158	45	160	18	7	3.22	0	1.067
Post All-Star			15	102.2	82	20	82	10	3	2.98	0	0.994

JOHN SMILEY   Age 31/L $18

His season turned around when he rubbed his arm with fur from the deceased Schottzie One. No, it's not a very pretty picture, but you can't argue with success. Don't be surprised if Her Margeship fires her pitching coach. Why carry that extra salary when you have the Hair of the Dog?

Year	Team	Lg.	G	IP	H	BB	SO	W	L	ERA	SV	Ratio
1992	Minnesota	AL	34	241.0	205	65	163	16	9	3.21	0	1.120
1993	Cincinnati	NL	18	105.2	117	31	60	3	9	5.62	0	1.401
1994	Cincinnati	NL	24	158.2	169	37	112	11	10	3.86	0	1.298
1995	Cincinnati	NL	28	176.2	173	39	124	12	5	3.46	0	1.200
Post All-Star			14	82.2	79	20	64	3	4	3.92	0	1.198

JOHN SMOLTZ   Age 28/R $16

Reclaimed his role as a solid No. 3 man in Braves rotation. Last year at this time rumors were flying that he might be traded. This year there's not been so much as a whisper—which probably means he'll be dealt by Opening Day.

Year	Team	Lg.	G	IP	H	BB	SO	W	L	ERA	SV	Ratio
1992	Atlanta	NL	35	246.2	206	80	215	15	12	2.85	0	1.159
1993	Atlanta	NL	35	243.2	208	100	208	15	11	3.62	0	1.264
1994	Atlanta	NL	21	134.2	120	48	113	6	10	4.14	0	1.248
1995	Atlanta	NL	29	192.2	166	72	193	12	7	3.18	0	1.235
Post All-Star			16	100.2	87	37	98	5	3	3.49	0	1.232

BILL SWIFT   Age 34/R $12

You invest big money in a starter, you expect big innings, don't you? For the second straight season, Swift has done DL time, and at his age you don't expect that to change. Too bad. If he and Saberhagen could manage to stay healthy a whole season, it wouldn't matter how many Reynosos and Freemans the Rockies had.

Year	Team	Lg.	G	IP	H	BB	SO	W	L	ERA	SV	Ratio
1992	San Francisco	NL	30	164.2	144	43	77	10	4	2.08	1	1.136
1993	San Francisco	NL	34	232.2	195	55	157	21	8	2.82	0	1.074
1994	San Francisco	NL	17	109.1	109	31	62	8	7	3.38	0	1.280
1995	Colorado	NL	19	105.2	122	43	68	9	3	4.94	0	1.562
Post All-Star			8	44.2	56	13	19	5	1	3.63	0	1.545

GREG SWINDELL   Age 31/L $5

He's shaped like Mickey Lolich. Too bad he doesn't pitch like him. The Astros have tried to put Swindell in every deal they've discussed in the last two years. Wanna buy a season ticket? Ya gotta take Swindell as part of the package. If anything stalls the Astros sale and removal to northern Virginia or wherever, it'll be because ya gotta take Swindell as part of the package.

Year	Team	Lg.	G	IP	H	BB	SO	W	L	ERA	SV	Ratio
1992	Cincinnati	NL	31	213.2	210	41	138	12	8	2.70	0	1.175
1993	Houston	NL	31	190.1	215	40	124	12	13	4.16	0	1.340
1994	Houston	NL	24	148.1	175	26	74	8	9	4.37	0	1.355
1995	Houston	NL	33	153.0	180	39	96	10	9	4.47	0	1.431
Post All-Star			19	75.1	96	20	46	4	6	4.78	0	1.540

KEVIN TAPANI   Age 32/R $4

Everybody thought that crumbling ERA the past couple of years came from pitching in the Humpdome. Everybody was wrong. The real cause came from pitching BP in game situations, thereby permitting opposing batters to hit .306 and score a lot of runs. This slump has lasted three seasons, and there's no good reason to expect him to come out of it.

Year	Team	Lg.	G	IP	H	BB	SO	W	L	ERA	SV	Ratio
1992	Minnesota	AL	34	220.0	226	48	138	16	11	3.97	0	1.245
1993	Minnesota	AL	36	225.2	243	57	150	12	15	4.43	0	1.329
1994	Minnesota	AL	24	156.0	181	39	91	11	7	4.62	0	1.410
1995	Minnesota	AL	20	133.2	155	34	88	6	11	4.92	0	1.414
1995	Los Angeles	NL	13	57.0	72	14	43	4	2	5.05	0	1.509
Post All-Star			17	84.2	112	21	59	6	4	5.10	0	1.571

Catchers
pp. 27-41

Corners
pp. 41-62

Infield
pp. 63-82

Outfield
pp. 83-113

DH
pp. 114-118

Starters
pp. 119-157

Relievers
pp. 157-193

TOM URBANI
Age 28/L **$4**

A modest plus for the Cardinals in a season filled with minuses.

Year	Team	Lg.	G	IP	H	BB	SO	W	L	ERA	SV	Ratio
1993	St. Louis	NL	18	62.0	73	26	33	1	3	4.65	0	1.597
1994	St. Louis	NL	20	80.1	98	21	43	3	7	5.15	0	1.481
1995	St. Louis	NL	24	82.2	99	21	52	3	5	3.70	0	1.452
Post All-Star			14	31.2	43	9	23	1	2	3.98	0	1.642

ISMAEL VALDES
Age 22/R **$16**

You can Call him Ismael. We prefer calling him a whale of a pitcher. Now, in addition to giving this young Mexican flamethrower the most glowing possible recommendation, we promise that hereinafter we will never, ever engage in cheap *Moby Dick* references again when talking about Sr. Valdes. He looks like he's got the stuff and the makeup to be a terrific pitcher for a lot of years, and that "Call me Ishmael" riff has already gotten trite. So that's it—you have our word.

Year	Team	Lg.	G	IP	H	BB	SO	W	L	ERA	SV	Ratio
1994	Los Angeles	NL	21	28.1	21	10	28	3	1	3.18	0	1.094
1995	Los Angeles	NL	33	197.2	168	51	150	13	11	3.05	1	1.108
Post All-Star			15	105.0	88	19	80	8	6	2.83	0	1.019

FERNANDO VALENZUELA
Age 35/L **$2**

The magic is there for only a few innings at a time now, but when he's moving the ball around, dinking screwballs here and cutting fastballs there, it makes the world feel young again.

Year	Team	Lg.	G	IP	H	BB	SO	W	L	ERA	SV	Ratio
1993	Baltimore	AL	32	178.2	179	79	78	8	10	4.94	0	1.444
1994	Philadelphia	NL	8	45.0	42	7	19	1	2	3.00	0	1.089
1995	San Diego	NL	29	90.1	101	34	57	8	3	4.98	0	1.494
Post All-Star			15	48.1	53	21	35	6	0	3.91	0	1.531

WILLIAM VAN LANDINGHAM
Age 25/R **$6**

Possesses best stuff on Giants staff, but—surprise, surprise—got hurt three different times last season. Until he puts together a full season or so, we see no reason to get particularly excited.

Year	Team	Lg.	G	IP	H	BB	SO	W	L	ERA	SV	Ratio
1994	San Francisco	NL	16	84.0	70	43	56	8	2	3.54	0	1.345
1995	San Francisco	NL	18	122.2	124	40	95	6	3	3.67	0	1.337
Post All-Star			11	81.1	75	25	59	5	1	3.32	0	1.230

PAUL WAGNER
Age 28/R **$1**

Advisory to all Rotisserie Ultra owners who had Paul Wagner active all season *except* for the week he pitched a one-hit shutout and won a second game while giving up just one earned run: the time and place of the next meeting of our support group will be posted presently.

Year	Team	Lg.	G	IP	H	BB	SO	W	L	ERA	SV	Ratio
1992	Pittsburgh	NL	6	13.0	9	5	5	2	0	0.69	0	1.077
1993	Pittsburgh	NL	44	141.1	143	42	114	8	8	4.27	2	1.309
1994	Pittsburgh	NL	29	119.2	136	50	86	7	8	4.59	0	1.554
1995	Pittsburgh	NL	33	165.0	174	72	120	5	16	4.80	1	1.491
Post All-Star			17	94.1	95	36	71	4	6	4.20	1	1.389

ALLEN WATSON   Age 25/L $4

He's been highly touted. He's been much anticipated. Now it looks like he may have been seriously overrated. Maybe Dave Duncan can help.

Year	Team	Lg.	G	IP	H	BB	SO	W	L	ERA	SV	Ratio
1993	St. Louis	NL	16	86.0	90	28	49	6	7	4.60	0	1.372
1994	St. Louis	NL	22	115.2	130	53	74	6	5	5.52	0	1.582
1995	St. Louis	NL	21	114.1	126	41	49	7	9	4.96	0	1.461
Post All-Star			14	82.1	81	32	37	5	7	4.26	0	1.372

DAVE WEATHERS   Age 26/R $1

Forecast calls for bad Weathers to continue indefinitely.

Year	Team	Lg.	G	IP	H	BB	SO	W	L	ERA	SV	Ratio
1992	Toronto	AL	2	3.1	5	2	3	0	0	8.10	0	2.100
1993	Florida	NL	14	45.2	57	13	34	2	3	5.12	0	1.533
1994	Florida	NL	24	135.0	166	59	72	8	12	5.27	0	1.667
1995	Florida	NL	28	90.1	104	52	60	4	5	5.98	0	1.727
Post All-Star			16	42.1	56	25	30	2	2	6.80	0	1.913

DAVID WELLS   Age 32/L $14

Did the job the Reds hired him to do in stretch run. Gritty, old-school competitor. If he stays, he gives the Reds the best 1-2-3 lefty combo in baseball. Figures to be a solid 15-game winner on this team.

Year	Team	Lg.	G	IP	H	BB	SO	W	L	ERA	SV	Ratio
1992	Toronto	AL	41	120.0	138	36	62	7	9	5.40	2	1.450
1993	Detroit	AL	32	187.0	183	42	139	11	9	4.19	0	1.203
1994	Detroit	AL	16	111.1	113	24	71	5	7	3.96	0	1.231
1995	Detroit	AL	18	130.1	120	37	83	10	3	3.04	0	1.205
1995	Cincinnati	NL	11	72.2	74	16	50	6	5	3.59	0	1.239
Post All-Star			14	95.0	93	22	67	8	5	3.51	0	1.211

DAVID WEST   Age 31/L $1

A Phillie, so naturally he spent his share of time on the DL. Underneath all that scar tissue is a live left arm, but it's never wise to bank on full recovery from a surgically repaired hurler on this star-crossed team.

Year	Team	Lg.	G	IP	H	BB	SO	W	L	ERA	SV	Ratio
1992	Minnesota	AL	9	28.1	32	20	19	1	3	6.99	0	1.835
1993	Philadelphia	NL	76	86.1	60	51	87	6	4	2.92	3	1.286
1994	Philadelphia	NL	31	99.0	74	61	83	4	10	3.55	0	1.364
1995	Philadelphia	NL	8	38.0	34	19	25	3	2	3.79	0	1.395
Post All-Star			0	0.0	0	0	0	0	0	0.00	0	0.000

TREVOR WILSON   Age 29/L $2

The poster boy for the modern Giants pitching legacy.

Year	Team	Lg.	G	IP	H	BB	SO	W	L	ERA	SV	Ratio
1992	San Francisco	NL	26	154.0	152	64	88	8	14	4.21	0	1.403
1993	San Francisco	NL	22	110.0	110	40	57	7	5	3.60	0	1.364
1995	San Francisco	NL	17	82.2	82	38	38	3	4	3.92	0	1.452
Post All-Star			6	28.0	28	17	14	0	1	4.18	0	1.607

Catchers
pp. 27-41

Corners
pp. 41-62

Infield
pp. 63-82

Outfield
pp. 83-113

DH
pp. 114-118

Starters
pp. 119-157

Relievers
pp. 157-193

AMERICAN LEAGUE

JIM ABBOTT   Age 28/L $9

The number one lefty in the league—alphabetically. Other than that he's a
sub-.500 pitcher whose career trajectory has flattened out after a great liftoff.
He was much better on the road once he joined the Angels, so watch where
he signs.

Year	Team	Lg.	G	IP	H	BB	SO	W	L	ERA	SV	Ratio
1992	California	AL	29	211.0	208	68	130	7	15	2.77	0	1.308
1993	New York	AL	32	214.0	221	73	95	11	14	4.37	0	1.374
1994	New York	AL	24	160.1	167	64	90	9	8	4.55	0	1.441
1995	Chicago	AL	17	112.1	116	35	45	6	4	3.36	0	1.344
1995	California	AL	13	84.2	93	29	41	5	4	4.15	0	1.441
Post All-Star			16	105.2	118	33	48	7	4	4.00	0	1.429

WILSON ALVAREZ   Age 26/L $15

Like most White Sox pitchers, he was maddeningly inconsistent until after
the All-Star break. Like most White Sox pitchers, he will rebound completely.
Alvarez didn't pitch in winter ball during the strike, didn't work out, and
reported to abbreviated spring training camp out of shape and overweight.
It cost him dearly. If he comes to camp in decent shape this spring, you
shouldn't have to wait until July for any good numbers.

Year	Team	Lg.	G	IP	H	BB	SO	W	L	ERA	SV	Ratio
1992	Chicago	AL	34	100.1	103	65	66	5	3	5.20	1	1.674
1993	Chicago	AL	31	207.2	168	122	155	15	8	2.95	0	1.396
1994	Chicago	AL	24	161.2	147	62	108	12	8	3.45	0	1.293
1995	Chicago	AL	29	175.0	171	93	118	8	11	4.32	0	1.509
Post All-Star			16	100.2	80	48	73	6	6	3.49	0	1.272

BRIAN ANDERSON   Age 23/L $2

We were all prepared to trot out the Bad Pitcher on a Good Team theory
and tell you to take a chance on Anderson, despite his scary numbers, on
the grounds that BPGTs are always good for some wins. Then we remembered how bad the Angels were over the last month and a half and went
back to the drawing board. Now we're recommending a modest investment
in Anderson because he's young and should get better—if last season didn't
prematurely age him.

Year	Team	Lg.	G	IP	H	BB	SO	W	L	ERA	SV	Ratio
1993	California	AL	4	11.1	11	2	4	0	0	3.97	0	1.147
1994	California	AL	18	101.2	120	27	47	7	5	5.22	0	1.446
1995	California	AL	18	99.2	110	30	45	6	8	5.87	0	1.405
Post All-Star			12	65.1	80	19	36	4	6	6.75	0	1.515

KEVIN APPIER   Age 28/R $23

One of the premier pitchers in the game. The Royals will probably move
him for several more building blocks for their reconstruction program, but
he's certainly young enough to build the new team around. Either way,
Appier's a terrific pitcher who would make a perfect ace for your staff.

Year	Team	Lg.	G	IP	H	BB	SO	W	L	ERA	SV	Ratio
1992	Kansas City	AL	30	208.1	167	68	150	15	8	2.46	0	1.128
1993	Kansas City	AL	34	238.2	183	81	186	18	8	2.56	0	1.106
1994	Kansas City	AL	23	155.0	137	63	145	7	6	3.83	0	1.290
1995	Kansas City	AL	31	201.1	163	80	185	15	10	3.89	0	1.207
Post All-Star			14	80.0	78	35	65	4	5	5.18	0	1.413

TIM BELCHER   Age 34/R $4

Another BPGT candidate—no, make that a *really* bad pitcher on a *really* good team. And this one is way beyond improving with age. But the Mariners have so much offense that a guy like Belcher can still be penciled in for 10 wins.

Year	Team	Lg.	G	IP	H	BB	SO	W	L	ERA	SV	Ratio
1992	Cincinnati	NL	35	227.2	201	80	149	15	14	3.91	0	1.234
1993	Chicago	AL	12	71.2	64	27	34	3	5	4.40	0	1.270
1993	Cincinnati	NL	22	137.0	134	47	101	9	6	4.47	0	1.321
1994	Detroit	AL	25	162.0	192	78	76	7	15	5.89	0	1.667
1995	Seattle	AL	28	179.1	188	88	96	10	12	4.52	0	1.539
Post All-Star			17	109.2	110	56	57	6	8	4.35	0	1.514

ANDY BENES   Age 28/R $11

For years he was the classic GPBT—Good Pitcher on a Bad Team. Or so we all thought. Good (but not great) ERA, good (but not great) Ratio, great (on occasion) stuff that made you think, hey, put him on a good team and he's a lock to be a big winner. Well, he did get the job done for the Mariners, winning seven and giving other teams someone to think about beyond Randy Johnson. But didn't those six earned runs a game constitute something of an overreaction to a new league, even one with a DH? Fortunately, those seven-plus runs a game his new teammates scored for Benes saved his bacon.

Year	Team	Lg.	G	IP	H	BB	SO	W	L	ERA	SV	Ratio
1992	San Diego	NL	34	231.1	230	61	169	13	14	3.35	0	1.258
1993	San Diego	NL	34	230.2	200	86	179	15	15	3.78	0	1.240
1994	San Diego	NL	25	172.1	155	51	189	6	14	3.86	0	1.195
1995	San Diego	NL	19	118.2	121	45	126	4	7	4.17	0	1.399
1995	Seattle	AL	12	63.0	72	33	45	7	2	5.86	0	1.667
Post All-Star			16	87.2	101	47	74	8	4	5.85	0	1.688

JASON BERE   Age 24/R $14

No doubt about it: 1995 was a bad year to pitch for the White Sox. But Bere was 22–7 with an ERA of 3.64 for the Chisox before last summer's debacle, so you have to figure he—and the team—will bounce back.

Year	Team	Lg.	G	IP	H	BB	SO	W	L	ERA	SV	Ratio
1993	Chicago	AL	24	142.2	109	81	129	12	5	3.47	0	1.332
1994	Chicago	AL	24	141.2	119	80	127	12	2	3.81	0	1.405
1995	Chicago	AL	27	137.2	151	106	110	8	15	7.19	0	1.867
Post All-Star			13	53.0	68	46	37	4	8	10.19	0	2.151

Catchers
pp. 27–41

Corners
pp. 41–62

Infield
pp. 63–82

Outfield
pp. 83–113

DH
pp. 114–118

Starters
pp. 119–157

Relievers
pp. 157–193

SEAN BERGMAN   Age 25/R $2

Every year is a bad year to pitch for the Tigers. Bergman's still young, but it doesn't look like he'll be allowed to age gracefully in Tiger Stadium.

Year	Team	Lg.	G	IP	H	BB	SO	W	L	ERA	SV	Ratio
1993	Detroit	AL	9	39.2	47	23	19	1	4	5.67	0	1.765
1994	Detroit	AL	3	17.2	22	7	12	2	1	5.60	0	1.642
1995	Detroit	AL	28	135.1	169	67	86	7	10	5.12	0	1.744
Post All-Star			15	72.2	86	38	49	4	5	5.33	0	1.706

MIKE BIELECKI   Age 36/R $1

Think of Bielecki as a nice sixth starter—for someone else's team.

Year	Team	Lg.	G	IP	H	BB	SO	W	L	ERA	SV	Ratio
1992	Atlanta	NL	19	80.2	77	27	62	2	4	2.57	0	1.289
1993	Cleveland	AL	13	68.2	90	23	38	4	5	5.90	0	1.646
1994	Atlanta	NL	19	27.0	28	12	18	2	0	4.00	0	1.481
1995	California	AL	22	75.1	80	31	45	4	6	5.97	0	1.473
Post All-Star			7	10.0	16	6	6	0	0	11.70	0	2.200

RICKY BONES   Age 26/R $4

Enjoyed best support on staff (5.61 runs a game), which is how he eked out those 10 wins. If you don't expect miracles, he's worth modest investment.

Year	Team	Lg.	G	IP	H	BB	SO	W	L	ERA	SV	Ratio
1992	Milwaukee	AL	31	163.1	169	48	65	9	10	4.57	0	1.329
1993	Milwaukee	AL	32	203.2	222	63	63	11	11	4.86	0	1.399
1994	Milwaukee	AL	24	170.2	166	45	57	10	9	3.43	0	1.236
1995	Milwaukee	AL	32	200.1	218	83	77	10	12	4.63	0	1.502
Post All-Star			17	100.2	127	44	41	6	5	5.45	0	1.699

CHRIS BOSIO   Age 32/R $2

Had roughly equal success facing righties or lefties last season, i.e., not very much (.312 and .313, respectively, if you're scoring at home). He was just awful last year. Belcher had more walks, but Bosio gave up 23 more hits in nine fewer innings. Stay away. Looked overweight, pitched over the hill.

Year	Team	Lg.	G	IP	H	BB	SO	W	L	ERA	SV	Ratio
1992	Milwaukee	AL	33	231.1	223	44	120	16	6	3.62	0	1.154
1993	Seattle	AL	29	164.1	138	59	119	9	9	3.45	1	1.199
1994	Seattle	AL	19	125.0	137	40	67	4	10	4.32	0	1.416
1995	Seattle	AL	31	170.0	211	69	85	10	8	4.92	0	1.647
Post All-Star			16	92.0	121	36	47	4	5	4.99	0	1.707

SHAWN BOSKIE
Age 29/R   **$1**

If Boskie lasts long enough in the majors, his name could go into the language as a synonym for "lousy pitcher." Flash forward to some Rotisserie auction draft of the future, and you'll hear an owner saying of some journeyman for Arizona or Tampa Bay: "No way I'm drafting this guy—he's a boskie." Guess it's better than not being remembered at all.

Year	Team	Lg.	G	IP	H	BB	SO	W	L	ERA	SV	Ratio
1992	Chicago	NL	23	91.2	96	36	39	5	11	5.01	0	1.440
1993	Chicago	NL	39	65.2	63	21	39	5	3	3.43	0	1.279
1994	Seattle	AL	2	2.2	4	1	0	0	1	6.75	0	1.875
1994	Chicago	NL	2	3.2	3	0	2	0	0	0.00	0	0.818
1994	Philadelphia	NL	18	84.1	85	29	59	4	6	5.23	0	1.352
1995	California	AL	20	111.2	127	25	51	7	7	5.64	0	1.361
Post All-Star			7	29.1	43	9	17	1	5	7.98	0	1.773

KEVIN BROWN
Age 31/R   **$12**

To have pitched that well and come away with only a 10–9 record speaks volumes about the kind of season it was in Camden Yards. This year has to be better, doesn't it?

Year	Team	Lg.	G	IP	H	BB	SO	W	L	ERA	SV	Ratio
1992	Texas	AL	35	265.2	262	76	173	21	11	3.32	0	1.272
1993	Texas	AL	34	233.0	228	74	142	15	12	3.59	0	1.296
1994	Texas	AL	26	170.0	218	50	123	7	9	4.82	0	1.576
1995	Baltimore	AL	26	172.1	155	48	117	10	9	3.60	0	1.178
Post All-Star			15	96.1	87	32	56	5	3	3.36	0	1.235

GIOVANNI CARRARA
Age 28/R   **$1**

Tonight, the role of Scungilli will be sung by . . . all right, we don't know if he sings, but he pitches like an opera singer. A soprano.

Year	Team	Lg.	G	IP	H	BB	SO	W	L	ERA	SV	Ratio
1995	Toronto	AL	12	48.2	64	25	27	2	4	7.21	0	1.829
Post All-Star			12	48.2	64	25	27	2	4	7.21	0	1.829

MARK CLARK
Age 27/R   **$3**

Another BPGT, but the team is so good you don't have to worry about overspending a few bucks for him. Clark clearly missed Phil Regan, who didn't exactly turn around that staff in Baltimore. If Regan comes to Cleveland as pitching coach, Clark is worth a tad more. Another plus: Clark had a good second half.

Year	Team	Lg.	G	IP	H	BB	SO	W	L	ERA	SV	Ratio
1992	St. Louis	NL	20	113.1	117	36	44	3	10	4.45	0	1.350
1993	Cleveland	AL	26	109.1	119	25	57	7	5	4.28	0	1.317
1994	Cleveland	AL	20	127.1	133	40	60	11	3	3.82	0	1.359
1995	Cleveland	AL	22	124.2	143	42	68	9	7	5.27	0	1.484
Post All-Star			13	83.2	85	25	43	5	4	4.20	0	1.315

ROGER CLEMENS
Age 33/R   **$19**

Clemens had his midlife crisis last year. He finally learned that he can no longer get by on what once was (and is no more) the liveliest heat in the league. The Rocket came into camp in bad shape, assuming he could just

Catchers
pp. 27–41

Corners
pp. 41–62

Infield
pp. 63–82

Outfield
pp. 83–113

DH
pp. 114–118

Starters
pp. 119–157

Relievers
pp. 157–193

get it going like he always did. It didn't happen, and his shoulder went sour. But he recovered to be his team's best pitcher the second half, despite the worst ERA of his career. One AL ump said he had the best forkball in the league. Mr. Rocket, meet Mr. Finesse.

Year	Team	Lg.	G	IP	H	BB	SO	W	L	ERA	SV	Ratio
1992	Boston	AL	32	246.2	203	62	208	18	11	2.41	0	1.074
1993	Boston	AL	29	191.2	175	67	160	11	14	4.46	0	1.263
1994	Boston	AL	24	170.2	124	71	168	9	7	2.85	0	1.143
1995	Boston	AL	23	140.0	141	60	132	10	5	4.18	0	1.436
Post All-Star			15	91.1	95	42	89	8	4	4.14	0	1.500

DAVID CONE   Age 33/R $24

Talk about your money pitchers—midway every other summer, Cone puts on a new uni and leads another team into the playoffs. His performance for the Yankees last season was botttom-line terrific. If he stays with them, expect a super season. Nobody handles that city like Cone. If he leaves, he'll still be great. Check out the length of his contract, though, because he talked about enjoying being a nomad.

Year	Team	Lg.	G	IP	H	BB	SO	W	L	ERA	SV	Ratio
1992	Toronto	AL	8	53.0	39	29	47	4	3	2.55	0	1.283
1992	New York	NL	27	196.2	162	82	214	13	7	2.88	0	1.241
1993	Kansas City	AL	34	254.0	205	114	191	11	14	3.33	0	1.256
1994	Kansas City	AL	23	171.2	130	54	132	16	5	2.94	0	1.072
1995	Toronto	AL	17	130.1	113	41	102	9	6	3.38	0	1.182
1995	New York	AL	13	99.0	82	47	89	9	2	3.82	0	1.303
Post All-Star			16	123.0	100	57	105	11	3	3.51	0	1.276

RHEAL CORMIER   Age 28/L $3

As a middle reliever and spot starter, Cormier is the Rheal dheal.

Year	Team	Lg.	G	IP	H	BB	SO	W	L	ERA	SV	Ratio
1992	St. Louis	NL	31	186.0	194	33	117	10	10	3.68	0	1.220
1993	St. Louis	NL	38	145.1	163	27	75	7	6	4.33	0	1.307
1994	St. Louis	NL	7	39.2	40	7	26	3	2	5.45	0	1.185
1995	Boston	AL	48	115.0	131	31	69	7	5	4.07	0	1.409
Post All-Star			23	59.0	76	18	37	4	4	4.73	0	1.593

TIM DAVIS   Age 25/L $1

A wiry lefty with hellacious stuff and some tasty minor league numbers, he didn't show much in five starts last season except a flare for walking people. But you may recall another hard-throwing Seattle left-hander who had trouble with his control early on, so keep Davis's name on your list of maybes.

Year	Team	Lg.	G	IP	H	BB	SO	W	L	ERA	SV	Ratio
1994	Seattle	AL	42	49.1	57	25	28	2	2	4.01	2	1.662
1995	Seattle	AL	5	24.0	30	18	19	2	1	6.38	0	2.000
Post All-Star			0	0.0	0	0	0	0	0	0.00	0	0.000

CAL ELDRED
Age 28/R   **$5**

Pitchers, even ones as rugged and gutsy as Eldred, typically need two years to come all the way back from major surgery. And Eldred is coming back to the Brewers. Worth a look at a low salary for next year. Really worth a look if he signs elsewhere.

Year	Team	Lg.	G	IP	H	BB	SO	W	L	ERA	SV	Ratio
1992	Milwaukee	AL	14	100.1	76	23	62	11	2	1.79	0	0.987
1993	Milwaukee	AL	36	258.0	232	91	180	16	16	4.01	0	1.252
1994	Milwaukee	AL	25	179.0	158	84	98	11	11	4.68	0	1.352
1995	Milwaukee	AL	4	23.2	24	10	18	1	1	3.42	0	1.437
Post All-Star			0	0.0	0	0	0	0	0	0.00	0	0.000

SCOTT ERICKSON
Age 28/R   **$12**

After two and half years on the down escalator, Erickson turned things around with a brilliant season-ending stint for the Orioles. Guess that means there's something to the old cliché about how a change of scenery might help.

Year	Team	Lg.	G	IP	H	BB	SO	W	L	ERA	SV	Ratio
1992	Minnesota	AL	32	212.0	197	83	101	13	12	3.40	0	1.321
1993	Minnesota	AL	34	218.2	266	71	116	8	19	5.19	0	1.541
1994	Minnesota	AL	23	144.0	173	59	104	8	11	5.44	0	1.611
1995	Minnesota	AL	15	87.2	102	32	45	4	6	5.95	0	1.529
1995	Baltimore	AL	17	108.2	111	35	61	9	4	3.89	0	1.344
Post All-Star			16	102.2	104	33	59	8	4	3.94	0	1.334

VAUGHN ESHELMAN
Age 26/L   **$4**

Another one of Dan Duquette's brilliant moves last year was plucking this guy from the Orioles farm system. A crafty (aren't they all?) left-hander, Eshelman kept the Red Sox near the top until Wakefield, Hanson, and Clemens came around to put them over. Then an injury spoiled the rest of his season. Worth a long look in spring training.

Year	Team	Lg.	G	IP	H	BB	SO	W	L	ERA	SV	Ratio
1995	Boston	AL	23	81.2	86	36	41	6	3	4.85	0	1.494
Post All-Star			12	39.2	38	12	18	3	1	3.18	0	1.261

ALEX FERNANDEZ
Age 26/R   **$18**

In one 10-game stretch at the end of last year, Fernandez went 7–1 with an ERA of 1.41. Whatever had been wrong, he fixed. The White Sox will come back to challenge the Indians, and Fernandez will be leading the charge. And he'll do it all year this time.

Year	Team	Lg.	G	IP	H	BB	SO	W	L	ERA	SV	Ratio
1992	Chicago	AL	29	187.2	199	50	95	8	11	4.27	0	1.327
1993	Chicago	AL	34	247.1	221	67	169	18	9	3.13	0	1.164
1994	Chicago	AL	24	170.1	163	50	122	11	7	3.86	0	1.250
1995	Chicago	AL	30	203.2	200	65	159	12	8	3.80	0	1.301
Post All-Star			16	116.2	105	28	92	8	2	2.39	0	1.140

Catchers
pp. 27–41

Corners
pp. 41–62

Infield
pp. 63–82

Outfield
pp. 83–113

DH
pp. 114–118

Starters
pp. 119–157

Relievers
pp. 157–193

CHUCK FINLEY

Age 33/L $14

Started out badly, pitched great for two months, and then finished up worse than he began. Sort of matched his team's performance, which is more than a coincidence. We had always wondered what Finley would do on a good team. Now we know. It was more fun to wonder.

Year	Team	Lg.	G	IP	H	BB	SO	W	L	ERA	SV	Ratio
1992	California	AL	31	204.1	212	98	124	7	12	3.96	0	1.517
1993	California	AL	35	251.1	243	82	187	16	14	3.15	0	1.293
1994	California	AL	25	183.1	178	71	148	10	10	4.32	0	1.358
1995	California	AL	32	203.0	192	93	195	15	12	4.21	0	1.404
Post All-Star			17	104.1	109	49	98	8	5	4.83	0	1.514

DAVE FLEMING

Age 26/L $1

Go ahead. Take a guy traded for Bob Milacki. Go ahead. Finish eighth.

Year	Team	Lg.	G	IP	H	BB	SO	W	L	ERA	SV	Ratio
1992	Seattle	AL	33	228.1	225	60	112	17	10	3.39	0	1.248
1993	Seattle	AL	26	167.1	189	67	75	12	5	4.36	0	1.530
1994	Seattle	AL	23	117.0	152	65	65	7	11	6.46	0	1.855
1995	Seattle	AL	16	48.0	57	34	26	1	5	7.50	0	1.896
1995	Kansas City	AL	9	32.0	27	19	14	0	1	3.66	0	1.438
Post All-Star			9	32.0	27	19	14	0	1	3.66	0	1.438

BRIAN GIVENS

Age 30/L $1

There are no givens in the big leagues. At least there didn't used to be. And if this Givens doesn't pitch better than he did last year, he won't be in the big leagues much longer.

Year	Team	Lg.	G	IP	H	BB	SO	W	L	ERA	SV	Ratio
1995	Milwaukee	AL	19	107.1	116	54	73	5	7	4.95	0	1.584
Post All-Star			15	89.2	88	44	59	5	5	4.42	0	1.472

TOM GORDON

Age 28/R $12

Had one of the ugliest box score lines in history in the last game of the year, a 17–7 loss to Cleveland (the Indians, not the Browns): 1 IP, 9 H, 4 BB, 10 ER. Deduct that last game and his 1995 ERA is a much more respectable 3.97. Somewhere out there in this great land of ours, there are Rotisserie owners who lost the pennant because of Gordon's final outing in 1995, and forevermore they will preface any mention of his name with a string of bleeping expletives. But there is a fairer, kinder way to treat Gordon's name, and that is as a synonym for curve. Aren't you tired of "yakker" and "Uncle Charlie" and "hook"? This guy has the best bender of his era, one of the best of all time, so why not henceforth call curveballs "gordons"? As in, "Old Lefty there has a gordon that drops off the table," or "Old Righty isn't afraid to come in with that big gordon of his on a 3–2 count."

Year	Team	Lg.	G	IP	H	BB	SO	W	L	ERA	SV	Ratio
1992	Kansas City	AL	40	117.2	116	55	98	6	10	4.59	0	1.453
1993	Kansas City	AL	48	155.2	125	77	143	12	6	3.58	1	1.298
1994	Kansas City	AL	24	155.1	136	87	126	11	7	4.35	0	1.436
1995	Kansas City	AL	31	189.0	204	89	119	12	12	4.43	0	1.550
Post All-Star			17	102.2	115	47	56	7	7	4.82	0	1.578

KEVIN GROSS

Gross!

Age 34/R $1

Year	Team	Lg.	G	IP	H	BB	SO	W	L	ERA	SV	Ratio
1992	Los Angeles	NL	34	204.2	182	77	158	8	13	3.17	0	1.265
1993	Los Angeles	NL	33	202.1	224	74	150	13	13	4.14	0	1.473
1994	Los Angeles	NL	25	157.1	162	43	124	9	7	3.60	1	1.303
1995	Texas	AL	31	183.2	200	89	106	9	15	5.54	0	1.574
Post All-Star			16	110.1	108	40	63	6	7	4.24	0	1.341

EDDIE GUARDADO

Age 25/L $1

As a spot starter and reliever for the Twins, he had as many blown saves as wins. That has to be some sort of record, doesn't it?

Year	Team	Lg.	G	IP	H	BB	SO	W	L	ERA	SV	Ratio
1993	Minnesota	AL	19	94.2	123	36	46	3	8	6.18	0	1.680
1994	Minnesota	AL	4	17.0	26	4	8	0	2	8.47	0	1.765
1995	Minnesota	AL	51	91.1	99	45	71	4	9	5.12	2	1.577
Post All-Star			31	42.2	41	23	38	4	2	4.22	2	1.500

MARK GUBICZA

Age 33/R $6

Good comeback from an old favorite.

Year	Team	Lg.	G	IP	H	BB	SO	W	L	ERA	SV	Ratio
1992	Kansas City	AL	18	111.1	110	36	81	7	6	3.72	0	1.311
1993	Kansas City	AL	49	104.1	128	43	80	5	8	4.66	2	1.639
1994	Kansas City	AL	22	130.0	158	26	59	7	9	4.50	0	1.415
1995	Kansas City	AL	33	213.1	222	62	81	12	14	3.75	0	1.331
Post All-Star			17	111.0	130	29	42	6	7	4.05	0	1.432

JUAN GUZMAN

Age 29/R $5

Guzman will probably be out of Toronto because GM Gord Ash seems to have given up on him. After a nice outing last September, Ash said "Great, but we need it regularly, and Juan hasn't done it." Blue Jays fans will find it hard to quarrel with that conclusion.

Year	Team	Lg.	G	IP	H	BB	SO	W	L	ERA	SV	Ratio
1992	Toronto	AL	28	180.2	135	72	165	16	5	2.64	0	1.146
1993	Toronto	AL	33	221.0	211	110	194	14	3	3.99	0	1.452
1994	Toronto	AL	25	147.1	165	76	124	12	11	5.68	0	1.636
1995	Toronto	AL	24	135.1	151	73	94	4	14	6.32	0	1.655
Post All-Star			13	74.1	75	36	62	2	9	5.57	0	1.493

CHRIS HANEY

Age 27/L $1

A herniated disc allowed for time to catch up on "Green Acres" reruns. This Mr. Haney must also be considered suspect.

Year	Team	Lg.	G	IP	H	BB	SO	W	L	ERA	SV	Ratio
1992	Kansas City	AL	7	42.0	35	16	27	2	3	3.86	0	1.214
1992	Montreal	NL	9	38.0	40	10	27	2	3	5.45	0	1.316
1993	Kansas City	AL	23	124.0	141	53	65	9	9	6.02	0	1.565
1994	Kansas City	AL	6	28.1	36	11	18	2	2	7.31	0	1.659
1995	Kansas City	AL	16	81.1	78	33	31	3	4	3.65	0	1.365
Post All-Star			1	2.0	6	3	1	0	1	27.00	0	4.500

Catchers
pp. 27–41

Corners
pp. 41–62

Infield
pp. 63–82

Outfield
pp. 83–113

DH
pp. 114–118

Starters
pp. 119–157

Relievers
pp. 157–193

ERIK HANSON Age 30/R $11

Along with Tim Wakefield, he carried the Red Sox while Clemens was recuperating, much of that time without the use of his fantastic curveball. Problem is, he's never more than one yakker, er, gordon away from a stint on the DL. Still, the Red Sox sure got their money's worth from a guy who started the spring in that camp for wayward ballplayers in Homestead, Fla.

Year	Team	Lg.	G	IP	H	BB	SO	W	L	ERA	SV	Ratio
1992	Seattle	AL	31	186.2	209	57	112	8	17	4.82	0	1.425
1993	Seattle	AL	31	215.0	215	60	163	11	12	3.47	0	1.279
1994	Cincinnati	NL	22	122.2	137	23	101	5	5	4.11	0	1.304
1995	Boston	AL	29	186.2	187	59	139	15	5	4.24	0	1.318
Post All-Star			15	99.1	101	38	62	8	3	4.80	0	1.399

MIKE HARKEY Age 29/R $1

There are still those who saw him pitch in Pittsfield, Mass., back in 1988 who swear he is the second coming of Bob Gibson. Subsequent evidence suggests that he is not.

Year	Team	Lg.	G	IP	H	BB	SO	W	L	ERA	SV	Ratio
1992	Chicago	NL	7	38.0	34	15	21	4	0	1.89	0	1.289
1993	Chicago	NL	28	157.1	187	43	67	10	10	5.26	0	1.462
1994	Colorado	NL	24	91.2	125	35	39	1	6	5.79	0	1.745
1995	Oakland	AL	14	66.0	75	31	28	4	6	6.27	0	1.606
1995	California	AL	12	61.1	80	16	28	4	3	4.55	0	1.565
Post All-Star			12	61.1	80	16	28	4	3	4.55	0	1.565

GREG W. HARRIS Age 32/R $1

Maybe he should try pitching left-handed, like that other Greg Harris.

Year	Team	Lg.	G	IP	H	BB	SO	W	L	ERA	SV	Ratio
1992	San Diego	NL	20	118.0	113	35	66	4	8	4.12	0	1.254
1993	San Diego	NL	22	152.0	151	39	83	10	9	3.67	0	1.250
1993	Colorado	NL	13	73.1	88	30	40	1	8	6.50	0	1.609
1994	Colorado	NL	29	130.0	154	52	82	3	12	6.65	1	1.585
1995	Minnesota	AL	7	32.2	50	16	21	0	5	8.82	0	2.020
Post All-Star			4	15.1	26	12	11	0	3	12.33	0	2.478

BUTCH HENRY Age 27/L $1

The Expos put him on waivers, figuring that no one would be interested in a pitcher who would be out a year recovering from Tommy John surgery. They figured wrong. The Red Sox snapped him up, calculating that in 1997 he will step right into their rotation and pick up where he left off last summer. A gamble? Sure, but it's the kind of smart, take-the-long-view approach that has become Bosox GM Dan Duquette's signature. And if it works for him, it can work for you: buy Henry for a buck, reserve him and call somebody else up, and welcome a $1 ace to your staff summer after next.

Year	Team	Lg.	G	IP	H	BB	SO	W	L	ERA	SV	Ratio
1992	Houston	NL	28	165.2	185	41	96	6	9	4.02	0	1.364
1993	Montreal	NL	10	18.1	18	4	8	1	1	3.93	0	1.200
1993	Colorado	NL	20	84.2	117	24	39	2	8	6.59	0	1.665
1994	Montreal	NL	24	107.1	97	20	70	8	3	2.43	1	1.090
1995	Montreal	NL	21	126.2	133	28	60	7	9	2.84	0	1.271
Post All-Star			7	46.1	51	9	25	4	2	1.36	0	1.295

PAT HENTGEN   Age 27/R $12

Hentgen went from being one of the best pitchers in the league to one of the worst. Like a lot of the pitchers (e.g., the White Sox) who had bad years, he finished strong, recovering the velocity on his fastball and the ability to get his good curveball over for strikes. Bank on a comeback.

Year	Team	Lg.	G	IP	H	BB	SO	W	L	ERA	SV	Ratio
1992	Toronto	AL	28	50.1	49	32	39	5	2	5.36	0	1.609
1993	Toronto	AL	34	216.1	215	74	122	19	9	3.87	0	1.336
1994	Toronto	AL	24	174.2	158	59	147	13	8	3.40	0	1.242
1995	Toronto	AL	30	200.2	236	90	135	10	14	5.11	0	1.625
Post All-Star			16	110.0	127	50	81	4	8	4.50	0	1.609

OREL HERSHISER   Age 37/R $14

He did everything the Indians could have wanted. He ate up innings and kept them in ball games. And he was steady when Dennis Martinez faltered. No reason he can't do it again.

Year	Team	Lg.	G	IP	H	BB	SO	W	L	ERA	SV	Ratio
1992	Los Angeles	NL	33	210.2	209	69	130	10	15	3.67	0	1.320
1993	Los Angeles	NL	33	215.2	201	72	141	12	14	3.59	0	1.266
1994	Los Angeles	NL	21	135.1	146	42	72	6	6	3.79	0	1.389
1995	Cleveland	AL	26	167.1	151	51	111	16	6	3.87	0	1.207
Post All-Star			14	90.2	82	30	62	11	2	3.67	0	1.235

KEN HILL   Age 30/R $18

After doing very little in St. Louis, Hill showed flashes of his Montreal brilliance in Cleveland. Could be great pitching for that team over a whole season—if they can afford to sign him.

Year	Team	Lg.	G	IP	H	BB	SO	W	L	ERA	SV	Ratio
1992	Montreal	NL	33	218.0	187	75	150	16	9	2.68	0	1.202
1993	Montreal	NL	28	183.2	163	74	90	9	7	3.23	0	1.290
1994	Montreal	NL	23	154.2	145	44	85	16	5	3.32	0	1.222
1995	St. Louis	NL	18	110.1	125	45	50	6	7	5.06	0	1.541
1995	Cleveland	AL	12	74.2	77	32	48	4	1	3.98	0	1.460
Post All-Star			14	84.1	93	39	55	5	2	4.70	0	1.565

STERLING HITCHCOCK   Age 24/L $6

With the emergence of Andy Pettitte, Hitchcock is no longer the best young lefty in the Bronx. He is, however, worth a modest investment.

Year	Team	Lg.	G	IP	H	BB	SO	W	L	ERA	SV	Ratio
1992	New York	AL	3	13.0	23	6	6	0	2	8.31	0	2.231
1993	New York	AL	6	31.0	32	14	26	1	2	4.65	0	1.484
1994	New York	AL	23	49.1	48	29	37	4	1	4.20	2	1.561
1995	New York	AL	27	168.1	155	68	121	11	10	4.70	0	1.325
Post All-Star			14	89.2	84	36	56	8	5	4.42	0	1.338

Catchers
pp. 27-41

Corners
pp. 41-62

Infield
pp. 63-82

Outfield
pp. 83-113

DH
pp. 114-118

Starters
pp. 119-157

Relievers
pp. 157-193

EDWIN HURTADO   **Age 26/R**   **$1**

Certainly pitched well enough to be given a shot at making Toronto's rotation this year. Did not pitch well enough to earn the nickname "The Big Hurtado."

Year	Team	Lg.	G	IP	H	BB	SO	W	L	ERA	SV	Ratio
1995	Toronto	AL	14	77.2	81	40	33	5	2	5.45	0	1.558
Post All-Star			12	73.2	75	40	29	5	2	5.62	0	1.561

JASON JACOME   **Age 25/L**   **$1**

A young lefty on an up-and-coming team, Jacome is worth a gamble. Just remember the Mets traded him for a player to be named in the next century.

Year	Team	Lg.	G	IP	H	BB	SO	W	L	ERA	SV	Ratio
1994	New York	NL	8	54.0	54	17	30	4	3	2.67	0	1.315
1995	New York	NL	5	21.0	33	15	11	0	4	10.29	0	2.286
1995	Kansas City	AL	15	84.0	101	21	39	4	6	5.36	0	1.452
Post All-Star			15	84.0	101	21	39	4	6	5.36	0	1.452

RANDY JOHNSON   **Age 32/L**   **$30**

More than Cal's big night, more than Mo's monster year, more than the Indians' amazing season, even more than Junior and his postseason dingers, the Big Unit deserves credit for turning America on to baseball again. That glorious six-day span in which he won three clutch games to send the Mariners into the ALCS galvanized the country. He was a warrior to the end, and his salute to the Seattle fans when he left the fifth playoff game against Cleveland in defeat was a study in grace and dignity. Oh, and one more thing—after you adjust for the DH factor in the AL, Johnson's season was every bit as good as Greg Maddux's. Thanks, Mr. Unit.

Year	Team	Lg.	G	IP	H	BB	SO	W	L	ERA	SV	Ratio
1992	Seattle	AL	31	210.1	154	144	241	12	14	3.77	0	1.417
1993	Seattle	AL	35	255.1	185	99	308	19	8	3.24	1	1.112
1994	Seattle	AL	23	172.0	132	72	204	13	6	3.19	0	1.186
1995	Seattle	AL	30	214.1	159	65	294	18	2	2.48	0	1.045
Post All-Star			14	105.0	69	31	142	9	1	2.06	0	0.952

SCOTT KAMIENIECKI   **Age 31/R**   **$2**

Likely the odd man out if Key and Perez can pitch, but still worth a buck or two at the end of the auction draft.

Year	Team	Lg.	G	IP	H	BB	SO	W	L	ERA	SV	Ratio
1992	New York	AL	28	188.0	193	74	88	6	14	4.36	0	1.420
1993	New York	AL	30	154.1	163	59	72	10	7	4.08	1	1.438
1994	New York	AL	22	117.1	115	59	71	8	6	3.76	0	1.483
1995	New York	AL	17	89.2	83	49	43	7	6	4.01	0	1.472
Post All-Star			15	84.1	76	44	40	7	5	3.74	0	1.423

SCOTT KARL   **Age 24/L**   **$3**

The most promising of several young Brewers pitchers given a shot last year.

Year	Team	Lg.	G	IP	H	BB	SO	W	L	ERA	SV	Ratio
1995	Milwaukee	AL	25	124.0	141	50	59	6	7	4.14	0	1.540
Post All-Star			17	99.2	116	39	45	5	7	4.52	0	1.555

JIMMY KEY

Age 34/L   **$6**

May be going the way of Frank Viola and Bruce Hurst. Too bad, because he has a heart as big as the Ritz. Worth a small flyer just because of the kind of guy and pitcher he is, but steel yourself for disappointment.

Year	Team	Lg.	G	IP	H	BB	SO	W	L	ERA	SV	Ratio
1992	Toronto	AL	33	216.2	205	59	117	13	13	3.53	0	1.218
1993	New York	AL	34	236.2	219	43	173	18	6	3.00	0	1.107
1994	New York	AL	25	168.0	177	52	97	17	4	3.27	0	1.363
1995	New York	AL	5	30.1	40	6	14	1	2	5.64	0	1.516
Post All-Star			0	0.0	0	0	0	0	0	0.00	0	0.000

RICK KRIVDA

Age 26/L   **$3**

A promising young lefty on a team that woefully underachieved last year. Orioles people believe the mistakes he made last year resulted from inexperience and that he has the stuff to be a good one.

Year	Team	Lg.	G	IP	H	BB	SO	W	L	ERA	SV	Ratio
1995	Baltimore	AL	13	75.1	76	25	53	2	7	4.54	0	1.341
Post All-Star			12	69.2	69	23	46	2	7	4.65	0	1.321

MARK LANGSTON

Age 35/L   **$15**

Had a strong two-thirds of a season year, then tanked along with the rest of the Angels. Bicep tendonitis caused him to miss a few starts at the end of the year, but he did pitch a very tough six-plus innings in the last series of the season against Oakland. Age does not seem to be an issue yet.

Year	Team	Lg.	G	IP	H	BB	SO	W	L	ERA	SV	Ratio
1992	California	AL	32	229.0	206	74	174	13	14	3.66	0	1.223
1993	California	AL	35	256.1	220	85	196	16	11	3.20	0	1.190
1994	California	AL	18	119.1	121	54	109	7	8	4.68	0	1.466
1995	California	AL	31	200.1	212	64	142	15	7	4.63	0	1.378
Post All-Star			16	102.2	118	33	75	7	6	5.08	0	1.471

AL LEITER

Age 30/L   **$9**

Gave up a ridiculous amount of walks but otherwise had a great year for a lifeless Blue Jay team that averaged just 3.64 runs scored when he was on the mound. If he'd gotten any run support at all, Leiter's record would have been something like 15–7. Paul White of *Baseball Weekly* suggested Leiter as a legitimate candidate for the Cy Young Award—and he wasn't kidding.

Year	Team	Lg.	G	IP	H	BB	SO	W	L	ERA	SV	Ratio
1992	Toronto	AL	1	1.0	1	2	0	0	0	9.00	0	3.000
1993	Toronto	AL	34	105.0	93	56	66	9	6	4.11	2	1.419
1994	Toronto	AL	20	111.2	125	65	100	6	7	5.08	0	1.701
1995	Toronto	AL	28	183.0	162	108	153	11	11	3.64	0	1.475
Post All-Star			15	107.0	94	51	90	6	7	3.45	0	1.355

Catchers pp. 27–41

Corners pp. 41–62

Infield pp. 63–82

Outfield pp. 83–113

DH pp. 114–118

Starters pp. 119–157

Relievers pp. 157–193

JOSE LIMA
Age 23/R   **$2**

Got belted around, especially by lefty hitters, but settled down and finished strong. Showed impressive poise for a rookie. Best thing about him: he didn't walk a lot of people.

Year	Team	Lg.	G	IP	H	BB	SO	W	L	ERA	SV	Ratio
1994	Detroit	AL	3	6.2	11	3	7	0	1	13.50	0	2.100
1995	Detroit	AL	15	73.2	85	18	37	3	9	6.11	0	1.398
Post All-Star			15	73.2	85	18	37	3	9	6.11	0	1.398

FELIPE LIRA
Age 23/R   **$1**

Reached the seventh inning in only 2 of 21 starts last year, but if the Tigers are ever going to go anywhere, they have to give kids like Lira and Lima a chance. They'll have some tough times, but at least they're not Mike Moore.

Year	Team	Lg.	G	IP	H	BB	SO	W	L	ERA	SV	Ratio
1995	Detroit	AL	37	146.1	151	56	89	9	13	4.31	1	1.415
Post All-Star			18	72.2	77	29	39	3	9	5.08	1	1.459

DENNIS MARTINEZ
Age 40/R   **$16**

Stamina showed signs of slipping, but El Presidente had all he needed when it counted the most. That final game against Seattle in the ALCS was a genuine work of art.

Year	Team	Lg.	G	IP	H	BB	SO	W	L	ERA	SV	Ratio
1992	Montreal	NL	32	226.1	172	60	147	16	11	2.47	0	1.025
1993	Montreal	NL	35	224.2	211	64	138	15	9	3.85	1	1.224
1994	Cleveland	AL	24	176.2	166	44	92	11	6	3.52	0	1.189
1995	Cleveland	AL	28	187.0	174	46	99	12	5	3.08	0	1.176
Post All-Star			14	92.0	82	30	51	4	5	3.82	0	1.217

BEN McDONALD
Age 28/R   **$9**

He's 56–53 over his career. He's an underachiever who doesn't seem willing to work to harness his considerable stuff. And he's developed a rep as a me-first kind of guy. At this point, it doesn't really matter that he wrestles alligators. What matters is that he still has that live arm and could turn out to be a late-bloomer in the maturity department. Or so the Orioles desperately hope.

Year	Team	Lg.	G	IP	H	BB	SO	W	L	ERA	SV	Ratio
1992	Baltimore	AL	35	227.0	213	74	158	13	13	4.24	0	1.264
1993	Baltimore	AL	34	220.1	185	86	171	13	14	3.39	0	1.230
1994	Baltimore	AL	24	157.1	151	54	94	14	7	4.06	0	1.303
1995	Baltimore	AL	14	80.0	67	38	62	3	6	4.16	0	1.313
Post All-Star			4	18.2	12	8	18	1	2	3.38	0	1.071

JACK McDOWELL
Age 30/R   **$18**

Flipping the bird to booing fans as he walked off the mound at Yankee Stadium in a July game last year didn't earn Black Jack any points as an ambassador for baseball. But let's put the dastardly deed in perspective. Was what he did anywhere near as bad as what the Lords of Baseball have been doing to baseball fans the last few years? Think about it. A high-strung, competitive athlete loses his cool and does something boorish. At least he does it in the heat of battle, on the field, and without giving it a PR spin that insults our intelligence. Plus, he apologized. No, he'll never be confused with Mr. Nice Guy. And he won't get many votes for Commissioner. But it'll be a long time before we'll forget the look on his face in the fifth game of the divisional playoffs when—hurting, tired, running on fumes—he came into the game and did heroic battle with Randy Johnson. He deserved to be carried out on his shield.

Year	Team	Lg.	G	IP	H	BB	SO	W	L	ERA	SV	Ratio
1992	Chicago	AL	34	260.2	247	75	178	20	10	3.18	0	1.235
1993	Chicago	AL	34	256.2	261	69	158	22	10	3.37	0	1.286
1994	Chicago	AL	25	181.0	186	42	127	10	9	3.73	0	1.260
1995	New York	AL	30	217.2	211	78	157	15	10	3.93	0	1.328
Post All-Star			15	111.0	101	43	82	9	5	3.32	0	1.297

ANGEL MIRANDA   Age 26/L $1

Read him his rights and move on.

Year	Team	Lg.	G	IP	H	BB	SO	W	L	ERA	SV	Ratio
1993	Milwaukee	AL	22	120.0	100	52	88	4	5	3.30	0	1.267
1994	Milwaukee	AL	8	46.0	39	27	24	2	5	5.28	0	1.435
1995	Milwaukee	AL	30	74.0	83	49	45	4	5	5.23	1	1.784
Post All-Star			15	21.0	22	12	13	0	2	5.14	1	1.619

JAMIE MOYER   Age 33/L $2

Well, you do need nine pitchers.

Year	Team	Lg.	G	IP	H	BB	SO	W	L	ERA	SV	Ratio
1993	Baltimore	AL	25	152.0	154	38	90	12	9	3.43	0	1.263
1994	Baltimore	AL	23	149.0	158	38	87	5	7	4.77	0	1.315
1995	Baltimore	AL	27	115.2	117	30	65	8	6	5.21	0	1.271
Post All-Star			12	61.2	71	12	34	4	3	6.42	0	1.346

MIKE MUSSINA   Age 27/R $26

There are a lot of reasons to love this guy, many of them having to do with the numbers he puts up, others having to do with what a tough competitor he is. But what we like most is the class and good humor he brings to the game. The final day of the season, in a meaningless game between Detroit and Baltimore at Camden Yards, Lou Whitaker and Alan Trammell—together for the last time—were batting one-two in the Tigers lineup. (Sparky would lift them after their first, and final, plate appearances.) Before making his first pitch, Mussina called catcher Chris Hoiles out to the mound: "Tell them nothing but fastballs. Tell them both." In a perfect, fantasy world, the two Tigers would both have hit home runs in their last major league at-bats. But in the real world, Mussina went on to pitch a two-hit shutout. One consolation, though: one of those hits was a single by Trammell.

Year	Team	Lg.	G	IP	H	BB	SO	W	L	ERA	SV	Ratio
1992	Baltimore	AL	32	241.0	212	48	130	18	5	2.54	0	1.079
1993	Baltimore	AL	25	167.2	163	44	117	14	6	4.46	0	1.235
1994	Baltimore	AL	24	176.1	163	42	99	16	5	3.06	0	1.163
1995	Baltimore	AL	32	221.2	187	50	158	19	9	3.29	0	1.069
Post All-Star			17	125.2	98	28	100	10	4	2.44	0	1.003

Catchers
pp. 27-41

Corners
pp. 41-62

Infield
pp. 63-82

Outfield
pp. 83-113

DH
pp. 114-118

Starters
pp. 119-157

Relievers
pp. 157-193

CHARLES NAGY
Age 28/R $18

How can you give up four and a half earned runs a game and still go 16–6? When your teammates score almost seven runs a game (6.83, to be exact) when you're on the mound. Not as sharp as he was the summer before last, but plenty good enough.

Year	Team	Lg.	G	IP	H	BB	SO	W	L	ERA	SV	Ratio
1992	Cleveland	AL	33	252.0	245	57	169	17	10	2.96	0	1.198
1993	Cleveland	AL	9	48.2	66	13	30	2	6	6.29	0	1.623
1994	Cleveland	AL	23	169.1	175	48	108	10	8	3.45	0	1.317
1995	Cleveland	AL	29	178.0	194	61	139	16	6	4.55	0	1.433
Post All-Star			15	90.2	114	33	72	9	2	5.46	0	1.621

CHAD OGEA
Age 25/R $10

Tough, hard-thower who should improve this year, his second as the Indians fifth starter. Could move up in the rotation if Martinez or Hershiser falters.

Year	Team	Lg.	G	IP	H	BB	SO	W	L	ERA	SV	Ratio
1994	Cleveland	AL	4	16.1	21	10	11	0	1	6.06	0	1.898
1995	Cleveland	AL	20	106.1	95	29	57	8	3	3.05	0	1.166
Post All-Star			11	53.0	58	18	31	3	2	3.91	0	1.434

DARREN OLIVER
Age 25/L $1

The talented Oliver left spring training last year as the Rangers' closer, then was shoved into the rotation, then went out with a rotator cuff. Surgery means this year is a washout, but grab him cheap and count on him to come back strong in 1997.

Year	Team	Lg.	G	IP	H	BB	SO	W	L	ERA	SV	Ratio
1993	Texas	AL	2	3.1	2	1	4	0	0	2.70	0	0.900
1994	Texas	AL	43	50.0	40	35	50	4	0	3.42	2	1.500
1995	Texas	AL	17	49.0	47	32	39	4	2	4.22	0	1.612
Post All-Star			0	0.0	0	0	0	0	0	0.00	0	0.000

STEVE ONTIVEROS
Age 35/R $10

No ERA title last season, but he pitched pretty well for a strictly mediocre team. These are tough times in Oakland, so don't expect much from this late-starting starter.

Year	Team	Lg.	G	IP	H	BB	SO	W	L	ERA	SV	Ratio
1993	Seattle	AL	14	18.0	18	6	13	0	2	1.00	0	1.333
1994	Oakland	AL	27	115.1	93	26	56	6	4	2.65	0	1.032
1995	Oakland	AL	22	129.2	144	38	77	9	6	4.37	0	1.404
Post All-Star			9	45.1	61	20	27	1	3	6.75	0	1.787

JOSE PARRA
Age 23/R $1

More like a triple bogey.

Year	Team	Lg.	G	IP	H	BB	SO	W	L	ERA	SV	Ratio
1995	Los Angeles	NL	8	10.1	10	6	7	0	0	4.35	0	1.548
1995	Minnesota	AL	12	61.2	83	22	29	1	5	7.59	0	1.703
Post All-Star			16	66.1	87	24	31	1	5	7.46	0	1.673

ROGER PAVLIK
Age 28/R   **$11**

Phenomenal comeback from major arm problems. Must master control problems to take the next step.

Year	Team	Lg.	G	IP	H	BB	SO	W	L	ERA	SV	Ratio
1992	Texas	AL	13	62.0	66	34	45	4	4	4.21	0	1.613
1993	Texas	AL	26	166.1	151	80	131	12	6	3.41	0	1.389
1994	Texas	AL	11	50.1	61	30	31	2	5	7.69	0	1.808
1995	Texas	AL	31	191.2	174	90	149	10	10	4.37	0	1.377
Post All-Star			16	109.2	80	51	88	5	6	3.45	0	1.195

MELIDO PEREZ
Age 30/R   **$6**

Fragile. If he can get healthy and stay that way, he can win games on a good team. Big if.

Year	Team	Lg.	G	IP	H	BB	SO	W	L	ERA	SV	Ratio
1992	New York	AL	33	247.2	212	93	218	13	16	2.87	0	1.231
1993	New York	AL	25	163.0	173	64	148	6	14	5.19	0	1.454
1994	New York	AL	22	151.1	134	58	109	9	4	4.10	0	1.269
1995	New York	AL	13	69.1	70	31	44	5	5	5.58	0	1.457
Post All-Star			1	1.0	1	0	0	0	0	0.00	0	1.000

ANDY PETTITTE
Age 23/L   **$14**

One half of the best trade that George Steinbrenner was ever prevented from making. In midsummer George wanted to send Pettitte to California as part of a package for Mark Langston. (Steinbrenner has always had this thing about Langston.) But Gene Michael threw his body in front of the train and refused to let it pull out of the station. If Stick hadn't blocked the deal, the Yankees probably wouldn't have won the wild card. That's probably why George gave Stick such a nice option at the end of the year: take a $200,000 pay cut as GM or get kicked downstairs to be chief scout. (For his own mental health, Michael took the demotion.) And Pettitte? He has the poise of a 10-year vet, the best pickoff move in the AL, and the makeup of a winner.

Year	Team	Lg.	G	IP	H	BB	SO	W	L	ERA	SV	Ratio
1995	New York	AL	31	175.0	183	63	114	12	9	4.17	0	1.406
Post All-Star			17	115.0	111	40	83	9	3	3.83	0	1.313

ARIEL PRIETO
Age 26/R   **$3**

You can't walk nearly five guys per nine innings and expect to live up to your advance billing as the best Cuban export since Macanudos. Last season this highly prized free agent signee didn't pitch worth a half-smoked El Producto. But we believe in second chances, provided that they come at the right price.

Year	Team	Lg.	G	IP	H	BB	SO	W	L	ERA	SV	Ratio
1995	Oakland	AL	14	58.0	57	32	37	2	6	4.97	0	1.534
Post All-Star			12	50.0	50	30	31	2	5	5.04	0	1.600

Catchers
pp. 27–41

Corners
pp. 41–62

Infield
pp. 63–82

Outfield
pp. 83–113

DH
pp. 114–118

Starters
pp. 119–157

Relievers
pp. 157–193

BRAD RADKE   Age 23/R $4

Survived his trial by fire last year, emerging only a little singed. The Twins
are a smart organization and will turn things around quickly. Radke will be
a part of the turnaround.

Year	Team	Lg.	G	IP	H	BB	SO	W	L	ERA	SV	Ratio
1995	Minnesota	AL	29	181.0	195	47	75	11	14	5.32	0	1.337
Post All-Star			15	104.0	95	28	39	6	7	4.76	0	1.183

ARTHUR RHODES   Age 26/L $1

You don't have to be a Rhodes scholar to figure out—finally—that there's
not going to be any delivery on that once-great promise.

Year	Team	Lg.	G	IP	H	BB	SO	W	L	ERA	SV	Ratio
1992	Baltimore	AL	15	94.1	87	38	77	7	5	3.63	0	1.325
1993	Baltimore	AL	17	85.2	91	49	49	5	6	6.51	0	1.634
1994	Baltimore	AL	10	52.2	51	30	47	3	5	5.81	0	1.538
1995	Baltimore	AL	19	75.1	68	48	77	2	5	6.21	0	1.540
Post All-Star			10	31.1	23	19	32	0	2	4.88	0	1.340

DAVE RIGHETTI   Age 37/L $1

The day McDowell flipped off the fans at Yankee Stadium, Righetti won his
end of a doubleheader there. Nice story, but it ended last year. Thanks for
all the memories to one of the all-time good guys.

Year	Team	Lg.	G	IP	H	BB	SO	W	L	ERA	SV	Ratio
1992	San Francisco	NL	54	78.1	79	36	47	2	7	5.06	3	1.468
1993	San Francisco	NL	51	47.1	58	17	31	1	1	5.70	1	1.585
1994	Oakland	AL	7	7.0	13	9	4	0	0	16.71	0	3.143
1994	Toronto	AL	13	13.1	9	10	10	0	1	6.75	0	1.425
1995	Chicago	AL	10	49.1	65	18	29	3	2	4.20	0	1.682
Post All-Star			10	49.1	65	18	29	3	2	4.20	0	1.682

SID ROBERSON   Age 24/L $3

Showed some very nice stuff in his 13 starts last year. Finished the season
in long relief. Should begin the year as the third starter and continue to
improve.

Year	Team	Lg.	G	IP	H	BB	SO	W	L	ERA	SV	Ratio
1995	Milwaukee	AL	26	84.1	102	37	40	6	4	5.76	0	1.648
Post All-Star			16	32.1	45	19	11	1	2	7.79	0	1.979

FRANK RODRIGUEZ   Age 23/R $2

The Red Sox couldn't decide if he was a starter or a closer, so he never did
much for them. The Twins see him as a starter, but he didn't do much for
them either. Still, you don't give up a Rick Aguilera unless you believe the
guy you're getting back can do something, so we're suggesting a long look-
see for Rodriguez, who needs some time to develop his control.

Year	Team	Lg.	G	IP	H	BB	SO	W	L	ERA	SV	Ratio
1995	Boston	AL	9	15.1	21	10	14	0	2	10.57	0	2.022
1995	Minnesota	AL	16	90.1	93	47	45	5	6	5.38	0	1.550
Post All-Star			15	87.1	90	45	42	5	5	5.26	0	1.546

KENNY ROGERS   Age 31/L $20

One of the best pitchers in the league. So good that we've stopped making stupid jokes about his knowing when to hold 'em and when to fold 'em. Pay a little more if he signs with a top team.

Year	Team	Lg.	G	IP	H	BB	SO	W	L	ERA	SV	Ratio
1992	Texas	AL	81	78.2	80	26	70	3	6	3.09	6	1.347
1993	Texas	AL	35	208.1	210	71	140	16	10	4.10	0	1.349
1994	Texas	AL	24	167.1	169	52	120	11	8	4.46	0	1.321
1995	Texas	AL	31	208.0	192	76	140	17	7	3.38	0	1.288
Post All-Star			16	113.2	102	39	76	9	3	3.64	0	1.240

BOB SCANLAN   Age 29/R $1

Give up your team first.

Year	Team	Lg.	G	IP	H	BB	SO	W	L	ERA	SV	Ratio
1992	Chicago	NL	69	87.1	76	30	42	3	6	2.89	14	1.214
1993	Chicago	NL	70	75.1	79	28	44	4	5	4.54	0	1.420
1994	Milwaukee	AL	30	103.0	117	28	65	2	6	4.11	2	1.408
1995	Milwaukee	AL	17	83.1	101	44	29	4	7	6.59	0	1.740
Post All-Star			8	33.0	48	16	11	1	3	8.45	0	1.939

AARON SELE   Age 25/R $13

His season ended after he developed shoulder tendinitis, but no surgery was needed. He should come back rested and ready to resume his position as Prince of Wales on the Boston staff. His auction price this year will be as low as it's going to go for the remainder of the century, so jump in.

Year	Team	Lg.	G	IP	H	BB	SO	W	L	ERA	SV	Ratio
1993	Boston	AL	18	111.2	100	48	93	7	2	2.74	0	1.325
1994	Boston	AL	22	143.1	140	60	105	8	7	3.83	0	1.395
1995	Boston	AL	6	32.1	32	14	21	3	1	3.06	0	1.423
Post All-Star			0	0.0	0	0	0	0	0	0.00	0	0.000

ZANE SMITH   Age 35/L $2

Time may have run out for this savvy, gritty, but oh-so-fragile lefty.

Year	Team	Lg.	G	IP	H	BB	SO	W	L	ERA	SV	Ratio
1992	Pittsburgh	NL	23	141.0	138	19	56	8	8	3.06	0	1.113
1993	Pittsburgh	NL	14	83.0	97	22	32	3	7	4.55	0	1.434
1994	Pittsburgh	NL	25	157.0	162	34	57	10	8	3.27	0	1.248
1995	Boston	AL	24	110.2	144	23	47	8	8	5.61	0	1.509
Post All-Star			12	50.1	55	11	22	5	3	5.54	0	1.311

STEVE SPARKS   Age 30/R $3

He's the league's second-best knuckleballer. Of course, there are only two.

Year	Team	Lg.	G	IP	H	BB	SO	W	L	ERA	SV	Ratio
1995	Milwaukee	AL	33	202.0	210	86	96	9	11	4.63	0	1.465
Post All-Star			19	113.0	138	45	50	4	8	5.58	0	1.619

Catchers
pp. 27-41

Corners
pp. 41-62

Infield
pp. 63-82

Outfield
pp. 83-113

DH
pp. 114-118

Starters
pp. 119-157

Relievers
pp. 157-193

DAVE STEWART
Age 39/R   No Price

We said goodbye to him in last year's book, because we didn't think he was coming back. He probably shouldn't have, but it gives us a chance to say goodbye again to one of the all-time great competitors.

Year	Team	Lg.	G	IP	H	BB	SO	W	L	ERA	SV	Ratio
1992	Oakland	AL	31	199.1	175	79	130	12	10	3.66	0	1.274
1993	Toronto	AL	26	162.0	146	72	96	12	8	4.44	0	1.346
1994	Toronto	AL	22	133.1	151	62	111	7	8	5.87	0	1.597
1995	Oakland	AL	16	81.0	101	39	58	3	7	6.89	0	1.728
Post All-Star			1	2.0	7	2	1	0	1	36.00	0	4.500

TODD STOTTLEMYRE
Age 30/R $10

Another LaRussa/Duncan project that paid off. Can he repeat now that they are in St. Louis? Probably.

Year	Team	Lg.	G	IP	H	BB	SO	W	L	ERA	SV	Ratio
1992	Toronto	AL	28	174.0	175	63	98	12	11	4.50	0	1.368
1993	Toronto	AL	30	176.2	204	69	98	11	12	4.84	0	1.545
1994	Toronto	AL	26	140.2	149	48	105	7	7	4.22	1	1.400
1995	Oakland	AL	31	209.2	228	80	205	14	7	4.55	0	1.469
Post All-Star			17	113.2	143	40	104	7	5	5.15	0	1.610

BOB TEWKSBURY
Age 35/R $5

Still has that amazing control, which is a doggone good thing, because he doesn't have much else.

Year	Team	Lg.	G	IP	H	BB	SO	W	L	ERA	SV	Ratio
1992	St. Louis	NL	33	233.0	217	20	91	16	5	2.16	0	1.017
1993	St. Louis	NL	32	213.2	258	20	97	17	10	3.83	0	1.301
1994	St. Louis	NL	24	155.2	190	22	79	12	10	5.32	0	1.362
1995	Texas	AL	21	129.2	169	20	53	8	7	4.58	0	1.458
Post All-Star			8	38.1	58	9	20	1	4	7.75	0	1.748

TODD VAN POPPEL
Age 24/R $5

Still young, although it seems like we've been talking about him forever. Occasionally pitched like the dominator he's supposed to be, but not often enough for you to take out a second mortgage on the family farm.

Year	Team	Lg.	G	IP	H	BB	SO	W	L	ERA	SV	Ratio
1993	Oakland	AL	16	84.0	76	62	47	6	6	5.04	0	1.643
1994	Oakland	AL	23	116.2	108	89	83	7	10	6.09	0	1.689
1995	Oakland	AL	36	138.1	125	56	122	4	8	4.88	0	1.308
Post All-Star			18	96.2	96	40	84	3	6	5.49	0	1.407

TIM WAKEFIELD
Age 29/R $19

Everybody knows that there were two Wakefields last year. One of them looked like a surefire Cy Young winner. The other one looked like he was throwing BP in Little League. But the Red Sox are getting smarter. They'll hire every living Niekro to work with Wakefield this spring. The goal: help him become more consistent. Just one problem—no one has a clue how to help a knuckleballer be more consistent. Want proof? Take a look at 1992, when he was terrific; at 1993, when he was awful; and at 1994, when he had the worst ERA of any regular starter in the *minor* leagues.

Year	Team	Lg.	G	IP	H	BB	SO	W	L	ERA	SV	Ratio
1992	Pittsburgh	NL	13	92.0	76	35	51	8	1	2.15	0	1.207
1993	Pittsburgh	NL	24	128.1	145	75	59	6	11	5.61	0	1.714
1995	Boston	AL	27	195.1	163	68	119	16	8	2.95	0	1.183
Post All-Star			17	117.0	104	46	77	9	7	3.85	0	1.282

BOBBY WITT   Age 31/R $1

Once upon a time, Witt was practically unhittable but walked about 10 guys a game. Last year, his control was perfectly respectable (slightly more than three BB per nine innings), but hitters beat him like a drum (.324 BA). We take this as a sign that it's time to give up on Mr. Witt.

Year	Team	Lg.	G	IP	H	BB	SO	W	L	ERA	SV	Ratio
1992	Oakland	AL	6	31.2	31	19	25	1	1	3.41	0	1.579
1992	Texas	AL	25	161.1	152	95	100	9	13	4.46	0	1.531
1993	Oakland	AL	35	220.0	226	91	131	14	13	4.21	0	1.441
1994	Oakland	AL	24	135.2	151	70	111	8	10	5.04	0	1.629
1995	Florida	NL	19	110.2	104	47	95	2	7	3.90	0	1.364
1995	Texas	AL	10	61.1	81	21	46	3	4	4.55	0	1.663
Post All-Star			15	98.0	109	35	85	4	5	3.67	0	1.469

STEVE WOJCIECHOWSKI   Age 25/R $1

Walk total as hard to look at as his name is to pronounce.

Year	Team	Lg.	G	IP	H	BB	SO	W	L	ERA	SV	Ratio
1995	Oakland	AL	14	48.2	51	28	13	2	3	5.18	0	1.623
Post All-Star			14	48.2	51	28	13	2	3	5.18	0	1.623

Out of the Bullpen

NATIONAL LEAGUE

TERRY ADAMS   Age 23/R $1

Lowest ERA in four minor league years prior to last season was 4.38. This suggests that you might not want to assign him a key role in your bullpen. But the Cubs see something there, and he could be of utility down the road as a middle reliever.

Year	Team	Lg.	G	IP	H	BB	SO	W	L	ERA	SV	Ratio
1995	Chicago	NL	18	18.0	22	10	15	1	1	6.50	1	1.778
Post All-Star			18	18.0	22	10	15	1	1	6.50	1	1.778

LUIS AQUINO   Age 30/R $2

A good enough pitcher, a guy with really okay stuff, who several times in his career has had stretches where you think, wow, he's going to break out of the pack and be worth something. So you get him, usually as a callup

Catchers
pp. 27–41

Corners
pp. 41–62

Infield
pp. 63–82

Outfield
pp. 83–113

DH
pp. 114–118

Starters
pp. 119–157

Relievers
pp. 157–193

rather than at the auction draft, and he goes sour, or hurts his arm, or disappears from his manager's radar screen entirely.

Year	Team	Lg.	G	IP	H	BB	SO	W	L	ERA	SV	Ratio
1992	Kansas City	AL	15	67.2	81	20	11	3	6	4.52	0	1.493
1993	Florida	NL	38	110.2	115	40	67	6	8	3.42	0	1.401
1994	Florida	NL	29	50.2	39	22	22	2	1	3.73	0	1.204
1995	Montreal	NL	29	37.1	47	11	22	0	2	3.86	2	1.554
1995	San Francisco	NL	5	5.0	10	2	4	0	1	14.40	0	2.400
Post All-Star			7	7.2	12	4	5	0	1	9.39	0	2.087

RENE AROCHA   Age 30/R $2

His stuff is too good for him not to be some kind of asset. The Cardinals are worried that he might be at least five years older than the age he's claiming to be, but that's not the problem. Even if he is half a decade older than he claims, he's still a spring chicken compared to the Cards' closer, Tom Henke. The problem with Arocha, who has already stubbed his toe as a starter, is the seven blown saves last season that lead you to believe that closing is not his thing, either. Maybe Tony LaRussa and Dave Duncan can straighten him out.

Year	Team	Lg.	G	IP	H	BB	SO	W	L	ERA	SV	Ratio
1993	St. Louis	NL	32	188.0	197	31	96	11	8	3.78	0	1.213
1994	St. Louis	NL	45	83.0	94	21	62	4	4	4.01	11	1.386
1995	St. Louis	NL	41	49.2	55	18	25	3	5	3.99	0	1.470
Post All-Star			7	9.1	11	1	6	0	1	5.79	0	1.286

ROGER BAILEY   Age 25/R $1

His future could be as a starter, though in Coors Field and with Don Baylor's managing, that line between starting and relieving gets pretty blurred.

Year	Team	Lg.	G	IP	H	BB	SO	W	L	ERA	SV	Ratio
1995	Colorado	NL	39	81.1	88	39	33	7	6	4.98	0	1.561
Post All-Star			12	42.0	48	15	14	4	2	5.14	0	1.500

SHAWN BARTON   Age 32/L $1

One of those left-handed relievers who will get lots of action and some garbage wins in a lucky season.

Year	Team	Lg.	G	IP	H	BB	SO	W	L	ERA	SV	Ratio
1992	Seattle	AL	14	12.1	10	7	4	0	1	2.92	0	1.378
1995	San Francisco	NL	52	44.1	37	19	22	4	1	4.26	1	1.263
Post All-Star			30	23.2	19	12	13	2	1	6.46	1	1.310

JOSE BAUTISTA   Age 31R $1

Didn't we read somewhere that this guy gives pretty good value for the small bucks you spend on him? Oops, we just remembered where we read it.

Year	Team	Lg.	G	IP	H	BB	SO	W	L	ERA	SV	Ratio
1993	Chicago	NL	58	111.2	105	27	63	10	3	2.82	2	1.182
1994	Chicago	NL	58	69.1	75	17	45	4	5	3.89	1	1.327
1995	San Francisco	NL	52	100.2	120	26	45	3	8	6.44	0	1.450
Post All-Star			27	37.2	50	6	19	1	4	7.88	0	1.487

ROD BECK   Age 27/R $35

Blew 10 saves, six of them on game-losing, sudden-death home runs. Just goes to show that the Candlestick Pitching Curse spares no one, not even one of the best relief pitchers in baseball.

Year	Team	Lg.	G	IP	H	BB	SO	W	L	ERA	SV	Ratio
1992	San Francisco	NL	65	92.0	62	15	87	3	3	1.76	17	0.837
1993	San Francisco	NL	76	79.1	57	13	86	3	1	2.16	48	0.882
1994	San Francisco	NL	48	48.2	49	13	39	2	4	2.77	28	1.274
1995	San Francisco	NL	60	58.2	60	21	42	5	6	4.45	33	1.381
Post All-Star			29	26.1	32	10	17	1	3	5.81	18	1.595

STEVE BEDROSIAN   Age 38/R   No Price

When he couldn't compete to his liking, when he couldn't rear back and fire the fastball past so-so hitters in middle-inning situations, when he felt he wasn't helping his team, he took one of baseball's classiest acts home for good. Bedrock will be missed.

Year	Team	Lg.	G	IP	H	BB	SO	W	L	ERA	SV	Ratio
1993	Atlanta	NL	49	49.2	34	14	33	5	2	1.63	0	0.966
1994	Atlanta	NL	46	46.0	41	18	43	0	2	3.33	0	1.283
1995	Atlanta	NL	29	28.0	40	12	22	1	2	6.11	0	1.857
Post All-Star			7	8.0	11	7	7	0	0	7.88	0	2.250

ANDRES BERUMEN   Age 24/R $3

Big-time stuff, 95-mph speed, but control right out of the Steve Blass School of Pitching. If he can harness the wildness just a little, he'll be another gun in what is becoming a frightening Padres bullpen arsenal. Definitely not for the faint of heart.

Year	Team	Lg.	G	IP	H	BB	SO	W	L	ERA	SV	Ratio
1995	San Diego	NL	37	44.1	37	36	42	2	3	5.68	1	1.647
Post All-Star			12	18.1	17	16	15	0	1	6.38	0	1.800

DOUG BOCHTLER   Age 25/R $2

A cut below Berumen in terms of pure stuff, but way ahead of him in command and control. Anybody who averages a strikeout an inning is worth paying attention to.

Year	Team	Lg.	G	IP	H	BB	SO	W	L	ERA	SV	Ratio
1995	San Diego	NL	34	45.1	38	19	45	4	4	3.57	1	1.257
Post All-Star			30	40.0	32	17	40	4	4	3.60	1	1.225

Catchers
pp. 27–41

Corners
pp. 41–62

Infield
pp. 63–82

Outfield
pp. 83–113

DH
pp. 114–118

Starters
pp. 119–157

Relievers
pp. 157–193

PEDRO BORBON   Age 28/L $2

What a year for the Borbon clan! Dad made one of the more stirring comebacks in recent history. Over a dozen years removed from active duty, he arrived in Cincinnati's replacement player camp, where his portly shape and feeble pitching condition caused Davey Johnson and his staff to double over with laughter. Meanwhile, Pedro the Junior proved himself to be a solid situational reliever for the Braves.

Year	Team	Lg.	G	IP	H	BB	SO	W	L	ERA	SV	Ratio
1992	Atlanta	NL	2	1.1	2	1	1	0	1	6.75	0	2.250
1993	Atlanta	NL	3	1.2	3	3	2	0	0	21.60	0	3.600
1995	Atlanta	NL	41	32.0	29	17	33	2	2	3.09	2	1.438
Post All-Star			24	20.2	23	15	21	2	1	3.05	0	1.839

TOBY BORLAND   Age 26/R $3

A little short on stuff, but his sidearm delivery gives right-handers fits.

Year	Team	Lg.	G	IP	H	BB	SO	W	L	ERA	SV	Ratio
1994	Philadelphia	NL	24	34.1	31	14	26	1	0	2.36	1	1.311
1995	Philadelphia	NL	50	74.0	81	37	59	1	3	3.77	6	1.595
Post All-Star			33	51.2	48	19	46	1	3	2.61	5	1.297

RICKY BOTTALICO   Age 26/R $12

Mark it down—he, not Heathcliff Slocumb, will be the Phillies closer this year. So why the cheap price? Because not everybody knows it yet. Shhhhh!

Year	Team	Lg.	G	IP	H	BB	SO	W	L	ERA	SV	Ratio
1994	Philadelphia	NL	3	3.0	3	1	3	0	0	0.00	0	1.333
1995	Philadelphia	NL	62	87.2	50	42	87	5	3	2.46	1	1.049
Post All-Star			33	51.0	28	23	55	2	2	2.82	0	1.000

JEFF BRANTLEY   Age 32/R $27

He doesn't inspire nicknames, he doesn't make any All-Star teams or Best lists, and hitters don't cringe away, shaking with fear. Nor does he fetch a premium price in Rotisserie auctions. All he does is pile up saves.

Year	Team	Lg.	G	IP	H	BB	SO	W	L	ERA	SV	Ratio
1992	San Francisco	NL	56	91.2	67	45	86	7	7	2.95	7	1.222
1993	San Francisco	NL	53	113.2	112	46	76	5	6	4.28	0	1.390
1994	Cincinnati	NL	50	65.1	46	28	63	6	6	2.48	15	1.133
1995	Cincinnati	NL	56	70.1	53	20	62	3	2	2.82	28	1.038
Post All-Star			27	29.2	23	9	26	0	1	2.73	14	1.079

DOUG BROCAIL   Age 28/R $2

Can spot start or long relieve in equally ho-hum fashion. Probably would get higher marks if his last name didn't remind us of broccoli.

Year	Team	Lg.	G	IP	H	BB	SO	W	L	ERA	SV	Ratio
1992	San Diego	NL	3	14.0	17	5	15	0	0	6.43	0	1.571
1993	San Diego	NL	24	128.1	143	42	70	4	13	4.56	0	1.442
1994	San Diego	NL	12	17.0	21	5	11	0	0	5.82	0	1.529
1995	Houston	NL	36	77.1	87	22	39	6	4	4.19	1	1.409
Post All-Star			19	49.0	50	17	26	4	4	4.22	0	1.367

HECTOR CARRASCO — Age 26/R — $4

The Reds thought that by now this bullet-thrower would be on the verge of big-time status. They didn't count on his inability to throw his bullets in the strike zone. Still, there's a pretty big upside here.

Year	Team	Lg.	G	IP	H	BB	SO	W	L	ERA	SV	Ratio
1994	Cincinnati	NL	45	56.1	42	30	41	5	6	2.24	6	1.278
1995	Cincinnati	NL	64	87.1	86	46	64	2	7	4.12	5	1.511
Post All-Star			35	41.0	37	24	38	0	4	5.05	0	1.488

LARRY CASIAN — Age 30/L — $1

A left-hander who appears in 42 games but pitches just 23⅓ innings is in there for just one thing, right? Get left-handed hitters out. That's his job. That's his only job. He's a specialist. So can somebody please explain how come lefties hit .308 against Casian last season while righties hit just .189? That's right, *.189*. He fared better against right-handed hitters than Greg Maddux, for Cy Young's sake. You look at the overall good year, the nifty ERA, and you think, maybe the Cubs should go to this guy a little more often. And maybe they should leave him in against a few more right-handers.

Year	Team	Lg.	G	IP	H	BB	SO	W	L	ERA	SV	Ratio
1992	Minnesota	AL	6	6.2	7	1	2	1	0	2.70	0	1.200
1993	Minnesota	AL	54	56.2	59	14	31	5	3	3.02	1	1.288
1994	Cleveland	AL	7	8.1	16	4	2	0	2	8.64	0	2.400
1994	Minnesota	AL	33	40.2	57	12	18	1	3	7.08	1	1.697
1995	Chicago	NL	42	23.1	23	15	11	1	0	1.93	0	1.629
Post All-Star			27	12.1	12	11	5	1	0	2.19	0	1.865

JASON CHRISTIANSEN — Age 26/L — $2

The Pirates think he has a chance to be something special. There is one big if: control. He has the stuff—look at the Ks and hits per IP—but hasn't learned to get it over. Yet.

Year	Team	Lg.	G	IP	H	BB	SO	W	L	ERA	SV	Ratio
1995	Pittsburgh	NL	63	56.1	49	34	53	1	3	4.15	0	1.473
Post All-Star			34	33.2	32	24	37	0	3	5.61	0	1.663

BRAD CLONTZ — Age 24/R — $4

Aided by Atlanta's ability to win late-inning games, the rookie earned a pile of garbage wins after being bumped from the closer's job. The Braves like to think he is a Dan Quisenberry clone and went so far as to have the Quiz come in to tutor Clontz on the art of the funky Laredo delivery. Alas, Quiz sprinkled his visit with his usual assortment of erudite one-liners, while Clontz mostly responded by saying "Huh?" These modern players just aren't as much fun. And maybe the Quiz isn't that great a pitching coach, because Clontz never got the hang of what every right-handed sidewinder must do to survive—get out lefty batters. He was hell on right-handers, who hit just .228 against him, but lefties ate his lunch, hitting .344.

Year	Team	Lg.	G	IP	H	BB	SO	W	L	ERA	SV	Ratio
1995	Atlanta	NL	59	69.0	71	22	55	8	1	3.65	4	1.348
Post All-Star			35	42.2	45	12	38	6	0	3.16	0	1.336

Catchers
pp. 27–41

Corners
pp. 41–62

Infield
pp. 63–82

Outfield
pp. 83–113

DH
pp. 114–118

Starters
pp. 119–157

Relievers
pp. 157–193

JOHN CUMMINGS   Age 26/L $1

Too far down on the depth chart to be of much interest.

Year	Team	Lg.	G	IP	H	BB	SO	W	L	ERA	SV	Ratio
1993	Seattle	AL	10	46.1	59	16	19	0	6	6.02	0	1.619
1994	Seattle	AL	17	64.0	66	37	33	2	4	5.63	0	1.609
1995	Seattle	AL	4	5.1	8	7	4	0	0	11.81	0	2.813
1995	Los Angeles	NL	35	39.0	38	10	21	3	1	3.00	0	1.231
Post All-Star			30	33.0	34	9	20	3	1	3.55	0	1.303

JERRY DiPOTO   Age 27/R $2

As the Mets improve, *e.g.,* developing the scoring punch to win games even
when their starters have off days, their middle innings and setup guys will
benefit: more chances for wins, more chances for three-inning saves. After
the first two months, when he was truly awful, DiPoto pitched pretty well
last year. He stranded 74% of the runners he inherited, second best to
Franco on the team. Not a bad pick for the eighth or ninth slot on your staff.

Year	Team	Lg.	G	IP	H	BB	SO	W	L	ERA	SV	Ratio
1993	Cleveland	AL	46	56.1	57	30	41	4	4	2.40	11	1.544
1994	Cleveland	AL	7	15.2	26	10	9	0	0	8.04	0	2.298
1995	New York	NL	58	78.2	77	29	49	4	6	3.78	2	1.347
Post All-Star			31	43.1	36	17	21	3	3	2.08	2	1.223

JIM DOUGHERTY   Age 28/R $1

Was in the right spot at the right time to pick up a bunch of wins. Don't
count on lightning striking twice. And by the way, the Astros would be
advised not to let this guy anywhere near left-handed hitters this year—they
hit a cool .425 off him last year.

Year	Team	Lg.	G	IP	H	BB	SO	W	L	ERA	SV	Ratio
1995	Houston	NL	56	67.2	76	25	49	8	4	4.92	0	1.493
Post All-Star			24	26.0	31	9	23	4	3	5.19	0	1.538

JOEY EISCHEN   Age 25/L $1

Take him over John Cummings if you absolutely, positively must have a
Dodger bullpen lefty. Why? He's a year younger. Aside from that, they're
the same pitcher, as far as we can tell.

Year	Team	Lg.	G	IP	H	BB	SO	W	L	ERA	SV	Ratio
1994	Montreal	NL	1	0.2	4	0	1	0	0	54.00	0	6.000
1995	Los Angeles	NL	17	20.1	19	11	15	0	0	3.10	0	1.475
Post All-Star			4	6.0	7	3	3	0	0	3.00	0	1.667

DON FLORENCE   Age 29/L $1

Could help somewhere for Mets and has distinction of being part of the All-
Italian cities team, an elite crew that includes Enrique Romo, Ed Napoleon,
Steve Palermo, Felix Milan, Al Salerno, etc.

Year	Team	Lg.	G	IP	H	BB	SO	W	L	ERA	SV	Ratio
1995	New York	NL	14	12.0	17	6	5	3	0	1.50	0	1.917
Post All-Star			14	12.0	17	6	5	3	0	1.50	0	1.917

BRYCE FLORIE
Age 25/R   **$2**

The best pitcher named "Bryce" ever to pitch in the majors. And one more of those promising young Padres relievers. Florie has particularly nasty stuff to go with serious heat. As soon as he figures out where home plate is, he'll be tough.

Year	Team	Lg.	G	IP	H	BB	SO	W	L	ERA	SV	Ratio
1994	San Diego	NL	9	9.1	8	3	8	0	0	0.96	0	1.179
1995	San Diego	NL	47	68.2	49	38	68	2	2	3.01	1	1.267
Post All-Star			22	31.0	26	15	32	0	2	3.77	1	1.323

TONY FOSSAS
Age 38/L   **$2**

The ultimate left-handed specialist—58 appearances but only 36⅔ innings pitched, facing lefty hitters almost exclusively and holding them to a .181 BA. Maybe Tony LaRussa and Dave Duncan will figure out a way to use him more.

Year	Team	Lg.	G	IP	H	BB	SO	W	L	ERA	SV	Ratio
1992	Boston	AL	60	29.2	31	14	19	1	2	2.43	2	1.517
1993	Boston	AL	71	40.0	38	15	39	1	1	5.18	0	1.325
1994	Boston	AL	44	34.0	35	15	31	2	0	4.76	1	1.471
1995	St. Louis	NL	58	36.2	28	10	40	3	0	1.47	0	1.036
Post All-Star			26	17.0	17	4	20	2	0	2.12	0	1.235

JOHN FRANCO
Age 35/L   **$29**

He was snappy when the Mets seemed to be drifting aimlessly into oblivion again, despondent and withdrawn when all the other veterans on the team were dealt away, and furious with himself—as always—every time he made a bad pitch. A real gang of fun to be around. But in the last seven weeks of the season, the old Franco spark came back. He emerged as team leader of one of baseball's up-and-coming clubs. He exuded boyish joy at playing—and winning. He was his old aggressive, competitive, energetic, funny, don't-mess-with-me-I'm-from-Brooklyn self. And not incidentally, he became again what he hadn't been for a while: one of the game's toughest closers. Look for a big year in what could be his New York farewell season.

Year	Team	Lg.	G	IP	H	BB	SO	W	L	ERA	SV	Ratio
1992	New York	NL	31	33.0	24	11	20	6	2	1.64	15	1.061
1993	New York	NL	35	36.1	46	19	29	4	3	5.20	10	1.789
1994	New York	NL	47	50.0	47	19	42	1	4	2.70	30	1.320
1995	New York	NL	48	51.2	48	17	41	5	3	2.44	29	1.258
Post All-Star			27	27.2	22	7	23	2	2	1.95	20	1.048

JOHN FRASCATORE
Age 26/R   **$2**

Hard thrower. Might start. Might relieve. Or you might take some young, milk-fed veal cutlets, pound until thin, and lightly coat with flour. Sauté chopped garlic in olive oil and cook veal until golden brown. Remove from heat to warm platter. Add lemon juice, capers, thinly cut portobello mushrooms, a splash of Balsamic vinegar, and salt and pepper to taste to sauté pan and cook until mushrooms are soft. Using slotted spoon, put mushroom mixture on top of cutlets. Garnish with Italian parsley, serve with penne (*al dente*, of course) lightly scented with pesto and steamed zucchini. Pour an amusing yet

Catchers
pp. 27-41

Corners
pp. 41-62

Infield
pp. 63-82

Outfield
pp. 83-113

DH
pp. 114-118

Starters
pp. 119-157

Relievers
pp. 157-193

unpretentious, glass of Valpolicella and—presto!—you have Veal Frascatore. Maybe Tony LaRussa and Dave Duncan will turn him into a pitcher.

Year	Team	Lg.	G	IP	H	BB	SO	W	L	ERA	SV	Ratio
1994	St. Louis	NL	1	3.1	7	2	2	0	1	16.20	0	2.700
1995	St. Louis	NL	14	32.2	39	16	21	1	1	4.41	0	1.684
Post All-Star			8	11.1	10	7	6	0	0	1.59	0	1.500

WILLIE FRASER   Age 31/R $1

A first-round draft pick in 1985. It's been a rocky road ever since.

Year	Team	Lg.	G	IP	H	BB	SO	W	L	ERA	SV	Ratio
1994	Florida	NL	9	12.1	20	6	7	2	0	5.84	0	2.108
1995	Montreal	NL	22	25.2	25	9	12	2	1	5.61	2	1.325
Post All-Star			22	25.2	25	9	12	2	1	5.61	2	1.325

JIM GOTT   Age 36/R $1

A lot of years, a lot of mileage, and his share of saves along the way. But time might have run out on a great competitor. No matter, he will always be remembered for one of the game's great moments. On September 6, 1995, he presented Ripken with the final-out ball from the first game of the Ripken streak. Gott had kept the ball because, it was also the final-out ball from his first major league win. "Somehow, I thought it was more important that Cal have it," said Gott. For the only time all night, Ripken wept, and tried to give the ball back to Gott. It doesn't get any better.

Year	Team	Lg.	G	IP	H	BB	SO	W	L	ERA	SV	Ratio
1992	Los Angeles	NL	68	88.0	72	41	75	3	3	2.45	6	1.284
1993	Los Angeles	NL	62	77.2	71	17	67	4	8	2.32	25	1.133
1994	Los Angeles	NL	37	36.1	46	20	29	5	3	5.94	2	1.817
1995	Pittsburgh	NL	25	31.1	38	12	19	2	4	6.03	3	1.596
Post All-Star			8	12.0	7	6	4	2	2	3.75	0	1.083

MARK GUTHRIE   Age 30/L $1

How do the Dodgers tell all those left-handers in their bullpen apart?

Year	Team	Lg.	G	IP	H	BB	SO	W	L	ERA	SV	Ratio
1992	Minnesota	AL	54	75.0	59	23	76	2	3	2.88	5	1.093
1993	Minnesota	AL	22	21.0	20	16	15	2	1	4.71	0	1.714
1994	Minnesota	AL	50	51.1	65	18	38	4	2	6.14	1	1.617
1995	Minnesota	AL	36	42.1	47	16	48	5	3	4.46	0	1.488
1995	Los Angeles	NL	24	19.2	19	9	19	0	2	3.66	0	1.424
Post All-Star			29	26.0	21	13	21	1	2	2.77	0	1.308

GREG HARRIS   Age 40/R $1

Aren't you glad that, after all these years of talking about it, he finally went ahead and pitched ambi in a game? And aren't you also glad that you're not Eddie Taubensee?

Year	Team	Lg.	G	IP	H	BB	SO	W	L	ERA	SV	Ratio
1992	Boston	AL	70	107.2	82	60	73	4	9	2.51	4	1.319
1993	Boston	AL	80	112.1	95	60	103	6	7	3.77	8	1.380
1994	Boston	AL	35	45.2	60	23	44	3	4	8.28	2	1.818
1994	New York	AL	3	5.0	4	3	4	0	1	5.40	0	1.400
1995	Montreal	NL	45	48.1	45	16	47	2	3	2.61	0	1.262
Post All-Star			28	27.2	21	13	27	1	3	2.28	0	1.229

DEAN HARTGRAVES
Age 29/L   **$2**

With a name like that he ought to be an academic leader of a small liberal arts college in the Midwest. With stuff like that—opposing batters hit just .227 against him, and he was just as tough against righties as he was against lefties—he ought to be exactly where he is, in a big-league bullpen. It took Hartgraves eight years of minor league ball before he finally hit the big time; now he looks like the lefty-of-choice in the Astros pen.

Year	Team	Lg.	G	IP	H	BB	SO	W	L	ERA	SV	Ratio
1995	Houston	NL	40	36.1	30	16	24	2	0	3.22	0	1.266
Post All-Star			26	22.2	20	11	16	2	0	3.57	0	1.368

BRYAN HARVEY
Age 32/R   **$5–25**

Pssst! Marlins people whisper that he's going to come all the way back from his arm problems and that he's once again going to be one of the game's stud closers. A risk? Absolutely. He's been "back" before, remember. A risk worth taking? Depends on the price, of course. If he pitches a lot this spring, he's sure to go near the high end of the range posted above. If he pitches only a little, well . . . as we said, it's a risk.

Year	Team	Lg.	G	IP	H	BB	SO	W	L	ERA	SV	Ratio
1992	California	AL	25	28.2	22	11	34	0	4	2.83	13	1.151
1993	Florida	NL	59	69.0	45	13	73	1	5	1.70	45	0.841
1994	Florida	NL	12	10.1	12	4	10	0	0	5.23	6	1.548
1995	Florida	NL	1	0.0	2	1	0	0	0	0.00	0	0.000
Post All-Star			0	0.0	0	0	0	0	0	0.00	64	0.000

TOM HENKE
Age 38/R   **$37**

An amazing pitcher who's never received sufficient credit for being one of the most automatic 35-save guys who's ever lived. Maybe Tony LaRussa and Dave Duncan can persuade him not to retire.

Year	Team	Lg.	G	IP	H	BB	SO	W	L	ERA	SV	Ratio
1992	Toronto	AL	57	55.2	40	22	46	3	2	2.26	34	1.114
1993	Texas	AL	66	74.1	55	27	79	5	5	2.91	40	1.103
1994	Texas	AL	37	38.0	33	12	39	3	6	3.79	15	1.184
1995	St. Louis	NL	52	54.1	42	18	48	1	1	1.82	36	1.104
Post All-Star			27	27.0	22	10	27	1	1	2.00	19	1.185

MIKE HENNEMAN
Age 34/R   **$22**

An Astros veteran, surveying the wreck of another late-season blown lead, was moved to observe, "Isn't it weird how every time Henny comes in to pitch lately, a team that hadn't hit all day, all of a sudden starts hitting?" Such coincidences always make you think the clock might be ticking for a pitcher of Henneman's age. But the Astros wouldn't have picked him up from the Tigers for the stretch drive if they had been completely happy with Todd Jones as a closer, so you have to figure—for now, at least—that Henneman is going to get the ball in save situations.

Year	Team	Lg.	G	IP	H	BB	SO	W	L	ERA	SV	Ratio
1992	Detroit	AL	60	77.1	75	20	58	2	6	3.96	24	1.228
1993	Detroit	AL	63	71.2	69	32	58	5	3	2.64	24	1.409
1994	Detroit	AL	30	34.2	43	17	27	1	3	5.19	8	1.731
1995	Detroit	AL	29	29.1	24	9	24	0	1	1.53	18	1.125
1995	Houston	NL	21	21.0	21	4	19	0	1	3.00	8	1.190
Post All-Star			25	26.0	25	5	23	0	1	2.42	9	1.154

Catchers
pp. 27-41

Corners
pp. 41-62

Infield
pp. 63-82

Outfield
pp. 83-113

DH
pp. 114-118

Starters
pp. 119-157

Relievers
pp. 157-193

DOUG HENRY   Age 32/R $6

One of the brightest spots in a Mets bullpen that started lousy and finished strong. Henry has been a closer before, and he showed last year that he could be one again. If Franco falters or has elbow problems, Henry will be the first guy Dallas Green turns to with the game on the line.

Year	Team	Lg.	G	IP	H	BB	SO	W	L	ERA	SV	Ratio
1992	Milwaukee	AL	68	65.0	64	24	52	1	4	4.02	29	1.354
1993	Milwaukee	AL	54	55.0	67	25	38	4	4	5.56	17	1.673
1994	Milwaukee	AL	25	31.1	32	23	20	2	3	4.60	0	1.755
1995	New York	NL	51	67.0	48	25	62	3	6	2.96	4	1.090
Post All-Star			28	40.0	26	17	37	2	3	2.25	2	1.075

WILSON HEREDIA   Age 24/R $1

As you can see below, he has a little control problem. Somebody let us know if he solves it.

Year	Team	Lg.	G	IP	H	BB	SO	W	L	ERA	SV	Ratio
1995	Texas	AL	6	12.0	9	15	6	0	1	3.75	0	2.000
Post All-Star			0	0.0	0	0	0	0	0	0.00	0	0.000

DUSTIN HERMANSON   Age 23/R $7

The Padres think he has a chance to be another Gossage, and so do a lot of Rotisserie owners, who made him a prime farm system pick. But he was so immature and so wild that they banished him to the minors after too many busted water coolers and too many walks. If he gets things under control—in every sense of the word—then he and Ron Villone could become a potent righty-lefty closer combo and permit the Pads to deal Trevor Hoffman.

Year	Team	Lg.	G	IP	H	BB	SO	W	L	ERA	SV	Ratio
1995	San Diego	NL	26	31.2	35	22	19	3	1	6.82	0	1.800
Post All-Star			14	19.2	20	11	14	0	0	5.95	0	1.576

JEREMY HERNANDEZ   Age 29/R $1

It would help to have access to his medical records. Barring that, pay close attention to his appearances this spring—the number of them more than the quality. A good pitcher, if he's able to pitch.

Year	Team	Lg.	G	IP	H	BB	SO	W	L	ERA	SV	Ratio
1992	San Diego	NL	26	36.2	39	11	25	1	4	4.17	1	1.364
1993	Cleveland	AL	49	77.1	75	27	44	6	5	3.14	8	1.319
1993	San Diego	NL	21	34.1	41	7	26	0	2	4.72	0	1.398
1994	Florida	NL	21	23.1	16	14	13	3	3	2.70	9	1.286
1995	Florida	NL	7	7.0	12	3	5	0	0	11.57	0	2.143
Post All-Star			2	1.1	2	0	1	0	0	20.25	0	1.500

XAVIER HERNANDEZ   Age 30/R $6

The X-Man is a horse—more Clydesdale than thoroughbred, but a horse nonetheless. You pitch 90 innings out of the bullpen for a good team, you're going to get a bunch of wins and even a few saves. He does. Nothing pretty about it, mind you, at least not last year. But Ray Knight will probably go to Hernandez about as often as Davey Johnson did, so once again you can count on a bunch of wins and even a few saves.

Year	Team	Lg.	G	IP	H	BB	SO	W	L	ERA	SV	Ratio
1992	Houston	NL	77	111.0	81	42	96	9	1	2.11	7	1.108
1993	Houston	NL	72	96.2	75	28	101	4	5	2.61	9	1.066
1994	New York	AL	31	40.0	48	21	37	4	4	5.85	6	1.725
1995	Cincinnati	NL	59	90.0	95	31	84	7	2	4.60	3	1.400
Post All-Star			26	42.2	52	11	34	2	1	5.06	0	1.477

BRYAN HICKERSON   Age 32/L $1

One of seven Rockies relievers who recorded saves last year. When that many guys get the call at the end of the game, it makes it a little tough to handicap a bullpen—except in the case of Hickerson, who definitely deserves to be No. 7 in your depth chart of Rockies relievers who recorded saves last year.

Year	Team	Lg.	G	IP	H	BB	SO	W	L	ERA	SV	Ratio
1992	San Francisco	NL	61	87.1	74	21	68	5	3	3.09	0	1.088
1993	San Francisco	NL	47	120.1	137	39	69	7	5	4.26	0	1.463
1994	San Francisco	NL	28	98.1	118	38	59	4	8	5.40	1	1.586
1995	Chicago	NL	38	31.2	36	15	28	2	3	6.82	1	1.611
1995	Colorado	NL	18	16.2	33	13	12	1	0	11.88	0	2.760
Post All-Star			25	20.2	38	16	15	1	0	10.89	0	2.613

TREVOR HOFFMAN   Age 28/R $33

Just scratching the surface of his considerable talent, but if Dustin Hermanson and Ron Villone pan out, the Padres will deal Hoffman to fill other holes. If so, they'll get a lot for him, because when he's on, he's one of the best. The problem, as evidenced by eight blown saves, is consistency.

Year	Team	Lg.	G	IP	H	BB	SO	W	L	ERA	SV	Ratio
1993	San Diego	NL	39	54.1	56	20	53	2	4	4.31	3	1.399
1993	Florida	NL	28	35.2	24	19	26	2	2	3.28	2	1.206
1994	San Diego	NL	47	56.0	39	20	68	4	4	2.57	20	1.054
1995	San Diego	NL	55	53.1	48	14	52	7	4	3.88	31	1.163
Post All-Star			29	27.2	22	6	27	3	2	3.58	20	1.012

DARREN HOLMES   Age 29/R $16

One of seven Rockies relievers who recorded saves last year, Holmes was so overused by Don Baylor that, by the end of the playoffs, he was shot-putting the ball toward home. But as with all Rockies relievers, the combination of grotesque starting pitching, that huge offense, and frequent rings of the bullpen phone gave him plenty of opportunities for wins and saves. If he ends up somewhere else, he could blossom into a major ace.

Year	Team	Lg.	G	IP	H	BB	SO	W	L	ERA	SV	Ratio
1992	Milwaukee	AL	41	42.1	35	11	31	4	4	2.55	6	1.087
1993	Colorado	NL	62	66.2	56	20	60	3	3	4.05	25	1.140
1994	Colorado	NL	29	28.1	35	24	33	0	3	6.35	3	2.082
1995	Colorado	NL	68	66.2	59	28	61	6	1	3.24	14	1.305
Post All-Star			37	32.2	32	15	32	1	1	3.86	8	1.439

Catchers
pp. 27-41

Corners
pp. 41-62

Infield
pp. 63-82

Outfield
pp. 83-113

DH
pp. 114-118

Starters
pp. 119-157

Relievers
pp. 157-193

JOHN HUDEK   Age 29/R $6

Houston won't know until late spring if he can come back. So you shouldn't make any decisions until they do.

Year	Team	Lg.	G	IP	H	BB	SO	W	L	ERA	SV	Ratio
1994	Houston	NL	42	39.1	24	18	39	0	2	2.97	16	1.068
1995	Houston	NL	19	20.0	19	5	29	2	2	5.40	7	1.200
Post All-Star			0	0.0	0	0	0	0	0	0.00	0	0.000

MIKE JACKSON   Age 31/R $8

He's always been one of our favorites. How the Giants could have let him go so easily is a mystery. But then again, how the people who make the Giants' pitching decisions keep their jobs is a mystery as well.

Year	Team	Lg.	G	IP	H	BB	SO	W	L	ERA	SV	Ratio
1992	San Francisco	NL	67	82.0	76	33	80	6	6	3.73	2	1.329
1993	San Francisco	NL	81	77.1	58	24	70	6	6	3.03	1	1.060
1994	San Francisco	NL	36	42.1	23	11	51	3	2	1.49	4	0.803
1995	Cincinnati	NL	40	49.0	38	19	41	6	1	2.39	2	1.163
Post All-Star			29	36.2	25	14	28	5	1	1.72	1	1.064

TODD JONES   Age 27/R $11

Has legit closer's stuff, but not the kind of control you like to see in the guy with the ball in his hands when a win is at stake—4.70 BB per 9 IP. Guess that's why Houston went out and got Henneman when it looked like the Astros had a shot at a playoff slot.

Year	Team	Lg.	G	IP	H	BB	SO	W	L	ERA	SV	Ratio
1993	Houston	NL	27	37.1	28	15	25	1	2	3.13	2	1.152
1994	Houston	NL	48	72.2	52	26	63	5	2	2.72	5	1.073
1995	Houston	NL	68	99.2	89	52	96	6	5	3.07	15	1.415
Post All-Star			35	45.2	50	33	45	1	4	4.53	9	1.818

DAVE LEIPER   Age 33/L $1

If the entire National League batted left-handed, Leiper would be a legitimate Cy Young candidate. Given its current configuration, he works to one or two batters per appearance, tops, so we don't see him getting many votes.

Year	Team	Lg.	G	IP	H	BB	SO	W	L	ERA	SV	Ratio
1994	Oakland	AL	26	18.2	13	6	14	0	0	1.93	1	1.018
1995	Oakland	AL	24	22.2	23	13	10	1	1	3.57	0	1.588
1995	Montreal	NL	26	22.0	16	6	12	0	2	2.86	2	1.000
Post All-Star			26	22.0	16	6	12	0	2	2.86	2	1.000

CURT LESKANIC   Age 27/R $12

One of seven Rockies relievers who recorded saves last season, Leskanic filled the hole left when Ruffin went down. If Ruffin comes back, something has to give, with either Holmes or Leskanic coming out with the short stick. Although he was never a closer in the minors or in brief previous stints in the majors, and the Rockies had him pegged for long relief, Leskanic has better control than Holmes, was harder to hit last year, and is two years younger. If it were our ball, we'd call in Curt and let Darren walk.

Year	Team	Lg.	G	IP	H	BB	SO	W	L	ERA	SV	Ratio
1993	Colorado	NL	18	57.0	59	27	30	1	5	5.37	0	1.509
1994	Colorado	NL	8	22.1	27	10	17	1	1	5.64	0	1.657
1995	Colorado	NL	76	98.0	83	33	107	6	3	3.40	10	1.184
Post All-Star			41	45.2	37	15	50	4	2	3.55	6	1.139

RICHIE LEWIS   Age 30/R $1

No thanks.

Year	Team	Lg.	G	IP	H	BB	SO	W	L	ERA	SV	Ratio
1992	Baltimore	AL	2	6.2	13	7	4	1	1	10.80	0	3.000
1993	Florida	NL	57	77.1	68	43	65	6	3	3.26	0	1.435
1994	Florida	NL	45	54.0	62	38	45	1	4	5.67	0	1.852
1995	Florida	NL	21	36.0	30	15	32	0	1	3.75	0	1.250
Post All-Star			9	18.1	16	10	14	0	0	2.95	0	1.418

PEDRO A. MARTINEZ   Age 27/L $2

Here's a hint. This is not the right-handed Pedro Martinez who hits a bunch
of people and throws bullets. This is the left-handed Pedro Martinez who
pitched lights out for San Diego in 1994 and couldn't get anybody out on
those infrequent occasions when he found the plate for Houston in 1995.

Year	Team	Lg.	G	IP	H	BB	SO	W	L	ERA	SV	Ratio
1993	San Diego	NL	32	37.0	23	13	32	3	1	2.43	0	0.973
1994	San Diego	NL	48	68.1	52	49	52	3	2	2.90	3	1.478
1995	Houston	NL	25	20.2	29	16	17	0	0	7.40	0	2.177
Post All-Star			1	1.0	0	1	0	0	0	0.00	0	1.000

TIM MAUSER   Age 29/R $1

Why are you reading about him?

Year	Team	Lg.	G	IP	H	BB	SO	W	L	ERA	SV	Ratio
1993	Philadelphia	NL	8	16.1	15	7	14	0	0	4.96	0	1.347
1993	San Diego	NL	28	37.2	36	17	32	0	1	3.58	0	1.407
1994	San Diego	NL	35	49.0	50	19	32	2	4	3.49	2	1.408
1995	San Diego	NL	5	5.2	4	9	9	0	1	9.53	0	2.294
Post All-Star			0	0.0	0	0	0	0	0	0.00	0	0.000

CHUCK McELROY   Age 28/L $3

What do you do with a good pitcher who has a bad year? Grab him cheap.

Year	Team	Lg.	G	IP	H	BB	SO	W	L	ERA	SV	Ratio
1992	Chicago	NL	72	83.2	73	51	83	4	7	3.55	6	1.482
1993	Chicago	NL	49	47.1	51	25	31	2	2	4.56	0	1.606
1994	Cincinnati	NL	52	57.2	52	15	38	1	2	2.34	5	1.162
1995	Cincinnati	NL	44	40.1	46	15	27	3	4	6.02	0	1.512
Post All-Star			27	26.1	32	10	18	2	2	6.49	0	1.595

Catchers
pp. 27–41

Corners
pp. 41–62

Infield
pp. 63–82

Outfield
pp. 83–113

DH
pp. 114–118

Starters
pp. 119–157

Relievers
pp. 157–193

GREG McMICHAEL

Age 29/R $6

Rotisserie owners who held onto him or bought him at stopper prices are still grinding their teeth in anger, but if you got him on the cheap for the setup work he has adapted to so well, you must be very happy. So are the Braves.

Year	Team	Lg.	G	IP	H	BB	SO	W	L	ERA	SV	Ratio
1993	Atlanta	NL	74	91.2	68	29	89	2	3	2.06	19	1.058
1994	Atlanta	NL	51	58.2	66	19	47	4	6	3.84	21	1.449
1995	Atlanta	NL	67	80.2	64	32	74	7	2	2.79	2	1.190
Post All-Star			36	39.0	32	20	36	2	2	2.31	1	1.333

CRAIG McMURTRY

Age 36/R $1

He needed the money because of a daughter's illnesss, so he did what he felt like he had to do and took the replacement player cash. Whatever your feelings might be on the general issue, you can understand what drove him to his own personal decision in the spring. But what was so bad about the whole thing late in the summer when he was called up by Houston was how it was handled by the Astros front office. The erstwhile owner, who is a neighbor of McMurtry's, wanted him recalled to stick it to the players. The baseball people in the front office went along with the idea, spicing things up with comments like "We won't have our inmates run the asylum" that threw gas on the fire. As a result, the players dug in their heels, people on both sides started yelling, and morale plummeted. The Astros lost 11 of the first 13 games after McMurtry was recalled, and that streak was the reason they didn't reach the playoffs. Was it McMurtry's fault? Of course not. But don't look for McMurtry on any rosters this year. After all, he didn't belong on one last year.

Year	Team	Lg.	G	IP	H	BB	SO	W	L	ERA	SV	Ratio
1995	Houston	NL	11	10.1	15	9	4	0	1	7.84	0	2.323
Post All-Star			11	10.1	15	9	4	0	1	7.84	0	2.323

DANNY MICELI

Age 25/R $14

The saves total says he's the Pirates closer. A lot of his other numbers—the .359 that lefties hit off him, the 4⅓ walks per nine innings, the 11 of 24 inherited runners who scored, the 6 blown saves in 27 chances—say that he's not, or at least not for long.

Year	Team	Lg.	G	IP	H	BB	SO	W	L	ERA	SV	Ratio
1993	Pittsburgh	NL	9	5.1	6	3	4	0	0	5.06	0	1.688
1994	Pittsburgh	NL	28	27.1	28	11	27	2	1	5.93	2	1.427
1995	Pittsburgh	NL	58	58.0	61	28	56	4	4	4.66	21	1.534
Post All-Star			31	32.0	38	22	30	3	1	5.06	11	1.875

BLAS MINOR

Age 30/R $1

Minor blahs.

Year	Team	Lg.	G	IP	H	BB	SO	W	L	ERA	SV	Ratio
1992	Pittsburgh	NL	1	2.0	3	0	0	0	0	4.50	0	1.500
1993	Pittsburgh	NL	65	94.1	94	26	84	8	6	4.10	2	1.272
1994	Pittsburgh	NL	17	19.0	27	9	17	0	1	8.05	1	1.895
1995	New York	NL	35	46.2	44	13	43	4	2	3.66	1	1.221
Post All-Star			12	19.1	17	4	16	1	0	2.79	1	1.086

MIKE MUNOZ   Age 30/L $1

One of seven Colorado relievers who earned saves last year, which should encourage every left-hander in America between the ages 16 and 46 to pull on their cleats, oil their gloves, and head straight to the Rockies' Spring Training camp at Hi Corbett Field in Tucson. How can you miss?

Year	Team	Lg.	G	IP	H	BB	SO	W	L	ERA	SV	Ratio
1992	Detroit	AL	65	48.0	44	25	23	1	2	3.00	2	1.438
1993	Detroit	AL	8	3.0	4	6	1	0	1	6.00	0	3.333
1993	Colorado	NL	21	18.0	21	9	16	2	1	4.50	0	1.667
1994	Colorado	NL	57	45.2	37	31	32	4	2	3.74	1	1.489
1995	Colorado	NL	64	43.2	54	27	37	2	4	7.42	2	1.855
Post All-Star			26	20.1	37	9	16	1	2	9.74	0	2.262

RANDY MYERS   Age 33/L $35

Saves games. Smashes cinder blocks with his bare hands. Defends honor of pitcher's mound from attack by deranged fans. We'd be proud to be in a foxhole with this guy. A little scared, but proud.

Year	Team	Lg.	G	IP	H	BB	SO	W	L	ERA	SV	Ratio
1992	San Diego	NL	66	79.2	84	34	66	3	6	4.29	38	1.481
1993	Chicago	NL	73	75.1	65	26	86	2	4	3.11	53	1.208
1994	Chicago	NL	38	40.1	40	16	32	1	5	3.79	21	1.388
1995	Chicago	NL	57	55.2	49	28	59	1	2	3.88	38	1.383
Post All-Star			28	25.2	27	15	26	1	1	5.61	17	1.636

ROBB NEN   Age 26/R $32

After an awful start, he got his mechanics straightened out and over the last two months was a flat-out automatic save machine. Expect big things from him this year. But expect things to get a little complicated if Bryan Harvey does come back.

Year	Team	Lg.	G	IP	H	BB	SO	W	L	ERA	SV	Ratio
1993	Texas	AL	9	22.2	28	26	12	1	1	6.35	0	2.382
1993	Florida	NL	15	33.1	35	20	27	1	0	7.02	0	1.650
1994	Florida	NL	44	58.0	46	17	60	5	5	2.95	15	1.086
1995	Florida	NL	62	65.2	62	23	68	0	7	3.29	23	1.294
Post All-Star			34	34.0	29	11	41	0	2	2.38	19	1.176

ANTONIO OSUNA   Age 22/R $6

Tommy Lasorda had him throw 78 pitches on opening night last year after an abbreviated Spring Training. Later on, Mr. Not-So-Slim-Fast would sit Osuna for 10 days at a stretch, destroying his confidence to the degree that he had to be sent to the minors to restore it. Look—the guy throws 95 mph and just needed to have his rough edges smoothed, but under Lasorda's inimical touch he had a year of his career wasted instead. For this and other such triumphs, Lasorda gets to come back for another season. But so will Osuna, who certainly has the talent to persevere. Let's just hope he has the emotional makeup.

Year	Team	Lg.	G	IP	H	BB	SO	W	L	ERA	SV	Ratio
1995	Los Angeles	NL	39	44.2	39	20	46	2	4	4.43	0	1.321
Post All-Star			28	30.1	21	9	37	1	2	2.67	0	0.989

Catchers
pp. 27-41

Corners
pp. 41-62

Infield
pp. 63-82

Outfield
pp. 83-113

DH
pp. 114-118

Starters
pp. 119-157

Relievers
pp. 157-193

LANCE PAINTER
Age 28/L   **$1**

One of seven Rockies relievers who recorded saves last year, Painter will forevermore be the answer to the trivia question "Who is the only player to make the last out of Game 1 of a playoff series and then throw the first pitch of Game 2 of the same playoff series?" (Somehow, we don't think Don Baylor will put this on his resumé.) Even though lefties are a notoriously wild breed, Painter was the control freak of the Rockies bullpen (1.99 BB per 9 IP). Good thing, because opposing hitters had their way with him (.296 BA, 9 HR).

Year	Team	Lg.	G	IP	H	BB	SO	W	L	ERA	SV	Ratio
1993	Colorado	NL	10	39.0	52	9	16	2	2	6.00	0	1.564
1994	Colorado	NL	15	73.2	91	26	41	4	6	6.11	0	1.588
1995	Colorado	NL	33	45.1	55	10	36	3	0	4.37	1	1.434
Post All-Star			28	39.1	44	6	32	3	0	2.97	1	1.271

JEFF PARRETT
Age 34/R   **$1**

Durable.

Year	Team	Lg.	G	IP	H	BB	SO	W	L	ERA	SV	Ratio
1992	Oakland	AL	66	98.1	81	42	78	9	1	3.02	0	1.251
1993	Colorado	NL	40	73.2	78	45	66	3	3	5.38	1	1.670
1995	St. Louis	NL	59	76.2	71	28	71	4	7	3.64	0	1.291
Post All-Star			29	40.1	32	13	38	2	5	2.45	0	1.116

ALEJANDRO PENA
Age 36/R   **$3**

Among Braves pitchers only Wohlers had a better K/9 IP ratio. In fact, among pitchers worked 25 innings or more, Peña was fourth in the league (after Wohlers and John Hudek) in K/9 IP. Not bad for a guy who didn't have a job when the season began—and had half a dozen (or so it seemed) before landing with the Braves for the stretch drive. Not at all clear where he fits in the greater scheme of things in Atlanta, but one thing is certain—he can still bring it.

Year	Team	Lg.	G	IP	H	BB	SO	W	L	ERA	SV	Ratio
1992	Atlanta	NL	41	42.0	40	13	34	1	6	4.07	15	1.262
1994	Pittsburgh	NL	22	28.2	22	10	27	3	2	5.02	7	1.116
1995	Boston	AL	17	24.1	33	12	25	1	1	7.40	0	1.849
1995	Florida	NL	13	18.0	11	3	21	2	0	1.50	0	0.778
1995	Atlanta	NL	14	13.0	11	4	18	0	0	4.15	0	1.154
Post All-Star			27	31.0	22	7	39	2	0	2.61	0	0.935

MIKE PEREZ
Age 31/R   **$4**

Has never become the ace closer we thought he would be, but still a solid setup man who will pick up a few saves along the way.

Year	Team	Lg.	G	IP	H	BB	SO	W	L	ERA	SV	Ratio
1992	St. Louis	NL	77	93.0	70	32	46	9	3	1.84	0	1.097
1993	St. Louis	NL	65	72.2	65	20	58	7	2	2.48	7	1.170
1994	St. Louis	NL	36	31.0	52	10	20	2	3	8.71	12	2.000
1995	Chicago	NL	68	71.1	72	27	49	2	6	3.66	2	1.388
Post All-Star			34	35.2	36	16	28	1	2	4.04	0	1.458

DAN PLESAC
Age 34/L **$4**

The quintessential crafty lefty. Once a big-time closer for the small-market Brewers, he is now a setup man/specialist-against-lefties/occasional closer for Jim Leyland and Ray Miller, which means he'll be used well and often as long as he continues to produce.

Year	Team	Lg.	G	IP	H	BB	SO	W	L	ERA	SV	Ratio
1992	Milwaukee	AL	44	79.0	64	35	54	5	4	2.96	1	1.253
1993	Chicago	NL	57	62.2	74	21	47	2	1	4.74	0	1.516
1994	Chicago	NL	54	54.2	61	13	53	2	3	4.61	1	1.354
1995	Pittsburgh	NL	58	60.1	53	27	57	4	4	3.58	3	1.326
Post All-Star			30	30.0	31	12	30	1	4	5.10	1	1.433

STEVE REED
Age 30/R **$5**

One of seven Rockies relievers who recorded saves last year, but Reed is not just another face in the crowd. He was the toughest pitcher on the entire staff to hit (.206 BA against him). He doesn't give up a lot of walks (2.25 per 9 innings). He pitches a lot of innings (second in the bullpen to Leskanic). He strands inherited runners (39 of 52). And he's good for a few wins and a few saves. A valuable pitcher.

Year	Team	Lg.	G	IP	H	BB	SO	W	L	ERA	SV	Ratio
1992	San Francisco	NL	18	15.2	13	3	11	1	0	2.30	0	1.021
1993	Colorado	NL	64	84.1	80	30	51	9	5	4.48	3	1.304
1994	Colorado	NL	61	64.0	79	26	51	3	2	3.94	3	1.641
1995	Colorado	NL	71	84.0	61	21	79	5	2	2.14	3	0.976
Post All-Star			39	49.0	34	13	39	4	1	2.02	0	0.959

MEL ROJAS
Age 29/R **$27**

Has the stuff to be a stud. Has the head to be a nightmare. Last season's signature Rojas moment came when he blew a save—which he did 25% of the time—and immediately disappeared into the trainer's room, whereupon Expos GM Kevin Malone asked sarcastically in front of a crowd of reporters, "Where's our closer, hiding somewhere to think up another excuse?" Malone is now gone from Montreal. So might Rojas be by the time you read this. Felipe Alou is definitely not amused by Rojas's approach to the game.

Year	Team	Lg.	G	IP	H	BB	SO	W	L	ERA	SV	Ratio
1992	Montreal	NL	68	100.2	71	34	70	7	1	1.43	10	1.043
1993	Montreal	NL	66	88.1	80	30	48	5	8	2.95	10	1.245
1994	Montreal	NL	58	84.0	71	21	84	3	2	3.32	16	1.095
1995	Montreal	NL	59	67.2	69	29	61	1	4	4.12	30	1.448
Post All-Star			30	33.1	38	13	30	0	1	4.32	16	1.530

Catchers
pp. 27–41

Corners
pp. 41–62

Infield
pp. 63–82

Outfield
pp. 83–113

DH
pp. 114–118

Starters
pp. 119–157

Relievers
pp. 157–193

JOHN ROPER   Age 24/R $1

Another brilliant Giants pitching move: they deal away a good starter (Mark
Portugal), a solid swingman (Dave Burba), and one of the top three defensive
center fielders in baseball (Darren Lewis) to Cincinnati for a 28-year-old
question mark with great stuff but no control (Scott Service), a football player
(Deion Sanders), and a Roper, who might never pitch again because of a
torn rotator cuff.

Year	Team	Lg.	G	IP	H	BB	SO	W	L	ERA	SV	Ratio
1993	Cincinnati	NL	16	80.0	92	36	54	2	5	5.63	0	1.600
1994	Cincinnati	NL	16	92.0	90	30	51	6	2	4.50	0	1.304
1995	Cincinnati	NL	2	7.0	13	4	6	0	0	10.29	0	2.429
1995	San Francisco	NL	1	1.0	2	2	0	0	0	27.00	0	4.000
Post All-Star			1	1.0	2	2	0	0	0	27.00	0	4.000

KIRK RUETER   Age 25/L $7

Took a little time in the minors to get straightened out, but now it appears
that 1994 was just a bump in the road, and that Rueter is going to deliver
on the promise he showed in 1993.

Year	Team	Lg.	G	IP	H	BB	SO	W	L	ERA	SV	Ratio
1993	Montreal	NL	14	85.2	85	18	31	8	0	2.73	0	1.202
1994	Montreal	NL	20	92.1	106	23	50	7	3	5.17	0	1.397
1995	Montreal	NL	9	47.1	38	9	28	5	3	3.23	0	0.993
Post All-Star			7	39.2	26	6	23	5	1	1.82	0	0.807

BRUCE RUFFIN   Age 32/L $12

One of seven Rockies relievers who recorded saves last year, Ruffin spent
much of the summer on the DL. If healthy, he forms half of a strong lefty-
righty closer platoon. But you always have to run up the caution flag when
you hear the word "if."

Year	Team	Lg.	G	IP	H	BB	SO	W	L	ERA	SV	Ratio
1992	Milwaukee	AL	25	58.0	66	41	45	1	6	6.67	0	1.845
1993	Colorado	NL	59	139.2	145	69	126	6	5	3.87	2	1.532
1994	Colorado	NL	56	55.2	55	30	65	4	5	4.04	16	1.527
1995	Colorado	NL	37	34.0	26	19	23	0	1	2.12	11	1.324
Post All-Star			22	18.0	16	11	10	0	1	3.00	3	1.500

JOHNNY RUFFIN   Age 24/R $2

Hellacious stuff, legal problems, arm trouble—a volatile mix.

Year	Team	Lg.	G	IP	H	BB	SO	W	L	ERA	SV	Ratio
1993	Cincinnati	NL	21	37.2	36	11	30	2	1	3.58	2	1.248
1994	Cincinnati	NL	51	70.0	57	27	44	7	2	3.09	1	1.200
1995	Cincinnati	NL	10	13.1	4	11	11	0	0	1.35	0	1.125
Post All-Star			4	7.1	0	3	7	0	0	0.00	0	0.409

TIM SCOTT

Age 29/R   **$5**

A consistent, tenacious, unappreciated performer.

Year	Team	Lg.	G	IP	H	BB	SO	W	L	ERA	SV	Ratio
1992	San Diego	NL	34	37.2	39	21	30	4	1	5.26	0	1.593
1993	Montreal	NL	32	34.0	31	19	35	5	2	3.71	1	1.471
1993	San Diego	NL	24	37.2	38	15	30	2	0	2.39	0	1.407
1994	Montreal	NL	40	53.1	51	18	37	5	2	2.70	1	1.294
1995	Montreal	NL	62	63.1	52	23	57	2	0	3.98	2	1.184
Post All-Star			31	32.0	29	10	27	2	0	3.09	0	1.219

RUDY SEANEZ

Age 27/R   **$1**

The John Littlefield of 1995. In a year when a lot of leagues held their auction drafts a couple of weeks into the season, Seanez got three saves in the first 10 games and fetched a handsome price all across the country. The rest of his year was pretty ugly.

Year	Team	Lg.	G	IP	H	BB	SO	W	L	ERA	SV	Ratio
1993	San Diego	NL	3	3.1	8	2	1	0	0	13.50	0	3.000
1994	Los Angeles	NL	17	23.2	24	9	18	1	1	2.66	0	1.394
1995	Los Angeles	NL	37	34.2	39	18	29	1	3	6.75	3	1.644
Post All-Star			11	12.2	15	12	10	0	1	9.95	0	2.132

HEATHCLIFF SLOCUMB

Age 29/R   **$12**

Fregosi and Podres nurtured Slocumb, gave him the ball, and reaped a rich harvest of saves through two thirds of the season. But then came control problems, blown saves, and a sharp decline in effectiveness. Most Phillies watchers believe that Bottalico will get the call from the git-go and that Slocumb will be relegated to setup work.

Year	Team	Lg.	G	IP	H	BB	SO	W	L	ERA	SV	Ratio
1992	Chicago	NL	30	36.0	52	21	27	0	3	6.50	1	2.028
1993	Cleveland	AL	20	27.1	28	16	18	3	1	4.28	0	1.610
1993	Chicago	NL	10	10.2	7	4	4	1	0	3.38	0	1.031
1994	Philadelphia	NL	52	72.1	75	28	58	5	1	2.86	0	1.424
1995	Philadelphia	NL	61	65.1	64	35	63	5	6	2.89	32	1.515
Post All-Star			29	31.2	40	17	34	4	6	3.69	12	1.800

UGUETH URBINA

Age 22/R   **$3**

A great name. A great arm. Possibly a great closer someday.

Year	Team	Lg.	G	IP	H	BB	SO	W	L	ERA	SV	Ratio
1995	Montreal	NL	7	23.1	26	14	15	2	2	6.17	0	1.714
Post All-Star			4	20.1	22	13	13	1	2	6.20	0	1.721

DAVE VERES

Age 29/R   **$9**

Without fanfare, he became one of the league's most consistent, most durable, most productive middle relievers. Guys like this can be more valuable than mediocre rotation starters, mainly because they more than make up in good ratio and ERA what they might lack in wins.

Year	Team	Lg.	G	IP	H	BB	SO	W	L	ERA	SV	Ratio
1994	Houston	NL	32	41.0	39	7	28	3	3	2.41	1	1.122
1995	Houston	NL	72	103.1	89	30	94	5	1	2.26	1	1.152
Post All-Star			37	51.2	49	15	51	2	0	2.79	1	1.239

Catchers
pp. 27–41

Corners
pp. 41–62

Infield
pp. 63–82

Outfield
pp. 83–113

DH
pp. 114–118

Starters
pp. 119–157

Relievers
pp. 157–193

RON VILLONE
Age 26/L $6

Another Randy Myers waiting to happen: mid-90s speed, hard slider, a lot of movement. Just where he fits among all those good young arms in the San Diego bullpen is a question right now, but he'll never be cheaper than this year.

Year	Team	Lg.	G	IP	H	BB	SO	W	L	ERA	SV	Ratio
1995	Seattle	AL	19	19.1	20	23	26	0	2	7.91	0	2.224
1995	San Diego	NL	19	25.2	24	11	37	2	1	4.21	1	1.364
Post All-Star			19	25.2	24	11	37	2	1	4.21	1	1.364

TURK WENDELL
Age 28/R $1

The eccentric behavior would be a lot more amusing if he were a lot better pitcher.

Year	Team	Lg.	G	IP	H	BB	SO	W	L	ERA	SV	Ratio
1993	Chicago	NL	7	22.2	24	8	15	1	2	4.37	0	1.412
1994	Chicago	NL	6	14.1	22	10	9	0	1	11.93	0	2.233
1995	Chicago	NL	43	60.1	71	24	50	3	1	4.92	0	1.575
Post All-Star			28	39.2	45	18	41	1	1	5.22	0	1.588

RICK WHITE
Age 27/R $1

Pirates aren't sure whether he's best suited to start or relieve. Our guess is neither.

Year	Team	Lg.	G	IP	H	BB	SO	W	L	ERA	SV	Ratio
1994	Pittsburgh	NL	43	75.1	79	17	38	4	5	3.82	6	1.274
1995	Pittsburgh	NL	15	55.0	66	18	29	2	3	4.75	0	1.527
Post All-Star			6	31.1	40	8	18	2	2	5.46	0	1.532

MIKE WILLIAMS
Age 27/R $3

Stayed healthy, which moved him up several notches on the Phillies staff even without taking into consideration his creditable work on the mound.

Year	Team	Lg.	G	IP	H	BB	SO	W	L	ERA	SV	Ratio
1992	Philadelphia	NL	5	28.2	29	7	5	1	1	5.34	0	1.256
1993	Philadelphia	NL	17	51.0	50	22	33	1	3	5.29	0	1.412
1994	Philadelphia	NL	12	50.1	61	20	29	2	4	5.01	0	1.609
1995	Philadelphia	NL	33	87.2	78	29	57	3	3	3.29	0	1.221
Post All-Star			19	53.2	45	15	33	3	1	2.52	0	1.118

MARK WOHLERS
Age 26/R $37

His fragile ego finally stabilized. Leo Mazzone smoothed out his delivery. His confidence grew and the ball was clocked regularly at 100 mph. One of the high points of a great season was Wohlers and Jose Mesa matching heat in Game 3 of the World Series. Until further notice, Wohlers is The Man in the NL.

Year	Team	Lg.	G	IP	H	BB	SO	W	L	ERA	SV	Ratio
1992	Atlanta	NL	32	35.1	28	14	17	1	2	2.55	4	1.189
1993	Atlanta	NL	46	48.0	37	22	45	6	2	4.50	0	1.229
1994	Atlanta	NL	51	51.0	51	33	58	7	2	4.59	1	1.647
1995	Atlanta	NL	65	64.2	51	24	90	7	3	2.09	25	1.160
Post All-Star			34	35.1	32	8	48	4	1	1.53	18	1.132

TODD WORRELL   Age 36/R $31

Lasorda hated him, for reasons that only Tommy can tell you, and usually that's the kiss of death for a Dodgers pitcher. But for an awfully long time last year, there was no more perfect a closer in baseball. There is still a lot of gas left in this tank.

Year	Team	Lg.	G	IP	H	BB	SO	W	L	ERA	SV	Ratio
1992	St. Louis	NL	67	64.0	45	25	64	5	3	2.11	3	1.094
1993	Los Angeles	NL	35	38.2	46	11	31	1	1	6.05	5	1.474
1994	Los Angeles	NL	38	42.0	37	12	44	6	5	4.29	11	1.167
1995	Los Angeles	NL	59	62.1	50	19	61	4	1	2.02	32	1.107
Post All-Star			32	34.0	38	14	35	2	1	3.44	20	1.529

ANTHONY YOUNG   Age 30/R $2

Useful.

Year	Team	Lg.	G	IP	H	BB	SO	W	L	ERA	SV	Ratio
1992	New York	NL	52	121.0	134	31	64	2	14	4.17	15	1.364
1993	New York	NL	39	100.1	103	42	62	1	16	3.77	3	1.445
1994	Chicago	NL	20	114.2	103	46	65	4	6	3.92	0	1.299
1995	Chaicago	NL	32	41.1	47	14	15	3	4	3.70	2	1.476
Post All-Star			28	33.0	38	9	10	3	2	3.00	1	1.424

AMERICAN LEAGUE

RICK AGUILERA   Age 34/R $34

Still one of the best. If he stays in Boston or signs with another contender, pay up. If he follows his heart and takes a pay cut back to the Twins, look elsewhere.

Year	Team	Lg.	G	IP	H	BB	SO	W	L	ERA	SV	Ratio
1992	Minnesota	AL	64	66.2	60	17	52	2	6	2.84	41	1.155
1993	Minnesota	AL	65	72.1	60	14	59	4	3	3.11	34	1.023
1994	Minnesota	AL	44	44.2	57	10	46	1	4	3.63	23	1.500
1995	Minnesota	AL	22	25.0	20	6	29	1	1	2.52	12	1.040
1995	Boston	AL	30	30.1	26	7	23	2	2	2.67	20	1.088
Post All-Star			29	29.1	25	7	22	2	2	2.76	19	1.091

PAUL ASSENMACHER   Age 35/L $6

Being a Situational Lefty has got to be one of the world's great jobs, particularly if you're as good at it as Assenmacher.

Year	Team	Lg.	G	IP	H	BB	SO	W	L	ERA	SV	Ratio
1992	Chicago	NL	70	68.0	72	26	67	4	4	4.10	8	1.441
1993	New York	AL	26	17.1	10	9	11	2	2	3.12	0	1.096
1993	Chicago	NL	46	38.2	44	13	34	2	1	3.49	0	1.474
1994	Chicago	AL	44	33.0	26	13	29	1	2	3.55	1	1.182
1995	Cleveland	AL	47	38.1	32	12	40	6	2	2.82	0	1.148
Post All-Star			28	24.2	24	7	26	4	0	3.28	0	1.257

Catchers
pp. 27–41

Corners
pp. 41–62

Infield
pp. 63–82

Outfield
pp. 83–113

DH
pp. 114–118

Starters
pp. 119–157

Relievers
pp. 157–193

BOBBY AYALA   Age 26/R $17

He lost his closing job to Charlton but he should still figure prominently in the Mariner bullpen. Piniella likes tough, competitive ballplayers and if Ayala learned anything by playing with Charlton he could come back as a closer soon. As a Red, Charlton had no trouble sharing.

Year	Team	Lg.	G	IP	H	BB	SO	W	L	ERA	SV	Ratio
1992	Cincinnati	NL	5	29.0	33	13	23	2	1	4.34	0	1.586
1993	Cincinnati	NL	43	98.0	106	45	65	7	10	5.60	3	1.541
1994	Seattle	AL	46	56.2	42	26	76	4	3	2.86	18	1.200
1995	Seattle	AL	63	71.0	73	30	77	6	5	4.44	19	1.451
Post All-Star			32	37.0	43	21	45	4	3	5.59	6	1.730

STAN BELINDA   Age 29/R $18

A great, unheralded comeback. Very few relievers had better years. And these numbers guarantee a return engagement in Boston.

Year	Team	Lg.	G	IP	H	BB	SO	W	L	ERA	SV	Ratio
1992	Pittsburgh	NL	59	71.1	58	29	57	6	4	3.15	18	1.220
1993	Kansas City	AL	23	27.1	30	6	25	1	1	4.28	0	1.317
1993	Pittsburgh	NL	40	42.1	35	11	30	3	1	3.61	19	1.087
1994	Kansas City	AL	37	49.0	47	24	37	2	2	5.14	1	1.449
1995	Boston	AL	63	69.2	51	28	57	8	1	3.10	10	1.134
Post All-Star			32	32.0	17	15	25	1	0	2.53	4	1.000

ARMANDO BENITEZ   Age 23/R $3

He's a fine minor league reliever. He hasn't made the jump to the majors, where our game is played. A year with Phil Regan should have produced something better than this. Move on.

Year	Team	Lg.	G	IP	H	BB	SO	W	L	ERA	SV	Ratio
1994	Baltimore	AL	3	10.0	8	4	14	0	0	0.90	0	1.200
1995	Baltimore	AL	44	47.2	37	37	56	1	5	5.66	2	1.552
Post All-Star			16	19.0	16	11	23	0	2	6.63	1	1.421

JOE BOEVER   Age 35/R $3

We asked around. Nobody knows why Boever is still playing. And this sport wants to expand?

Year	Team	Lg.	G	IP	H	BB	SO	W	L	ERA	SV	Ratio
1992	Houston	NL	81	111.1	103	45	67	3	6	2.51	2	1.329
1993	Detroit	AL	19	23.0	14	11	14	2	1	2.74	3	1.087
1993	Oakland	AL	42	79.1	87	33	49	4	2	3.86	0	1.513
1994	Detroit	AL	46	81.1	80	37	49	9	2	3.98	3	1.439
1995	Detroit	AL	60	98.2	128	44	71	5	7	6.39	3	1.743
Post All-Star			30	51.1	80	28	33	1	3	8.24	0	2.104

MARK BRANDENBURG   Age 25/R $5

Good control in his major league stint last year. Worth a gamble in a wide-open Texas bullpen.

Year	Team	Lg.	G	IP	H	BB	SO	W	L	ERA	SV	Ratio
1995	Texas	AL	11	27.1	36	7	21	0	1	5.93	0	1.573
Post All-Star			11	27.1	36	7	21	0	1	5.93	0	1.573

BILLY BREWER
Age 27/L   **$9**

Forget last year. Brewer will be a leading vulture this year and could even grab some serious saves if Montgomery is gone.

Year	Team	Lg.	G	IP	H	BB	SO	W	L	ERA	SV	Ratio
1993	Kansas City	AL	46	39.0	31	20	28	2	2	3.46	0	1.308
1994	Kansas City	AL	50	38.2	28	16	25	4	1	2.56	3	1.138
1995	Kansas City	AL	48	45.1	54	20	31	2	4	5.56	0	1.632
Post All-Star			18	22.2	28	11	10	1	2	6.35	0	1.721

JOHN BRISCOE
Age 28/R   **$2**

Hurt most of last year but is worth looking at due to the LaRussa/Duncan factor.

Year	Team	Lg.	G	IP	H	BB	SO	W	L	ERA	SV	Ratio
1992	Oakland	AL	2	7.0	12	9	4	0	1	6.43	0	3.000
1993	Oakland	AL	17	24.2	26	26	24	1	0	8.03	0	2.108
1994	Oakland	AL	37	49.1	31	39	45	4	2	4.01	1	1.419
1995	Oakland	AL	16	18.1	25	21	19	0	1	8.35	0	2.509
Post All-Star			16	18.1	25	21	19	0	1	8.35	0	2.509

MIKE BUTCHER
Age 29/R   **$7**

If the Angels bounce back from last year's collapse, Butcher should continue to get some nice wins in middle relief.

Year	Team	Lg.	G	IP	H	BB	SO	W	L	ERA	SV	Ratio
1992	California	AL	19	27.2	29	13	24	2	2	3.25	0	1.518
1993	California	AL	23	28.1	21	15	24	1	0	2.86	8	1.271
1994	California	AL	33	29.2	31	23	19	2	1	6.67	1	1.820
1995	California	AL	40	51.1	49	31	29	6	1	4.73	0	1.558
Post All-Star			15	26.0	25	14	16	1	0	3.12	0	1.500

TONY CASTILLO
Age 33/L   **$12**

Salary assumes the Blue Jays go out and improve the team. Even if they don't do much, Castillo is still a nice little pitcher.

Year	Team	Lg.	G	IP	H	BB	SO	W	L	ERA	SV	Ratio
1993	Toronto	AL	51	50.2	44	22	28	3	2	3.38	0	1.303
1994	Toronto	AL	41	68.0	66	28	43	5	2	2.51	1	1.382
1995	Toronto	AL	55	72.2	64	24	38	1	5	3.22	13	1.211
Post All-Star			26	30.1	25	14	14	1	3	3.86	10	1.286

NORM CHARLTON
Age 33/L   **$29**

Charlton's comeback was helped immeasurably by playing for a kindred soul in Lou Piniella. A subtle Rotisserie point: when evaluating players, try to figure out if there is any kind of relationship between the player and manager. Piniella and Kevin Kennedy are good examples of managers who go with "their guys." Charlton will continue to thrive as a Mariner because he would go through a wall for Piniella. Actually, he probably has.

Year	Team	Lg.	G	IP	H	BB	SO	W	L	ERA	SV	Ratio
1992	Cincinnati	NL	64	81.1	79	26	90	4	2	2.99	26	1.291
1993	Seattle	AL	34	34.2	22	17	48	1	3	2.34	18	1.125
1995	Philadelphia	NL	25	22.0	23	15	12	2	5	7.36	0	1.727
1995	Seattle	AL	30	47.2	23	16	58	2	1	1.51	14	0.818
Post All-Star			30	47.2	23	16	58	2	1	1.51	14	0.818

Catchers
pp. 27–41

Corners
pp. 41–62

Infield
pp. 63–82

Outfield
pp. 83–113

DH
pp. 114–118

Starters
pp. 119–157

Relievers
pp. 157–193

MIKE CHRISTOPHER   Age 32/R $7

That rarest of cats, a promising Tiger reliever.

Year	Team	Lg.	G	IP	H	BB	SO	W	L	ERA	SV	Ratio
1992	Cleveland	AL	10	18.0	17	10	13	0	0	3.00	0	1.500
1993	Cleveland	AL	9	11.2	14	2	8	0	0	3.86	0	1.371
1995	Detroit	AL	36	61.1	71	14	34	4	0	3.82	1	1.386
Post All-Star			33	57.2	70	14	31	2	0	4.06	1	1.457

TERRY CLARK   Age 35/R $1

Nice symmetry in his stats for runs, earned runs, and walks. However, 15 of each in 39 innings, to go along with 40 hits, is not going to help you much.

Year	Team	Lg.	G	IP	H	BB	SO	W	L	ERA	SV	Ratio
1995	Atlanta	NL	3	3.2	3	5	2	0	0	4.91	0	2.182
1995	Baltimore	AL	38	39.0	40	15	18	2	5	3.46	1	1.410
Post All-Star			24	26.2	30	12	13	1	4	4.72	1	1.575

JIM CORSI   Age 34/R $3

Nice ERA but little else of interest.

Year	Team	Lg.	G	IP	H	BB	SO	W	L	ERA	SV	Ratio
1992	Oakland	AL	32	44.0	44	18	19	4	2	1.43	0	1.409
1993	Florida	NL	15	20.1	28	10	7	0	2	6.64	0	1.869
1995	Oakland	AL	38	45.0	31	26	26	2	4	2.20	2	1.267
Post All-Star			17	18.0	16	10	11	0	1	3.00	0	1.444

ROB DIBBLE   Age 32/R $1

Worth a try if he ends up in Seattle. Otherwise, it's over.

Year	Team	Lg.	G	IP	H	BB	SO	W	L	ERA	SV	Ratio
1992	Cincinnati	NL	63	70.1	48	31	110	3	5	3.07	25	1.123
1993	Cincinnati	NL	45	41.2	34	42	49	1	4	6.48	19	1.824
1995	Chicago	AL	16	14.1	7	27	16	0	1	6.28	1	2.372
1995	Milwaukee	AL	15	12.0	9	19	10	1	1	8.25	0	2.333
Post All-Star			16	13.0	9	23	12	1	1	8.31	0	2.462

JOHN DOHERTY   Age 28/R $8

Filled in admirably when Henneman left. Still, guys like Doherty make you realize why Sparky left town.

Year	Team	Lg.	G	IP	H	BB	SO	W	L	ERA	SV	Ratio
1992	Detroit	AL	47	116.0	131	25	37	7	4	3.88	3	1.345
1993	Detroit	AL	32	184.2	205	48	63	14	11	4.44	0	1.370
1994	Detroit	AL	18	101.1	139	26	28	6	7	6.48	0	1.628
1995	Detroit	AL	48	113.0	130	37	46	5	9	5.10	6	1.478
Post All-Star			26	54.0	55	13	21	1	6	4.67	5	1.259

DENNIS ECKERSLEY

Age 41/R   **$26**

Had a great year for a mediocre team. Still, if LaRussa leaves, we bet Eck retires. If he stays, just remember that's he's a one-category pitcher. (Okay, maybe two, but that ratio is over 50 innings and doesn't help that much.)

Year	Team	Lg.	G	IP	H	BB	SO	W	L	ERA	SV	Ratio
1992	Oakland	AL	69	80.0	62	11	93	7	1	1.91	51	0.913
1993	Oakland	AL	64	67.0	67	13	80	2	4	4.16	36	1.194
1994	Oakland	AL	45	44.1	49	13	47	5	4	4.26	19	1.398
1995	Oakland	AL	52	50.1	53	11	40	4	6	4.83	29	1.272
Post All-Star			24	21.1	24	8	22	2	4	7.17	11	1.500

ALAN EMBREE

Age 26/L   **$12**

Hard thrower who will emerge this year as the best lefty in the Cleveland bullpen.

Year	Team	Lg.	G	IP	H	BB	SO	W	L	ERA	SV	Ratio
1992	Cleveland	AL	4	18.0	19	8	12	0	2	7.00	0	1.500
1995	Cleveland	AL	23	24.2	23	16	23	3	2	5.11	1	1.581
Post All-Star			23	24.2	23	16	23	3	2	5.11	1	1.581

MIKE FETTERS

Age 31/R   **$22**

It wasn't pretty, but 22 saves for this team is still nice pitching. Chances are the Brewers will be unFettered this year so he could end up on a good team.

Year	Team	Lg.	G	IP	H	BB	SO	W	L	ERA	SV	Ratio
1992	Milwaukee	AL	50	62.2	38	24	43	5	1	1.87	2	0.989
1993	Milwaukee	AL	45	59.1	59	22	23	3	3	3.34	0	1.365
1994	Milwaukee	AL	42	46.0	41	27	31	1	4	2.54	17	1.478
1995	Milwaukee	AL	40	34.2	40	20	33	0	3	3.38	22	1.731
Post All-Star			22	19.0	23	14	16	0	3	4.74	12	1.947

LEE GUETTERMAN

Age 36/L   **$1**

Again, this sport wants to expand?

Year	Team	Lg.	G	IP	H	BB	SO	W	L	ERA	SV	Ratio
1992	New York	AL	15	22.2	35	13	5	1	1	9.53	0	2.118
1992	New York	NL	43	43.1	57	14	15	3	4	5.82	2	1.638
1993	St. Louis	NL	40	46.0	41	16	19	3	3	2.93	1	1.239
1995	Seattle	AL	23	17.0	21	11	11	0	0	6.88	1	1.882
Post All-Star			13	11.1	9	9	3	0	0	5.56	1	1.588

ERIC GUNDERSON

Age 30/L   **$2**

Time for the annual reminder that lefties die hard in this game.

Year	Team	Lg.	G	IP	H	BB	SO	W	L	ERA	SV	Ratio
1992	Seattle	AL	9	9.1	12	5	2	2	1	8.68	0	1.821
1994	New York	NL	14	9.0	5	4	4	0	0	0.00	0	1.000
1995	New York	NL	30	24.1	25	8	19	1	1	3.70	0	1.356
1995	Boston	AL	19	12.1	13	9	9	2	1	5.11	0	1.784
Post All-Star			27	17.2	22	12	14	2	1	4.08	0	1.925

Catchers
pp. 27–41

Corners
pp. 41–62

Infield
pp. 63–82

Outfield
pp. 83–113

DH
pp. 114–118

Starters
pp. 119–157

Relievers
pp. 157–193

DARREN HALL   Age 31/L $1

If there was such a thing as "Rotisserie DL," the Blue Jays would be a team to watch. Hall's elbow surgery means you should look elsewhere.

Year	Team	Lg.	G	IP	H	BB	SO	W	L	ERA	SV	Ratio
1994	Toronto	AL	30	31.2	26	14	28	2	3	3.41	17	1.263
1995	Toronto	AL	17	16.1	21	9	11	0	2	4.41	3	1.837
Post All-Star			3	5.0	3	4	4	0	0	1.80	0	1.400

ROBERTO HERNANDEZ   Age 31/R $33

The rebound we expect in Chicago will extend to the bullpen, too.

Year	Team	Lg.	G	IP	H	BB	SO	W	L	ERA	SV	Ratio
1992	Chicago	AL	43	71.0	45	20	68	7	3	1.65	12	0.915
1993	Chicago	AL	70	78.2	66	20	71	3	4	2.29	38	1.093
1994	Chicago	AL	45	47.2	44	19	50	4	4	4.91	14	1.322
1995	Chicago	AL	60	59.2	63	28	84	3	7	3.92	32	1.525
Post All-Star			32	32.0	36	14	46	1	4	3.66	20	1.563

RICK HONEYCUTT   Age 41/L $5

Honeycutt had some nice numbers last year because LaRussa used him in the right spots. On the Yankees he could become a one-batter specialist, and those guys don't do much, Rotisserie-wise.

Year	Team	Lg.	G	IP	H	BB	SO	W	L	ERA	SV	Ratio
1992	Oakland	AL	54	39.0	41	10	32	1	4	3.69	3	1.308
1993	Oakland	AL	52	41.2	30	20	21	1	4	2.81	1	1.200
1994	Texas	AL	42	25.0	37	9	18	1	2	7.20	1	1.840
1995	Oakland	AL	49	44.2	37	9	21	5	1	2.42	2	1.030
1995	New York	AL	3	1.0	2	1	0	0	0	27.00	0	3.000
Post All-Star			29	24.0	14	7	11	1	0	2.63	1	0.875

STEVE HOWE   Age 38/L $3

The numbers aren't horrible but they aren't enough to get excited about. By the end of June, Showalter had no confidence in him. Eventually, the Yankees went out and got Honeycutt for the last 10 days of the season. Back to the ticket booth for one of the great jerks.

Year	Team	Lg.	G	IP	H	BB	SO	W	L	ERA	SV	Ratio
1992	New York	AL	20	22.0	9	3	12	3	0	2.45	6	0.545
1993	New York	AL	51	50.2	58	10	19	3	5	4.97	4	1.342
1994	New York	AL	40	40.0	28	7	18	3	0	1.80	15	0.875
1995	New York	AL	56	49.0	66	17	28	6	3	4.96	2	1.694
Post All-Star			27	26.0	38	7	11	3	0	5.54	1	1.731

JOE HUDSON   Age 25/R $5

Had a decent year in AA last year and has a decent shot at contributing to the major league club this year. Pitching coach Al Nipper likes him and that counts for something in Boston.

Year	Team	Lg.	G	IP	H	BB	SO	W	L	ERA	SV	Ratio
1995	Boston	AL	39	46.0	53	23	29	0	1	4.11	1	1.652
Post All-Star			31	38.2	42	19	23	0	1	3.72	1	1.578

MIKE IGNASIAK

Age 30/L $5

Vulture wins but nothing else.

Year	Team	Lg.	G	IP	H	BB	SO	W	L	ERA	SV	Ratio
1993	Milwaukee	AL	27	37.0	32	21	28	1	1	3.65	0	1.432
1994	Milwaukee	AL	23	47.2	51	13	24	3	1	4.53	0	1.343
1995	Milwaukee	AL	25	39.2	51	23	26	4	1	5.90	0	1.866
Post All-Star			11	13.2	26	6	8	1	0	8.56	0	2.341

MIKE JAMES

Age 28/R $7

A good young pitcher on a good young team. Last year was relief wins and a nice ERA. Look for improvement this year.

Year	Team	Lg.	G	IP	H	BB	SO	W	L	ERA	SV	Ratio
1995	California	AL	46	55.2	49	26	36	3	0	3.88	1	1.347
Post All-Star			27	31.1	28	18	23	3	0	3.45	1	1.468

DOUG JONES

Age 38/R $19

Not a great ERA for a closer, so the saves are impressive. Remember that few players have a more tenuous grasp on their jobs, so take him only if there are no other closers out there.

Year	Team	Lg.	G	IP	H	BB	SO	W	L	ERA	SV	Ratio
1992	Houston	NL	80	111.2	96	17	93	11	8	1.85	36	1.012
1993	Houston	NL	71	85.1	102	21	66	4	10	4.54	26	1.441
1994	Philadelphia	NL	47	54.0	55	6	38	2	4	2.17	27	1.130
1995	Baltimore	AL	52	46.2	55	16	42	0	4	5.01	22	1.521
Post All-Star			20	16.2	24	8	19	0	2	7.56	8	1.920

RICARDO JORDAN

Age 25/L $1

The fact that he's not coming off surgery gives him a distinct advantage over most of his fellow Blue Jay relievers.

Year	Team	Lg.	G	IP	H	BB	SO	W	L	ERA	SV	Ratio
1995	Toronto	AL	15	15.0	18	13	10	1	0	6.60	1	2.067
Post All-Star			10	9.2	10	7	8	1	0	6.52	1	1.759

MATT KARCHNER

Age 28/R $10

Pick him up. After last year's impressive debut, Karchner will be a big factor in the White Sox bullpen this year.

Year	Team	Lg.	G	IP	H	BB	SO	W	L	ERA	SV	Ratio
1995	Chicago	AL	31	32.0	33	12	24	4	2	1.69	0	1.406
Post All-Star			31	32.0	33	12	24	4	2	1.69	0	1.406

GRAEME LLOYD

Age 28/L $1

Should have claimed he had the same mosquito-borne illness that plagued teammate and fellow Australian Dave Nilsson. Otherwise, these numbers are hard to justify. With his name, maybe he should just join a Moody Blues cover band and get out of baseball.

Year	Team	Lg.	G	IP	H	BB	SO	W	L	ERA	SV	Ratio
1993	Milwaukee	AL	55	63.2	64	13	31	3	4	2.83	0	1.209
1994	Milwaukee	AL	43	47.0	49	15	31	2	3	5.17	3	1.362
1995	Milwaukee	AL	33	32.0	28	8	13	0	5	4.50	4	1.125
Post All-Star			6	5.0	3	1	3	0	0	1.80	0	0.800

Catchers
pp. 27–41

Corners
pp. 41–62

Infield
pp. 63–82

Outfield
pp. 83–113

DH
pp. 114–118

Starters
pp. 119–157

Relievers
pp. 157–193

ALBIE LOPEZ Age 24/R $1

Limited but decent major league numbers last year, but he was lousy for Buffalo in AAA. Last year was a step backward for this hard-throwing prospect.

Year	Team	Lg.	G	IP	H	BB	SO	W	L	ERA	SV	Ratio
1993	Cleveland	AL	9	49.2	49	32	25	3	1	5.98	0	1.631
1994	Cleveland	AL	4	17.0	20	6	18	1	2	4.24	0	1.529
1995	Cleveland	AL	6	23.0	17	7	22	0	0	3.13	0	1.043
Post All-Star			5	18.1	13	6	17	0	0	3.44	0	1.036

BOB MACDONALD Age 30/L $5

Could see more work with Steve Howe no longer in the picture.

Year	Team	Lg.	G	IP	H	BB	SO	W	L	ERA	SV	Ratio
1992	Toronto	AL	27	47.1	50	16	26	1	0	4.37	0	1.394
1993	Detroit	AL	68	65.2	67	33	39	3	3	5.35	3	1.523
1995	New York	AL	33	46.1	50	22	41	1	1	4.86	0	1.554
Post All-Star			18	25.1	22	10	19	0	0	3.20	0	1.263

MIKE MADDUX Age 34/R $8

Gave the Red Sox nearly 100 great innings at the end of the year. Maddux should be a steady middle reliever this year. Greg always said his brother would eventually put it together.

Year	Team	Lg.	G	IP	H	BB	SO	W	L	ERA	SV	Ratio
1992	San Diego	NL	50	79.2	71	24	60	2	2	2.37	5	1.192
1993	New York	NL	58	75.0	67	27	57	3	8	3.60	5	1.253
1994	New York	NL	27	44.0	45	13	32	2	1	5.11	2	1.318
1995	Pittsburgh	NL	8	9.0	14	3	4	1	0	9.00	0	1.889
1995	Boston	AL	36	89.2	86	15	65	4	1	3.61	1	1.126
Post All-Star			21	58.2	56	11	41	3	0	3.99	0	1.142

MIKE MAGNANTE Age 30/R $2

A bad habit among sports commentators is to add an *s* to the last name of a player when making a general point about the sport. As in "The Mike Magnantes of the world mean nothing in Rotisserie." It's a bad habit because there is, in this case, only one Mike Magnante.

Year	Team	Lg.	G	IP	H	BB	SO	W	L	ERA	SV	Ratio
1992	Kansas City	AL	44	89.1	115	35	31	4	9	4.94	0	1.679
1993	Kansas City	AL	7	35.1	37	11	16	1	2	4.08	0	1.358
1994	Kansas City	AL	36	47.0	55	16	21	2	3	4.60	0	1.511
1995	Kansas City	AL	28	44.2	45	16	28	1	1	4.23	0	1.366
Post All-Star			27	43.1	43	16	27	1	1	4.15	0	1.362

JOSIAS MANZANILLO Age 28/R $1

Former Red Sox farmhand finished the year on the Yankees' disabled list. When he pitched, he did well enough but not enough to help your team.

Year	Team	Lg.	G	IP	H	BB	SO	W	L	ERA	SV	Ratio
1993	Milwaukee	AL	10	17.0	22	10	10	1	1	9.53	1	1.882
1993	New York	NL	6	12.0	8	9	11	0	0	3.00	0	1.417
1994	New York	NL	37	47.1	34	13	48	3	2	2.66	2	0.993
1995	New York	NL	12	16.0	18	6	14	1	2	7.88	0	1.500
1995	New York	AL	11	17.1	19	9	11	0	0	2.08	0	1.615
Post All-Star			0	0.0	0	0	0	0	0	0.00	3	0.000

BRIAN MAXCY
Age 24/R $1

He did a lot of damage in 52 innings.

Year	Team	Lg.	G	IP	H	BB	SO	W	L	ERA	SV	Ratio
1995	Detroit	AL	41	52.1	61	31	20	4	5	6.88	0	1.758
Post All-Star			23	31.1	39	18	12	0	4	8.62	0	1.819

JAMIE McANDREW
Age 28/R $1

Aside from the occasional relief appearance, McAndrew will stink up the joint in a start now and then.

Year	Team	Lg.	G	IP	H	BB	SO	W	L	ERA	SV	Ratio
1995	Milwaukee	AL	10	36.1	37	12	19	2	3	4.71	0	1.349
Post All-Star			10	36.1	37	12	19	2	3	4.71	0	1.349

KIRK McCASKILL
Age 34/R $9

McCaskill could be in the right place at the right time. The White Sox will be in the hunt next year and he could do a lot of nice things along the way.

Year	Team	Lg.	G	IP	H	BB	SO	W	L	ERA	SV	Ratio
1992	Chicago	AL	34	209.0	193	95	109	12	13	4.18	0	1.378
1993	Chicago	AL	30	113.2	144	36	65	4	8	5.23	2	1.584
1994	Chicago	AL	40	52.2	51	22	37	1	4	3.42	3	1.386
1995	Chicago	AL	55	81.0	97	33	50	6	4	4.89	2	1.605
Post All-Star			25	41.2	48	13	29	2	2	4.75	1	1.464

ROGER McDOWELL
Age 35/R $9

See Kirk McCaskill.

Year	Team	Lg.	G	IP	H	BB	SO	W	L	ERA	SV	Ratio
1992	Los Angeles	NL	65	83.2	103	42	50	6	10	4.09	14	1.733
1993	Los Angeles	NL	54	68.0	76	30	27	5	3	2.25	2	1.559
1994	Los Angeles	NL	32	41.1	50	22	29	0	3	5.23	0	1.742
1995	Texas	AL	64	85.0	86	34	49	7	4	4.02	4	1.412
Post All-Star			32	43.0	45	17	26	3	3	3.98	3	1.442

RUSTY MEACHAM
Age 28/R $5

Just another middle reliever.

Year	Team	Lg.	G	IP	H	BB	SO	W	L	ERA	SV	Ratio
1992	Kansas City	AL	64	101.2	88	21	64	10	4	2.74	2	1.072
1993	Kansas City	AL	15	21.0	31	5	13	2	2	5.57	0	1.714
1994	Kansas City	AL	36	50.2	51	12	36	3	3	3.73	4	1.243
1995	Kansas City	AL	49	59.2	72	19	30	4	3	4.98	2	1.525
Post All-Star			22	32.2	38	12	17	2	1	5.51	2	1.531

PAUL MENHART
Age 27/R $1

Paul NoHeart is more like it. He put up surprisingly similar numbers in AAA. What were the Jays expecting? Expect big changes in Toronto, from Cito Gaston on down, and don't expect Menhart to survive them.

Year	Team	Lg.	G	IP	H	BB	SO	W	L	ERA	SV	Ratio
1995	Toronto	AL	21	78.2	72	47	50	1	4	4.92	0	1.513
Post All-Star			13	63.1	58	31	32	0	3	3.84	0	1.405

Catchers
pp. 27–41

Corners
pp. 41–62

Infield
pp. 63–82

Outfield
pp. 83–113

DH
pp. 114–118

Starters
pp. 119–157

Relievers
pp. 157–193

JOSE MERCEDES   Age 25/R $1

Jose Yugo is more like it.

Year	Team	Lg.	G	IP	H	BB	SO	W	L	ERA	SV	Ratio
1994	Milwaukee	AL	19	31.0	22	16	11	2	0	2.32	0	1.226
1995	Milwaukee	AL	5	7.1	12	8	6	0	1	9.82	0	2.727
Post All-Star			0	0.0	0	0	0	0	0	0.00	0	0.000

JOSE MESA   Age 29/R $40

Here's a guy who never did much and then became the best reliever in
baseball. In most leagues last year, Mesa went for a song because he was
one of those former phenoms and he was 28 and he hadn't done anything.
Who cared about Jose Mesa last year? Just a little reminder to file away the
names of former phenoms in case they stick around long enough to get it
together. Mesa is also a reminder that many pitchers bloom after leaving
their original teams. By the way, we fully expect Mesa to dominate the
league again.

Year	Team	Lg.	G	IP	H	BB	SO	W	L	ERA	SV	Ratio
1992	Baltimore	AL	13	67.2	77	27	22	3	8	5.19	0	1.537
1992	Cleveland	AL	15	93.0	92	43	40	4	4	4.16	0	1.452
1993	Cleveland	AL	34	208.2	232	62	118	10	12	4.92	0	1.409
1994	Cleveland	AL	51	73.0	71	26	63	7	5	3.82	2	1.329
1995	Cleveland	AL	62	64.0	49	17	58	3	0	1.13	46	1.031
Post All-Star			35	34.2	26	9	33	2	0	0.52	25	1.010

MIKE MOHLER   Age 27/L $5

He had two wins and five saves in the minors as well as what you see here.
Add the stats together and you have a nice, complementary reliever, which
is what he will be this year.

Year	Team	Lg.	G	IP	H	BB	SO	W	L	ERA	SV	Ratio
1993	Oakland	AL	42	64.1	57	44	42	1	6	5.60	0	1.570
1994	Oakland	AL	1	2.1	2	2	4	0	1	7.71	0	1.714
1995	Oakland	AL	28	23.2	16	18	15	1	1	3.04	1	1.437
Post All-Star			28	23.2	16	18	15	1	1	3.04	1	1.437

JEFF MONTGOMERY   Age 34/R $32

Still one of the best closers in the game, though he is bound to be playing
elsewhere this year. Nice comeback in ERA and ratio indicates that Montgomery may have made adjustments that will allow him to age gracefully.

Year	Team	Lg.	G	IP	H	BB	SO	W	L	ERA	SV	Ratio
1992	Kansas City	AL	65	82.2	61	27	69	1	6	2.18	39	1.065
1993	Kansas City	AL	69	87.1	65	23	66	7	5	2.27	45	1.008
1994	Kansas City	AL	42	44.2	48	15	50	2	3	4.03	27	1.410
1995	Kansas City	AL	54	65.2	60	25	49	2	3	3.43	31	1.294
Post All-Star			29	37.0	37	15	31	2	2	3.41	17	1.405

OSCAR MUNOZ   Age 26/R $3

Pitched reasonably well as a starter in AAA, so pay a little more if the Twins
put him in the rotation.

Year	Team	Lg.	G	IP	H	BB	SO	W	L	ERA	SV	Ratio
1995	Minnesota	AL	10	35.1	40	17	25	2	1	5.60	0	1.613
Post All-Star			10	35.1	40	17	25	2	1	5.60	0	1.613

MIKE MYERS   Age 26/L $1

Why he left "Saturday Night Live" to pitch for the Tigers is a mystery.

Year	Team	Lg.	G	IP	H	BB	SO	W	L	ERA	SV	Ratio
1995	Florida	NL	2	2.0	1	3	0	0	0	0.00	0	2.000
1995	Detroit	AL	11	6.1	10	4	4	1	0	9.95	0	2.211
Post All-Star			11	6.1	10	4	4	1	0	9.95	0	2.211

JEFF NELSON   Age 29/R $14

An above-average setup man, pitching for a manager who likes him and knows how to use him. Expect similar numbers this year and maybe even more saves.

Year	Team	Lg.	G	IP	H	BB	SO	W	L	ERA	SV	Ratio
1992	Seattle	AL	66	81.0	71	44	46	1	7	3.44	6	1.420
1993	Seattle	AL	71	60.0	57	34	61	5	3	4.35	1	1.517
1994	Seattle	AL	28	42.1	35	20	44	0	0	2.76	0	1.299
1995	Seattle	AL	62	78.2	58	27	96	7	3	2.17	2	1.081
Post All-Star			33	42.2	37	10	59	4	2	2.74	1	1.102

GREGG OLSON   Age 29/R $6

Interesting comeback from injury. Keep your eye on Olson in the spring because if Montgomery leaves, this bullpen is as wide open as any in the league.

Year	Team	Lg.	G	IP	H	BB	SO	W	L	ERA	SV	Ratio
1992	Baltimore	AL	60	61.1	46	24	58	1	5	2.05	36	1.141
1993	Baltimore	AL	50	45.0	37	18	44	0	2	1.60	29	1.222
1994	Atlanta	NL	16	14.2	19	13	10	0	2	9.20	1	2.182
1995	Cleveland	AL	3	2.2	5	2	0	0	0	13.50	0	2.625
1995	Kansas City	AL	20	30.1	23	17	21	3	3	3.26	3	1.319
Post All-Star			20	30.1	23	17	21	3	3	3.26	3	1.319

MIKE OQUIST   Age 27/R $2

Spare part.

Year	Team	Lg.	G	IP	H	BB	SO	W	L	ERA	SV	Ratio
1993	Baltimore	AL	5	11.2	12	4	8	0	0	3.86	0	1.371
1994	Baltimore	AL	15	58.1	75	30	39	3	3	6.17	0	1.800
1995	Baltimore	AL	27	54.0	51	41	27	2	1	4.17	0	1.704
Post All-Star			8	12.1	11	12	3	1	1	2.92	38	1.865

JESSE OROSCO   Age 39/L $2

Still useful in the major leagues but carries no great Rotisserie value.

Year	Team	Lg.	G	IP	H	BB	SO	W	L	ERA	SV	Ratio
1992	Milwaukee	AL	59	39.0	33	13	40	3	1	3.23	1	1.179
1993	Milwaukee	AL	57	56.2	47	17	67	3	5	3.18	8	1.129
1994	Milwaukee	AL	40	39.0	32	26	36	3	1	5.08	0	1.487
1995	Baltimore	AL	65	49.2	28	27	58	2	4	3.26	3	1.107
Post All-Star			36	30.0	15	18	33	1	3	3.60	3	1.100

Catchers
pp. 27-41

Corners
pp. 41-62

Infield
pp. 63-82

Outfield
pp. 83-113

DH
pp. 114-118

Starters
pp. 119-157

Relievers
pp. 157-193

BOB PATTERSON
Age 36/L $5

Still useful in the major leagues and carries a little Rotisserie value. Would have had even nicer numbers last year if not for the Angels descent into hell in August and September.

Year	Team	Lg.	G	IP	H	BB	SO	W	L	ERA	SV	Ratio
1992	Pittsburgh	NL	60	64.2	59	23	43	6	3	2.92	9	1.268
1993	Texas	AL	52	52.2	59	11	46	2	4	4.78	1	1.329
1994	California	AL	47	42.0	35	15	30	2	3	4.07	1	1.190
1995	California	AL	62	53.1	48	13	41	5	2	3.04	0	1.144
Post All-Star			34	24.1	22	5	17	1	0	4.07	0	1.110

TROY PERCIVAL
Age 26/R $10

Pick him up as a long-term investment in a closer. We steadfastly refuse to predict the demise of Lee Arthur Smith, but when it happens we predict that Percival gets the job.

Year	Team	Lg.	G	IP	H	BB	SO	W	L	ERA	SV	Ratio
1995	California	AL	62	74.0	37	26	94	3	2	1.95	3	0.851
Post All-Star			33	41.0	16	14	50	2	2	1.54	3	0.732

HIPOLITO PICHARDO
Age 26/R $10

Another year like this and there may be a bunch of little Hipolitos running around Missouri. Okay, maybe not.

Year	Team	Lg.	G	IP	H	BB	SO	W	L	ERA	SV	Ratio
1992	Kansas City	AL	31	143.2	148	49	59	9	6	3.95	0	1.371
1993	Kansas City	AL	30	165.0	183	53	70	7	8	4.04	0	1.430
1994	Kansas City	AL	45	67.2	82	24	36	5	3	4.92	3	1.567
1995	Kansas City	AL	44	64.0	66	30	43	8	4	4.36	1	1.500
Post All-Star			20	29.1	35	15	21	3	1	4.91	0	1.705

JEFF PIERCE
Age 26/R $5

Mike Maddux will probably get the spot starts and long relief stints for which Pierce is suited. May need another year of seasoning in AAA but is still a decent prospect.

Year	Team	Lg.	G	IP	H	BB	SO	W	L	ERA	SV	Ratio
1995	Boston	AL	12	15.0	16	14	12	0	3	6.60	0	2.000
Post All-Star			0	0.0	0	0	0	0	0	0.00	0	0.000

ERIC PLUNK
Age 32/R $11

When role players accept their roles, it's a beautiful thing.

Year	Team	Lg.	G	IP	H	BB	SO	W	L	ERA	SV	Ratio
1992	Cleveland	AL	58	71.2	61	38	50	9	6	3.64	4	1.381
1993	Cleveland	AL	70	71.0	61	30	77	4	5	2.79	15	1.282
1994	Cleveland	AL	41	71.0	61	37	73	7	2	2.54	3	1.380
1995	Cleveland	AL	56	64.0	48	27	71	6	2	2.67	2	1.172
Post All-Star			26	30.0	27	13	32	2	1	3.60	1	1.333

JIM POOLE
Age 29/L $5

An average reliever in Cleveland is better than average.

Year	Team	Lg.	G	IP	H	BB	SO	W	L	ERA	SV	Ratio
1992	Baltimore	AL	6	3.1	3	1	3	0	0	0.00	0	1.200
1993	Baltimore	AL	55	50.1	30	21	29	2	1	2.15	2	1.013
1994	Baltimore	AL	38	20.1	32	11	18	1	0	6.64	0	2.115
1995	Cleveland	AL	42	50.1	40	17	41	3	3	3.75	0	1.132
Post All-Star			21	24.2	20	8	19	2	0	4.01	0	1.135

SCOTT RADINSKY — Age 28/L — $9

First of all, on underacheiving teams middle relievers don't do much. Secondly, he's another year recovered from leukemia. Pick him up and look for numbers like he posted in 1993.

Year	Team	Lg.	G	IP	H	BB	SO	W	L	ERA	SV	Ratio
1992	Chicago	AL	68	59.1	54	34	48	3	7	2.73	15	1.483
1993	Chicago	AL	73	54.2	61	19	44	8	2	4.28	4	1.463
1995	Chicago	AL	46	38.0	46	17	14	2	1	5.45	1	1.658
Post All-Star			20	15.1	17	4	8	0	0	4.11	0	1.370

AL REYES — Age 24/R — $2

Pitched a nice 33 innings last year. Double it and he'll be worth something.

Year	Team	Lg.	G	IP	H	BB	SO	W	L	ERA	SV	Ratio
1995	Milwaukee	AL	27	33.1	19	18	29	1	1	2.43	1	1.110
Post All-Star			2	2.2	1	3	2	1	0	0.00	0	1.500

CARLOS REYES — Age 26/R — $1

May be good in a foot reyes but not in an arms reyes.

Year	Team	Lg.	G	IP	H	BB	SO	W	L	ERA	SV	Ratio
1994	Oakland	AL	27	78.0	71	44	57	0	3	4.15	1	1.474
1995	Oakland	AL	40	69.0	71	28	48	4	6	5.09	0	1.435
Post All-Star			21	35.0	39	18	26	4	5	6.43	0	1.629

BILL RISLEY — Age 28/R — $9

The Mariners have a pretty good bullpen, don't they?

Year	Team	Lg.	G	IP	H	BB	SO	W	L	ERA	SV	Ratio
1992	Montreal	NL	1	5.0	4	1	2	1	0	1.80	0	1.000
1993	Montreal	NL	2	3.0	2	2	2	0	0	6.00	0	1.333
1994	Seattle	AL	37	52.1	31	19	61	9	6	3.44	0	0.955
1995	Seattle	AL	45	60.1	55	18	65	2	1	3.13	1	1.210
Post All-Star			23	28.2	31	9	24	1	0	5.02	0	1.395

JEFF RUSSELL — Age 34/R — $20

A nice year, but Johnny Oates was pretty close to closing by committee last year and that won't change. Not nearly the same guy he was the last time he was home on the Rangers.

Year	Team	Lg.	G	IP	H	BB	SO	W	L	ERA	SV	Ratio
1992	Oakland	AL	8	9.2	4	3	5	2	0	0.00	2	0.724
1992	Texas	AL	51	56.2	51	22	43	2	3	1.91	28	1.288
1993	Boston	AL	51	46.2	39	14	45	1	4	2.70	33	1.136
1994	Boston	AL	29	28.0	30	13	18	0	5	5.14	12	1.536
1994	Cleveland	AL	13	12.2	13	3	10	1	1	4.97	5	1.263
1995	Texas	AL	37	32.2	36	9	21	1	0	3.03	20	1.378
Post All-Star			18	15.0	17	5	10	0	0	3.00	8	1.467

Catchers
pp. 27–41

Corners
pp. 41–62

Infield
pp. 63–82

Outfield
pp. 83–113

DH
pp. 114–118

Starters
pp. 119–157

Relievers
pp. 157–193

KEN RYAN   Age 27/R $5

Played in AA and the majors last year but in the wrong order. Without significant improvement, Ryan will soon be someone else's problem.

Year	Team	Lg.	G	IP	H	BB	SO	W	L	ERA	SV	Ratio
1992	Boston	AL	7	7.0	4	5	5	0	0	6.43	1	1.286
1993	Boston	AL	47	50.0	43	29	49	7	2	3.60	1	1.440
1994	Boston	AL	42	48.0	46	17	32	2	3	2.44	13	1.313
1995	Boston	AL	28	32.2	34	24	34	0	4	4.96	7	1.776
Post All-Star			2	3.2	1	0	0	0	0	0.00	22	0.273

JEFF SHAW   Age 29/R $1

This Jeff's a mutt.

Year	Team	Lg.	G	IP	H	BB	SO	W	L	ERA	SV	Ratio
1992	Cleveland	AL	2	7.2	7	4	3	0	1	8.22	0	1.435
1993	Montreal	NL	55	95.2	91	32	50	2	7	4.14	0	1.286
1994	Montreal	NL	46	67.1	67	15	47	5	2	3.88	1	1.218
1995	Montreal	NL	50	62.1	58	26	45	1	6	4.62	3	1.368
1995	Chicago	AL	9	9.2	12	1	6	0	0	6.52	0	1.345
Post All-Star			29	29.2	31	11	0	15	2	4.85	1	1.416

LEE SMITH   Age 38/R $34

We learned our le: ⅂. The big guy had 17 saves after the All-Star break for a team that had ɑ ⱶrrible second half. If he's slowing down, he's hiding it from us. In golf, it s ɑn achievement to shoot your age. Last year, Smith had a save for each year. Look for 38 this year.

Year	Team	Lg.	G	IP	H	BB	SO	W	L	ERA	SV	Ratio
1992	St. Louis	NL	70	75.0	62	26	60	4	9	3.12	43	1.173
1993	New York	AL	8	8.0	4	5	11	0	0	0.00	3	1.125
1993	St. Louis	NL	55	50.0	49	9	49	2	4	4.50	43	1.160
1994	Baltimore	AL	41	38.1	34	11	42	1	4	3.29	33	1.174
1995	California	AL	52	49.1	42	25	43	0	5	3.47	37	1.358
Post All-Star			28	27.0	24	9	22	0	3	3.67	17	1.222

MIKE STANTON   Age 28/L $12

If Stanton regains some of the form he showed in Atlanta, his acquisition could be remembered as Dan Duquette's finest hour. If the Sox let Aguilera go, it will mean they think Stanton is the answer. Pay more if that's the case.

Year	Team	Lg.	G	IP	H	BB	SO	W	L	ERA	SV	Ratio
1992	Atlanta	NL	65	63.2	59	20	44	5	4	4.10	8	1.241
1993	Atlanta	NL	63	52.0	51	29	43	4	6	4.67	27	1.538
1994	Atlanta	NL	49	45.2	41	26	35	3	1	3.55	3	1.467
1995	Atlanta	NL	26	19.1	31	6	13	1	1	5.59	1	1.914
1995	Boston	AL	22	21.0	17	8	10	1	0	3.00	0	1.190
Post All-Star			26	23.2	26	8	12	1	0	3.42	1	1.437

DAVE STEVENS   Age 26/R $18

Stepped in as closer when Aguilera left and did a decent job. We think he'll rise to the occasion and have a good year on a lousy team.

Year	Team	Lg.	G	IP	H	BB	SO	W	L	ERA	SV	Ratio
1994	Minnesota	AL	24	45.0	55	23	24	5	2	6.80	0	1.733
1995	Minnesota	AL	56	65.2	74	32	47	5	4	5.07	10	1.614
Post All-Star			30	30.1	37	18	24	2	4	4.45	9	1.813

JULIAN TAVAREZ   Age 22/R $12

He was our rookie of the year. He'll spend another year or two as a middle man and then become a closer or a starter. His stuff is too good for him not to have a more important role at some point.

Year	Team	Lg.	G	IP	H	BB	SO	W	L	ERA	SV	Ratio
1993	Cleveland	AL	8	37.0	53	13	19	2	2	6.57	0	1.784
1994	Cleveland	AL	1	1.2	6	1	0	0	1	21.60	0	4.200
1995	Cleveland	AL	57	85.0	76	21	68	10	2	2.44	0	1.141
Post All-Star			31	39.1	40	11	34	5	2	3.89	0	1.297

SCOTT TAYLOR   Age 29/R $1

Has shown some consistency. He was a poor minor league starter and a lousy major league reliever. To be fair, he had an ERA of 3.66 in 118 innings for a weak Oklahoma City team last year. Still, no matter how many pitching questions your team has, Scott Taylor is not the answer to any of them.

Year	Team	Lg.	G	IP	H	BB	SO	W	L	ERA	SV	Ratio
1995	Texas	AL	3	15.1	25	5	10	1	2	9.39	0	1.957
Post All-Star			3	15.1	25	5	10	1	2	9.39	0	1.957

MIKE TIMLIN   Age 30/R $9

If the Blue Jays turn it around this year, Timlin will have a chance at posting some nice numbers. We think they will and he will.

Year	Team	Lg.	G	IP	H	BB	SO	W	L	ERA	SV	Ratio
1992	Toronto	AL	26	43.2	45	20	35	0	2	4.12	1	1.489
1993	Toronto	AL	54	55.2	63	27	49	4	2	4.69	1	1.617
1994	Toronto	AL	34	40.0	41	20	38	0	1	5.18	2	1.525
1995	Toronto	AL	31	42.0	38	17	36	4	3	2.14	5	1.310
Post All-Star			13	19.2	17	7	17	1	2	0.46	2	1.220

ED VOSBERG   Age 34/L $10

Vosberg was arrested at last year's All-Star game for scalping his tickets. That's good. You don't want certain relievers to be distracted by having a working brain.

Year	Team	Lg.	G	IP	H	BB	SO	W	L	ERA	SV	Ratio
1994	Oakland	AL	16	13.2	16	5	12	0	2	3.95	0	1.537
1995	Texas	AL	44	36.0	32	16	36	5	5	3.00	4	1.333
Post All-Star			22	16.0	15	9	15	2	3	3.38	2	1.500

DUANE WARD   Age 31/R $1

A more complete physical breakdown would be hard to find. Still, baseball is a sport that welcomes resurrections, so Duane "Surgical" Ward might be worth the tiniest investment. He will not help this year, though. That's for sure, but next year that buck could throw a nice dividend.

Year	Team	Lg.	G	IP	H	BB	SO	W	L	ERA	SV	Ratio
1992	Toronto	AL	79	101.1	76	39	103	7	4	1.95	12	1.135
1993	Toronto	AL	71	71.2	49	25	97	2	3	2.13	45	1.033
1995	Toronto	AL	4	2.2	11	5	3	0	1	27.00	0	6.000
Post All-Star			0	0.0	0	0	0	0	0	0.00	0	0.000

Catchers
pp. 27–41

Corners
pp. 41–62

Infield
pp. 63–82

Outfield
pp. 83–113

DH
pp. 114–118

Starters
pp. 119–157

Relievers
pp. 157–193

BOB WELLS   Age 29/R $2

Wells forego.

Year	Team	Lg.	G	IP	H	BB	SO	W	L	ERA	SV	Ratio
1994	Seattle	AL	1	4.0	4	1	3	1	0	2.25	0	1.250
1994	Philadelphia	NL	6	5.0	4	3	3	1	0	1.80	0	1.400
1995	Seattle	AL	30	76.2	88	39	38	4	3	5.75	0	1.657
Post All-Star			15	34.0	36	21	14	2	0	4.76	0	1.676

DON WENGERT   Age 26/R $1

Moving right along . . .

Year	Team	Lg.	G	IP	H	BB	SO	W	L	ERA	SV	Ratio
1995	Oakland	AL	19	29.2	30	12	16	1	1	3.34	0	1.416
Post All-Star			14	21.0	21	12	10	0	0	3.00	0	1.571

JOHN WETTELAND   Age 29/R $30

Will probably take his salt-encrusted cap back to the National League because he just didn't cut it in the American. The numbers were passable, but
if you saw him pitch you rarely saw the confident closer that he was in
Montreal. He's no Mark Davis, but he simply didn't perform as expected.
His last pitch of the season was a grand slam to Edgar Martinez, so the
$5 million man sat while Jack McDowell tried to hold off the Mariners in
the divisional playoffs. 'Nuff said.

Year	Team	Lg.	G	IP	H	BB	SO	W	L	ERA	SV	Ratio
1992	Montreal	NL	67	83.1	64	36	99	4	4	2.92	37	1.200
1993	Montreal	NL	70	85.1	58	28	113	9	3	1.37	43	1.008
1994	Montreal	NL	52	63.2	46	21	68	4	6	2.83	25	1.052
1995	New York	AL	60	61.1	40	14	66	1	5	2.93	31	0.880
Post All-Star			34	32.2	20	8	36	0	4	3.31	19	0.857

MATT WHITESIDE   Age 28/R $8

The departure of Kevin Kennedy allowed Whiteside to bloom. Look for
more improvement this year.

Year	Team	Lg.	G	IP	H	BB	SO	W	L	ERA	SV	Ratio
1992	Texas	AL	20	28.0	26	11	13	1	1	1.93	4	1.321
1993	Texas	AL	60	73.0	78	23	39	2	1	4.32	1	1.384
1994	Texas	AL	47	61.0	68	28	37	2	2	5.02	1	1.574
1995	Texas	AL	40	53.0	48	19	46	5	4	4.08	3	1.264
Post All-Star			22	25.2	27	9	21	3	2	4.91	2	1.403

SEAN WHITESIDE   Age 24/L $1

Will probably start the year in AAA, but pay attention. Whiteside is one of
many good young Tigers pitching prospects. In fact, GM Joe Klein did such
fine work in rebuilding the Tigers minor league system, his job was in jeopardy. That's baseball.

Year	Team	Lg.	G	IP	H	BB	SO	W	L	ERA	SV	Ratio
1995	Detroit	AL	2	3.2	7	4	2	0	0	14.73	0	3.000
Post All-Star			0	0.0	0	0	0	0	0	0.00	0	0.000

BOB WICKMAN

Age 27/R   **$12**

Last year was a tough one in the Bronx for a lot of people. Count on Wickman to bounce back.

Year	Team	Lg.	G	IP	H	BB	SO	W	L	ERA	SV	Ratio
1992	New York	AL	8	50.1	51	20	21	6	1	4.11	0	1.411
1993	New York	AL	41	140.0	156	69	70	14	4	4.63	4	1.607
1994	New York	AL	53	70.0	54	27	56	5	4	3.09	6	1.157
1995	New York	AL	63	80.0	77	33	51	2	4	4.05	1	1.375
Post All-Star			33	37.0	45	14	24	0	2	4.38	1	1.595

WOODY WILLIAMS

Age 29/R   **$2**

Nice ninth pitcher whose ERA won't kill you.

Year	Team	Lg.	G	IP	H	BB	SO	W	L	ERA	SV	Ratio
1993	Toronto	AL	30	37.0	40	22	24	3	1	4.38	0	1.676
1994	Toronto	AL	38	59.1	44	33	56	1	3	3.64	0	1.298
1995	Toronto	AL	23	53.2	44	28	41	1	2	3.69	0	1.342
Post All-Star			1	1.1	3	2	1	0	0	13.50	0	3.750

Catchers
pp. 27–41

Corners
pp. 41–62

Infield
pp. 63–82

Outfield
pp. 83–113

DH
pp. 114–118

Starters
pp. 119–157

Relievers
pp. 157–193

AUCTION DRAFT UPDATE? YOU BETCHA!

See page 268 to find out how to get your free *Rotisserie Hot List*

3

By the Numbers

1996 Rotisserie Stat-Pak:
Never Leave for the Auction
Draft Without It

A certain kind of Rotisserie owner breezes into the auction draft without so much as pencil or notepad. The night before, he went to the movies. The week before, he went snorkeling in the Caribbean and didn't see a single newspaper for six days. The month before, he re-read all of Raymond Chandler and the new James Lee Burke. Preparation? Well, he rented *Major League* on Super Bowl Sunday and watched it instead of the game. While other owners at the table are frantically rearranging their lists, agonizing over which of seven alternative strategies to pursue, and trying to remember their own names, he leans back, folds his arms over his chest, and, with a dreamy look in his eyes, asks of no one in particular, "I wonder how much Bobby Bonds will go for?" Six months later, *he*'s the one taking the Yoo-Hoo shower.

We hate that guy.

But we have to admit he may be on to something. Maybe you really don't need to show up at the auction draft with the *Baseball Register*, all the spring training box scores from *USA Today*, Bill James, the last six months of *Baseball America* and *Baseball Weekly*, a stack of computer print-outs, all of John Benson's newsletters for the past year, a well-thumbed copy of *Nine Innings*, and your original 1948 Cleveland Indians cap. Maybe all you need is the Rotisserie Stat-Pak.

The Rotisserie Stat-Pak is the nearest thing in this book to a grand-slam homer. Here you get the top performers in all the Rotissecategories (plus Runs Scored for batters and Strikeouts and Net Wins for pitchers). You also get the *worst* performers in ERA, Ratio, and BA so you can find out in an instant who might hurt you. And for batters, you get the top performers in each category by position. Plus, this year you get Post All-Star stats so you can scope out who finished strong (and otherwise) last season.

So forget all that other stuff. Just tear out this chapter and travel light. You can wear your lucky Indians cap. But remember to take it off just before they pour the Yoo-Hoo.

LEAGUE LEADERS, 1995

NATIONAL LEAGUE PITCHERS

RATIO
(Minimum 75 Innings Pitched)

1. Maddux, G.	0.811	15. DeLucia, R.	1.202	29. Ashby, A.	1.256
2. Reed, S.	0.976	16. Perez, C.	1.203	30. Hampton, M.	1.261
3. Bottalico, R.	1.049	17. Williams, M.	1.221	31. Hammond, C.	1.267
4. Schilling, C.	1.052	18. Sanders, S.	1.222	32. Neagle, D.	1.269
5. Nomo, H.	1.056	19. Leiter, M.	1.227	33. Astacio, P.	1.269
6. Schourek, P.	1.067	20. Harnisch, P.	1.227	34. Henry, B.	1.271
7. Valdes, I.	1.108	21. Castillo, F.	1.229	35. Morgan, M.	1.272
8. Martinez, P.	1.151	22. Reynolds, S.	1.231	36. Foster, K.	1.276
9. Veres, D.	1.152	23. Smoltz, J.	1.235	37. Isringhausen, J.	1.280
10. Mathews, T.	1.173	24. Petkovsek, M.	1.245	38. Candiotti, T.	1.287
11. Leskanic, C.	1.184	25. Martinez, R.	1.246	39. Osborne, D.	1.288
12. McMichael, G.	1.190	26. Navarro, J.	1.248	40. Parrett, J.	1.291
13. Hamilton, J.	1.199	27. Glavine, T.	1.248		
14. Smiley, J.	1.200	28. Avery, S.	1.252		

WORST RATIOS
(Minimum 75 Innings Pitched)

1. Banks, W.	1.809	15. Brewington, J.	1.500	29. Swindell, G.	1.431
2. Weathers, D.	1.727	16. Valenzuela, F.	1.494	30. Quantrill, P.	1.428
3. Freeman, M.	1.722	17. Wagner, P.	1.491	31. Dishman, G.	1.423
4. Jackson, D.	1.669	18. Ericks, J.	1.491	32. Jones, T.	1.415
5. Reynoso, A.	1.634	19. Parris, S.	1.488	33. Brocail, D.	1.409
6. Greene, T.	1.585	20. Fassero, J.	1.487	34. Burkett, J.	1.407
7. Swift, B.	1.562	21. Gardner, M.	1.485	35. Mercker, K.	1.406
8. Bailey, R.	1.561	22. Mimbs, M.	1.478	36. Drabek, D.	1.400
9. Jarvis, K.	1.557	23. Kile, D.	1.472	37. Hernandez, X.	1.400
10. Trachsel, S.	1.556	24. Watson, A.	1.461	38. Rekar, B.	1.400
11. Hill, K.	1.541	25. Wilson, T.	1.452	39. Benes, A.	1.399
12. Mulholland, T.	1.530	26. Urbani, T.	1.452	40. Rapp, P.	1.398
13. Carrasco, H.	1.511	27. Bautista, J.	1.450		
14. Loaiza, E.	1.506	28. Bullinger, J.	1.447		

EARNED RUN AVERAGE
(Minimum 75 Innings Pitched)

1. Maddux, G.	1.63	15. Castillo, F.	3.21	29. Morgan, M.	3.56
2. Reed, S.	2.14	16. Schourek, P.	3.22	30. Schilling, C.	3.57
3. Veres, D.	2.26	17. Navarro, J.	3.28	31. Parrett, J.	3.64
4. Bottalico, R.	2.46	18. Williams, M.	3.29	32. Martinez, R.	3.66
5. Nomo, H.	2.54	19. Hampton, M.	3.35	33. Van Landingham	3.67
6. McMichael, G.	2.79	20. Mathews, T.	3.38	34. Harnisch, P.	3.68
7. Isringhausen, J.	2.81	21. DeLucia, R.	3.39	35. Perez, C.	3.69
8. Henry, B.	2.84	22. Leskanic, C.	3.40	36. Urbani, T.	3.70
9. Ashby, A.	2.94	23. Neagle, D.	3.43	37. DiPoto, J.	3.78
10. Valdes, I.	3.05	24. Rapp, P.	3.44	38. Hammond, C.	3.80
11. Jones, T.	3.07	25. Smiley, J.	3.46	39. Osborne, D.	3.81
12. Glavine, T.	3.08	26. Reynolds, S.	3.47	40. Leiter, M.	3.82
13. Hamilton, J.	3.08	27. Candiotti, T.	3.50		
14. Smoltz, J.	3.18	28. Martinez, P.	3.51		

WORST EARNED RUN AVERAGES
(Minimum 75 Innings Pitched)

1. Bautista, J.	6.44	15. Valenzuela, F.	4.98	29. Gardner, M.	4.49
2. Weathers, D.	5.98	16. Bailey, R.	4.98	30. Swindell, G.	4.47
3. Jackson, D.	5.90	17. Rekar, B.	4.98	31. Blair, W.	4.34
4. Freeman, M.	5.89	18. Kile, D.	4.96	32. Fassero, J.	4.33
5. Mulholland, T.	5.80	19. Watson, A.	4.96	33. Heredia, G.	4.31
6. Jarvis, K.	5.70	20. Swift, B.	4.94	34. Burkett, J.	4.30
7. Banks, W.	5.66	21. Wagner, P.	4.80	35. Sanders, S.	4.30
8. Parris, S.	5.38	22. Drabek, D.	4.77	36. Mlicki, D.	4.26
9. Reynoso, A.	5.32	23. Avery, S.	4.67	37. Astacio, P.	4.24
10. Greene, T.	5.31	24. Quantrill, P.	4.67	38. Ritz, K.	4.21
11. Loaiza, E.	5.16	25. Hernandez, X.	4.60	39. Brocail, D.	4.19
12. Trachsel, S.	5.15	26. Ericks, J.	4.58	40. Jones, B.	4.19
13. Hill, K.	5.06	27. Brewington, J.	4.54		
14. Dishman, G.	5.01	28. Foster, K.	4.51		

WINS

1. Maddux, G.	19	16. Bullinger, J.	12	31. Mlicki, D.	9
2. Schourek, P.	18	17. Foster, K.	12	32. Hampton, M.	9
3. Martinez, R.	17	18. Portugal, M.	11	33. Mimbs, M.	9
4. Glavine, T.	16	19. Ritz, K.	11	34. Isringhausen, J.	9
5. Burkett, J.	14	20. Castillo, F.	11	35. Valenzuela, F.	8
6. Navarro, J.	14	21. Quantrill, P.	11	36. DeLucia, R.	8
7. Martinez, P.	14	22. Drabek, D.	10	37. Greene, T.	8
8. Rapp, P.	14	23. Swindell, G.	10	38. Clontz, B.	8
9. Fassero, J.	13	24. Leiter, M.	10	39. Dougherty, J.	8
10. Neagle, D.	13	25. Burba, D.	10	40. Loaiza, E.	8
11. Valdes, I.	13	26. Reynolds, S.	10	41. Morgan, M.	7
12. Nomo, H.	13	27. Jones, B.	10	42. Candiotti, T.	7
13. Smiley, J.	12	28. Perez, C.	10	43. Saberhagen, B.	7
14. Smoltz, J.	12	29. Swift, B.	9	44. Schilling, C.	7
15. Ashby, A.	12	30. Hammond, C.	9	45. Hernandez, X.	7

Catchers
pp. 27–41

Corners
pp. 41–62

Infield
pp. 63–82

Outfield
pp. 83–113

DH
pp. 114–118

Starters
pp. 119–157

Relievers
pp. 157–193

SAVES

#	Player		#	Player		#	Player	
1.	Myers, R.	38	20.	Carrasco, H.	5	39.	Borbon, P.	2
2.	Henke, T.	36	21.	Henry, D.	4	40.	McMichael, G.	2
3.	Beck, R.	33	22.	Clontz, B.	4	41.	DiPoto, J.	2
4.	Worrell, T.	32	23.	Gott, J.	3	42.	Walker, M.	1
5.	Slocumb, H.	32	24.	Plesac, D.	3	43.	Frey, S.	1
6.	Hoffman, T.	31	25.	Hernandez, X.	3	44.	Gardner, M.	1
7.	Rojas, M.	30	26.	Seanez, R.	3	45.	Veres, R.	1
8.	Franco, J.	29	27.	Shaw, J.	3	46.	Stanton, M.	1
9.	Brantley, J.	28	28.	Mathews, T.	3	47.	Heredia, G.	1
10.	Wohlers, M.	25	29.	Reed, S.	3	48.	Hickerson, B.	1
11.	Nen, R.	23	30.	Leiper, D.	2	49.	Perez, Y.	1
12.	Miceli, D.	21	31.	Aquino, L.	2	50.	Wagner, P.	1
13.	Jones, T.	15	32.	Jackson, M.	2	51.	Minor, B.	1
14.	Holmes, D.	14	33.	Fraser, W.	2	52.	Barton, S.	1
15.	Ruffin, B.	11	34.	Ritz, K.	2	53.	Brocail, D.	1
16.	Leskanic, C.	10	35.	Munoz, M.	2	54.	Painter, L.	1
17.	Henneman, M.	8	36.	Perez, M.	2			
18.	Hudek, J.	7	37.	Scott, T.	2			
19.	Borland, T.	6	38.	Young, A.	2			

STRIKEOUTS

#	Player		#	Player		#	Player	
1.	Nomo, H.	236	15.	Martinez, R.	138	29.	Trachsel, S.	117
2.	Smoltz, J.	193	16.	Castillo, F.	135	30.	Hampton, M.	115
3.	Maddux, G.	181	17.	Leiter, M.	129	31.	Schilling, C.	114
4.	Reynolds, S.	175	18.	Navarro, J.	128	32.	Kile, D.	113
5.	Martinez, P.	174	19.	Glavine, T.	127	33.	Leskanic, C.	107
6.	Fassero, J.	164	20.	Jones, B.	127	34.	Perez, C.	106
7.	Schourek, P.	160	21.	Burkett, J.	126	35.	Quantrill, P.	103
8.	Ashby, A.	150	22.	Benes, A.	126	36.	Mercker, K.	102
9.	Neagle, D.	150	23.	Hammond, C.	126	37.	Rapp, P.	102
10.	Valdes, I.	150	24.	Smiley, J.	124	38.	Saberhagen, B.	100
11.	Foster, K.	146	25.	Mlicki, D.	123	39.	Portugal, M.	96
12.	Drabek, D.	143	26.	Hamilton, J.	123	40.	Swindell, G.	96
13.	Candiotti, T.	141	27.	Ritz, K.	120			
14.	Avery, S.	141	28.	Wagner, P.	120			

NET WINS

#	Player		#	Player		#	Player	
1.	Maddux, G.	17	16.	Smoltz, J.	5	31.	Barton, S.	3
2.	Schourek, P.	11	17.	Hernandez, X.	5	32.	Reed, S.	3
3.	Martinez, R.	10	18.	Holmes, D.	5	33.	Hoffman, T.	3
4.	Glavine, T.	9	19.	Neagle, D.	5	34.	Painter, L.	3
5.	Navarro, J.	8	20.	McMichael, G.	5	35.	Leskanic, C.	3
6.	Smiley, J.	7	21.	Wohlers, M.	4	36.	Van Landingham	3
7.	Rapp, P.	7	22.	Bullinger, J.	4	37.	Florence, D.	3
8.	Clontz, B.	7	23.	Martinez, P.	4	38.	Pena, A.	2
9.	Nomo, H.	7	24.	Daal, O.	4	39.	Franco, J.	2
10.	Isringhausen, J.	7	25.	Veres, D.	4	40.	Service, S.	2
11.	Swift, B.	6	26.	Dougherty, J.	4	41.	Schilling, C.	2
12.	Burba, D.	6	27.	Hook, C.	4	42.	Tapani, K.	2
13.	Valenzuela, F.	5	28.	Worrell, T.	3	43.	Blair, W.	2
14.	Fernandez, S.	5	29.	Fossas, T.	3	44.	Ashby, A.	2
15.	Jackson, M.	5	30.	Hammond, C.	3	45.	Scott, T.	2

NATIONAL LEAGUE POSITION PLAYERS

HOME RUNS

1. Bichette, D.	40	15. Conine, J.	25	29. King, J.	18
2. Walker, L.	36	16. Hill, G.	24	30. Carreon, M.	17
3. Sosa, S.	36	17. Justice, D.	24	31. Gilkey, B.	17
4. Bonds, B.	33	18. Williams, M.	23	32. Abbott, K.	17
5. Castilla, V.	32	19. Colbrunn, G.	23	33. Grace, M.	16
6. Karros, E.	32	20. Klesko, R.	23	34. Sheffield, G.	16
7. Piazza, M.	32	21. Jones, C.	23	35. Larkin, B.	15
8. Galarraga, A.	31	22. Biggio, C.	22	36. Hundley, T.	15
9. Gant, R.	29	23. Jordan, B.	22	37. Merced, O.	15
10. Sanders, R.	28	24. Brogna, R.	22	38. Boone, B.	15
11. McGriff, F.	27	25. Bagwell, J.	21	39. Pendleton, T.	14
12. Caminiti, K.	26	26. Kent, J.	20	40. Dunston, S.	14
13. Mondesi, R.	26	27. Bonilla, B.	18		
14. Lankford, R.	25	28. Parent, M.	18		

RUNS BATTED IN

1. Bichette, D.	128	15. Colbrunn, G.	89	29. Biggio, C.	77
2. Sosa, S.	119	16. Gant, R.	88	30. Brogna, R.	76
3. Galarraga, A.	106	17. Mondesi, R.	88	31. Klesko, R.	70
4. Conine, J.	105	18. King, J.	87	32. Dunston, S.	69
5. Karros, E.	105	19. Bagwell, J.	87	33. Gilkey, B.	69
6. Bonds, B.	104	20. Hill, G.	86	34. Gonzalez, L.	69
7. Walker, L.	101	21. Bell, D.	86	35. Segui, D.	68
8. Sanders, R.	99	22. Jones, C.	86	36. Boone, B.	68
9. Caminiti, K.	94	23. Hayes, C.	85	37. Larkin, B.	66
10. McGriff, F.	93	24. Merced, O.	83	38. Williams, M.	65
11. Piazza, M.	93	25. Lankford, R.	82	39. Carreon, M.	65
12. Grace, M.	92	26. Jordan, B.	81	40. Kent, J.	65
13. Gwynn, T.	90	27. Pendleton, T.	78		
14. Castilla, V.	90	28. Justice, D.	78		

STOLEN BASES

1. Veras, Q.	56	15. Lansing, M.	27	29. Cangelosi, J.	21
2. Larkin, B.	51	16. Mondesi, R.	27	30. Roberts, B.	20
3. DeShields, D.	39	17. Hill, G.	25	31. Martin, A.	20
4. Finley, S.	36	18. Carr, C.	25	32. Fonville, C.	20
5. Sanders, R.	36	19. White, R.	25	33. Kelly, R.	19
6. Young, E.	35	20. Mouton, J.	25	34. Sheffield, G.	19
7. Sosa, S.	34	21. Sanders, D.	24	35. Gwynn, T.	17
8. Biggio, C.	33	22. Lankford, R.	24	36. Howard, T.	17
9. Butler, B.	32	23. Clayton, R.	24	37. Walker, L.	16
10. Lewis, D.	32	24. Jordan, B.	24	38. Ausmus, B.	16
11. Bonds, B.	31	25. Tarasco, T.	24	39. Weiss, W.	15
12. Grissom, M.	29	26. Hunter, B.	24	40. Kingery, M.	13
13. McRae, B.	27	27. Gant, R.	23		
14. Bell, D.	27	28. Brumfield, J.	22		

Catchers
pp. 27–41

Corners
pp. 41–62

Infield
pp. 63–82

Outfield
pp. 83–113

DH
pp. 114–118

Starters
pp. 119–157

Relievers
pp. 157–193

RUNS SCORED

1. Biggio, C.	123	15. Jones, C.	87	29. Caminiti, K.	74
2. Bonds, B.	109	16. Veras, Q.	86	30. Justice, D.	73
3. Finley, S.	104	17. McGriff, F.	85	31. Gilkey, B.	73
4. Bichette, D.	102	18. Karros, E.	83	32. Conine, J.	72
5. Larkin, B.	98	19. Jordan, B.	83	33. Brogna, R.	72
6. Grace, M.	97	20. Gwynn, T.	82	34. Hill, G.	71
7. Walker, L.	96	21. Castilla, V.	82	35. Pendleton, T.	70
8. McRae, B.	92	22. Piazza, M.	82	36. Colbrunn, G.	70
9. Sanders, R.	91	23. Lankford, R.	81	37. Martin, A.	70
10. Mondesi, R.	91	24. Grissom, M.	80	38. Jefferies, G.	69
11. Galarraga, A.	89	25. Bell, J.	79	39. Offerman, J.	69
12. Sosa, S.	89	26. Gant, R.	79	40. Gonzalez, L.	69
13. Bagwell, J.	88	27. Butler, B.	78		
14. White, R.	87	28. Merced, O.	75		

BATTING AVERAGE
(Minimum 225 At Bats)

1. Gwynn, T.	.368	15. Castilla, V.	.309	29. Merced, O.	.300
2. Piazza, M.	.346	16. Segui, D.	.309	30. Eusebio, T.	.299
3. Bichette, D.	.340	17. Mabry, J.	.307	31. Gilkey, B.	.298
4. Williams, M.	.336	18. Jefferies, G.	.306	32. Karros, E.	.298
5. Bell, D.	.334	19. Sanders, R.	.306	33. Finley, S.	.297
6. Grace, M.	.326	20. Walker, L.	.306	34. Jordan, B.	.296
7. Bonilla, B.	.325	21. Roberts, B.	.304	35. Dunston, S.	.296
8. Larkin, B.	.319	22. Howard, T.	.302	36. White, R.	.295
9. Berry, S.	.318	23. Caminiti, K.	.302	37. Bonds, B.	.294
10. Young, E.	.317	24. Conine, J.	.302	38. Garcia, C.	.294
11. Eisenreich, J.	.316	25. Hunter, B.	.302	39. Ausmus, B.	.293
12. Lopez, J.	.315	26. Biggio, C.	.302	40. Pendleton, T.	.290
13. Magadan, D.	.313	27. Carreon, M.	.301		
14. Klesko, R.	.310	28. Butler, B.	.300		

WORST BATTING AVERAGES
(Minimum 225 At Bats)

1. Phillips, J.	.195	15. Daulton, D.	.249	29. Everett, C.	.260
2. Nieves, M.	.205	16. Tarasco, T.	.249	30. Branson, J.	.260
3. Cedeno, A.	.210	17. Lewis, D.	.250	31. Weiss, W.	.260
4. Blauser, J.	.211	18. Manwaring, K.	.251	32. Williams, E.	.260
5. Stocker, K.	.218	19. Johnson, C.	.251	33. Veras, Q.	.261
6. Thompson, R.	.223	20. Thompson, R.	.251	34. Mouton, J.	.262
7. Cromer, T.	.226	21. Justice, D.	.253	35. Girardi, J.	.262
8. Carr, C.	.227	22. Lemke, M.	.253	36. Bell, J.	.262
9. Cooper, S.	.230	23. Abbott, K.	.255	37. Miller, O.	.262
10. Parent, M.	.234	24. Lansing, M.	.255	38. Shipley, C.	.263
11. Clayton, R.	.244	25. Reed, J.	.256	39. Hill, G.	.264
12. Hernandez, J.	.245	26. DeShields, D.	.256	40. Dykstra, L.	.264
13. Grudzielanek, M.	.245	27. Dawson, A.	.257		
14. Zeile, T.	.246	28. Grissom, M.	.258		

AMERICAN LEAGUE PITCHERS

RATIO
(Minimum 75 Innings Pitched)

1. Johnson, R.	1.045	15. Rogers, K.	1.288	29. Langston, M.	1.378
2. Mussina, M.	1.069	16. Fernandez, A.	1.301	30. Abbott, J.	1.386
3. Nelson, J.	1.081	17. Van Poppel, T.	1.308	31. Ontiveros, S.	1.404
4. Maddux, M.	1.126	18. McDonald, B.	1.313	32. Finley, C.	1.404
5. Tavarez, J.	1.141	19. Hanson, E.	1.318	33. Anderson, B.	1.405
6. Ogea, C.	1.166	20. Hitchcock, S.	1.325	34. Pettitte, A.	1.406
7. Martinez, D.	1.176	21. McDowell, J.	1.328	35. Cormier, R.	1.409
8. Brown, K.	1.178	22. Gubicza, M.	1.331	36. McDowell, R.	1.412
9. Wakefield, T.	1.183	23. Radke, B.	1.337	37. Tapani, K.	1.414
10. Wells, D.	1.205	24. Krivda, R.	1.341	38. Lira, F.	1.415
11. Appier, K.	1.207	25. Boskie, S.	1.361	39. Erickson, S.	1.426
12. Hershiser, O.	1.207	26. Haney, C.	1.365	40. Nagy, C.	1.433
13. Cone, D.	1.234	27. Wickman, B.	1.375		
14. Moyer, J.	1.271	28. Pavlik, R.	1.377		

WORST RATIOS
(Minimum 75 Innings Pitched)

1. Bere, J.	1.867	15. Hentgen, P.	1.625	29. Keyser, B.	1.527
2. Moore, M.	1.862	16. Rodriguez, F.	1.618	30. Trombley, M.	1.526
3. Klingenbeck, S.	1.795	17. McCaskill, K.	1.605	31. Menhart, P.	1.513
4. Bergman, S.	1.744	18. Harkey, M.	1.586	32. Smith, Z.	1.509
5. Boever, J.	1.743	19. Givens, B.	1.584	33. Alvarez, W.	1.509
6. Scanlan, B.	1.740	20. Guardado, E.	1.577	34. Bones, R.	1.502
7. Stewart, D.	1.728	21. Gross, K.	1.574	35. Eshelman, V.	1.494
8. Fleming, D.	1.712	22. Hurtado, E.	1.558	36. Clark, M.	1.484
9. Wells, B.	1.657	23. Mahomes, P.	1.553	37. Doherty, J.	1.478
10. Guzman, J.	1.655	24. Gordon, T.	1.550	38. Leiter, A.	1.475
11. Roberson, S.	1.648	25. Karl, S.	1.540	39. Bielecki, M.	1.473
12. Bosio, C.	1.647	26. Rhodes, A.	1.540	40. Kamieniecki, S.	1.472
13. Darwin, D.	1.636	27. Belcher, T.	1.539		
14. Darling, R.	1.635	28. Bohanon, B.	1.533		

EARNED RUN AVERAGE
(Minimum 75 Innings Pitched)

1. Nelson, J.	2.17	15. Abbott, J.	3.70	29. Finley, C.	4.21
2. Tavarez, J.	2.44	16. Gubicza, M.	3.75	30. Hanson, E.	4.24
3. Johnson, R.	2.48	17. Fernandez, A.	3.80	31. Lira, F.	4.31
4. Wakefield, T.	2.95	18. Hershiser, O.	3.87	32. Alvarez, W.	4.32
5. Wells, D.	3.04	19. Appier, K.	3.89	33. Pavlik, R.	4.37
6. Ogea, C.	3.05	20. McDowell, J.	3.93	34. Ontiveros, S.	4.37
7. Martinez, D.	3.08	21. Kamieniecki, S.	4.01	35. Gordon, T.	4.43
8. Mussina, M.	3.29	22. McDowell, R.	4.02	36. Belcher, T.	4.52
9. Rogers, K.	3.38	23. Wickman, B.	4.05	37. Krivda, R.	4.54
10. Cone, D.	3.57	24. Cormier, R.	4.07	38. Stottlemyre, T.	4.55
11. Brown, K.	3.60	25. Karl, S.	4.14	39. Nagy, C.	4.55
12. Maddux, M.	3.61	26. McDonald, B.	4.16	40. Tewksbury, B.	4.58
13. Leiter, A.	3.64	27. Pettitte, A.	4.17		
14. Haney, C.	3.65	28. Clemens, R.	4.18		

Catchers
pp. 27–41

Corners
pp. 41–62

Infield
pp. 63–82

Outfield
pp. 83–113

DH
pp. 114–118

Starters
pp. 119–157

Relievers
pp. 157–193

WORST EARNED RUN AVERAGES
(Minimum 75 Innings Pitched)

1.	Moore, M.	7.53	15.	Anderson, B.	5.87	29.	Guardado, E.	5.12
2.	Darwin, D.	7.45	16.	Roberson, S.	5.76	30.	Bergman, S.	5.12
3.	Bere, J.	7.19	17.	Wells, B.	5.75	31.	Hentgen, P.	5.11
4.	Klingenbeck, S.	7.12	18.	Boskie, S.	5.64	32.	Doherty, J.	5.10
5.	Stewart, D.	6.89	19.	Trombley, M.	5.62	33.	Keyser, B.	4.97
6.	Scanlan, B.	6.59	20.	Smith, Z.	5.61	34.	Givens, B.	4.95
7.	Boever, J.	6.39	21.	Gross, K.	5.54	35.	Bosio, C.	4.92
8.	Mahomes, P.	6.37	22.	Bohanon, B.	5.54	36.	Menhart, P.	4.92
9.	Guzman, J.	6.32	23.	Hurtado, E.	5.45	37.	Tapani, K.	4.92
10.	Darling, R.	6.23	24.	Harkey, M.	5.44	38.	McCaskill, K.	4.89
11.	Rhodes, A.	6.21	25.	Jacome, J.	5.36	39.	Van Poppel, T.	4.88
12.	Rodriguez, F.	6.13	26.	Radke, B.	5.32	40.	Eshelman, V.	4.85
13.	Bielecki, M.	5.97	27.	Clark, M.	5.27			
14.	Fleming, D.	5.96	28.	Moyer, J.	5.21			

WINS

1.	Mussina, M.	19	16.	Gubicza, M.	12	31.	Pavlik, R.	10
2.	Cone, D.	18	17.	Gordon, T.	12	32.	Tavarez, J.	10
3.	Johnson, R.	18	18.	Fernandez, A.	12	33.	Gross, K.	9
4.	Rogers, K.	17	19.	Pettitte, A.	12	34.	Ontiveros, S.	9
5.	Hershiser, O.	16	20.	Leiter, A.	11	35.	Clark, M.	9
6.	Nagy, C.	16	21.	Abbott, J.	11	36.	Lira, F.	9
7.	Wakefield, T.	16	22.	Hitchcock, S.	11	37.	Sparks, S.	9
8.	Langston, M.	15	23.	Radke, B.	11	38.	Smith, Z.	8
9.	Finley, C.	15	24.	Clemens, R.	10	39.	Tewksbury, B.	8
10.	McDowell, J.	15	25.	Bosio, C.	10	40.	Moyer, J.	8
11.	Hanson, E.	15	26.	Brown, K.	10	41.	Harkey, M.	8
12.	Appier, K.	15	27.	Belcher, T.	10	42.	Alvarez, W.	8
13.	Stottlemyre, T.	14	28.	Wells, D.	10	43.	Belinda, S.	8
14.	Erickson, S.	13	29.	Bones, R.	10	44.	Pichardo, H.	8
15.	Martinez, D.	12	30.	Hentgen, P.	10	45.	Bere, J.	8

SAVES

1.	Mesa, J.	46	20.	Timlin, M.	5	39.	Nelson, J.	2
2.	Smith, L.	37	21.	McDowell, R.	4	40.	Guardado, E.	2
3.	Aguilera, R.	32	22.	Vosberg, E.	4	41.	Benitez, A.	2
4.	Hernandez, R.	32	23.	Lloyd, G.	4	42.	Guetterman, L.	1
5.	Montgomery, J.	31	24.	Orosco, J.	3	43.	Maddux, M.	1
6.	Wetteland, J.	31	25.	Boever, J.	3	44.	Dibble, R.	1
7.	Eckersley, D.	29	26.	Olson, G.	3	45.	Clark, T.	1
8.	Jones, D.	22	27.	Mahomes, P.	3	46.	Lee, M.	1
9.	Fetters, M.	22	28.	Whiteside, M.	3	47.	Wickander, K.	1
10.	Russell, J.	20	29.	Hall, D.	3	48.	Grimsley, J.	1
11.	Ayala, B.	19	30.	Percival, T.	3	49.	Radinsky, S.	1
12.	Henneman, M.	18	31.	Howe, S.	2	50.	Bohanon, B.	1
13.	Charlton, N.	14	32.	Honeycutt, R.	2	51.	Christopher, M.	1
14.	Castillo, T.	13	33.	Wegman, B.	2	52.	Springer, R.	1
15.	Belinda, S.	10	34.	McCaskill, K.	2	53.	Pichardo, H.	1
16.	Stevens, D.	10	35.	Plunk, E.	2	54.	Groom, B.	1
17.	Ryan, K.	7	36.	Corsi, J.	2	55.	Risley, B.	1
18.	Doherty, J.	6	37.	Cook, D.	2			
19.	Henry, D.	5	38.	Meacham, R.	2			

STRIKEOUTS

1. Johnson, R.	294	15. Hentgen, P.	135	29. Belcher, T.	96
2. Stottlemyre, T.	205	16. Clemens, R.	132	30. Nelson, J.	96
3. Finley, C.	195	17. Van Poppel, T.	122	31. Sparks, S.	96
4. Cone, D.	191	18. Hitchcock, S.	121	32. Guzman, J.	94
5. Appier, K.	185	19. Gordon, T.	119	33. Percival, T.	94
6. Fernandez, A.	159	20. Wakefield, T.	119	34. Lira, F.	89
7. Mussina, M.	158	21. Alvarez, W.	118	35. Tapani, K.	88
8. McDowell, J.	157	22. Brown, K.	117	36. Abbott, J.	86
9. Leiter, A.	153	23. Pettitte, A.	114	37. Bergman, S.	86
10. Pavlik, R.	149	24. Hershiser, O.	111	38. Bosio, C.	85
11. Langston, M.	142	25. Bere, J.	110	39. Hernandez, R.	84
12. Rogers, K.	140	26. Gross, K.	106	40. Wells, D.	83
13. Hanson, E.	139	27. Erickson, S.	106		
14. Nagy, C.	139	28. Martinez, D.	99		

NET WINS

1. Johnson, R.	16	16. McDowell, J.	5	31. Finley, C.	3
2. Hershiser, O.	10	17. Appier, K.	5	32. Maddux, M.	3
3. Cone, D.	10	18. Benes, A.	5	33. Patterson, B.	3
4. Rogers, K.	10	19. Butcher, M.	5	34. Mesa, J.	3
5. Hanson, E.	10	20. Ogea, C.	5	35. Hill, K.	3
6. Nagy, C.	10	21. Honeycutt, R.	4	36. Abbott, J.	3
7. Mussina, M.	10	22. Plunk, E.	4	37. Mills, A.	3
8. Langston, M.	8	23. Assenmacher, P.	4	38. Erickson, S.	3
9. Wakefield, T.	8	24. Fernandez, A.	4	39. Ignasiak, M.	3
10. Tavarez, J.	8	25. Christopher, M.	4	40. Kiefer, M.	3
11. Martinez, D.	7	26. Nelson, J.	4	41. James, M.	3
12. Wells, D.	7	27. Pichardo, H.	4	42. Eshelman, V.	3
13. Stottlemyre, T.	7	28. Howe, S.	3	43. Pettitte, A.	3
14. Belinda, S.	7	29. Ontiveros, S.	3	44. Hurtado, E.	3
15. Clemens, R.	5	30. McDowell, R.	3	45. Black, B.	2

Catchers
pp. 27–41

Corners
pp. 41–62

Infield
pp. 63–82

Outfield
pp. 83–113

DH
pp. 114–118

Starters
pp. 119–157

Relievers
pp. 157–193

AMERICAN LEAGUE POSITION PLAYERS

HOME RUNS

1. Belle, A.	50	15. Phillips, T.	27	29. Berroa, G.	22
2. Buhner, J.	40	16. Gonzalez, J.	27	30. Murray, E.	21
3. Thomas, F.	40	17. Valentin, J.	27	31. Curtis, C.	21
4. McGwire, M.	39	18. Ventura, R.	26	32. Davis, C.	20
5. Palmeiro, R.	39	19. Carter, J.	25	33. Jaha, J.	20
6. Vaughn, M.	39	20. Sorrento, P.	25	34. Sierra, R.	19
7. Gaetti, G.	35	21. Thome, J.	25	35. Hoiles, C.	19
8. Salmon, T.	34	22. Baines, H.	24	36. Stanley, M.	18
9. Edmonds, J.	33	23. Canseco, J.	24	37. Munoz, P.	18
10. Tettleton, M.	32	24. Snow, J.	24	38. Sprague, E.	18
11. Fielder, C.	31	25. Cordova, M.	24	39. Williams, B.	18
12. Martinez, T.	31	26. Puckett, K.	23	40. Ripken, C.	17
13. Ramirez, M.	31	27. Blowers, M.	23		
14. Martinez, E.	29	28. O'Neill, P.	22		

RUNS BATTED IN

1. Belle, A.	126	15. O'Neill, P.	96	29. Murray, E.	82
2. Vaughn, M.	126	16. Blowers, M.	96	30. Gonzalez, J.	82
3. Buhner, J.	121	17. Ventura, R.	93	31. Williams, B.	82
4. Martinez, E.	113	18. Clark, W.	92	32. Canseco, J.	81
5. Thomas, F.	111	19. McGwire, M.	90	33. Fryman, T.	81
6. Martinez, T.	111	20. Baerga, C.	90	34. Sorrento, P.	79
7. Ramirez, M.	107	21. Ripken, C.	88	35. Tettleton, M.	78
8. Edmonds, J.	107	22. Berroa, G.	88	36. Carter, J.	76
9. Salmon, T.	105	23. Davis, C.	86	37. Greenwell, M.	76
10. Palmeiro, R.	104	24. Sierra, R.	86	38. Sprague, E.	74
11. Valentin, J.	102	25. Cordova, M.	84	39. Surhoff, B.	73
12. Snow, J.	102	26. Joyner, W.	83	40. Thome, J.	73
13. Puckett, K.	99	27. Stanley, M.	83		
14. Gaetti, G.	96	28. Fielder, C.	82		

STOLEN BASES

1. Lofton, K.	54	15. Amaral, R.	21	29. Molitor, P.	12
2. Nixon, O.	50	16. Valentin, J.	20	30. Carter, J.	12
3. Goodwin, T.	50	17. Cordova, M.	20	31. White, D.	11
4. Knoblauch, C.	46	18. Cora, J.	18	32. Hamilton, D.	11
5. Coleman, V.	42	19. Diaz, A.	18	33. Baerga, C.	11
6. Johnson, L.	40	20. Tinsley, L.	18	34. Bordick, M.	11
7. Javier, S.	36	21. Durham, R.	18	35. Vaughn, M.	11
8. Henderson, R.	32	22. Valentin, J.	16	36. Alexander, M.	11
9. Alomar, R.	30	23. Hulse, D.	15	37. Polonia, L.	10
10. Vizquel, O.	29	24. Raines, T.	13	38. Vaughn, G.	10
11. Curtis, C.	27	25. Phillips, T.	13	39. Kirby, W.	10
12. Anderson, B.	26	26. Hudler, R.	13	40. Meares, P.	10
13. Goodwin, C.	22	27. Alicea, L.	13		
14. McLemore, M.	21	28. Listach, P.	13		

RUNS SCORED

1. Martinez, E.	121	15. Martinez, T.	92	29. Javier, S.	81
2. Belle, A.	121	16. Thome, J.	92	30. Cordova, M.	81
3. Edmonds, J.	120	17. Palmeiro, R.	89	31. Snow, J.	80
4. Phillips, T.	119	18. Nixon, O.	87	32. Ventura, R.	79
5. Salmon, T.	111	19. Berroa, G.	87	33. Fryman, T.	79
6. Anderson, B.	108	20. Vizquel, O.	87	34. Sprague, E.	77
7. Valentin, J.	108	21. Baerga, C.	87	35. Gaetti, G.	76
8. Knoblauch, C.	107	22. Buhner, J.	86	36. Boggs, W.	76
9. Thomas, F.	102	23. Clark, W.	85	37. Tettleton, M.	76
10. Johnson, L.	98	24. Ramirez, M.	85	38. McGwire, M.	75
11. Vaughn, M.	98	25. Puckett, K.	83	39. McLemore, M.	73
12. Curtis, C.	96	26. O'Neill, P.	82	40. Sierra, R.	73
13. Williams, B.	93	27. Raines, T.	81		
14. Lofton, K.	93	28. Davis, C.	81		

BATTING AVERAGE
(Minimum 225 At Bats)

1. Martinez, E.	.356	15. Jaha, J.	.313	29. Canseco, J.	.306
2. Bonilla, B.	.333	16. Seitzer, K.	.311	30. Rodriguez, I.	.303
3. Knoblauch, C.	.333	17. Palmeiro, R.	.310	31. Clark, W.	.302
4. Salmon, T.	.330	18. Lofton, K.	.310	32. Munoz, P.	.301
5. Boggs, W.	.324	19. Joyner, W.	.310	33. O'Neill, P.	.300
6. Murray, E.	.323	20. Thomas, F.	.308	34. Vaughn, M.	.300
7. Lockhart, K.	.321	21. O'Leary, T.	.308	35. Alomar, R.	.300
8. Anderson, G.	.321	22. Ramirez, M.	.308	36. Henderson, R.	.300
9. Surhoff, B.	.320	23. Williams, B.	.307	37. Baines, H.	.299
10. Davis, C.	.318	24. Naehring, T.	.307	38. Valentin, J.	.298
11. Belle, A.	.317	25. Martinez, D.	.307	39. Cora, J.	.297
12. Baerga, C.	.314	26. DiSarcina, G.	.307	40. Greenwell, M.	.297
13. Thome, J.	.314	27. Johnson, L.	.306		
14. Puckett, K.	.314	28. Devereaux, M.	.306		

WORST BATTING AVERAGES
(Minimum 225 At Bats)

1. Bautista, D.	.203	15. Tartabull, D.	.236	29. Leius, S.	.247
2. Easley, D.	.216	16. Kelly, P.	.237	30. Diaz, A.	.248
3. Karkovice, R.	.217	17. Becker, R.	.237	31. Guillen, O.	.248
4. Listach, P.	.219	18. Tettleton, M.	.238	32. Hoiles, C.	.250
5. Valentin, J.	.219	19. Barberie, B.	.241	33. Hulse, D.	.251
6. Gil, B.	.219	20. Gonzalez, A.	.243	34. Mayne, B.	.251
7. Gomez, C.	.223	21. Fielder, C.	.243	35. Mieske, M.	.251
8. Higginson, B.	.224	22. Flaherty, J.	.243	36. Carter, J.	.253
9. Vaughn, G.	.224	23. Howard, D.	.243	37. Gates, B.	.254
10. Macfarlane, M.	.225	24. Sprague, E.	.244	38. Gagne, G.	.256
11. Paquette, C.	.226	25. Bass, K.	.244	39. Manto, J.	.256
12. Pagliarulo, M.	.232	26. Nunnally, J.	.244	40. Durham, R.	.257
13. Sorrento, P.	.235	27. Fernandez, T.	.245		
14. Alexander, M.	.236	28. Fabregas, J.	.247		

Catchers
pp. 27–41

Corners
pp. 41–62

Infield
pp. 63–82

Outfield
pp. 83–113

DH
pp. 114–118

Starters
pp. 119–157

Relievers
pp. 157–193

PRESEASON CHECKLIST

✓ 1. Call Roti•Stats for info about stats service: 800-676-7684.
✓ 2. Join the RLBA (see page 266).
✓ 3. Send in for Free Opening Day Update (see page 266).
✓ 4. Outfit entire neighborhood in Rotisserie Caps and T-shirts (see page 267).
✓ 5. Cancel all business and social plans for two weeks prior to auction draft.

TOP POSITION PLAYERS, 1995

NL CATCHERS
(20 Games or More)

HOME RUNS

1. Piazza, M.	32	11. Taubensee, E.	9	21. Hemond, S.	3
2. Parent, M.	18	12. Girardi, J.	8	22. Decker, S.	3
3. Hundley, T.	15	13. Wilkins, R.	7	23. Laker, T.	3
4. Lopez, J.	14	14. Eusebio, T.	6	24. Johnson, B.	3
5. Servais, S.	13	15. Sheaffer, D.	5	25. Pagnozzi, T.	2
6. Santiago, B.	11	16. Ausmus, B.	5	26. Berryhill, D.	2
7. Fletcher, D.	11	17. Manwaring, K.	4	27. Hernandez, C.	2
8. Johnson, C.	11	18. Borders, P.	4	28. Encarnacion, A.	2
9. Daulton, D.	9	19. Webster, L.	4	29. Spehr, T.	1
10. O'Brien, C.	9	20. Stinnett, K.	4	30. Tucker, S.	1

BATTING AVERAGE

1. Piazza, M.	.346	11. Reed, J.	.266	21. Sheaffer, D.	.231
2. Lopez, J.	.315	12. Servais, S.	.265	22. O'Brien, C.	.227
3. Slaught, D.	.304	13. Girardi, J.	.262	23. Encarnacion, A.	.226
4. Eusebio, T.	.299	14. Spehr, T.	.257	24. Decker, S.	.226
5. Ausmus, B.	.292	15. Johnson, B.	.251	25. Stinnett, K.	.219
6. Santiago, B.	.286	16. Johnson, C.	.251	26. Pagnozzi, T.	.215
7. Fletcher, D.	.286	17. Manwaring, K.	.250	27. Borders, P.	.208
8. Taubensee, E.	.284	18. Daulton, D.	.249	28. Wilkins, R.	.203
9. Hundley, T.	.280	19. Laker, T.	.234	29. Berryhill, D.	.183
10. Webster, L.	.267	20. Parent, M.	.234	30. Hernandez, C.	.149

RUNS BATTED IN

1. Piazza, M.	93	11. Johnson, C.	39	21. Pagnozzi, T.	15
2. Eusebio, T.	58	12. Parent, M.	38	22. Webster, L.	14
3. Daulton, D.	55	13. Manwaring, K.	36	23. Slaught, D.	13
4. Girardi, J.	55	14. Ausmus, B.	34	24. Borders, P.	13
5. Hundley, T.	51	15. Sheaffer, D.	30	25. Decker, S.	13
6. Lopez, J.	51	16. Johnson, B.	29	26. Berryhill, D.	11
7. Servais, S.	47	17. O'Brien, C.	23	27. Encarnacion, A.	10
8. Fletcher, D.	45	18. Laker, T.	20	28. Reed, J.	9
9. Santiago, B.	44	19. Wilkins, R.	19	29. Hemond, S.	9
10. Taubensee, E.	44	20. Stinnett, K.	18	30. Hernandez, C.	8

STOLEN BASES

1. Ausmus, B.	16	7. Stinnett, K.	2
2. Daulton, D.	3	8. Manwaring, K.	1
3. Girardi, J.	3	9. Hundley, T.	1
4. Santiago, B.	2	10. Decker, S.	1
5. Taubensee, E.	2	11. Piazza, M.	1
6. Servais, S.	2	12. Encarnacion, A.	1

RUNS SCORED

1. Piazza, M.	82	11. Lopez, J.	37	21. Encarnacion, A.	18
2. Girardi, J.	63	12. Taubensee, E.	32	22. Pagnozzi, T.	17
3. Eusebio, T.	46	13. Parent, M.	30	23. Laker, T.	17
4. Daulton, D.	44	14. Wilkins, R.	30	24. Borders, P.	15
5. Ausmus, B.	44	15. Sheaffer, D.	24	25. Slaught, D.	13
6. Fletcher, D.	42	16. Stinnett, K.	23	26. Reed, J.	12
7. Santiago, B.	40	17. Manwaring, K.	21	27. Decker, S.	12
8. Johnson, C.	40	18. Johnson, B.	20	28. Hemond, S.	11
9. Hundley, T.	39	19. O'Brien, C.	18	29. Berryhill, D.	6
10. Servais, S.	38	20. Webster, L.	18	30. Spehr, T.	4

AL CATCHERS
(20 Games or More)

HOME RUNS

1. Hoiles, C.	19	10. Myers, G.	9	19. Zaun, G.	3
2. Stanley, M.	18	11. Wilson, D.	9	20. Martinez, S.	2
3. Steinbach, T.	15	12. Leyritz, J.	7	21. LaValliere, M.	1
4. Macfarlane, M.	15	13. Pena, T.	5	22. Kreuter, C.	1
5. Karkovice, R.	13	14. Haselman, B.	5	23. Merullo, M.	1
6. Oliver, J.	12	15. Parrish, L.	4	24. Mayne, B.	1
7. Rodriguez, I.	12	16. Tingley, R.	4	25. Walbeck, M.	1
8. Flaherty, J.	11	17. Allanson, A.	3	26. Fabregas, J.	1
9. Alomar Jr, S.	10	18. Knorr, R.	3		

BATTING AVERAGE

1. Rodriguez, I.	.303	11. Zaun, G.	.260	21. Martinez, S.	.241
2. Alomar Jr, S.	.300	12. Walbeck, M.	.257	22. Valle, D.	.240
3. Merullo, M.	.282	13. Mercedes, H.	.256	23. Kreuter, C.	.227
4. Steinbach, T.	.278	14. Mayne, B.	.251	24. Tingley, R.	.226
5. Wilson, D.	.278	15. Hoiles, C.	.250	25. Macfarlane, M.	.225
6. Oliver, J.	.273	16. Matheny, M.	.247	26. Karkovice, R.	.217
7. Leyritz, J.	.269	17. Fabregas, J.	.247	27. Knorr, R.	.212
8. Stanley, M.	.268	18. LaValliere, M.	.245	28. Parrish, L.	.202
9. Pena, T.	.262	19. Haselman, B.	.243	29. Allanson, A.	.171
10. Myers, G.	.260	20. Flaherty, J.	.243	30. Helfand, E.	.163

RUNS BATTED IN

1. Stanley, M.	83	11. Myers, G.	38	21. Matheny, M.	21
2. Rodriguez, I.	67	12. Leyritz, J.	37	22. LaValliere, M.	19
3. Steinbach, T.	65	13. Alomar Jr, S.	35	23. Tingley, R.	18
4. Hoiles, C.	58	14. Pena, T.	28	24. Knorr, R.	16
5. Karkovice, R.	51	15. Merullo, M.	27	25. Zaun, G.	14
6. Macfarlane, M.	51	16. Mayne, B.	27	26. Allanson, A.	10
7. Oliver, J.	51	17. Martinez, S.	25	27. Mercedes, H.	9
8. Wilson, D.	51	18. Haselman, B.	23	28. Kreuter, C.	8
9. Walbeck, M.	44	19. Parrish, L.	22	29. Helfand, E.	7
10. Flaherty, J.	40	20. Fabregas, J.	22	30. Valle, D.	5

STOLEN BASES

1. Alomar Jr, S.	3	6. Wilson, D.	2	11. Stanley, M.	1
2. Walbeck, M.	3	7. Matheny, M.	2	12. Hoiles, C.	1
3. Karkovice, R.	2	8. Pena, T.	1	13. Leyritz, J.	1
4. Macfarlane, M.	2	9. Valle, D.	1	14. Zaun, G.	1
5. Oliver, J.	2	10. Steinbach, T.	1		

Catchers
pp. 27–41

Corners
pp. 41–62

Infield
pp. 63–82

Outfield
pp. 83–113

DH
pp. 114–118

Starters
pp. 119–157

Relievers
pp. 157–193

RUNS SCORED

1. Stanley, M.	63	11. Leyritz, J.	37	21. Parrish, L.	15
2. Rodriguez, I.	56	12. Myers, G.	35	22. Tingley, R.	14
3. Hoiles, C.	53	13. Alomar Jr, S.	32	23. Matheny, M.	13
4. Macfarlane, M.	45	14. Pena, T.	25	24. Kreuter, C.	12
5. Karkovice, R.	44	15. Fabregas, J.	24	25. Martinez, S.	12
6. Steinbach, T.	43	16. Mayne, B.	23	26. Helfand, E.	9
7. Oliver, J.	43	17. Haselman, B.	22	27. Valle, D.	7
8. Wilson, D.	40	18. Merullo, M.	19	28. LaValliere, M.	7
9. Walbeck, M.	40	19. Knorr, R.	18	29. Mercedes, H.	7
10. Flaherty, J.	39	20. Zaun, G.	18	30. Allanson, A.	5

NL CORNERS
(20 Games or More)

HOME RUNS

1. Castilla, V.	32	16. Zeile, T.	14	31. Johnson, H.	7
2. Karros, E.	32	17. Berry, S.	14	32. Oliva, J.	7
3. Galarraga, A.	31	18. Hernandez, J.	13	33. Young, K.	6
4. McGriff, F.	27	19. Johnson, M.	13	34. Livingstone, S.	5
5. Caminiti, K.	26	20. Williams, E.	12	35. Cianfrocco, A.	5
6. Williams, M.	23	21. Segui, D.	12	36. Mabry, J.	5
7. Colbrunn, G.	23	22. Branson, J.	12	37. Alfonzo, E.	4
8. Jones, C.	23	23. Jefferies, G.	11	38. Coles, D.	3
9. Brogna, R.	22	24. Morris, H.	11	39. Shipley, C.	3
10. Bagwell, J.	21	25. Hayes, C.	11	40. Benjamin, M.	3
11. King, J.	18	26. Scarsone, S.	11	41. Cooper, S.	3
12. Carreon, M.	17	27. Wallach, T.	9	42. Lewis, M.	3
13. Grace, M.	16	28. Simms, M.	9	43. Arias, A.	3
14. Merced, O.	15	29. Phillips, J.	9	44. Huskey, B.	3
15. Pendleton, T.	14	30. Andrews, S.	8	45. Petagine, R.	3

BATTING AVERAGE

1. Lewis, M.	.339	18. Brogna, R.	.289	35. Simms, M.	.256
2. Livingstone, S.	.337	19. Hansen, D.	.287	36. Aude, R.	.248
3. Williams, M.	.335	20. McGriff, F.	.280	37. Zeile, T.	.247
4. Grace, M.	.326	21. Galarraga, A.	.280	38. Grudzielanek, M.	.245
5. Berry, S.	.318	22. Morris, H.	.278	39. Hernandez, J.	.245
6. Magadan, D.	.313	23. Alfonzo, E.	.278	40. Petagine, R.	.234
7. Segui, D.	.309	24. Colbrunn, G.	.276	41. Young, K.	.232
8. Castilla, V.	.309	25. Hayes, C.	.276	42. Cooper, S.	.230
9. Mabry, J.	.307	26. Arias, A.	.269	43. McCarty, D.	.227
10. Jefferies, G.	.306	27. Wallach, T.	.266	44. Coles, D.	.225
11. Caminiti, K.	.302	28. Scarsone, S.	.266	45. Benjamin, M.	.220
12. Carreon, M.	.300	29. King, J.	.265	46. Hunter, B.	.215
13. Merced, O.	.300	30. Jones, C.	.265	47. Andrews, S.	.214
14. Karros, E.	.298	31. Shipley, C.	.263	48. Johnson, M.	.208
15. Pendleton, T.	.291	32. Cianfrocco, A.	.263	49. Harris, L.	.208
16. Bagwell, J.	.290	33. Williams, E.	.260	50. Johnson, H.	.195
17. Bogar, T.	.290	34. Branson, J.	.260		

RUNS BATTED IN

1. Galarraga, A.	106	18. Jefferies, G.	56	35. Phillips, J.	28		
2. Karros, E.	105	19. Berry, S.	55	36. Johnson, M.	28		
3. Caminiti, K.	94	20. Zeile, T.	52	37. Arias, A.	26		
4. McGriff, F.	93	21. Magadan, D.	51	38. Shipley, C.	24		
5. Grace, M.	92	22. Morris, H.	51	39. Simms, M.	24		
6. Castilla, V.	90	23. Williams, E.	47	40. Johnson, H.	22		
7. Colbrunn, G.	89	24. Branson, J.	45	41. Young, K.	22		
8. King, J.	87	25. Mabry, J.	41	42. Bogar, T.	21		
9. Bagwell, J.	87	26. Alfonzo, E.	41	43. Oliva, J.	20		
10. Jones, C.	86	27. Cooper, S.	40	44. Grudzielanek, M.	20		
11. Hayes, C.	85	28. Hernandez, J.	40	45. Aude, R.	19		
12. Merced, O.	83	29. Wallach, T.	38	46. Petagine, R.	17		
13. Pendleton, T.	78	30. Livingstone, S.	32	47. Coles, D.	16		
14. Brogna, R.	76	31. Cianfrocco, A.	31	48. Harris, L.	16		
15. Segui, D.	68	32. Andrews, S.	31	49. Hansen, D.	14		
16. Williams, M.	65	33. Lewis, M.	30	50. Benjamin, M.	12		
17. Carreon, M.	65	34. Scarsone, S.	29				

STOLEN BASES

1. Galarraga, A.	12	15. Johnson, M.	5	29. Morris, H.	1
2. Caminiti, K.	12	16. Karros, E.	4	30. Zeile, T.	1
3. Bagwell, J.	12	17. McGriff, F.	3	31. Simms, M.	1
4. Benjamin, M.	11	18. Berry, S.	3	32. Hernandez, J.	1
5. Colbrunn, G.	11	19. Scarsone, S.	3	33. Arias, A.	1
6. Harris, L.	10	20. Magadan, D.	2	34. Young, K.	1
7. Jefferies, G.	9	21. Williams, M.	2	35. Bogar, T.	1
8. Jones, C.	8	22. Segui, D.	2	36. McCarty, D.	1
9. Grudzielanek, M.	8	23. Hunter, B.	2	37. Phillips, J.	1
10. King, J.	7	24. Livingstone, S.	2	38. Huskey, B.	1
11. Merced, O.	7	25. Castilla, V.	2	39. Aude, R.	1
12. Shipley, C.	6	26. Branson, J.	2	40. Andrews, S.	1
13. Grace, M.	6	27. Johnson, H.	1	41. Alfonzo, E.	1
14. Hayes, C.	5	28. Pendleton, T.	1		

RUNS SCORED

1. Grace, M.	97	18. Carreon, M.	53	35. Livingstone, S.	26
2. Galarraga, A.	89	19. Morris, H.	53	36. Alfonzo, E.	26
3. Bagwell, J.	88	20. Zeile, T.	50	37. Lewis, M.	25
4. Jones, C.	87	21. Magadan, D.	44	38. Wallach, T.	24
5. McGriff, F.	85	22. Branson, J.	43	39. Shipley, C.	23
6. Karros, E.	83	23. Berry, S.	38	40. Cianfrocco, A.	22
7. Castilla, V.	82	24. Hernandez, J.	37	41. Arias, A.	22
8. Merced, O.	75	25. Williams, E.	35	42. Benjamin, M.	19
9. Caminiti, K.	74	26. Mabry, J.	35	43. Hansen, D.	19
10. Brogna, R.	72	27. Scarsone, S.	33	44. Bogar, T.	17
11. Pendleton, T.	70	28. Harris, L.	32	45. Oliva, J.	15
12. Colbrunn, G.	70	29. Johnson, M.	32	46. Petagine, R.	15
13. Jefferies, G.	69	30. Cooper, S.	29	47. Simms, M.	14
14. Segui, D.	68	31. Phillips, J.	27	48. Coles, D.	13
15. King, J.	61	32. Andrews, S.	27	49. Young, K.	13
16. Hayes, C.	58	33. Grudzielanek, M.	27	50. McCarty, D.	11
17. Williams, M.	53	34. Johnson, H.	26		

Catchers
pp. 27–41

Corners
pp. 41–62

Infield
pp. 63–82

Outfield
pp. 83–113

DH
pp. 114–118

Starters
pp. 119–157

Relievers
pp. 157–193

AL CORNERS
(20 Games or More)

HOME RUNS

1. Thomas, F.	40	15. Jaha, J.	20	29. Mattingly, D.	7
2. McGwire, M.	39	16. Sprague, E.	18	30. Hollins, D.	7
3. Palmeiro, R.	39	17. Manto, J.	17	31. Giambi, J.	6
4. Vaughn, M.	39	18. Brosius, S.	17	32. Boggs, W.	5
5. Gaetti, G.	35	19. Clark, W.	16	33. Seitzer, K.	5
6. Fielder, C.	31	20. Fryman, T.	15	34. Martinez, D.	5
7. Martinez, T.	31	21. Surhoff, B.	13	35. Coomer, R.	5
8. Bonilla, B.	28	22. Paquette, C.	13	36. Pagliarulo, M.	4
9. Phillips, T.	27	23. Samuel, J.	12	37. Aldrete, M.	4
10. Ventura, R.	26	24. Joyner, W.	12	38. Leius, S.	4
11. Sorrento, P.	25	25. Naehring, T.	10	39. Gomez, L.	4
12. Thome, J.	25	26. Palmer, D.	9	40. Reboulet, J.	4
13. Snow, J.	24	27. Cirillo, J.	9		
14. Blowers, M.	23	28. Olerud, J.	8		

BATTING AVERAGE

1. Palmer, D.	.336	18. Reboulet, J.	.292	35. Coomer, R.	.257
2. Bonilla, B.	.329	19. Olerud, J.	.291	36. Manto, J.	.256
3. Boggs, W.	.324	20. Snow, J.	.289	37. Giambi, J.	.256
4. Surhoff, B.	.320	21. Mattingly, D.	.288	38. Espinoza, A.	.252
5. Perry, H.	.315	22. Cirillo, J.	.277	39. Stubbs, F.	.250
6. Thome, J.	.314	23. Davis, R.	.275	40. Huson, J.	.249
7. Jaha, J.	.313	24. Fryman, T.	.275	41. Leius, S.	.247
8. Seitzer, K.	.311	25. McGwire, M.	.274	42. Sprague, E.	.244
9. Palmeiro, R.	.311	26. Strange, D.	.271	43. Fielder, C.	.243
10. Joyner, W.	.310	27. Aldrete, M.	.269	44. Clark, T.	.238
11. Thomas, F.	.308	28. Stahoviak, S.	.266	45. Masteller, D.	.237
12. Martinez, D.	.307	29. Donnels, C.	.265	46. Gomez, L.	.236
13. Naehring, T.	.307	30. Samuel, J.	.263	47. Sorrento, P.	.235
14. Clark, W.	.302	31. Brosius, S.	.262	48. Worthington, C.	.233
15. Vaughn, M.	.300	32. Gaetti, G.	.261	49. Pagliarulo, M.	.232
16. Ventura, R.	.295	33. Phillips, T.	.261	50. Ortiz, L.	.231
17. Martinez, T.	.293	34. Blowers, M.	.257		

RUNS BATTED IN

1. Vaughn, M.	126	18. Thome, J.	73	35. Hollins, D.	26
2. Thomas, F.	111	19. Seitzer, K.	69	36. Giambi, J.	25
3. Martinez, T.	111	20. Jaha, J.	65	37. Aldrete, M.	24
4. Palmeiro, R.	104	21. Boggs, W.	63	38. Palmer, D.	24
5. Snow, J.	102	22. Phillips, T.	61	39. Reboulet, J.	23
6. Bonilla, B.	99	23. Naehring, T.	57	40. Stahoviak, S.	23
7. Gaetti, G.	96	24. Olerud, J.	54	41. Perry, H.	23
8. Blowers, M.	96	25. Mattingly, D.	49	42. Strange, D.	21
9. Ventura, R.	93	26. Paquette, C.	49	43. Masteller, D.	21
10. Clark, W.	92	27. Brosius, S.	46	44. Stubbs, F.	19
11. McGwire, M.	90	28. Leius, S.	45	45. Huson, J.	19
12. Joyner, W.	83	29. Samuel, J.	39	46. Coomer, R.	19
13. Fielder, C.	82	30. Cirillo, J.	39	47. Ortiz, L.	18
14. Fryman, T.	81	31. Manto, J.	38	48. Espinoza, A.	17
15. Sorrento, P.	79	32. Martinez, D.	37	49. Donnels, C.	13
16. Sprague, E.	74	33. Owen, S.	28	50. Gomez, L.	12
17. Surhoff, B.	73	34. Pagliarulo, M.	27	51. Davis, R.	12

STOLEN BASES

1. Phillips, T.	13	12. Brosius, S.	4	23. Snow, J.	2
2. Vaughn, M.	11	13. Thome, J.	4	24. Giambi, J.	2
3. Martinez, D.	8	14. Gaetti, G.	3	25. Boggs, W.	1
4. Surhoff, B.	7	15. Owen, S.	3	26. McGwire, M.	1
5. Cirillo, J.	7	16. Joyner, W.	3	27. Palmer, D.	1
6. Samuel, J.	6	17. Palmeiro, R.	3	28. Sorrento, P.	1
7. Huson, J.	5	18. Thomas, F.	3	29. Hollins, D.	1
8. Paquette, C.	5	19. Seitzer, K.	2	30. Reboulet, J.	1
9. Stahoviak, S.	5	20. Blowers, M.	2	31. Perry, H.	1
10. Ventura, R.	4	21. Leius, S.	2	32. Masteller, D.	1
11. Fryman, T.	4	22. Jaha, J.	2		

RUNS SCORED

1. Phillips, T.	119	18. Fielder, C.	70	35. Palmer, D.	30
2. Thomas, F.	102	19. Joyner, W.	69	36. Stahoviak, S.	28
3. Vaughn, M.	98	20. Brosius, S.	69	37. Pagliarulo, M.	27
4. Bonilla, B.	96	21. Naehring, T.	61	38. Giambi, J.	27
5. Martinez, T.	92	22. Mattingly, D.	59	39. Huson, J.	24
6. Thome, J.	92	23. Blowers, M.	59	40. Perry, H.	23
7. Palmeiro, R.	89	24. Jaha, J.	59	41. Masteller, D.	21
8. Clark, W.	85	25. Cirillo, J.	57	42. Aldrete, M.	19
9. Snow, J.	80	26. Seitzer, K.	56	43. Strange, D.	19
10. Ventura, R.	79	27. Leius, S.	51	44. Owen, S.	17
11. Fryman, T.	79	28. Sorrento, P.	50	45. Donnels, C.	17
12. Sprague, E.	77	29. Martinez, D.	49	46. Gomez, L.	16
13. Gaetti, G.	76	30. Hollins, D.	48	47. Espinoza, A.	15
14. Boggs, W.	76	31. Paquette, C.	42	48. Coomer, R.	15
15. McGwire, M.	75	32. Reboulet, J.	39	49. Davis, R.	14
16. Surhoff, B.	72	33. Samuel, J.	31	50. Stubbs, F.	13
17. Olerud, J.	72	34. Manto, J.	31		

NL MIDDLE INFIELDERS
(20 Games or More)

HOME RUNS

1. Biggio, C.	22	15. Bates, J.	8	29. Alfonzo, E.	4
2. Kent, J.	20	16. Duncan, M.	6	30. Benjamin, M.	3
3. Abbott, K.	17	17. Morandini, M.	6	31. Vizcaino, J.	3
4. Larkin, B.	15	18. Cedeno, A.	6	32. Sanchez, R.	3
5. Boone, B.	15	19. Garcia, C.	6	33. Silvestri, D.	3
6. Dunston, S.	14	20. Young, E.	6	34. Arias, A.	3
7. Bell, J.	13	21. Liriano, N.	5	35. Mordecai, M.	3
8. Hernandez, J.	13	22. Lemke, M.	5	36. Oquendo, J.	2
9. Blauser, J.	12	23. Clayton, R.	5	37. Roberts, B.	2
10. Branson, J.	12	24. Cromer, T.	5	38. Caraballo, R.	2
11. Cordero, W.	10	25. Miller, O.	5	39. Holbert, R.	2
12. Lansing, M.	10	26. Veras, Q.	5	40. Bell, D.	2
13. Thompson, R.	8	27. Reed, J.	4		
14. DeShields, D.	8	28. Offerman, J.	4		

Catchers
pp. 27–41

Corners
pp. 41–62

Infield
pp. 63–82

Outfield
pp. 83–113

DH
pp. 114–118

Starters
pp. 119–157

Relievers
pp. 157–193

BATTING AVERAGE

1. Larkin, B.	.318	18. Kent, J.	.277	35. Bell, D.	.247
2. Young, E.	.317	19. Gutierrez, R.	.276	36. Grudzielanek, M.	.245
3. Roberts, B.	.304	20. Arias, A.	.269	37. Hernandez, J.	.245
4. Biggio, C.	.302	21. Pena, G.	.267	38. Clayton, R.	.244
5. Dunston, S.	.295	22. Boone, B.	.267	39. Cromer, T.	.226
6. Garcia, C.	.294	23. Bates, J.	.267	40. Silvestri, D.	.226
7. Bogar, T.	.290	24. Bell, J.	.262	41. Thompson, R.	.223
8. Duncan, M.	.287	25. Miller, O.	.262	42. Belliard, R.	.222
9. Vizcaino, J.	.287	26. Veras, Q.	.261	43. Benjamin, M.	.220
10. Offerman, J.	.287	27. Weiss, W.	.260	44. Stocker, K.	.219
11. Cordero, W.	.286	28. Branson, J.	.260	45. Blauser, J.	.211
12. Liriano, N.	.286	29. Reed, J.	.256	46. Cedeno, A.	.210
13. Morandini, M.	.283	30. DeShields, D.	.256	47. Oquendo, J.	.209
14. Mordecai, M.	.280	31. Browne, J.	.255	48. Patterson, J.	.205
15. Fonville, C.	.278	32. Lansing, M.	.255	49. Caraballo, R.	.202
16. Sanchez, R.	.278	33. Abbott, K.	.255	50. Smith, O.	.199
17. Alfonzo, E.	.278	34. Lemke, M.	.253		

RUNS BATTED IN

1. Biggio, C.	77	18. Hernandez, J.	40	35. Bogar, T.	21
2. Dunston, S.	69	19. Liriano, N.	38	36. Grudzielanek, M.	20
3. Boone, B.	68	20. Lemke, M.	38	37. Bell, D.	19
4. Larkin, B.	66	21. DeShields, D.	37	38. Cromer, T.	18
5. Kent, J.	65	22. Duncan, M.	36	39. Oquendo, J.	17
6. Lansing, M.	62	23. Young, E.	36	40. Browne, J.	17
7. Abbott, K.	60	24. Miller, O.	36	41. Fonville, C.	16
8. Clayton, R.	58	25. Offerman, J.	33	42. Patterson, J.	14
9. Vizcaino, J.	56	26. Stocker, K.	32	43. Benjamin, M.	12
10. Bell, J.	55	27. Veras, Q.	32	44. Gutierrez, R.	12
11. Garcia, C.	50	28. Blauser, J.	31	45. Smith, O.	11
12. Morandini, M.	49	29. Cedeno, A.	31	46. Silvestri, D.	11
13. Cordero, W.	49	30. Sanchez, R.	27	47. Mordecai, M.	11
14. Bates, J.	46	31. Arias, A.	26	48. Elster, K.	9
15. Branson, J.	45	32. Roberts, B.	25	49. Pena, G.	8
16. Alfonzo, E.	41	33. Weiss, W.	25	50. Belliard, R.	7
17. Reed, J.	40	34. Thompson, R.	23	51. Stankiewicz, A.	7

STOLEN BASES

1. Veras, Q.	56	18. Grudzielanek, M.	8	35. Belliard, R.	2
2. Larkin, B.	51	19. Reed, J.	6	36. Bell, J.	2
3. DeShields, D.	39	20. Sanchez, R.	6	37. Liriano, N.	2
4. Young, E.	35	21. Stocker, K.	6	38. Lemke, M.	2
5. Biggio, C.	33	22. Cedeno, A.	5	39. Offerman, J.	2
6. Lansing, M.	27	23. Boone, B.	5	40. Branson, J.	2
7. Clayton, R.	24	24. Gutierrez, R.	5	41. Silvestri, D.	2
8. Roberts, B.	20	25. Smith, O.	4	42. Oquendo, J.	1
9. Fonville, C.	20	26. Patterson, J.	4	43. Duncan, M.	1
10. Weiss, W.	15	27. Stankiewicz, A.	4	44. Browne, J.	1
11. Benjamin, M.	11	28. Abbott, K.	4	45. Thompson, R.	1
12. Dunston, S.	10	29. Holbert, R.	4	46. Hernandez, J.	1
13. Morandini, M.	9	30. Pena, G.	3	47. Arias, A.	1
14. Cordero, W.	9	31. Kent, J.	3	48. Bogar, T.	1
15. Blauser, J.	8	32. Caraballo, R.	3	49. Bell, D.	1
16. Vizcaino, J.	8	33. Miller, O.	3	50. Alfonzo, E.	1
17. Garcia, C.	8	34. Bates, J.	3		

RUNS SCORED

1. Biggio, C.	123	18. Sanchez, R.	57	35. Liriano, N.	29		
2. Larkin, B.	98	19. Clayton, R.	56	36. Patterson, J.	27		
3. Veras, Q.	86	20. Thompson, R.	51	37. Grudzielanek, M.	27		
4. Bell, J.	79	21. Lansing, M.	47	38. Alfonzo, E.	26		
5. Offerman, J.	69	22. Branson, J.	43	39. Arias, A.	22		
6. Young, E.	68	23. Fonville, C.	43	40. Gutierrez, R.	22		
7. Vizcaino, J.	66	24. Lemke, M.	42	41. Browne, J.	21		
8. DeShields, D.	66	25. Cedeno, A.	42	42. Pena, G.	20		
9. Weiss, W.	65	26. Stocker, K.	42	43. Benjamin, M.	19		
10. Morandini, M.	65	27. Bates, J.	42	44. Bogar, T.	17		
11. Kent, J.	65	28. Garcia, C.	41	45. Smith, O.	16		
12. Cordero, W.	64	29. Roberts, B.	40	46. Silvestri, D.	16		
13. Boone, B.	63	30. Hernandez, J.	37	47. Bell, D.	13		
14. Blauser, J.	60	31. Duncan, M.	36	48. Belliard, R.	12		
15. Abbott, K.	60	32. Cromer, T.	36	49. Elster, K.	11		
16. Dunston, S.	58	33. Miller, O.	36	50. Holbert, R.	11		
17. Reed, J.	58	34. Oquendo, J.	31				

AL MIDDLE INFIELDERS
(20 Games or More)

HOME RUNS

1. Valentin, J.	27	16. Durham, R.	7	31. Cedeno, D.	4
2. Ripken, C.	17	17. Gagne, G.	6	32. Cora, J.	3
3. Baerga, C.	15	18. Hudler, R.	6	33. Alexander, M.	3
4. Whitaker, L.	14	19. Alicea, L.	6	34. Vina, F.	3
5. Alomar, R.	13	20. Vizquel, O.	6	35. Trammell, A.	2
6. Meares, P.	12	21. Lockhart, K.	6	36. Espinoza, A.	2
7. Knoblauch, C.	11	22. Fernandez, T.	5	37. Barberie, B.	2
8. Valentin, J.	11	23. McLemore, M.	5	38. Martin, N.	2
9. Gomez, C.	11	24. DiSarcina, G.	5	39. Fletcher, S.	1
10. Gonzalez, A.	10	25. Gates, B.	5	40. Owen, S.	1
11. Gil, B.	9	26. Rodriguez, A.	5	41. Guillen, O.	1
12. Cirillo, J.	9	27. Kelly, P.	4	42. Huson, J.	1
13. Bordick, M.	8	28. Reboulet, J.	4	43. Grebeck, C.	1
14. Velarde, R.	7	29. Frye, J.	4	44. Perez, T.	1
15. Sojo, L.	7	30. Easley, D.	4	45. Caceres, E.	1

BATTING AVERAGE

1. Knoblauch, C.	.333	18. Vizquel, O.	.266	35. Barberie, B.	.240
2. Lockhart, K.	.321	19. Hudler, R.	.265	36. Caceres, E.	.239
3. Baerga, C.	.314	20. Bordick, M.	.264	37. Kelly, P.	.237
4. DiSarcina, G.	.307	21. Ripken, C.	.262	38. Cedeno, D.	.236
5. Alomar, R.	.300	22. McLemore, M.	.261	39. Lind, J.	.236
6. Valentin, J.	.298	23. Grebeck, C.	.260	40. Alexander, M.	.236
7. Cora, J.	.297	24. Vina, F.	.257	41. Gallego, M.	.233
8. Whitaker, L.	.293	25. Durham, R.	.257	42. Rodriguez, A.	.232
9. Reboulet, J.	.292	26. Gagne, G.	.256	43. Fletcher, S.	.231
10. Sojo, L.	.289	27. Gates, B.	.254	44. Owen, S.	.229
11. Velarde, R.	.278	28. Espinoza, A.	.252	45. Gomez, C.	.223
12. Frye, J.	.278	29. Huson, J.	.249	46. Gil, B.	.219
13. Cirillo, J.	.277	30. Guillen, O.	.248	47. Valentin, J.	.219
14. Alicea, L.	.270	31. Fernandez, T.	.245	48. Listach, P.	.219
15. Trammell, A.	.269	32. Perez, T.	.245	49. Beltre, E.	.217
16. Meares, P.	.269	33. Howard, D.	.243	50. Easley, D.	.216
17. Martin, N.	.269	34. Gonzalez, A.	.242		

Catchers
pp. 27–41

Corners
pp. 41–62

Infield
pp. 63–82

Outfield
pp. 83–113

DH
pp. 114–118

Starters
pp. 119–157

Relievers
pp. 157–193

RUNS BATTED IN

1. Valentin, J.	102	18. Bordick, M.	44	35. Trammell, A.	23
2. Baerga, C.	90	19. Gonzalez, A.	42	36. Reboulet, J.	23
3. Ripken, C.	88	20. Guillen, O.	41	37. Alexander, M.	23
4. Alomar, R.	66	21. McLemore, M.	41	38. Huson, J.	19
5. Knoblauch, C.	63	22. DiSarcina, G.	41	39. Howard, D.	19
6. Vizquel, O.	56	23. Cora, J.	39	40. Rodriguez, A.	19
7. Gates, B.	56	24. Sojo, L.	39	41. Grebeck, C.	18
8. Durham, R.	51	25. Cirillo, J.	39	42. Fletcher, S.	17
9. Gomez, C.	50	26. Easley, D.	35	43. Espinoza, A.	17
10. Gagne, G.	49	27. Lockhart, K.	33	44. Martin, N.	17
11. Valentin, J.	49	28. Kelly, P.	29	45. Caceres, E.	17
12. Meares, P.	49	29. Frye, J.	29	46. Fermin, F.	15
13. Velarde, R.	46	30. Vina, F.	29	47. Cedeno, D.	14
14. Gil, B.	46	31. Owen, S.	28	48. Gallego, M.	8
15. Fernandez, T.	45	32. Hudler, R.	27	49. Perez, T.	8
16. Whitaker, L.	44	33. Barberie, B.	25	50. Lind, J.	7
17. Alicea, L.	44	34. Listach, P.	25	51. Beltre, E.	7

STOLEN BASES

1. Knoblauch, C.	46	18. DiSarcina, G.	7	35. Owen, S.	3
2. Alomar, R.	30	19. Cirillo, J.	7	36. Barberie, B.	3
3. Vizquel, O.	29	20. Fernandez, T.	6	37. Frye, J.	3
4. McLemore, M.	21	21. Guillen, O.	6	38. Gates, B.	3
5. Valentin, J.	20	22. Howard, D.	6	39. Fermin, F.	2
6. Cora, J.	18	23. Vina, F.	6	40. Gil, B.	2
7. Durham, R.	18	24. Velarde, R.	5	41. Caceres, E.	2
8. Valentin, J.	16	25. Huson, J.	5	42. Fletcher, S.	1
9. Hudler, R.	13	26. Easley, D.	5	43. Reboulet, J.	1
10. Alicea, L.	13	27. Martin, N.	5	44. Ripken, C.	0
11. Listach, P.	13	28. Whitaker, L.	4	45. Espinoza, A.	0
12. Baerga, C.	11	29. Sojo, L.	4	46. Gallego, M.	0
13. Bordick, M.	11	30. Gomez, C.	4	47. Lind, J.	0
14. Alexander, M.	11	31. Gonzalez, A.	4	48. Grebeck, C.	0
15. Meares, P.	10	32. Rodriguez, A.	4	49. Beltre, E.	0
16. Kelly, P.	8	33. Trammell, A.	3	50. Cedeno, D.	0
17. Lockhart, K.	8	34. Gagne, G.	3	51. Perez, T.	0

RUNS SCORED

1. Valentin, J.	108	18. Cirillo, J.	57	35. Hudler, R.	30
2. Knoblauch, C.	107	19. Gonzalez, A.	51	36. Trammell, A.	28
3. Vizquel, O.	87	20. Guillen, O.	50	37. Huson, J.	24
4. Baerga, C.	87	21. Sojo, L.	50	38. Howard, D.	23
5. McLemore, M.	73	22. Gomez, C.	49	39. Fermin, F.	21
6. Ripken, C.	71	23. Bordick, M.	46	40. Fletcher, S.	19
7. Alomar, R.	71	24. Vina, F.	46	41. Grebeck, C.	19
8. Durham, R.	68	25. Lockhart, K.	41	42. Cedeno, D.	18
9. Cora, J.	64	26. Reboulet, J.	39	43. Owen, S.	17
10. Alicea, L.	64	27. Frye, J.	38	44. Martin, N.	17
11. Valentin, J.	62	28. Whitaker, L.	36	45. Espinoza, A.	15
12. DiSarcina, G.	61	29. Gil, B.	36	46. Rodriguez, A.	15
13. Velarde, R.	60	30. Listach, P.	35	47. Caceres, E.	13
14. Gates, B.	60	31. Easley, D.	35	48. Perez, T.	12
15. Gagne, G.	58	32. Alexander, M.	35	49. Gallego, M.	11
16. Fernandez, T.	57	33. Kelly, P.	32	50. Lind, J.	9
17. Meares, P.	57	34. Barberie, B.	32	51. Beltre, E.	7

NL OUTFIELDERS
(20 Games or More)

HOME RUNS

1. Bichette, D.	40	26. Grissom, M.	12	51. Pegues, S.	6
2. Walker, L.	36	27. Segui, D.	12	52. Anthony, E.	5
3. Sosa, S.	36	28. Whiten, M.	12	53. Mabry, J.	5
4. Bonds, B.	33	29. McRae, B.	12	54. Hollandsworth, T.	5
5. Gant, R.	29	30. Everett, C.	12	55. Clark, D.	4
6. Sanders, R.	28	31. Jefferies, G.	11	56. Brumfield, J.	4
7. Mondesi, R.	26	32. Devereaux, M.	11	57. Buford, D.	4
8. Lankford, R.	25	33. Eisenreich, J.	10	58. Newfield, M.	4
9. Conine, J.	25	34. Finley, S.	10	59. Mouton, J.	4
10. Hill, G.	24	35. Cordero, W.	10	60. Smith, D.	3
11. Justice, D.	24	36. Gwynn, T.	9	61. Howard, T.	3
12. Klesko, R.	23	37. Plantier, P.	9	62. Bullett, S.	3
13. Jones, C.	23	38. May, D.	9	63. Marsh, T.	3
14. Jordan, B.	22	39. Dawson, A.	8	64. Longmire, T.	3
15. Carreon, M.	17	40. Kingery, M.	8	65. Kelly, M.	3
16. Gilkey, B.	17	41. Walton, J.	8	66. Thompson, M.	2
17. Sheffield, G.	16	42. Jones, C.	8	67. Cangelosi, J.	2
18. Merced, O.	15	43. Bell, D.	8	68. Dykstra, L.	2
19. Burks, E.	14	44. Ashley, B.	8	69. Roberts, B.	2
20. Alou, M.	14	45. Timmons, O.	8	70. Polonia, L.	2
21. Nieves, M.	14	46. Kelly, R.	7	71. Carr, C.	2
22. Tarasco, T.	14	47. Thompson, R.	7	72. Flora, K.	2
23. Gonzalez, L.	13	48. Van Slyke, A.	6	73. Clark, P.	2
24. Martin, A.	13	49. Gregg, T.	6	74. Rodriguez, H.	2
25. White, R.	13	50. Sanders, D.	6	75. Cummings, M.	2

BATTING AVERAGE

1. Gwynn, T.	.368	26. Santangelo, F.	.296	51. Sanders, D.	.268
2. Longmire, T.	.356	27. White, R.	.295	52. Sosa, S.	.268
3. Bichette, D.	.340	28. Bonds, B.	.294	53. Burks, E.	.266
4. Bell, D.	.334	29. Marsh, T.	.293	54. Jones, C.	.265
5. Sheffield, G.	.324	30. Walton, J.	.290	55. Dykstra, L.	.264
6. Cangelosi, J.	.318	31. Tavarez, J.	.290	56. Hill, G.	.264
7. Eisenreich, J.	.315	32. McRae, B.	.288	57. Timmons, O.	.263
8. Klesko, R.	.310	33. Cordero, W.	.286	58. Mouton, J.	.262
9. Segui, D.	.309	34. Mondesi, R.	.286	59. Polonia, L.	.261
10. Wehner, J.	.309	35. Orsulak, J.	.283	60. Everett, C.	.259
11. Mabry, J.	.307	36. May, D.	.282	61. Grissom, M.	.258
12. Jefferies, G.	.306	37. Martin, A.	.282	62. Dawson, A.	.257
13. Walker, L.	.306	38. Clark, D.	.281	63. Browne, J.	.255
14. Sanders, R.	.306	39. Jones, C.	.280	64. Plantier, P.	.254
15. Roberts, B.	.304	40. Kelly, R.	.278	65. Justice, D.	.253
16. Howard, T.	.303	41. Lankford, R.	.277	66. Varsho, G.	.252
17. Conine, J.	.302	42. Parker, R.	.276	67. Smith, D.	.252
18. Hunter, B.	.302	43. Gonzalez, L.	.276	68. Thompson, R.	.251
19. Butler, B.	.300	44. Gant, R.	.275	69. Lewis, D.	.250
20. Carreon, M.	.300	45. Alou, M.	.273	70. Tarasco, T.	.249
21. Merced, O.	.300	46. Bullett, S.	.273	71. Pegues, S.	.246
22. Devereaux, M.	.299	47. Brumfield, J.	.271	72. Cummings, M.	.243
23. Gilkey, B.	.298	48. Battle, A.	.271	73. Whiten, M.	.241
24. Finley, S.	.297	49. Kingery, M.	.269	74. Rodriguez, H.	.239
25. Jordan, B.	.296	50. Anthony, E.	.269	75. Cedeno, R.	.238

Catchers
pp. 27-41

Corners
pp. 41-62

Infield
pp. 63-82

Outfield
pp. 83-113

DH
pp. 114-118

Starters
pp. 119-157

Relievers
pp. 157-193

RUNS BATTED IN

1. Bichette, D.	128	26. Jefferies, G.	56	51. Ashley, B.	27
2. Sosa, S.	119	27. Eisenreich, J.	55	52. Mouton, J.	27
3. Conine, J.	105	28. Everett, C.	54	53. Howard, T.	26
4. Bonds, B.	104	29. May, D.	50	54. Brumfield, J.	26
5. Walker, L.	101	30. Burks, E.	49	55. Roberts, B.	25
6. Sanders, R.	99	31. Cordero, W.	49	56. Van Slyke, A.	24
7. Gwynn, T.	90	32. McRae, B.	48	57. Clark, D.	24
8. Gant, R.	88	33. Whiten, M.	47	58. Lewis, D.	24
9. Mondesi, R.	88	34. Sheffield, G.	46	59. Anthony, E.	23
10. Hill, G.	86	35. Finley, S.	44	60. Walton, J.	22
11. Bell, D.	86	36. Grissom, M.	42	61. Bullett, S.	22
12. Jones, C.	86	37. Martin, A.	41	62. Smith, D.	21
13. Merced, O.	83	38. Mabry, J.	41	63. Newfield, M.	21
14. Lankford, R.	82	39. Tarasco, T.	40	64. Gregg, T.	20
15. Jordan, B.	81	40. Butler, B.	38	65. Carr, C.	20
16. Justice, D.	78	41. Nieves, M.	38	66. Thompson, M.	19
17. Klesko, R.	70	42. Dawson, A.	37	67. Longmire, T.	19
18. Gilkey, B.	69	43. Orsulak, J.	37	68. Cangelosi, J.	18
19. Gonzalez, L.	69	44. Kingery, M.	37	69. Dykstra, L.	18
20. Segui, D.	68	45. Plantier, P.	34	70. Browne, J.	17
21. Carreon, M.	65	46. Jones, C.	31	71. Polonia, L.	17
22. Devereaux, M.	63	47. Thompson, R.	31	72. Kelly, M.	17
23. Alou, M.	58	48. Sanders, D.	28	73. Pegues, S.	16
24. Kelly, R.	57	49. Hunter, B.	28	74. Marsh, T.	15
25. White, R.	57	50. Timmons, O.	28	75. Rodriguez, H.	15

STOLEN BASES

1. Finley, S.	36	25. Kelly, R.	19	49. Gonzalez, L.	6
2. Sanders, R.	36	26. Sheffield, G.	19	50. May, D.	5
3. Sosa, S.	34	27. Gwynn, T.	17	51. Klesko, R.	5
4. Butler, B.	32	28. Howard, T.	17	52. Thompson, M.	4
5. Lewis, D.	32	29. Walker, L.	16	53. Justice, D.	4
6. Bonds, B.	31	30. Kingery, M.	13	54. Alou, M.	4
7. Grissom, M.	29	31. Polonia, L.	13	55. Clark, D.	3
8. McRae, B.	27	32. Bichette, D.	13	56. Gregg, T.	3
9. Bell, D.	27	33. Gilkey, B.	12	57. Wehner, J.	3
10. Mondesi, R.	27	34. Eisenreich, J.	10	58. Thompson, R.	3
11. Hill, G.	25	35. Dykstra, L.	10	59. Pride, C.	3
12. Carr, C.	25	36. Walton, J.	10	60. Timmons, O.	3
13. White, R.	25	37. Buford, D.	10	61. Battle, A.	3
14. Mouton, J.	25	38. Jefferies, G.	9	62. Varsho, G.	2
15. Sanders, D.	24	39. Cordero, W.	9	63. Anthony, E.	2
16. Lankford, R.	24	40. Devereaux, M.	8	64. Segui, D.	2
17. Jordan, B.	24	41. Whiten, M.	8	65. Conine, J.	2
18. Tarasco, T.	24	42. Bullett, S.	8	66. Jones, C.	2
19. Hunter, B.	24	43. Jones, C.	8	67. Nieves, M.	2
20. Gant, R.	23	44. Van Slyke, A.	7	68. Everett, C.	2
21. Brumfield, J.	22	45. Burks, E.	7	69. Hollandsworth, T.	2
22. Cangelosi, J.	21	46. Merced, O.	7	70. Otero, R.	2
23. Roberts, B.	20	47. Kelly, M.	7		
24. Martin, A.	20	48. Tavarez, J.	7		

RUNS SCORED

1. Bonds, B.	109	25. Segui, D.	68	49. Orsulak, J.	41		**Catchers**	
2. Finley, S.	104	26. Kingery, M.	66	50. Burks, E.	41		pp. 27–41	
3. Bichette, D.	102	27. Lewis, D.	66	51. Roberts, B.	40		**Corners**	
4. Walker, L.	96	28. Brumfield, J.	64	52. Thompson, R.	39		pp. 41–62	
5. McRae, B.	92	29. Cordero, W.	64	53. Dykstra, L.	37			
6. Sanders, R.	91	30. Tarasco, T.	64	54. Mabry, J.	35		**Infield**	
7. Mondesi, R.	91	31. Bell, D.	63	55. Plantier, P.	33		pp. 63–82	
8. Sosa, S.	89	32. Kelly, R.	58	56. Jones, C.	33			
9. White, R.	87	33. Devereaux, M.	55	57. Van Slyke, A.	32		**Outfield**	
10. Jones, C.	87	34. Carr, C.	54	58. Walton, J.	32		pp. 83–113	
11. Jordan, B.	83	35. Carreon, M.	53	59. Nieves, M.	32		**DH**	
12. Gwynn, T.	82	36. Hunter, B.	52	60. Tavarez, J.	31		pp. 114–118	
13. Lankford, R.	81	37. Whiten, M.	51	61. Dawson, A.	30			
14. Grissom, M.	80	38. Sanders, D.	48	62. Clark, D.	30		**Starters**	
15. Gant, R.	79	39. Alou, M.	48	63. Buford, D.	30		pp. 119–157	
16. Butler, B.	78	40. Klesko, R.	48	64. Timmons, O.	30			
17. Merced, O.	75	41. Everett, C.	48	65. Kelly, M.	26		**Relievers**	
18. Justice, D.	73	42. Eisenreich, J.	46	66. Browne, J.	21		pp. 157–193	
19. Gilkey, B.	73	43. Cangelosi, J.	46	67. Longmire, T.	21			
20. Conine, J.	72	44. Sheffield, G.	46	68. Gregg, T.	20			
21. Hill, G.	71	45. May, D.	44	69. Anthony, E.	19			
22. Martin, A.	70	46. Polonia, L.	43	70. Bullett, S.	19			
23. Jefferies, G.	69	47. Howard, T.	42					
24. Gonzalez, L.	69	48. Mouton, J.	42					

AL OUTFIELDERS
(20 Games or More)

HOME RUNS

1. Belle, A.	50	26. Surhoff, B.	13	51. Ward, T.	4
2. Buhner, J.	40	27. Paquette, C.	13	52. Goodwin, T.	4
3. Salmon, T.	34	28. Greer, R.	13	53. Hiatt, P.	4
4. Edmonds, J.	33	29. Raines, T.	12	54. Hammonds, J.	4
5. Tettleton, M.	32	30. Nilsson, D.	12	55. Tomberlin, A.	4
6. Ramirez, M.	31	31. Mieske, M.	12	56. Tucker, M.	4
7. Bonilla, B.	28	32. White, D.	10	57. Clark, J.	3
8. Phillips, T.	27	33. Johnson, L.	10	58. Hulse, D.	3
9. Carter, J.	25	34. O'Leary, T.	10	59. Diaz, A.	3
10. Cordova, M.	24	35. Henderson, R.	9	60. Bragg, D.	3
11. Puckett, K.	23	36. Maldonado, C.	9	61. Smith, M.	3
12. O'Neill, P.	22	37. Javier, S.	8	62. Hosey, D.	3
13. Berroa, G.	22	38. Velarde, R.	7	63. Masteller, D.	3
14. Curtis, C.	21	39. Lofton, K.	7	64. Damon, J.	3
15. Sierra, R.	19	40. Tinsley, L.	7	65. McGee, W.	2
16. Munoz, P.	18	41. Bautista, D.	7	66. James, D.	2
17. Williams, B.	18	42. Hudler, R.	6	67. Stubbs, F.	2
18. Griffey Jr, K.	17	43. Williams, G.	6	68. Amaral, R.	2
19. Brosius, S.	17	44. Bass, K.	5	69. Voigt, J.	2
20. Anderson, B.	16	45. McLemore, M.	5	70. Becker, R.	2
21. Anderson, G.	16	46. Coleman, V.	5	71. Young, E.	2
22. Greenwell, M.	15	47. Martinez, D.	5	72. Steverson, T.	2
23. Green, S.	15	48. Hamilton, D.	5	73. Nevin, P.	2
24. Higginson, B.	14	49. Newson, W.	5		
25. Nunnally, J.	14	50. Mouton, L.	5		

BATTING AVERAGE

1. Cole, A.	.342	25. Goodwin, T.	.288	49. Anderson, B.	.262
2. Clark, J.	.339	26. Green, S.	.288	50. Steverson, T.	.262
3. Hosey, D.	.338	27. James, D.	.287	51. McLemore, M.	.261
4. Salmon, T.	.330	28. McGee, W.	.285	52. Newson, W.	.261
5. Bonilla, B.	.329	29. Raines, T.	.285	53. Stairs, M.	.261
6. Anderson, G.	.321	30. Tinsley, L.	.285	54. Phillips, T.	.261
7. Surhoff, B.	.320	31. White, D.	.283	55. Tucker, M.	.260
8. Belle, A.	.317	32. Amaral, R.	.282	56. Griffey Jr, K.	.258
9. Puckett, K.	.314	33. Damon, J.	.282	57. Carter, J.	.253
10. Lofton, K.	.310	34. Javier, S.	.278	58. Hulse, D.	.251
11. O'Leary, T.	.308	35. Berroa, G.	.278	59. Mieske, M.	.251
12. Ramirez, M.	.308	36. Velarde, R.	.278	60. Stubbs, F.	.250
13. Martinez, D.	.307	37. Nilsson, D.	.277	61. Diaz, A.	.248
14. Williams, B.	.307	38. Cordova, M.	.277	62. Williams, G.	.247
15. Johnson, L.	.307	39. Hamilton, D.	.271	63. Bass, K.	.244
16. Gallagher, D.	.306	40. Greer, R.	.271	64. Nunnally, J.	.244
17. Mouton, L.	.302	41. Curtis, C.	.268	65. Howard, D.	.243
18. Munoz, P.	.300	42. Hudler, R.	.265	66. Herrera, J.	.243
19. Henderson, R.	.300	43. Ward, T.	.264	67. Hammonds, J.	.241
20. O'Neill, P.	.300	44. Maldonado, C.	.263	68. Tettleton, M.	.238
21. Greenwell, M.	.297	45. Sierra, R.	.263	69. Becker, R.	.237
22. Nixon, O.	.295	46. Goodwin, C.	.263	70. Masteller, D.	.237
23. Edmonds, J.	.291	47. Brosius, S.	.262		
24. Coleman, V.	.288	48. Buhner, J.	.262		

RUNS BATTED IN

1. Belle, A.	126	26. Henderson, R.	54	51. Hudler, R.	27
2. Buhner, J.	121	27. Green, S.	54	52. Diaz, A.	27
3. Ramirez, M.	107	28. White, D.	53	53. Bautista, D.	27
4. Edmonds, J.	107	29. Lofton, K.	53	54. Mouton, L.	27
5. Salmon, T.	105	30. Nilsson, D.	53	55. James, D.	26
6. Puckett, K.	99	31. O'Leary, T.	49	56. Goodwin, C.	24
7. Bonilla, B.	99	32. Paquette, C.	49	57. Hammonds, J.	23
8. O'Neill, P.	96	33. Mieske, M.	48	58. Damon, J.	23
9. Berroa, G.	88	34. Hulse, D.	47	59. Masteller, D.	21
10. Sierra, R.	86	35. Velarde, R.	46	60. Stubbs, F.	19
11. Cordova, M.	84	36. Brosius, S.	46	61. Howard, D.	19
12. Williams, B.	82	37. Nixon, O.	45	62. Amaral, R.	19
13. Tettleton, M.	78	38. Hamilton, D.	44	63. Stairs, M.	17
14. Carter, J.	76	39. Higginson, B.	43	64. Tucker, M.	17
15. Greenwell, M.	76	40. Griffey Jr, K.	42	65. Ward, T.	16
16. Surhoff, B.	73	41. Nunnally, J.	42	66. McGee, W.	15
17. Anderson, G.	69	42. McLemore, M.	41	67. Clark, J.	15
18. Raines, T.	67	43. Tinsley, L.	41	68. Newson, W.	15
19. Curtis, C.	67	44. Martinez, D.	37	69. Smith, M.	15
20. Anderson, B.	64	45. Becker, R.	33	70. Cole, A.	14
21. Phillips, T.	61	46. Bass, K.	32	71. Kirby, W.	14
22. Greer, R.	61	47. Maldonado, C.	30	72. Nevin, P.	13
23. Munoz, P.	58	48. Coleman, V.	29	73. Gallagher, D.	12
24. Johnson, L.	57	49. Goodwin, T.	28	74. Hiatt, P.	12
25. Javier, S.	56	50. Williams, G.	28	75. Bragg, D.	12

STOLEN BASES

1. Lofton, K.	54	26. Bragg, D.	9	51. Williams, G.	4		
2. Nixon, O.	50	27. Bass, K.	8	52. Hammonds, J.	4		
3. Goodwin, T.	50	28. Martinez, D.	8	53. Tomberlin, A.	4		
4. Coleman, V.	42	29. Williams, B.	8	54. Bautista, D.	4		
5. Johnson, L.	40	30. Becker, R.	8	55. Puckett, K.	3		
6. Javier, S.	36	31. Surhoff, B.	7	56. Clark, J.	3		
7. Henderson, R.	32	32. Berroa, G.	7	57. Smith, M.	3		
8. Curtis, C.	27	33. Damon, J.	7	58. Greer, R.	3		
9. Anderson, B.	26	34. Ward, T.	6	59. Cuyler, M.	2		
10. Goodwin, C.	22	35. Howard, D.	6	60. Newson, W.	2		
11. McLemore, M.	21	36. Ramirez, M.	6	61. Nilsson, D.	2		
12. Amaral, R.	21	37. Anderson, G.	6	62. Mieske, M.	2		
13. Cordova, M.	20	38. Hosey, D.	6	63. Tucker, M.	2		
14. Diaz, A.	18	39. Higginson, B.	6	64. Steverson, T.	2		
15. Tinsley, L.	18	40. Nunnally, J.	6	65. Maldonado, C.	1		
16. Hulse, D.	15	41. McGee, W.	5	66. O'Neill, P.	1		
17. Raines, T.	13	42. Sierra, R.	5	67. Huff, M.	1		
18. Phillips, T.	13	43. Velarde, R.	5	68. Cole, A.	1		
19. Hudler, R.	13	44. Belle, A.	5	69. Amaro, R.	1		
20. Frazier, L.	13	45. Salmon, T.	5	70. Hiatt, P.	1		
21. Carter, J.	12	46. O'Leary, T.	5	71. Edmonds, J.	1		
22. White, D.	11	47. Paquette, C.	5	72. Green, S.	1		
23. Hamilton, D.	11	48. James, D.	4	73. Mouton, L.	1		
24. Kirby, W.	10	49. Griffey Jr, K.	4	74. Nevin, P.	1		
25. Greenwell, M.	9	50. Brosius, S.	4	75. Masteller, D.	1		

RUNS SCORED

1. Belle, A.	121	26. Brosius, S.	69	51. Newson, W.	34		
2. Edmonds, J.	120	27. Henderson, R.	67	52. Williams, G.	33		
3. Phillips, T.	119	28. Greenwell, M.	67	53. Bass, K.	32		
4. Salmon, T.	111	29. Coleman, V.	66	54. McGee, W.	32		
5. Anderson, B.	108	30. White, D.	61	55. Damon, J.	32		
6. Johnson, L.	98	31. Tinsley, L.	61	56. Hudler, R.	30		
7. Bonilla, B.	96	32. Higginson, B.	61	57. Kirby, W.	29		
8. Curtis, C.	96	33. Velarde, R.	60	58. Maldonado, C.	28		
9. Williams, B.	93	34. O'Leary, T.	60	59. Bautista, D.	28		
10. Lofton, K.	93	35. Greer, R.	58	60. Frazier, L.	25		
11. Nixon, O.	87	36. Hamilton, D.	54	61. Howard, D.	23		
12. Berroa, G.	87	37. Griffey Jr, K.	52	62. Tucker, M.	23		
13. Buhner, J.	86	38. Green, S.	52	63. Mouton, L.	23		
14. Ramirez, M.	85	39. Nunnally, J.	51	64. James, D.	22		
15. Puckett, K.	83	40. Anderson, G.	50	65. Masteller, D.	21		
16. O'Neill, P.	82	41. Martinez, D.	49	66. Bragg, D.	20		
17. Raines, T.	81	42. Hulse, D.	46	67. Hosey, D.	20		
18. Javier, S.	81	43. Munoz, P.	45	68. Ward, T.	19		
19. Cordova, M.	81	44. Amaral, R.	45	69. Hammonds, J.	18		
20. Tettleton, M.	76	45. Becker, R.	45	70. Clark, J.	17		
21. McLemore, M.	73	46. Diaz, A.	44	71. Cuyler, M.	15		
22. Sierra, R.	73	47. Mieske, M.	42	72. Tomberlin, A.	15		
23. Surhoff, B.	72	48. Paquette, C.	42	73. Huff, M.	14		
24. Goodwin, T.	72	49. Nilsson, D.	41	74. Stubbs, F.	13		
25. Carter, J.	70	50. Goodwin, C.	40	75. Gallagher, D.	13		

Catchers
pp. 27–41

Corners
pp. 41–62

Infield
pp. 63–82

Outfield
pp. 83–113

DH
pp. 114–118

Starters
pp. 119–157

Relievers
pp. 157–193

AL DESIGNATED HITTERS
(20 Games or More)

HOME RUNS

1. Thomas, F.	40	10. Murray, E.	21	19. Tartabull, D.	8
2. Tettleton, M.	32	11. Davis, C.	20	20. Hamelin, B.	7
3. Fielder, C.	31	12. Sierra, R.	19	21. Vitiello, J.	7
4. Martinez, E.	29	13. Munoz, P.	18	22. Jefferson, R.	5
5. Gonzalez, J.	27	14. Vaughn, G.	17	23. Tucker, M.	4
6. Baines, H.	24	15. Molitor, P.	15	24. Winfield, D.	2
7. Canseco, J.	24	16. Raines, T.	12	25. James, D.	2
8. Puckett, K.	23	17. Samuel, J.	12	26. Kruk, J.	2
9. Berroa, G.	22	18. Gibson, K.	9	27. Hale, C.	2

BATTING AVERAGE

1. Martinez, E.	.356	10. Gonzalez, J.	.295	19. Gibson, K.	.260
2. Murray, E.	.323	11. Jefferson, R.	.289	20. Tucker, M.	.260
3. Davis, C.	.318	12. James, D.	.287	21. Vitiello, J.	.254
4. Puckett, K.	.314	13. Raines, T.	.285	22. Fielder, C.	.243
5. Kruk, J.	.308	14. Berroa, G.	.278	23. Tettleton, M.	.238
6. Thomas, F.	.308	15. Molitor, P.	.271	24. Tartabull, D.	.236
7. Canseco, J.	.306	16. Samuel, J.	.263	25. Vaughn, G.	.225
8. Munoz, P.	.300	17. Sierra, R.	.263	26. Winfield, D.	.191
9. Baines, H.	.299	18. Hale, C.	.262	27. Hamelin, B.	.168

RUNS BATTED IN

1. Martinez, E.	113	10. Canseco, J.	81	19. Tartabull, D.	35
2. Thomas, F.	111	11. Tettleton, M.	78	20. James, D.	26
3. Puckett, K.	99	12. Raines, T.	67	21. Jefferson, R.	26
4. Berroa, G.	88	13. Baines, H.	63	22. Hamelin, B.	25
5. Davis, C.	86	14. Molitor, P.	60	23. Kruk, J.	23
6. Sierra, R.	86	15. Vaughn, G.	59	24. Vitiello, J.	21
7. Murray, E.	82	16. Munoz, P.	58	25. Hale, C.	18
8. Fielder, C.	82	17. Samuel, J.	39	26. Tucker, M.	17
9. Gonzalez, J.	82	18. Gibson, K.	35	27. Winfield, D.	4

STOLEN BASES

1. Raines, T.	13	9. James, D.	4
2. Molitor, P.	12	10. Canseco, J.	4
3. Vaughn, G.	10	11. Martinez, E.	4
4. Gibson, K.	9	12. Davis, C.	3
5. Berroa, G.	7	13. Puckett, K.	3
6. Samuel, J.	6	14. Thomas, F.	3
7. Murray, E.	5	15. Tucker, M.	2
8. Sierra, R.	5	16. Winfield, D.	1

RUNS SCORED

1. Martinez, E.	121	10. Murray, E.	68	19. Samuel, J.	31
2. Thomas, F.	102	11. Vaughn, G.	67	20. Tucker, M.	23
3. Berroa, G.	87	12. Canseco, J.	64	21. James, D.	22
4. Puckett, K.	83	13. Molitor, P.	63	22. Jefferson, R.	21
5. Raines, T.	81	14. Baines, H.	60	23. Hamelin, B.	20
6. Davis, C.	81	15. Gonzalez, J.	57	24. Kruk, J.	13
7. Tettleton, M.	76	16. Munoz, P.	45	25. Vitiello, J.	13
8. Sierra, R.	73	17. Gibson, K.	37	26. Winfield, D.	11
9. Fielder, C.	70	18. Tartabull, D.	34	27. Hale, C.	10

POST All-STAR LEADERS

NATIONAL LEAGUE PITCHERS

EARNED RUN AVERAGES—Post All-Star
(Minimum 50 Innings Pitched)

1. Maddux, G.	1.623	12. Van Landingham	3.320	22. Portugal, M.	3.700
2. Heredia, G.	2.077	13. Fernandez, S.	3.340	23. Osborne, D.	3.745
3. Rapp, P.	2.282	14. Castillo, F.	3.473	24. Burkett, J.	3.757
4. Ashby, A.	2.593	15. Smoltz, J.	3.487	25. Petkovsek, M.	3.767
5. Martinez, R.	2.660	16. Wells, D.	3.505	26. Pulsipher, B.	3.772
6. Glavine, T.	2.700	17. Neagle, D.	3.529	27. Smiley, J.	3.919
7. Isringhausen, J.	2.806	18. Leiter, M.	3.632	28. Martinez, P.	4.014
8. Valdes, I.	2.829	19. Hampton, M.	3.669	29. Juden, J.	4.021
9. Schourek, P.	2.981	20. Burba, D.	3.670	30. Perez, C.	4.106
10. Nomo, H.	3.030	21. Navarro, J.	3.678		
11. Hamilton, J.	3.280				

WORST EARNED RUN AVERAGES—Post All-Star
(Minimum 50 Innings Pitched)

1. Dishman, G.	5.831	11. Rekar, B.	4.976	21. Foster, K.	4.448
2. Saberhagen, B.	5.774	12. Bullinger, J.	4.883	22. Mlicki, D.	4.410
3. Reynoso, A.	5.500	13. Hammond, C.	4.862	23. Watson, A.	4.263
4. Jones, B.	5.480	14. Ritz, K.	4.846	24. Morgan, M.	4.215
5. Mulholland, T.	5.420	15. Swindell, G.	4.779	25. Reynolds, S.	4.208
6. Loaiza, E.	5.196	16. Drabek, D.	4.716	26. Wagner, P.	4.198
7. Avery, S.	5.153	17. Fassero, J.	4.707	27. Candiotti, T.	4.183
8. Ericks, J.	5.143	18. Parris, S.	4.617	28. Mercker, K.	4.165
9. Tapani, K.	5.102	19. Mimbs, M.	4.552	29. Banks, W.	4.154
10. Quantrill, P.	5.007	20. Brewington, J.	4.540	30. Blair, W.	4.113

AMERICAN LEAGUE PITCHERS

EARNED RUN AVERAGES—Post All-Star
(Minimum 50 Innings Pitched)

1. Johnson, R.	2.057	11. Hershiser, O.	3.673	21. Clemens, R.	4.139
2. Fernandez, A.	2.391	12. Witt, B.	3.673	22. Clark, M.	4.195
3. Mussina, M.	2.435	13. Kamieniecki, S.	3.735	23. Gross, K.	4.242
4. McDowell, J.	3.324	14. Martinez, D.	3.815	24. Belcher, T.	4.350
5. Brown, K.	3.363	15. Pettitte, A.	3.835	25. Givens, B.	4.416
6. Pavlik, R.	3.447	16. Wakefield, T.	3.846	26. Hitchcock, S.	4.416
7. Leiter, A.	3.449	17. Ogea, C.	3.906	27. Hentgen, P.	4.500
8. Alvarez, W.	3.487	18. Erickson, S.	3.945	28. Karl, S.	4.515
9. Cone, D.	3.512	19. Abbott, J.	4.003	29. Harkey, M.	4.549
10. Rogers, K.	3.642	20. Gubicza, M.	4.054	30. Krivda, R.	4.651

Catchers
pp. 27–41

Corners
pp. 41–62

Infield
pp. 63–82

Outfield
pp. 83–113

DH
pp. 114–118

Starters
pp. 119–157

Relievers
pp. 157–193

WORST EARNED RUN AVERAGES—Post All-Star
(Minimum 50 Innings Pitched)

1. Bere, J.	10.189	11. Van Poppel, T.	5.493	21. Lira, F.	5.078
2. Parra, J.	7.462	12. Nagy, C.	5.460	22. Prieto, A.	5.040
3. Anderson, B.	6.750	13. Bones, R.	5.454	23. Bosio, C.	4.989
4. Moyer, J.	6.422	14. Jacome, J.	5.357	24. Finley, C.	4.831
5. Lima, J.	6.109	15. Bergman, S.	5.326	25. Gordon, T.	4.821
6. Benes, A.	5.852	16. Rodriguez, F.	5.256	26. Hanson, E.	4.802
7. Hurtado, E.	5.620	17. Appier, K.	5.175	27. Radke, B.	4.760
8. Sparks, S.	5.575	18. Keyser, B.	5.159	28. Cormier, R.	4.729
9. Guzman, J.	5.570	19. Stottlemyre, T.	5.147	29. Hill, K.	4.696
10. Smith, Z.	5.543	20. Langston, M.	5.084	30. Krivda, R.	4.651

NATIONAL LEAGUE CATCHERS

BATTING AVERAGE—Post All-Star
(Minimum 150 At Bats)

1. Lopez, J.	.361	4. Fletcher, D.	.294	7. Manwaring, K.	.254
2. Piazza, M.	.327	5. Eusebio, T.	.287	8. Girardi, J.	.229
3. Ausmus, B.	.299	6. Santiago, B.	.269		

NATIONAL LEAGUE CORNERS

BATTING AVERAGE—Post All-Star
(Minimum 150 At Bats)

1. Jefferies, G.	.342	9. Mabry, J.	.307	17. McGriff, F.	.279
2. Bagwell, J.	.333	10. Castilla, V.	.302	18. Galarraga, A.	.270
3. Berry, S.	.333	11. Brogna, R.	.301	19. Wallach, T.	.260
4. Magadan, D.	.327	12. Karros, E.	.289	20. King, J.	.260
5. Caminiti, K.	.316	13. Segui, D.	.288	21. Hayes, C.	.252
6. Grace, M.	.314	14. Pendleton, T.	.285	22. Branson, J.	.235
7. Carreon, M.	.313	15. Jones, C.	.282	23. Zeile, T.	.207
8. Morris, H.	.309	16. Colbrunn, G.	.280		

JOIN THE RLBA!
1-800-676-7684

NATIONAL LEAGUE MIDDLE INFIELDERS

BATTING AVERAGE—Post All-Star
(Minimum 150 At Bats)

1. Young, E.	.344	10. Morandini, M.	.285	19. Boone, B.	.260
2. Larkin, B.	.343	11. Lansing, M.	.281	20. Reed, J.	.255
3. Biggio, C.	.322	12. Weiss, W.	.281	21. Abbott, K.	.251
4. Garcia, C.	.310	13. Fonville, C.	.278	22. Thompson, R.	.244
5. Vizcaino, J.	.304	14. DeShields, D.	.273	23. Sanchez, R.	.237
6. Bell, J.	.292	15. Cordero, W.	.270	24. Clayton, R.	.235
7. Veras, Q.	.288	16. Offerman, J.	.264	25. Stocker, K.	.229
8. Kent, J.	.285	17. Lemke, M.	.262	26. Blauser, J.	.188
9. Liriano, N.	.285	18. Dunston, S.	.260	27. Cedeno, A.	.173

NATIONAL LEAGUE OUTFIELDERS

BATTING AVERAGE—Post All-Star
(Minimum 150 At Bats)

1. Gwynn, T.	.372	15. Jordan, B.	.299	29. Hill, G.	.269
2. Butler, B.	.345	16. Walker, L.	.293	30. Whiten, M.	.263
3. Bichette, D.	.344	17. McRae, B.	.289	31. Sosa, S.	.262
4. Bell, D.	.330	18. Howard, T.	.288	32. Mouton, J.	.256
5. Martin, A.	.329	19. Gilkey, B.	.287	33. Mondesi, R.	.256
6. Finley, S.	.314	20. Lankford, R.	.286	34. Gant, R.	.256
7. Tavarez, J.	.311	21. Conine, J.	.285	35. Plantier, P.	250
8. White, R.	.307	22. Klesko, R.	.284	36. Kingery, M.	250
9. Gonzalez, L.	.305	23. Bonds, B.	.283	37. Lewis, D.	.245
10. Devereaux, M.	.304	24. Sanders, D.	.279	38. Van Slyke, A.	.240
11. Eisenreich, J.	.301	25. Everett, C.	.276	39. Justice, D.	.238
12. Sanders, R.	.300	26. Kelly, R.	.272	40. Carr, C.	.230
13. May, D.	.299	27. Brumfield, J.	.272	41. Grissom, M.	.229
14. Merced, O.	.299	28. Hunter, B.	.270	42. Tarasco, T.	.219

AMERICAN LEAGUE CATCHERS

BATTING AVERAGE—Post All-Star
(Minimum 150 At Bats)

1. Steinbach, T.	.300	5. Rodriguez, I.	.281	9. Macfarlane, M.	.247
2. Mayne, B.	.291	6. Alomar Jr, S.	.279	10. Martinez, S.	.238
3. Hoiles, C.	.291	7. Stanley, M.	.275	11. Karkovice, R.	.226
4. Wilson, D.	.290	8. Walbeck, M.	.272	12. Flaherty, J.	.192

AMERICAN LEAGUE CORNERS

BATTING AVERAGE—Post All-Star
(Minimum 150 At Bats)

1. Boggs, W.	.348	11. Mattingly, D.	.298	21. Leius, S.	.266
2. Bonilla, B.	.340	12. Thomas, F.	.294	22. Cirillo, J.	.263
3. Olerud, J.	.336	13. Brosius, S.	.294	23. Gaetti, G.	.255
4. Palmeiro, R.	.334	14. Surhoff, B.	.293	24. Phillips, T.	.244
5. Joyner, W.	.322	15. Ventura, R.	.291	25. Fielder, C.	.230
6. Clark, W.	.317	16. Martinez, T.	.288	26. Sprague, E.	.226
7. Vaughn, M.	.309	17. Blowers, M.	.281	27. Paquette, C.	.218
8. Jaha, J.	.308	18. Fryman, T.	.277	28. Sorrento, P.	.213
9. Seitzer, K.	.300	19. Snow, J.	.274		
10. Thome, J.	.300	20. Naehring, T.	.273		

AMERICAN LEAGUE MIDDLE INFIELDERS

BATTING AVERAGE—Post All-Star
(Minimum 150 At Bats)

1. Knoblauch, C.	.351	10. Howard, D.	.278	19. Ripken, C.	.241
2. Valentin, J.	.312	11. Vizquel, O.	.274	20. Easley, D.	.235
3. Cora, J.	.309	12. Gates, B.	.272	21. Listach, P.	.226
4. Sojo, L.	.303	13. Bordick, M.	.259	22. Kelly, P.	.220
5. Baerga, C.	.301	14. Meares, P.	.258	23. Gonzalez, A.	.220
6. Lockhart, K.	.299	15. Vina, F.	.250	24. Guillen, O.	.218
7. Alicea, L.	.297	16. Durham, R.	.249	25. Gomez, C.	.209
8. Velarde, R.	.290	17. Fernandez, T.	.249	26. Gil, B.	.193
9. Alomar, R.	.284	18. Gagne, G.	.247		

Catchers
pp. 27–41

Corners
pp. 41–62

Infield
pp. 63–82

Outfield
pp. 83–113

DH
pp. 114–118

Starters
pp. 119–157

Relievers
pp. 157–193

AMERICAN LEAGUE OUTFIELDERS

BATTING AVERAGE—Post All-Star
(Minimum 150 At Bats)

1. Salmon, T.	.364	15. Greenwell, M.	.294	29. Anderson, B.	.265
2. Williams, B.	.350	16. Edmonds, J.	.290	30. Sierra, R.	.261
3. Puckett, K.	.347	17. Cordova, M.	.289	31. Curtis, C.	.255
4. Anderson, G.	.339	18. McGee, W.	.286	32. Griffey Jr, K.	.255
5. Johnson, L.	.338	19. Nilsson, D.	.286	33. Buhner, J.	.253
6. Martinez, D.	.337	20. Goodwin, T.	.286	34. Mieske, M.	.237
7. Henderson, R.	.325	21. Damon, J.	.282	35. Becker, R.	.237
8. Green, S.	.323	22. Greer, R.	.282	36. Carter, J.	.228
9. Belle, A.	.322	23. Coleman, V.	.281	37. McLemore, M.	.227
10. Mouton, L.	.313	24. Hamilton, D.	.279	38. Hulse, D.	.222
11. Lofton, K.	.306	25. O'Leary, T.	.271	39. Nunnally, J.	.212
12. Nixon, O.	.302	26. Raines, T.	.271	40. Higginson, B.	.204
13. Javier, S.	.296	27. O'Neill, P.	.269	41. Goodwin, C.	.175
14. Ramirez, M.	.296	28. White, D.	.268		

AMERICAN LEAGUE DESIGNATED HITTERS

BATTING AVERAGE—Post All-Star
(Minimum 150 At Bats)

1. Martinez, E.	.351	5. Gonzalez, J.	.307	9. Berroa, G.	.286
2. Canseco, J.	.325	6. Molitor, P.	.298	10. Vaughn, G.	.275
3. Murray, E.	.324	7. Baines, H.	.290	11. Tettleton, M.	.254
4. Munoz, P.	.311	8. Davis, C.	.288		

STATS INK

All the stats in the Scouting Report (Chapter 2) plus all the stats in the Rotisserie Stat-Pak (Chapter 3) that you've just finished memorizing come from STATS, Inc., a band of merry number noodlers whose client list reads like a Who's Who of baseball publications: *Sports Illustrated, The Sporting News,* ESPN, *USA Today,* and, yours truly, *Rotisserie League Baseball.*

STATS, Inc. also publishes several books that belong in every Rotisserie owner's library. Among them:

- *Major League Handbook.* The first baseball annual to hit the bookstores every year (November 1), with player stats for the year just ended plus projections by Bill James for the year coming up.
- *Minor League Handbook.* An essential tool for building your farm system. Year-by-year data for AAA and AA players, plus Bill James's "Major League Equivalencies."
- *Player Profiles.* Detailed situational analyses, including month-by-month performance breakdowns.
- *Matchups!* A compendium of batter vs. pitcher matchups that gives you the lowdown on the game within the game.
- *The Scouting Report.* A mix of stats and analysis, this hardy annual includes "Stars, Bums, and Sleepers," a look at who's on the way up and who's on the way down.

And that's only for starters! For a complete catalog of STATS, Inc. publications and fantasy games (including something called "football"), call the STATS inksters at 800-63-STATS.

4

Down on the Farm

A Long Night's Journey into Day

The 1996 Minor League Report
by John Benson

Last year's farm report opened with a long statement—okay, a list of ex-cuses—about why major upheavals in the 1994 season, *i.e.*, the continuing impact of expansion and then the Strike, made forecasting so difficult in 1995. Every change, I wrote, has a ripple effect, and the more unusual the change, the bigger the ripples.

Guess what. The change was even bigger than we thought it was a year ago. The same old ripples grew larger in 1995. And we experienced the phenomenon of new and overlapping multidirectional ripples, a concept that can be quickly grasped by anyone who has ever taken a small boat into a large lake and, having steadied the boat to ride out a series of waves, watches helplessly as a 500-horsepower cruiser speeds by, creating a wake that mea-sures 10 on the tsunami scale.

Down here on the farm we do indeed have a large lake and a small boat, and our neighbors Bud and Donald both have huge cruisers that speed past us too frequently, too closely, and too carelessly. And now the weather forecast brings another small craft warning due to further expansion coming just over the horizon, and new neighbors by the name of Diamondback and some other family bringing more of those big boats with large wakes. Shall we head for dock and wait for all this to pass? No way! It's our farm and our lake, too. We just have to get adjusted to the age of never-ending change, and maybe invest in a slightly larger boat.

(And while we're at it, we'll definitely have to get a new metaphor, because this one has sprung a leak.)

The 1995 season was even more unusual than the 1994 season that ended so cruelly and prematurely. At least the 1994 season was "normal" until shortly before the Strike hit, except for those abnormalities resulting from expansion, talent dilution, and the "rushing 'em" syndrome. But in 1995 we still had all these expansion/dilution effects, *plus* a new wave of repercussions resulting from the longest winter in baseball history—the hot stove league went stone cold—followed by the shortest spring training in baseball history.

First there was the false spring, featuring the most disturbing sights and sounds: sights like Pedro Borbon *Senior* collapsing while trying to pick up a slow roller back to the mound, sounds like the tape-recorded message of a major league media office announcing, "Nobody works here anymore."

And then there was Homestead, Florida, the first-ever work fair for unemployed major leaguers, which came and went so quickly that many attendees never did find jobs. And some of those who did successfully land a job, like ex–Phillie first baseman Ricky Jordan, who went to the Angels, spent so little time in Homestead that they could suffer an injury like a torn rotator cuff without anyone even noticing—in Jordan's case, certainly not the Angels.

The real spring training of 1995 was so short, the "regular season" began with spring training–style games still being played in major league stadiums with major league crowds. Come to think of it, maybe they weren't really major league crowds—the smallish numbers and many low-priced tickets added to the spring training aura. The game on the field in early May certainly seemed like some form of preseason play: rosters were expanded to spread the workload among more players with less physical conditioning, and rules were introduced to allow starting pitchers to get a win with less than five innings of work. If all of that didn't sound like spring training, the creaking joints and popping hamstrings sure did.

Finally, the "real" regular season did arrive. And when the longest winter and the shortest spring were over, the game of baseball had changed yet again. It doesn't seem so long ago that anyone harping about how much baseball had changed could be labeled an old-timer. Now the fans who talk about rapid change may be coming from any frame of reference: prewar, postwar, the fifties, the dead-ball/high-mound sixties, the dawn of the DH, the year Cal Ripken was a rookie, or born yesterday—they all sense rapid change in the most conservative of games.

So, with the joy of knowing that we have plenty of company—not just the growing crew of thinkers and tinkerers here at Diamond Library, but also the expanding population of Rotisserians worldwide, and most of the baseball fan community—this farming business must go on, come hail or high water. We embrace the task warmly, with rolled-up sleeves and fingers strongly callused by years of honest sowing and reaping. The good news is that this year's farm report is chock-full of new insights, innovative theories, offbeat strategies, and the longest list of prospects ever to make these pages.

And the bad news? This spring, for the first time in a while, there is no bad news.

The New World Order

The chaotic nature of the game has made us philosophical. As others begin to see just how crazy the baseball world has become, forgive us here at the Farm Bureau for feeling a little prescient about our philosophical outlook. Life is imitating art. In this case the highest form of life, baseball, is imitating the highest art form, Rotisserie baseball. Rotisseowners have understood from day one that honest competition on a level playing field must be founded on sound principles of personnel management within a fixed payroll . . . a salary cap, if you will.

Even if you hate the notion of a salary cap, take joy in the observation that baseball is becoming a perfect example of the free market at work. Major league owners (a growing number of them, anyway) now understand that they have a finite amount of money—even more finite because of sagging attendance and vanishing television revenue. For every free agent who gets a big-money deal, now there's another who takes a hit in the shorts. In addition to looking for new customers for their product, owners (having dropped the pretense that they are just a bunch of philanthropic sportsmen) are now openly searching for cheap labor.

And just where is that cheap labor going to come from? The same place it always has been when big-city bigwigs want someone to do their dirty work: down on the farm. More minor leaguers are coming up faster for the simple reason that they're willing to work for lower wages than experienced veterans.

Finally, most MLB owners have finally grasped the concept that baseball is show business. And since it's a live show, not a film, the model is more like a Broadway play than a Hollywood extravaganza. Instead of a blockbuster movie with an all-star cast, baseball (as a business) is better served when the stage is used to showcase one headline star (or maybe two or three) surrounded by a supporting cast of hard-working hopefuls making union-scale wages.

The result of this new understanding is a rush of players rising from the minors to the majors in roles such as middle reliever, utility infielder, and backup catcher. Some of them are Rule Five draft picks plucked from the lower minors and thrust into roles of varying sizes.

Want some evidence? Eight of the 13 players who were designated here last year with our one-star (*) long-term rating ("Good Idea for 1996–97") had already reached the majors by mid-September 1995.

Every year we learn something in our quest for the Yoo-Hooly Grail, and you can learn too, unless your name is Bud or Donald. Last year we clued you in on such gems of Rotissewisdom as the Jason Jacome Rule. (Yes, Jacome once again had fun with hitters who hadn't seen him before, by moving to the American League after getting crushed in the National, but that AL fun will also end soon.)

This year we offer another set of postulates, each with a decent chance of maturing into conventional wisdom. Take them to heart, if not to the bank.

---

1. **The Jody Reed Phenomenon.** You remember Jody Reed. Well, you should, he was still in the majors, with the San Diego Padres, in 1995. The difference is that where he used to feel comfortable turning down multimillion-dollar contracts, he now has to go hat-in-hand to his job interviews. The days of million-dollar mediocrity are over.

2. **The Andy Tomberlin Phenomenon.** Because the off-season lasted from August to April last year, too many players spent too much time sitting around negotiating sessions and then washing down Big Macs with glasses of vodka (we have reliable eyewitnesses) instead of working out. Then, with the short spring training, it became increasingly clear that some of them couldn't possibly get into shape before the "regular" season started. That squeeze created opportunities for some longtime minor leaguers who, because they were not on 40-man rosters, had gone through a normal minor league spring training. They moved up from Triple-A, joining their major league teams near the end of their abbreviated spring training—if the manager had a discerning eye and quick mind like Tony LaRussa did in the case of Tomberlin—or getting the call after Opening Day if it took longer for the manager to catch on.

   One reason why so many Tomberlin types are hanging around the high minors is to play Crash Davis for the Ebby Lalooshes on their way up. Vets who are no longer legitimate prospects also make wonderful role models. They're allowed to hang around long after passing the prospect stage because most are early-to-bed, early-to-the-park, hard-working players with good off-field habits who can tell the real prospects what it's like to be in the majors. Organizations pick such players carefully, assigning roster spots to these ex–major leaguers often as low as the Double-A level, where the best prospects reside. Ask the Expos what it meant for them to have Rafael Bournigal at Harrisburg and Ottawa last year.

3. **The Juan Acevedo Phenomenon.** The reasoning behind jumping Acevedo from Double-A to the major league rotation was simple: here's a minor league pitcher in shape (see Tomberlin), who did well early in the minors, who's low on the pay scale, and who actually shouldn't be any worse than the fifth-best alternative on the major league roster.

   This effect was even more pronounced for middle relievers than for the starters, but I am naming it after Acevedo for personal reasons. During the Strike last summer, while scouting a game at New Haven, I smuggled my son down from the grandstand to the front row behind home plate, where he sat between me and Acevedo, who was charting pitches. I told my son in no uncertain terms that he should remember Acevedo as someone bound for the majors. I had no idea, of course, that Acevedo would arrive so soon, but I'd like to maintain my son's illusion, as long as possible, about his father's ability to see the future.

   The Acevedo theory did work for the starting rotations of two teams, only one of which was owned by a guy named Bud. The Brewers tried a no-name rotation of Steve Sparks, Scott Karl, Sid Roberson, and Brian Givens. Another small-market team, the Pittsburgh/Northern Virginia Pirates, liked (Steve) Parris in the springtime, when it drizzled, and in the summer, when he sizzled. The Bucs also found it just as effective to start Esteban Loaiza and John Ericks in place of the fading, higher-priced veterans they had been sending out there earlier.

4. **The Jon Nunnally Phenomenon.** Nothing complicated here. Take a guy who batted .267 with 125 strikeouts in A-ball but who has some power (22 home runs) and some speed (23 steals). Stick him in the lineup. Then watch the second time around the league when the pitchers start feeding him breaking stuff, and get him out of the lineup before his average falls into Mendoza country. Honorable mention to Tomas Perez and Freddy Garcia.

5. **The Ron Villone Phenomenon.** Because almost anyone with a live arm qualifies as a major league pitcher these days, it makes sense in the New World Order to promote any hard-throwing short relievers, especially high draft picks, even if they're not ready. Thus were Villone and Dustin Hermanson, for example, given major league roles in 1995. They couldn't be trusted as closers, not right away. But if you snapped them up last summer and hung on through their ups and downs, you could be very happy this season.

6. **The Johnny Damon Phenomenon.** This one also could be called The Bob Boone Effect, or The Vince Coleman Corollary. It was first isolated by trend spotters when Kansas City manager Boone realized he could lose with talented veterans delivering halfhearted efforts—or he could still lose with untested rookies putting out their best efforts on every play. Thus did Damon and Joe Vitiello and Brent Cookson get surprise shots last summer with the Royals. And talking about surprises, the Royals actually won games with their kids, hanging in there all summer in the chase for a wild card playoff berth.

Damon received one star in this chapter last year, but it was a very big one. Pardon us as we pat ourselves on the back for writing a year ago, "For the long term, you won't find a better prospect."

That's a perfect lead-in for us to brag a little bit about how good our advice was in last year's book—and to eat a little crow. Consider this three-star assessment of Garret Anderson: "Those who viewed Jim Edmonds's arrival as meteoric will be even more impressed with Anderson, who is two years younger than Edmonds." You read it here first.

But then there was Denny Hocking, also rated three stars, who we said was "better than all the other Twins shortstop options." Would someone please ask Tom Kelly to read this book?

The best 1995 rookies whom we missed—more correctly, didn't include, for all of them were in contention until we made the final cut to our short list—were Roberson, Hermanson, Villone, Detroit's Bobby Higginson and Felipe Lira, Minnesota's Brad Radke, the Yankees' Andy Pettitte, Colorado's Jason Bates and Roger Bailey, Montreal's Carlos Perez, and the Mets' Jason Isringhausen.

That list tells you two things: we still haven't perfected the art of picking the right pitching prospects, and you wouldn't go far with a team comprised of the prospects we miss. Remember this long-standing Rotisserule in your major league auction draft—avoid rookies, especially rookie pitchers.

To satisfy your rookie habit without putting your major league roster at risk, and to fill your minor league slots wisely, pay attention to the list that follows. Remember that because of all the phenomena we listed above, this year's crop will get more opportunity to play than their counterparts did in years past. That can be good, but only if they play well. Our basic advice is still to let the other owners overbid and live with their rookie struggles this year, then jump on the young players in their second or third major league seasons. We can't guarantee that all of the players listed eventually will become major league stars, or even regulars, but they do come with our highest recommendation for being useful someday.

Overall, our record was pretty good again last year. All of our three-star players got to the majors. Eleven of them became regulars, and just about all of the others are good bets to be playing regularly in 1996. Six of our two-star picks and one of our one-star long-term recommendations (Quilvio Veras) ended up as regulars, often via the trade route.

Veras illustrates the point that trades, either of the prospect or of the player blocking his path, can change a rookie's status. We even said as much for Roberto Petagine ("He might get an outfielder's glove, or get traded") and Brian L. Hunter ("What will the Astros do with Steve Finley?") and Salomon Torres ("Worth a shot if he's traded"). Others on our 1995 list who have benefited from inter-team deals were Carl Everett, Jose Oliva, Luis Ortiz, Marc Newfield, David Bell, Phil Nevin, Scott Klingenbeck, Chris Stynes, Andrew Lorraine, and Lyle Mouton.

About 80 percent of the players we listed reached the majors in 1995. Injuries prevented some from having much impact—among them were Alan Benes, Darren Dreifort, Luis Raven, and Brien Taylor. You also see some useful players on the list we printed of 1994 rookies who were sent down just before the strike so they could keep playing. It included Lorraine, Petagine, Jacome, Armando Benitez, Chad Ogea, Sean Bergman, Dwayne Hosey, Dave Stevens, Sterling Hitchcock, Ernie Young, Mike Kelly, Steve Trachsel, Orlando Miller, James Mouton, Ismail Valdes, Ricky Bottalico, Bryce Florie, and William Van Landingham.

Sometimes we qualify our statements, stumbling into foresight. On Nigel Wilson: "He could be on the way from prospect to suspect." On Jacome: "Don't expect more stats like those he had in 1994." On Albie Lopez: "If he visits the salad bar instead of the dessert cart occasionally, he'll be just fine." We asked a coach in the American Association why Lopez struggled at Buffalo in 1995. His response: "He looks heavy to me."

Finally, there were a number of players who were on our list last year whom we're not including again here this year, even though they spent most of last summer in the minors. Hey, you buy a new book, you deserve some new names. Also, some of them made enough of an impact to earn mention in Chapter 2, Scouting Report. We still like these players: Carlos Delgado, Tony Clark, David Bell, Butch Huskey, Roger Cedeño, Ray McDavid, Michael Tucker, Ernie Young, Brian Barber, Bill Pulsipher, Paul Shuey, Curtis Goodwin, and Todd Hollandsworth.

1996 Farm System Prospects

Most members of this Class of 1996 will make it to the majors sooner or later. We've tried to give you an idea of which ones will get there sooner—and which ones will have a major impact once they arrive. Owners in leagues with large farm systems, owners in Ultra leagues, and anyone building with a focus on the long-term future will want to pay special attention to the players with one-star ratings. Players ages are stated as of April 1, 1996. Profiles do not include 1995 major league stats (if any), which appear in the Appendix (pages 315–340).

RATING GUIDE

* * * Ready to be a productive regular now.
* * Fine talent, should make it to the majors in 1996.
* Good idea for 1997 or 1998.

CATCHERS

RAUL CASANOVA PADRES Age 23/B *

"Papo" Casanova's 1994 season in the California League was nearly as good as fellow phenom Todd Greene's. And Casanova's the better catcher. Ankle injuries slowed the Latin lover in 1995, and Brad Ausmus blocks the way. But if Casanova continues to develop, Ausmus becomes trade bait.

Team	Level	AB	HR	RBI	SB	BA
Memphis	AA	306	12	44	4	.271

ALBERTO CASTILLO METS Age 26/R * *

Through two years in rookie ball and five years in Class A, Castillo seemed stuck behind succeeding generations of Brook Fordyces in the Mets' organization. The wonder last season was how New York could keep him down so long, given his considerable behind-the-plate skills. He's always had a reputation as a strong-armed thrower and good handler of pitchers. Finally, in 1995, he began to show signs that he could swing the bat.

Team	Level	AB	HR	RBI	SB	BA
Norfolk	AAA	217	4	31	2	.267

RAMON CASTRO ASTROS Age 20/R *

The first Puerto Rico–born player ever drafted in the first round, Castro struggled a bit in the Florida State League, but was a tough out in the New York–Penn circuit. He can throw, but needs to concentrate on the everyday routine of catching rather than its flashier aspects—in other words, more Al Lopez and less Benito Santiago.

Team	Level	AB	HR	RBI	SB	BA
Kissimmee	A	120	0	8	0	.208
Auburn	A	224	9	49	0	.299

SAL FASANO ROYALS Age 23/R * *

In 1994 Fasano tore up the Midwest League, but then struggled some when he started 1995 still at the "A" level. No matter. He got back on track in Double-A. When Kansas City called up a catcher late last season, they went for Mike Sweeney, a better defensive backstop, but the Royals are likely to find room somewhere for Fasano's bat, and soon.

Team	Level	AB	HR	RBI	SB	BA
Wilmington	A	88	2	7	0	.227
Wichita	AA	317	20	66	3	.290

TODD GREENE ANGELS Age 23/R * *

What a resumé! MVP of the Northwest League in 1993. MVP of the California League in 1994. The first minor leaguer in 10 years to hit 40 home runs in a season in 1995. His arrival in the majors probably should be preceded by a cram course at third base during the off-season and maybe a little live action at the hot corner in Triple-A, just in case. But the Angels aren't exactly stacked behind the plate, so Greene may get to skip that part of his education.

Team	Level	AB	HR	RBI	SB	BA
Midland	AA	318	26	57	3	.327
Vancouver	AAA	168	14	35	1	.250

SCOTT HATTEBERG RED SOX Age 26/L * *

Hatteberg is a solid defensive catcher whose bat finally showed signs of life last year. His hitting will determine whether he ever achieves a higher station in life than he had as Aaron Sele's college batterymate at Washington State.

Team	Level	AB	HR	RBI	SB	BA
Pawtucket	AAA	251	7	27	2	.271

JASON KENDALL PIRATES Age 21/R * *

Fred Kendall hung around for 12 major league seasons, with a career average of .234. His son just came close to leading the Southern League in batting. Which proves: (a) hitting isn't all in the genes, or (b) Jason's mother swings a mean bat.

Team	Level	AB	HR	RBI	SB	BA
Carolina	AA	429	8	71	10	.326

PAUL KONERKO DODGERS Age 20/R *

Advisory to (really) long-range planners: Konerko, the Dodgers' 1994 first-round draft pick, is in the fast lane to arrive in Chavez Ravine in 1998, when the script calls for him to push Mike Piazza to first or third.

Team	Level	AB	HR	RBI	SB	BA
San Bernardino	A	448	19	77	3	.277

JORGE POSADA YANKEES Age 23/B * * *

Posada's 1995 debut was delayed while he was on the disabled list with a strained lower back. That was after a broken left ankle ended his 1994 season. Injuries are the only thing that might hold back this switch-hitting catcher with a strong and accurate throwing arm.

Team	Level		AB	HR	RBI	SB	BA
Columbus	AAA		368	8	51	4	.255

JASON VARITEK   MARINERS   Age 23/B   * *

First the Twins, then the Mariners, tried and failed to sign Varitek after drafting him in the first round. Only after he stubbornly signed with an independent team did Seattle finally come up with enough money to get his John Hancock. Varitek isn't ready yet, but he's a can't-miss power prospect, not to mention a heckuva tough-nosed negotiator.

Team	Level		AB	HR	RBI	SB	BA
Port City	AA		352	10	44	0	.224

GEORGE WILLIAMS   ATHLETICS   Age 26/B   * *

Many catching prospects have come and gone through Oakland in recent years, none of whom could budge Terry Steinbach from his post. Meanwhile, all Williams did was hit in the lower minors, then hit even more as he moved closer to the majors, paying his dues every step of the way. Could be his timing is just about right.

Team	Level		AB	HR	RBI	SB	BA
Edmonton	AAA		290	13	55	0	.310

FIRST BASEMEN

DAN CHOLOWSKY   CARDINALS   Age 25/R   * *

One of baseball's Philip Nolans: A Man Without a Position. Cholowsky has played outfield, third, and second in addition to first. He can run well for a first-sacker, which is a bonus. But Triple-A pitchers found holes in his big swing, which is cause for pause. If he could work his way back into the middle infield, he'd have a lot more Rotisserie value.

Team	Level		AB	HR	RBI	SB	BA
Arkansas	AA		190	7	35	7	.311
Louisville	AAA		238	7	25	10	.218

1996 ROOKIE ALL-STAR TEAM—AMERICAN LEAGUE

C	Todd Greene (Angels)	OF	Robert Perez (Blue Jays)
1B	Tony Clark (Tigers)	OF	Jose Herrera (Athletics)
2B	Arquimedez Pozo (Mariners)	OF	Jason McDonald (Athletics)
3B	Antone Williamson (Brewers)	P	Rocky Coppinger (Orioles)
SS	Nomar Garciaparra (Red Sox)	P	Wolcott (Mariners)

STEVE COX   ATHLETICS   Age 21/L   *

The California League is a hitters' paradise, but nobody else drove in 110 runs there last year. Keep an eye on how he adapts to grown-up curveballs as he climbs the minor league ladder.

Team	Level	AB	HR	RBI	SB	BA
Modesto	A	483	30	110	5	.298

KEVIN GRIJAK   BRAVES   Age 25/L   * *

Grijak grew up to hit the way you'd expect from a kid whose parents built him a batting cage in his own yard. The only negative was that he didn't face many lefties in that cage.

Team	Level	AB	HR	RBI	SB	BA
Greenville	AA	74	2	11	0	.432
Richmond	AAA	309	12	56	1	.298

DERREK LEE   PADRES   Age 20/R   *

San Diego is not going to rush their 1993 first-round draft choice. At 6'5" and 205 pounds, Lee is still agile enough to steal bases and play some at third. And he's this year's most legitimate prospect from our favorite minor league town, Rancho Cucamonga.

Team	Level	AB	HR	RBI	SB	BA
Rancho Cucamonga	A	502	23	95	14	.301
Memphis	AA	9	0	1	0	.111

ALDO PECORILLI   BRAVES   Age 25/R   * *

Too bad that Lee falls alphabetically between Pecorilli and Grijak, because the latter two are like twins. They were born a month apart, grew up together, and spent their formative years in Grijak's batting cage. A trade reunited them in 1995, and they platooned at first base for Atlanta's top farm team. Pecorilli has tried other positions but will have to rely on his hitting to become a major league success. This is a make-or-break year for him.

Team	Level	AB	HR	RBI	SB	BA
Greenville	AA	265	7	42	2	.385
Richmond	AAA	127	6	17	0	.260

CHRIS PRITCHETT   ANGELS   Age 26/L   * *

Pritchett is a contact hitter with line drive power. He's also an excellent defensive first baseman. His problem is that he's stuck behind a young major league star (J. T. Snow) who's only two years older. A trade is a possibility, so watch the off-season transaction wire.

Team	Level	AB	HR	RBI	SB	BA
Vancouver	AAA	434	8	53	2	.276

JASON THOMPSON   PADRES   Age 24/L   * *

No, old-timers, not *that* Jason Thompson. Jason II's numbers suffered after going from the California and Texas leagues to the Southern League, but the power numbers are better than they look. Only two players hit more homers in the Southern League in 1995.

Team	Level	AB	HR	RBI	SB	BA
Memphis	AA	475	20	64	7	.272

DARYLE WARD   TIGERS   Age 20/L   *

The Tigers' major cash crop has been first basemen—Rico Brogna, Tony Clark, and a failed crop, Ivan Cruz, preceded Ward. The 1994 15th-round draft pick is young enough to develop even more power. If Clark can't turn Cecil Fielder into a full-time DH, Ward will.

Team	Level	AB	HR	RBI	SB	BA
Fayetteville	A	524	14	106	1	.284

SECOND BASEMEN

JEFF BERBLINGER   CARDINALS   Age 25/R   * *

Berblinger is a heads-up player. The road to second base in St. Louis is arrow straight and free of traffic. If he doesn't make it as a player, Berblinger has the knowledge and personality to make a good coach. But that's getting way ahead of our story.

Team	Level	AB	HR	RBI	SB	BA
Arkansas	AA	332	5	29	16	.319

HOMER BUSH   PADRES   Age 23/R   * *

Aside from a .234 season in the Sally League in 1992, Bush has always hit well—even in Australia. He has serious speed, and he'll become an even better hitter when he learns to be more patient at the plate.

Team	Level	AB	HR	RBI	SB	BA
Memphis	AA	432	5	37	34	.280

FELIPE CRESPO   BLUE JAYS   Age 23/B   * * *

Having another switch-hitting second baseman waiting in the wings could ease Toronto's mourning period if Roberto Alomar leaves as a free agent. Crespo is no Alomar, but who is? Even though he doesn't have the speed or the glove, Crespo can sure swing a bat.

Team	Level	AB	HR	RBI	SB	BA
Syracuse	AAA	347	13	41	12	.294

EDWIN DIAZ   RANGERS   Age 21/R   *

Middle infield prospects—what the heck, any kind of prospects—have been scarcer than humility in Texas in recent years. Diaz could find himself alongside the most recent Rangers prospect, Benji Gil, in a couple of years.

Team	Level	AB	HR	RBI	SB	BA
Charlotte	A	450	8	56	8	.284

DAVID DOSTER   **PHILLIES**   **Age 25/R**   * *

The Phils have a couple of second base prospects with good bats and iffy gloves. Doster is borderline too old to be taken seriously as a prospect, but if he does make it, he will become a Rotisserie celebrity, one of the few power sources among National League middle infielders.

Team	Level		AB	HR	RBI	SB	BA
Reading	AA		551	21	79	11	.265

KEVIN JORDAN   **PHILLIES**   **Age 26/R**   * *

Standing in Doster's way is Jordan. The Phils toyed with the idea of moving the former Yankees farmhand to third base before they reacquired Charlie Hayes. Even more than for Doster, the age factor makes 1996 a make-it or break-it year for Jordan. And with Mickey Morandini coming off a solid season, second base is not exactly a top Phillies priority, considering how many other holes they have.

Team	Level		AB	HR	RBI	SB	BA
Scranton	AAA		410	5	60	3	.310

RALPH MILLIARD   **MARLINS**   **Age 22/R**   * *

The total package: good defense, some pop, a little speed, and the patience to walk more often than he strikes out. Milliard is on track to supplant Hensley Meulens as the most successful player ever produced in the Netherlands Antilles.

Team	Level		AB	HR	RBI	SB	BA
Portland	AA		464	11	40	22	.267

BOBBY MORRIS   **CUBS**   **Age 23/L**   *

Hal Morris's younger brother, with even less power. But little Bobby is growing into a decent hitting prospect, and he does play a position where power is not the prime consideration.

Team	Level		AB	HR	RBI	SB	BA
Daytona	A		344	2	55	22	.308

ERIC OWENS   **REDS**   **Age 25/R**   * *

Owens, the American Association MVP, led the league in a number of offensive categories. In truth, it wasn't a very good year for the league, but it was by far Owens's best year to date—the season before, he hit just .254 at Chattanooga. Was 1995 a portent of the future—or a career year? That's the kind of question that keeps the old ticker pumping.

Team	Level		AB	HR	RBI	SB	BA
Indianapolis	AAA		427	12	63	33	.314

ARQUIMEDEZ POZO   **MARINERS**   **Age 22/R**   * *

In this book, Pozo functions like a galaxy: he just keeps adding stars. He was a one-star player in our 1995 book. This year he gets two. If he spends this summer in the minors, he's a sure bet for—you guessed it—three stars next year. A big talent, but he needs a nickname to make it in the majors.

When I asked him what he likes to be called, he explained simply, "Everybody calls me Pozo." If he makes it, Chris Berman will certainly change that.

Team	Level	AB	HR	RBI	SB	BA
Tacoma	AAA	450	10	62	3	.300

ADAM RIGGS DODGERS Age 23/R *

Here's a 1994 22nd-round draft pick who puts up big-time offensive numbers while playing second base. And with the Dodgers, it won't matter that he's not a good fielder. Riggs is a fine pick for an Ultra roster.

Team	Level	AB	HR	RBI	SB	BA
San Bernardino	A	542	24	106	31	.362

STEVE RODRIGUEZ TIGERS Age 25/R * *

It is not true that Boston had to put him on waivers because of a rule limiting the number of players named Rodriguez in any one organization. (There were four Rodriguezes at Pawtucket in 1995, and two others the year before.) But it is true that the Tigers (who have a Rodriguez shortage compared to Boston) quickly snatched him up. Steve, voted the International League's best defensive second baseman, is a heady player in the Red Sox tradition of Marty Barrett and Jody Reed.

Team	Level	AB	HR	RBI	SB	BA
Pawtucket	AAA	324	1	24	12	.241

TODD WALKER TWINS Age 22/L * * *

With Chuck Knoblauch in the way at second, Walker could become the solution to the Twins' third base problem. He has the bat to play a corner position; he set a season record for home runs at New Britain's Beehive Field.

Team	Level	AB	HR	RBI	SB	BA
Hardware City	AA	513	21	85	23	.290

THIRD BASEMEN

GEORGE ARIAS ANGELS Age 24/R * *

Arias and Todd Greene were about the best one-two punch in baseball last year. Don't let the low SB total fool you. Arias had enough speed to leg out 11 triples a year ago.

Team	Level	AB	HR	RBI	SB	BA
Midland	AA	520	30	104	3	.279

LINO DIAZ ROYALS Age 25/R *

Diaz hit well in the Midwest and Carolina leagues the last two years, then hit even better in the Texas League. He's from the former major league city (Union Association, 1884) of Altoona, PA. The main problem is his age.

Team	Level	AB	HR	RBI	SB	BA
Wilmington	A	173	2	23	0	.301
Wichita	AA	226	6	43	0	.350

SCOTT ROLEN PHILLIES Age 20/R *

Wrist surgery cut short Rolen's season, but he made the most of his limited time. He batted .294 in the Sally League in 1994, then .290 and .289 as he moved up last year. He's still very young and on track to be about a .285 hitter with power in the majors.

Team	Level	AB	HR	RBI	SB	BA
Clearwater	A	238	10	39	4	.290
Reading	AA	76	3	15	1	.289

ANTONE WILLIAMSON BREWERS Age 22/L * * *

Milwaukee made Williamson their first draft pick in 1994 out of Arizona State. The Brewers have this thing about converting all sorts of people into third basemen. But starting next year, Milwaukee fans can settle back for a cold one and watch Williamson at the hot corner as long as the team stays in their town.

Team	Level	AB	HR	RBI	SB	BA
El Paso	AA	392	7	90	3	.309

SHORTSTOPS

RICH AURILIA GIANTS Age 24/R * *

According to *Baseball America*, Aurilia was the Texas League's best defensive shortstop in 1995. Not a bad hitter, either, even when he stepped up to Triple-A.

Team	Level	AB	HR	RBI	SB	BA
Shreveport	AA	226	4	42	10	.327
Phoenix	AAA	258	5	34	2	.279

NOMAR GARCIAPARRA RED SOX Age 22/R * *

Too big to play shortstop? Humbug! That's what they said about Cal Ripken, and he's even bigger than Garciaparra. Ripken also is a stronger hitter, but there may not be a player in the game today who can match Garciaparra's defensive potential. He bears an uncanny resemblance to Dave Concepcion, and could be that good.

Team	Level	AB	HR	RBI	SB	BA
Trenton	AA	513	8	47	35	.267

WILTON GUERRERO DODGERS Age 21/R * *

On the other hand, there's this skinny kid (5'11", 145) who hits for a higher average than Garciaparra, but can't carry his glove defensively.

Team	Level	AB	HR	RBI	SB	BA
San Antonio	AA	382	0	26	21	.348
Albuquerque	AAA	49	0	2	2	.327

MARK LORETTA   BREWERS   Age 24/R   * *

The man can hit, but there are many questions about Loretta's glove.

Team	Level		AB	HR	RBI	SB	BA
New Orleans	AAA		479	7	79	8	.286

REY ORDONEZ   METS   Age 23/B   *

Likely to be 1996's classic example of a player worth more in "real" baseball than in Rotisserie. Ordonez can handle a glove like Ozzie Smith ... and a bat like Mario Mendoza. Think of 500 at bats and a .210 average, and you get an idea of Ordonez's value. That's today. In two or three years, he could hit .250 and drive in 50 runs, so wait a while.

Team	Level		AB	HR	RBI	SB	BA
Norfolk	AAA		439	2	50	11	.214

DONNIE SADLER   RED SOX   Age 20/R   *

Here's a rarity for you: a Boston farmhand who can run. You'll see the term "spark plug" used in articles describing this 5'7" ball of fire. He knows how to work the count and draw a walk, too, so he's a natural leadoff hitter.

Team	Level		AB	HR	RBI	SB	BA
Michigan	A		438	9	55	41	.283

OUTFIELDERS

JEFF ABBOTT   WHITE SOX   Age 23/R   *

A 1994 fourth-round pick out of the University of Kentucky, Abbott has done nothing but put dents in baseballs since turning pro. The bad news is that his average has slipped as he has shot up through the Chicago organization. The good news is that the slippage has been from .467 to .393 to .348 to .320. Most Rotisserie owners could live with that. One of those rare birds who throws left and bats right.

Team	Level		AB	HR	RBI	SB	BA
Prince William	A		264	4	47	7	.348
Birmingham	AA		197	3	28	1	.320

BOB ABREU   ASTROS   Age 22/L   * *

After spending his youth near the top of the roll call in school, Abreu now rates high among Houston's prospects. Consistency has marked his career—in five seasons, his averages all have been between .283 and last year's .304, and his stolen bases totals have ranged from 10 to 16. He also had the highest RBI total of his career in 1995. Good and improving.

Team	Level		AB	HR	RBI	SB	BA
Tucson	AAA		415	10	75	16	.304

BRUCE AVEN   INDIANS   Age 24/R   *

Proof positive that scouting is an inexact science, Aven was a 30th-round draft pick out of Lamar University. Now he's a legitimate power/speed prospect.

Team	Level	AB	HR	RBI	SB	BA
Kinston	A	479	23	69	15	.261

YAMIL BENITEZ   EXPOS   Age 23/R   * *

Benitez has an unforgettable name, and it will be hard for baseball fans to forget his feats on the field over the next decade or more.

Team	Level	AB	HR	RBI	SB	BA
Ottawa	AAA	474	18	69	14	.259

JAMES BETZSOLD   INDIANS   Age 23/R   *

With Aven, Betzsold, and playoff MVP Richie Sexson in Kinston's lineup, it's little wonder the aspiring Indians were the Carolina League champions. However, all three big sticks have big holes in their swings. It will require less mortaring and spackling to fill in the gaps for Aven and Betzsold.

Team	Level	AB	HR	RBI	SB	BA
Kinston	A	455	25	71	3	.268

JOHNNY DAMON   ROYALS   Age 22/L   * * *

Damon surpassed even our expectations last season, when we said he'd be a good bet for 1996 or 1997. Turned out he was a good bet for late 1995. You can put your money on him again this year. A blue-chipper all the way.

Team	Level	AB	HR	RBI	SB	BA
Wichita	AA	318	16	54	26	.343

JUAN ENCARNACION   TIGERS   Age 20/R   *

A PA announcer's dream. Can't you just imagine Bob Sheppard at Yankee Stadium intoning: "Now batting, numbah twwentty-one, Whan En-car-nah-see-own, numbah twwentty-one." You won't have to wait long to hear it.

Team	Level	AB	HR	RBI	SB	BA
Fayetteville	A	457	16	72	5	.282

KARIM GARCIA   DODGERS   Age 20/L   * * *

Either LA has done an excellent job of scouting young talent, or the prospects are telling whoppers about their ages. Garcia, who skipped from the Florida State League to the Pacific Coast League, may have surpassed the old man ahead of him, 21-year-old Roger Cedeño.

Team	Level	AB	HR	RBI	SB	BA
Albuquerque	AAA	474	20	90	12	.319

STEVE GIBRALTER   REDS   Age 23/R   * * *

Gibralter had a couple of mediocre seasons after tearing apart the Midwest League in 1992. He returned last year to tear up the American Association before tearing up ligaments in his left thumb. He'll be OK, though. Talk about his injury, then bid.

Team	Level	AB	HR	RBI	SB	BA
Indianapolis	AAA	263	18	63	0	.316

VLADIMIR GUERRERO EXPOS Age 20/R *

Won't it be fun when Vladimir and Yamil are patrolling the outfield in Montreal, or wherever the Expos are by then? Especially if they have Moises to lead them out of the wilderness. Vladimir's arm makes him the right fielder.

Team	Level	AB	HR	RBI	SB	BA
Albany	A	421	16	63	12	.333

JOSE HERRERA ATHLETICS Age 23/L * * *

There was some concern when Herrera didn't immediately step into the majors after being acquired for Rickey Henderson in 1993. When he did make it, he held his own, despite skipping over Triple-A.

Team	Level	AB	HR	RBI	SB	BA
Huntsville	AA	358	6	45	9	.282

RICHARD HIDALGO ASTROS Age 20/R * *

Gap power and one of the minors' best arms are the starting points in the raves about Hidalgo. Both skills will be extremely helpful in the Astrodome.

Team	Level	AB	HR	RBI	SB	BA
Jackson	AA	489	14	59	8	.266

DAMON HOLLINS BRAVES Age 21/R *

Hollins's numbers slipped only slightly when he moved from the Carolina League up to the Southern League. He's another of those throws-left, bats-right rarities. Maybe it's a fin-de-siècle trend.

Team	Level	AB	HR	RBI	SB	BA
Greenville	AA	466	18	77	6	.247

ROBIN JENNINGS CUBS Age 23/L * *

Jennings is a pure line-drive hitter with a rifle arm. He has done it all the way through the minors so far, and there's no reason to believe he'll stop.

Team	Level	AB	HR	RBI	SB	BA
Orlando	AA	490	17	79	7	.296

ANDRUW JONES BRAVES Age 18/R *

Those aren't typos. Jones has a U in his first name, and he is just 18 years old. Before he could vote—well, actually we're not sure what the voting age is in Curaçao—he was destroying South Atlantic League pitching. He tailed off, but still turned in some of the best overall numbers in the minors. One thing holding him back could be the Braves' wealth of outfield talent. Then again, he might be the best of the bunch on their farm. Did we mention he also was voted the Sally League's best defensive outfielder, and *Baseball America*'s Player of the Year? He will be around long enough to win the latter honor again, but not the former.

Team	Level		AB	HR	RBI	SB	BA
Macon	A		537	25	100	56	.277

BROOKS KIESCHNICK   CUBS   Age 23/L   * * *

In college, he was a Certs All-Star: Kieschnick is a pitcher; no, he's a designated hitter. In the National League, he has to find a position, so the Cubs have settled on left field. The American Association home run champ will be addressing a lot of baseballs to Sheffield and Waveland Avenues in Chicago.

Team	Level		AB	HR	RBI	SB	BA
Iowa	AAA		505	23	73	2	.295

GATOR McBRIDE   BRAVES   Age 22/R   *

McBride proved he wasn't really an infielder defensively, so the Braves threw him into their crowd of talented outfielders. His powerful bat could get him to Atlanta as soon as any of the others. And when he arrives, he'll already have a colorful, wonderful nickname.

Team	Level		AB	HR	RBI	SB	BA
Durham	A		360	13	59	11	.236

QUINTON McCRACKEN   ROCKIES   Age 26/B   * *

The speedy McCracken was disappointed about starting his second consecutive season in Double-A, so he did something about it: he earned an in-season promotion to Triple-A.

Team	Level	AB	HR	RBI	SB	BA
New Haven	AA	221	1	26	26	.357
Colorado Springs	AAA	244	3	28	17	.361

JASON McDONALD   ATHLETICS   Age 24/B   * *

An excellent offensive table setter and base stealer, McDonald had defensive problems as a middle infielder. Oakland now projects him as a center fielder. With 110 walks and 109 runs scored to go with those 70 SB, he has "leadoff" written all over him.

Team	Level		AB	HR	RBI	SB	BA
Modesto	A		493	6	50	70	.262

BILLY McMILLON   MARLINS   Age 24/L   * *

The All-McSomething outfield is crowded, but McMillon could well be the number three hitter in its lineup. He's an RBI machine.

Team	Level		AB	HR	RBI	SB	BA
Portland	AA		518	14	93	15	.313

TROT NIXON   RED SOX   Age 22/L   *

There's only one question about Nixon's potential. Will a recurring back problem rob him of his awesome power? He also has been a good enough athlete to play center field. But the injury prevented him from taking the fast track through the Arizona Fall League in 1994, and his struggles in Double-A last year indicate he may not be ready until 1997.

Team	Level	AB	HR	RBI	SB	BA
Sarasota	A	264	5	39	7	.303
Trenton	AA	94	2	8	2	.160

ALEX OCHOA   METS   Age 24/R   * *

Panicking at the trade deadline as division rivals improved themselves, the Orioles finally relented and included Ochoa in the Bobby Bonilla deal. Gong! It wasn't Bonilla's fault that the deal didn't work out, but Orioles will be cursing the trade for a long time to come. Scouts are in love with Ochoa's arm—and sometimes he falls in love with it as well, trying to throw out everybody in the ballpark. He has enough of a gun from right field to keep runners from taking an extra base, but has to learn to reduce his errors rather than try to pad his assists total. Oh, and Ochoa also has line-drive power and fine speed.

Team	Level	AB	HR	RBI	SB	BA
Rochester	AAA	336	8	46	17	.274
Norfolk	AAA	123	2	15	7	.309

JAY PAYTON   METS   Age 23/R   * * *

With Payton, Varitek, and Garciaparra on the same team, Georgia Tech still did no better than second in the 1994 College World Series. That says something about the Yellowjackets' pitching. Payton will be the center fielder at Shea Stadium for years to come. The only question is whether he'll bat leadoff or third. Based on Gerry Hunsicker's three-word scouting report ("born to hit") we predict he will eventually settle into the three slot.

Team	Level	AB	HR	RBI	SB	BA
Binghamton	AA	357	14	54	16	.345
Norfolk	AAA	196	4	30	11	.240

ROBERT PEREZ   BLUE JAYS   Age 26/R   * * *

Perez may not need any more .300 seasons in the International League—he's had two, plus a .294 mark in 1993—to advance to the majors. His average led the International League a year ago. His arm is good enough for right field, but his glove may limit him to left and/or DH.

Team	Level	AB	HR	RBI	SB	BA
Syracuse	AAA	502	9	66	7	.343

RUBEN RIVERA   YANKEES   Age 22/R   * *

No current prospect has had the hype that Rivera inspired during the last couple of years. No, he's not the next Mantle, but he's probably better than the next Bobby Murcer, which isn't shabby. After his bat, his greatest asset is his arm. The greatest negative is his tendency to strike out.

Team	Level	AB	HR	RBI	SB	BA
Norwich	AA	256	9	39	16	.293
Columbus	AAA	174	15	35	8	.270

CHRIS SHEFF   MARLINS   Age 25/R   * *

Sheff and McMillon formed a potent one-two punch for the Eastern League's best team. The gang of outfield prospects the Marlins took in the expansion draft didn't pan out so well. Their home-grown duo, Sheff and McMillon, should fare better.

Team	Level	AB	HR	RBI	SB	BA
Portland	AA	471	12	91	23	.276

DUANE SINGLETON   BREWERS   Age 23/L   * *

Singleton won't hit for power, but he can cause trouble on the base paths. Has been held back by a reputation as a head case, but maybe it's just a question of immaturity.

Team	Level	AB	HR	RBI	SB	BA
New Orleans	AAA	355	4	29	31	.268

DEMOND SMITH   ATHLETICS   Age 23/B   *

The simple advice is "See the ball, hit the ball." Smith was having trouble seeing the ball until he had an eye exam. Now he is hitting the ball well enough that Oakland gave up Mike Aldrete to get Smith from the Angels. Okay, so it wasn't exactly a king's ransom, but you don't give up a useful major leaguer for a prospect lightly. Smith was also voted the Midwest League's best base runner in the *Baseball America* poll.

Team	Level	AB	HR	RBI	SB	BA
Lake Elsinore	A	148	7	26	14	.351
Cedar Rapids	A	317	7	41	37	.341
West Michigan	A	32	2	3	3	.313

BUBBA TRAMMELL   TIGERS   Age 23/R   *

With a name like Bubba, you figure he can hit. With a name like Trammell, you figure he's got to be a Tiger. No relation to Alan, but Bubba will soon be ready, so the Trammell name won't be absent from Detroit box scores for long.

Team	Level	AB	HR	RBI	SB	BA
Lakeland	A	454	16	72	13	.284

PAT WATKINS   REDS   Age 23/R   *

Before last season, speculation about Watkins focused on how much his power stats would fall off after his 27-homer 1994 season at the Winston-Salem hitters' haven. Quite a bit, as it turned out, but Watkins still is a solid offensive and defensive prospect.

Team	Level	AB	HR	RBI	SB	BA
Chattanooga	AA	358	12	57	5	.291

KEITH WILLIAMS   GIANTS   Age 23/R   * *

Williams has risen rapidly through the San Francisco organization. He'll slow down now, because his defensive limitations limit him to left field, and that position is taken.

Team	Level		AB	HR	RBI	SB	BA
Shreveport	AA		275	9	55	5	.305
Phoenix	AAA		83	2	14	0	.301

PITCHERS

ALAN BENES   CARDINALS   Age 24/R   * * *

After going 17–3 at four levels in 1994 and surging in early 1995, this "other" member of the pitching Benes family seemed headed for an early callup. But then his elbow started acting up. Was he fully recovered at season's end? Well, in the minor league playoffs he threw 18 innings, allowing just one run, six hits, two walks, and 13 strikeouts—and that was against top opponents.

Team	Level		W	L	ERA	IP	H	BB	K
Louisville	AAA		4	2	2.41	56.0	37	14	54

JAIME BLUMA   ROYALS   Age 23/R   *

Ain't alphabetical order great? This case gives me a chance to get right up on my soapbox and warn you not to go overboard on minor league relief aces. Call it the Mike Draper Syndrome: 37 saves at Triple-A in 1992, then zero saves in the majors in 1993 despite spending a whole year in the Mets bullpen and getting a fair amount of work. Yet people keep calling me and asking my opinion of this or that minor league reliever who has 25 saves in July. "Isn't he being groomed as a closer?" they ask me. Maybe he is, but minor league work comes early in the process of developing a closer. Would you go to a college freshman when you need a medical doctor? The real professional school for soon-to-be major league relief aces is the major league setup corps, and only the best of them graduate. Draper didn't even make it to a second year of apprentice work; he was released at the end of 1993. (And to think you just saved two bucks a minute by reading that here instead of listening to me say it on the phone!) Back to Bluma: he's got his own personal warning label, in the form of a strikeout/walk ratio that plummeted when he reached the Triple-A level. So pay attention to that and discount the 26 saves he tallied last year.

Team	Level		W	L	ERA	IP	H	BB	K
Wichita	AA		4	3	3.09	55.0	38	9	31
Omaha	AAA		0	0	3.04	23.2	21	14	12

BARTOLO COLON   INDIANS   Age 20/R   *

Colon is one more in the long line of exceptional Indians pitching prospects that includes fellow Dominican Julian Tavarez. Colon's season ended early because of an arm bruise, but *Baseball America*'s poll said he had the Carolina League's best fastball, and that he was an even better prospect than our next entry.

Team	Level		W	L	ERA	IP	H	BB	K
Kinston	A		13	3	1.96	128.2	91	39	152

ROCKY COPPINGER   ORIOLES   Age 22/R   * *

Though rated below Colon overall in that poll by our friends at *Baseball America*, good old Rocky Cop won the vote for best breaking pitch in the Carolina League in the same poll. Coppinger also went farther up his organization last season, and could stay a step or two ahead of Colon in 1996.

Team	Level	W	L	ERA	IP	H	BB	K
Frederick	A	7	1	1.57	69.0	46	24	98
Bowie	AA	6	2	2.69	37.1	25	18	30
Rochester	AAA	3	0	1.04	34.2	23	17	19

JEFF D'AMICO   BREWERS   Age 20/R   * *

D'Amico, a first-round pick by Milwaukee in 1993, missed all of that season because of a shoulder problem, then all of 1994 after undergoing elbow surgery. But then in the Midwest League 1995, the 6'7", 250-pounder rapidly made up for much of that lost time, conceivably because there was nothing left to cut on.

Team	Level	W	L	ERA	IP	H	BB	K
Beloit	A	13	3	2.39	132.0	102	31	119

MATT DREWS   YANKEES   Age 21/R   * *

Even D'Amico has to look up to the 6'8" Drews, the Yankees' first draft pick in 1993 and the Florida State League's best pitching prospect in 1995. And if you are getting the idea that being tall and being a top pitching prospect are somehow correlated, they are—scouts love height. Especially, so help me Randy Johnson, in righties.

Team	Level	W	L	ERA	IP	H	BB	K
Tampa	A	15	7	2.27	182.0	142	58	140

ALAN EMBREE   INDIANS   Age 26/L   * * *

Embree's career appeared to be in serious jeopardy after arm surgery. Or wouldn't you call 16 losses and a 5.50 ERA in the Eastern League in 1994 serious jeopardy? But then last year Embree's fastball was back, both in terms of 90-plus velocity and movement. He also moved to the bullpen, where he could become an awesome left-handed complement to Jose Mesa.

Team	Level	W	L	ERA	IP	H	BB	K
Buffalo	AAA	3	4	0.89	41.0	31	19	56

1996 ROOKIE ALL-STAR TEAM—NATIONAL LEAGUE

C Jason Kendall (Pirates)	OF Bob Abreu (Astros)
1B Dan Cholowsky (Cardinals)	OF Alex Ochoa (Mets)
2B Homer Bush (Padres)	OF Steve Gibralter (Reds)
3B Scott Rolen (Phillies)	P Alan Benes (Cardinals)
SS Wilton Guerrero (Dodgers)	P Billy Wagner (Astros)

STEVE FALTEISEK   EXPOS   Age 24/R   • •

Falteisek is a big guy (6'2", 200) who depends more on changeups than power pitches to get out left-handers. He also tries to keep the ball away from right-handers with a tailing fastball. When Falteisek has control of his off-speed pitches, he is very hard to beat.

Team	Level	W	L	ERA	IP	H	BB	K
Harrisburg	AA	9	6	2.95	168.0	112	64	152
Ottawa	AAA	2	0	1.17	23.0	17	5	18

TOM FORDHAM   WHITE SOX   Age 22/L   • •

A year ago, the Chisox organization seemed loaded with pitching prospects. After so many failed when exposed to the major leagues in 1995, Fordham's chances of getting his own shot in the Windy City sometime during 1996 improved greatly.

Team	Level	W	L	ERA	IP	H	BB	K
Prince William	A	9	0	2.04	84.0	66	35	78
Birmingham	AA	6	3	3.38	82.2	79	28	61

JIMMY HAYNES   ORIOLES   Age 23/R   • •

The baby-faced Haynes can barely grow a mustache, but his pitching presence in the International League in 1995 was imposing, the lack of facial hair notwithstanding. He led the league in strikeouts.

Team	Level	W	L	ERA	IP	H	BB	K
Rochester	AAA	12	8	3.29	167.0	162	49	140

ROD HENDERSON   EXPOS   Age 25/R   • •

Henderson doesn't look much older than Haynes, but Montreal has been concerned with the slow maturing of their 1992 first-round pick. After winning 17 games in 1993, Henderson was rushed to the majors briefly the next season. He's been just 11–16 the last two years. His control was much improved last season, so he could be about to turn the corner.

Team	Level	W	L	ERA	IP	H	BB	K
Harrisburg	AA	3	6	4.31	56.1	51	18	53

RICH HUNTER   PHILLIES   Age 21/R   •

An exception to the Phillies organization's tendency to have players who are older than their competition at every level. Hunter is not over-age for his level, but he is close to being over-talented.

Team	Level	W	L	ERA	IP	H	BB	K
Piedmont	A	10	2	2.77	104.0	79	19	80
Reading	AA	3	0	2.05	22.0	14	6	17

MARTY JANZEN   BLUE JAYS   Age 22/R   • •

The key acquisition in the David Cone trade with the Yankees, Janzen may turn out to be yet another in the long line of prospects the Yankees have dealt away. He has a good hard sinker and the mentality of a winner. He may not equal the value of Jeff Kent and Ryan Thompson, whom the Jays traded to get Cone in the first place, but Janzen should be on the building blocks in the reconstruction of the Blue Jays.

Team	Level	W	L	ERA	IP	H	BB	K
Tampa	A	10	3	2.61	114.0	102	30	104
Norwich	AA	1	2	4.95	20.0	17	7	16
Knoxville	AA	5	1	2.63	48.0	35	14	44

CALVIN MADURO   ORIOLES   Age 21/R   *

Maduro was just too good a pitcher to be floundering as he was at Frederick early in 1995. He proved that when he turned his season around with a 7–0 streak that earned him a promotion to Double-A.

Team	Level	W	L	ERA	IP	H	BB	K
Frederick	A	8	5	2.94	122.0	109	34	120
Bowie	AA	0	6	5.09	35.1	39	27	26

ALLEN McDILL   ROYALS   Age 24/L   * *

The key factor is that letter *L* after "Age 24" on the line above. McDill has a good, live arm, and it's his left arm. That's why Kansas City traded to get him from the Mets organization.

Team	Level	W	L	ERA	IP	H	BB	K
St. Lucie	A	4	2	1.64	49.0	36	13	28
Binghamton	AA	3	5	4.56	73.0	69	38	44
Wichita	AA	1	0	2.11	21.1	16	5	20

RAFAEL ORELLANO   RED SOX   Age 22/L   * *

Orellano takes McDill one better by being left-handed and *really* throwing smoke. If he can avoid childhood illnesses—he was felled by chicken pox last season—he could become the left-hander the Red Sox have been looking for since Mel Parnell. (Yes, I know that's said of just about anybody in the Bosox organization with a left arm, but I like the idea of a younger generation of Rotisserie owners scurrying to their *Baseball Encyclopedia* to find out who Mel Parnell was.)

Team	Level	W	L	ERA	IP	H	BB	K
Trenton	AA	11	7	2.99	186.2	146	72	160

BILLY PERCIBAL   ORIOLES   Age 22/R   *

Percibal was voted the best pitching prospect in the California League, and looked good in Double-A before an elbow problem shut him down. Not to be confused with Troy Percival, Billy's name ends in *B-A-L*, as in the first three letters in Baltimore, his destination in the near future.

Team	Level	W	L	ERA	IP	H	BB	K
High Desert	A	7	6	3.23	128.0	123	55	105
Bowie	AA	1	0	0.00	14.0	7	7	7

JAY POWELL   MARLINS   Age 24/R   * *

Originally from the Orioles' farm, Powell was traded to Florida for Bret Barberie. A move to the bullpen helped Powell, a former first-round pick. With 24 saves, he was voted the league's number one reliever, on its number one team. While you know my feelings about minor league saves (see JAIME BLUMA, above), there are plenty of other reasons to watch Powell closely, not the least of which is the state of the Orioles' bullpen.

Team	Level	W	L	ERA	IP	H	BB	K
Portland	AA	5	4	1.87	53.0	42	15	53

GARY RATH   DODGERS   Age 23/L   * *

Rath's assignment, should he decide to accept it, is to prove that he's not just another Ben Vanryn, who dominated the Texas League but couldn't get over the hump in the Pacific Coast League. Rath is not overpowering, so he needs to throw strikes and hit spots to be effective.

Team	Level	W	L	ERA	IP	H	BB	K
San Antonio	AA	13	3	2.77	117.0	96	48	96
Albuquerque	AAA	3	5	5.08	39.0	46	20	23

BRANDON REED   TIGERS   Age 21/R   *

Reed was only okay as a starting pitcher in Rookie ball. After the Tigers moved him to the bullpen last year, he recorded 41 saves, breaking John Hiller's season record for the organization. Reed also was the Rolaids Relief Man Award winner for the entire minor leagues. But ... does the name Mike Draper ring a bell?

Team	Level	W	L	ERA	IP	H	BB	K
Fayetteville	A	3	0	0.97	64.2	40	18	78

BRYAN REKAR   ROCKIES   Age 23/R   * * *

Okay, so Rekar was nearly unhittable at New Haven, where every pitcher has an advantage. But how can we explain his success in Colorado, where hitters get to continue their batting practice long after the cage is removed from the field? In a word: slider. Bruce Ruffin got the idea in early 1994, from watching videotape of visiting pitchers who had shut down the Rockies at home. Ruffin, long a Rotisserie nemesis, turned his career around by shifting his repertoire heavily toward the slider. (In doing so, Ruffin apparently turned his elbow around too, but that's another story.) Of course, you have to throw that slider to precise spots, not leaving it high and over the plate. Guess what? Rekar has pinpoint control.

Team	Level	W	L	ERA	IP	H	BB	K
New Haven	AA	6	3	2.13	90.1	65	16	80
Colorado Springs	AAA	4	2	1.49	48.1	29	13	39

RAY RICKEN   YANKEES   Age 22/R   *

A very encouraging sign for any prospect is an in-season promotion followed by success at the higher level. When a player can move up twice in one season, that's an even better sign.

Team	Level	W	L	ERA	IP	H	BB	K
Greensboro	A	3	2	2.23	65.0	42	16	77
Tampa	A	3	4	2.15	75.0	47	27	58
Norwich	AA	4	2	2.72	53.0	44	24	43

MARIANO RIVERA   YANKEES   Age 26/R   * * *

The only advantage the more advanced Sterling Hitchcock and Andy Pettitte have over Rivera is that they're left-handed, a special plus at Yankee Stadium. Rivera is a blow-'em-away strikeout pitcher, pure and simple, who showed a lot of guts in his playoff appearances last fall. If John Wetteland gets run out of town on a rail by Boss George, Rivera could be instantly elevated to the closer role.

Team	Level	W	L	ERA	IP	H	BB	K
Columbus	AAA	2	2	2.10	30.0	25	3	30

JOE ROA   INDIANS   Age 24/R   * *

Roa has had the misfortune of getting lost in a crowd of flashier pitching prospects with both the Mets and the Indians. He doesn't break any radar guns; all he does is throw strikes and win.

Team	Level	W	L	ERA	IP	H	BB	K
Buffalo	AAA	17	3	3.50	164.2	168	28	93

GLENDON RUSCH   ROYALS   Age 21/L   *

Along with Colon and Coppinger, Rusch was one of the three best pitching prospects in the Carolina League last year. In the *Baseball America* poll, Rusch was voted the best control pitcher. But more important, when he threw the ball over the plate, batters couldn't hit it. He and Coppinger tied for the lowest opponents' batting averages in the minors (.187, which is nothing short of phenomenal).

Team	Level	W	L	ERA	IP	H	BB	K
Wilmington	A	14	6	1.74	165.2	110	34	147

MARINO SANTANA   MARINERS   Age 23/R   *

Santana was also among the stingiest pitchers in giving up hits last year, holding opposing batters to a .195 average. Santana's control weakened after he got promoted to the California League, and that's not good, because he survives mainly on guile and an excellent slider and changeup.

Team	Level	W	L	ERA	IP	H	BB	K
Wisconsin	A	8	3	1.77	97.0	57	25	110
Riverside	A	3	5	6.19	48.0	44	25	57

CURT SCHMIDT   EXPOS   Age 26/R   * *

If he can prove himself as a successful setup man in the majors, the side-arming Schmidt might actually find himself emerging as a less expensive alternative to Mel Rojas for ninth-inning work.

Team	Level	W	L	ERA	IP	H	BB	K
Ottawa	AAA	5	0	2.22	52.2	40	18	38

JASON SCHMIDT   BRAVES   Age 23/R   * *

The raw material is good: a 90-mph fastball, breaking stuff, and decent control. Schmidt just needs more refining to become a valuable commodity.

Team	Level	W	L	ERA	IP	H	BB	K
Richmond	AAA	8	6	2.25	116.0	97	48	95

TODD SCHMITT   PADRES   Age 26/R   * *

Hello, Schmidt, Schmidt, and Schmitt, Attorneys at Law. Mr. Schmidt, please. *Sorry, he's out.* Then I'll speak with Mr. Schmidt. *Sorry, he's on the phone.* What about Mr. Schmitt? *Well, he was voted the Southern League's best reliever last year, but he struggled after graduating to the PCL. He needs to pitch well right out of the box in Triple-A if he is to continue to be considered a prospect.* Fine, is he in? *Who?* Mr. Schmidt, Mr. Schmidt, or Mr. Schmitt?

Team	Level	W	L	ERA	IP	H	BB	K
Memphis	AA	0	0	1.30	18.0	28	11	27
Las Vegas	AAA	0	2	7.82	12.2	16	9	6

DAN SERAFINI   TWINS   Age 22/L   * *

The only pitching prospect surnamed Serafini in the history of baseball. (I'm guessing on this one. Prove me wrong and win a free copy of next year's book.) A first-round draft pick in 1992, he was a staff ace last year, but his numbers were helped by working in a pitcher's park. He's not far from getting a major league shot.

Team	Level	W	L	ERA	IP	H	BB	K
Hardware City	AA	12	9	3.38	162.2	155	72	123
Salt Lake	AAA	0	0	6.75	4.0	4	1	4

JEFF SUPPAN   RED SOX   Age 21/R   * *

If he's on the Opening Day roster, Suppan will be bid out of sight in Rotisserie auctions in New England by fans thinking too much about his potential and not enough about struggles when he got above Double-A last year. He'll be fine, but pitching takes time to develop. Suppan supplements his fastball and curve with a foshball, an off-speed forkball.

Team	Level	W	L	ERA	IP	H	BB	K
Trenton	AA	6	2	2.36	99.0	86	26	88
Pawtucket	AAA	2	3	5.32	45.2	50	9	32

AMAURY TELEMACO   CUBS   Age 22/R   * *

The Cubs' best pitching prospect is a strikeout pitcher, and that's good. If opponents can't hit the ball, fans in the bleachers won't have to throw it back onto the field.

Team	Level	W	L	ERA	IP	H	BB	K
Orlando	AA	8	8	3.29	147.2	112	42	151

BILLY WAGNER   ASTROS   Age 24/L   * * *

Whoooooooooosh! That's the sound of an average major league fastball. Whoosh! That was Randy Johnson, almost too quick to time. Whoooosh! That was a Wagner fastball going by. You get the idea. This guy can throw hard, almost as hard as the Big Unit. And he's a lefty. And his mother team plays indoors. Beyond that, it's way premature to extend the comparison.

Team	Level	W	L	ERA	IP	H	BB	K
Jackson	AA	2	2	2.57	70.0	49	36	77
Tucson	AAA	5	3	3.18	76.1	70	32	80

JOHN WASDIN   ATHLETICS   Age 23/R   * *

A first-round draft pick in 1993, Wasdin has advanced rapidly, and could be in the Oakland rotation in 1996. From his 1995 line, the biggest concern is his low strikeouts/innings ratio, rather than his high hits/innings. Ground balls often get through the hard infields in the Pacific Coast League, inflating hits and ERAs. But a swing and a miss works about the same on all types of fields.

Team	Level	W	L	ERA	IP	H	BB	K
Edmonton	AAA	12	8	5.52	174.1	193	38	111

DOUG WEBB   BREWERS   Age 22/R   *

The best reliever in the California League struggled in the Texas League, the main problem being his control, though he did manage eight saves at El Paso. Remember the Caveat Rotissemptor, though, when it comes to minor league saves.

Team	Level	W	L	ERA	IP	H	BB	K
Stockton	A	0	0	1.70	37.0	17	8	34
El Paso	AA	2	1	4.42	18.1	11	13	11

MATT WHISENANT   MARLINS   Age 24/L   * *

Here's how much Whisenant likes baseball: he can't wait to get home after a game to watch "Baseball Tonight." Oh, he can pitch, too. So it won't be long before he sees himself on ESPN.

Team	Level	W	L	ERA	IP	H	BB	K
Portland	AA	10	6	3.50	128.2	106	65	107

PAUL WILSON   METS   Age 23/R   * * *

After being taken first overall in the 1994 draft, Wilson was 0–7 in the low minors. What a difference a winter of rest made! First Bill Pulsipher, then Jason Isringhausen handled the job of staff ace at Norfolk. Wilson stepped right in after their departures, and didn't miss a beat.

Team	Level	W	L	ERA	IP	H	BB	K
Binghamton	AA	6	3	2.17	120.0	89	24	127
Norfolk	AAA	5	3	2.85	66.1	59	20	67

LARRY WIMBERLY   PHILLIES   Age 20/L   *

Fairly tall (6'2"), hard-throwing, and left-handed—that's a Trifecta we always like to see. Wimberly has plenty of time to develop, too.

Team	Level	W	L	ERA	IP	H	BB	K
Piedmont	A	10	3	2.67	135.0	99	44	139

BOB WOLCOTT   MARINERS   Age 22/R   * * *

Wolcott got his 1995 wake-up call with the Port City Roosters. By the time he settled down for the night, he was pitching in Seattle. His gutsy performance in the first playoff game against the Indians—walking the first three batters in the first inning, getting out without giving up a run, then hanging in there for seven innngs to get the win—amounted to more than just a huge win for Seattle. It was one of the groundswell of wonderful things that happened in the second half of last season that made us all realize—happily, joyously—that baseball was really back.

Team	Level	W	L	ERA	IP	H	BB	K
Port City	AA	7	3	2.20	86.0	60	13	53
Tacoma	AAA	6	3	4.08	79.0	94	16	43

BEST LONG-TERM PROSPECTS

C	Jason Varitek (Mariners)	OF	Karim Garcia (Dodgers)
C	Ramon Castro (Astros)	OF	Andruw Jones (Braves)
1B	Steve Cox (Athletics)	OF	Jay Payton (Mets)
1B	Derrek Lee (Padres)	OF	Ruben Rivera (Yankees)
2B	Arquimedez Pozo (Mariners)	P	Paul Wilson (Mets)
2B	Todd Walker (Twins)	P	Jeff D'Amico (Brewers)
3B	Antone Williamson (Brewers)	P	Jimmy Haynes (Orioles)
SS	Nomar Garciaparra (Red Sox)	P	Alan Benes (Cardinals)
OF	Johnny Damon (Royals)		

5

Front Office

How to Keep Score

Once upon a time, the entire front office complex of Rotisserie League Baseball consisted of Beloved Founder and Former Commissioner-for-Life Daniel Okrent. There is a fading daguerreotype of Marse Dan, one hand clinching an unfiltered Camel, the other slowly stroking his abacus, sitting alone in his Berkshire woodshed, from which post he spewed out—we use the word advisedly—our fledgling league's biweekly standings every third fortnight or so. We were having too much fun to know any better that first season, but eventually we got smart and figured that the BFFCL would never compile and distribute the standings in a timely fashion until his team, the hapless Fenokees, got themselves in a pennant race and gave him something to crow about. Not willing to wait 'til the end of time or hell froze over, whichever came first, we fired him.

That single, surgical act marked the yawning of a new Rotisserie Era.

You can still do your league's stats by hand, of course—if the task required a mathematical genius, we'd still be waiting for our first standings report for the 1980 season. All you need is a calculator and about four hours of free time a week, every week of the season. (You're going to want weekly standings, whether you know it now or not.) But it's tiresome, tedious work, the only thing about Rotisserie League Baseball that isn't a whole gang of fun. We don't recommend keeping score by hand, but if you want to give it a shot, we'll be happy to send you a simple "Keeping Score" pamphlet for free; just write **Rotisserie League Baseball Association, 82 Wall Street, Suite 1105, New York, NY 10005.**

You can hire someone to do the stats by hand for you. We did that from 1981 through 1983, and our first (and only) Director of Statistical Services, Sandra Krempasky, was immortalized by election to the Rotisserie Hall of Fame on the first ballot in recognition of her yeowoman's effort. Problem is, Sandra retired (actually, she was phased out by a computer), and you're never going to find anyone as good as she was.

You can develop your own computer program for crunching Rotisserie stats and put the family computer to better use than prepping for the SATs, keeping track of the family fortune, or playing "Jeopardy." At least we think you can. When it comes to computers, the Founding Fathers are still trying to figure out why the light in the refrigerator comes on when you open the

---

door. Other people say it can be done, though—something to do with spreading sheets, we think.

The *best* thing you can do, of course, is to have **Roti•Stats** compile and compute your league's stats. **Roti•Stats** is now the exclusive, officially authorized stats service for Rotisserie League Baseball—the *only* stats service sanctioned by the Founding Fathers of the game. Most important, it's the *best* stats service in the business.

We know. Last year, after a decade of running our own stats service, we decided to hang up our spikes. We went looking for a new stats service. We examined them all, and we liked what we saw in **Roti•Stats**. They've been in business just about as long as Rotisserie League Baseball, and they have an unparalleled record for accuracy and timeliness. We were delighted with their performance. We think you will be, too. Find out for yourself what they can do for your league. Call **Roti•Stats** toll-free at **800-676-7684.**

Roti•Stats!
(You Play. Let Roti•Stats Do the Hard Stuff.)

Each week **Roti•Stats** records your transactions, computes your standings, and rushes a report via first-class mail to your league secretary. (Fax, overnight express, and modem service available for the terminally anxious.) Each weekly report contains the standings, up-to-the-minute rosters for all teams, a list of free agents, and a transactions update. Your league can make free, unlimited transactions that may be made retroactively at any time. Player salaries, contract status, and positions are tracked at no additional cost. No hidden charges. Just one flat fee at the beginning of the season.

- *Quick Turnaround of Opening Day Rosters!* Reports are available after the *first* week of play. Most services make you wait two to three weeks for your first standings report. **Roti•Stats** knows how anxious your owners are to find out where they stand from the first crack of the bat.
- *Free Agent List!* Each weekly report includes a list of unowned players in your league, complete with weekly and year-to-date stats for *every* player in the league.
- *Free Custom Comment Page!* You may add an extra page to your weekly report containing important information for your league members. Many leagues use this page to reflect up-to-the-minute waiver information or to conduct general business among league members.
- *How Your Team Stacks Up Nationwide!* Periodically you'll receive special reports such as "Top Teams" in the country, "Tightest Pennant Races," and much more (see pages 270–271). You'll see how well

your team and league stack up against other **Roti•Stats** leagues nationwide.

- *Additional Stat Categories!* Want more than the original eight scoring categories? No problem. Their state-of-the art software lets you include any alternative scoring categories you want—at no extra charge.

- *Same Day & Overnight Fax Service!* Reduced fax charges permit your owners to receive their standings reports the fastest and most efficient way possible—the same day they are generated. (Monday for AL and Mixed; Tuesday for NL).

- *Player Value and Position Eligibility Reports!* Player values are generated by **Roti•Stats'** own proven formulas based on stats for the last two years for each player (by position). An invaluable tool on Auction Draft Day. Also free: a Position Eligibility Report that shows all positions for which each player is eligible to be drafted.

- *League-at-a-Glance Report!* Includes all team rosters with position, salary, and contract information. Great when you're pondering trades.

- *Free League Administration Software!* You can use this program to submit moves to **Roti•Stats** each week or just use it to track your league fees. The fee reports alone make this a tremendous aid for your secretary.

- *The Roti•Tiller Newsletter!* Dig the latest dirt in Rotisserie baseball with **Roti•Stats'** highly unofficial, semi-irregular, not-always-polite newsletter called **The Roti•Tiller.** Designed to keep the Rotissespirit alive in your league, **The Roti•Tiller** spreads gossip, stirs up rumors, and occasionally even dispenses nuggets of useful information. Don't be surprised to see your name in headlines!

- *Multiple League Discounts!* Play in more than one league? The RLBA will discreetly provide you with a list of counselors in your region who might be able to help. Better still, **Roti•Stats** will provide significant discounts when all your leagues sign up for the best service in the game.

- *Championship Hat & Certificate!* The winning owner(s) in your league will receive the coveted Roti•Stats Championship Hat, as well as a Championship Certificate suitable for framing.

- *800 Number for Transactions!* Call in your transactions toll-free.

For complete information about **Roti•Stats**, the only stats service officially authorized by the Founding Fathers of Rotisserie League Baseball, call toll-free: **800-676-7684.** You'll get a sign-up kit, sample standings and special reports, and a lot more reasons why **Roti•Stats** should be *your* stats service. Did you get that number? It's still **800-676-7684**.

The RLBA Wants You!

You've collared a roomful of other baseball fanatics, memorized this book, subscribed to *Baseball America*, made *USA Today* a daily habit, found a newsstand that carries *USA Today Baseball Weekly*, bought every baseball mag on the racks, and appointed someone else to bring chow for your first Auction Draft Day. What's next? Membership in the **Rotisserie League Baseball Association**. Join now and beat the Christmas rush. Here's what your league gets with membership in the **RLBA**:

1. ***Commissioner's Services.*** No need for your league to be rent asunder by rules disputes and internecine fighting: one Civil War was quite enough, thank you. For member leagues of the **RLBA,** we adjudicate disputes, interpret rules, issue Solomonic judgments, and otherwise maintain law and order so you can concentrate on playing the game.

2. ***Position Eligibility List.*** Complete and up-to-date. Updated every month during the season.

3. ***Quarterly Updates.*** Information on rules changes, news from other leagues, baseball gossip, and happenings around the Rotisseworld.

4. ***Opening Day Rosters.*** Official 25-man rosters, complete with last-minute disabled list moves and minor league promotions and demotions. Mailed to you Opening Day.

5. ***Championship Certificate.*** Signed by Beloved Founder and Former Commissioner-for-Life Daniel Okrent, this suitable-for-framing certificate is the perfect grace note for your pennant winner's rec room wall.

6. ***Company Store.*** The right to purchase an astonishing range of Rotisserie products at full retail price. (See the following pages.)

7. ***Yoo-Hoo.*** If you live outside the Yoo-Hoo belt, we'll send you a bottle of the precious nectar to pour over your pennant winner's head, in solemn observance of that most sacred of Rotisserituals.

How does your league join? Easy. Just fill out the form on page 274 and send it with your league's check or money order for $50 (only $25 for renewals) to the **Rotisserie League Baseball Association, 82 Wall Street, Suite 1105, New York, NY 10005.**

Rotisserie Baseball—The Video!
"Great!"—Siskel "Terrible!"—Ebert

That's right. We made a video. Go ahead and laugh. But hey—it works for Madonna, why not us?

Hosted by Reggie Jackson (yeah, *that* Reggie Jackson), **Rotisserie Baseball—The Video** is 30 minutes of rollicking, swashbuckling, gut-wrenching excitement, with enough car chases, frontal nudity, and violence to satisfy even Peter "Sudden Pete" Gethers ("Two thumbs!"). It features Glen "Iron Horse" Waggoner ("Two cheeseburgers!"), Harry Stein ("Not since *Gone with the Wind*..."), BFFCL Daniel Okrent ("Not since *Deep Throat*..."), and all the fun-loving Rotissegang, talking about the game they love so well.

For people new to The Greatest Game etc., **Rotisserie Baseball—The Video** is an informative, vaguely useful overview of the obsession that will soon take over their lives. For veteran Rotisserie players, it's a handy way to explain what the game is all about to people who don't know a baseball from a bass fiddle. (Just invite them over, cook up a tubful of popcorn, and pop The Video into the old VCR. They'll never be able to thank you enough, so they probably won't even try.) It's also a perfect gift idea for weddings, anniversaries, divorces, bar mitzvahs, and M-O-T-H-E-R on *Her* Day!

Just $15 plus postage and handling. See order form on page 274.

Rotisserie Ready-to-Wear!

Even if you draft like a Pollet Burro, there's no reason you can't dress like a pennant winner. Just order a few dozen official **Rotisserie T-shirts**. Available in a variety of designer colors, all of them white, this top-quality 100% cotton shirt has the famous Rotisserie coat-of-arms emblazoned across the chest in four dazzling colors. Perfect for any social occasion, but especially suitable for Auction Draft Day. A trifling $15 (plus postage and handling). Get a couple in case you slop mustard on yourself at the ballpark.

And what's an official Rotisserie T-shirt without an official **Rotisserie Cap**? Only half a uniform, that's what. The Rotisserie Cap is a top-quality number in breathtaking white with the famous four-color Rotisserie logo. Only $18 (plus postage and handling)—and get this: One size fits all! See page 274 for information on how to order.

Free Opening Day *Rotisserie Hot List!*

Get all the lowdown on late spring training cuts, last-minute deals, nagging injuries, rising and falling stars, rookies who are going to make the club, and much, much more—all just in time for your auction draft!

We'll tell you who's going to be in every rotation (plus the guys in line to step in if somebody falters or gets hurt). We'll tell you which middle-innings relievers have the best shot at picking up 8–10 garbage wins. We'll tab the fourth and fifth outfielders who will pick up 10–15 SB. We'll identify the second-string catchers most likely to deliver five homers for your one-buck investment. We'll go through every bullpen and tell you who's going to get the saves. Trade talk! Rumors! Buzz!

What you get is a news-packed, eight-page newsletter filled with all the up-to-the-minute inside stuff you need to put the finishing touches on your auction draft strategy—*free*! All you have to do is send us your name, your address, and $2.95 to cover postage and handling. We'll ship your official *Rotisserie Hot List* by first-class mail on Thursday, March 28. After that, same-day service on all *Rotisserie Hot List* requests.

Order your *Rotisserie Hot List* now. Send your name, address, and $2.95 to cover postage and handling to **Rotisserie Hot List, 82 Wall Street, Suite 1105, New York, NY 10005.**

ROTISSERIE HOOPS!

ROTISSERIE LEAGUE

BASKETBALL

- Compete in eight offensive and defensive categories based on the Official Rule Book.

- Categories include Total Points, Field Goal Percentage, 3-pointers, Free Throws Made, Assists, Rebounds, Steals, and Blocked Shots.

- Designate weekly lineups.

- Make trades. Shaq for the Admiral, anyone?

- Form your own league and we'll track it for you.

- Weekly standings reports and transactions.

- -

Yes, send me information about the Greatest Game for Basketball Fans Since Basketball!

Name _____

Address _____

City _____ State _____ Zip _____

Telephone _____

Mail to:
Rotisserie League Basketball Association
82 Wall Street, Suite 1105,
New York, NY 10005

ROTI·STATS TOP TEAMS OF 1995

Here are some of the top 1995 Rotisserie teams around the country as tracked by Roti· Stats. These teams managed to capture the highest percentage of their leagues' possible points. Is your team here? It could be next year!

NATIONAL LEAGUES

#	%	TEAM	LEAGUE	TEAMS	CAT	HR	RBI	SB	AVG	W	SV	ERA	RTO
1.	100.0	Titans	Original Indy League	12	8	224	909	194	.287	85	74	3.49	1.239
2.	95.8	Karlin Black Labels	Knickerbocker Pioneer	12	8	231	848	177	.283	62	57	3.63	1.284
3.	95.0	Two Baggers	Freeway	10	8	221	848	184	.282	82	78	3.53	1.255
4.	93.8	Zeligs	Boys of Summer League	8	8	274	982	251	.285	76	90	3.59	1.298
5.	93.4	Boston Black Sox	National Biohazard	12	12	196	758	167	.291	68	52	3.09	1.220
6.	93.3	Whiners	Great Desert Roti League	12	10	207	817	182	.279	85	62	3.56	1.260
7.	92.5	Kiss Of Death	Gibbosity	10	8	223	851	140	.275	95	78	3.34	1.250
8.	92.3	Pop's Lumber	Tomahawk League	11	10	199	855	183	.296	84	59	3.63	1.299
9.	92.0	Whack Pack	CDPARL	7	8	186	715	161	.296	67	64	3.12	1.203
10.	91.3	Marksmen	Orange County (Not So) Big 12	12	10	165	706	144	.277	79	49	3.38	1.242

AMERICAN LEAGUES

#	%	TEAM	LEAGUE	TEAMS	CAT	HR	RBI	SB	AVG	W	SV	ERA	RTO
1.	98.2	Lollygaggers	The Tarney League	10	12	251	980	123	.280	68	68	4.45	1.339
2.	94.6	Timtations	Barristers' Trust Roto League	11	10	237	954	160	.286	69	73	3.88	1.282
3.	94.4	Wild Boars	AeroVironment	9	8	269	980	162	.285	76	99	4.00	1.377
4.	94.3	Custer's Ballbusters	Renegade League	11	8	230	883	146	.290	81	56	3.79	1.282
5.	92.5	Watson's Weiners	Blue Springs Bar-B-Que	12	10	226	895	153	.278	83	63	4.13	1.373
6.	92.4	Comeback Kids	Bourbon Boys	9	8	201	831	136	.282	65	54	3.79	1.269
7.	91.7	Tommies Boys	Cannon Ball Jacuzzi League	6	8	226	864	128	.279	82	56	4.29	1.419
8.	91.7	Glendale Rajes	R&P Refugees	9	8	235	926	124	.289	88	65	3.57	1.263
9.	91.5	The Microbrewers	American Peacock Roto League	8	8	244	1002	151	.279	85	57	4.13	1.342
10.	91.4	Holme Boys	Left Coast Fantasy League	7	10	280	1015	172	.282	73	82	4.24	1.371

MIXED LEAGUES

#	%	TEAM	LEAGUE	TEAMS	CAT	HR	RBI	SB	AVG	W	SV	ERA	RTO
1.	96.3	Golden Monikers	Strawberries League	10	8	289	1092	208	.286	98	105	3.47	1.212
2.	95.3	Dodgems	Capital League of D.C.	12	8	280	1105	196	.298	82	97	3.42	1.168
3.	94.6	Devastation Inc.	Coast to Coast	12	10	319	1106	186	.287	91	88	3.35	1.187
4.	90.1	Pinstripe Pride	Not Ready For Prime Time Players	10	10	290	1161	176	.296	73	57	3.62	1.208
5.	90.1	Mashers	The Cavalier Baseball League	5	12	358	1234	199	.300	94	91	3.56	1.211
6.	90.0	Thomaston Threat	NYBL Gotham	5	10	155	744	153	.260	81	44	4.07	1.341
7.	90.0	The Rooster Crows	All In The Family	10	10	340	1160	198	.292	105	88	3.34	1.214
8.	89.7	Halrox	Smog League	15	10	224	849	195	.284	87	87	3.82	1.265
9.	87.5	Humm Babies	The Black Sox League	5	8	345	1235	109	.293	121	0	3.78	1.255
10.	87.5	Whoopie Wizards	American Baseball Assoc.	8	10	309	1111	176	.291	79	114	3.57	1.223

ROTI·STATS TIGHTEST PENNANT RACES OF 1995

Talk about close pennant races! Here are some of the most competitive leagues around the country as tracked by Roti·Stats. The "RATING" figure refers to the average point difference among the top five teams in a league.

NATIONAL LEAGUES

#	RATING	LEAGUE	LEADER	TEAMS	CAT	1ST	2ND	3RD	4TH	5TH
1.	1.13	Fools in the Field	Brewers	9	8	47.5	47.0	45.0	44.5	43.0
2.	1.25	Miller & Martin Rotisserie League	The Yahoos	9	8	51.0	50.0	50.0	46.5	46.0
3.	1.25	The Black Sheep League	Mucho Sheepish	9	12	63.0	60.5	59.0	58.5	58.0
4.	1.50	Columbus Rotisserie League	Ric Martin Team	11	8	57.0	53.0	52.5	52.5	51.0
5.	1.75	Oly League	Duncan Yo-Yo's	11	8	58.0	55.0	54.5	52.0	51.0
6.	2.00	Golden State League	Bruins	8	10	54.5	54.0	54.0	47.0	46.5
7.	2.00	National Sou Cakalaki	Sharecroppers	6	8	32.0	31.0	30.0	28.0	24.0
8.	2.25	Illinois Loanmakers	Smegma	8	10	57.5	54.0	53.5	49.0	48.5
9.	2.25	Ship of Fools	Cardiff Reefers	10	10	69.5	69.0	65.5	64.5	60.5
10.	2.25	Front Range Back Burner League	Wolfson Sheeps Clothing	10	10	67.0	63.5	62.5	60.5	58.0

AMERICAN LEAGUES

#	RATING	LEAGUE	LEADER	TEAMS	CAT	1ST	2ND	3RD	4TH	5TH
1.	1.63	American Hot Shots	Corona Club	10	8	57.0	55.0	55.0	54.0	50.5
2.	1.63	W.I.N. (What's In a Name)	Huff's Heroes	12	8	69.5	66.5	64.0	63.0	63.0
3.	1.88	Boys of Sommer	Legion of Doom	8	12	59.0	56.5	53.0	52.0	51.5
4.	2.00	Lawyer and Banker Rotisserie Guild	Hinkle's Hosers	9	8	53.0	48.0	48.0	46.0	45.0
5.	2.25	Wildcat Sin	Rad's Bad Boys	11	8	29.0	25.5	23.5	22.0	20.0
6.	2.38	Orange Coast League	Vegas Wise Guys	9	8	52.5	51.0	45.0	43.0	43.0
7.	2.38	SuperFreak	Dan's Clan	11	8	68.5	66.0	63.0	59.0	59.0
8.	2.50	Over the Hill Dreamers	Perfect Prospects	8	10	55.0	52.5	51.5	50.0	45.0
9.	2.50	Wildcat Sin	True Amateurs	11	8	60.5	57.5	57.0	56.0	50.5
10.	2.63	Michael Jack Schmidt League	Waimea Waves	9	10	63.5	58.0	56.5	55.0	53.0

MIXED LEAGUES

#	RATING	LEAGUE	LEADER	TEAMS	CAT	1ST	2ND	3RD	4TH	5TH
1.	1.13	Brooklyn Ballbusters Baseball Assoc.	Crazy Horse	10	12	83.0	81.5	81.0	80.0	78.5
2.	1.25	Seventh Inning Stretch	Roti-Sluts	10	10	61.5	59.5	57.5	57.0	56.5
3.	2.00	Kids League	Junkyard Dogs	7	8	40.0	35.0	34.0	33.0	32.0
4.	2.00	Alexandria Fantasy League	Go-Nads	14	8	78.0	77.0	72.5	72.0	70.0
5.	2.25	I Met Scott Bankhead's Wife RBA	Wantabees	9	8	55.0	50.0	48.5	48.0	46.0
6.	2.38	George Craig's League	Glen Ridge Pirates	6	8	33.0	33.0	32.0	24.0	23.5
7.	2.50	Virgin Americans	Chester Peeks	11	8	61.0	57.0	56.0	52.0	51.0
8.	2.63	L & R Rotisserie	Buckhead Braves	14	8	83.0	78.5	78.0	77.5	72.5
9.	2.63	Sacratomato	Crafty Clerks	12	8	71.0	67.0	64.5	61.5	60.5
10.	2.88	Card Sharks II	Team Beckett	9	10	62.0	60.0	56.5	55.0	50.5

ROTISSERIE LEAGUE, 1995

FINAL STANDINGS

1. EISENBURG FURRIERS	80.0		7. SKLAR GAZERS	51.0
2. LOVIN' SPOONFULS	76.0		8. CARY NATIONS	41.5
3. SMOKED FISH	62.0		9. WULF GANG	38.0
4. OKRENT FENOKEES	61.0		10. POLLET BURROS	38.0
5. GLENWAG GONERS	58.5		11. STEIN BRENNERS	37.0
6. FLEDER MICE	54.0		12. ABEL BAKERS	27.0

PITCHING RECORDS

EARNED RUN AVERAGE			RATIO		
FLEDER MICE	3.64	12.0	EISENBURG FURRIERS	1.296	12.0
SMOKED FISH	3.76	11.0	LOVIN' SPOONFULS	1.299	11.0
LOVIN' SPOONFULS	3.92	10.0	FLEDER MICE	1.301	10.0
EISENBURG FURRIERS	4.00	9.0	SMOKED FISH	1.311	9.0
OKRENT FENOKEES	4.04	8.0	ABEL BAKERS	1.328	8.0
WULF GANG	4.07	7.0	OKRENT FENOKEES	1.358	7.0
ABEL BAKERS	4.07	6.0	CARY NATIONS	1.363	6.0
CARY NATIONS	4.18	5.0	WULF GANG	1.388	5.0
POLLET BURROS	4.31	4.0	STEIN BRENNERS	1.397	4.0
GLENWAG GONERS	4.40	3.0	GLENWAG GONERS	1.400	3.0
SKLAR GAZERS	4.56	2.0	SKLAR GAZERS	1.408	2.0
STEIN BRENNERS	4.56	1.0	POLLET BURROS	1.420	1.0

SAVES			WINS		
POLLET BURROS	70	12.0	STEIN BRENNERS	77	12.0
LOVIN' SPOONFULS	67	11.0	EISENBURG FURRIERS	74	11.0
EISENBURG FURRIERS	55	10.0	GLENWAG GONERS	71	10.0
SMOKED FISH	44	9.0	SKLAR GAZERS	66	9.0
FLEDER MICE	38	8.0	SMOKED FISH	65	8.0
GLENWAG GONERS	37	6.5	OKRENT FENOKEES	62	7.0
CARY NATIONS	37	6.5	ABEL BAKERS	58	6.0
OKRENT FENOKEES	36	5.0	POLLET BURROS	56	5.0
SKLAR GAZERS	31	4.0	WULF GANG	55	4.0
WULF GANG	17	3.0	FLEDER MICE	54	3.0
ABEL BAKERS	13	2.0	LOVIN' SPOONFULS	53	2.0
STEIN BRENNERS	7	1.0	CARY NATIONS	51	1.0

(Continued)

BATTING RECORDS

RUNS BATTED IN			STOLEN BASES		
GLENWAG GONERS	843	12.0	LOVIN' SPOONFULS	197	12.0
LOVIN' SPOONFULS	785	11.0	SKLAR GAZERS	165	11.0
EISENBURG FURRIERS	737	10.0	GLENWAG GONERS	157	10.0
SMOKED FISH	712	9.0	EISENBURG FURRIERS	143	9.0
OKRENT FENOKEES	706	8.0	OKRENT FENOKEES	123	8.0
WULF GANG	600	7.0	CARY NATIONS	119	7.0
CARY NATIONS	599	6.0	POLLET BURROS	118	6.0
SKLAR GAZERS	598	5.0	WULF GANG	115	5.0
FLEDER MICE	574	4.0	FLEDER MICE	90	4.0
POLLET BURROS	530	3.0	STEIN BRENNERS	89	3.0
STEIN BRENNERS	453	2.0	SMOKED FISH	81	2.0
ABEL BAKERS	445	1.0	ABEL BAKERS	73	1.0

HOME RUNS			BATTING AVERAGE		
LOVIN' SPOONFULS	193	12.0	STEIN BRENNERS	.287	12.0
EISENBURG FURRIERS	184	11.0	SKLAR GAZERS	.279	11.0
GLENWAG GONERS	182	10.0	FLEDER MICE	.276	10.0
OKRENT FENOKEES	169	9.0	OKRENT FENOKEES	.276	9.0
SMOKED FISH	151	8.0	EISENBURG FURRIERS	.274	8.0
SKLAR GAZERS	142	7.0	LOVIN' SPOONFULS	.273	7.0
WULF GANG	137	6.0	SMOKED FISH	.272	6.0
CARY NATIONS	135	5.0	CARY NATIONS	.272	5.0
POLLET BURROS	117	4.0	GLENWAG GONERS	.270	4.0
FLEDER MICE	111	3.0	POLLET BURROS	.269	3.0
STEIN BRENNERS	102	2.0	ABEL BAKERS	.268	2.0
ABEL BAKERS	100	1.0	WULF GANG	.268	1.0

TEAR OUT THIS PAGE!

YES! Enroll our league immediately in the **Rotisserie League Baseball Association** and send us the official **1996 Position Eligibility List** by return mail! Enclosed is our check or money order for $50 payable to **RLBA.** (Renewal leagues, send $25.)

HOLD ON! We're not sure yet, we haven't had our organizational meeting, and all we want right now is information about **Roti•Stats,** the **RLBA's** officially authorized stats service.

(Please Print)

Name of League _____

c/o Commissioner _____

Address _____

City _____ State _____ Zip _____

Telephone _____ AL/NL _____

ROTISSERIE T-SHIRTS

Size	Quantity	Price
Small	_____	$15 each
Medium	_____	2 for $28
Large	_____	3 for $39
X-Large	_____	4 for $48
XX-Large	_____	5+ $10 each

ROTISSERIE CAPS

Size	Quantity	Price
One size fits all	_____	$18 each

ROTISSERIE VIDEOS

	Quantity	Price
	_____	$15 each

Guarantee
If not completely satisfied with any Official Rotisserie product, send it back. We'll replace it or refund your money.

Shirts	$_____
Caps	$_____
Videos	$_____
Postage/Hdlg.	$ 3.50
Total	$_____ *

($US only; Check or M/O)
*NY residents add sales tax.

Name _____

Address_____

City _____ State _____ Zip _____

Mail to:
Rotisserie League Baseball Association
82 Wall Street, Suite 1105
New York, NY 10005

6

Ground Rules

OFFICIAL CONSTITUTION OF ROTISSERIE LEAGUE BASEBALL

Preamble

We,

the People of the Rotisserie League, in order
to spin a more perfect Game, drive Justice
home, kiss
domestic Tranquility good-bye, promote the
general Welfare in Tidewater—where it's been
tearing up
the International League—and secure the
Blessings of Puberty to ourselves and those
we've left on Base,
do ordain and establish this
Constitution for Rotisserie League Baseball,
and also finish this run-on sentence.

ARTICLE I. OBJECT

To assemble a lineup of 23 National League or American League baseball players whose cumulative statistics during the regular season, compiled and measured by the methods described in these rules, exceed those of all other teams in the League.

ARTICLE II. TEAMS

There are 12 teams in a duly constituted Rotisserie League composed of either National League or American League players.

> **NOTE:** If you choose to play with fewer teams, be sure to make necessary adjustments so that you acquire approximately 80% of all available players at your auction draft. You could have a six-team league using American League players, for example, and draft only from among your seven favorite AL teams. Unless you reduce the available player pool proportionately to reflect a reduced number of teams, you'll never learn to appreciate the value of a good bench.

> **NOTE:** Do *not* mix the two leagues. It's unrealistic and silly, it's not the way the big leagues do it, it means you end up using only All-Stars and established regulars, and it's fattening. (On the other hand, if you *do* mix leagues, we're not going to call out the Rotisserie National Guard or anything.)

ARTICLE III. ROSTER

A team's active roster consists of the following players:

1. **NATIONAL LEAGUE PLAYERS**
   Five outfielders, two catchers, one second baseman, one shortstop, one middle infielder (either second baseman or shortstop), one first baseman, one third baseman, one corner man (either first baseman or third baseman), one utility player (who may play any nonpitching position), and nine pitchers.

2. **AMERICAN LEAGUE PLAYERS**
   The same, except that the utility player is called a designated hitter, consistent with the AL's insistence on perpetuating that perversion of the game.

ARTICLE IV. AUCTION DRAFT DAY

A **Major League Player Auction** is conducted on the first weekend after Opening Day of the baseball season. Each team must acquire 23 players at a total cost not to exceed $260. A team need not spend the maximum. The League by general agreement determines the order in which teams may nominate players for acquisition. The team bidding first opens with a minimum salary bid of $1 for any eligible player, and the bidding proceeds around the room at minimum increments of $1 until only one bidder is left. That team acquires the player for that amount and announces the roster position the player will fill. The process is repeated, with successive team owners introducing players to be bid on, until every team has a squad of 23 players, by requisite position.

- Don't get hung up on the bidding order; it's irrelevant. Do allow plenty of time; your first draft will take all day.
- Players eligible at more than one position may be shifted during the course of the draft.
- No team may make a bid for a player it cannot afford. For example, a team with $3 left and two openings on its roster is limited to a maximum bid of $2 for one player.
- No team may bid for a player who qualifies only at a position that the team has already filled. For example, a team that has acquired two catchers, and whose utility or DH slot is occupied, may not enter the bidding for any player who qualifies *only* at catcher.
- Players who commence the season on a major league team's disabled list *are* eligible to be drafted. If selected, they may be reserved and replaced upon completion of the auction draft. (See **Article XII**, page 285.)

NOTE: Final Opening Day rosters for all National League or American League teams will be needed on Auction Draft Day. Because some teams don't make their final roster moves until the last minute, even *USA Today*'s rosters, published on Opening Day, have holes. The best way to get the most complete, updated rosters is with membership in the **Rotisserie League Baseball Association**. (See page 266 for information on how to join.)

A **Minor League Player Draft** is conducted immediately following the major league auction, in which each Rotisserie League team may acquire players (a) who are not on any National/American League team's active roster; and (b) who still have official rookie status, as defined by major league baseball.

NOTE: The major league rule reads: "A player shall be considered a rookie unless, during a previous season or seasons, he has (a) exceeded 130 at-bats or 50 innings pitched in the major leagues; or (b) accumulated more than 45 days on the active roster of a major league club or clubs during the period of a 25-player limit (excluding time in the military service)."

- Selection takes place in two rounds of a simple draft, not an auction.
- In the first season, the selection order shall be determined by drawing paired numbers from a hat (that is, positions 1 and 24, 2 and 23, and so on in a 12-team league).
- In subsequent years, the selection order in each of the two rounds is determined by the order in which the teams finished in the previous

season. In leagues with 12 teams, the 6th place team selects first, proceeding in descending order to the 12th place team, which is in turn followed by the 5th, 4th, 3rd, 2nd, and 1st place teams.

- The price and subsequent salary upon activation of each farm system player drafted is $10.
- See **Article XIII**, page 287, for rules governing farm systems.

NOTE: The order of selection stated above represents a change from early years of Rotisserie baseball, when teams selected in reverse order of the final standings of the preceding season's pennant race. By awarding the first selection to the highest finisher among second-division teams instead of the last-place team, we seek to offer an incentive to teams to keep plugging and a disincentive to finish last (i.e., in the past, a last place finish would be "rewarded" with the first farm system draft pick).

ARTICLE V. POSITION ELIGIBILITY

A player may be assigned to any position at which he appeared in 20 or more games in the preceding season. If a player did not appear in 20 games at a single position, he may be drafted only at the position at which he appeared most frequently. The 20 games/most games measure is used only to determine the position(s) at which a player may be drafted. Once the season is under way (but after Auction Draft Day), a player becomes eligible for assignment to any position at which he has appeared at least once. In American League versions, players selected as DHs may qualify at any position (i.e., they need not have appeared in 20 games as DH the preceding season). In National League versions, players selected for the utility slot may qualify at any position.

NOTE: Two official major league sources for determining player eligibility are the National League's *Green Book* and the American League's *Red Book*. Both list appearances by position under fielding averages. The *Red Book* lists all players who appeared as designated hitters the preceding season. Circulating an eligibility list by position before Auction Draft Day saves a lot of time. Prepare one yourself in March, when the *Green Book* and *Red Book* are published. Or obtain it with membership in the **Rotisserie League Baseball Association**—our list is available at least five months earlier, so you'll be able to spend the winter doing something worthwhile (see page 266 for details). Spend a few minutes before your auction to settle eligibility questions and assign eligibility to rookies. When in doubt, use common sense (instead of knives) to resolve disputes.

ARTICLE VI. FEES

The Rotisserie League has a schedule of fees covering all player personnel moves. No money passes directly from team to team. No bets are made on the outcome of any game. All fees are payable into the prize pool and are subsequently distributed to the top four teams in the final standings. (See **Articles VIII** and **IX**, page 282.)

1. **BASIC:** The cumulative total of salaries paid for acquisition of a 23-man roster on Auction Draft Day may not exceed $260.

2. **TRANSACTIONS:** $10 per trade (no matter how many players are involved) or player activation (from reserve list or farm system). In a trade, the team that pays the fee is subject to negotiation.

3. **CALL-UP FROM FREE AGENT POOL:** $25 for each player called up from the free agent pool.

4. **RESERVE:** $10 for each player placed on a team's reserve list (see **Article XII**, page 285).

5. **FARM SYSTEM:** $10 for each player in a team's farm system (see **Article XIII**, page 287).

6. **ACTIVATION:** $10 for each player activated from the reserve list or farm system.

7. **WAIVERS:** $10 for each player claimed on waivers (see **Article XV**, page 290).

8. **SEPTEMBER ROSTER EXPANSION:** $50 (see **Article XVI**, page 291).

ARTICLE VII. PLAYER SALARIES

The salary of a player is determined by the time and means of his acquisition and does not change unless the player becomes a free agent or is signed to a guaranteed long-term contract. (See **Article XVII**, page 291.)

- The salary of a player acquired in the major league draft is his auction price.
- The salary of a player called up from the free agent pool during the season is $10.
- The salary of a player activated from a team's farm system during the season is $10.
- The salary of a player claimed on waivers is $10.
- The salary of a player called up during September Roster Expansion to supplement the 23-man roster is $25 if he is drawn from the free agent pool. (See **Article XVI**, page 291.)

NOTE: Because you can commit only $260 for salaries on Auction Draft Day, and because you will keep some of your players from one season to the next, salaries are *extremely* important, particularly after the first season ends and winter trading begins. Would you trade Albert Belle for Paul O'Neill? The Indians wouldn't, not even if Blowhard George threw in Yankee Stadium (which he would be only too happy to do, outfield monuments and all). But a smart Rotisserie League owner just might make such a deal *in the off-season*, because the $15-plus difference between Belle's and O'Neill's auction price is enough to buy a front-line starter.

Maintaining accurate, centralized player-personnel records of salary and contract status is *the most important* task of the League Secretary, who deserves hosannas from the other owners for all the work he does.

NOTE: The $260 salary limit pertains to Auction Draft Day *only*. After Auction Draft Day, free agent signings and acquisition of high-priced players in trades may well drive a team's payroll above $260.

ARTICLE VIII. PRIZE MONEY

All fees shall be promptly collected by the League Treasurer, who is empowered to subject owners to public humiliation and assess fines as needed to ensure that payments are made to the League in a timely fashion. The interest income from this investment can be used to defray the cost of a gala postseason awards ceremony and banquet. The principal shall be divided among the first four teams in the final standings as follows:

- 1st place—50%
- 2nd place—20%
- 3rd place—15%
- 4th place—10%
- 5th place—5%

ARTICLE IX. STANDINGS

The following criteria are used to determine team performance:

- Composite batting average (BA)
- Total home runs (HR)
- Total runs batted in (RBI)
- Total stolen bases (SB)
- Composite earned run average (ERA)
- Total wins (W)
- Total saves (S)
- Composite ratio: walks (BB) + hits (H) ÷ innings pitched (IP)

Teams are ranked from first to last in each of the eight categories and given points for each place. For example, in a 12-team league, the first-place team in a category receives 12 points, the second-place team 11, and so on down to 1 point for last place. The team with the most total points wins the pennant.

THE FENOKEE IP REQUIREMENT. A team must pitch a total of 900 innings to receive points in ERA and ratio. A team that does not pitch 900 innings maintains its place in ERA and ratio ranking but receives zero points in both of these categories. (Thus, a team that finished third in ERA but did not have 900 IP would receive no points in that category. The fourth-place team in ERA would still receive 9 points.) This rule was passed in 1988 in response to an "all-relief" strategy attempted by the Okrent Fenokees in the 1987 season. The strategy was not successful because Swampmaster Dan Okrent abandoned it after six weeks or so. But it might have worked, in more disciplined hands. Hence the new rule.

THE FENOKEE AB REQUIREMENT. A team must have 4250 at bats in the season. A team that does not have 4250 at bats maintains its place in the batting average ranking but receives zero points in that category. This rule was passed in 1991 in response to an "all-pitching" strategy attempted by the Okrent Fenokees in 1990. This time, the Beloved Founder and Former Commissioner-for-Life assembled an all-star pitching staff, Tony Gwynn, and 13 Ken Oberkfells (i.e., guys who didn't play enough to bring down Gwynn's "team" BA). The BFFCL hoped to amass 40 pitching points, 10 BA points, and 3 points in the other offensive categories to squeeze into the first division. The strategy was not successful because the Swampmaster abandoned it after six weeks or so. But it might have worked, in more disciplined hands. Hence the new rule.

- Pitchers' offensive stats are *not* counted, mainly because they don't appear weekly in *USA Today*. Nor are the pitching stats of the occasional position player called in to pitch when the score is 16–1 after five innings and the relief corps is hiding under the stands.
- In cases of ties in an individual category, the tied teams are assigned points by totaling points for the rankings at issue and dividing the total by the number of teams tied.
- In cases of ties in total points, final places in the standings are determined by comparing placement of teams in individual categories. Respective performances are calculated and a point given to each team for bettering the other. Should one team total more points than the other, that team is declared the winner.
- Should the point totals still be equal, the tie is broken by adding each team's *total at-bats* at season's end, plus *triple the number of its innings pitched.* The team that scores a higher total by this measure wins the pennant.

ARTICLE X. STATS

The weekly player-performance summaries published in *USA Today* beginning in late April constitute the official data base for the computation of standings in Rotisserie League Baseball.

NOTE: When we first started out, we used *The Sporting News*. That was when *TSN* cared more about baseball than about all the Stanley

Cup skate-offs, NBA playoffs, and NFL summer camping rolled into one (which, by the way, is what the Rotisserie League's Founding Fathers believe should be done with them). Not for nothing was the Holy Bible known to baseball people as *The Sporting News* of religion. But that was then, and this is now. *The Sporting News* has passed from the last Spink to new owners who seem intent on taking the "Sporting" part seriously—that is, covering other sports at the expense of baseball.

- The effective date of any transaction for purposes of statistical calculation is the Monday (AL) or Tuesday (NL) *before* the commencement of play on those days. This is because weekly stats appear in *USA Today* on Tuesday for AL games through the preceding Sunday and on Wednesday for NL games through the preceding Monday.
- Reporting deadlines should be established as close to these breaks as possible but not later than the start of any game at the beginning of a new reporting period. Noon on Monday (AL) or Tuesday (NL) makes sense.
- Transactions recorded *on* Auction Draft Day, including trades and call-ups to replace disabled players, are effective retroactive to Opening Day. Transactions occurring *after* Auction Draft Day but *before* the closing date of the first cumulative summaries to appear in *USA Today* in April are effective the Monday (AL) or Tuesday (NL) immediately after the first closing date.
- Performance stats of a player shall be assigned to a Rotisserie League team *only* when he is on the active 23-man roster of that team. It is common for a player to appear on the roster of more than one Rotisserie League team during the season because of trades and waiver-list moves. Even a player who is not traded may spend time on a team's reserve list, during which period any numbers he might compile for his major league team do not count for his Rotisserie League team.
- Standings shall be tabulated and issued in a regular and timely fashion, as determined by the League owners.

NOTE: Keeping score (see pages 263–264) is the only part of Rotisserie League Baseball that isn't any fun. Unless you're computerized, it's tedious and time-consuming. And even if your league does have a computer wonk on board, it still means he or she can't take a vacation between Opening Day and early October. (God forbid your league should go a week without standings!) The best solution: Let the official stat service authorized by the Founding Fathers do all the heavy lifting for you (see page 264).

ARTICLE XI. TRADES

From the completion of the auction draft until August 31, Rotisserie League teams are free to make trades of any kind without limit, except as stipulated below, *so long as the active rosters of both teams involved in a trade reflect the required position distribution upon completion of the transaction.* No trades are permitted from September 1 through the end of the season. Trades made from the day after the season ends until rosters are frozen on

April 2 prior to Auction Draft Day are *not* bound by the position distribution requirement.

> **NOTE:** This means that if Team A wants to swap David Justice to Team B for José Rijo anytime between Auction Draft Day and the trade deadline, Team A will have to throw in a bum pitcher and Team B a duff outfielder to make the deal. During the off-season, the two could be dealt even-up.

- Trades do not affect the salaries or contract status of players.
- Each trade is subject to the $10 transaction fee. The fee is not affected by the number of players involved in the trade.
- Unless you want knife fights to break out among owners, prohibit all trades involving cash, "players to be named later," or "future considerations." Trust us.

NOTE ON DUMPING: "Dumping" is the inelegant but scientifically precise term used to describe what happens when a team out of contention gives up on the season and trades to a contending team its most expensive talent and its players who will be lost to free agency at the end of the year, typically for inexpensive players who can be kept the following season. A "dumping" trade is always unbalanced, sometimes egregiously so, with the contending team giving up far less than it gets, and the noncontending team giving up much more in order to acquire a nucleus for the following season. While this strategy makes sense for both clubs, extreme cases can potentially undermine the results of the auction draft, which should always be the primary indicator of an owner's ability to put together a successful team.

To guard against this, we have in the past employed rigid and restrictive Anti-Dumping measures to control trades between contenders and noncontenders. But in light of major shifts in international politics and economics in recent years, we decided in 1993 that these restrictive measures tended to inhibit rather than enhance the playing of the game.

Accordingly, we swept away all Anti-Dumping legislation in 1993. We did so with some trepidation, but we felt the benefits of a free market would outweigh the potential for abuses. We were right. Let freedom ring.

ARTICLE XII. THE RESERVE LIST

A team may replace any player on its 23-man roster who is:

- placed on the **disabled list,**
- **released,**
- **traded** to the other league, or
- **sent down** to the minors by his major league team.

To replace such a player, a Rotisserie League team must first release him outright or place him on its reserve list. A team reserves a player by notifying the League Secretary and paying the $10 transaction fee. A reserved player is removed from a team's active roster at the end of the stat week (on Monday or Tuesday)—when formal notification is given—and placed on the team's reserve list. There is no limit to the number of players a team may have on its reserve list. Reserving a player protects a team's rights to that player.

A team has two weeks to take action once a player is placed on the disabled list, released, traded to the other league, or sent to the minors by his major league team. If no action is taken, the position is frozen open until the original player's return, and no replacement may be made.

> • *A suspended player may not be reserved, released, or replaced.*

NOTE: When we first wrote that, we were thinking about the old-fashioned things players might do to get themselves suspended—Bill Madlock hitting an umpire (1980), say, or Gaylord Perry throwing a spitter (1962 to 1983), although he was suspended for doing it only once (1982). Then came the drug suspensions of 1984 and afterward. We have decided to consider players suspended for substance abuse as if they were on the disabled list, and allow teams to replace them.

- Once a specific action has been taken to remove a player from its 23-man roster (via release or placing him on the reserve list), a team is then free to select any eligible player from the free agent pool of players not already owned by another Rotisserie League team. The salary assigned to a player so selected from the free agent pool is $10; the call-up fee is $25 (see **Article VI**, page 281).
- If the same player is claimed by more than one team in a given week, he goes to the team ranking lowest in the most recent standings.
- Every reserve move must be accompanied by a concomitant replacement move (i.e., a team may not reserve a player without replacing him).
- Placing a player *on* the reserve list and activating a player *from* the reserve list are *each* subject to a $10 transaction fee.
- The call-up takes effect as soon as it is recorded by the League Secretary, although the player's stats do not begin to accrue to his new team until Monday (AL) or Tuesday (NL) of the week the League Secretary records the call-up.
- A player on a Rotisserie League reserve list may not be traded *unless* the replacement player linked to him is also traded. Thus, a team might trade Andy Van Slyke (on reserve) and Midre Cummings (called up to replace him) for Derrick May.
- A replacement player may be traded or otherwise replaced (e.g., in case of injury, he could be reserved and a free agent called up to fill his slot). In such a case, the newly acquired player becomes linked to the original reserved player. To avoid even the appearance of collusion, a replacement player traded from one team to another may not be traded back to his original team for three reporting periods.
- When a player on a reserve list returns to active major league duty, he must be **reinstated** to the active 23-man roster of his Rotisserie League team *two weeks* after his activation or be **waived**. Failure to

notify the League Secretary shall be considered a waiver of the player on the reserve list. A player may not be **reinstated** or **waived** until he has been activated by his major league team.

NOTE: Intended to prevent stockpiling of players, this rule is tricky to monitor. Daily newspaper transaction columns and telephone sports-information lines don't always catch every single major league roster move. The clock starts ticking when the League Secretary *is made aware of* a player being reactivated. By the way, "two weeks" means two full reporting periods and may actually be as much as two weeks plus six days (as in the case of a player being reactivated the day after a reporting deadline). In fairness, and because this is not full-contact karate but a game played among friends, an owner should be given warning by the League Secretary that time is up and he will lose a player if he doesn't make a move. Especially if there are extenuating circumstances (i.e., anything from retracing Livingston's steps in Africa to just plain laziness).

- When a player is reinstated to the active 23-man Rotisserie League roster from a team's reserve list, the player originally called up to replace him must be waived, unless the replacement player *or* the original player can be shifted to another natural opening on the roster for which he qualifies.
- If the replacement player is replaced (e.g., he is injured, put on reserve, and a free agent is called up), then *his* replacement becomes linked to the original player on the reserve list.
- A player reinstated from the reserve list may not displace any active player on the Rotisserie League team's 23-man roster *other than* his original replacement (or his successor).

NOTE: The intent of all this is to minimize the benefit a team might derive from an injury. Say Jeff Bagwell breaks his wrist (nah, could never happen again) and you call up the inevitable Dave Magaden to replace him. Bagwell comes back. What you'd like to do is activate Bagwell, keep Magadan, and waive your other corner man, Phil Clark, who hasn't had more than 10 at-bats a week since the season began. Our rules say you can't, on the premise that *a team is not ordinarily helped by an injury to a key player.* We know the big leagues don't handle it this way, but art doesn't always imitate life. Without some restriction, an owner might never have to pay the price for his bad judgment in drafting Phil Clark in the first place.

ARTICLE XIII. FARM SYSTEM

If a farm system player is promoted to the active roster of a major league team at any time during the regular season *prior to* September 1 (when major league rosters may expand to 40), his Rotisserie League team has *two weeks* after his promotion to **activate** him (at any position for which he qualifies) *or* **waive** him.

- The fee for activating a player from a team's farm system is $10.
- If a farm system player is activated, the player displaced from the 23-

man roster to make room for him must be placed on waivers, *unless* the farm system player can be activated into a natural opening, in which case no waiver is required. **Example:** One of your pitchers is placed on a major league disabled list; you reserve him and activate a pitcher from your farm system who has been called up by his major league team.

- Once brought up from its farm system by a Rotisserie League team, a player may not be returned to it, although he may be placed on a team's reserve list in the event he is returned to the minor leagues by his major league club.
- A farm system player not brought up to a team's 23-man roster during the season of his initial selection may be kept within the farm system in subsequent seasons upon payment of an additional $10 per year, so long as he retains official rookie status and the League Secretary is duly notified on April 1 each year, when rosters are frozen. (See also **Article XVIII**, page 293.)
- A team may have no more than three players in its farm system.
- A farm system player may be traded during authorized trading periods, subject to prevailing rules governing transactions, as may a team's selection rights in the minor league draft.

NOTE: This means that a team could acquire and exercise as many as three farm system draft picks, providing that it does not exceed the maximum of three players in its farm system at a given time.

ARTICLE XIV. SIGNING FREE AGENTS

Active major league players not on any Rotisserie League team's roster at the conclusion of the auction draft become free agents. During the course of the season the pool of free agents may also include minor league players not in any Rotisserie League's farm system (see **Article XIII**, page 293) who are promoted to an active major league roster; waived players who are not claimed; and players traded from the "other" major league. Such players may be signed in the following manner.

From Opening Day Until the All-Star Game. Free agents may be called up to replace players placed on a Rotisserie League team's reserve list as outlined in **Article XII** (see page 285). The only exception to **Article XII**'s provisions for signing free agents during this period is that a player traded into the league from the "other" major league or signed by a team within the league as a free agent may be signed by a Rotisserie League team with its **Free Agent Acquisition Budget (FAAB)**, as described below.

After the All-Star Game. From the All-Star Game until the last weekly transaction deadline before September 1, free agents may be signed, without limit in number, but within the limitations of a Rotisserie League team's **Free Agent Acquisition Budget:**

- Each team shall have, for the purpose of acquiring free agents during the course of the season, a supplementary budget of $100.

- At the deadline established by each league for recording weekly transactions, a team may submit a *sealed* bid for one or more free agents.
- The minimum bid shall be $5; the maximum shall be the amount remaining in a team's **FAAB**.
- A free agent so selected goes to the highest bidder. If more than one team bids the same amount on a player, and if that amount is the highest bid, the player goes to the team that is lowest in the most recently compiled standings.
- The salary of a free agent signed in this manner is his acquisition price. His contract status is that of a first-year player.
- In addition to the player's acquisition price, a team signing a free agent must pay the $25 transaction fee for calling up free agents as set forth in **Article VI** (page 281).
- For each free agent that it signs, a team *must* at the same time waive or release a player at the same position from its *active* roster. If on a major league team's *active* roster, such a player is *waived*. If he has been placed on a major league team's disabled list, released, traded to the "other" league, or demoted to the minors, such a player is *released* and may not be acquired by a Rotisserie League team until he is once again on a major league roster.)
- A free agent signed for a salary in excess of $10 (i.e., more than the customary call-up fee for replacement players) is deemed to have a guaranteed two-year contract. If such a player is not protected the following season (i.e., if he is released into the free agent pool at the time rosters are frozen on April 1), then a contract buyout fee in the amount of twice his salary or $100, whichever is greater, shall be paid by the team owning his contract at the time.
- If a Rotisserie League team loses a player to the "other" league in an interleague trade, then the team's available **FAAB** dollars are increased by an amount equal to the lost player's salary.

NOTE: If a team wishes to replace an injured player and reserve him, it must use the mechanism described in **Article XII** (page 285); it may *not* use the FAAB process without releasing an active player.

NOTE: The provision regarding players acquired for a sum in excess of the customary $10 call-up fee is intended to discourage frivolous bidding for free agents. It is also intended to make teams who are most likely to benefit from signing costly free agents—that is, teams still in the race for the first division—pay for it dearly, by making such players expensive to dump the following spring.

NOTE: Set up a simple, common-sense mechanism for handling the "sealed bid" part of the **FAAB** process. Nothing elaborate is needed. Price, Waterhouse need not be called in. Don't permit bidders to make contingency bids (e.g., "If I don't get Ruth at $29, then I'll bid $25 for Gehrig, and if I don't get Gehrig...") unless your League Secretary doesn't have a day job.

ARTICLE XV. WAIVERS

Under certain conditions, a Rotisserie League player may be waived.

- When a player on a Rotisserie League team's reserve list is activated by his major league team, either he or the player called up earlier to replace him *must* be placed on waivers (see **Article XII**, page 285).
- When a team activates a player from its farm system, except into a natural opening (see **Article XIII**, page 287), the player dropped from the 23-man roster to make room for him *must* be placed on waivers.
- A player no longer on the active roster of his major league team and whose Rotisserie League position is taken by a player activated from the reserve list or farm system may not be placed on waivers but *must* be released outright.

NOTE: This is to prevent a team from picking up a disabled list player on waivers merely for the purpose of releasing him and replacing him with a player of higher quality from the free agent pool.

- The waiver period begins at noon on the Monday (AL) or Tuesday (NL) after the League Secretary has been notified that a player has been waived and lasts one week, at the end of which time the player shall become the property of the lowest-ranked team to have claimed him. To make room on its roster, the team acquiring a player on waivers must assign the player to a natural opening or waive a player at the same position played by the newly acquired player.
- Waiver claims take precedence over the replacement of an injured, released, or demoted player who has been put on reserve. That is, a player on waivers may be signed by a team with a roster opening at his position only if no other team lower in the standings claims the player on waivers.
- A team may acquire on waivers *no more* than one player in a given week, but there is no limit to the number of players a team may acquire on waivers during the season.
- A player who clears waivers—that is, is not claimed by any team—returns to the free agent pool.
- The fee for acquiring a player on waivers is $10. The salary of a player acquired on waivers shall be $10 or his current salary, whichever is greater. His contract status shall remain the same.
- A player with a guaranteed long-term contract may *not* be waived during the season. He may, however, be released and replaced if he is traded to the "other" league.
- A player may be given his outright release *only* if he is
    - (a) unconditionally released,
    - (b) placed on the "designated for assignment" list,
    - (c) sent to the minors,
    - (d) placed on the "disqualified" list,
    - (e) traded to the "other" major league, or
    - (f) placed on the disabled list.

ARTICLE XVI. SEPTEMBER ROSTER EXPANSION

If it chooses, a team may expand its roster for the pennant drive by calling up additional players after September 1 from the free agent pool, its own reserve list, or its own farm system. A team may call up as many players as it wishes, subject to payment of appropriate fees as outlined below, except that at no time may the number of active players on its roster exceed 40.

- The order of selection for September Roster Expansion is determined by the most recent standings, with the last-place team having first selection, and so on. During this 24-hour period, September Roster Expansion claims take precedence over waiver claims and routine call-ups to replace players who are disabled, released, or traded to the other league by their major league teams. This selection order pertains until midnight, September 2, *only*, after which time a team forfeits its order in the selection process, though *not* its right to make a selection. Selection after midnight, September 2, is on a first-come, first-served basis. Also, after midnight, September 2, waiver claims and routine call-ups to fill natural openings take precedence over September Roster Expansion claims.
- The performance stats of players called up during September Roster Expansion start to accrue on the Monday (AL) or Tuesday (NL) after the League Secretary has been notified of the player's selection.
- The fee for expanding the roster in September is $50 per player.
- The salary assigned to a September call-up from the free agent pool is $25. The salary of a September call-up from a team's reserve list or farm system is the salary established at the time he was previously acquired (on Auction Draft Day, or subsequently from the free agent pool, or via waivers).

NOTE: A device for heightening the excitement for contending teams and for sweetening the kitty at their expense, September Roster Expansion will generally not appeal to second-division clubs (who should, however, continue to watch the waiver wire in the hope of acquiring "keepers" for next season at a $10 salary).

ARTICLE XVII. THE OPTION YEAR AND GUARANTEED LONG-TERM CONTRACTS

A player who has been under contract at the same salary during two consecutive seasons and whose service has been uninterrupted (that is, he has not been waived or released, although he may have been traded) must, prior to the freezing of rosters in his third season, be released; signed at the same salary for his option year; or signed to a guaranteed long-term contract.

If **released**, the player returns to the free agent pool and becomes available to the highest bidder at the next auction draft. If signed at the same salary for an **option year**, the player must be released back into the free agent pool at the end of that season. If signed to a **guaranteed long-term contract**, the player's salary in each year covered by the new contract

---

(which commences with the option year) shall be the sum of his current salary plus $5 for each additional year beyond the option year. In addition, a signing bonus, equal to one half the total value of the long-term contract, but not less than $5, shall also be paid.

NOTE: This rule is intended to prevent blue-chippers, low-priced rookies who blossom into superstars, and undervalued players from being tied up for the duration of their careers by the teams who originally drafted them. It guarantees periodic transfusions of top-flight talent for Auction Draft Day and provides rebuilding teams something to rebuild with. And it makes for some interesting decisions at roster-freeze time two years down the pike.

Here's how it works. Let's say you drafted Manny Ramirez of the Cleveland Indians for $13 in 1994, a fair price then for a rookie with only 53 major league at-bats under his belt. Sure, everybody said he was a can't-miss slugger, but how many guys like that have you seen miss *a lot* when switched to a diet of major league curveballs? So you pay your 13 bucks and you cross your fingers. Flash forward to the spring of 1996 and you count your lucky stars. Your can't-miss phenom didn't miss. He's now one of the premier sluggers in baseball. And he's still only 23. It's now the spring of 1996. You could let Ramirez play one more season for you and get a tremendous return on your 13 bucks, but taking a longer view, you daydream about Manny's power numbers, assess your needs, project what's likely to be available in the upcoming draft, cross your fingers—and sign him to a four-year guaranteed contract. Ramirez's salary zooms to $28 ($13 + $5 + $5 + $5), but he's yours through the 1999 season. His signing bonus, which does not count against your $260 Auction Draft Day limit, is $42 (one half of 3 × $28). If he continues to mature as a ballplayer, you've got a huge bargain. And if you balk at pulling the trigger, just remember: this is the way the 1995 Cleveland Indians were built.

- In determining a player's status, "season" is understood to be a full season or any fraction thereof. Thus, a player called up from the free agent pool in the middle of the 1993 season and subsequently retained at the same salary without being released in 1994 (even though he may have been traded) enters his option year in 1995 and must be released, signed at the same salary for an option year, or signed to a long-term contract.
- A team may sign a player to only one long-term contract, at the end of which he becomes a free agent.
- Option-year and long-term contracts are entirely transferable, both in rights and obligations; the trade of a player in no way affects his contract status.
- If, during the course of a long-term contract, a player is traded from the National League to the American League (or vice versa), the contract is rendered null and void. The team that loses the player's services shall be under no further financial obligations.
- In all other cases—specifically *including* sudden loss of effectiveness—a team must honor the terms of a long-term contract, as follows: A player with such a contract *may* be released back into the free agent

pool (that is, not protected on a team's roster prior to Auction Draft Day), but a team that chooses to do so must pay into the prize pool, above the $260 Auction Draft Day limit, a sum equal to *twice* the remaining value of the player's contract or $100, whichever is greater.

ARTICLE XVIII. ROSTER PROTECTION

For the first three seasons of the League's existence, each team must retain, from one season to the next, *no fewer than* **7** but *no more than* **15** of the players on its 23-man roster. After three seasons, this minimum requirement is eliminated, the maximum retained. The minimum is removed because, after three seasons, a team might find it impossible to retain a specific minimum because too many players have played out their option.

- The names of players being retained must be recorded with the League Secretary by midnight, April 1. Specific notice must also be made at that time of any guaranteed long-term contract signings and farm system renewals.
- The cumulative salaries of players protected prior to Auction Draft Day are deducted from a team's $260 expenditure limit, and the balance is available for acquisition of the remaining players needed to complete the team's 23-man roster.
- The League Secretary should promptly notify all teams in the League of each team's protected roster, including player salaries, contract status, and amount available to spend on Auction Draft Day.
- Failure to give notice of a guaranteed long-term contract for a player in his option year will result in his being continued for one season at his prior year's salary and then released into the free agent pool. Failure to renew a farm system player's minor league contract will result in his becoming available to all other teams in the subsequent minor league draft.
- A farm system player whose minor league contract is renewed on April 1 and who subsequently makes his major league team's active roster may, at his Rotisserie League owner's option, be added to the protected list of players on Auction Draft Day (and another player dropped, if necessary, to meet the 15-player limit), or he may be dropped and made available in the auction draft. He may not be retained in his Rotisserie League team's farm system.

NOTE: The April 1 roster-protection deadline was originally set to correspond with the end of the major leagues' spring interleague trading period, a rite of spring that no longer exists. We've stuck to April 1 anyway, because it gives us a week or so to fine-tune draft strategies. Until you know who the other teams are going to keep, you won't know for sure who's going to be available. And until you know how much they will have to spend on Auction Draft Day, you won't be able to complete your own pre-draft budget. So April 1 it is; don't fool with it.

ARTICLE XIX. GOVERNANCE

The Rotisserie League is governed by a Committee of the Whole consisting of all team owners. The Committee of the Whole may designate as many League officials as from time to time it deems appropriate, although only two—the League Secretary and the League Treasurer—ever do any work. The Committee of the Whole also designates annually an Executive Committee composed of three team owners in good standing. The Executive Committee has the authority to interpret playing rules and to handle all necessary and routine League business. All decisions, rulings, and interpretations by the Executive Committee are subject to veto by the Committee of the Whole. Rule changes, pronouncements, and acts of whimsy are determined by majority vote of the Committee of the Whole. Member leagues of the **Rotisserie League Baseball Association** (see page 266) may appeal to the RLBA for adjudication of disputes and interpretation of rules. The Rotisserie League has three official meetings each year: Auction Draft Day (the first weekend after Opening Day), the Midsummer Trade Meeting (at the All-Star break), and the Gala Postseason Banquet and Awards Ceremony. Failure to attend at least two official meetings is punishable by trade to the Minnesota Twins.

ARTICLE XX. YOO-HOO

To consecrate the bond of friendship that unites all Rotisserie League owners in their pursuit of the pennant, to symbolize the eternal verities and values of the Greatest Game for Baseball Fans Since Baseball, and to soak the head of the League champion with a sticky brown substance before colleagues and friends duly assembled, the **Yoo-Hoo Ceremony** is hereby ordained as the culminating event of the baseball season. Each year, at the awards ceremony and banquet, the owner of the championship team shall have a bottle of Yoo-Hoo poured over his or her head by the preceding year's pennant winner. The Yoo-Hoo Ceremony shall be performed with the dignity and solemnity appropriate to the occasion.

> **NOTE:** If Yoo-Hoo, the chocolate-flavored beverage once endorsed by soft-drink connoisseur Yogi Berra, is not available in your part of the country, you have two options: (a) send up an alternative beverage, one chosen in the Yoo-Hoo spirit, as a pinch-hitter, or (b) move.

STILL CONFUSED?

Call Roti-Stats, the best Rotisserie stats service in the business, for clarifications, explanations, salutations, a current weather report, and a hard sell.

800-676-7684

ROTISSERIE ULTRA
The Rules of Play

Turn Up the Volume

Rotisserie Ultra requires more scouting, more planning, more wheeling, and more dealing. You move players off and onto your active roster as often as you want to. You ride guys on hot streaks, then ditch them when they go cold. You buy free agents. You bring along youngsters all the way from the low minors. You swing complicated, multiplayer deals. You build a strong bench with waiver moves to carry you through injuries and slumps.

Does playing Rotisserie Ultra mean giving up all pretense of having a normal life? No, you should keep up that pretense as long as you can. It does mean that you're not going to have a lot of time for scuba diving the Great Barrier Reef, reading Joyce, learning to play the saxophone, paneling the rec room, or having a catch with your kid this summer. You're going to be busy, Bucky—or you're going to be in the second division.

Remember that the Sturgeon General himself—Peter Gethers, owner of Peter's Famous Smoked Fish—has warned that playing Rotisserie Ultra *before you're ready* can lead to "sensory overload, stress-related insomnia, pattern baldness, hot flashes, and premature ejaculation."

We recommend that fledgling leagues play the regular version of the game, become acclimated to its demands and pressures, and shake out owners who can't stand the heat of a pennant race before moving on to Ultra. Stay within yourselves, walk before you run, take it one game at a time, and floss regularly. Only then should you consider Ultra. After all, we can't have everybody in America having too much fun all at once.

Editor's Note: *Many of the rules in the Official Constitution of Rotisserie League Baseball also apply to Rotisserie Ultra, so we decided not to repeat every line of fine print that applies to both, except as needed for clarity. That means that the "Rules of Play" that follow for Rotisserie Ultra should be read together with the original Constitution. If you can't handle that assignment, you're going to have* real *trouble with Rotisserie Ultra.*

ULTRA I. THE ROTATION DRAFT

After the conclusion of the auction draft, in which teams acquire their 23-man active rosters for a sum not to exceed $260, owners successively draft up to 17 additional players in 17 separate rounds of selection. Initially, players acquired in this fashion comprise a team's reserve roster.

- Any baseball player is eligible for this draft. *Exception:* In National

League versions, no player on the roster or in the minor league organization of an American League team may be selected; and, in American League versions, the opposite is true. Eligible players include (in the NL version, by way of example) previously undrafted NL players, NL-owned minor leaguers, unsigned players, Japanese players, high-school or college players, and the kid down the block with the great arm.

- In the rotation draft, owners are not required to select players by position. They may select all pitchers, all position players, or a mix.
- The order of selection for each of the 17 rounds is determined by the order of finish in the previous season. In leagues with 12 teams, the 6th place team selects first, proceeding in descending order to the 12th place team, followed by the 5th, 4th, 3rd, 2nd, and 1st place teams.

NOTE: For leagues switching over from Rotisserie League rules to Rotisserie League Ultra rules, the first two rounds of the rotation draft follow the order of the former farm system draft. Only players who have rookie status and are not on a major league 25-man roster or disabled list may be selected in these two rounds. This protects the property rights of teams that may have acquired additional farm system draft picks or improved their draft position via trades prior to the shift to Rotisserie League Ultra.

ULTRA II. THE RESERVE ROSTER

A team's reserve roster consists of those players acquired through the rotation draft, through trades, through demotions from the active roster, or through waiver claims. Any transaction (e.g., trade, demotion, waiver claim) that increases the size of the reserve roster beyond 17 players must be accompanied by a concomitant transaction (e.g., trade, promotion, waiver) that simultaneously returns the reserve roster to its maximum 17.

ULTRA III. FEES

1. **Basic:** The cumulative total of salaries paid for acquisition of a 23-man active roster on Auction Draft Day may not exceed $260.

2. **Reserve Roster:** There are no fees payable for the acquisition of players for the 17-man reserve roster.

3. **Transactions:** $10 per trade (no matter how many players are involved), $10 per player activation or demotion.

4. **Waivers:** $10 for each player claimed on waivers.

5. **September Roster Expansion:** $50 for each player added to a team's active roster after September 1.

ULTRA IV. PLAYER SALARIES

The salary of a player is determined by the time and means of his acquisition and does not change unless the player becomes a free agent by means of release or is signed to a guaranteed long-term contract.

THE TENTH PITCHER OPTION

As everybody in the baseball world knows, a Rotisserie team is composed of 9 pitchers and 14 position players (see **Article III,** page 278). Except, of course, when it's not.

A couple of years back we experimented with a slight variation on the traditional roster configuration and permitted a team to carry 10 pitchers and 13 position players.

Most major league teams carry 10 pitchers and 15 position players. But some (e.g., the Detroit Tigers in April and May in recent years) carry only 9 pitchers, while others (e.g., the Oakland A's) carry 11. It comes down to a GM's assessment of the team's needs, its personnel, and the schedule.

If this flexibility is good for the American and National leagues, why not for the third major league—the Rotisserie League? So a couple of years back we decided to let teams fill the utility slot with a position player *or* a pitcher. The result? An unqualified success.

The Tenth Pitcher Option allows a GM to realize the full potential of Ultra. Let's say you have the usual 9 pitchers and 14 position players on your active roster, and your team starts slipping in wins. Presto! You send down the outfielder hitting .227 in your utility slot and promote a good middle innings guy from your reserve roster. In AL leagues, you must still have a DH, two catchers, and three middle infielders, so the 10th pitcher must come at the expense of a corner or an outfielder.

The Tenth Pitcher Option provides more action, sweetens the pot through additional transaction fees, and is simple to administer and monitor. You can change the mix back and forth as frequently as you wish, provided only that the total number of active players does not exceed 23, and that at no time do you have more than 14 active position players or more than 10 active pitchers.

After hearing from leagues around the country regarding their experience with the Tenth Pitcher Option, we decided to leave it as just that—an option. Some leagues, particularly those using AL players, found it awkward to implement because of the DH. Others thought it was okay for Ultra but not regular Rotisserie. Still others simply didn't like it. Many made the transition smoothly.

Hey, that's why we call it an *Option.*

- The salary of a player acquired in the auction draft is his auction price.
- The salary of a player acquired in the rotation draft is determined as follows: If the player was selected in the first round, $15; rounds 2–6, $10; rounds 7–12, $5; rounds 13–17, $2.
- The salary of a player claimed on waivers is $10 or his previous salary, whichever is greater. His contract status remains the same.

ULTRA V. TRADES

From the completion of the rotation draft until noon on the Monday (AL) or Tuesday (NL) on or following August 31, teams are free to make trades of any kind without limit (except as indicated in **Ultra VI**, below). However, at no time can any team have on its active roster more players at a particular position than allowed under the rules of the auction draft (see **Article III**, page 278 of the Official Constitution of Rotisserie League Baseball). A team may, however, be underrepresented at a position. So long as these strictures are adhered to in the immediate wake of a trade, teams may trade any number of players, at any position, irrespective of the number or position of players being received in such trade (except, again, as indicated below in **Ultra VI**).

- At no point may a team have more than 17 players on its reserve roster or more than 40 players on its active and reserve rosters combined.
- At no point may a team have more than 23 players on its active roster, except during the September Roster Expansion period (see **Ultra X**, page 300).
- No trades of any kind may be made between September 1 and October 15, nor between April 2 (Roster Freeze Day) and the conclusion of the rotation draft on Auction Draft Day.

ULTRA VI. ANTI-DUMPING

Players in the last year of a guaranteed contract or playing out their option year and players with a salary of $25 or more are considered "asterisk" players. Such players may be traded only under the following conditions:

- One team may trade asterisk players to another team provided that for each asterisk player traded, one is received in the same deal.
- The above notwithstanding, a team may trade *one* asterisk player to another team without an asterisk player coming in return or receive *one* asterisk player without giving one up, but may make only *one* such unbalanced trade in the course of the season.
- Between October 15 and Roster Freeze Day, asterisk players on winter rosters may be traded without restrictions whatsoever.

ULTRA VI-A. ANTI-DUMPING REPEALED

Effective Opening Day, 1993, Article **Ultra VI** (above) was repealed. The text of **Ultra VI** is left in place so that newcomers to **Ultra** will know just what is being done away with.

ULTRA VII. MOVEMENT BETWEEN ACTIVE ROSTER AND RESERVE ROSTER

An owner may demote a player from the active roster to the reserve roster, or promote a player in the reverse direction, at any time and for any reason, such promotions to take effect with the subsequent stat deadline (Monday noon for AL leagues, Tuesday noon for NL leagues). However, no player may be demoted without being replaced on the active roster by an eligible player—that is, a player who fulfills position eligibility requirements (which may include shifting another active player into the demoted player's position and the promoted player into the shifted player's position) *and* who is currently on a major league roster and not on a major league disabled list.

- **Exception:** If the acquisition of an active player in a trade places the acquiring team's active roster above the positional limit (e.g., more than two catchers), a player at that position may be sent down without the need for the recall of another player.
- A player acquired by trade from another team's active roster is considered active with the acquiring team on the effective date of the trade, unless the acquiring team chooses (or is compelled by roster restrictions) to demote him. Similarly, a player acquired in a trade from another team's reserve roster is considered to be reserved with the acquiring team, unless the acquiring team promotes him.

ULTRA VIII. SIGNING FREE AGENTS

Active major league players not on any Rotisserie League team's active roster or reserve roster at the conclusion of the auction draft become free agents. During the course of the season the pool of free agents may also include minor league players not on any Rotisserie League team's reserve roster who are promoted to an active major league roster; players traded from the "other" major league; and waived players who are not claimed. Beginning one week after the first standings report, and continuing through the season until the last weekly transaction deadline before September 1, such free agents may be signed, without limit, in the following manner:

- Each team shall have, for the purpose of acquiring free agents during the course of the season, a supplementary budget of $100, known as its **Free Agent Acquisition Budget (FAAB).**
- At the deadline established by each Rotisserie League for recording weekly transactions, a Rotisserie League team may submit a *sealed* bid for one or more free agents.
- The minimum bid shall be $5; the maximum shall be the amount remaining in a team's **FAAB.**
- A free agent so selected goes to the highest bidder. If more than one team bids the same amount on a player, and if that amount is the highest bid, the player goes to the team that is lowest in the most recently compiled standings.
- The salary of a free agent signed in this manner is his acquisition price. His contract status is that of a first-year player.
- For each free agent that it signs, a team *must* at the same time waive or release a player from its *active* roster.
- If a free agent signed for a salary of $25 or more is not protected on the subsequent April 1 Roster Freeze, then the owner of his contract at the time must pay into the prize pool a buyout fee of twice his salary or $100, whichever is greater.

NOTE: The reason for the pre–September 1 deadline is to prevent a Rotisserie League team from completely restocking with $5 players when the major leagues expand their rosters to 40 in September.

NOTE: The mechanics of the "sealed bid" process will vary from league to league. Where practicable, as in leagues that have weekly meetings, the sealed bid should be just that—a bid sealed in an envelope that is opened at the meeting. In other cases, it may be more efficient to recruit a disinterested party to record all bids and report them to the League Secretary for action. Whatever mechanism you devise, keep matters in perspective. These aren't the secrets to nuclear fusion, for Einstein's sake! So try to balance the gee of security with the haw of mutual trust.

ULTRA IX. WAIVERS

Players are placed on waivers (a) when they cannot be accommodated on a team's active or reserve roster, because of space and/or positional limitations; and (b) under the rules governing the winter roster (see **Ultra XI**, page 301).

- The waiver period commences at noon on the Monday (AL) or Tuesday (NL) immediately following the team's notification of waiver to the League Secretary and extends for one full reporting period (i.e., one week). At the conclusion of that week, if the player is unclaimed, he goes into the free agent pool, and may be acquired by a team only as outlined in **Ultra VIII**, above.
- Waiver claims are honored according to the inverse order of the standings effective the week before the close of the waiver period.
- A team may reclaim a player it has waived only if all other teams in the league decline to claim him.
- The fee for acquiring a player on waivers is $10. The salary of a player acquired on waivers shall be $10 or his current salary, whichever is greater; and his contract status shall remain the same.
- Only a player currently on a 25-man major league roster (i.e., not on a disabled list) may be claimed on waivers.
- A player traded to the "other" league may not be placed on waivers.
- A player on a guaranteed long-term contract may not be placed on waivers, even in the final year of his contract.

ULTRA X. SEPTEMBER ROSTER EXPANSION

If it chooses, a team may expand its roster for the pennant drive by promoting from its reserve roster an *unlimited* number of players, as the post–September 1 active-roster size expands to a maximum of 40 players. Such players may play any position.

- September expansions can be effective no earlier than noon on the Monday (AL) or Tuesday (NL) immediately following August 31.

Expansions made later in September become effective the subsequent Monday or Tuesday at noon.

- A fee of $50 must be paid for every promotion that increases the active-roster size beyond 23. Player salaries are not affected by such promotions.

ULTRA XI. WINTER ROSTER

Effective October 15, each owner is required to submit to the League Secretary a list of 23 players, irrespective of position, taken from its combined active and reserve rosters, but one not including any players who have concluded their option year or the last year of a guaranteed long-term contract. This group of players becomes the winter roster.

- Immediately after the submission of winter rosters, a waiver period concluding at noon, November 1, begins. By inverse order of the final standings in the season just ended, teams may select no more than one player from that group of players not protected on a winter roster, again with the exception of players who have concluded their option year or the final year of a guaranteed long-term contract. On claiming such a player, the claiming team must, in turn, waive a player from its own winter roster. Players thus waived become eligible for a second round of waiver claims, for a period of one week, that are conducted in the same fashion. (Unclaimed players from the first waiver period are no longer eligible.) The process continues until there is a week in which no one is claimed.
- All winter-waiver claims cost the claiming team $10, to be paid into the league treasury for the coming season.
- The salary of a player claimed on winter waivers is $10 (or his current salary, whichever is greater), and he shall be deemed to be commencing the first year of a new contract with the coming season.
- After October 23, winter rosters may exceed or fall below 23 players through trading action. Whatever size the roster, however, any successful claim of a player on waivers must be accompanied by the placing of another player from the claiming team on waivers.

ULTRA XII. ROSTER PROTECTION

Roster protection in Rotisserie League and Rotisserie League Ultra is identical (see **Article XVIII**, page 293), except as follows:

- The cumulative salaries of frozen players are deducted from a team's $260 expenditure limit in the auction draft, and the balance is available for the acquisition of the remainder of a team's active roster. However, salaries of players frozen on April 1 who are not on 25-man major league rosters on Auction Draft Day do not count against the $260 limit.
- Frozen players not on 25-man major league rosters count against the limit of 17 players on draft day reserve rosters, and the salaries they carry must be paid into the league treasury on draft day.

- In addition to the 15 players that a team may protect from its winter roster of active and reserve roster players, a team may also protect an additional 3 players on its reserve roster, provided that such players have rookie status and have never been active on a Rotisserie League team.
- Players frozen may include players who have spent the entire previous season on a reserve roster—typically because they played only in the minor leagues. Even so, such players who are subsequently frozen are deemed to be in the *second* year of their contract with their Rotisserie League Ultra team.
- Assignment of frozen players to a reserve roster position is at the owner's discretion. That is, an owner with a $10 minor leaguer carried over from the preceding year might, for strategic reasons, assign that player to the 17th position in the rotation draft, thus forgoing a $2 pick. Or the owner might assign the player to the first round and forgo a $15 pick. The assignment of frozen players by all teams will be made before the rotation draft commences.

NOTE: Some Ultra Leagues believe that the clock on minor leaguers should not start ticking until they are promoted to the majors, as in Rotisserie Regular. We feel this would tie up too many players and eventually undermine the auction draft. Effective in 1991, we increased the number of $2 and $5 players in the rotation draft (see **Ultra IV**, page 296). That should facilitate building a farm system and encourage protection of key players without providing the blanket protection of freezing the clock. This is called a compromise.

Let There Be Lite!

Great ideas often have implausibly pedestrian beginnings.

Isaac Newton was sitting under an apple tree, thinking he would like something sweet but tart and loaded with vitamin A, when the principle of gravity fell in his lap. A man who loved martinis a bit too well, Eli Whitney got his big inspiration when his wife yelled from the kitchen, "Keep your cotton-picking hands off that gin!" And because somebody else was picking up the tab, Daniel Okrent, down from his rustic estate in western Massachusetts to join Manhattan friends for lunch, found himself eating snails and making history over a decade ago in the then-fashionable East Side bistro La Rôtisserie Française, instead of wolfing down a grease-on-white-with-mayo at his favorite New York restaurant—and thus the world was deprived of Blimpie League Baseball.

Maybe there's something in the water up there in the Berkshire Mountains, or maybe there's just nothing else to do, but a few years back yet another bucolic Edison stumbled out of the backwoods with a new widget. Fortunately, BFFCL Okrent recognized his nearby neighbor's creation as an inspired variation on a great theme, an ingenious mechanism for filling an important sociocultural need, a cleverly constructed design with possible commercial potential.

So we stole it.

That's how we are able to bring you the newest version of The Greatest Game for Baseball Fans Since Youknowwhat, Rotisserie Lite! But before we do, common courtesy requires us to say a few words about the country bumpk . . . ah, *squire* who we city-slickered into giving away his invention for a handful of T-shirts and the promise to spell his name right.

Tony Lake (that's L-A-K-E) is a man for all seasons, though he definitely prefers summer. A hardscrabble farmer then biding his time between crops as a circuit-riding professor of international politics at several pricey New England colleges, Farmer-Professor Lake is currently President Clinton's National Security Adviser and the highest-ranking Rotisserian in the world. He is a terminal Boston Red Sox fan who started playing Rotisserie League Baseball almost a decade ago, when BFFCL Okrent sold him a copy of the rules for 40 acres and a mule. Farmer-Professor Lake says the idea for Rotisserie Lite came to him one day near the end of the 1989 season when he was sitting on his tractor thinking about the Middle East situation.

"Late that season I suddenly found myself going sane," the tiller-scholar recalls. "I caught myself reading boxscores to find out who won, not just to see how my players had done. Some days I even read the front page first. Clearly, I was in trouble."

The academic-agrarian attacked the problem by identifying what he liked best and least about Rotisserie Ultra play in the League of Nations, where his team—the Smuts Peddlers—had always been a strong contender. "I like boxscores, and I like listening to games on the radio," he says. "I don't like the lure of trading, because it appeals to extreme type-A personalities like Okrent. I was spending too much time thinking about trades instead of about foreign policy or that funny sound my tractor was making."

While unwilling to go cold turkey (he still plays in the League of Nations), Farmer-Professor Lake did go looking for a halfway house. He found it when he founded the Washington Slo-Pitch League, a six-team outfit whose owners hail mostly from the nation's capital. (The mayor of the founder's hometown was awarded a one-third ownership in a franchise as a hedge against local tax increases. So far it's worked.)

"I see the game we play in Slo-Pitch as a halfway house in either direction," Farmer-Professor Lake says. "If you've never played Rotisserie before, it's a great way to learn what it's all about. And if you've been playing it too hard or too long, it helps you recapture the whimsy, and whimsy is the whole point of Rotisserie in the first place."

Thanks, Tony. We needed that.

ROTISSERIE LITE
The Rules of Play

Same Auction Draft!
Same Stat Categories!
Same Yoo-Hoo!

No Farm System!
No Reserve List!
No Money!

Editor's Note: *The following rules were lifted from the unwritten constitution of the Washington Slo-Pitch League, with several embellishments and alterations of our own to give them a bogus air of originality. Please note that we were too lazy to repeat all the pertinent rules of Rotisserie Regular that also apply in Rotisserie Lite. That means you'll have to go back and read the* **Official Constitution of Rotisserie League Baseball** *(pages 277–294) to figure out what we're talking about.*

LITE I. FEWER TEAMS

A Rotisserie Lite League using National League or American League players is composed of six teams.

- With only six teams, Rotisserie Lite Leagues have shorter (and probably more orderly) auction drafts, fewer friendships to wreck, and less trouble squeezing into a telephone booth.

LITE II. ONE DIVISION ONLY

A Rotisserie Lite League uses players from only *one* NL or AL division.

- Resist the temptation to draw players from an entire league or—worse still—to mix the two leagues. "Lite" doesn't mean "soft." By restricting the talent pool to players of one division, Lite owners will need to scout as diligently as do Rotisserie Regular and Rotisserie Ultra owners. You'll have to learn which middle innings relievers can be counted on for the greatest number of quality innings, which non-regular corner men will get the most at-bats, and which fourth outfielders will deliver 40 or more RBI. In other words, you'll have to become a better, more knowledgeable fan. And isn't that the Rotisserie Way?
- Using players from only one division helps an owner new to the world of Rotisserie to draw on his or her strength. After all, we all start out as fans of a particular team, which means that we enter the Rotisserie

world knowing and liking one team—and one division—better than others. What better place to start?

LITE III. NO MONEY

Each team has 23 Lite Dollars (L$) to spend at the auction draft to acquire a full roster of 23 active major league players, with a minimum salary and minimum bidding increments of 10 cents. But real money is not used.

- "The intensity of feeling in Rotisserie is unrelated to money anyhow," sez Farmer-Professor Lake. "If you play for traditional Rotissestakes— 260 real dollars for 23 real players—it's enough to be irritating if you lose, but not enough to buy a new car if you win. So what's the point?"
- Using L$ still requires an owner to manage the team budget and cope with the exigencies of free market competition for the services of Matt Williams, Mo Vaughn, and other superstars at the auction draft. Farmer-Professor Lake promises that your throat goes dry and your heart palpitates when the bidding hits L$2.70 for Greg Maddux, the same as when it crosses $30 for baseball's best pitcher in regular Rotisserie. This means that a kid owner can have just as much Rotissefun as a parent owner without having to beg for an advance against the next six months of allowances.
- Playing for L$ also makes a team owner feel a little less hysterical when the *Baseball America* and *Baseball Weekly* subs come due.

LITE IV. MONTHLY TRANSACTIONS

Transaction Day occurs once a month, on the Monday (AL) or Tuesday (NL) before stats appear in *USA Today*. The first Transaction Day falls on the first Monday or Tuesday in May. Except for the All-Star Break Trading Period described below, all Rotisserie Lite roster moves are restricted to Transaction Day.

- On Transaction Day, a Rotisserie Lite team may release players (a) placed on a major league disabled list; (b) demoted to the minor leagues; (c) traded to the other division or to the other major league; or (d) released by their major league team, *without limit* from its current roster and replace them with players from the free agent pool who qualify at the same position. Players may not be reserved. Even players on major league disabled lists must be released if their Rotisserie Lite owner chooses to replace them. Released players go into the free agent pool and may be claimed on the *next* Transaction Day.
- Player moves on Transaction Day shall take place in reverse order of the most recent standings, with the lowest team in the standings having the right of first claim on a player from the free agent pool. While there is no limit on the number of players a team may release and replace, a team may make only one transaction at a time. That is, the last-place team in a six-team league may not make a second

transaction until all other teams in the league have had an opportunity to make a transaction.

- As there is no reserve list in Rotisserie Lite, an owner whose star player is on his major league team's disabled list and isn't scheduled to come off for another two weeks will have to make a strategic call: Ride out the injury and retain the player under contract; or release him into the free agent pool and call up a replacement immediately.
- The salary of a player claimed from the free agent pool on Transaction Day is L$1.

LITE V. TRADE RESTRICTIONS

Except for a two-week trading period ending with the last out of the All-Star Game, no trades are permitted in Rotisserie Lite.

- All trades during the trading period take effect on the first pitch of the first regular season game after the All-Star Game.
- A Rotisserie Lite team may trade only one player with a salary of L$2 or more to any one team.

LITE VI. SAME SCORING CATEGORIES

Standings shall be determined on the same basis as in Rotisserie Regular and Rotisserie Ultra—that is, according to each team's cumulative performance over the course of a full season in eight statistical categories: home runs, RBI, stolen bases, and batting average for batters; wins, saves, ERA, and ratio (hits plus walks divided by innings pitched) for pitchers.

- A team receives points in each category according to its relative position. In a six-team league, the leader in home runs would receive six points, the second-place team five points, and so on. The team with the highest point total wins the Rotisserie Lite pennant.
- Standings should be compiled and distributed weekly. As keeping score is no more fun in Lite than in Regular or Ultra, new Lite leagues should consider the special deal offered by **Roti·Stats**. As transactions only take place monthly, **Roti·Stats** is able to provide timely, accurate weekly stat reports for Rotisserie Lite Leagues at a deep discount from its regular low rates. (See pages 264–265 for details.)

LITE VII. LONG-TERM CONTRACTS

The same rules governing the option year and long-term contracts that complicate an owner's life in Rotisserie Regular and Rotisserie Ultra shall also pertain in Rotisserie Lite. (See **Article XVII** of the Official Constitution, page 291.)

- **Exception:** A player under a long-term contract in Rotisserie Lite may be released and replaced at any time without penalty, subject only to the restrictions regarding player transactions.

LITE VIII. ROSTER PROTECTION

On April 1, each team may protect a certain number of players according to the following schedule: The team that finished first the preceding year may protect a maximum of seven players; all other teams, a maximum of ten players. There is no minimum requirement.

- Yes, this makes it a lot harder to build a dynasty. But trust us: One Harry Stein loose on the land is more than enough.
- Trading is not permitted over the winter on the grounds that Rotisserie Lite owners have better things to do with their time. Particularly those who also play Rotisserie Regular or Rotisserie Ultra.

LITE IX. YOO-HOO

As there is no prize pool to divvy up in Rotisserie Lite, the Yoo-Hoo running down a Rotisserie Lite pennant winner's face and trickling into the corners of his or her mouth will taste all the sweeter, if you can imagine such a thing.

Editor's Postscript: *As you play Rotisserie Lite, let us know what you think. It takes a long time to turn a piece of coal into a diamond, and it may take us a couple of seasons to get Lite exactly rite. We particularly want to hear from you about new wrinkles, adaptations, and changes that we might scarf up for next year's book. Just remember:* Keep it Lite!

ROTI•STATS
THE BEST
CALL 800-676-7684

7

Postgame Shower

A Yoo-Hoo to Arms

Editor's Note: *We ended our first book ten years ago with the following dispatch from Maestro Steve Wulf of the Wulfgang. We ended all our other books the same way. It's how we're ending this book. And it's the way we'll end our next book. That's because tradition is everything in Rotisserie League Baseball . . . unless you have to throw it into a deal for a stud power hitter.*

Unseen hands hold you, force your head down, and pour water, dairy whey, corn sweetener, nonfat milk, sugar, coconut oil, cocoa, sodium caseinate, salt, sodium bicarbonate, dipotassium phosphates, calcium phosphates, guar gum, natural flavors, xanthan gum, vanillin (an artificial flavor), sodium ascorbate, ferric orthophosphate, palmitate, niacinamide, vitamin D, and, yes, *riboflavin* all over your hair. The bizarre ritual is a Yoo-Hoo shampoo, and it is what you get for winning the Rotisserie League pennant.

The chocolate-flavored rinse will not leave your locks radiant and soft to the touch, and squirrels will probably follow you around for a day or two. All in all, the ritual is pretty distasteful. But there's not a member of the Rotisserie League who wouldn't gladly suffer the rite so long as it came at the end of a championship season.

Since we traditionally end each Rotisseseason with an outpouring of the chocolate drink of our youth, we figured we may as well end the book the same way. Besides, as the beverage company's former executive vice president for promotions, Lawrence Peter Berra, once noted, or at least we think he noted, "Yoo-Hoo tastes good. And it's good for you, too."

Yoo-Hoo does taste good if your taste buds also happen to be impressed with the nose on strawberry fizzies. To sophisticated palates, Yoo-Hoo tastes a little like the runoff in the gutter outside a Carvel store.

As for Yoo-Hoo being good for you, well, Yogi says he let his kids drink it, and one of them grew up to be the .255-hitting shortstop for the Pittsburgh Pirates. But then, maybe if Dale *hadn't* touched the stuff, he might actually be worth more than the $7 the Fleder Mice paid for him in 1983.

Yoo-Hoo is not unlike the Rotisserie League. Both of them taste good, and both of them are good for you. Just don't tell anybody that. Whenever one of us tries to explain just what the Rotisserie League is, we all get the same kind of look. It's the look one might get from a bartender if one ordered, say, a Kahlua and Yoo-Hoo. The look says, "Aren't you a little too old to be partaking of that stuff?" Our look invariably replies, "But it tastes good, and it's good for you."

Yoo-Hoo's current slogan is "Yoo-Hoo's Got Life." Catchy, isn't it? But then, Yogi Berra used to be a catchy. The Rotisserie League's got life, too. It enlivens not only boxscores, but "Kiner's Korner," as well. Why, the game adds color to every fiber of your being, it gives you a sense of purpose in this crazy, cockeyed world, it puts a spring in your step and a song in your heart, and it makes you care, deeply care, for your fellow man, especially if your fellow man's name is Biff Pocoroba. So the Rotisserie League is childish, is it? Yoo-Hoo and a bottle of rum, barkeep.

In case you're wondering where Yoo-Hoo comes from, we thought we'd tell you. It comes from Carlstadt, N.J. Yoo-Hoo also goes back to the days of Ruth and Gehrig. It first arrived on the American scene as a fruit drink named after a popular greeting of that day. Founder Natale Olivieri was obsessed with making a stable chocolate drink, and after years of experimentation, he hit upon the idea of heating the chocolate. The rest is soft-drink history.

In the '50s, Yoo-Hoo's Golden Age, the product came to be associated with Yogi. A billboard of Yogi and a bottle of Yoo-Hoo greeted fans in Yankee Stadium. And Yogi wasn't the only Yankee who endorsed Yoo-Hoo— Whitey, Mickey, and the Moose could all be seen on the insides of Yoo-Hoo bottle caps. Nowadays, nobody inhabits the inside of the bottle cap. However, if you turn the cap upside down, it reads, "ooh-ooy," which is Yiddish for Rod Scurry's ERA.

Yoo-Hoo is also like baseball: You don't want to know too much about it. In the interests of this chapter, we sent an envoy out to Yankee Stadium to talk to Yogi. Yes, you've read all those funny Berra quotes over the years, about how it's not over until it's over, and about how nobody goes to that restaurant anymore because it's too crowded. To tell you the truth, Yogi is not the man that people suppose him to be. He is actually two different people, depending on his mood. When he is on guard, he is full of monosyllables, and when he is relaxed, he can be genuinely engaging. But the star of "The Hathaways"* he is not.

We—actually, it was only one of us, who shall remain nameless, and if the *New Yorker* can do it, why can't we—asked Yogi if he would mind talking about Yoo-Hoo. He said, "Sorry, I can't." This caught us by surprise, but being quick on our tongue, we asked, "You can't?" Yogi said, "Nope. Ask Cerone."

At which point, we approached Rick Cerone, the catcher who took Yogi's place as executive vice president for promotions. For all their sterling qualities, Berra and Cerone do not strike us as being pillars of the corporate structure, but Yoo-Hoo obviously saw through to their executive talents. We asked Cerone if he would mind talking about Yoo-Hoo. He said, "I can't." This time, we asked, "Why?" and Cerone said, "Because I'm suing them, that's why."

*Does anybody remember who "The Hathaways" were? We've forgotten.

As it turns out, the company has changed hands, and Cerone claims that Yoo-Hoo never paid him for certain appearances. Yogi ran into similar problems, but he settled out of court. So that's why Yoo-Hoo is just like baseball: if you look too closely, it can get ugly on you.

We went back to Yogi and pleaded with him. All we cared about, we said, were the old days of Yoo-Hoo. He warmed to the subject in much the same way Natale Olivieri warmed Yoo-Hoo—slowly. Through his grunts and moans, we determined that Yogi thought Yoo-Hoo tasted good, that his kids drank it, that he wishes he had some money invested in it, and that people still link him with Yoo-Hoo, and vice versa. Then he said, "What's this for, anyway?"

We explained to him about the Rotisserie League and the book. When we said, "Then, at the end of the year, we pour Yoo-Hoo over the head of the winner," Yogi—dripping tobacco juice out of the left side of his mouth—gave us a look of partial disgust and said something like "ooh-ooy."

So, if you decide to take up baseball as played by the Rotisserie League, be warned. People will look at you funny. Pay them no mind. Just pay the Treasurer.

We hate long good-byes. When we meet again, perhaps at a theater near you showing *The Rotisserie League Goes to Japan*, let's just say, "Yoo-Hoo."

Final 1995 Averages

NATIONAL LEAGUE: BATTERS

NL Batter	Team	BA	HR	RBI	SB	CS	G	AB	R	BB	OBP
Abbott, K.	Fla	.255	17	60	4	3	120	420	60	36	.318
Alfonzo, E.	NYN	.278	4	41	1	1	101	335	26	12	.301
Alou, M.	Mon	.273	14	58	4	3	93	344	48	29	.342
Andrews, S.	Mon	.214	8	31	1	1	84	220	27	17	.271
Anthony, E.	Cin	.269	5	23	2	1	47	134	19	13	.327
Arias, A.	Fla	.269	3	26	1	0	94	216	22	22	.337
Ashley, B.	LA	.237	8	27	0	0	81	215	17	25	.320
Aude, R.	Pit	.248	2	19	1	2	42	109	10	6	.287
Aurilia, R.	SF	.474	2	4	1	0	9	19	4	1	.476
Ausmus, B.	SD	.293	5	34	16	5	103	328	44	31	.353
Bagwell, J.	Hou	.290	21	87	12	5	114	448	88	79	.399
Barry, J.	NYN	.133	0	0	0	0	15	15	2	1	.188
Bates, J.	Col	.267	8	46	3	6	116	322	42	42	.355
Battle, A.	StL	.271	0	2	3	3	61	118	13	15	.358
Bean, B.	SD	.000	0	0	0	0	4	7	1	1	.000
Bell, D.	StL	.250	2	19	1	2	39	144	13	4	.278
Bell, D.	Hou	.334	8	86	27	9	112	452	63	33	.385
Bell, J.	Pit	.262	13	55	2	5	138	530	79	55	.336
Belliard, R.	Atl	.222	0	7	2	2	75	180	12	6	.255
Benard, M.	SF	.382	1	4	1	0	13	34	5	1	.400
Benitez, Y.	Mon	.385	2	7	0	2	14	39	8	1	.400
Benjamin, M.	SF	.220	3	12	11	1	68	186	19	8	.256
Bennett, G.	Phi	.000	0	0	0	0	1	1	0	0	.000
Benzinger, T.	SF	.200	1	2	0	0	9	10	2	2	.308
Berry, S.	Mon	.318	14	55	3	8	103	314	38	25	.367
Berryhill, D.	Cin	.183	2	11	0	0	34	82	6	10	.260
Bichette, D.	Col	.340	40	128	13	9	139	579	102	22	.364
Biggio, C.	Hou	.302	22	77	33	8	141	553	123	80	.406
Blauser, J.	Atl	.211	12	31	8	5	115	431	60	57	.319
Bogar, T.	NYN	.290	1	21	1	0	78	145	17	9	.329
Bonds, B.	SF	.294	33	104	31	10	144	506	109	120	.431
Bonilla, B.	NYN	.325	18	53	0	3	80	317	49	31	.385
Boone, B.	Cin	.267	15	68	5	1	138	513	63	41	.326
Borders, P.	Hou	.114	0	0	0	0	11	35	1	2	.162
Bradshaw, T.	StL	.227	0	2	1	2	19	44	6	2	.261
Branson, J.	Cin	.260	12	45	2	1	122	331	43	44	.345
Brito, J.	Col	.216	0	7	1	0	18	51	5	2	.259
Brogna, R.	NYN	.289	22	76	0	0	134	495	72	39	.342
Browne, J.	Fla	.255	1	17	1	1	77	184	21	25	.346
Brumfield, J.	Pit	.271	4	26	22	12	116	402	64	37	.339
Brumley, M.	Hou	.056	1	2	1	0	18	18	1	0	.056
Buechele, S.	ChN	.189	1	9	0	0	32	106	10	11	.265
Buford, D.	NYN	.235	4	12	7	7	44	136	24	19	.346
Bullett, S.	ChN	.273	3	22	8	3	104	150	19	12	.331
Burks, E.	Col	.266	14	49	7	3	103	278	41	39	.359
Busch, M.	LA	.235	3	6	0	0	13	17	3	0	.235
Butler, B.	LA	.274	0	13	11	1	39	146	24	24	.368
Butler, B.	NYN	.311	1	25	21	7	90	367	54	43	.381

NL Batter	Team	BA	HR	RBI	SB	CS	G	AB	R	BB	OBP
Caminiti, K.	SD	.302	26	94	12	5	143	526	74	69	.380
Cangelosi, J.	Hou	.318	2	18	21	5	90	201	46	48	.457
Caraballo, R.	StL	.202	2	3	3	2	34	99	10	6	.269
Carr, C.	Fla	.227	2	20	25	11	105	308	54	46	.330
Carreon, M.	SF	.301	17	65	0	1	117	396	53	23	.343
Castellano, P.	Col	.000	0	0	0	0	4	5	0	2	.000
Castilla, V.	Col	.309	32	90	2	8	139	527	82	30	.347
Castillo, A.	NYN	.103	0	0	1	0	13	29	2	3	.212
Castro, J.	LA	.250	0	0	0	0	11	4	0	1	.400
Cedeno, A.	SD	.210	6	31	5	3	120	390	42	28	.271
Cedeno, R.	LA	.238	0	3	1	0	40	42	4	3	.283
Cianfrocco, A.	SD	.263	5	31	0	2	51	118	22	11	.333
Clark, D.	Pit	.281	4	24	3	3	77	196	30	24	.359
Clark, P.	SD	.216	2	7	0	2	75	97	12	8	.278
Clayton, R.	SF	.244	5	58	24	9	138	509	56	38	.298
Colbrunn, G.	Fla	.277	23	89	11	3	138	528	70	22	.311
Coles, D.	StL	.225	3	16	0	0	63	138	13	16	.316
Conine, J.	Fla	.302	25	105	2	0	133	483	72	66	.379
Cooper, S.	StL	.230	3	40	0	3	118	374	29	49	.321
Cordero, W.	Mon	.286	10	49	9	5	131	514	64	36	.341
Counsell, C.	Col	.000	0	0	0	0	3	1	0	1	.000
Cromer, T.	StL	.226	5	18	0	0	105	345	36	14	.261
Cummings, M.	Pit	.243	2	15	1	0	59	152	13	13	.303
Daulton, D.	Phi	.249	9	55	3	0	98	342	44	55	.359
Dawson, A.	Fla	.257	8	37	0	0	79	226	30	9	.305
Decker, S.	Fla	.226	3	13	1	0	51	133	12	19	.318
DeShields, D.	LA	.256	8	37	39	14	127	425	66	63	.353
Devereaux, M.	Atl	.255	1	8	2	0	29	55	7	2	.281
Diaz, M.	Fla	.230	1	6	0	0	49	87	5	1	.239
Donnels, C.	Hou	.300	0	2	0	0	19	30	4	3	.364
Duncan, M.	Cin	.290	3	13	0	1	29	69	16	5	.329
Duncan, M.	Phi	.286	3	23	1	2	52	196	20	0	.285
Dunston, S.	ChN	.296	14	69	10	5	127	477	58	10	.317
Dykstra, L.	Phi	.264	2	18	10	5	62	254	37	33	.353
Eisenreich, J.	Phi	.316	10	55	10	0	129	377	46	38	.375
Elster, K.	Phi	.208	1	9	0	0	26	53	10	7	.302
Encarnacion, A.	Pit	.226	2	10	1	1	58	159	18	13	.285
Eusebio, T.	Hou	.299	6	58	0	2	113	368	46	31	.354
Everett, C.	NYN	.260	12	54	2	5	79	289	48	39	.352
Faneyte, R.	SF	.198	0	4	1	0	46	86	7	11	.289
Finley, S.	SD	.297	10	44	36	12	139	562	104	59	.366
Fletcher, D.	Mon	.286	11	45	0	1	110	350	42	32	.351
Flora, K.	Phi	.213	2	7	1	0	24	75	12	4	.253
Floyd, C.	Mon	.130	1	8	3	0	29	69	6	7	.221
Foley, T.	Mon	.208	0	2	1	0	11	24	2	2	.269
Fonville, C.	LA	.276	0	16	20	5	88	308	41	23	.328
Fonville, C.	Mon	.333	0	0	0	2	14	12	2	0	.333
Fordyce, B.	NYN	.500	0	0	0	0	4	2	1	1	.667
Franco, M.	ChN	.294	0	1	0	0	16	17	3	0	.294
Frazier, L.	Mon	.190	0	3	4	0	35	63	6	8	.297
Galarraga, A.	Col	.280	31	106	12	2	143	554	89	32	.331
Gallagher, D.	Phi	.318	1	12	0	0	62	157	12	16	.379
Gant, R.	Cin	.276	29	88	23	8	119	410	79	74	.386
Garcia, C.	Pit	.294	6	50	8	4	104	367	41	25	.340

NL Batter	Team	BA	HR	RBI	SB	CS	G	AB	R	BB	OBP
Garcia, F.	Pit	.140	0	1	0	1	42	57	5	8	.246
Garcia, K.	LA	.200	0	0	0	0	13	20	1	0	.200
Giannelli, R.	StL	.091	0	0	0	0	9	11	0	3	.286
Gibralter, S.	Cin	.333	0	0	0	0	4	3	0	0	.333
Gilkey, B.	StL	.298	17	69	12	6	121	480	73	42	.358
Giovanola, E.	Atl	.071	0	0	0	0	13	14	2	3	.235
Girardi, J.	Col	.262	8	55	3	3	125	462	63	29	.308
Goff, J.	Hou	.154	1	3	0	0	12	26	2	4	.267
Gonzalez, L.	ChN	.290	7	34	5	5	77	262	34	39	.384
Gonzalez, L.	Hou	.258	6	35	1	3	56	209	35	18	.322
Grace, M.	ChN	.326	16	92	6	2	143	552	97	65	.395
Greene, W.	Cin	.105	0	0	0	0	8	19	1	3	.227
Gregg, T.	Fla	.237	6	20	3	1	72	156	20	16	.313
Grissom, M.	Atl	.258	12	42	29	9	139	551	80	47	.317
Grudzielanek, M.	Mon	.245	1	20	8	3	78	269	27	14	.300
Gutierrez, R.	Hou	.276	0	12	5	0	52	156	22	10	.321
Gwynn, C.	LA	.214	1	10	0	0	67	84	8	6	.272
Gwynn, T.	SD	.368	9	90	17	5	135	535	82	35	.404
Hajek, D.	Hou	.000	0	0	1	0	5	2	0	1	.000
Haney, T.	ChN	.411	2	6	0	0	25	73	11	7	.463
Hansen, D.	LA	.287	1	14	0	0	100	181	19	28	.384
Harris, L.	Cin	.208	2	16	10	1	101	197	32	14	.259
Hayes, C.	Phi	.276	11	85	5	1	141	529	58	50	.340
Hemond, S.	StL	.144	3	9	0	0	57	118	11	12	.233
Hernandez, C.	LA	.149	2	8	0	0	45	94	3	7	.216
Hernandez, J.	ChN	.245	13	40	1	0	93	245	37	13	.281
Hill, G.	SF	.264	24	86	25	5	132	497	71	39	.317
Holbert, R.	SD	.178	2	5	4	0	63	73	11	8	.277
Hollandsworth, T.	LA	.233	5	13	2	1	41	103	16	10	.304
Hollins, D.	Phi	.229	7	25	1	1	65	205	46	53	.393
Howard, T.	Cin	.302	3	26	17	8	113	281	42	20	.350
Hubbard, M.	ChN	.174	0	1	0	0	15	23	2	2	.240
Hubbard, T.	Col	.310	3	9	2	1	24	58	13	8	.394
Hulett, T.	StL	.182	0	0	0	0	4	11	0	0	.182
Hundley, T.	NYN	.280	15	51	1	0	90	275	39	42	.382
Hunter, B.	Cin	.215	1	9	2	1	40	79	9	11	.312
Hunter, B.	Hou	.302	2	28	24	7	78	321	52	21	.346
Huskey, B.	NYN	.189	3	11	1	0	28	90	8	10	.267
Hyers, T.	SD	.000	0	0	0	0	6	5	0	0	.000
Ingram, G.	LA	.200	0	3	3	0	44	55	5	9	.313
Jefferies, G.	Phi	.306	11	56	9	5	114	480	69	35	.349
Johnson, B.	SD	.251	3	29	0	0	68	207	20	11	.287
Johnson, C.	Fla	.251	11	39	0	2	97	315	40	46	.351
Johnson, H.	ChN	.195	7	22	1	1	87	169	26	34	.330
Johnson, M.	Pit	.208	13	28	5	2	79	221	32	37	.326
Jones, C.	Atl	.265	23	86	8	4	140	524	87	73	.353
Jones, C.	NYN	.280	8	31	2	1	79	182	33	13	.327
Jordan, B.	StL	.296	22	81	24	9	131	490	83	22	.339
Jordan, K.	Phi	.185	2	6	0	0	24	54	6	2	.228
Justice, D.	Atl	.253	24	78	4	2	120	411	73	73	.365
Karros, E.	LA	.298	32	105	4	4	143	551	83	61	.369
Kelly, M.	Atl	.190	3	17	7	3	97	137	26	11	.258
Kelly, R.	LA	.279	6	48	15	7	112	409	47	15	.306
Kelly, R.	Mon	.274	1	9	4	3	24	95	11	7	.337
Kent, J.	NYN	.278	20	65	3	3	125	472	65	29	.327

FINAL 1995 AVERAGES •

NL Batter	Team	BA	HR	RBI	SB	CS	G	AB	R	BB	OBP
King, J.	Pit	.265	18	87	7	4	122	445	61	55	.342
Kingery, M.	Col	.269	8	37	13	5	119	350	66	45	.351
Klesko, R.	Atl	.310	23	70	5	4	107	329	48	47	.396
Kmak, J.	ChN	.245	1	6	0	0	19	53	7	6	.328
Kowitz, B.	Atl	.167	0	3	0	1	10	24	3	2	.259
Laker, T.	Mon	.234	3	20	0	1	64	141	17	14	.306
Lampkin, T.	SF	.276	1	9	2	0	65	76	8	9	.360
Lankford, R.	StL	.277	25	82	24	8	132	483	81	63	.360
Lansing, M.	Mon	.255	10	62	27	4	127	467	47	28	.299
Larkin, B.	Cin	.319	15	66	51	5	131	496	98	61	.394
Ledesma, A.	NYN	.242	0	3	0	0	21	33	4	6	.359
Lee, M.	StL	1.000	0	0	0	0	1	1	1	0	1.000
Lemke, M.	Atl	.253	5	38	2	2	116	399	42	44	.325
Leonard, M.	SF	.190	1	4	0	0	14	21	4	5	.346
Lewis, D.	Cin	.245	0	8	11	11	58	163	19	17	.324
Lewis, D.	SF	.252	1	16	21	7	74	309	47	17	.303
Lewis, M.	Cin	.339	3	30	0	3	81	171	25	21	.407
Lieberthal, M.	Phi	.255	0	4	0	0	16	47	1	5	.327
Liriano, N.	Pit	.286	5	38	2	2	107	259	29	24	.347
Livingstone, S.	SD	.337	5	32	2	1	99	196	26	15	.380
Longmire, T.	Phi	.356	3	19	1	1	59	104	21	11	.419
Lopez, J.	Atl	.315	14	51	0	1	100	333	37	14	.344
Mabry, J.	StL	.307	5	41	0	3	129	388	35	24	.347
Magadan, D.	Hou	.313	2	51	2	1	127	348	44	71	.428
Manwaring, K.	SF	.251	4	36	1	0	118	379	21	27	.314
Marsh, T.	Phi	.294	3	15	0	1	43	109	13	4	.316
Martin, A.	Pit	.282	13	41	20	11	124	439	70	44	.351
May, D.	Hou	.301	8	41	5	0	78	206	29	19	.358
McCarty, D.	SF	.250	0	2	1	0	12	20	1	2	.318
McCracken, Q.	Col	.000	0	0	0	0	3	1	0	0	.000
McDavid, R.	SD	.176	0	0	1	1	11	17	2	2	.263
McGriff, F.	Atl	.280	27	93	3	6	144	528	85	65	.361
McRae, B.	ChN	.288	12	48	27	8	137	580	92	47	.348
Mejia, R.	Col	.154	1	4	0	1	23	52	5	0	.167
Merced, O.	Pit	.300	15	83	7	2	132	487	75	52	.365
Miller, O.	Hou	.262	5	36	3	4	92	324	36	22	.319
Mondesi, R.	LA	.285	26	88	27	4	139	536	91	33	.328
Morandini, M.	Phi	.283	6	49	9	6	127	494	65	42	.350
Mordecai, M.	Atl	.280	3	11	0	0	69	75	10	9	.353
Morman, R.	Fla	.278	3	7	0	0	34	72	9	3	.316
Morris, H.	Cin	.279	11	51	1	1	101	359	53	29	.333
Mouton, J.	Hou	.262	4	27	25	8	104	298	42	25	.326
Munoz, N.	LA	.000	0	0	0	0	2	1	0	0	.000
Natal, B.	Fla	.233	2	6	0	0	16	43	2	1	.244
Nevin, P.	Hou	.117	0	1	1	0	18	60	4	7	.221
Newfield, M.	SD	.309	1	7	0	0	21	55	6	2	.333
Nieves, M.	SD	.205	14	38	2	3	98	234	32	19	.276
Nokes, M.	Col	.182	0	0	0	0	10	11	1	1	.250
O'Brien, C.	Atl	.227	9	23	0	1	67	198	18	29	.343
Ochoa, A.	NYN	.297	0	0	1	0	11	37	7	2	.333
Offerman, J.	LA	.287	4	33	2	7	119	429	69	69	.389
Oliva, J.	Atl	.156	5	12	0	0	48	109	7	7	.207
Oliva, J.	StL	.122	2	8	0	0	22	74	8	5	.195
Oquendo, J.	StL	.209	2	17	1	1	88	220	31	35	.316

• FINAL 1995 AVERAGES

NL Batter	Team	BA	HR	RBI	SB	CS	G	AB	R	BB	OBP
Orsulak, J.	NYN	.283	1	37	1	3	108	290	41	19	.323
Otero, R.	NYN	.137	0	1	2	1	35	51	5	3	.185
Owens, E.	Cin	1.000	0	1	0	0	2	2	0	0	1.000
Owens, J.	Col	.244	4	12	0	0	18	45	7	2	.286
Pagnozzi, T.	StL	.215	2	15	0	1	62	219	17	11	.254
Parent, M.	ChN	.250	3	5	0	0	12	32	5	3	.314
Parent, M.	Pit	.232	15	33	0	0	69	233	25	23	.301
Parker, R.	LA	.276	0	4	1	1	27	29	3	2	.323
Patterson, J.	SF	.205	1	14	4	2	95	205	27	14	.294
Pegues, S.	Pit	.246	6	16	1	2	82	171	17	4	.263
Pena, G.	StL	.267	1	8	3	2	32	101	20	16	.367
Pendleton, T.	Fla	.290	14	78	1	2	133	513	70	38	.339
Perez, E.	Atl	.308	1	4	0	0	7	13	1	0	.308
Perry, G.	StL	.165	0	5	0	0	65	79	4	6	.224
Petagine, R.	SD	.234	3	17	0	0	89	124	15	26	.367
Phillips, J.	SF	.195	9	28	1	1	92	231	27	19	.256
Piazza, M.	LA	.346	32	93	1	0	112	434	82	39	.400
Plantier, P.	Hou	.250	4	15	0	0	22	68	12	11	.349
Plantier, P.	SD	.257	5	19	1	1	54	148	21	17	.333
Polonia, L.	Atl	.264	0	2	3	0	28	53	6	3	.304
Pratt, T.	ChN	.133	0	4	0	0	25	60	3	6	.209
Pride, C.	Mon	.175	0	2	3	2	48	63	10	5	.235
Prince, T.	LA	.200	1	4	0	0	18	40	3	4	.273
Pulliam, H.	Col	.400	1	3	0	0	5	5	1	0	.400
Pye, E.	LA	.000	0	0	0	0	7	8	0	0	.000
Ready, R.	Phi	.138	0	0	0	1	23	29	3	3	.219
Reed, J.	SF	.265	0	9	0	0	66	113	12	20	.376
Reed, J.	SD	.256	4	40	6	4	131	445	58	59	.348
Rhodes, K.	ChN	.125	0	2	0	0	13	16	2	0	.118
Roberson, K.	ChN	.184	4	6	0	1	32	38	5	6	.311
Roberts, B.	SD	.304	2	25	20	2	73	296	40	17	.346
Rodriguez, H.	LA	.262	1	10	0	1	21	80	6	5	.306
Rodriguez, H.	Mon	.207	1	5	0	0	24	58	7	6	.277
Sabo, C.	StL	.154	0	3	1	0	5	13	0	1	.214
Sanchez, R.	ChN	.278	3	27	6	4	114	428	57	14	.301
Sanders, D.	Cin	.240	1	10	16	3	33	129	19	9	.296
Sanders, D.	SF	.285	5	18	8	6	52	214	29	18	.346
Sanders, R.	Cin	.306	28	99	36	12	133	484	91	69	.397
Santangelo, F.	Mon	.296	1	9	1	1	35	98	11	12	.384
Santiago, B.	Cin	.286	11	44	2	2	81	266	40	24	.351
Sasser, M.	Pit	.154	0	0	0	0	14	26	1	0	.154
Scarsone, S.	SF	.266	11	29	3	2	80	233	33	18	.333
Schall, G.	Phi	.231	0	5	0	0	24	65	2	6	.306
Schofield, D.	LA	.100	0	0	0	0	9	10	0	1	.182
Sefcik, K.	Phi	.000	0	0	0	0	5	4	1	0	.000
Segui, D.	Mon	.305	10	57	1	4	97	383	59	28	.355
Segui, D.	NYN	.329	2	11	1	3	33	73	9	12	.420
Servais, S.	ChN	.286	12	35	2	1	52	175	31	23	.371
Servais, S.	Hou	.225	1	12	0	1	28	89	7	9	.300
Sharperson, M.	Atl	.143	0	2	0	0	7	7	1	0	.143
Sheaffer, D.	StL	.231	5	30	0	0	76	208	24	23	.306
Sheffield, G.	Fla	.324	16	46	19	4	63	213	46	55	.467
Shipley, C.	Hou	.263	3	24	6	1	92	232	23	8	.291
Siddall, J.	Mon	.300	0	1	0	0	7	10	4	3	.500
Silvestri, D.	Mon	.264	2	7	2	0	39	72	12	9	.341

NL Batter	Team	BA	HR	RBI	SB	CS	G	AB	R	BB	OBP
Simms, M.	Hou	.256	9	24	1	2	50	121	14	13	.341
Slaught, D.	Pit	.304	0	13	0	0	35	112	13	9	.361
Smith, D.	Atl	.252	3	21	0	3	103	131	16	13	.327
Smith, O.	StL	.199	0	11	4	3	44	156	16	17	.282
Sosa, S.	ChN	.268	36	119	34	7	144	564	89	58	.340
Spehr, T.	Mon	.257	1	3	0	0	41	35	4	6	.366
Spiers, B.	NYN	.208	0	11	0	1	63	72	5	12	.314
Stankiewicz, A.	Hou	.115	0	7	4	2	43	52	6	12	.281
Stinnett, K.	NYN	.219	4	18	2	0	77	196	23	29	.338
Stocker, K.	Phi	.218	1	32	6	1	125	412	42	43	.304
Sweeney, M.	StL	.273	2	13	1	1	37	77	5	10	.348
Tarasco, T.	Mon	.249	14	40	24	3	126	438	64	51	.329
Tatum, J.	Col	.235	0	4	0	0	34	34	4	1	.257
Taubensee, E.	Cin	.284	9	44	2	2	80	218	32	22	.354
Tavarez, J.	Fla	.289	2	13	7	5	63	190	31	16	.346
Thompson, M.	Hou	.220	2	19	4	2	92	132	14	14	.297
Thompson, R.	SF	.223	8	23	1	2	95	336	51	42	.317
Thompson, R.	NYN	.251	7	31	3	1	75	267	39	19	.306
Timmons, O.	ChN	.263	8	28	3	0	77	171	30	13	.314
Treadway, J.	LA	.118	0	3	0	0	17	17	2	0	.118
Treadway, J.	Mon	.240	0	10	0	1	41	50	4	5	.309
Tucker, S.	Hou	.286	1	1	0	0	5	7	1	0	.286
Van Slyke, A.	Phi	.243	3	16	7	0	63	214	26	28	.333
Vanderwal, J.	Col	.347	5	21	1	1	105	101	15	16	.432
Varsho, G.	Phi	.252	0	11	2	0	72	103	7	7	.310
Veras, Q.	Fla	.261	5	32	56	21	124	440	86	80	.384
Vizcaino, J.	NYN	.287	3	56	8	3	135	509	66	35	.332
Walker, L.	Col	.306	36	101	16	3	131	494	96	49	.381
Wallach, T.	LA	.266	9	38	0	0	97	327	24	27	.326
Walton, J.	Cin	.290	8	22	10	7	102	162	32	17	.368
Webster, L.	Phi	.267	4	14	0	0	49	150	18	16	.337
Webster, M.	LA	.179	1	3	0	0	54	56	6	4	.246
Wehner, J.	Pit	.308	0	5	3	1	52	107	13	10	.361
Weiss, W.	Col	.260	1	25	15	3	137	427	65	98	.403
White, R.	Mon	.295	13	57	25	5	130	474	87	41	.356
Whiten, M.	Phi	.269	11	37	7	0	60	212	38	31	.365
Whitmore, D.	Fla	.190	1	2	0	0	27	58	6	5	.250
Wilkins, R.	ChN	.191	6	14	0	0	50	162	24	36	.340
Wilkins, R.	Hou	.250	1	5	0	0	15	40	6	10	.392
Williams, E.	SD	.260	12	47	0	0	97	296	35	23	.320
Williams, M.	SF	.336	23	65	2	0	76	283	53	30	.399
Williams, R.	LA	.091	0	1	0	0	15	11	2	2	.231
Wilson, N.	Cin	.000	0	0	0	0	5	7	0	0	.000
Worthington, C.	Cin	.278	1	2	0	0	10	18	1	2	.350
Young, E.	Col	.317	6	36	35	12	120	366	68	49	.404
Young, K.	Pit	.232	6	22	1	3	56	181	13	8	.268
Zeile, T.	ChN	.227	9	30	0	0	79	299	34	16	.271
Zeile, T.	StL	.291	5	22	1	0	34	127	16	18	.378
Zosky, E.	Fla	.200	0	0	0	0	6	5	0	0	.200

NATIONAL LEAGUE: PITCHERS

NL Pitcher	Team	W	L	SV	ERA	Ratio	GS	IP	H	BB	K
Abbott, K.	Phi	2	0	0	3.81	1.553	0	28.1	28	16	21
Acevedo, J.	Col	4	6	0	6.44	1.645	11	65.2	82	20	40
Adams, T.	ChN	1	1	1	6.50	1.778	0	18.0	22	10	15
Alvarez, T.	Mon	1	5	0	6.75	1.688	8	37.1	46	14	17
Aquino, L.	Mon	0	2	2	3.86	1.634	0	37.1	47	11	22
Aquino, L.	SF	0	1	0	14.40	2.400	0	5.0	10	2	4
Arocha, R.	StL	3	5	0	3.99	1.530	0	49.2	55	18	25
Ashby, A.	SD	12	10	0	2.94	1.313	31	192.2	180	62	150
Astacio, P.	LA	7	8	0	4.24	1.308	11	104.0	103	29	80
Avery, S.	Atl	7	13	0	4.67	1.287	29	173.1	165	52	141
Bailey, C.	StL	0	0	0	7.36	1.091	0	3.2	2	2	5
Bailey, R.	Col	7	6	0	4.98	1.574	6	81.1	88	39	33
Banks, W.	ChN	0	1	0	15.43	3.343	0	11.2	27	12	9
Banks, W.	LA	0	2	0	4.03	1.828	6	29.0	36	16	23
Banks, W.	Fla	2	3	0	4.32	1.480	9	50.0	43	30	30
Barber, B.	StL	2	1	0	5.22	1.602	4	29.1	31	16	27
Barton, S.	SF	4	1	1	4.26	1.308	0	44.1	37	19	22
Bautista, J.	SF	3	8	0	6.44	1.500	6	100.2	120	26	45
Beck, R.	SF	5	6	33	4.45	1.415	0	58.2	60	21	42
Bedrosian, S.	Atl	1	2	0	6.11	1.893	0	28.0	40	12	22
Benes, A.	StL	1	2	0	8.44	1.813	3	16.0	24	4	20
Benes, A.	SD	4	7	0	4.17	1.433	19	118.2	121	45	126
Berumen, A.	SD	2	3	1	5.68	1.714	0	44.1	37	36	42
Birkbeck, M.	NYN	0	1	0	1.63	0.867	4	27.2	22	2	14
Blair, W.	SD	7	5	0	4.34	1.395	12	114.0	112	45	83
Bochtler, D.	SD	4	4	1	3.57	1.257	0	45.1	38	19	45
Borbon, P.	Atl	2	2	2	3.09	1.469	0	32.0	29	17	33
Borland, T.	Phi	1	3	6	3.77	1.662	0	74.0	81	37	59
Bottalico, R.	Phi	5	3	1	2.46	1.095	0	87.2	50	42	87
Bowen, R.	Fla	2	0	0	3.78	2.100	3	16.2	23	12	15
Brantley, J.	Cin	3	2	28	2.82	1.052	0	70.1	53	20	62
Brewington, J.	SF	6	4	0	4.54	1.553	13	75.1	68	45	45
Brocail, D.	Hou	6	4	1	4.19	1.461	7	77.1	87	22	39
Bruske, J.	LA	0	0	1	4.50	1.700	0	10.0	12	4	5
Bullinger, J.	ChN	12	8	0	4.14	1.507	24	150.0	152	65	93
Burba, D.	Cin	6	2	0	3.27	1.232	9	63.1	52	26	50
Burba, D.	SF	4	2	0	4.98	1.454	0	43.1	38	25	46
Burgos, E.	SF	0	0	0	8.64	2.520	0	8.1	14	6	12
Burkett, J.	Fla	14	14	0	4.30	1.439	30	188.1	208	57	126
Byrd, P.	NYN	2	0	0	2.05	1.182	0	22.0	18	7	26
Candiotti, T.	LA	7	14	0	3.50	1.335	30	190.1	187	58	141
Carrasco, H.	Cin	2	7	5	4.12	1.534	0	87.1	86	46	64
Carter, A.	Phi	0	0	0	6.14	0.955	0	7.1	4	2	6
Casian, L.	ChN	1	0	0	1.93	1.629	0	23.1	23	15	11
Castillo, F.	ChN	11	10	0	3.21	1.261	29	188.0	179	52	135
Charlton, N.	Phi	2	5	0	7.36	1.864	0	22.0	23	15	12
Christiansen, J.	Pit	1	3	0	4.15	1.527	0	56.1	49	34	53
Clark, T.	Atl	0	0	0	4.91	2.182	0	3.2	3	5	2
Clontz, B.	Atl	8	1	4	3.65	1.406	0	69.0	71	22	55
Cornelius, R.	Mon	0	0	0	8.00	2.000	0	9.0	11	5	4
Cornelius, R.	NYN	3	7	0	5.15	1.561	10	57.2	64	25	35
Courtright, J.	Cin	0	0	0	9.00	2.000	0	1.0	2	0	0
Creek, D.	StL	0	0	0	0.00	0.750	0	6.2	2	3	10
Cummings, J.	LA	3	1	0	3.00	1.231	0	39.0	38	10	21

NL Pitcher	Team	W	L	SV	ERA	Ratio	GS	IP	H	BB	K
Daal, O.	LA	4	0	0	7.20	2.250	0	20.0	29	15	11
DeLeon, J.	Mon	0	1	0	7.56	1.800	0	8.1	7	7	12
DeLucia, R.	StL	8	7	0	3.39	1.239	1	82.1	63	36	76
Deshaies, J.	Phi	0	1	0	20.25	3.000	2	5.1	15	1	6
Dewey, M.	SF	1	0	0	3.13	1.484	0	31.2	30	17	32
DiPoto, J.	NYN	4	6	2	3.78	1.398	0	78.2	77	29	49
Dishman, G.	SD	4	8	0	5.01	1.464	16	97.0	104	34	43
Dougherty, J.	Hou	8	4	0	4.92	1.537	0	67.2	76	25	49
Drabek, D.	Hou	10	9	0	4.77	1.443	31	185.0	205	54	143
Dunbar, M.	Fla	0	1	0	11.57	3.429	0	7.0	12	11	5
Dyer, M.	Pit	4	5	0	4.34	1.554	0	74.2	81	30	53
Edens, T.	ChN	1	0	0	6.00	3.000	0	3.0	6	3	2
Eischen, J.	LA	0	0	0	3.10	1.574	0	20.1	19	11	15
Elliott, D.	SD	0	0	0	0.00	1.500	0	2.0	2	1	3
Ericks, J.	Pit	3	9	0	4.58	1.509	18	106.0	108	50	80
Estes, S.	SF	0	3	0	6.75	1.269	3	17.1	16	5	14
Eversgerd, B.	Mon	0	0	0	5.14	1.524	0	21.0	22	9	8
Fassero, J.	Mon	13	14	0	4.33	1.497	30	189.0	207	74	164
Fernandez, S.	Phi	6	1	0	3.34	1.082	11	64.2	48	21	79
Fletcher, P.	Phi	1	0	0	5.40	1.875	0	13.1	15	9	10
Florence, D.	NYN	3	0	0	1.50	1.917	0	12.0	17	6	5
Florie, B.	SD	2	2	1	3.01	1.325	0	68.2	49	38	68
Fossas, T.	StL	3	0	0	1.47	1.064	0	36.2	28	10	40
Foster, K.	ChN	12	11	0	4.51	1.312	28	167.2	149	65	146
Franco, J.	NYN	5	3	29	2.44	1.258	0	51.2	48	17	41
Frascatore, J.	StL	1	1	0	4.41	1.745	4	32.2	39	16	21
Fraser, W.	Mon	2	1	2	5.61	1.442	0	25.2	25	9	12
Freeman, M.	Col	3	7	0	5.89	1.743	18	94.2	122	41	61
Frey, S.	Phi	0	0	1	0.84	0.469	0	10.2	3	2	2
Frey, S.	SF	0	1	0	4.26	1.421	0	6.1	7	2	5
Garces, R.	ChN	0	0	0	3.27	1.273	0	11.0	11	3	6
Garces, R.	Fla	0	2	0	5.40	1.650	0	13.1	14	8	16
Gardner, M.	Fla	5	5	1	4.49	1.534	11	102.1	109	43	87
Glavine, T.	Atl	16	7	0	3.08	1.273	29	198.2	182	66	127
Gomez, P.	SF	0	0	0	5.14	2.000	0	14.0	16	12	15
Gott, J.	Pit	2	4	3	6.03	1.628	0	31.1	38	12	19
Grace, M.	Phi	1	1	0	3.18	1.235	2	11.1	10	4	7
Grahe, J.	Col	4	3	0	5.08	1.747	9	56.2	69	27	27
Green, T.	Phi	8	9	0	5.31	1.614	25	140.2	157	66	85
Greene, T.	Phi	0	5	0	8.29	2.020	6	33.2	45	20	24
Greer, K.	SF	0	2	0	5.25	1.750	0	12.0	15	5	7
Groom, B.	Fla	1	2	0	7.20	2.133	0	15.0	26	6	12
Grott, M.	Cin	0	0	0	21.60	3.600	0	1.2	6	0	2
Gunderson, E.	NYN	1	1	0	3.70	1.397	0	24.1	25	8	19
Guthrie, M.	LA	0	2	0	3.66	1.475	0	19.2	19	9	19
Habyan, J.	StL	3	2	0	2.88	1.180	0	40.2	32	15	35
Hamilton, J.	SD	6	9	0	3.08	1.253	30	204.1	189	56	123
Hammond, C.	Fla	9	6	0	3.80	1.323	24	161.0	157	47	126
Hampton, M.	Hou	9	8	0	3.35	1.288	24	150.2	141	49	115
Hancock, L.	Pit	0	0	0	1.93	0.857	0	14.0	10	2	6
Hansell, G.	LA	0	1	0	7.45	1.914	0	19.1	29	6	13
Harnisch, P.	NYN	2	8	0	3.68	1.255	18	110.0	111	24	82
Harris, G.	Phi	2	2	0	4.26	1.421	0	19.0	19	8	9
Harris, G.	Mon	2	3	0	2.61	1.283	0	48.1	45	16	47

• FINAL 1995 AVERAGES

NL Pitcher	Team	W	L	SV	ERA	Ratio	GS	IP	H	BB	K
Hartgraves, D.	Hou	2	0	0	3.22	1.266	0	36.1	30	16	24
Harvey, B.	Fla	0	0	0	0.00	0.00	0	0.0	2	1	0
Henke, T.	StL	1	1	36	1.82	1.104	0	54.1	42	18	48
Henneman, M.	Hou	0	1	8	3.00	1.286	0	21.0	21	4	19
Henry, B.	Mon	7	9	0	2.84	1.287	21	126.2	133	28	60
Henry, D.	NYN	3	6	4	2.96	1.104	0	67.0	48	25	62
Heredia, G.	Mon	5	6	1	4.31	1.370	18	119.0	137	21	74
Hermanson, D.	SD	3	1	0	6.82	1.832	0	31.2	35	22	19
Hernandez, J.	Fla	0	0	0	11.57	2.286	0	7.0	12	3	5
Hernandez, X.	Cin	7	2	3	4.60	1.444	0	90.0	95	31	84
Hickerson, B.	ChN	2	3	1	6.82	1.611	0	31.2	36	15	28
Hickerson, B.	Col	1	0	0	11.88	2.820	0	16.2	33	13	12
Hill, K.	StL	6	7	0	5.06	1.541	18	110.1	125	45	50
Hoffman, T.	SD	7	4	31	3.88	1.163	0	53.1	48	14	52
Holmes, D.	Col	6	1	14	3.24	1.320	0	66.2	59	28	61
Hook, C.	SF	5	1	0	5.50	1.662	0	52.1	55	29	40
Hope, J.	Pit	0	0	0	30.86	6.429	0	2.1	8	4	2
Hudek, J.	Hou	2	2	7	5.40	1.200	0	20.0	19	5	29
Isringhausen, J.	NYN	9	2	0	2.81	1.301	14	93.0	88	31	55
Jackson, D.	StL	2	12	0	5.90	1.728	19	100.2	120	48	52
Jackson, M.	Cin	6	1	2	2.39	1.184	0	49.0	38	19	41
Jacome, J.	NYN	0	4	0	10.29	2.333	5	21.0	33	15	11
Jarvis, K.	Cin	3	4	0	5.70	1.595	11	79.0	91	32	33
Johnstone, J.	Fla	0	0	0	3.86	1.929	0	4.2	7	2	3
Jones, B.	NYN	10	10	0	4.19	1.375	30	195.2	209	53	127
Jones, T.	Hou	6	5	15	3.07	1.475	0	99.2	89	52	96
Juden, J.	Phi	2	4	0	4.02	1.420	10	62.2	53	31	47
Karp, R.	Phi	0	0	0	4.50	2.000	0	2.0	1	3	2
Kile, D.	Hou	4	12	0	4.96	1.567	21	127.0	114	73	113
Konuszewski, D.	Pit	0	0	0	54.00	12.000	0	0.1	3	1	0
Kroon, M.	SD	0	1	0	10.80	1.800	0	1.2	1	2	2
Krueger, B.	SD	0	0	0	7.04	2.217	0	7.2	13	4	6
Leiper, D.	Mon	0	2	2	2.86	1.000	0	22.0	16	6	12
Leiter, M.	SF	10	12	0	3.82	1.313	29	195.2	185	55	129
Leskanic, C.	Col	6	3	10	3.40	1.184	0	98.0	83	33	107
Lewis, R.	Fla	0	1	0	3.75	1.278	1	36.0	30	15	32
Lieber, J.	Pit	4	7	0	6.32	1.665	12	72.2	103	14	45
Loaiza, E.	Pit	8	9	0	5.16	1.535	31	172.2	205	55	85
Lomon, K.	NYN	0	1	0	6.75	2.357	0	9.1	17	5	6
Maddux, G.	Atl	19	2	0	1.63	0.830	28	209.2	147	23	181
Maddux, M.	Pit	1	0	0	9.00	1.889	0	9.0	14	3	4
Mantei, M.	Fla	0	1	0	4.72	1.875	0	13.1	12	13	15
Manzanillo, J.	NYN	1	2	0	7.88	1.500	0	16.0	18	6	14
Manzanillo, R.	Pit	0	0	0	4.91	1.636	0	3.2	3	2	1
Martinez, P.	Mon	14	10	0	3.51	1.207	30	194.2	158	66	174
Martinez, P.	Hou	0	0	0	7.40	2.274	0	20.2	29	16	17
Martinez, R.	LA	17	7	0	3.66	1.270	30	206.1	176	81	138
Mathews, T.	StL	1	1	2	1.52	1.079	0	29.2	21	11	28
Mathews, T.	Fla	4	4	3	3.38	1.185	0	82.2	70	27	72
Mauser, T.	SD	0	1	0	9.53	2.294	0	5.2	4	9	9
May, D.	Atl	0	0	0	11.25	2.500	0	4.0	10	0	1
McCurry, J.	Pit	1	4	1	5.02	1.918	0	61.0	82	30	27
McElroy, C.	Cin	3	4	0	6.02	1.537	0	40.1	46	15	27

NL Pitcher	Team	W	L	SV	ERA	Ratio	GS	IP	H	BB	K
McMichael, G.	Atl	7	2	2	2.79	1.190	0	80.2	64	32	74
McMurtry, C.	Hou	0	1	0	7.84	2.419	0	10.1	15	9	4
Mercker, K.	Atl	7	8	0	4.15	1.427	26	143.0	140	61	102
Miceli, D.	Pit	4	4	21	4.66	1.603	0	58.0	61	28	56
Mimbs, M.	Phi	9	7	1	4.15	1.522	19	136.2	127	75	93
Minor, B.	NYN	4	2	1	3.66	1.243	0	46.2	44	13	43
Mintz, S.	SF	1	2	0	7.45	2.069	0	19.1	26	12	7
Mlicki, D.	NYN	9	7	0	4.26	1.357	25	160.2	160	54	123
Morel, R.	Pit	0	1	0	2.84	1.263	0	6.1	6	2	3
Morgan, M.	ChN	2	1	0	2.19	1.176	4	24.2	19	9	15
Morgan, M.	StL	5	6	0	3.88	1.350	17	106.2	114	25	46
Mulholland, T.	SF	5	13	0	5.80	1.557	24	149.0	190	38	65
Munoz, B.	Phi	0	2	0	5.74	1.723	3	15.2	15	9	6
Munoz, M.	Col	2	4	2	7.42	1.878	0	43.2	54	27	37
Murphy, R.	LA	0	1	0	12.60	1.800	0	5.0	6	3	2
Murphy, R.	Fla	1	1	0	9.82	1.773	0	7.1	8	5	5
Murray, M.	Atl	0	2	0	6.75	1.500	1	10.2	10	5	3
Myers, M.	Fla	0	0	0	0.00	2.000	0	2.0	1	3	0
Myers, R.	ChN	1	2	38	3.88	1.383	0	55.2	49	28	59
Nabholz, C.	ChN	0	1	0	5.40	1.543	0	23.1	22	14	21
Navarro, J.	ChN	14	6	0	3.28	1.263	29	200.1	194	56	128
Neagle, D.	Pit	13	8	0	3.43	1.283	31	209.2	221	45	150
Nen, R.	Fla	0	7	23	3.29	1.310	0	65.2	62	23	68
Nichols, R.	Atl	0	0	0	5.40	2.850	0	6.2	14	5	3
Nied, D.	Col	0	0	0	20.77	3.231	0	4.1	11	3	3
Nitkowski, C.	Cin	1	3	0	6.12	1.794	7	32.1	41	15	18
Nomo, H.	LA	13	6	0	2.54	1.082	28	191.1	124	78	236
Olivares, O.	Phi	0	1	0	5.40	1.400	0	10.0	11	2	7
Olivares, O.	Col	1	3	0	7.39	2.116	6	31.2	44	21	15
Osborne, D.	StL	4	6	0	3.81	1.306	19	113.1	112	34	82
Osuna, A.	LA	2	4	0	4.43	1.343	0	44.2	39	20	46
Painter, L.	Col	3	0	1	4.37	1.478	1	45.1	55	10	36
Palacios, V.	StL	2	3	0	5.80	1.711	5	40.1	48	19	34
Park, C.	LA	0	0	0	4.50	1.000	1	4.0	2	2	7
Parra, J.	LA	0	0	0	4.35	1.645	0	10.1	10	6	7
Parrett, J.	StL	4	7	0	3.64	1.304	0	76.2	71	28	71
Parris, S.	Pit	6	6	0	5.38	1.573	15	82.0	89	33	61
Pena, A.	Atl	0	0	0	4.15	1.154	0	13.0	11	4	18
Pena, A.	Fla	2	0	0	1.50	0.778	0	18.0	11	3	21
Pennington, B.	Cin	0	0	0	5.59	2.172	0	9.2	9	11	7
Perez, C.	Mon	10	8	0	3.69	1.238	23	141.1	142	28	106
Perez, M.	ChN	2	6	2	3.66	1.444	0	71.1	72	27	49
Perez, Y.	Fla	2	6	1	5.21	1.393	0	46.2	35	28	47
Person, R.	NYN	1	0	0	0.75	0.583	1	12.0	5	2	10
Petkovsek, M.	StL	6	6	0	4.00	1.289	21	137.1	136	35	71
Plesac, D.	Pit	4	4	3	3.58	1.343	0	60.1	53	27	57
Portugal, M.	Cin	6	5	0	3.82	1.326	14	77.2	79	22	33
Portugal, M.	SF	5	5	0	4.15	1.365	17	104.0	106	34	63
Powell, J.	Fla	0	0	0	1.08	1.800	0	8.1	7	6	4
Powell, R.	Hou	0	0	0	11.00	3.000	0	9.0	16	11	8
Powell, R.	Pit	0	2	0	5.23	1.548	3	20.2	20	10	12
Pugh, T.	Cin	6	5	0	3.84	1.353	12	98.1	100	32	38
Pulsipher, B.	NYN	5	7	0	3.98	1.350	17	126.2	122	45	81
Quantrill, P.	Phi	11	12	0	4.67	1.461	29	179.1	212	44	103

NL Pitcher	Team	W	L	SV	ERA	Ratio	GS	IP	H	BB	K
Rapp, P.	Fla	14	7	0	3.44	1.440	28	167.1	158	76	102
Reed, R.	Cin	0	0	0	5.82	1.235	3	17.0	18	3	10
Reed, S.	Col	5	2	3	2.14	0.988	0	84.0	61	21	79
Rekar, B.	Col	4	6	0	4.98	1.435	14	85.0	95	24	60
Remlinger, M.	Cin	0	0	0	9.00	5.000	0	1.0	2	3	1
Remlinger, M.	NYN	0	1	0	6.35	1.588	0	5.2	7	2	6
Reynolds, S.	Hou	10	11	0	3.47	1.241	30	189.1	196	37	175
Reynoso, A.	Col	7	7	0	5.32	1.688	18	93.0	116	36	40
Ricci, C.	Phi	1	0	0	1.80	1.300	0	10.0	9	3	9
Rijo, J.	Cin	5	4	0	4.17	1.420	14	69.0	76	22	62
Ritz, K.	Col	11	11	2	4.21	1.396	28	173.1	171	65	120
Rivera, R.	ChN	0	0	0	5.40	2.000	0	5.0	8	2	2
Rodriguez, F.	LA	1	1	0	2.53	1.500	0	10.2	11	5	5
Rodriguez, R.	StL	0	0	0	0.00	0.000	0	1.2	0	0	0
Rojas, M.	Mon	1	4	30	4.12	1.552	0	67.2	69	29	61
Roper, J.	Cin	0	0	0	10.29	2.429	2	7.0	13	4	6
Roper, J.	SF	0	0	0	27.00	4.000	0	1.0	2	2	0
Rosselli, J.	SF	2	1	0	8.70	1.967	5	30.0	39	20	7
Rueter, K.	Mon	5	3	0	3.23	1.014	9	47.1	38	9	28
Ruffin, B.	Col	0	1	11	2.12	1.324	0	34.0	26	19	23
Ruffin, J.	Cin	0	0	0	1.35	1.125	0	13.1	4	11	11
Saberhagen, B.	NYN	5	5	0	3.35	1.182	16	110.0	105	20	71
Saberhagen, B.	Col	2	1	0	6.28	1.814	9	43.0	60	13	29
Sager, A.	Col	0	0	0	7.36	1.773	0	14.2	19	7	10
Sanders, S.	SD	5	5	0	4.30	1.244	15	90.0	79	31	88
Scheid, R.	Fla	0	0	0	6.10	2.032	0	10.1	14	7	10
Schilling, C.	Phi	7	5	0	3.57	1.078	17	116.0	96	26	114
Schmidt, C.	Mon	0	0	0	6.97	2.516	0	10.1	15	9	7
Schmidt, J.	Atl	2	2	0	5.76	1.840	2	25.0	27	18	19
Schourek, P.	Cin	18	7	0	3.22	1.109	29	190.1	158	45	160
Scott, T.	Mon	2	0	2	3.98	1.279	0	63.1	52	23	57
Seanez, R.	LA	1	3	3	6.75	1.673	0	34.2	39	18	29
Service, S.	SF	3	1	0	3.19	1.290	0	31.0	18	20	30
Shaw, J.	Mon	1	6	3	4.62	1.396	0	62.1	58	26	45
Slocumb, H.	Phi	5	6	32	2.89	1.531	0	65.1	64	35	63
Small, A.	Fla	1	0	0	1.42	2.053	0	6.1	7	6	5
Smiley, J.	Cin	12	5	0	3.46	1.223	27	176.2	173	39	124
Smith, P.	Cin	1	2	0	6.66	1.562	2	24.1	30	7	14
Smoltz, J.	Atl	12	7	0	3.18	1.256	29	192.2	166	72	193
Springer, D.	Phi	0	3	0	4.84	1.388	4	22.1	21	9	15
Springer, R.	Phi	0	0	0	3.71	1.275	0	26.2	22	10	32
Stanton, M.	Atl	1	1	1	5.59	1.966	0	19.1	31	6	13
Sturtze, T.	ChN	0	0	0	9.00	1.500	0	2.0	2	1	0
Sullivan, S.	Cin	0	0	0	4.91	1.636	0	3.2	4	2	2
Swartzbaugh, D.	ChN	0	0	0	0.00	1.091	0	7.1	5	3	5
Swift, B.	Col	9	3	0	4.94	1.571	19	105.2	122	43	68
Swindell, G.	Hou	10	9	0	4.47	1.444	26	153.0	180	39	96
Tabaka, J.	Hou	1	0	0	2.22	1.192	0	24.1	17	12	19
Tabaka, J.	SD	0	0	0	7.11	2.368	0	6.1	10	5	6
Tapani, K.	LA	4	2	0	5.05	1.526	11	57.0	72	14	43
Telgheder, D.	NYN	1	2	0	5.61	1.597	4	25.2	34	7	16
Thobe, J.	Mon	0	0	0	9.00	2.250	0	4.0	6	3	0
Thobe, T.	Atl	0	0	0	10.80	2.100	0	3.1	7	0	2
Thompson, M.	Col	2	3	0	6.53	1.882	5	51.0	73	22	30
Torres, S.	SF	0	1	0	9.00	2.500	1	8.0	13	7	2
Trachsel, S.	ChN	7	13	0	5.15	1.556	29	160.2	174	76	117

NL Pitcher	Team	W	L	SV	ERA	Ratio	GS	IP	H	BB	K
Urbani, T.	StL	3	5	0	3.70	1.476	13	82.2	99	21	52
Urbina, U.	Mon	2	2	0	6.17	1.714	4	23.1	26	14	15
Valdes, I.	LA	13	11	1	3.05	1.113	27	197.2	168	51	150
Valdes, M.	Fla	0	0	0	14.14	3.857	3	7.0	17	9	2
Valdez, C.	SF	0	1	0	6.14	1.909	0	14.2	19	8	7
Valdez, S.	SF	4	5	0	4.75	1.477	11	66.1	78	17	29
Valenzuela, F.	SD	8	3	0	4.98	1.494	15	90.1	101	34	57
Van Landingham	SF	6	3	0	3.67	1.353	18	122.2	124	40	95
Veres, D.	Hou	5	1	1	2.26	1.190	0	103.1	89	30	94
Veres, R.	Fla	4	4	1	3.88	1.418	0	48.2	46	22	31
Villone, R.	SD	2	1	1	4.21	1.364	0	25.2	24	11	37
Viola, F.	Cin	0	1	0	6.28	1.605	3	14.1	20	3	4
Wade, T.	Atl	0	1	0	4.50	1.750	0	4.0	3	4	3
Wagner, B.	Hou	0	0	0	0.00	0.000	0	0.1	0	0	0
Wagner, P.	Pit	5	16	1	4.80	1.533	25	165.0	174	72	120
Walker, M.	ChN	1	3	1	3.22	1.545	0	44.2	45	24	20
Walker, P.	NYN	1	0	0	4.58	1.642	0	17.2	24	5	5
Wall, D.	Hou	3	1	0	5.55	1.562	5	24.1	33	5	16
Watson, A.	StL	7	9	0	4.96	1.504	19	114.1	126	41	49
Weathers, D.	Fla	4	5	0	5.98	1.782	15	90.1	104	52	60
Wells, D.	Cin	6	5	0	3.59	1.239	11	72.2	74	16	50
Wendell, T.	ChN	3	1	0	4.92	1.608	0	60.1	71	24	50
West, D.	Phi	3	2	0	3.79	1.421	8	38.0	34	19	25
White, G.	Mon	1	2	0	7.01	1.403	1	25.2	26	9	25
White, R.	Pit	2	3	0	4.75	1.564	9	55.0	66	18	29
Williams, B.	SD	3	10	0	6.00	1.736	6	72.0	79	38	75
Williams, M.	Phi	3	3	0	3.29	1.255	8	87.2	78	29	57
Williams, T.	LA	2	2	0	5.12	1.345	0	19.1	19	7	8
Wilson, G.	Pit	0	1	0	5.02	1.395	0	14.1	13	5	8
Wilson, T.	SF	3	4	0	3.92	1.500	17	82.2	82	38	38
Witt, B.	Fla	2	7	0	3.90	1.383	19	110.2	104	47	95
Wohlers, M.	Atl	7	3	25	2.09	1.175	0	64.2	51	24	90
Woodall, B.	Atl	1	1	0	6.10	2.032	0	10.1	13	8	5
Worrell, T.	SD	1	0	0	4.72	1.725	0	13.1	16	6	13
Worrell, T.	LA	4	1	32	2.02	1.123	0	62.1	50	19	61
Young, A.	ChN	3	4	2	3.70	1.548	1	41.1	47	14	15

AMERICAN LEAGUE: BATTERS

AL Batter	Team	BA	HR	RBI	SB	CS	G	AB	R	BB	OBP
Aldrete, M.	Cal	.250	0	3	0	0	18	24	1	0	.240
Aldrete, M.	Oak	.272	4	21	0	0	60	125	18	19	.367
Alexander, M.	Bal	.236	3	23	11	4	94	242	35	20	.299
Alicea, L.	Bos	.270	6	44	13	10	132	419	64	63	.367
Allanson, A.	Cal	.171	3	10	0	1	35	82	5	7	.244
Alomar, R.	Tor	.300	13	66	30	3	130	517	71	47	.354
Alomar Jr, S.	Cle	.300	10	35	3	1	66	203	32	7	.332
Amaral, R.	Sea	.282	2	19	21	2	90	238	45	21	.342
Amaro, R.	Cle	.200	1	7	1	3	28	60	5	4	.273
Anderson, B.	Bal	.262	16	64	26	7	143	554	108	87	.371
Anderson, G.	Cal	.321	16	69	6	2	106	374	50	19	.352

AL Batter	Team	BA	HR	RBI	SB	CS	G	AB	R	BB	OBP
Baerga, C.	Cle	.314	15	90	11	2	135	557	87	35	.355
Baines, H.	Bal	.299	24	63	0	2	127	385	60	70	.403
Barberie, B.	Bal	.241	2	25	3	3	90	237	32	36	.351
Bass, K.	Bal	.244	5	32	8	8	111	295	32	24	.303
Battle, H.	Tor	.200	0	0	1	0	9	15	3	4	.368
Bautista, D.	Det	.203	7	27	4	1	89	271	28	12	.237
Becker, R.	Min	.237	2	33	8	9	106	392	45	34	.303
Bell, D.	Cle	.000	0	0	0	0	2	2	0	0	.000
Bell, J.	Bos	.154	1	2	0	0	17	26	7	2	.207
Belle, A.	Cle	.317	50	126	5	2	143	546	121	73	.401
Beltre, E.	Tex	.217	0	7	0	0	54	92	7	4	.250
Berroa, G.	Oak	.278	22	88	7	4	141	546	87	63	.351
Blowers, M.	Sea	.257	23	96	2	1	134	439	59	53	.335
Boggs, W.	NYA	.324	5	63	1	1	126	460	76	74	.412
Bonilla, B.	Bal	.333	10	46	0	2	61	237	47	23	.392
Borders, P.	KC	.231	4	13	0	0	52	143	14	7	.267
Bordick, M.	Oak	.264	8	44	11	3	126	428	46	35	.325
Brady, D.	ChA	.190	0	3	0	1	12	21	4	2	.261
Bragg, D.	Sea	.234	3	12	9	0	52	145	20	18	.331
Brito, B.	Min	.200	1	1	0	0	5	5	1	0	.333
Brosius, S.	Oak	.262	17	46	4	2	123	389	69	41	.342
Brown, J.	Bal	.148	0	1	1	1	18	27	2	7	.324
Buechele, S.	Tex	.125	0	0	0	0	9	24	0	4	.250
Buford, D.	Bal	.063	0	2	3	1	24	32	6	6	.205
Buhner, J.	Sea	.262	40	121	0	1	126	470	86	60	.343
Burnitz, J.	Cle	.571	0	0	0	0	9	7	4	0	.571
Caceres, E.	KC	.239	1	17	2	2	55	117	13	8	.291
Cameron, M.	ChA	.184	1	2	0	0	28	38	4	3	.244
Canseco, J.	Bos	.306	24	81	4	0	102	396	64	42	.378
Carter, J.	Tor	.253	25	76	12	1	139	558	70	37	.300
Cedeno, D.	Tor	.236	4	14	0	1	51	161	18	10	.289
Chamberlain, W.	Bos	.119	1	1	1	0	19	42	4	3	.178
Cirillo, J.	Mil	.277	9	39	7	2	125	328	57	47	.371
Clark, J.	Min	.339	3	15	3	0	36	109	17	2	.354
Clark, T.	Det	.238	3	11	0	0	27	101	10	8	.294
Clark, W.	Tex	.302	16	92	0	1	123	454	85	68	.389
Cole, A.	Min	.342	1	14	1	3	28	79	10	8	.409
Coleman, V.	KC	.287	4	20	26	9	75	293	39	27	.348
Coleman, V.	Sea	.290	1	9	16	7	40	162	27	10	.335
Cookson, B.	KC	.143	0	5	1	0	22	35	2	2	.189
Coomer, R.	Min	.257	5	19	0	1	37	101	15	9	.324
Cora, J.	Sea	.297	3	39	18	7	120	427	64	37	.359
Cordova, M.	Min	.277	24	84	20	7	137	512	81	52	.352
Correia, R.	Cal	.238	0	3	0	0	14	21	3	0	.238
Cruz, F.	Oak	.217	0	5	1	1	8	23	0	3	.286
Curtis, C.	Det	.268	21	67	27	15	144	586	96	70	.349
Cuyler, M.	Det	.205	0	5	2	1	41	88	15	8	.271
Dalesandro, M.	Cal	.100	0	0	0	0	11	10	1	0	.100
Damon, J.	KC	.282	3	23	7	0	47	188	32	12	.324
Davis, C.	Cal	.318	20	86	3	3	119	424	81	89	.429
Davis, R.	NYA	.276	2	12	0	0	40	98	14	10	.349
Delgado, C.	Tor	.165	3	11	0	0	37	91	7	6	.212
Devarez, C.	Bal	.000	0	0	0	0	6	4	0	0	.000
Devereaux, M.	ChA	.306	10	55	6	6	92	333	48	25	.352
Diaz, A.	Sea	.248	3	27	18	8	103	270	44	13	.286
DiSarcina, G.	Cal	.307	5	41	7	4	99	362	61	20	.344

AL Batter	Team	BA	HR	RBI	SB	CS	G	AB	R	BB	OBP
Donnels, C.	Bos	.253	2	11	0	0	40	91	13	9	.317
Dunn, S.	Min	.000	0	0	0	0	5	6	0	1	.000
Durham, R.	ChA	.257	7	51	18	5	125	471	68	31	.309
Easley, D.	Cal	.216	4	35	5	2	114	357	35	32	.288
Edmonds, J.	Cal	.290	33	107	1	4	141	558	120	51	.352
Eenhoorn, R.	NYA	.143	0	2	0	0	5	14	1	1	.200
Elster, K.	NYA	.118	0	0	0	0	10	17	1	1	.167
Espinoza, A.	Cle	.252	2	17	0	2	66	143	15	2	.264
Fabregas, J.	Cal	.247	1	22	0	2	73	227	24	17	.298
Fermin, F.	Sea	.195	0	15	2	0	73	200	21	6	.232
Fernandez, T.	NYA	.245	5	45	6	6	108	384	57	42	.322
Fielder, C.	Det	.243	31	82	0	1	136	494	70	75	.346
Flaherty, J.	Det	.243	11	40	0	0	112	354	39	18	.284
Fletcher, S.	Det	.231	1	17	1	0	67	182	19	19	.312
Flora, K.	Cal	.000	0	0	0	0	2	1	1	0	.000
Fox, E.	Tex	.000	0	0	0	0	10	15	2	3	.000
Frazier, L.	Tex	.212	0	8	9	1	49	99	19	7	.278
Frye, J.	Tex	.278	4	29	3	3	90	313	38	24	.335
Fryman, T.	Det	.275	15	81	4	2	144	567	79	63	.347
Gaetti, G.	KC	.261	35	96	3	3	137	514	76	47	.329
Gagne, G.	KC	.256	6	49	3	5	120	430	58	38	.316
Gallagher, D.	Cal	.188	0	0	0	0	11	16	1	2	.278
Gallego, M.	Oak	.233	0	8	0	1	43	120	11	9	.292
Gates, B.	Oak	.254	5	56	3	3	136	524	60	46	.308
Giambi, J.	Oak	.256	6	25	2	1	54	176	27	28	.364
Gibson, K.	Det	.260	9	35	9	2	70	227	37	33	.358
Gil, B.	Tex	.219	9	46	2	4	130	415	36	26	.266
Giles, B.	Cle	.556	1	3	0	0	6	9	6	0	.556
Gomez, C.	Det	.223	11	50	4	1	123	431	49	41	.292
Gomez, L.	Bal	.236	4	12	0	1	53	127	16	18	.336
Gonzales, R.	Cal	.333	1	3	0	0	30	18	1	0	.333
Gonzalez, A.	Tor	.243	10	42	4	4	111	367	51	44	.322
Gonzalez, J.	Tex	.295	27	82	0	0	90	352	57	17	.324
Goodwin, C.	Bal	.263	1	24	22	4	87	289	40	15	.301
Goodwin, T.	KC	.287	4	28	50	18	133	480	72	38	.346
Grebeck, C.	ChA	.260	1	18	0	0	53	154	19	21	.360
Green, S.	Tor	.288	15	54	1	2	121	379	52	20	.326
Greenwell, M.	Bos	.297	15	76	9	5	120	481	67	38	.349
Greer, R.	Tex	.271	13	61	3	1	131	417	58	55	.355
Griffey Jr, K.	Sea	.258	17	42	4	2	72	260	52	52	.379
Grotewold, J.	KC	.278	1	6	0	0	15	36	4	9	.422
Guillen, O.	ChA	.248	1	41	6	7	122	415	50	13	.270
Hale, C.	Min	.262	2	18	0	0	69	103	10	11	.333
Hall, J.	Det	.133	0	0	0	0	7	15	2	2	.235
Hamelin, B.	KC	.168	7	25	0	1	72	208	20	26	.278
Hamilton, D.	Mil	.271	5	44	11	1	112	398	54	47	.350
Hammonds, J.	Bal	.242	4	23	4	2	57	178	18	9	.279
Hare, S.	Tex	.250	0	2	0	0	18	24	2	4	.357
Harper, B.	Oak	.000	0	0	0	0	2	7	0	0	.000
Haselman, B.	Bos	.243	5	23	0	2	64	152	22	17	.322
Hatcher, B.	Tex	.083	0	0	0	0	6	12	2	1	.154
Hatteberg, S.	Bos	.500	0	0	0	0	2	2	1	0	.500
Helfand, E.	Oak	.163	0	7	0	0	38	86	9	11	.265
Henderson, R.	Oak	.300	9	54	32	10	112	407	67	72	.407

AL Batter	Team	BA	HR	RBI	SB	CS	G	AB	R	BB	OBP
Herrera, J.	Oak	.243	0	2	1	3	33	70	9	6	.299
Hiatt, P.	KC	.204	4	12	1	0	52	113	11	9	.262
Higginson, B.	Det	.224	14	43	6	4	131	410	61	62	.329
Hocking, D.	Min	.200	0	3	1	0	9	25	4	2	.259
Hoiles, C.	Bal	.250	19	58	1	0	114	352	53	67	.373
Hollins, D.	Bos	.154	0	1	0	0	5	13	2	4	.353
Horn, S.	Tex	.111	0	0	0	0	11	9	0	1	.200
Hosey, D.	Bos	.338	3	7	6	0	24	68	20	8	.408
Howard, D.	KC	.243	0	19	6	1	95	255	23	24	.310
Hudler, R.	Cal	.265	6	27	13	0	84	223	30	10	.310
Huff, M.	Tor	.232	1	9	1	1	61	138	14	22	.337
Hulse, D.	Mil	.251	3	47	15	3	119	339	46	18	.285
Huson, J.	Bal	.248	1	19	5	4	66	161	24	15	.315
Ingram, R.	Min	.125	0	1	0	0	4	8	0	2	.300
Jaha, J.	Mil	.313	20	65	2	1	88	316	59	36	.389
James, C.	Bos	.167	0	1	0	0	16	24	2	1	.200
James, C.	KC	.310	2	7	1	0	26	58	6	6	.373
James, D.	NYA	.287	2	26	4	1	85	209	22	20	.346
Javier, S.	Oak	.278	8	56	36	5	130	442	81	49	.353
Jefferson, R.	Bos	.289	5	26	0	0	46	121	21	9	.333
Jeter, D.	NYA	.250	0	7	0	0	15	48	5	3	.294
Johnson, L.	ChA	.306	10	57	40	6	142	607	98	32	.341
Jose, F.	KC	.133	0	1	0	0	9	30	2	2	.188
Joyner, W.	KC	.310	12	83	3	2	131	465	69	69	.394
Karkovice, R.	ChA	.217	13	51	2	3	113	323	44	39	.306
Kelly, P.	NYA	.237	4	29	8	3	89	270	32	23	.307
Kirby, W.	Cle	.207	1	14	10	3	101	188	29	13	.260
Knoblauch, C.	Min	.333	11	63	46	18	136	538	107	78	.424
Knorr, R.	Tor	.212	3	16	0	0	45	132	18	11	.273
Kreuter, C.	Sea	.227	1	8	0	0	26	75	12	5	.293
Kruk, J.	ChA	.308	2	23	0	1	45	159	13	26	.399
LaValliere, M.	ChA	.245	1	19	0	0	46	98	7	9	.303
Lawton, M.	Min	.317	1	12	1	1	21	60	11	7	.414
Leius, S.	Min	.247	4	45	2	1	117	372	51	49	.335
Levis, J.	Cle	.333	0	3	0	0	12	18	1	1	.333
Leyritz, J.	NYA	.269	7	37	1	1	77	264	37	37	.374
Lind, J.	Cal	.163	0	1	0	0	15	43	5	3	.217
Lind, J.	KC	.268	0	6	0	1	29	97	4	3	.290
Listach, P.	Mil	.219	0	25	13	3	101	334	35	25	.276
Lockhart, K.	KC	.321	6	33	8	1	94	274	41	14	.355
Lofton, K.	Cle	.310	7	53	54	15	118	481	93	40	.362
Loretta, M.	Mil	.260	1	3	1	1	19	50	13	4	.327
Lyons, B.	ChA	.266	5	16	0	0	27	64	8	4	.304
Maas, K.	Min	.193	1	5	0	0	22	57	5	7	.281
Macfarlane, M.	Bos	.225	15	51	2	1	115	364	45	38	.319
Mahay, R.	Bos	.200	1	3	0	0	5	20	3	1	.273
Maldonado, C.	Tex	.233	2	5	0	1	13	30	6	7	.378
Maldonado, C.	Tor	.269	7	25	1	1	61	160	22	25	.368
Manto, J.	Bal	.256	17	38	0	3	89	254	31	24	.325
Martin, N.	ChA	.269	2	17	5	0	72	160	17	3	.281
Martinez, C.	Cal	.180	1	9	0	0	26	61	7	6	.265
Martinez, D.	ChA	.307	5	37	8	2	118	303	49	32	.371
Martinez, E.	Sea	.356	29	113	4	3	145	511	121	116	.479

FINAL 1995 AVERAGES •

AL Batter	Team	BA	HR	RBI	SB	CS	G	AB	R	BB	OBP
Martinez, S.	Tor	.241	2	25	0	0	62	191	12	7	.270
Martinez, T.	Sea	.293	31	111	0	0	141	519	92	62	.369
Marzano, J.	Tex	.333	0	0	0	0	2	6	1	0	.333
Masteller, D.	Min	.237	3	21	1	2	71	198	21	18	.303
Matheny, M.	Mil	.247	0	21	2	1	80	166	13	12	.306
Mattingly, D.	NYA	.288	7	49	0	2	128	458	59	40	.341
May, D.	Mil	.248	1	9	0	1	32	113	15	5	.286
Mayne, B.	KC	.251	1	27	0	1	110	307	23	25	.313
McCarty, D.	Min	.218	0	4	0	1	25	55	10	4	.279
McGee, W.	Bos	.285	2	15	5	2	67	200	32	9	.311
McGinnis, R.	KC	.000	0	0	0	0	3	5	1	1	.000
McGwire, M.	Oak	.274	39	90	1	1	104	317	75	88	.441
McLemore, M.	Tex	.261	5	41	21	11	129	467	73	59	.346
Meares, P.	Min	.269	12	49	10	4	116	390	57	15	.311
Mercedes, H.	KC	.256	0	9	0	0	23	43	7	8	.370
Merullo, M.	Min	.282	1	27	0	1	76	195	19	14	.335
Mieske, M.	Mil	.251	12	48	2	4	117	267	42	27	.323
Miller, K.	KC	.333	1	3	0	0	9	15	2	2	.412
Molitor, P.	Tor	.270	15	60	12	0	130	525	63	61	.350
Mota, J.	KC	.000	0	0	0	0	2	2	0	0	.000
Mouton, L.	ChA	.302	5	27	1	0	58	179	23	19	.373
Munoz, P.	Min	.301	18	58	0	3	104	376	45	19	.338
Murray, E.	Cle	.323	21	82	5	1	113	436	68	39	.375
Myers, G.	Cal	.260	9	38	0	1	85	273	35	17	.304
Naehring, T.	Bos	.307	10	57	0	2	126	433	61	77	.415
Nevin, P.	Det	.219	2	12	0	0	29	96	9	11	.318
Newfield, M.	Sea	.188	3	14	0	0	24	85	7	3	.225
Newson, W.	ChA	.235	3	9	1	1	51	85	19	23	.404
Newson, W.	Sea	.292	2	6	1	0	33	72	15	16	.420
Nilsson, D.	Mil	.278	12	53	2	0	81	263	41	24	.337
Nixon, O.	Tex	.295	0	45	50	21	139	589	87	58	.357
Nokes, M.	Bal	.122	2	6	0	0	26	49	4	4	.185
Norman, L.	KC	.225	0	4	0	1	24	40	6	6	.326
Nunnally, J.	KC	.244	14	42	6	4	119	303	51	51	.357
O'Leary, T.	Bos	.308	10	49	5	3	112	399	60	29	.355
O'Neill, P.	NYA	.300	22	96	1	2	127	460	82	71	.387
Obando, S.	Bal	.263	0	3	1	0	16	38	0	2	.293
Olerud, J.	Tor	.291	8	54	0	0	135	492	72	84	.398
Oliver, J.	Mil	.273	12	51	2	4	97	337	43	27	.332
Ortiz, L.	Tex	.231	1	18	0	1	41	108	10	6	.270
Owen, S.	Cal	.229	1	28	3	2	82	218	17	18	.288
Pagliarulo, M.	Tex	.232	4	27	0	0	86	241	27	15	.277
Palmeiro, O.	Cal	.350	0	1	0	0	15	20	3	1	.381
Palmeiro, R.	Bal	.310	39	104	3	1	143	554	89	62	.380
Palmer, D.	Tex	.336	9	24	1	1	36	119	30	21	.448
Paquette, C.	Oak	.226	13	49	5	2	105	283	42	12	.256
Parrish, L.	Tor	.202	4	22	0	0	70	178	15	15	.265
Pemberton, R.	Det	.300	0	3	0	0	12	30	3	1	.344
Pena, T.	Cle	.262	5	28	1	0	91	263	25	14	.302
Penn, S.	Det	.333	0	0	0	0	3	9	0	1	.400
Perez, E.	Cal	.169	1	7	0	2	29	71	9	12	.302
Perez, R.	Tor	.188	1	3	0	0	17	48	2	0	.188
Perez, T.	Tor	.245	1	8	0	1	41	98	12	7	.292
Perry, H.	Cle	.315	3	23	1	3	52	162	23	13	.376
Phillips, T.	Cal	.261	27	61	13	10	139	525	119	113	.394

• FINAL 1995 AVERAGES

AL Batter	Team	BA	HR	RBI	SB	CS	G	AB	R	BB	OBP
Pirkl, G.	Sea	.235	0	0	0	0	10	17	2	1	.278
Polonia, L.	NYA	.261	2	15	10	4	67	238	37	25	.326
Posada, J.	NYA	.000	0	0	0	0	1	0	0	0	.000
Pozo, A.	Sea	.000	0	0	0	0	1	1	0	0	.000
Puckett, K.	Min	.314	23	99	3	2	137	538	83	56	.379
Raabe, B.	Min	.214	0	1	0	0	6	14	4	1	.267
Raines, T.	ChA	.285	12	67	13	2	133	502	81	70	.374
Ramirez, M.	Cle	.308	31	107	6	6	137	484	85	75	.402
Randa, J.	KC	.171	1	5	0	1	34	70	6	6	.237
Reboulet, J.	Min	.292	4	23	1	2	87	216	39	27	.373
Rhodes, K.	Bos	.080	0	1	0	0	10	25	2	3	.179
Ripken, B.	Cle	.412	2	3	0	0	8	17	4	0	.412
Ripken, C.	Bal	.262	17	88	0	1	144	550	71	52	.324
Rivera, R.	NYA	.000	0	0	0	0	5	1	0	0	.000
Rodriguez, A.	Sea	.232	5	19	4	2	48	142	15	6	.264
Rodriguez, C.	Bos	.333	0	5	0	0	13	30	5	2	.394
Rodriguez, I.	Tex	.303	12	67	0	2	130	492	56	16	.327
Rodriguez, S.	Bos	.125	0	0	1	0	6	8	1	1	.222
Rodriguez, S.	Det	.194	0	0	1	2	12	31	4	5	.306
Rowland, R.	Bos	.172	0	1	0	0	14	29	1	0	.172
Sabo, C.	ChA	.254	1	8	2	0	20	71	10	3	.295
Salmon, T.	Cal	.330	34	105	5	5	143	537	111	91	.429
Samuel, J.	Det	.281	10	34	5	4	76	171	28	24	.376
Samuel, J.	KC	.176	2	5	1	0	15	34	3	5	.282
Schofield, D.	Cal	.250	0	2	0	0	12	20	1	4	.375
Seitzer, K.	Mil	.311	5	69	2	0	132	492	56	64	.395
Shumpert, T.	Bos	.234	0	3	3	1	21	47	6	4	.294
Sierra, R.	NYA	.260	7	44	1	0	56	215	33	22	.322
Sierra, R.	Oak	.265	12	42	4	4	70	264	40	24	.323
Silvestri, D.	NYA	.095	1	4	0	0	17	21	4	4	.259
Singleton, D.	Mil	.065	0	0	1	0	13	31	0	1	.094
Smith, M.	Bal	.231	3	15	3	0	37	104	11	12	.314
Snopek, C.	ChA	.324	1	7	1	0	22	68	12	9	.403
Snow, J.	Cal	.289	24	102	2	1	143	544	80	52	.353
Sojo, L.	Sea	.289	7	39	4	2	102	339	50	23	.335
Sorrento, P.	Cle	.235	25	79	1	1	104	323	50	51	.336
Sprague, E.	Tor	.244	18	74	0	0	144	521	77	58	.333
Stahoviak, S.	Min	.266	3	23	5	1	94	263	28	30	.341
Stairs, M.	Bos	.261	1	17	0	1	39	88	8	4	.298
Stanley, M.	NYA	.268	18	83	1	1	118	399	63	57	.360
Steinbach, T.	Oak	.278	15	65	1	3	114	406	43	25	.322
Steverson, T.	Det	.262	2	6	2	0	30	42	11	6	.340
Stewart, S.	Tor	.211	0	1	2	0	12	38	2	5	.318
Strange, D.	Sea	.271	2	21	0	3	74	155	19	10	.323
Strawberry, D.	NYA	.276	3	13	0	0	32	87	15	10	.364
Stubbs, F.	Det	.250	2	19	0	1	62	116	13	19	.358
Stynes, C.	KC	.171	0	2	0	0	22	35	7	4	.256
Surhoff, B.	Mil	.320	13	73	7	3	117	415	72	37	.378
Sweeney, M.	KC	.250	0	0	0	0	4	4	1	0	.250
Tartabull, D.	NYA	.224	6	28	0	0	59	192	25	33	.335
Tartabull, D.	Oak	.261	2	7	0	2	24	88	9	10	.337
Tettleton, M.	Tex	.238	32	78	0	0	134	429	76	107	.396
Thomas, F.	ChA	.308	40	111	3	2	145	493	102	136	.454
Thome, J.	Cle	.314	25	73	4	3	137	452	92	97	.438
Thurman, G.	Sea	.320	0	3	5	2	13	25	3	1	.333

AL Batter	Team	BA	HR	RBI	SB	CS	G	AB	R	BB	OBP
Tingley, R.	Det	.226	4	18	0	1	54	124	14	15	.307
Tinsley, L.	Bos	.284	7	41	18	8	100	341	61	39	.359
Tomberlin, A.	Oak	.212	4	10	4	1	46	85	15	5	.256
Trammell, A.	Det	.269	2	23	3	1	74	223	28	27	.345
Tremie, C.	ChA	.167	0	0	0	0	10	24	0	1	.200
Tucker, M.	KC	.260	4	17	2	3	62	177	23	18	.332
Tucker, S.	Cle	.000	0	0	0	0	17	20	2	5	.000
Turner, C.	Cal	.100	0	1	0	0	5	10	0	0	.100
Unroe, T.	Mil	.250	0	0	0	0	2	4	0	0	.250
Valentin, J.	Bos	.298	27	102	20	5	135	520	108	81	.399
Valentin, J.	Mil	.219	11	49	16	8	112	338	62	37	.293
Valle, D.	Tex	.240	0	5	1	0	36	75	7	6	.305
Van Slyke, A.	Bal	.159	3	8	0	0	17	63	6	5	.221
Vaughn, G.	Mil	.224	17	59	10	4	108	392	67	55	.317
Vaughn, M.	Bos	.300	39	126	11	4	140	550	98	68	.388
Velarde, R.	NYA	.278	7	46	5	1	111	367	60	55	.375
Ventura, R.	ChA	.295	26	93	4	3	135	492	79	75	.384
Vina, F.	Mil	.257	3	29	6	3	113	288	46	22	.327
Vitiello, J.	KC	.254	7	21	0	0	53	130	13	8	.317
Vizquel, O.	Cle	.266	6	56	29	11	136	542	87	59	.333
Voigt, J.	Bal	1.000	0	0	0	0	3	1	1	0	1.000
Voigt, J.	Tex	.161	2	8	0	0	33	62	8	10	.274
Walbeck, M.	Min	.257	1	44	3	1	115	393	40	25	.302
Ward, T.	Mil	.264	4	16	6	1	44	129	19	14	.338
Whitaker, L.	Det	.293	14	44	4	0	84	249	36	31	.372
White, D.	Det	.188	0	2	1	0	39	48	3	0	.188
White, D.	Tor	.283	10	53	11	2	101	427	61	29	.334
Whiten, M.	Bos	.185	1	10	1	0	32	108	13	8	.239
Widger, C.	Sea	.200	1	2	0	0	23	45	2	3	.245
Williams, B.	NYA	.307	18	82	8	6	144	563	93	75	.392
Williams, G.	Oak	.291	3	14	0	0	29	79	13	11	.383
Williams, G.	NYA	.247	6	28	4	2	100	182	33	22	.327
Wilson, D.	Sea	.278	9	51	2	1	119	399	40	33	.336
Winfield, D.	Cle	.191	2	4	1	0	46	115	11	14	.285
Worthington, C.	Tex	.221	2	6	0	0	26	68	4	7	.293
Young, E.	Oak	.200	2	5	0	0	26	50	9	8	.310
Zaun, G.	Bal	.260	3	14	1	1	40	104	18	16	.358

AMERICAN LEAGUE: PITCHERS

AL Pitcher	Team	W	L	SV	ERA	Ratio	GS	IP	H	BB	K
Abbott, J.	Cal	5	4	0	4.15	1.453	13	84.2	93	29	41
Abbott, J.	ChA	6	4	0	3.36	1.353	17	112.1	116	35	45
Acre, M.	Oak	1	2	0	5.71	1.577	0	52.0	52	28	47
Aguilera, R.	Bos	2	2	20	2.67	1.088	0	30.1	26	7	23
Aguilera, R.	Min	1	1	12	2.52	1.080	0	25.0	20	6	29
Ahearne, P.	Det	0	2	0	11.70	2.500	3	10.0	20	5	4
Alberro, J.	Tex	0	0	0	7.40	1.887	0	20.2	26	12	10
Alvarez, W.	ChA	8	11	0	4.32	1.520	29	175.0	171	93	118
Anderson, B.	Cal	6	8	0	5.87	1.435	17	99.2	110	30	45
Anderson, S.	KC	1	0	0	5.33	1.500	4	25.1	29	8	6
Andujar, L.	ChA	2	1	0	3.26	1.352	5	30.1	26	14	9

AL Pitcher	Team	W	L	SV	ERA	Ratio	GS	IP	H	BB	K
Appier, K.	KC	15	10	0	3.89	1.247	31	201.1	163	80	185
Assenmacher, P.	Cle	6	2	0	2.82	1.226	0	38.1	32	12	40
Ausanio, J.	NYA	2	0	1	5.73	1.726	0	37.2	42	23	36
Ayala, B.	Sea	6	5	19	4.44	1.535	0	71.0	73	30	77
Baker, S.	Oak	0	0	0	9.82	3.000	0	3.2	5	5	3
Baldwin, J.	ChA	0	1	0	12.89	2.795	4	14.2	32	9	10
Bankhead, S.	NYA	1	1	0	6.00	1.538	1	39.0	44	16	20
Bark, B.	Bos	0	0	0	0.00	1.286	0	2.1	2	1	0
Belcher, T.	Sea	10	12	0	4.52	1.567	28	179.1	188	88	96
Belinda, S.	Bos	8	1	10	3.10	1.191	0	69.2	51	28	57
Benes, A.	Sea	7	2	0	5.86	1.698	12	63.0	72	33	45
Benitez, A.	Bal	1	5	2	5.66	1.657	0	47.2	37	37	56
Bennett, E.	Cal	0	0	0	0.00	0.000	0	0.1	0	0	0
Bere, J.	ChA	8	15	0	7.19	1.910	27	137.2	151	106	110
Bergman, S.	Det	7	10	0	5.12	1.773	28	135.1	169	67	86
Bertotti, M.	ChA	1	1	0	12.56	2.581	4	14.1	23	11	15
Bielecki, M.	Cal	4	6	0	5.97	1.513	11	75.1	80	31	45
Black, B.	Cle	4	2	0	6.85	1.669	10	47.1	63	16	34
Blomdahl, B.	Det	0	0	1	7.77	2.014	0	24.1	36	13	15
Boehringer, B.	NYA	0	3	0	13.75	2.660	3	17.2	24	22	10
Boever, J.	Det	5	7	3	6.39	1.774	0	98.2	128	44	71
Bohanon, B.	Det	1	1	1	5.54	1.571	10	105.2	121	41	63
Bolton, R.	ChA	0	2	0	8.18	2.136	3	22.0	33	14	10
Bones, R.	Mil	10	12	0	4.63	1.522	31	200.1	218	83	77
Borowski, J.	Bal	0	0	0	1.23	1.227	0	7.1	5	4	3
Bosio, C.	Sea	10	8	0	4.92	1.676	31	170.0	211	69	85
Boskie, S.	Cal	7	7	0	5.64	1.424	20	111.2	127	25	51
Brandenburg, M.	Tex	0	1	0	5.93	1.610	0	27.1	36	7	21
Brewer, B.	KC	2	4	0	5.56	1.676	0	45.1	54	20	31
Briscoe, J.	Oak	0	1	0	8.35	2.618	0	18.1	25	21	19
Bronkey, J.	Mil	0	0	0	3.65	1.703	0	12.1	15	6	5
Brown, K.	Bal	10	9	0	3.60	1.230	26	172.1	155	48	117
Browning, T.	KC	0	2	0	8.10	1.800	2	10.0	13	5	3
Bunch, M.	KC	1	3	0	5.63	1.400	5	40.0	42	14	19
Burrows, T.	Tex	2	2	1	6.45	1.813	3	44.2	60	19	22
Butcher, M.	Cal	6	1	0	4.73	1.578	0	51.1	49	31	29
Campbell, K.	Min	0	0	0	4.66	1.345	0	9.2	8	5	5
Carmona, R.	Sea	2	4	1	5.66	1.909	3	47.2	55	34	28
Carrara, G.	Tor	2	4	0	7.21	1.849	7	48.2	64	25	27
Castillo, T.	Tor	1	5	13	3.22	1.252	0	72.2	64	24	38
Charlton, N.	Sea	2	1	14	1.51	0.839	0	47.2	23	16	58
Christopher, M.	Det	4	0	1	3.82	1.418	0	61.1	71	14	34
Clark, M.	Cle	9	7	0	5.27	1.516	21	124.2	143	42	68
Clark, T.	Bal	2	5	1	3.46	1.436	0	39.0	40	15	18
Clemens, R.	Bos	10	5	0	4.18	1.536	23	140.0	141	60	132
Cone, D.	NYA	9	2	0	3.82	1.313	13	99.0	82	47	89
Cone, D.	Tor	9	6	0	3.38	1.220	17	130.1	113	41	102
Converse, J.	KC	1	0	0	5.84	1.622	0	12.1	12	8	5
Converse, J.	Sea	0	3	1	7.36	2.182	1	11.0	16	8	9
Cook, D.	Cle	0	0	0	6.39	2.132	0	12.2	16	10	13
Cook, D.	Tex	0	2	2	4.00	1.422	1	45.0	47	16	40
Cormier, R.	Bos	7	5	0	4.07	1.435	12	115.0	131	31	69
Cornett, B.	Tor	0	0	0	9.00	2.600	0	5.0	9	3	4
Corsi, J.	Oak	2	4	2	2.20	1.311	0	45.0	31	26	26
Cox, D.	Tor	1	3	0	7.40	2.022	0	45.0	57	33	38
Crabtree, T.	Tor	0	2	0	3.09	1.406	0	32.0	30	13	21

AL Pitcher	Team	W	L	SV	ERA	Ratio	GS	IP	H	BB	K
Cummings, J.	Sea	0	0	0	11.81	2.813	0	5.1	8	7	4
Darling, R.	Oak	4	7	0	6.23	1.673	21	104.0	124	46	69
Darwin, D.	Tex	2	2	0	7.15	1.412	4	34.0	40	7	22
Darwin, D.	Tor	1	8	0	7.62	1.815	11	65.0	91	24	36
Davis, T.	Sea	2	1	0	6.38	2.000	5	24.0	30	18	19
Davison, S.	Sea	0	0	0	6.23	1.846	0	4.1	7	1	3
Dedrick, J.	Bal	0	0	0	2.35	1.957	0	7.2	8	6	3
DeLeon, J.	ChA	5	3	0	5.19	1.389	0	67.2	60	28	53
DeSilva, J.	Bal	1	0	0	7.27	1.846	2	8.2	8	7	1
Dettmer, J.	Tex	0	0	0	27.00	6.000	0	0.1	2	0	0
Dibble, R.	ChA	0	1	1	6.28	2.581	0	14.1	7	27	16
Dibble, R.	Mil	1	1	0	8.25	2.333	0	12.0	9	19	10
Doherty, J.	Det	5	9	6	5.10	1.531	2	113.0	130	37	46
Eckersley, D.	Oak	4	6	29	4.83	1.291	0	50.1	53	11	40
Eddy, C.	Oak	0	0	0	7.36	3.000	0	3.2	7	2	2
Edenfield, K.	Cal	0	0	0	4.26	1.579	0	12.2	15	5	6
Eiland, D.	NYA	1	1	0	6.30	2.000	1	10.0	16	3	6
Eldred, C.	Mil	1	1	0	3.42	1.479	4	23.2	24	10	18
Embree, A.	Cle	3	2	1	5.11	1.581	0	24.2	23	16	23
Erickson, S.	Bal	9	4	0	3.89	1.353	16	108.2	111	35	61
Erickson, S.	Min	4	6	0	5.95	1.574	15	87.2	102	32	45
Eshelman, V.	Bos	6	3	0	4.85	1.506	14	81.2	86	36	41
Fajardo, H.	Tex	0	0	0	7.80	1.667	0	15.0	19	5	9
Farrell, J.	Cle	0	0	0	3.86	1.500	0	4.2	7	0	4
Fermin, R.	Oak	0	0	0	13.50	3.750	0	1.1	4	1	0
Fernandez, A.	ChA	12	8	0	3.80	1.301	30	203.2	200	65	159
Fernandez, S.	Bal	0	4	0	7.39	1.893	7	28.0	36	17	31
Fetters, M.	Mil	0	3	22	3.38	1.731	0	34.2	40	20	33
Finley, C.	Cal	15	12	0	4.21	1.438	32	203.0	192	93	195
Fleming, D.	KC	0	1	0	3.66	1.500	5	32.0	27	19	14
Fleming, D.	Sea	1	5	0	7.50	1.896	7	48.0	57	34	26
Fortugno, T.	ChA	1	3	0	5.59	1.267	0	38.2	30	19	24
Frey, S.	Sea	0	3	0	4.76	2.029	0	11.1	16	6	7
Gardiner, M.	Det	0	0	0	14.59	2.351	0	12.1	27	2	7
Givens, B.	Mil	5	7	0	4.95	1.612	19	107.1	116	54	73
Gohr, G.	Det	1	0	0	0.87	1.161	0	10.1	9	3	12
Gordon, T.	KC	12	12	0	4.43	1.571	31	189.0	204	89	119
Grimsley, J.	Cle	0	0	1	6.09	2.088	2	34.0	37	32	25
Groom, B.	Det	1	3	1	7.52	2.041	4	40.2	55	26	23
Gross, K.	Tex	9	15	0	5.54	1.617	30	183.2	200	89	106
Guardado, E.	Min	4	9	2	5.12	1.577	5	91.1	99	45	71
Gubicza, M.	KC	12	14	0	3.75	1.359	33	213.1	222	62	81
Guetterman, L.	Sea	0	0	1	6.88	2.059	0	17.0	21	11	11
Gunderson, E.	Bos	2	1	0	5.11	1.946	0	12.1	13	9	9
Guthrie, M.	Min	5	3	0	4.46	1.512	0	42.1	47	16	48
Guzman, J.	Tor	4	14	0	6.32	1.677	24	135.1	151	73	94
Habyan, J.	Cal	1	2	0	4.13	1.500	0	32.2	36	12	25
Hall, D.	Tor	0	2	3	4.41	1.837	0	16.1	21	9	11
Hammaker, A.	ChA	0	0	0	12.79	3.158	0	6.1	11	8	3
Haney, C.	KC	3	4	0	3.65	1.389	13	81.1	78	33	31
Hanson, E.	Bos	15	5	0	4.24	1.323	29	186.2	187	59	139
Harikkala, T.	Sea	0	0	0	16.20	2.400	0	3.1	7	1	1
Harkey, M.	Cal	4	3	0	4.55	1.582	8	61.1	80	16	28

AL Pitcher	Team	W	L	SV	ERA	Ratio	GS	IP	H	BB	K
Harkey, M.	Oak	4	6	0	6.27	1.652	12	66.0	75	31	28
Harris, G.	Bal	0	0	0	4.50	1.250	0	4.0	4	1	4
Harris, G.	Min	0	5	0	8.82	2.020	6	32.2	50	16	21
Hartley, M.	Bal	1	0	0	1.29	0.857	0	7.0	5	1	4
Hartley, M.	Bos	0	0	0	9.00	1.714	0	7.0	8	2	2
Hawkins, L.	Min	2	3	0	8.67	1.926	6	27.0	39	12	9
Haynes, J.	Bal	2	1	0	2.25	0.958	3	24.0	11	12	22
Helling, R.	Tex	0	2	0	6.57	2.189	3	12.1	17	8	5
Henneman, M.	Det	0	1	18	1.53	1.125	0	29.1	24	9	24
Henry, D.	Det	1	0	5	6.23	2.423	0	8.2	11	10	9
Hentgen, P.	Tor	10	14	0	5.11	1.650	30	200.2	236	90	135
Heredia, W.	Tex	0	1	0	3.75	2.000	0	12.0	9	15	6
Hernandez, R.	ChA	3	7	32	3.92	1.575	0	59.2	63	28	84
Hershiser, O.	Cle	16	6	0	3.87	1.237	26	167.1	151	51	111
Hill, K.	Cle	4	1	0	3.98	1.473	11	74.2	77	32	48
Hitchcock, S.	NYA	11	10	0	4.70	1.354	27	168.1	155	68	121
Holzemer, M.	Cal	0	1	0	5.40	2.280	0	8.1	11	7	5
Honeycutt, R.	NYA	0	0	0	27.00	3.000	0	1.0	2	1	0
Honeycutt, R.	Oak	5	1	2	2.42	1.052	0	44.2	37	9	21
Horsman, V.	Min	0	0	0	7.00	1.778	0	9.0	12	4	4
Howard, C.	Tex	0	0	0	0.00	1.000	0	4.0	3	1	2
Howe, S.	NYA	6	3	2	4.96	1.776	0	49.0	66	17	28
Hudson, J.	Bos	0	1	1	4.11	1.696	0	46.0	53	23	29
Huisman, R.	KC	0	0	0	7.45	1.552	0	9.2	14	1	12
Hurtado, E.	Tor	5	2	0	5.45	1.622	10	77.2	81	40	33
Ignasiak, M.	Mil	4	1	0	5.90	1.916	0	39.2	51	23	26
Jacome, J.	KC	4	6	0	5.36	1.464	14	84.0	101	21	39
James, M.	Cal	3	0	1	3.88	1.401	0	55.2	49	26	36
Johns, D.	Oak	5	3	0	4.61	1.372	9	54.2	44	26	25
Johnson, R.	Sea	18	2	0	2.48	1.073	30	214.1	159	65	294
Johnston, J.	Bos	0	1	0	11.25	1.500	0	4.0	2	3	4
Jones, D.	Bal	0	4	22	5.01	1.564	0	46.2	55	16	42
Jordan, R.	Tor	1	0	1	6.60	2.200	0	15.0	18	13	10
Kamieniecki, S.	NYA	7	6	0	4.01	1.506	16	89.2	83	49	43
Karchner, M.	ChA	4	2	0	1.69	1.438	0	32.0	33	12	24
Karl, S.	Mil	6	7	0	4.14	1.565	18	124.0	141	50	59
Key, J.	NYA	1	2	0	5.64	1.516	5	30.1	40	6	14
Keyser, B.	ChA	5	6	0	4.97	1.549	10	92.1	114	27	48
Kiefer, M.	Mil	4	1	0	3.44	1.289	0	49.2	37	27	41
King, K.	Sea	0	0	0	12.27	2.455	0	3.2	7	1	3
Klingenbeck, S.	Bal	2	2	0	4.88	1.596	5	31.1	32	18	15
Klingenbeck, S.	Min	0	2	0	8.57	2.007	4	48.1	69	24	27
Krivda, R.	Bal	2	7	0	4.54	1.394	13	75.1	76	25	53
Krueger, B.	Sea	2	1	0	5.85	2.050	5	20.0	37	4	10
Langston, M.	Cal	15	7	0	4.63	1.393	31	200.1	212	64	142
Lee, M.	Bal	2	0	1	4.86	1.500	0	33.1	31	18	27
Leiper, D.	Oak	1	1	0	3.57	1.632	0	22.2	23	13	10
Leiter, A.	Tor	11	11	0	3.64	1.508	28	183.0	162	108	153
Lilliquist, D.	Bos	2	1	0	6.26	1.565	0	23.0	27	9	9
Lima, J.	Det	3	9	0	6.11	1.452	15	73.2	85	18	37
Linton, D.	KC	0	1	0	7.25	1.522	2	22.1	22	10	13
Lira, F.	Det	9	13	1	4.31	1.469	22	146.1	151	56	89
Lloyd, G.	Mil	0	5	4	4.50	1.125	0	32.0	28	8	13
Looney, B.	Bos	0	1	0	17.36	3.429	1	4.2	12	4	2

AL Pitcher	Team	W	L	SV	ERA	Ratio	GS	IP	H	BB	K
Lopez, A.	Cle	0	0	0	3.13	1.087	2	23.0	17	7	22
Lorraine, A.	ChA	0	0	0	3.38	0.750	0	8.0	3	2	5
MacDonald, B.	NYA	1	1	0	4.86	1.576	0	46.1	50	22	41
Maddux, M.	Bos	4	1	1	3.61	1.149	4	89.2	86	15	65
Magnante, M.	KC	1	1	0	4.23	1.410	0	44.2	45	16	28
Mahomes, P.	Min	4	10	3	6.37	1.574	7	94.2	100	47	67
Manzanillo, J.	NYA	0	0	0	2.08	1.731	0	17.1	19	9	11
Marquez, I.	ChA	0	1	0	6.75	1.650	0	6.2	9	2	8
Martinez, D.	Cle	12	5	0	3.08	1.241	28	187.0	174	46	99
Maxcy, B.	Det	4	5	0	6.88	1.796	0	52.1	61	31	20
Mcandrew, J.	Mil	2	3	0	4.71	1.376	4	36.1	37	12	19
McCaskill, K.	ChA	6	4	2	4.89	1.667	1	81.0	97	33	50
McDonald, B.	Bal	3	6	0	4.16	1.350	13	80.0	67	38	62
McDowell, J.	NYA	15	10	0	3.93	1.351	30	217.2	211	78	157
McDowell, R.	Tex	7	4	4	4.02	1.482	0	85.0	86	34	49
Meacham, R.	KC	4	3	2	4.98	1.542	0	59.2	72	19	30
Mecir, J.	Sea	0	0	0	0.00	1.500	0	4.2	5	2	3
Menhart, P.	Tor	1	4	0	4.92	1.589	9	78.2	72	47	50
Mercedes, J.	Mil	0	1	0	9.82	2.727	0	7.1	12	8	6
Mesa, J.	Cle	3	0	46	1.13	1.031	0	64.0	49	17	58
Mills, A.	Bal	3	0	0	7.43	2.174	0	23.0	30	18	16
Miranda, A.	Mil	4	5	1	5.23	1.784	10	74.0	83	49	45
Mohler, M.	Oak	1	1	1	3.04	1.437	0	23.2	16	18	15
Monteleone, R.	Cal	1	0	0	2.00	1.222	0	9.0	8	3	5
Montgomery, J.	KC	2	3	31	3.43	1.325	0	65.2	60	25	49
Moore, M.	Det	5	15	0	7.53	1.877	25	132.2	179	68	64
Moyer, J.	Bal	8	6	0	5.21	1.297	18	115.2	117	30	65
Munoz, O.	Min	2	1	0	5.60	1.642	3	35.1	40	17	25
Murray, M.	Bos	0	1	0	18.90	4.200	1	3.1	11	3	1
Mussina, M.	Bal	19	9	0	3.29	1.074	32	221.2	187	50	158
Myers, M.	Det	1	0	0	9.95	2.526	0	6.1	10	4	4
Nagy, C.	Cle	16	6	0	4.55	1.466	29	178.0	194	61	139
Nelson, J.	Sea	7	3	2	2.17	1.157	0	78.2	58	27	96
Nichting, C.	Tex	0	0	0	7.03	2.055	0	24.1	36	13	6
Nitkowski, C.	Det	1	4	0	7.09	1.932	11	39.1	53	20	13
Ogea, C.	Cle	8	3	0	3.05	1.176	14	106.1	95	29	57
Oliver, D.	Tex	4	2	0	4.22	1.633	7	49.0	47	32	39
Olson, G.	Cle	0	0	0	13.50	2.625	0	2.2	5	2	0
Olson, G.	KC	3	3	3	3.26	1.319	0	30.1	23	17	21
Ontiveros, S.	Oak	9	6	0	4.37	1.434	22	129.2	144	38	77
Oquist, M.	Bal	2	1	0	4.17	1.741	0	54.0	51	41	27
Orosco, J.	Bal	2	4	3	3.26	1.128	0	49.2	28	27	58
Parra, J.	Min	1	5	0	7.59	1.735	12	61.2	83	22	29
Patterson, B.	Cal	5	2	0	3.04	1.163	0	53.1	48	13	41
Patterson, J.	NYA	0	0	0	2.70	1.800	0	3.1	3	3	3
Pavlas, D.	NYA	0	0	0	3.18	1.412	0	5.2	8	0	3
Pavlik, R.	Tex	10	10	0	4.37	1.398	31	191.2	174	90	149
Pena, A.	Bos	1	1	0	7.40	1.849	0	24.1	33	12	25
Pennington, B.	Bal	0	1	0	8.10	2.100	0	6.2	3	11	10
Percival, T.	Cal	3	2	3	1.95	0.865	0	74.0	37	26	94
Perez, M.	NYA	5	5	0	5.58	1.471	12	69.1	70	31	44
Pettitte, A.	NYA	12	9	0	4.17	1.411	26	175.0	183	63	114
Phoenix, S.	Oak	0	0	0	32.40	3.600	0	1.2	3	3	3
Pichardo, H.	KC	8	4	1	4.36	1.563	0	64.0	66	30	43

AL Pitcher	Team	W	L	SV	ERA	Ratio	GS	IP	H	BB	K
Pierce, J.	Bos	0	3	0	6.60	2.000	0	15.0	16	14	12
Pittsley, J.	KC	0	0	0	13.50	2.400	1	3.1	7	1	0
Plunk, E.	Cle	6	2	2	2.67	1.234	0	64.0	48	27	71
Poole, J.	Cle	3	3	0	3.75	1.172	0	50.1	40	17	41
Prieto, A.	Oak	2	6	0	4.97	1.621	9	58.0	57	32	37
Radinsky, S.	ChA	2	1	1	5.45	1.658	0	38.0	46	17	14
Radke, B.	Min	11	14	0	5.32	1.359	28	181.0	195	47	75
Rasmussen, D.	KC	0	1	0	9.00	2.100	1	10.0	13	8	6
Reyes, A.	Mil	1	1	1	2.43	1.200	0	33.1	19	18	29
Reyes, C.	Oak	4	6	0	5.09	1.507	1	69.0	71	28	48
Rhodes, A.	Bal	2	5	0	6.21	1.540	9	75.1	68	48	77
Righetti, D.	ChA	3	2	0	4.20	1.682	9	49.1	65	18	29
Rightnowar, R.	Mil	2	1	1	5.40	1.582	0	36.2	35	18	22
Risley, B.	Sea	2	1	1	3.13	1.227	0	60.1	55	18	65
Rivera, M.	NYA	5	3	0	5.51	1.537	10	67.0	71	30	51
Roa, J.	Cle	0	1	0	6.00	1.833	1	6.0	9	2	0
Roberson, S.	Mil	6	4	0	5.76	1.743	13	84.1	102	37	40
Robertson, R.	Min	2	0	0	3.83	1.529	4	51.2	48	31	38
Robinson, K.	Tor	1	2	0	3.69	1.256	0	39.0	25	22	31
Rodriguez, F.	Bos	0	2	0	10.57	2.022	2	15.1	21	10	14
Rodriguez, F.	Min	5	6	0	5.38	1.605	16	90.1	93	47	45
Rogers, J.	Tor	2	4	0	5.70	1.648	0	23.2	21	18	13
Rogers, K.	Tex	17	7	0	3.38	1.298	31	208.0	192	76	140
Ruffcorn, S.	ChA	0	0	0	7.88	3.125	0	8.0	10	13	5
Russell, J.	Tex	1	0	20	3.03	1.378	0	32.2	36	9	21
Ryan, K.	Bos	0	4	7	4.96	1.806	0	32.2	34	24	34
Sanderson, S.	Cal	1	3	0	4.12	1.373	7	39.1	48	4	23
Sanford, M.	Min	0	0	0	5.30	1.821	0	18.2	16	16	17
Scanlan, B.	Mil	4	7	0	6.59	1.824	14	83.1	101	44	29
Schullstrom, E.	Min	0	0	0	6.89	1.894	0	47.0	66	22	21
Sele, A.	Bos	3	1	0	3.06	1.515	6	32.1	32	14	21
Shaw, J.	ChA	0	0	0	6.52	1.448	0	9.2	12	1	6
Shepherd, K.	Bos	0	0	0	36.00	6.000	0	1.0	4	2	0
Shuey, P.	Cle	0	2	0	4.26	1.579	0	6.1	5	5	5
Simas, B.	ChA	1	1	0	2.57	1.857	0	14.0	15	10	16
Sirotka, M.	ChA	1	2	0	4.19	1.631	6	34.1	39	17	19
Slusarski, J.	Mil	1	1	0	5.40	1.933	0	15.0	21	6	6
Smith, L.	Cal	0	5	37	3.47	1.378	0	49.1	42	25	43
Smith, Z.	Bos	8	8	0	5.61	1.518	21	110.2	144	23	47
Sodowsky, C.	Det	2	2	0	5.01	1.800	6	23.1	24	18	14
Sparks, S.	Mil	9	11	0	4.63	1.490	27	202.0	210	86	96
Springer, R.	Cal	1	2	1	6.10	1.742	6	51.2	60	25	38
Stanton, M.	Bos	1	0	0	3.00	1.190	0	21.0	17	8	10
Stevens, D.	Min	5	4	10	5.07	1.629	0	65.2	74	32	47
Stewart, D.	Oak	3	7	0	6.89	1.753	16	81.0	101	39	58
Stottlemyre, T.	Oak	14	7	0	4.55	1.498	31	209.2	228	80	205
Suppan, J.	Bos	1	2	0	5.96	1.500	3	22.2	29	5	19
Tapani, K.	Min	6	11	0	4.92	1.444	20	133.2	155	34	88
Tavarez, J.	Cle	10	2	0	2.44	1.176	0	85.0	76	21	68
Taylor, S.	Tex	1	2	0	9.39	1.957	3	15.1	25	5	10
Tewksbury, B.	Tex	8	7	0	4.58	1.481	21	129.2	169	20	53
Thomas, L.	ChA	0	0	0	1.32	1.024	0	13.2	8	6	12
Thomas, M.	Mil	0	0	0	0.00	2.250	0	1.1	2	1	0
Timlin, M.	Tor	4	3	5	2.14	1.357	0	42.0	38	17	36
Torres, D.	KC	1	2	0	6.09	1.669	2	44.1	56	17	28

AL Pitcher	Team	W	L	SV	ERA	Ratio	GS	IP	H	BB	K
Torres, S.	Sea	3	8	0	6.00	1.819	13	72.0	87	42	45
Trombley, M.	Min	4	8	0	5.62	1.556	18	97.2	107	42	68
Van Poppel, T.	Oak	4	8	0	4.88	1.337	14	138.1	125	56	122
Vanegmond, T.	Bos	0	1	0	9.45	2.250	1	6.2	9	6	5
Villone, R.	Sea	0	2	0	7.91	2.276	0	19.1	20	23	26
Vosberg, E.	Tex	5	5	4	3.00	1.333	0	36.0	32	16	36
Wakefield, T.	Bos	16	8	0	2.95	1.229	27	195.1	163	68	119
Ward, D.	Tor	0	1	0	27.00	6.375	0	2.2	11	5	3
Ware, J.	Tor	2	1	0	5.47	1.899	5	26.1	28	21	18
Wasdin, J.	Oak	1	1	0	4.67	1.038	2	17.1	14	3	6
Watkins, S.	Min	0	0	0	5.40	1.523	0	21.2	22	11	11
Wegman, B.	Mil	5	7	2	5.35	1.599	4	70.2	89	21	50
Wells, B.	Sea	4	3	0	5.75	1.696	4	76.2	88	39	38
Wells, D.	Det	10	3	0	3.04	1.220	18	130.1	120	37	83
Wengert, D.	Oak	1	1	0	3.34	1.449	0	29.2	30	12	16
Wetteland, J.	NYA	1	5	31	2.93	0.880	0	61.1	40	14	66
Whiteside, M.	Tex	5	4	3	4.08	1.283	0	53.0	48	19	46
Whiteside, S.	Det	0	0	0	14.73	3.000	0	3.2	7	4	2
Wickander, K.	Det	0	0	1	2.60	1.615	0	17.1	18	9	9
Wickander, K.	Mil	0	0	0	0.00	0.667	0	6.0	1	3	2
Wickman, B.	NYA	2	4	1	4.05	1.438	1	80.0	77	33	51
Williams, M.	Cal	1	2	0	6.75	3.375	0	10.2	13	21	9
Williams, W.	Tor	1	2	0	3.69	1.379	3	53.2	44	28	41
Willis, C.	Min	0	0	0	94.50	15.000	0	0.2	5	5	0
Witt, B.	Tex	3	4	0	4.55	1.679	10	61.1	81	21	46
Wojciechowski, S.	Oak	2	3	0	5.18	1.644	7	48.2	51	28	13
Wolcott, B.	Sea	3	2	0	4.42	1.609	6	36.2	43	14	19